Thomas Cook

NORTH AMERICAN

RAIL AND BUS GUIDE

1994

GW00370927

Published by Thomas Cook Publishing
The Thomas Cook Group Ltd.
PO Box 227
PETERBOROUGH PE3 6SB
United Kingdom

☎(Sales): 0733 268943
☎(Editorial): 0733 269610

ISBN 0 906273 48 X

While every care has been taken in compiling this publication, using the most up-to-date information available at the time of going to press, the publishers cannot accept any liability whatsoever arising from errors or omissions, howsoever caused. Views and opinions expressed in this book are not necessarily those of the Thomas Cook Group Ltd.

Edited by John Gage. Compiled by Peter Tremlett and John Gage. Maps and plans by John Gage. Additional research by Christopher J Bane.

Contributor: John Pitt

Typeset by Thomas Cook Publishing and output by Riverhead Typesetting, Grimsby.

Printed in Great Britain by Bell & Bain Ltd, Glasgow

Front cover photograph: An *AMTRAK* train passes through suburban California.
Reproduced by kind permission of Tony Stone.

CONTENTS

Page

IMPORTANT NOTE

New schedules for the current year are not released by some operators until early summer, and even then they can still sometimes be subject to confirmation.

The timetables on pages 63–135 are based wherever possible on 1994 schedules received from operators; these are provisional in some cases. In instances where we have not received 1994 information from operators, the timetables have been based on 1993 schedules. The notes on pages 56-57 contain latest advance information received from operators at the time of going to press, together with predictions of new schedules based on the actual experience of services in 1993. Readers are therefore strongly advised:

(a)   To read the notes on pages 56–57 in conjunction with the timetables themselves.

(b)   To reconfirm actual times and dates of services before each journey during their trip.

Whilst every care has been taken in the compilation of this guide to provide the most accurate up-to-date or predicted information, the publishers cannot hold themselves responsible for the consequences of either changes or inaccuracies. The inclusion of a fare does not imply that Thomas Cook can supply tickets at the rate shown, or at all.

INTRODUCTION

Welcome to the new *Thomas Cook North American Rail & Bus Guide!* We'd like to tell you a little bit about it and why we've published it . . .

More and more people visit Canada and the USA each year. Hardly surprising really, as both these large and diverse countries contain thousands of places and attractions for the visitor to explore.

Fly-drive and coach tour holidays have become very popular in recent years, but with over 150 years experience in arranging holidays, and as experts in **all** methods of travel, we at Thomas Cook know that our customers are as diverse as the types of travel and holidays we arrange for them. We know that for many, much of the enjoyment of travel is meeting and mixing with the local population and getting the real 'feel' of the country, an experience frequently missed by those cocooned in their cars and coaches.

But is there any alternative to fly-drives or coach tours? After all, it's a well-known fact, isn't it, that there's no public transport to speak of in Canada or the USA because they all have cars and jump into them for any journey over 100 yards (or sometimes even less), so they don't need buses or trains? Except, of course, for the subway in New York – everyone's heard of that. And the cable cars in San Francisco which they run for the tourists. And for long journeys, they fly everywhere. Don't they?

Well, like most preconceptions gleaned from afar, there's an element of truth and also a great deal of myth in all this. Car ownership in Canada and the USA **is** very high, compared to many areas of the world. And the North Americans certainly like their cars – one look at the freeways in cities such as Los Angeles will confirm this. But not everybody drives. And contrary to the popular myth, Canada and the USA have excellent public transport systems, which can be both an economical and enjoyable way to get around these countries.

In most cities you will find a comprehensive urban transit system, with a combination of buses, subways, trolleys (trams), suburban rail networks and rapid transit systems. For longer distance travel, there are the national railroad networks (VIA Rail in Canada and **AMTRAK** in the USA), plus a number of smaller operators. Buses, too, have nationwide networks such as Greyhound Lines of Canada, and Greyhound and Trailways in the USA, and also many smaller, more localised companies. Or, if you are pushed for time and don't mind missing a bit of the scenery, you can cover the longer distances by air.

The choice is yours. This guide incorporates the timetables of all the main North American long-distance rail and bus operators which are published every two months in the *Thomas Cook Overseas Timetable* (available on subscription or as single copies from Thomas Cook Publishing). With its comprehensive index and easy-to-use route maps, it helps you to find the services you need in order to plan your own itinerary and go **where** you want to go **when** you want to go.

The entertaining article 'Travelling North America' by John Pitt on pages 6–11 of this book offers first-hand knowledge on how to get the most out of your trip, and how to avoid the pitfalls.

To help you find your feet when you arrive, we've featured main gateway cities, with information about airports and connections to the downtown areas and other places of interest.

We haven't included air timetables, partly because the network is incredibly intensive (most North American cities have daily connections with many other North American cities by hop-on, hop-off, turn-up-and-board flights which don't require any advance reservations) and partly because airline schedules can change quite often, so it's best to ring the airport or airline a few days beforehand for the latest information. We've included telephone numbers for all airports in the 'Gateway Cities' section of this guide; the airport information service will be able to tell you which airlines fly to your intended destination and give you the number to ring to check schedules etc.

Likewise, rail and bus timetables can change, and furthermore there are some cases where the operators have not yet published their Summer '94 schedules. In these situations, we either show the latest available schedules, those in operation for Summer '93, or in some instances we have predicted the service for Summer '94, according to what we consider will most accurately reflect the likely pattern of service. So it's sensible to always follow the golden rule of travel by public transport, and check with the operator for latest timings before setting out on a particular trip. All **AMTRAK** services we show are taken from their 1994 schedules (and were correct at the time of going to press) but even these can change. Canadians and Americans are a decidedly 'phone-and-check-first' society (that's why 'Freefone' numbers are so abundant!) and wouldn't dream of doing anything else. We've shown the telephone numbers of transport operators in the footnotes of each timetable.

Now for the crunch question. Surely it must work out more expensive to put together a trip like this, rather than buy an 'off the peg' package? The answer to this one is that by being in control yourself, your holiday can be as cheap or expensive as you care to make it. If you are on a tight budget, you can save on accommodation costs by travelling overnight (although this does require a bit of stamina after a while!). You can choose to have 5-course meals in up-market restaurants, or snacks or take-aways from the many economical fast food chain outlets. Instead of buying individual tickets for each sector of your trip, you can invest in one (or more) of the almost bewildering array of rail, bus and air passes there are to choose from – this guide tells you about them and helps you to pick those best suited to your needs.

With careful planning, using the **Thomas Cook North American Rail & Bus Guide**, you can have the holiday **you** want, visiting the places **you** want to see, at a price **you** can afford.

TRAVELLING NORTH AMERICA
by John Pitt

North America is a vast and diverse continent but there are many ways to see it, each with particular advantages. Flying is quickest, though travelling above the clouds means you lose contact with the landscape. Some of the time saved in the air is eaten up by tedious journeys to and from airports or by hanging around in departure lounges. Car hire is cheap – and the highways impressive – but driving long distances can still be tiring and no one can park in downtown New York.

Luckily there are ways to travel which keep you in touch with the scenery, require no real exertion and are remarkably inexpensive. **AMTRAK** passenger trains go to more than five hundred destinations in the United States and VIA Rail serves all the big Canadian cities. Overseas visitors can buy passes giving access to all or part of both networks. Buses go to even more places, with Greyhound and Trailways alone operating over 100,000 miles of routes in all the continental States and Canada. Add to these the many local, city and regional services and it's easy to plan almost any desired itinerary.

Trains are best for very long distances or for overnight travel. They're less crowded, quieter and the seats are bigger and more comfortable. Sleeping accommodation is usually available. If you get restless you can take a stroll to the dining car or observation lounge. On the other hand, buses operate more frequently, go to many more destinations and are an ideal way to get to know 'real' Americans. Ticket prices tend to be slightly lower and travelling times slightly longer for buses than for trains, since speeds are kept down to improve fuel economy. Travelling cross-country by bus takes at least three days.

To see as much of the country as possible in a short time, especially on a limited budget, it's a good idea to combine buses with trains. This is easily done because schedules are arranged to facilitate transfers between routes. Travel on **AMTRAK**'s Thruway buses can be booked at the same time as your train ticket, so you might go to Seattle on the Empire Builder, for instance, before continuing immediately by bus to Vancouver in Canada. Thruway bus connections are guaranteed and offer a direct service to or from many rail destinations.

Other Thruway buses link one **AMTRAK** train with another or go to places not served by passenger trains at all. **AMTRAK** also acts as selling agent for Interline services such as Greyhound and Gray Line, including airport buses, sightseeing tours and travel to the Mexican border. Some Interline services are run by local transport authorities. Most regional and city services are designed for commuters and suburb dwellers but offer an alternative way for the tourist to visit smaller towns near the major cities. Services are usually fast and frequent and may be cheaper than **AMTRAK** or Greyhound. Information and timetables can be obtained from the individual carriers or from city tourist centres.

Greyhound buses have been cruising North American highways for most of this century, appearing in films like 'It Happened One Night' and 'Bus Stop', on their way to becoming classics in their own right. Over 2,600 of them travel almost 40 million miles a year. Buses are air conditioned with wide tinted windows and at night the interior lights are dimmed so that you can relax in a reclining seat complete with headrest and reading lamp. Stops are made every few hours, scheduled as close to normal meal times as possible. A restroom is located at the rear. Newer buses have a retractable front entry step to make boarding easier for the elderly or disabled.

You can check in two pieces of luggage (total weight less than 100 lbs) for which liability is limited to $250. When a bus is filled, the company adds a second one, so make sure your bags are loaded on to the one you board. Don't lose the claim check. For security reasons you should take valuables such as cash or travel documents with you if you leave the bus for rest or meal stops. No smoking is allowed on Greyhound or most other buses. *AMTRAK* permits cigarette smoking in designated coaches, sleeping accommodation and some areas of lounge or club cars. Whichever way you travel you should take care not to disturb other passengers. Earphones or headphones must be used when listening to radios, tape-players or portable TVs, and the volume kept down to avoid 'leakage'.

Apart from Greyhound, other bus companies include Bonanza, New England's Jack Rabbit Lines, Peerless Stage, Raz Transportation, Peter Pan Lines and the Skylark Company. Buses go to all the main cities as well as to National Parks like Yosemite and Yellowstone, often travelling round the clock. Schedules are subject to late changes, so you should check your selected departure one day ahead. Arrive at the terminal at least thirty minutes before departure time to locate the appropriate boarding bay and check your luggage at coach side. Some depots are unsafe at night so try to arrange your arrival and departure at sensible hours. Bus companies usually won't accept responsibility for delays or inconvenience caused by accidents, breakdowns or failure to make connections.

An Ameripass (not available for purchase in the USA) entitles you to travel Greyhound's entire system in the United States plus the routes of lines such as Blue Star and Colonial Trailways (about 75 in all). A similar Canada Pass operates north of the border. Since reservations aren't required a pass lets you travel spontaneously, departing when and where you wish and reboarding at any time and in any direction. Greyhound and Trailways also offer discounts for senior citizens and the disabled. Accompanied children under five ride free and those between five and eleven pay half fare. Often there are reduced rate excursion fares.

Many people integrate the Ameripass/Canada Pass or *AMTRAK*/VIA Rail pass with city bus tours. Travel by night and you can arrive in the morning at your desired tour point, join the tour bus or explore on a more freewheeling basis, then reboard the train or bus to your next destination. This can be exhausting after a while but it saves on hotel bills. Local buses are often the most economic way to go sightseeing, with passes lasting one or more days. Sometimes, as in Seattle, the downtown buses are free.

An excellent example of how to mix buses, trains and local transport is the route from New York down to the Florida Keys. New York City is well served by the Metropolitan Transit Authority and the MTA subway is the quickest way to get around Manhattan. Despite clean-up campaigns some subway stations remain dirty and dangerous at night, so buses are safer and cleaner.

Hundreds of Metro North trains operate daily to suburbs and Connecticut from the romantically elegant Grand Central Terminal. The more modern Pennsylvania Station – a labyrinthine building beneath Madison Square Garden – is used by PATH trains to New Jersey and by the Long Island Railroad. Penn Station has shops, restaurants, snack bars, a baggage room and a subway stop. Nearby on 8th Avenue is the Port Authority Terminal used by Greyhound and other bus lines. The PAT is a resort for the city's homeless so beware of pickpockets and bag snatchers and avoid the restrooms if possible.

AMTRAK's New York trains operate out of Pennsylvania Station and the Silver Meteor, one of several going down to Florida, takes 26 hours to reach Miami. The equivalent Greyhound journey lasts a day and a half. Trains from other northeastern cities connect with the Silver Meteor in New York and one through coach travels all the way from Chicago. You should arrive at least half an hour before departure to allow time to find your train and get on board. Being early also gives you more chance of a window seat away from the sometimes noisy doors.

A check-in baggage service allows up to three items weighing no more than 150 lbs in total. Liability is limited to $500 but you can buy more insurance if required. If you need special assistance with luggage you should let *AMTRAK* know when making your reservation. Porters are called Redcaps (for the obvious reason) and will provide free help, though it's ususal to tip one dollar per bag. Get a receipt in case your luggage is mislaid and never accept help from anyone other than a Redcap. Some stations have handcarts for which a small charge is made, refunded when you return the cart to a vending machine.

The Silver Meteor leaves Pennsylvania Station mid-afternoon by means of a 2½ mile tunnel, heading south through New Jersey along part of the Northeast Corridor. This is *AMTRAK*'s busiest route and the only section of the network where the corporation owns its own tracks (the rest belong to freight railroads). This means *AMTRAK*'s timekeeping is to some extent at the mercy of others so occasional delays are unavoidable. Allow at least an hour between trains when planning connections. Times shown in the timetables are local, taking full account of zone changes en route.

People often come on board loaded with food, cooler boxes and giant bags of potato chips as well as sodas and cans of beer, though except in sleeping cars you're not supposed to consume your own supplies of alcohol. Dining car meals are reasonable value at around $10, often with specials such as freshly-caught trout on the menu. Meals are also available for children, vegetarians and those on kosher or low salt diets. Sandwiches, snacks, coffee and iced Coke can be bought at any time in the lounge car. In the licensed bar you can meet other passengers and perhaps join a poker game lasting until dawn.

One of the nicest things about trains is the way you are cossetted by the staff, most of whom act as if auditioning for bit parts in a 1930s movie. The conductor is in charge of the crew and is responsible for safety as well as collecting tickets. The chief of on-board services looks after service personnel. The man (or more likely woman) you see most of is your car attendant, who helps with boarding, 'detraining', allocating seats and making sure everything goes smoothly. Tipping of *AMTRAK* personnel isn't required but most people reward bar staff, waiters and sleeping car attendants for any extra services.

In Philadelphia, the Silver Meteor stops at the recently restored 30th Street Station, close to Greyhound's terminal. Philadelphia can be reached more cheaply from New York by travelling on a New Jersey Transit train to Trenton, then boarding a SEPTA commuter train. *AMTRAK* ticket holders can travel free by commuter train from 30th Street to the downtown Penn Center Station. Philadelphia is best explored on foot or with the Fairmount Trolley, which takes in most historic sights. SEPTA also runs buses and a subway.

The Silver Meteor continues south during the evening through Delaware and Maryland to Baltimore and Washington DC, where the splendid Union Station is as impressive as the capital's other buildings. Renovations has made it one of

AMTRAK's showpieces, with dozens of shops, restaurants and cinema screens, and a waiting room inspired by ancient Rome's Baths of Diocletian. Most places of interest are within walking distance. The station has a subway stop giving access to an ultra-modern Metrorail system which features the longest escalator in the western world. Weekend passes and tickets can be bought with transfers between subway and Metrobus, operating throughout the city as well as into Maryland and northern Virginia. The Greyhound/Trailways terminal, six blocks north of Union Station, has frequent services to nearby cities.

The Silver Meteor leaves past the Pentagon building, travelling by night through Virginia and North Carolina to reach Charleston, South Carolina, early in the morning. Like most long distance trains the Meteor requires reservations. These should be made as far in advance as possible, especially during summer, and can be obtained through ticket offices or designated travel agents (including those abroad).
Alternatively, you can call 1-800-872-7245 and be given a reservation number enabling you to collect your tickets before a certain date. Coach seats on unreserved trains are not guaranteed so it pays to be early.

AMTRAK's Charleston station is actually in North Charleston, seven miles from downtown, but there are frequent buses. *AMTRAK* offers one-day sightseeing tours in many cities across the country, including Charleston and Washington. South Carolina Electric & Gas buses operate throughout Charleston and the Downtown Area Shuttle (DASH) runs on weekdays with free transfers to other SCE & G services. The Greyhound depot is some distance from downtown, with a local bus stop outside.

After Charleston the Meteor crosses the Ashley and Edisto Rivers as it travel along the coastal plain to arrive in Savannah, Georgia, two hours later. The station is a five mile taxi ride from downtown but Greyhound's terminal is handier and Chatham Area Transit (CAT) buses operate in the city. Bus tours are available from the Historic Foundation to visit some of Savannah's one thousand restored buildings. The C & H bus goes to nearby Tybee Island beach.

The Silver Meteor continues into Florida, stopping for about half an hour at sprawling Jacksonville. Greyhound buses connect here with Talahassee and New Orleans, where *AMTRAK* and Greyhound share the same terminal. When taking a break on the platform you should stay within sight and sound of the train and listen for announcements. Trains don't necessarily stop as long as the timetable indicates and getting left behind can be a problem when the next one isn't due for a day or more.

Arrival and departure times can be checked by calling 1-800-USA-RAIL.

Part of the Silver Meteor splits off at Jacksonville to travel to Florida's west coast by way of Orlando, home of Disney world. The rest of the Meteor crosses the Kissimmee River, skirts Everglades National Park then runs down through the east coast resorts to reach Miami by late afternoon. Metro-Dade buses operate throughout the metropolitan area and the L bus for Miami Beach leaves from outside *AMTRAK*'s station. Close by is Metrorail's Northside station, with free transfers to Metrobus.

Greyhound is at 99 NE 4th Street, from where two buses each day travel to Key West along an Overseas Highway stretching a hundred breathtaking miles across the Keys. The base for this spectacular road was once the right of way for a part of the Florida East Coat Railway destroyed by hurricane in 1936. Look out for egrets and ospreys and many miles of bridging, including Seven Mile Bridge (one of the world's longest).

The bus stops at Coral Gables, Key Largo and Big Pine Key, and there are regular mile markers along the route. If you prefer to get off at one of these the man behind the wheel may be open to persuasion, since Greyhound's drivers have instructions to provide every assistance to passengers 'according to circumstances'. Drivers are smart and cheerful and consider themselves as much part of America's heritage as the Fourth of July and Mom's apple pie. Most have been in the business for years and handle their responsibilities with cool, sometimes sardonic professionalism. They also have a sixth sense which tells them exactly what's going on behind them on the bus, even if they occasionally turn a blind eye. When you arrive in Key West you'll find two public buses, one running clockwise round the island and the other anti-clockwise.

Countless other rail and bus routes can be linked effectively throughout the US and Canada. for example, the Southwest Chief train out of Chicago stops at Lamy, where Lamy Shuttle buses connect with Santa Fe and other buses continue to the pueblos of Taos. At Flagstaff, Arizona, there are Nava-Hopi buses to the southern rim of the Grand Canyon, Monument Valley, the Painted Desert and the Petrified Forest. Other Nava-Hopi buses go from **AMTRAK**'s Flagstaff station to Phoenix. The Southwest Chief eventually reaches a beautiful Spanish-style station in Los Angeles, where buses and trains fan out to the rest of California, DASH buses link the station with Chinatown and RTD buses go to jmost of the city's attractions, including Hollywood. **AMTRAK**'s San Joaquin stations such as Bakersfield and Martinez have direct train/Thruway bus transfers, including connections to may off-line cities in southern California, the Sacramento Valley, the Bay Area and northern California.

Information is available from **AMTRAK** agents or by writing to Timetable, c/o. Caltrans, Division of Rail, PO Box 942874, Sacramento, CA 94274-0001.

The California Zephyr train makes a dazzling journey over the Rocky Mountains, with side trips possible by bus to Colorado Springs and Lake Tahoe. At Oakland a shuttle bus crosses the bay to San Francisco and serves the Cal Tran station. From here Southern Pacific trains go to **AMTRAK**'s San Jose station, with stops at intermediate cities. Bay Area Rapid Transit (BART) provides fast, inexpensive trains between Market Street station and Oakland, Berkley and Concord. San Francisco is best seen on foot or by cable car or by using buses and the MUNI Metro, a light railway running partly underground.

The Texas Eagle takes two and a half days to get from Chicago to Los Angeles by way of Dallas, San Antonio and the Texas plains. Riding any US long distance train is a great experience and like most of those west of the Mississippi the Eagle has gleaming, twin-decked aluminium Superliner coaches. The big padded seats have leg and foot rests, folding trays and personal reading lights. Luggage can be left at the lower level when you board or kept on the rack above your seat. Restroom facilities include toilet, wash basin, mirror, infant changing table, soap, tissues and a 120V AC electric point. Massive lounge car windows extend part way over the roof for panoramic views. Sometimes a historian or Native American guide joins the train to point out places of interest. In the evening there's often a video movie. Superliners are too large for most routes in the East, so trains there usually have Amfleet or Heritage coaches. Some of these characterful affairs predate **AMTRAK** and are preferred for their smooth ride.

Sleeping is no problem given a generous reclining seat and a pillow from the attendant. As on the bus, you should take a blanket or coat to ward off fierce night-time air conditioning. Overnight trains also have sleeping cars where accommodation ranges from single 'roomettes' to family bedrooms sleeping four people. Some incorporate private restrooms and are miracles of ingenuity, with fold-down bunks, sliding seats and disappearing wash basins. They can feel rather cramped, so it's best to leave most of your luggage in the storage area and take only a small bag of essentials into the room. The most luxurious accommodation includes all meals in the dining car as well as coffee and a newspaper each morning. Some bedrooms are adapted for disabled passengers.

Like the USA, Canada has many impressive landscapes easily explored by bus and train. One of the best and most accessible is the journey through rural Ontario from Toronto to Ottawa by Voyageur Colonial bus. Other long distance carriers include Grey Goose in Manitoba and Maverick Coach in British Columbia. Greyhound Lines of Canada is the country's largest bus operator and runs a cross-country service between Toronto and Vancouver.

Canada's **AMTRAK** equivalent is VIA Rail, set up by the government to take over most passenger train services. VIA Rail has its own locomotives and personnel but uses tracks belonging Canadian Pacific and Canadian National. The equipment, though sometimes older than **AMTRAK**'s, has been refurbished to a comfortable standard and newer coaches are being introduced.

VIA joins **AMTRAK** in running several trains which link with US cities (the Adirondack, Montrealer, Maple Leaf and International. Connecting bus and ferry services include those between Edmonton and Calgary and between Truro in Nova Scotia and St. John's, Newfoundland.

Three trains a week travel each way between Vancouver and Toronto, completing the trip in three days and four nights. The route crosses Saskatchewan's farms and prairies as well as Jasper National Park's mountains and river gorges. The Hudson Bay train travels a thousand miles out of Winnipeg, going north to Churchill and polar bear country along a route opened to export grain from the prairies. The British Columbia Railway operates between its own stations in Vancouver and Prince George, with summer steam trains along the coast of Howe Sound.

The Rocky Mountaineer, run by the Great Canadian Railtour Company, makes a two-day journey among the mountains, rivers and waterfalls of the Canadian Rockies via Yoho and Glacier National Parks. Other Canadian railways include the Algoma Central through Ontario's forests and mountains, giving terrific views of the Agawa Canyon. The autumn foliage season is very popular with 'leaf peepers' so you should plan a weekday trip if possible. Northland Railway trains travel between Toronto's splendid Union Station and Cochrane via North Bay. No passenger trains run in the Northwest Territories or the Yukon but buses go as far north as Hay River and White Horse.

Besides being ecologically sound and a fine way to see the country, North American trains and buses offer some of the world's greatest travel bargains. Train fares vary depending on distance travelled and standard of service provided, with special offers, seasonal rates and excursion deals often bringing substantial reductions. Children aged under 2 travel free and those between 2 and 15 pay half fare. Seniors get 25% discount off one-way tickets.

*John Pitt has toured extensively in Europe and North America, where he has travelled over 50,000 miles by bus and train. He is the author of **U.S.A. by Rail plus Canada** (Bradt Publications, £10.95 – available from bookshops, or by post at £12.90 (inc. p. & p.) from Thomas Cook Publishing). This describes 28 long-distance routes in detail and includes all the essential information about stations, sightseeing and accommodation.*

ATLANTIC AIRDEALS

In this section we aim to provide some practical information on air travel both to and from North America, and within the countries themselves. Crossing the Atlantic affords some of the cheapest air fares in the world, on a cost-per-kilometre basis. Due to the number of carriers available on these routes, competition is fierce, and prices low, which can only be good news for consumers. Practically all travel agents now offer competitive fares, but it can still pay to shop around and obtain quotes. Remember, though, that some 'bucket shop' operators can (and do) suddenly go bust, and you could end up with no flight; worse still, you could also lose your money. Payment by credit card may safeguard you against this, but check with your credit card company. If you book with an ABTA bonded agent, you will at least receive compensation should the carrier or agent fail. Thomas Cook act as an official consolidator for various airlines, often providing the most competitive fares, so you can book in full confidence without the risk of worrying whether or not your tickets will actually turn up.

FLYING THE ATLANTIC

Before deciding which airline to opt for, we would advise you to work out the itinerary for your holiday in advance. This will then dictate the most suitable type of ticket for you. For example, if you intend to start and finish your holiday in New York, and do not intend to use any internal US flights during your stay, then the cheapest possible return ticket to New York would be the best for you. You may, though, decide to fly into New York, travel by train to San Francisco, and then return to the UK from there, in which case you would require an 'open-jaw' ticket. This enables you to fly into one destination and return from another, although you must specify which cities at the time of booking. Another itinerary may consist of flying to and returning from the same city, but combining internal airline flights with rail or bus travel within the USA. One of the most cost-effective ways to do this is to buy a series of air coupons before you go, which allows you to travel on your chosen carrier's domestic network; however, many carriers require you to fly the Atlantic with them in order to qualify for these coupons at lower cost rates. If you intend to visit both the USA and Canada, then Continental Airlines offer the best option, because their airpass coupons are also valid on the flights of Air Canada. Travel agents are more likely to view you seriously as a potential client if you present a detailed (but flexible) itinerary than if you just wander in and ask about the cheapest ticket. When planning your itinerary, bear in mind that flights are generally cheaper mid-week than at weekends, and that from October 1 1994, passengers departing UK airports on intercontinental flights will be subject to a £10 departure tax.

The airlines flying the Atlantic fall into three basic categories: US, British and Others. Some of the cheapest point-to-point fares are with such carriers as Air India and Kuwait Airlines, who fly from their own country to the USA and Canada via London. The US and Canadian carriers view their transatlantic routes as showpieces and often place their most highly trained crews and best equipment on them. Whilst their main aim is undoubtedly to attract the business-class passenger, they still aim to provide an above average level of service and comfort to all clients.

Spending 7 or more hours in an aeroplane on a long-haul flight is nobody's idea of fun. TWA, who fly from Gatwick to St. Louis, have substantially increased the seat space and provided footrests in their economy class cabins, renaming it 'comfort class.' This really does produce noticeably more space, and is worth considering if you find ordinary airline seats too small. Another advantage offered by TWA is that anyone flying on a full-price economy ticket will be upgraded to Ambassador Class.

One of the major hassles involved in transatlantic flights is faced on arrival, namely the time it takes to clear customs and immigration for non-US or Canadian residents.

Often this takes at least the best part of an hour, and at peak times even longer. There is nothing worse than rushing to be one of the first off the aeroplane, only to find that a jumbo jet arrived moments before yours, so that you end up joining the back of a queue stretching into infinity.

United Airlines, however, offer a solution to this. When you check in at Heathrow, details from your passport are fed into an Advance Passenger Information System (APIS). This is then transmitted to the immigration authorities in the US, and upon arrival you can proceed through the blue lane, normally set aside for green card holders. At the counter the immigration official will already have all the details he or she needs; the end result is that you clear customs and immigration in half the time it normally takes.

Continental seem to make an extra special effort to make sure you enjoy your trip. If you are flying with them to New York, you will land at Newark airport which offers faster journey times into New York City than JFK, and also speedier passage through customs and immigration because of the smaller numbers of passengers.

British Airways and Virgin Atlantic both offer excellent transatlantic products. Wherever you are in the world, stepping onto a BA aircraft is always a guarantee of a warm welcome, and Virgin are supreme with their efforts to make what is actually a very tiring journey as enjoyable as possible. Often you will find entertainers and magicians passing down the aisles keeping passengers amused.

At the end of the day, the carrier which will suit you best is often a matter of personal preference. If your transatlantic flight is to be followed immediately by a connecting domestic flight, it's worthwhile considering using the same airline for both, as apart from the possible financial advantages, the transfer from one to the other will almost certainly be smoother and probably within the same terminal.

Whichever airline you fly, you may wish to consider joining its frequent flyer club. Even if you only intend to make one transatlantic trip, your accumulated points stay valid for a long time (often indefinitely). Normally it takes only two roundtrip transatlantic journeys before you qualify for an award. Even if you don't plan to return to the USA, you may change your mind at a later stage and regret not having joined. The other major advantage is that members of frequent flyer clubs don't get 'bumped' in the event of the flight being 'full'.

Being 'bumped' is trade slang for 'denied boarding' (due to overbooking), and the practice is becoming more common. Officially, the 'error' is invariably the fault of the ubiquitous computer; in reality the widespread practice of overbooking by a certain percentage is quite deliberate, and is calculated on the average number of 'no-shows' for that flight. The airlines cannot really be blamed for protecting themselves against those who are too inconsiderate to cancel unwanted reservations, but this is of little comfort to you if you arrive holding a valid ticket and have a reservation, but are denied boarding. One compensating factor is that US airlines often award worthwhile cash sums to passengers willing to give up their seats in this situation. A mini-auction may take place, whereby the airline starts by offering compensation of $50 to any passenger willing to give up their seat, and some people come forward. If there are still too many people wanting to fly, they increase the compensation to $100, and so on. If you are not in a rush to travel it may be worth your while to take advantage of this. You get a guaranteed seat on the next available flight, and if this involves an overnight wait, hotel accommodation will be provided for you.

DOMESTIC AIRLINES

Internal flights in North America are cheap by world standards. They are readily affordable by all sectors of the community, and for this reason are often called flying buses. Constant price cutting appears to be the norm and many of the major carriers are only operating under the protection of the US Chapter 11 bankruptcy laws, which protect them from their creditors. In January this year Northwest Airlines cut their fares, in some cases, by as much as 45%. Other carriers soon followed, but not in all areas. As well as the major carriers, smaller airlines have appeared; these usually offer basic services (i.e. cheap flights without meals or any other frills). Good examples of these include Kiwi, Reno, Morris Air and Valujet. Look out for these names as they offer excellent value-for-money point-to-point fares. Two larger domestic carriers offering greater route networks are SouthWest Air and America West.

Flying in America is quite informal; you generally just turn up at the airport and get on the next flight heading where you want to go, like using a bus or a train. You don't have to book in advance using a travel agent, as the airlines have competitive 'walk-up' fares (some of the smaller 'value' carriers actually charge extra to those booking by telephone). With the smaller carriers you may not even receive a boarding pass, let alone a seat number. You just turn up at the aircraft and sit wherever there is a spare seat. Morris Air have taken this a stage further and abolished the actual ticket itself. You telephone a reservations number and quote your credit card. You are then given a reference number to quote at the airport, where you just show up, quote this number and provide identification and board the aircraft.

Of the major carriers, Continental offer some of the most competitive fares, so-called 'Peanut Fares'. The only inflight catering is peanuts, hence the name. Unless you are travelling alone, you should take advantage of their 'Add-a-penny, add-a-pal' fares, where, in effect, two travel for the price of one. Travelling offpeak hours is one of the major qualifications for this type of ticket, which for the leisure traveller should not prove to be too inconvenient.

Airports in America can be very confusing. The terminal you need will generally depend on the carrier used, but can also be influenced by your destination and whether you are arriving or departing, so always check in advance from which terminal your flight is leaving. New York's JFK, for instance, has no fewer than nine separate terminal buildings. A United flight may arrive at one terminal and a connecting United flight may leave from another. Airport codes on baggage tags can also sometimes be obscure. 'MIA' easily suggests Miami, and 'LAX' is only slightly less obviously Los Angeles (there is an increasing tendency to refer to the airport itself as 'LAX' – much less of a mouthful than 'Los Angeles International Airport'); however, 'ORD' does not immediately shriek 'Chicago' at you unless you have flown there, or work in the travel industry. Air buffs will know that Chicago O'Hare used to be called Orchard Field and hence the code, but not everybody is an air buff. Most airline timetables list the airport codes somewhere, and it's a good idea be aware of them so that you can ensure that your checked luggage has been correctly labelled.

If you are planning to take several internal flights and are using a system of airpass coupons, do check that the cities you wish to visit are included on the carrier's domestic route network. This particularly applies to some smaller towns. Sometimes the major carriers have a separate 'feeder' airline, which normally employs small propellor-driven aircraft between major 'hubs' and local airports within the catchment area. Examples are Continental Airlines (who use Continental Express) and American Airlines (American Eagle). You may find that each area only has one feeder service carrier. Even the major carriers don't serve everywhere; US Air, for example, is very thin on the ground in the north-west, so when you buy an airline's airpass coupons, make sure that the airline (or its subsidiary) actually flies where you want to go. Your local travel agent should be able to assist you in making the best choice.

The United States and Canada are vast countries, and travelling by air allows you to explore further; however, it does inevitably deny you many of the sights which can only be appreciated at ground level. Bus and rail may be amongst the best ways to see the continent, but it takes much longer to cover the same ground. The decision is yours . . .

US AND CANADIAN DOMESTIC FLIGHT COUPONS AND PASSES (1994)

AIRLINE	NUMBER OF FLIGHT COUPONS PURCHASED						SEASON
	3	4	5	6	7	8	
DELTA (rate for Delta transatlantic clients)	£242	£312	£381	£402	£423	£444	All
(rate for other transatlantic clients)	£312	£381	£451	£472	£492	£513	All
	Standby Passes		(30-day pass £347; 60-day pass £555)				All
AMERICA WEST	N/A	£219	£251	£283	£315	£348	All
UNITED (travel to the USA must be with United, BA or Virgin)	£235	£290	£345	£395	£450	£505	off peak
	£270	£335	£405	£470	£540	£605	peak *
CONTINENTAL/AIR CANADA (travel to the USA/Canada must be with one of these two carriers)	£240	£300	£360	£410	£430	£450	off peak
	£270	£340	£410	£430	£450	£470	peak *
US AIR (travel to the USA must be with BA or Virgin)	£237	£303	£369	£389	£409	£428	off peak
	£257	£323	£389	£409	£428	£448	peak *
CANADIAN (travel to Canada must be with Canadian)	CA$436	CA$486	CA$536	CA$586	CA$636	CA$686	off peak
	CA$474	CA$534	CA$594	CA$654	CA$714	CA$774	peak *

* Peak periods are as follows: **United:** June 1–September 6; November 22–28; December 15–January 10 1995. **Continental/Air Canada:** July 1–August 31. **US Air:** July 1–August 31 **Canadian:** June 27–August 31.

DEALS ON WHEELS

The various passes mentioned in this section can mostly be purchased only outside North America. They are available from official International Sales Agents; in the UK you can contact Long Haul Leisurail, PO Box 113, PETERBOROUGH PE3 8HY; ☎(0733) 335599, or your local Thomas Cook shop. These outlets convert dollar prices (where shown) into Pounds Sterling using exchange rates applicable at the time of booking.

RAIL PASSES – AMTRAK

AMTRAK is the US nationwide passenger rail network. **AMTRAK** rail passes are available to anyone who is permanently resident outside the United States. A variety of different options is available which covers the entire system and smaller geographical areas. A complete set of prices and options is given below. The passes are valid for travel in ordinary Coach Class; however, upgrades are available on payment of the appropriate supplement.

To use the pass, you must take it to an **AMTRAK** ticket desk in the station, where you will be given a ticket for the journey of your choice. It is also advisable to purchase any upgrades at this stage, rather than from the conductor on the train. You must obtain a valid ticket before starting your journey (the pass itself is not actually a ticket – it merely entitles you to one). Without a valid ticket you will be charged the regular fare on the train and may have to pay a surcharge for being without a ticket.

The National pass covers the entire **AMTRAK** network. The dividing line between the East and West passes is the Chicago–Memphis–New Orleans rail line, which is covered on either pass. Another option is the Far West pass, which covers an area to the west of an imaginary line stretching from Wolf Point to El Paso. The two remaining passes cover only the coastal routes. Coastal West, all points between Seattle and San Diego, and Coastal East from Montreal to Miami, to which the Jacksonville–New Orleans line has now been added, making this even more of a bargain. The adult prices shown below are valid during the 1994 season. Peak period rates apply May 30–Aug. 28. Children aged 2–15 pay 50% of the adult price.

AMTRAK	Off-peak		Peak	
	15 days	30 days	15 days	30 days
National Rail Pass	$218	$319	$318	$399
Far West Rail Pass	$168	$219	$188	$239
West Rail Pass	$198	$269	$238	$299
East Rail Pass	$168	$219	$188	$239
Coastal Pass East	n/a	$189	n/a	$209
Coastal Pass West	n/a	$189	n/a	$209

AIR-RAIL PASSES – AMTRAK

AMTRAK also feature an Air-Rail Travel Plan in association with United Airlines. This can be purchased either before you go or after you have arrived in the USA, and offers one air sector (at start or end of trip; connections allowed, but not stopovers) plus up to 3 rail sectors (with stopovers).

The Travel Plan is very flexible; the USA is divided into 4 zones (different to those for the **AMTRAK** Rail Pass) and you can buy a Plan for one zone, or for a permutation of two zones. So, for instance, on the Transcontinental Plan, you could catch the train from New York to Seattle, on to Portland, San Francisco and Los Angeles, then fly back to New York. Or on the East Coast Plan, fly from Boston to Miami and return by train stopping off at Orlando, Washington DC and New York. Prices depend on the arrangement and date of your Plan; they start from $314. Further information and prices can be obtained from your **AMTRAK** Sales Agent outside the States, or from within the USA from **AMTRAK**'s Great American Vacations on ☎ 1-800-321-8684, or from United Airlines.

RAIL PASSES – VIA RAIL

Canadian **VIA Rail** offers the system-wide 'CANRAILPASS', which as its name implies covers all of VIA's services. It entitles you only to Coach Class travel, but you can upgrade to VIA 1 or to a sleeping car on payment of the appropriate supplement. The pass is valid for twelve days' actual travel within a period of thirty days. To qualify for one of these passes you must be permanently resident outside Canada. Included with the CANRAILPASS is a 'HELLO! phone pass', worth $20 in long-distance calls, and also discounts at any of the 174 hotels in the Choice Hotels Canada chain. Special rates apply for seniors 60 and over and young adventurers between 2 and 24.

New for 1994 is an upgrade option in association with Hertz Rent-a-car. This includes 3 days' car hire in a mid-sized vehicle within the same 30-day period as the validity of the pass. This upgrade is only available to those over 21.

Passengers intending to use one of these passes should note that they are not valid for travel on certain specified dates within the Easter, Christmas, and New Year holiday periods. If you are just intending to travel across Canada from east to west or vice versa, it still works out cheaper to purchase a system-wide pass, compared with the Coach Class single fare. For 1994 the peak season will apply June 1 – Sept. 30.

Discounts can be obtained on regular Coach Class tickets by travelling off-peak, avoiding Fridays and Sundays; this can reduce ordinary fares by between 25% and 40%. These may need to be purchased 5–7 days in advance.

VIA RAIL 12 days rail travel in a 30 day period		Off-peak	Peak
Adult	*Canrailpass*	$349	$510
Youth/Senior		$319	$460
Adult	*Canrailpass + Hertz*	$493	$654
Youth/Senior		$463	$604

BUS PASSES – GREYHOUND LINES

An Ameripass (not for sale in the USA) entitles you to travel over Greyhound's entire route system in the United States plus the routes of many connecting bus lines. It's also valid for Canada on the routes of Greyhound Lines of Canada and for Greyhound routes from Seattle to Vancouver, Fargo to Winnipeg and Boston or New York to Montréal. Prices are as shown in the grid below; children under 11 pay half these rates. Daily extensions (£12 per day) must be bought at the same time as the Ameripass. A 4-day ticket costing £50 is valid only from Monday to Thursday.

GREYHOUND AMERIPASS	
7 days	£90
15 days	£135
30 days	£180

BUS PASSES – GREYHOUND LINES OF CANADA

Greyhound's Canada Pass permits unlimited travel on all scheduled services of Greyhound Lines of Canada plus Voyageur Colonial's routes between Montréal, Toronto and Ottawa, Gray Coach from Toronto to Niagara Falls and Buffalo, Brewsters between Banff and Jasper, Arctic Frontier Carriers between Hay River and Yellowknife, and Adirondack Trailways from New York to Toronto. Prices are shown below. The All-Canada Pass allows travel on the above routes plus those of Orleans Express (Montréal–Québec City–Rivière du Loup), Acadian Lines (Amhurst–Truro–Halifax) and SMT Lines (Rivière du Loup–Edmunston–St. John's, NB). No daily extensions or child reductions are available on the Canada Passes.

GREYHOUND CANADA PASSES		
	Canada	All Canada
7 days	£92	n/a
15 days	£120	£150
30 days	£165	£200

BUS PASSES – GENERAL INFORMATION

All passes are for use by the purchaser only and tickets are not transferable. You may be asked to show identification such as a passport or driving licence. A pass allows you to stop off anywhere just as often or as long as you wish, provided travel is completed within the time limit. Initially, the pass must be presented to a terminal or station ticket agent, who will validate it when he/she issues your first ticket.

TRAIN AND BUS ACCOMMODATION

AMTRAK

Two different types of rolling stock are to be found operating **AMTRAK**'s long-distance trains. The more modern, double-deck 'Superliners' were introduced back in 1979, and have proved to be exceptionally popular with the American public. The older 'Heritage' fleet has recently undergone major refurbishment to bring it up to date. Due to loading gauge restrictions, Superliners are used exclusively west of the Mississippi; the Heritage fleet covers all points to the east.

There is considerable debate as to which is the premier fleet. Whilst the Superliners are undoubtedly luxurious, it is believed that the Heritage cars offer a smoother, more comfortable ride. **AMTRAK** has recently ordered more Superliners, which are now entering service; it is intended to start replacing the Heritage stock with new Viewliner cars in late 1994.

In New York, Chicago, Philadelphia and Washington DC, **AMTRAK**'s Metropolitan Lounges are available for use by Club service and sleeping car passengers. These private waiting lounges provide an oasis of calm in which to relax before commencing your journey.

COACH SEATING
Most coaches now have reclining seats, folding trays and personal reading lights. Long-distance trains often have footrests as well. Coach passengers are entitled to use the dining car, but may have to pay a supplement to gain access to the lounge or dome cars. At least one WC is available in each car, situated at the end (or on the lower levels on the Superliners). Metroliners are fast commuter trains, which feature all the facilities of coach class seating and in addition have footrests and legrests which fold out from under each seat.

CLUB SERVICE
Selected Northeast corridor and Metroliner services often feature 'club service'. Wider than normal seats are available, which can be individually reserved in advance. An at-seat service of complimentary beverages and meals further enhances the service. It is designed in many ways to compete with the business service of the airlines, and special touches such as newspapers, mints and hot towels are also provided.

ROOMETTE (HERITAGE)
A Roomette is a first-class enclosed compartment for use by one adult. An armchair by day converts to a single bed that folds out from the wall for night-time use. The room contains bathroom facilities (to use the WC at night the bed must be raised) and storage space for two average-sized suitcases.
Meals and complimentary tea or coffee are included. Room size: 2m x 1.1m

BEDROOM (HERITAGE)
Private first-class compartments designed for use by two adults (or one adult and two small children). Bedrooms have two fold-down beds, one above the other (access to the upper berth is by ladder), containing enclosed bathroom facilities which include a sink, mirror, and hanging space. Storage is available to accommodate three average-sized suitcases.
Meals and complimentary tea or coffee are included. Room size: 2.3m x 1.6m

SINGLE SLUMBERCOACH (HERITAGE)

Slumbercoach rooms are designed for budget-minded travellers who require sleeping car privacy and comfort. A single slumbercoach provides one seat for daytime travel, with a bed which folds down from the wall for sleeping. Bathroom facilities are included, as well as a mirror and reading lights. Storage space is minimal with room for two small suitcases only.

Meals are **not** included. Room size 1.3m x 1.1m

DOUBLE SLUMBERCOACH (HERITAGE)

This enclosed room provides two single seats (facing each other) for daytime use, and two bunk beds which fold down from the wall.

Facilities included as per single slumbercoach. Room size 1.8m x 1.1m

ECONOMY BEDROOM (SUPERLINER)

Designed for use by one or two adults, and located on both upper and lower levels of the car. The room features two windowside reclining seats for daytime travel, which slide together to form the lower berth, and an upper berth which folds out of the wall. Other features include a large picture window, fold-down table, wardrobe, mirrors, and reading lights. There are no WC facilities within the room, but they can be found on the lower level of the car. The room can only accommodate two small overnight bags which will fit under the seats. Larger suitcases can be stored in a baggage area on the lower level.

Meals and complimentary beverages are included. Room size 2m x 1.1m

DELUXE BEDROOM (SUPERLINER)

The largest accommodation on the Superliners, located on the upper level, and providing comfortable facilities for two adults. All have large picture windows, and by day a sofa and single armchair. At night a berth folds down out of the wall, and the sofa converts into a wider sleeping berth. The room also features WC facilities and a shower. Storage space is available for two average-sized suitcases.

Meals and complimentary beverages are included. Room size 2m x 2.3m

FAMILY BEDROOM (SUPERLINER)

There is one family bedroom in each carriage, extending the full width of the car, with windows on both sides. Each family bedroom will accommodate two adults and two children. The room contains a long sofa and two child seats for daytime use. These convert to an upper and lower berth for adults and two short berths for the children. Additional facilities include a fold-down table and hanging space. There are no WC facilities within the room, but they are located only a short distance away.

Meals and complimentary tea and coffee are included. Room size 1.6m x 2.9m

SPECIAL BEDROOM (SUPERLINER)

There is one special bedroom in each Superliner sleeping car, designed to accommodate a disabled passenger and a travelling companion. There is ample space for access by a wheelchair throughout — including the WC. The special bedroom is located on the lower level and extends the full width of the car. It contains two reclining seats which face each other during the day, with two single berths folding out of the wall for sleeping.

Bathroom facilities are located at one end of the room, separated by a curtain. Also provided: fold-down tray, attendant call button, and storage space for two suitcases. Meals are included and will be brought to the room by the car attendant if required. Room size 2.9m x 2m

LOUNGE AND BAR CARS

These cars have been designed especially for sightseeing, and have large picture windows which extend partly over the roof. They are often the point of social focus, and a meeting place for passengers. A video may be shown, or a local guide may provide commentary about the area you are passing through. Alcoholic drinks may be purchased from the bar, most of which have a 'happy hour'.

DINING CARS

A full meal service is available on all long-distance trains, and the quality can be of a very high standard, often featuring specialities of the region. Special dietary requirements can be catered for, although you are required to give 72 hours notice to **AMTRAK** by telephoning ☎ 1-800-USA-RAIL. These arrangements can only be made in the USA. Advance dinner reservations are normally taken so that the meal is ready to be served on your arrival in the dining car.

OTHER INFORMATION

Reservations: **AMTRAK** advise passengers to reserve all types of accommodation as far in advance as possible, and provide a toll-free reservations number (☎ 1-800-USA-RAIL). Reservations are mandatory on certain services shown in this guide, and for all club and sleeping car passengers.

Checked Baggage: Passengers are allowed to check in up to 150lb of baggage free of charge, provided no single item exceeds 75lb. Special items such as surf boards, scuba equipment, musical instruments etc. are normally subject to a $5 handling charge. Free assistance with baggage is provided at most major stations by Redcaps, although most expect a cash tip.

Smoking: Cigars and pipe tobacco are prohibited at all times. Cigarettes may be smoked only in private sleeping car accommodations or in specially designated areas of either the lounge or coach car. Smoking accommodation is limited and passengers are requested to vacate the area if they do not wish to smoke in order to allow access to others. Smoking is generally prohibited altogether on trains whose total journey time is less than about 6 hours.

VIA RAIL

COACH CLASS

Coaches have reclining seats, and folding trays, with WC facilities located at the end of the car. They provide a good basic standard of accommodation, with plenty of legroom and panoramic window views. There are normally four seats per row (two either side of the centre aisle).

VIA 1

VIA 1 is only available within the Quebec City – Windsor corridor. This first class travel provides wider, more comfortable reclining seats and full at-seat meal service with complimentary alcoholic beverages. VIA 1 panorama lounges are also available before boarding in Montréal, Toronto and Ottawa.

ROOMETTE

A one-person room which affords individual privacy. A seat for day travel is converted into a sleeping berth for the night, and basic bathroom facilities are also provided. A shower is situated at the end of the car, and towels, shampoo, soap etc. are available in the roomette.

BEDROOM

This accommodation is more spacious than the roomette and is designed for two adults. Seating is again converted into a berth for the night, as well as a bed which folds out from the wall. Basic WC facilities are inside the room; a shower is located at the end of the car. The same toiletries are provided as in the roomette.

SECTION

During the day a section is two couch-style seats facing each other, and at night they convert to an upper and lower berth, with a heavy-duty curtain screen for privacy. A section can be purchased separately as an upper or lower berth for one person. A washroom is available at the end of each car.

SILVER AND BLUE CLASS

This is the new level of first-class accommodation available on the route of the *Canadian*, a train which has recently been restored to its original sleek 1950's style, and conveys a unique atmosphere of train travel during that era. Passengers travel in the Park Car, which is divided into three separate areas. The Dome provides spectacular views from the observation deck; below this are the Bullet Lounge and Mural Lounge, where passengers can relax in comfortable armchairs. During the night passengers retire to one of the sleeping cars described above.

OTHER INFORMATION

Reservations: Many of VIA's principal services are heavily patronised; reservations are recommended for coach class travel, and are essential for VIA 1 and sleeping car passengers. These should be made as far in advance as possible by telephoning ☎ 1-800-561-8630 (toll free), or from outside Canada + 1 416 366 8411.

Checked Baggage: If you are travelling with heavy luggage and will not need access to it during your journey, you may use the checked baggage facility available at most stations. You may check up to 45kg per adult without any charge. You must, however, check baggage at least 30 minutes before the scheduled departure of the train. *VIA Rail* employees may refuse to lift any single article in excess of 34kg.

Smoking: *VIA Rail* does not permit smoking on any of its trains travelling wholly within the Quebec City–Windsor corridor or in any dining car. Smoking is permitted on long-distance trains in specified areas of the coach or lounge cars, and within fully-enclosed sleeping car accommodation. Smoking is banned in most stations.

BUSES

There are hundreds of bus operators in North America, but many are quite small, local companies serving a relatively compact area. Obviously vehicle types vary according to the operator, but with the vast majority of fleets, buses are comfortable and are equipped with modern conveniences, which enable you to travel round the clock. Rest stops are still made every few hours, to stretch your legs, and meal stops are scheduled as near as possible to normal dining times.

OTHER INFORMATION

Generally, reservations are not required, and you simply turn up, preferably about half an hour before the bus leaves. Many long-distance journeys involve a change (or several changes) of vehicle en route. From New York to Los Angeles for example, the bus you board in New York, although signed 'Los Angeles' will not go through all the way. Bear this in mind and make sure your luggage gets transferred onto the same bus as you at change points.

COUNTRY INFORMATION

CANADA

Passports: Required by all except nationals of France (residing in and entering from St. Pierre & Miquelon) and USA, and residents of Greenland entering from Greenland. **N.B.** British Visitor's Passports and passports issued by the All Palestine Government or by Bophuthatswana, Ciskei, Transkei or Venda are not valid for entry into Canada.

Visas: Required by all except nationals of Andorra, Antigua & Barbuda, Argentina, Australia, Bahamas, Barbados, Belgium, Belize, Bermuda, Botswana, Brunei, Cayman Is., Costa Rica, Cyprus, Denmark, Dominica, Eire, Falkland Is., Finland, France, Germany, Gibraltar, Greece, Grenada, Hong Kong, Iceland, Israel, Italy, Japan, Kenya, Kiribati, Lesotho, Liechtenstein, Luxembourg, Malawi, Malaysia, Malta, México, Monaco, Montserrat, Nauru, Netherlands, New Zealand, Nicaragua, Norway, Papua New Guinea, Paraguay, Pitcairn Is., St. Helena, St. Kitts & Nevis, St. Lucia, St. Vincent, Samoa (Western), San Marino, Saudi Arabia, Seychelles, Singapore, Solomon Is., Spain, Suriname, Swaziland, Sweden, Switzerland, Tonga, Trinidad & Tobago, Turks & Caicos Is., UK, USA, Uruguay, Vanuatu, Vatican, Venezuela, Virgin Is. (British), Zambia and Zimbabwe, or persons who are in transit through Canada on a flight which stops in Canada solely for the purpose of refuelling.

Documentation: Varies with nationality of applicant. All visitors must hold onward or return tickets.

Health: No vaccinations required. Tap water safe to drink.

Climate: Basically continental, with severe winters (especially inland and in the North) and warm summers. Rainfall can be heavy on the Pacific Coast.

Public holidays: National: ⑦; Jan. 1; July 1; Nov. 11; Dec. 25, 26 except NW Territories, Nova Scotia, Québec and Yukon); also Good Friday, Easter Monday, Victoria Day (penultimate ① in May), Labour Day (first ① in Sept.) and Thanksgiving (second ① in Oct.). Additional regional holidays: Alberta - Heritage Day*. British Columbia - British Columbia Day*. Manitoba, New Brunswick, North West Territories, Ontario, Saskatchewan - Civic Holiday*. Newfoundland - St. Patrick's Day (① prior to Mar. 18), St. George's Day (nearest ① to Apr. 24), Discovery Day (① prior to July 5), Orangeman's Day (④ prior to July 16). Québec - June 24. Yukon - Discovery Day (① prior to Aug. 22).
– First ① in Aug.

Currency: 100 Cents = 1 Canadian Dollar (CAD). 1.98 = GBP1; 1.33 = USD1.

Principal languages: English, French.

Postage abroad: Postcard or airmail letter to USA (up to 30g) 43¢; elsewhere (up to 20g) 74¢. Post boxes are red.

Standard time: Newfoundland (Island) GMT-2½ (GMT-3½ from Oct. 30); Atlantic Zone GMT-3 (GMT-4 from Oct. 30); Eastern Québec GMT-4; Eastern Zone GMT-4 (GMT-5 from Oct. 30); Western Ontario GMT-5; Central Zone GMT-5 (GMT-6 from Oct. 30); Saskatchewan GMT-6; Mountain Zone GMT-6 (GMT-7 from Oct. 30); Alberta and part of NE British Columbia GMT-7; Pacific and Yukon Zone GMT-7 (GMT-8 from Oct. 30); British Columbia around Creston and Yahk GMT-8. For extent of zones see map 1.

✔ : 110v 60Hz AC.

☎: Calgary 403, Edmonton 403, Halifax 902, Montréal 514, Niagara Falls 416, Ottawa 613, Québec 418, Toronto 416, Vancouver 604, Victoria 604, Winnipeg 204. Call boxes (internal calls and calls to USA only – colour varies with province/territory) accept 5-, 10- and 25-¢ coins.

🚗 : Own national licence required. Imported vehicles must be accompanied by the registration documents, and in the case of rented vehicles, the rental agreement or letter of authorisation from the owner. Third-party insurance compulsory. Vehicles imported from overseas must have the underside steam-cleaned or high-pressure water washed in the country of origin immediately prior to shipment.The wearing of seat belts by driver and all passengers is compulsory, except in N.W.Territories and Yukon. The use of dipped headlamps during certain hours of daylight is mandatory in some provinces and territories. Drive on the RIGHT. Speed limit 50 km/h in urban areas, 80 km/h on main roads, 100 km/h on motorways (highways).

ℹ : Tourism Canada, 235 Queen St., Ottawa, PQ, K1A 0H6. ☎(613) 954 3830. Tourism Canada offices. Police officers (blue uniform).
TCWN: Thomas Cook Group (Canada) Ltd., Scotia Plaza, 100 Yonge St., 15th Floor, Toronto. Ontario M5C 2W1. ☎ 359-3700. Fax: 359-3670.

BBC : 1100-1745 and 2100-0730 on 15260 15220 15205 15070 12095 11820 11775 9915 9740 9640 9590 9515 6175 5975 and 5965 kHz.

UNITED STATES OF AMERICA

Passports: Required by all except persons carrying valid Alien Registration Card.

Visas: Required by all except citizens of Canada, nationals of México holding US Border Crossing Cards (form I-186), nationals of Sweden arriving by air for tourism purposes, UK subjects resident in Bermuda or Canada who hold valid UK passports and, in the case of Canada, have the status of 'landed immigrants', and UK citizens who hold unexpired full British Passports and whose National Status is shown in their passport as 'British Citizen' (passports showing status 'British Subject' must be endorsed 'Holder has the right of abode in the United Kingdom' to qualify) who are travelling on holiday or business purposes for a stay in the USA for a maximum of 90 days and who hold valid non-refundable return tickets issued by a participating carrier. The foregoing also applies to British Passports issued by the Falkland Islands and Dependencies, Guernsey and Dependencies, Jersey, and the Isle of Man, but **not** to British Dependent Territories. Travellers without visas must present a completed and signed Visa Waiver Form (I-791) on entry. This form is obtainable from most travel agencies and all participating carriers.

Documentation: 1 photograph for visa.

Health: No mandatory requirements. Tap water safe to drink.

Climate: Varies greatly throughout the country with cold winters (severe inland) and warm (hot and humid in North East) summers in the North, mild wet winters and hot humid summers in the South East and mild winters and hot dry summers in the South West.

Public holidays: ⑦; Jan. 1; July 4; Nov. 11; Dec. 25; also Martin Luther King's Birthday (third ① in Jan.), Washington's Birthday (third ① in Feb.), Memorial Day (last ① in May), Labor Day (first ① in Sept.), Columbus Day (second ① in Oct.), and Thanksgiving Day (fourth ④ in Nov.); these apply to all states and territories. A large number of additional holidays are observed in various states and cities, especially Lincoln's Birthday (Feb. 12), which is widely observed in the North and largely ignored in the South.

Currency: 100 Cents = 1 US Dollar (USD). 1.49 = GBP1.

Principal language: English.

Postage abroad: Postcard ❖. Airmail letter ❖. Post boxes are blue.

Standard time: Eastern Zone GMT-4 (GMT-5 from Oct. 30); Indiana GMT-5; Central Zone GMT-5 (GMT-6 from Oct. 30); Mountain Zone GMT-6 (GMT-7 from Oct. 30); Arizona GMT-7; Pacific Zone GMT-7 (GMT-8 from Oct. 30); Alaska (Mainland and Eastern Aleutian Islands) GMT-8 (GMT-9 from Oct. 30); Alaska (Western Aleutian Islands) GMT-9 (GMT-10 from Oct. 30); Hawaii GMT-10. For extent of zones see Map 1.

✔ : 110-120v 60Hz AC.

☎: Boston 617, Chicago 312, Fort Lauderdale 305, Honolulu 808, Los Angeles 213, Miami 305, New Orleans 504, New York City (Manhattan and Bronx) 212, Richmond (VA) 804, San Diego 619, San Francisco 415, Tampa 813, Washington (DC) 202. Call boxes are blue. 5- 10- and 25¢ coins accepted.

🚗 : International Permit or own national licence valid. Drive on the RIGHT. Speed limit 88 km/h.

ℹ : US Travel & Tourism Administration. Police officers (black uniform). TCWN: Thomas Cook Travel, 100 Cambridge Park Drive, P.O.Box 9104, Cambridge MA 02140. ☎(617) 354-5060. Fax: (617) 349-1097.

BBC : 1100-1745 and 2100-0730 on 15260 15220 15205 15070 12095 11820 11775 9915 9740 9640 9590 9515 6175 5975 and 5965 kHz.

KEY TO SYMBOLS ON THIS PAGE

✔ = **Electricity supply.** (v = Voltage; Hz = Hertz [cycles]).

☎ = **Telephones.** Principal area codes.

🚗 = **Driving.** Documentation required to drive a car. Principal maximum speed limits in kilometres per hour (km/h). (To convert to miles per hour use the conversion table on page 60).

ℹ = **Tourist assistance and information.** National tourist board network. Main offices of the Thomas Cook Worldwide Network (TCWN); other office addresses and telephone numbers can be obtained by calling the main office, or a full list is available from Operational Integrity Procedures, Thomas Cook Group Ltd., P.O.Box 36, Peterborough PE3 6SB, U.K.

BBC = **BBC World Service.** Details of times and frequencies of BBC World Service Radio Broadcasts in English. Times are given in GMT; frequencies in kHz. It should be noted that although we show all frequencies used, broadcasts are generally only transmitted on selected frequencies at any given time. Full details can be obtained by writing to BBC World Service, P.O. Box 76, Bush House, Strand, LONDON WC2B 4PH, England.

GATEWAY AIRPORTS

This section contains details of the main airports through which most visitors to Canada and the USA arrive, and also includes some of the main hubs for onward connections or for separate internal flights.

BOSTON

Logan International Airport,
East Boston, Massachusetts, USA

Situation: 4.8km/3 miles north-east of Boston
Airport Code: BOS
Time zone: GMT-5 (GMT-4 Apr–Sept)
Telephone number: (617) 567-1830
Telefax number: (617) 567-1830

AIRPORT AND TOURIST INFORMATION
The information booth at Terminal A is open 0730–2300, Terminal C 0730–2300, Terminal E 1000–2100 or the last flight arrival.

BANKS AND BUREAUX DE CHANGE
There are automatic cashpoint machines at the airport access road and at Terminals A, B, C, and E. In Terminal C there is a foreign currency exchange office open daily 0800–1900 and in Terminal E 0800④ (1130⑥⑦) –2130. Full-service banking facilities are located in Terminal E, open 0900④ (1130⑥) –1500.

FACILITIES FOR DISABLED TRAVELLERS
Restrooms, lifts, amplified telephones, ramps. A free service between airport terminals is provided for handicapped people. ☎561 1770. Available daily 0730–2300.

LOST PROPERTY & LEFT LUGGAGE
Lockers are located beyond security in Terminals B, C and E and are open 24 hours. Charge per day: US$0.75. The baggage offices of individual airlines also provide left luggage facilities.

CATERING FACILITIES
There are cafeteria facilities on the upper levels of all terminals. Terminal A also has a cocktail lounge, Terminal B an à la carte restaurant, Terminal C a seafood restaurant and ice cream shop and Terminal E a bar and grill, ice cream shop and the *Port of Boston* restaurant.

POST OFFICE
The airport mail facility is open 0800–2400④, 0800–1700⑥ and 1000–1400⑦.

SHOPS & DUTY-FREE FACILITIES
Shopping facilities can be found on the upper levels of all terminals. All contain news and gift shops; additionally wines and spirits, fragrances and cosmetics, tobacco, luxury and sundry goods and also a stamp machine are available in Terminal B; bookshops, news, gifts and all standard duty-free items are available in terminals C and E.

AIRLINE REPRESENTATION
Terminal A: *Continental, Continental Express, Trump Shuttle.* Terminal B: *American, American Eagle, America West, Cape Air, HubExpress, Midway, Midwest Express, Mohawk Airlines, Qantas, Sabena* (departures only), *USAir, Virgin Atlantic.*
Terminal C: *Delta Airlines, Skymaster, TWA* (except international arrivals), *United.*
Terminal D: Charter flights. (May also operate to/from other terminals.)
Terminal E: *Aer Lingus, Air Alliance, Air Atlantic, Air Canada, Air France, Air Nova, Alitalia, British Airways, El Al, Lufthansa, Northeast Express, Northwest, Sabena* (international arrivals only), *Swissair, TAP Air Portugal, TWA* (international arrivals only).

PUBLIC TRANSPORT
Within the Airport: *MBTA (Massachusetts Bay Transportation Authority)* operates free shuttle bus **11** which connects all terminals.

To Downtown Boston: *Airport Water Shuttle* operates Logan Airport Dock to Downtown Boston (Rowes Wharf). 0600–2000 every 15 mins.④; 1200–2000 every 30 mins.†; no service on ⑥, July 4, Thanksgiving, Christmas or New Year's Day. Journey 7 mins (plus max. 9 mins. shuttle bus); fare US$8 (including bus) *MBTA* free shuttle bus (**22** from Terminals A and B, **33** from Terminals C, D and E) available to metro station for *MBTA* Blue Line Metro to downtown 0530–0030 every 10 mins. journey (inc. bus) 20–30 mins; fare US$ 0.85. Taxis available from all terminals 24 hours per day; journey time to downtown 15–20 mins.; fare US$ 12.00–15.00 plus 0.50 airport surcharge
To Boston Suburbs: Bus lines **116, 117, 120, 121** run to out of town suburban destinations. Available 0515–2400, every 10☆/12⑦ mins. Fare US$0.75; three-, five- and seven-day visitors passes available at station. *Logan Express Bus* to Framingham (Western suburbs) and Braintree (South Shore) at 30 min intervals peak travel times, hourly off-peak. Other motorcoach and transportation services available. For information, free (in Boston area only) telephone 1-800-23 LOGAN.

CHICAGO

Chicago O'Hare International Airport,
PO Box 66142, Chicago, Illinois 60666, USA

Situation: 27 km/16 miles north-west of the city centre.
Airport Code: CHI/ORD
Time Zone: GMT-6 (-5 Apr–Sept)
Telephone Number: (312) 686-2200
Flight enquiries: contact specific airlines
Telefax number: (312) 686-4980

AIRPORT & TOURIST INFORMATION
Airport information desks are located in all terminals and are staffed by multi-lingual representatives; open 0800–2000 daily ☎686-2304.
Airport tourism booths are situated on the lower levels of all domestic terminals and in Terminal 4; ☎686-7965.

BANKS & BUREAUX DE CHANGE
A foreign currency exchange is sited in the lower level of Terminal 4; open 1000 (0800⑤⑥)–2000 daily.
Automatic cash dispensers are available in Terminals 1, 2 and 3.

FACILITIES FOR DISABLED TRAVELLERS

Special telephones (TDD) for the hearing-impaired persons; restrooms, catering facilities and telephones are accessible to wheelchairs and all levels of the terminal buildings as well as the rapid transit station can be accessed by lift (elevator).

LOST PROPERTY & LEFT LUGGAGA

The lost property office is staffed 24 hours per day; ☎ 686-2201. There are left luggage lockers in Terminals 2, 3 and 4.

CATERING FACILITIES

The airport has snack bars, food malls, cocktail lounges and restaurants in the concourses on the airside of the terminals. In the Rotunda Building (between Terminals 2 and 3) and in the Carson's Building. There is an international restaurant and cocktail lounge on the landside of Terminal 4.

POST OFFICE

Located in Terminal 2 and open 0700–1900ⓐ.

SHOPS & DUTY-FREE FACILITIES

Duty-free shops are in the Departures area of Terminal 4. Satellite duty-free shop is located in Terminal 3. Other shops are to be found on the airside upper levels of Terminals 1, 2 and 3 and on the ground level of Terminal 4.

AIRLINE REPRESENTATION

Terminals 1, 2 and 3 (domestic): *American Airlines, American Eagle, American Trans Air, Continental Airlines, Continental Express, Delta, Great Lakes Aviation, Northwest, TWA, United Airlines, USAir, United Express.*
Terminal 4 (International): *Air Canada, Air France, ALIA Royal Jordanian, Alitalia, British Airways, El Al, Ecuatoriana, Iberia, JAT, KLM, Korean Air, LOT Polish Airlines, Lufthansa, Mexicana, Philippine Airlines, Sabena, SAS, Swissair.*

PUBLIC TRANSPORT

Taxis are available from 0600 to 0100. Journey time to downtown Chicago approx. 40–50 mins.; fare US$18 – US$22 (shared-ride rate US$12).

Chicago Transit Authority operate rail services (O'Hare Rapid Transit) between O'Hare Airport and downtown Chicago 24 hours per day. Service interval 0100–0500 every 30 mins.; 0500–0100 every 5–10 mins. Journey time to downtown Chicago (Dearborn Street) approx. 35 mins.; fare US$1.25. O'Hare Station is located under Terminal 4 and is reached by pedestrian tunnels/moving walkways from the lower levels of Terminals 1, 2 and 3 and from the lobby of Terminal 4.

Airport–City Bus Service. There are frequent bus services between the airport and downtown Chicago, the city suburbs and to and from city hotels. Airport–downtown journey time approx. 50-60 mins. but longer during weekday rush hour periods; fare approx. US$10.50.

Continental Air Transport run an Airport Express service connecting O'Hare with a number of city hotels. Information is available on ☎ 454-7800, 454-7799. Journey time to hotels in downtown Chicago averages 45 mins.; fare US$12.50.

There are a number of direct suburban and regional bus services operating from the Rotunda Bus Terminal including those run by *Continental, Greyhound, Indian Trails, Pace, Peoria-Rockford, Swallow Shuttle, Tri State* and *United Limo.* Among places served are Dekalb, Elkhart, Evanston, Gary, Hammond, Indianapolis, Joliet, Kalamazoo, Kenosha,

LOS ANGELES

Los Angeles International Airport,
PO Box 92216, Los Angeles, CA 90009–2216, USA

Situation: 27 km/17 miles south-west of downtown Los Angeles
Airport Code: LAX
Time Zone: GMT-8 (GMT-7 Apr–Sept)
Telephone Number: (213) 646 5252
Telefax number: (213) 646 0523, 646 1894
Telex: 653413

AIRPORT & TOURIST INFORMATION

There is an information centre at the International (Tom Bradley) Terminal as well as information display telephones. Tourist information is available on ☎ 689 8822 between 0830 and 1700.

BANKS & BUREAUX DE CHANGE

Currency exchange facilities are available in all terminals serving international flights and there are automatic cashpoint machines.

FACILITIES FOR DISABLED TRAVELLERS

Ramps, lifts, special toilets, telephone booths and restaurant facilities which accommodate wheelchairs, telecommunication devices for the hard of hearing and for those with speech impairments – ☎ 417 0439 for information. Restrooms equipped for the disabled can be found on the Departures levels of Terminals 2 and 6. Free shuttle service for disabled persons in wheelchairs between parking lot C and the terminals; a number of shuttle buses running between the terminals and 'remote' car parks are fitted with lifts accessible to persons in wheelchairs.

LOST PROPERTY & LEFT LUGGAGE

Airport Police (☎ 417 0440) handle all items of lost property with the exception of luggage.
Left luggage lockers can be hired at the International Terminal and at business centres in Terminals 1, 4 and 7.

CATERING FACILITIES

Cafeterias and bars can be found in all terminals. The main restaurant is the *California Place Restaurant and Theme Room* at the Theme Building which is open 1100–2200✕, 1000–1430 and 1700–2200⑦.

POST OFFICE

The post office in the International Terminal is open 0900–1700 daily.

SHOPS & DUTY–FREE FACILITIES

A great variety of goods and food can be purchased from the 20 gift shops and 7 duty-free shops at the airport's nine terminals, including tobacco, cigarettes & lighters, wines & spirits, cosmetics, watches and jewellery, writing equipment, souvenirs, clothing and electronic items.

AIRLINE REPRESENTATION

Airlines operate as follows from the nine terminals.
International (Tom Bradley) Terminal: *Aero California, Aerolineas Argentinas, Aeromexico, Aeroquetzal, Air France, Air LA* (arrivals), *Air New Zealand, Alitalia, American Trans Air, All Nippon Airways, Aviateca, Britannia, British Airways, Canadian Airlines International, Cathay Pacific, China Airlines, Ecuatoriana, Egyptair, El Al, Finnair, Garuda Indonesia, Iberia, Japan Airlines, JAT, KLM, Korean Air, LACSA, Lan Chile, LTU, Lufthansa, Malaysia Airlines, Mexicana, Nationair Canada, Philippine Airlines, Qantas, SAS, Singapore Airlines, Swissair, TACA, Thai Airways International, UTA, Varig, Virgin Atlantic* (arrivals).
Terminal 1: *America West, Southwest, USAir* and *USAir Express (StatesWest).*

Terminal 2: *Air Canada*, *Air China*, *Avianca*, *Hawaiian Air*, *LOT Polish Airlines*, *Northwest*.
Terminal 3: *Alaska Airlines*, *Midway*, *Midwest Express*, *TWA*.
Terminal 4: *American Airlines* and *American Eagle*.
Terminal 5: *Delta*.
Terminal 6: *Continental, Skywest (Delta Connection)*.
Terminal 7: *United* and *United Express*, *Virgin Atlantic* (departures).
Imperial Terminal: *Air LA* (departures), *Alpha*, *Grand*, *MGM Grand Air*, *Pacific Coast*.
There is also a Heliport operating from Parking Structure 4 from which Helitrans and L.A. Helicopter operate.

PUBLIC TRANSPORT

Taxis to downtown Los Angeles and the surrounding areas are freely available with fares dependent on the distance travelled – approx. US$26 to downtown LA.

Ground transportation information desks are situated outside the baggage reclaim area of each terminal and are open 0800 to 2400 daily. A free LAX Shuttle service operates between the various terminals.

A Super Shuttle service links the airport with Los Angeles Union Station.

Southern California Rapid Transit District operate bus services calling at the airport and serving the city and surrounding region. The airport–city centre fare is US$1.15 and the journey takes approx. 1 hour.

MIAMI

Miami International Airport,
PO Box 592075, Miami, Florida 33159, USA

Situation: 8 km/5 miles north-west of the city
Airport Code: MIA
Time zone: GMT-5 (GMT-4 Apr–Sept)
Telephone Number: (305) 876-7000
Telefax number: (305) 876-0819

AIRPORT & TOURIST INFORMATION

The airport information center is situated at Departures Level, Concourse E and is open 0630–2230 – ☎876-7579.
There are courtesy information phones sited throughout the terminal.

BANKS & BUREAUX DE CHANGE

Barnett Bank on Concourse C (Departures Level) operates a full banking service during normal business hours (①–⑤). There are five currency exchange locations throughout the terminal; the Concourse E *Bank America* outlet is open 24 hours per day.

FACILITIES FOR DISABLED TRAVELLERS

Restrooms equipped for disabled persons; automatic doors, ramps and lifts; accessible telephones and water fountains; phones for the hard-of-hearing (at the central information counter on Concourse E and passenger service center at Concourse C); accommodation for disabled persons available at the hotel located at the terminal complex.

LOST PROPERTY & LEFT LUGGAGE

The airport lost and found office is at the Departures Level of Concourse E and is open 1000–1800 daily.
Left luggage rooms are sited at the Departures Level of Concourse B and Arrivals Level of Concourse G; left luggage lockers can be found throughout the terminal complex and offer 24-hour storage.

CATERING FACILITIES

Snack bars, restaurants, coffee shops and bars available throughout the terminal complex and passenger concourses.

Top of the Port Restaurant and Lounge on the 7th and 8th floors (Miami International Airport Hotel) is open 0700–2300 daily. The pharmacy at Concourses D and F are open 24 hours a day for food and beverages.

POST OFFICE

Located at Concourse B, Arrivals Level and open 0830–2100④ and 0930–1300⑥. Postal boxes throughout the terminal; postage stamps can be purchased at most gift shops and at the passenger service center on Concourse C.

SHOPS & DUTY–FREE FACILITIES

Shops sell a variety of goods, including toys, gifts, souvenirs and speciality items. 12 duty-free shops stock perfume and cosmetics, wines and spirits, cigarettes and tobacco goods, watches and jewellery, electronic equipment, clothes and leather goods, lighters, pens and writing equipment, confectionery and gourmet food.

AIRLINE REPRESENTATION

One terminal serves all international and domestic US flights.

PUBLIC TRANSPORT

Taxi journey to downtown Miami takes approx. 15 mins.; fare US$13.20. Other sample taxi fares: to Miami Springs and Miracle Mile US$8.40, to Seaport US$14, to Miami Beach (Lincoln Road) US$18, to Key Biscayne US$24, to Fort Lauderdale US$45. An Airport Region Taxi Service operates on a two-zone system to hotels and destinations near the airport. Zone A flat-rate fare is US$5 and Zone B US$8.

Metro-Dade Transit operate local bus services to downtown Miami, South Miami, Miami Springs, Miami Beach, Hialeah and Coral Gables.

Metrobus route 7 to downtown Miami operates 20④/14⑥ journeys per day. Journey time is approx. 25 mins.; fare US$1.25. The service also calls at Miami Springs.

Route 37 connects the airport with Hialeah, Coral Gables and South Miami; Route 42 calls at Coral Gables Bus Terminal, Douglas Road Metrorail Station and Opa–Locka; Route J links the airport with Miami Beach and Coral Gables Bus Terminal calling at Douglas Road & Allapattah Metrorail stations.

A *Tri–Rail* Shuttle bus service connects the airport with Miami Airport Tri-Rail station and from here with Hialeah Metro Rail, Fort Lauderdale Airport, Fort Lauderdale, Palm Beach Airport and West Palm Beach stations.

MONTRÉAL

Montréal–Mirabel Airport,
PO Box 1000, Mirabel, Quebec, Canada

Situation: 53 km/33 miles north-west of Montréal
Airport Code: YMQ–YMX
Time zone: GMT-5 (GMT-4 Apr–Oct)
Telephone Number: (514) 476–2875; 1–800–465–1213 (within Canada)
Flight enquiries: (514) 476–3010; (514) 633–3105 for Dorval International Airport
Telefax number: (514) 476–3178
Telex: 05–822544

AIRPORT & TOURIST INFORMATION

Transport Canada traveller's information desk is located in the arrivals zone on the main level of the terminal ☎ 476-3010. *INFO Tourisme Montréal* are on ☎476-9734.

BANKS & BUREAUX DE CHANGE

National Bank, open 24 hours a day, operate an automatic cash dispenser. *Banque d'Amerique* is open for all international flights. *Thomas Cook* have four bureaux de change desks located around the airport ☎636 3582.

FACILITIES FOR DISABLED TRAVELLERS

Lifts, mobile ramps, level surfaces and wide door clearances, wheelchair-accessible washrooms, toilets, telephones and drinking fountains, telephones for those with impaired hearing.

LOST PROPERTY AND LEFT LUGGAGE

The lost property office is open 0800–2300, ☎476–3086. Left luggage facilities open 24 hours per day.

CATERING FACILITIES

Restaurant is open 1200–2300 and the cafeteria 24 hours daily.

Snack bars/coffee shop open 0530–2300. Most of the bars are open all hours excepting the period 2300–0300/0500. Catering facilities are situated on the main and mezzanine levels.

POST OFFICE

No post office at the airport; postage stamps available at the insurance counter 1400–2400.

SHOPS & DUTY–FREE FACILITIES

Shops sited in the mezzanine and waiting areas sell souvenirs, toys, arts and crafts, newspapers and books, pharmaceutical items, cigarettes and tobacco goods etc.; there is a beauty salon and a dry cleaners.

AIRLINE REPRESENTATION

There is only one terminal from which all international flights depart. Canadian and American Domestic flights use Montreal Dorval Airport.

PUBLIC TRANSPORT

Taxi journey time to downtown Montréal is 20–25 mins.; approx. fare C$56; to Dorval Airport C$53 (fares include tax).

Aeroplus provides a bus service between the airport and downtown Montréal, calling in Montréal at Central Station (corner of Lagauchetière and University) and the *Voyageur* bus terminal (505 de Maisonneuve Blvd. East), with stops at major hotels en route. Departures (approx.) from airport at 0000, 0100, 0400, 0600, 0800, 0900, 1000, 1100, 1200; then every 30 mins. to 2000; 2100, 2200, 2300. Journey time approx. 45 mins.; fare C$12.25.

Aeroplus also operate a service 0900-2320 between Mirabel and Dorval airports. Service interval every 20 mins.; journey time 35 mins.; fare C$10.25. (This service is free to in-transit passengers with less than 7 hours between connections).

Aerocar and *Voyageur* run a bus service between the airport and Ottawa; journey approx. 2 hours; fare *(Voyageur)* C$15; fare *(Aerocar)* C$23.50 (door-to-door service available).

NEW ORLEANS

New Orleans International Airport, PO Box 20007,
New Orleans, Louisiana 70141, USA

Situation: 16 km/10 miles west of New Orleans
Airport Code: MSY
Time zone: GMT-6 (GMT-5 Apr–Sept)
Telephone Number: (504) 464-0831
Telefax number: (504) 465-1264

AIRPORT & TOURIST INFORMATION

Travel & Tourism Administration Gateway Receptionist desks in the West Lobby ☎464-2752, and the East Lobby ☎465-8852 – both open 0800–2100 daily. Tourist information desk of the Greater New Orleans Tourist and Convention Commission is located on the lower level of the terminal near baggage reclaim ☎ 467-9276. There are multi-lingual receptionists at all the above desks.

BANKS & BUREAUX DE CHANGE

Whitney National Bank is sited in the ticket counter lobby area and offer all normal banking facilities including automatic cash dispensers; open 0830–1530①–④; 0830–1730⑥. Currency exchange facilities are also offered by *Mutual of Omaha* Business Service Center (open 0600–1900 daily) and *American Express* have cash/travellers cheques dispensers; all these facilities are situated in the West lobby.

FACILITIES FOR DISABLED TRAVELLERS

All toilets/restrooms are adapted for handicapped persons. Telephone Display Device is located at the tourist information desk near the car rental desks. Sky Caps are available with wheelchairs. Ramps and lifts conveniently placed for disabled persons, parking spaces in the parking garage. Guide dogs are allowed free access throughout the terminal.

LOST PROPERTY & LEFT LUGGAGE

Lost Property Office can be found on the lower level of the West lobby of the terminal in the Airport Operations Office; open 24 hours a day. ☎464-2671, 464-3500 Left luggage lockers are sited on all four concourses ☎ 464-2672

CATERING FACILITIES

In the West lobby of the terminal there is a 24-hour snack bar, the *Coffee House* self-service restaurant and *Coffee & Beignet Shop* open 0600–1900, *Mardi Gras Lounge/Oyster Bar* open 1030–2000/2100, the *Grove Natural Snack Shop* open 0800–2000/2130 and the *Haagen Dazs* ice cream and confectionery shop. In the East lobby there is the *French Quarter* fast food cafe and bar open 1000–2230, *Pizza Perfecto* open 0830–2030 and further branches of *Haagen Dazs/Cookie Time* and *Grove Natural Snack Shop*. Other facilities include **Croissant Bakery Cart**, mobile carts with complete beverage service and snack/liquor bars, generally open early morning to mid-evening.

POST OFFICE

Located in the ticket counter lobby area and open 0830–1630 Ⓐ. There are posting boxes and a postage stamp machine in the East lobby near the water fountain.

SHOPS & DUTY–FREE FACILITIES

Shops at the airport sell a variety of goods including chocolate, confectionery and foodstuffs, newspapers, magazines and books, gifts, souvenirs and local arts & crafts, toys. There is a Louisiana State Tax Free Refund Center where refunds of state and local sales taxes can be received by international visitors.

AIRLINE REPRESENTATION

Concourse A: **American Airlines**, **Northwest** and **USAir**.

Concourse B: **American**, **Continental**, **Midway**, **Southwest** and **TWA**.
Concourse C: **Aeromexico**, **Aviateca**, Central American airlines, **LACSA**, **Sahsa**, **Taca International** and **United**.
Concourse D: **Delta** and **L'Express**.
General Aviation, **Ground Services Inc.** and **Transit Aviation** are ground handling agents for charter flights. **Ground Services Inc.** are also agents for several Central American airlines and **Continental** for **Aviateca**, **Midway** and **TWA**.

PUBLIC TRANSPORT

Taxi journey to the central business district of New Orleans takes approx. 25–30 mins.; fare US$21 for up to 3 persons, US$8 per person for 4 or more passengers.

Jefferson Transit/Louisiana Transit Authority operate airport bus services. The Airlines Highway bus runs approx. every 15–20 mins. on Ⓐ; every 30 mins. on Ⓒ. Journey time is about 45

NEW YORK: JOHN F. KENNEDY

John F. Kennedy International Airport, Jamaica, NY, 11430, USA.

Situation: 24km/14 miles south-east of New York City
Airport Code: NYC
Time zone: GMT-5 (GMT-4 Apr–Sept)
Telephone Number: (718) 656-4520
Flight enquiries: (718) 656-4520
Telefax number: (212) 466-7467

AIRPORT & TOURIST INFORMATION

A centrally located information counter staffed by multi-lingual personnel is on the first floor of the main lobby of the International Arrivals Building, ☎ 656-7990. Information desks can also be found in most other terminals. For general information, ☎656-4520.

BANKS & BUREAUX DE CHANGE

Foreign currency exchanges, cash point machines and banks can be found at Kennedy International in every terminal. **Thomas Cook** bureaux de change offices are located throughout the airport ☎656 8444.

FACILITIES FOR DISABLED TRAVELLERS

Reserved parking spaces, Autolink (an on-demand transportation service), lifts, restrooms, telephones

LOST PROPERTY & LEFT LUGGAGE

Left luggage facilities are located in Terminal 1A 0700–2300 and United Terminal 0700–2200. At the International Arrivals Building there are two baggage storage areas to be found on the second level in both the East and West wings, open 0700–2200. For lost property ☎(718) 656-4120.

CATERING FACILITIES

Cafeterias, cocktail bars and coffee shops are available in all terminals. Restaurants are also located throughout except in the United Airlines Terminal.

POST OFFICE

Post boxes and stamp vending machines are to be found in all airline terminals. There is a post office in the Air Mail Facility, Building 250 on North Boundary Road in the cargo area ☎ 917-1438.

SHOPS & DUTY-FREE FACILITIES

Duty-free shops selling wine and spirits, fragrances and cosmetics, tobacco goods, luxury and sundry goods can be found in every terminal as can newsstands. There are gourmet shops located throughout except in Terminal Three, Terminal 1A and the TWA International Terminal A.

AIRLINE REPRESENTATION

International Arrivals Building: **Aer Lingus**, **Aerolineas Argentinas**, **Air Afrique**, **Air Europa**, **Air France**, **Air India**, **Air Jamaica**, **Alitalia**, **American Transair**, **Austrian Airlines**, **Avensa** (arrivals), **Balair**, **Cayman**, **Condor**, **Dominicana**, **Egyptair**, **El Al**, **Guyana**, **Iberia**, **Icelandair**, **Japan Airlines**, **JAT Yugoslav**, **Key**, **KLM**, **Korean**, **Kuwait Air**, **Lacsa**, **Ladeco**, **Lan Chile**, **Latur**, **LOT Polish**, **LTU**, **Lufthansa**, **Mexicana**, **Nigeria**, **North American**, **Olympic**, **PIA Pakistan International Airlines**, **Royal Air Maroc**, **Royal Jordanian**, **Sabena**, **South African Airways**, **Spanair**, **Surinam**, **Swissair**, **TACA**, **TAESA**, **TAP**, **Turkish Air**, **Varig**, **Virgin Atlantic**.
American Airlines Terminal: **American Airlines**, **American Eagle**, **Ecuatoriana**, **Finnair**.
Terminal One: **America West**, **American Transair** (departures), **Avensa** (departures), **Key**, **Ladeco**, **MGM Grand Air**, **North American**, **Surinam**, **Tower**.
Terminal 1A: **Carnival Airlines**, **Saudia**, **Tarom** (departures).
Terminal Three: **American Airlines**, **American Eagle**, **American Transair**, **Northwest**.
TWA International Terminal A: **Ecuatoriana**, **NY Helicopter**, **TWA**, **TW Express**.
British Airways Terminal: **British Airways**.
Delta Terminal: **Aeroflot**, **All Nippon**, **Air China**, **Czechoslovak Airlines**, **Delta**, **JES Air**, **Malev Hungarian**, **Tarom** (arrivals).

PUBLIC TRANSPORT

To all destinations: Taxis are available at each terminal. Use authorised yellow cabs only. Fares between the airport terminals range from about US$2–$6. Journey time to LaGuardia Airport about 30 mins., fare US$16–$20; to mid-Manhattan about 45 mins, fare US$25–$30 plus tolls. (There is a surcharge of 50 cents per trip between 2000 and 0600 and all day on ⑦). To Newark International Airport 1¼ hours, fare approx. US$50–$55. Uniformed taxi dispatchers are on duty at the International Arrivals building and other Central Terminal Area buildings during normal peak travel hours to provide multilingual taxi information. For taxi lost and found information ☎ 212 221-TAXI.

Within the Airport: The Port Authority operates an Airline Connection bus between the nine air terminals. Service runs 24 hours per day; frequency every 5-15 mins. Journey time 5-30 mins. (depending on terminals); free service.

To other airports – direct links: (connections also possible by transferring in Manhattan – see under each airport heading for details to/from Manhattan).
La Guardia: Carey (☎ (718) 632-0500/9) operate a scheduled bus service 0530-2300 every 30 mins. Journey time 30-45 mins. Fare: US$11.
Newark International: Princeton Airporter (☎(609) 587-6600) operate a frequent service 0700–1900. Journey time 60–75 mins. Fare US$19.

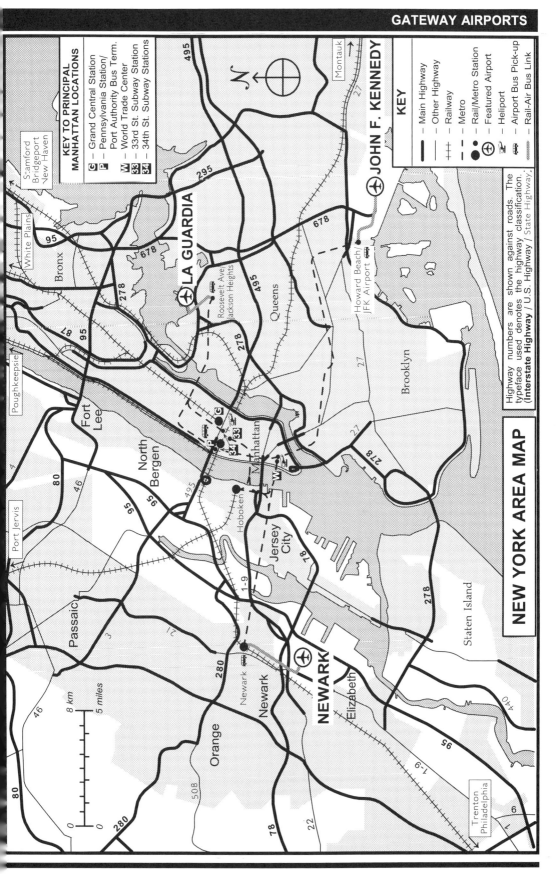

NEW YORK AREA MAP

KEY TO PRINCIPAL MANHATTAN LOCATIONS

- **G** – Grand Central Station
- **P** – Pennsylvania Station/ Port Authority Bus Term.
- **W** – World Trade Center
- **33** – 33rd St. Subway Station
- **34** – 34th St. Subway Stations

KEY

- ▬ – Main Highway
- ▬ – Other Highway
- ╫ – Railway
- ┉ – Metro
- ● – Rail/Metro Station
- ✈ – Featured Airport
- ⬡ – Heliport
- 🚌 – Airport Bus Pick-up
- ∿ – Rail-Air Bus Link

Highway numbers are shown against roads. The typeface used denotes the highway classification. (**Interstate Highway** / U.S. Highway / State Highway).

JOHN F. KENNEDY

LA GUARDIA

NEWARK

To New York City (Manhattan): *New York Helicopter* (☎ 1-800 645-3494) operates frequent flights throughout the day (every 30 mins. in afternoon) from TWA International Terminal/Gate 37 to East 34th Street Heliport. Journey time 15-20 mins.; fare US$62 (reduced rates available for connections with some airlines; group rates also available). *Carey Airport Express* (☎ (718) 632-0500/9) operates from all JFK terminals 0600-0000 every 30 mins. to Grand Central Terminal/Park Ave. and the Port Authority Bus Terminal. Journey time approx. 45–65 mins.; fare US$9.50. A shuttle bus service to the New York Hilton, Sheraton City Squire, Marriott Marquis and the Holiday Inn Crowne Plaza is available from Park Avenue 0715–2215 daily, every 20 mins.; inclusive fare from Airport US$11. *Gray Line Air Shuttle* (☎ (212) 757-6840) operates on demand 0800-2300 to anywhere between 23rd and 63rd Streets. Journey time 40-60 mins; fare US$14. *Carey Transportation* (☎ (718) 632-0500/9) operate a shuttle bus 0530-2300 every 30 mins. to connect with *Long Island Railroad* (☎ (718) 217-5477) trains to Penn station. Journey time (total) 60-70 mins; fare (bus) US$5, (rail) US$3–US$4.25. *NYC Subway* (☎ (718) 330-1234) to Manhattan or Brooklyn can be accessed by taking the brown and white long-term parking lot bus (which departs every 15 mins. from all terminals) to Howard Beach Station, then by the 'A' train from there. Journey time approx. 60–75 mins. from JFK to mid-Manhattan; fare: (bus) free, (subway) US$1.15. (Passengers travelling by subway **to** JFK should ensure that they board the 'A' train destined for Far Rockaway, and alight at Howard Beach).

To New York City Suburbs: *Q10/Green Bus Lines* (☎ (718) 995-4700) operates a local service to Queens (Lefferts Blvd. and Kew Gardens) for connections with *NYC Subway* system. Fare US$1.15 (exact change required). *Q3/N.Y.C.T.A.* (☎ (718) 330-1234) operates a local service to Queens (169th St.

and Hillside Ave.) for connections with *NYC Subway* system (F and R trains), other local bus services along its route, and *Long Island Rail Road* (Hollis or Locust Manor Stations). Fare: US$1.15 (exact change required). *Carey Transportation* (☎ (718) 632-0500/9) to Queens every 30 mins. 0530–2300 stopping at *Long Island Rail Road* Jamaica Station, Sutphin Blvd, and Archer Avenue. Journey time approx. 20 mins; fare US$5. To Brooklyn: every 60 mins. 0830–2030 calling at Ashland and Hanson Place near the Williamsburg Bank. Journey time approx. 30 mins; fare US$9.50.

To Long Island: *Carey Transportation* (☎ (718) 632-0500/9) operate a shuttle bus 0530-2300 every 30 mins. to connect with *Long Island Railroad* (☎ (718) 217-5477).

To Upstate New York, Pennsylvania, New Jersey, Connecticut – direct links:- *Trans-Bridge Lines* (☎ (215) 868-6001) operate services to West Allentown, Easton, Bethlehem and Allentown. Departures from JFK (International Arrivals Building – Gate B) at 1230, 1440, 1740 and 2040; from Allentown at 0730, 1030, 1330 and 1530. Journey time 4 hours. Fare: US$20.75. *Princeton Airporter* (☎ (609) 587-6600) operate a scheduled service to Middlesex, Morris and Mercer Counties. Fares range from $24 to $27.

Connections:- *Carey Airport Express* to Manhattan, then; *AMTRAK* (☎ (212) 582 6875) or *Metro North Commuter Railroad* (☎ (212) 532-4900) for rail services from Grand Central Station to destinations in Connecticut, Westchester and Upstate New York; *Port Authority Bus Terminal* (☎ (212) 564-8484) for details of bus services to destinations in New Jersey, Upstate New York and Pennsylvania.

NEW YORK: LA GUARDIA

New York (La Guardia) Airport,
Flushing, NY 11371, USA

Situation: 13km/8 miles north-east of New York City
Airport Code: LGA
Time zone: GMT-5 (GMT-4 Apr–Sept)
Telephone number: (718) 476-5000
Flight enquiries: (718) 656-4520
Telefax number: (718) 476-5029
Telex: 424747 PANYNJ

AIRPORT & TOURIST INFORMATION

The 'AppleAide' information desk, staffed by volunteers, is centrally located in the departures level of the Main Terminal. Open 0900–2000①–③ and ⑤; 0900–1700④ and 1400–1800⑦. Airport staff at the Manager's office 0900–1700①–⑤ (☎ 476-5000) and at the Operations office 24 hours per day (☎ 476-5072) are available to answer questions about the Airport.

BANKS & BUREAUX DE CHANGE

Foreign Currency exchange offices, automatic cash dispensers and banks are located throughout the main Terminal and departure hall.

FACILITIES FOR DISABLED TRAVELLERS

Wheelchairs, special restrooms, parking facilities, telephones, elevators, controlled access roadway.

LOST PROPERTY & LEFT LUGGAGE

Lost and Found office is at the Airport's Port Authority Police Headquarters ☎ 476-5115. Baggage can be stored at *Mutual of Omaha* travel insurance counters, located on the second

floor of the Main Terminal and the Delta Terminal building Open 0600–2000⑥; 0700–1530©. ☎ 651-6725. Lockers are available in departures.

CATERING FACILITIES

There are restaurants, bars, coffee shops and cafeterias throughout the Main Terminal and the departures hall. The *Terrace Restaurant* is located on the fourth floor.

POST OFFICE

A post office is located on the lower level of the Main Terminal in the central lobby area. Open 0900–1500①②; 0900–1600③④⑤ ☎ 429-5689. There are post boxes and stamp vending machines throughout the Main Terminal.

SHOPS & DUTY-FREE FACILITIES

There are duty-free shops in Fingers 1, 2 and 4 which sell wine and spirits, fragrances and cosmetics, luxury and sundry goods. A pharmacy selling Disney products, American arts and crafts and travellers accessories can also be found. In departures there is a book and gift shop and another which specialises in cutlery. There is also a newsstand. The recently completed restaurant, food shop and deli complex is located in the Central Terminal's west end.

AIRLINE REPRESENTATION

Main Terminal: *American Airlines*, *Air Canada*, *Tropical Sea Airlines*, *Continental Airlines*, *TWA*, *United Airlines*, *Midwest Express Airways*, *USAir*.
Delta Terminal: *Delta Air Lines*, *Northwest Airlines*.
Trump Shuttle Terminal: *Air Botnia*.
Marine Terminal: *Long Island Airlines Ltd*.

PUBLIC TRANSPORT

To all destinations: Taxis are available outside each terminal. Use authorised yellow cabs only. Approx fare to mid Manhattan US$14–$20. Group taxi rides to Manhattan are provided by Taxicab Dispatch Services, Inc. at airport taxi stands. Group fares to Manhattan approx. US$7–$9.

Within the Airport: Free bus service between the terminals and the parking lots is provided 0500–0200 every 10–15 minutes. The Port Authority operates a free bus between the Marine Air Terminal and all terminal buildings 0600–2330Ⓐ; 0630–2200Ⓒ; 0730–2330Ⓓ.

To other airports – direct links: (connections also possible by transferring in Manhattan – see under each airport heading for details to/from Manhattan).

John F. Kennedy: *Carey Transportation* operate an inter-airport connection to and from JFK airport 0630–2300, every 30 mins. Journey time 30–45 mins; fare: US$11.

Newark International: No direct link; connection may be made by transfer in Manhattan. See below for travel La Guardia – Manhattan, and under 'New York: Newark' entry for travel Manhattan–Newark.

To New York City (Manhattan): *Carey Airport Express* (☎ (718) 632-0500/9) operates 0645-0000 every 20 mins. to Grand Central Terminal/Park Ave. and the Port Authority Bus Terminal. Journey time approx. 30–45 mins; fare US$9.50. A shuttle bus service to the New York Hilton, Sheraton City Squire, Marriott Marquis and the Holiday Inn Crowne Plaza is available from Park Avenue 0715–2215 daily, every 20 mins.; inclusive fare from Airport US$11. *Gray Line Air Shuttle* (☎ (212) 757-6840) operates on demand 0800-2300 to anywhere between 23rd and 63rd Streets. Journey time 30-45 mins; fare US$14. *Carey Transportation* (☎ (718) 632-0500/9) operate a shuttle bus 0630-2300 every 30 mins. to connect with *Long Island Rail Road* (☎ (718) 217-5477) trains to Penn station. Journey time (total) 60-70 mins; fare (bus) US$5, (rail) US$3–

US$4.25. *Two Borough QT Express Bus* (☎ (718) 335-1000) operates from all terminals 0630-2240 about every 20 mins to 21st Queensbridge Station for *NYC Subway* (☎ (718) 330-1234) 'Q' or 'B' trains to Manhattan. Journey time 30-45 mins; fare: (bus) US$5, (subway) US$1.15.

To New York City (suburbs): *Triboro coach* (☎ 335-1000) Bus Q-33 operates to Queens and to IRT and BMT subway stations on Roosevelt Avenue at 82nd Street and at 74th Street, 24 hours per day, every 10–20 mins. *Metropolitan Transportation Authority* bus Q-48 operates 0530–0030, every 15 mins to Queens and to *Long Island Rail Road* (☎ (718) 217-5477) station at Flushing. *Carey Transportation* (☎ (718) 632-0500/9) operate a shuttle bus to Queens 0630–2300, every 30 mins, and to Brooklyn 0915–2115, every 60 min. Fare: $5 return to Queens, $7.50 return to Brooklyn.

To Long Island: *Carey Transportation* (☎ (718) 632-0500/9) operate a shuttle bus 0630-2300 every 30 mins. to connect with *Long Island Rail Road* (☎ (718) 217-5477).

To Upstate New York, Pennsylvania, New Jersey, Connecticut – connecting services: *Carey Airport Express* to Manhattan, then: *AMTRAK* (☎ (212) 582 6875) or *Metro North Commuter Railroad* (☎ (212) 532-4900) for rail services from Grand Central Station to destinations in Connecticut, Westchester and Upstate New York; *Port Authority Bus Terminal* (☎ (212) 564-8484) for details of bus services to destinations in New Jersey, Upstate New York and Pennsylvania.

NEW YORK: NEWARK

Newark International Airport,
Newark, New Jersey, 07114, USA.

Ground Handling Agents: *Butler Aviation*, *Ogden Allied*, *AMR*.

Situation: 28km/16 miles from New York City. 5km/3 miles from Newark
Airport Code: NYC/EWR
Time Zone: GMT-5 (GMT-4 Apr–Sept)
Telephone Number: (201) 961-6000
Flight Enquiries: Contact individual airlines
Telefax Number: (201) 961-6259

AIRPORT & TOURIST INFORMATION

Airport Aides are available to supply information in the International Facility. Information regarding non-international flights can be obtained from the respective airlines. For general airport information ☎(201) 961-6000.

BANKS & BUREAUX DE CHANGE

First Fidelity Bank is open 0900–1500 and has an automatic cash dispenser. Currency Exchange Desks are located in each terminal

FACILITIES FOR THE DISABLED

Lifts, reserved parking spaces at reduced rate, curb cuts, transportation via specially designed vans, amplified phones

LOST PROPERTY & LEFT LUGGAGE

Each airline has its own Lost and Found office. The Newark International Airport Police are also available to offer assistance.

CATERING FACILITIES

All three terminals have bars and restaurants.

AIRLINE REPRESENTATION

Terminal A: *American*, *America West*, *TWA*, *United*, *Mid-West Express*, *USAir*.
Terminal B: International Flights, *Delta*, *Northwest*.
Terminal C: *Continental*.

PUBLIC TRANSPORT

Within the Airport: An Airline Connection Bus operates between Terminals A, B and C, 24 hours per day, every 10 mins. Journey time 5 mins, free service.

To other airports – direct links: (connections also possible by transferring in Manhattan – see under each airport heading for details to/from Manhattan).

John F. Kennedy: *New York Helicopter* (☎ 1-800-645-3494) operates a frequent service from Terminal C – call for details. Journey time 20 mins; fare US$ 62.00. *Princeton Airporter* (☎ (609) 587-6600) operate a frequent minibus service 0700–1900. Journey 60–75 mins; fare US$ 19.00.

La Guardia: No direct link; connection may be made by transfer in Manhattan. See below for travel Newark – Manhattan, and under 'New York: La Guardia' entry for travel Manhattan–La Guardia.

To New York City (Manhattan): *New York Helicopter* operates a frequent service from Terminal C to East 34th Street Heliport – call ☎ 1-800-645-3494 for details. Journey time 15-20 mins.; fare US$62 (reduced rates available for connections with some airlines; group rates also available). *NJ Transit* (☎ (201) 460-8444) Express Bus no. **300** operates 0600–0100 every 10–15 mins; 0100–0600 every 30-60 mins to the Port Authority Bus Terminal at 42nd St/8th Ave. Journey time 30 mins (longer in peaks); fare US$ 7.00. *Gray Line Air Shuttle* (☎ (212) 757-6840) operates on demand 0800-2300 to anywhere between 23rd and 63rd Streets. Journey time 55 mins; fare US$16. *Olympia Trails* (☎ NY (212) 964-6233; NJ (908) 354-3330) operate two Express Bus services; to downtown Manhattan (One World Trade Center – West St) 0700–2200 every 20–30 mins Ⓐ; 0715–2245 every 30 mins Ⓒ; journey time 20–40 mins; fare US$ 7.00; to mid-Manhattan (Grand Central Station and Penn Station) 0615–2300 every 20–30 mins; journey time 30–60 mins; fare US$ 7.00. *NJ Transit* (☎ (201) 460-8444) Airlink bus no. **302** operates from the North Terminal (calling at Terminal A, Terminal B, Terminal C, Penn Station Lane 1, PSE & G Building, Quality Inn and Broad St. Station) to Newark Penn Station (for onward journey to Manhattan by *PATH* (☎ 201) 659 8823) / *NJ Transit* (☎ (201) 762 5100 / *AMTRAK* (☎ (212) 582 6875) trains). Service operates 0605–0140 every 20-30 mins Ⓐ; 0625–0155 every 30 mins Ⓒ. Journey time (total) 45 mins to downtown Manhattan; 60 mins to mid-Manhattan; fare US$ 4.00 (exact fare only) Newark Airport – Newark Penn, then US$ 1.00 (PATH), US$ 3.00 (NJ Transit), US$ 5.50 (**AMTRAK**) to Manhattan.

To New Jersey destinations: *NJ Transit* trains operate from Newark Penn Station for the North Jersey Coast Line, the Northeast Corridor Line and the Raritan Valley Line; from Newark Broad Street for the Gladstone Branch, Montclair Branch and Morristown Line. Bus services connect to Newark–Willowbrook Mall, Broad–Clinton, Mt. Prospect, Newark–Montclair, Bloomfield Ave., Chancellor Ave. Kearny Ave., Kearny-Port Newark, Park Ave.-Elizabeth Ave. *NJ Transit* Newark City Subway No. 7 provides a connecting subway

service from Newark Penn Station. **Path Train Service** (☎ 963-2558) connects from Penn Station to Harrison, Hoboken Jersey City and New York (World Trade Centre or 33rd Street)

To all destinations: *AMTRAK* train service (☎ (800) 872-7245 connects from Penn Station to Philadelphia and othe destinations nationwide.

Taxi stands are located on the lower (arrivals) level a Terminals A, B and C. Journey time to Newark 10 mins. to Manhattan 25 mins. Taxi fares are $14 to Newark, $27–$30 plus tolls to Manhattan. For destinations on the East side of Manhattan above 14th Street taxi drivers charge an additiona $2. There is an extra charge of $1 for large items of luggage over 24 inches in length.

ORLANDO

Orlando International Airport,
Orlando, Florida, USA.

Situation: 13 km/8 miles south-east of Orlando.
Airport Code: MCO
Time zone: GMT–5 (–4 Apr–Sept)
Telephone number: (404) 825-2001
Flight enquiries: contact individual airlines
Telefax number: (407) 857-4079

AIRPORT & TOURIST INFORMATION
Centrally located kiosks on level 3 have multi-lingual assistants and visual and audio information on the airport and central Florida.

BANKS & BUREAU DE CHANGE
The *Sun Bank* Airport Office, 24 hour automatic cash dispensers and the *Lifeco* Travel Counter are all located in the main Terminal, Level 3.

FACILITIES FOR DISABLED TRAVELLERS
Ramps, wide lifts, TDD telephones, multi-user flight information systems with colour displays, wide entryways into restrooms, wheelchair assistance.

LOST PROPERTY & LEFT LUGGAGE
Locker facilities are available on Level 2.

CATERING FACILITIES
Restaurants, an American Buffet Bar, continental bistro snackbars, seafood bar and ice cream parlour are all located on Level 3.

POST OFFICE
24 hour self-service postal facilities are available in the mai terminal.

SHOPS & DUTY-FREE FACILITIES
Duty-free shops can be found in the airside buildings and o level 3. Further shops on level 3 stock gifts and souvenirs, toy and camera supplies, newspapers, magazines, books an jewellery.

AIRLINE REPRESENTATION
Gate 1–29: **American, Continental, TWA.**
Gates 30–59: **All Nippon Airways, Bahamasair, Midway Northwest, United, USAir.**
Gates 60–99: **Aeropostal, British Airways, ComAir, Delta KLM, TransBrasil, Virgin Atlantic.**

PUBLIC TRANSPORT
Tri-County Transit Route **11** operates a daily service from th airport to Orlando. Departures every hour from both sides of the airport. Fare US$0.75.
By taxi from Airport to city centre; journey time 20–30 mins fare US$24.00. A limousine service is available.

PHILADELPHIA

Philadelphia International Airport,
Philadelphia, Pennsylvania, USA.

Situation: 12km/7 miles south-west of Philadelphia
Airport Code: PHL
Time Zone: GMT-5 (GMT-4 Apr–Sept.)
Telephone Number: (215) 937 6800
Flight Enquiries: (215) 937 6937
Telefax Number: (215) 937 0124

AIRPORT & TOURIST INFORMATION
There is an information desk at Terminal A, open 1300–2300ⓐ; 0800–2300ⓒ.

BANKS & BUREAU DE CHANGE
Bureau de Change are located in Terminal A, open 0600–2000, Terminal B, open 0600–1800 and in Terminals D and E, open 0600–2000. Automatic cash dispensers are available in Terminal C.

FACILITIES FOR DISABLED TRAVELLERS
Ramps, lifts, wheelchairs, specially equipped toilets an telephones.

LOST PROPERTY & LEFT LUGGAGE
Lost Property should be reported to the respective airline. Th lost property office is located in the communication centr which is in the departure area of Terminal C, lower leve Luggage lockers can be found by the security checkpoints i each of the 5 terminals. Charges per 24 hours: Terminal A US$1.00, Terminals B, C, D, E.: US$0.75

CATERING FACILITIES
In Terminal A, the *Food Court Snack & Bar* is open 0600 1900, in Terminals B and C 0630–2000, in Terminal D 0630 1930, and in Terminal E 0545–2030 ①②③ⓒ; 0545–2000 ④ⓒ There are various other cocktail bars and cafeterias locate throughout all 5 terminals

POST OFFICE
There is a post office in Terminal C.

HOPS & DUTY-FREE FACILITIES

ewstand and gift shops are available in all terminals. Opening
mes in Terminals A and E 0600–2100; B, C and D 0615–
200. In Terminal D there are also various other shops
cluding a Boutique (open 0800–1800), card shop (open 0800–
000) and a sports shop (open 0800–1930).

AIRLINE REPRESENTATION

he following International airlines fly from Terminal A
Overseas): Swissair, Air Jamaica, British Airways, Lufthansa,
WA. The following airlines fly from Terminal B: American,
Continental, Delta, Midway, Midwest Express, Northwest, TWA,
nited, USAir. All other charter and commuter airlines fly out of
erminals C, D and E.
erminal A: *Air Jamaica*, *American*, *American Eagle*, *British
Airways*, *Lufthansa*, *Swissair*.
erminal B: *USAir*, *USAir Express*.
erminal C: *Continental*, *Continental Express*, *Midwest*,
Midwest Express, *USAir*.

Terminal D: *Mohawk*, *United*, *Wings*.
Terminal E: *Delta*, *Delta Connection*, *Northwest*, *Northwest
Airlink*, *TWA*.

PUBLIC TRANSPORT

Within the Airport: *LaidLaw Bus* operate a parking lot bus
with services every 10 mins. commencing from the terminals to
Atlantic Aviation, the Employee Parking Lot, the Remote
Parking Lot, the last bus shelter at the Overseas Parking Lot
then returning to the terminals.

To downtown Philadelphia: *SEPTA* (☎ 580 7800) Airport
Rail Line R1 operates a commuter rail service from Terminals
B, C, D and E to 30th Street, Penn and Market East Stations
0600–0000 every 30 mins. Journey time about 20 mins; fare
US$ 4.75.

Taxis are available to the city centre. Approx journey time: 20
mins.

SAN FRANCISCO

*San Francisco International Airport,
PO Box 8097, San Francisco,
California, 94128, USA.*

Situation: 19km/11.5 miles South of
San Francisco
Airport Code: SFO
Time Zone: GMT-8 (GMT-7 Apr–Sept)
Telephone Number: (415) 876-2421
Flight Enquiries: Contact individual
airlines.
Telefax number: (415) 876-7875
Telex: 509520

AIRPORT & TOURIST INFORMATION

formation desks available in the Upper level of both North and
outh Terminals and in the lower level of the International
erminal. Open 0900–2100.

BANKS & BUREAUX DE CHANGE

Thomas Cook (☎ 583 4029) bureaux de change offices are
vailable throughout the airport,.
ull service *Bank of America* branches are located on the
orth Terminal mezzanine level and in the International
erminal, open 0830–1700ⓐ. Foreign exchange services are
the *Bank of America* International Terminal branch, open
700–2300 daily, and in Boarding Area D, open 0800–2000
aily. Automatic cash dispensers are located throughout the
rport.

FACILITIES FOR DISABLED TRAVELLERS

amps, wheelchairs, rest rooms, telephones equipped with
mplifiers for those of impaired hearing, handicapped parking
cilities.

LOST PROPERTY & LEFT LUGGAGE

he lost and found property office is located at the Police desk
ext to the China Airlines ticket counter in the International
erminal. Lockers can be found in the boarding areas of all
rminals. Long-term luggage storage facilities are available for
rger baggage or for extended storage.

CATERING FACILITIES

orth Terminal: three full-service restaurants (*Terrace Room
estaurant and Cocktail Lounge*, *North Beach Deli*, *Crab
ot Seafood Restaurant*). There is also a self-service
staurant in Boarding Area F and various snack bars and
cktail lounges are located in every other boarding area.
ternational Terminal and South Terminal: cocktail bars and
feteria style restaurants available throughout both terminals.

POST OFFICE

Located in the lower level of the North Terminal, open 0600–
0000. There are also postage machines located in the upper
levels of all terminals and available 24 hours daily.

SHOPS & DUTY-FREE FACILITIES

Various shops stocking a wide range of gifts, souvenirs and
sports goods are located on the departure level of each
terminal. Duty-free shops are on the upper level of the
International Terminal and in the International flight departure
area. Small duty-free trolleys are available at Air Canada
boarding gates when international flights depart.

AIRLINE REPRESENTATION

International Terminal: *Air France*, *Balair*, *British Airtours*,
British Airways, *CAAC*, *Canadian Pacific*, *Cathay Pacific*,
China Airlines, *Condor*, *Hawaiian Air*, *Japan Air Lines*,
Korean Air Lines, *LTU International*, *Lufthansa*, *Mexicana
Airlines*, *Minerve*, *Northwest*, *Philippine Airlines*, *Qantas*,
Singapore Airlines, *TACA*, *United*, *UTA French Airlines*.
North Terminal: Domestic.
South Terminal: Domestic.

PUBLIC TRANSPORT

Within the Airport: A free shuttle bus connects all terminals
0530–0100 every 5 mins; to outlying facilities/long-stay parking
0000–0600 every 10–15 mins; 0600–0000 every 5–7 mins.
To downtown San Francisco: *SFO Airporter* (☎ (415) 673–
2433) services depart from the blue column, lower level of all
terminals. Route **1** runs 0610–2350 every 20 mins, calling at
Meridien, Grand Hyatt, Westin, St. Francis, Hilton Nikko, Parc
55 and Marriott hotels. Journey time 30–40 mins; fare US$
7.00. Route **2** runs 0620–0001 every 20 mins, calling at Sir
Francis Drake, Holiday Inn Union Square, Hilton Nikko,
Sheraton Palace, Hyatt Regency and Westin St. Francis hotels.
Journey times/fares as for route **1**. *Samtrans* (☎ 761–7000/
367–1500) services depart from the upper level between the
South and International Terminals, and the upper level of the
North Terminal. Route **7F** (express – carries passengers
without luggage only) to Transbay Terminal (calling at 8th/
Mission) departs 0055, 0600ⓐ, 0618ⓐ, 0701ⓐ, 0715ⓒ, 0736ⓐ,
0800, then every 30 mins until 1900, 1953, 2048, 2148, 2248,
2348. Journey time 22 mins to 8th/Mission, 30 mins to
Transbay Terminal; fare US$ 1.25. Route **7B** (local) to
Transbay Terminal (calling at 7th/Mission) departs 0021, 0121,
0543, 0613ⓐ, 0633, 0725ⓐ, 0745, then every 30 mins until
1845, 1913, then every 30 mins until 2313. Journey time
approx 43 mins to 7th/Mission, 50 mins to Transbay Terminal;
fare US$ 1.00.
Connecting services also possible by taking *Samtrans* Route
3B (every 30–60 mins – no evening service) to Daly City and
transferring to *BART (Bay Area Rapid Transit)* (☎ 788-2278)
train to various downtown stations.
To North Bay area (services depart from the blue column,

lower level of all terminals): **Marin Airporter** (☎ 461-4222) operates to Sausalito, Mill Valley and Larkspur (departures on the hour continue to Terra Linda, Ignacio and Novato) at 0000, 0600 and every 30 mins until 2300. Journey time/fares: Sausalito 35 mins/US$ 8.00; Larkspur 50 mins/US$ 9.00; Novato 1 hr 20 mins/US$ 12.00. **Santa Rosa Airporter** (☎ (415) 898-8888 / (707) 545-8015) operates to Mill Valley, Corta Madera, San Rafael, Terra Linda, Marin Wood and Novato at 0645 and hourly until 2345. Journey times/fares: Mill Valley 40 mins/US$ 10.00; San Rafael 55 mins/US$ 12.00; Novato 1 hr 25 mins/US$ 14.00. Also to Petaluma, Rohnert Park and Santa Rosa at 0630 and hourly until 2330 (departures at 1030, 1330 and 1830 continue to Healdsburg, Cloverdale, Hopland and Ukiah). Journey times/fares: Petaluma 1 hr 5 mins/US$ 15.00; Santa Rosa 1 hr 15 mins/US$ 15.00; Ukiah 2 hrs 45 mins/US$ 30.00. **Sonoma Airporter** (☎ (707) 938-4246) operates to Sonoma (calling at Temelec, Sears Point, Glen Ellen, Kenwood, Boyes Hot Springs and Blackpoint) at 0805, 0945ⓐ, 1220, 1445ⓐ, 1740. Journey time 1 hr 35 mins; fare US$ 20.00. **Sonoma County Airport Express** (☎ (800) 327-2024) operates to Petaluma, Rohnert Park and Santa Rosa at 0600 and hourly until 0000. Journey times: Petaluma 1hr 15 mins, Santa Rosa 1 hr 45 mins; fare US$ 12.00.

To East Bay (North) area (services depart from the blue column, lower level of all terminals): **Bay Area Bus Service** (☎ (415) 632-5506) operates to Oakland Airport (calling at Oakland and Treasure Island) 0700 and hourly to 0000. Journey time 55 mins; fare US$ 7.00. **Bay Area Shuttle** (☎ (800) 345-8687) operates to Emeryville, Berkeley and Claremont 0600 and hourly until 1300, then every 30 mins until 2230. (Reduced service on major holidays). Journey time 55 mins; fare US$ 10.00. **Capitol City Commuter** (☎ (916) 371-8151) operates to Davis and Sacramento at 0830ⓐ, 1200, 1830ⓐ, 2300ⓒ. Journey times: Davis 1 hr 55 mins, Sacramento 2½–3 hrs; fare US$ 25.00. **Evans Airport Service** (☎ (707) 255-1559) operates to Vallejo and Napa at 0630ⓐ, 0815, 1000, 1145, 1345, 1515, 1645, 1815, 2000, 2130, 2245ⓑ. Journey times/fares: Vallejo 1–1½ hrs/US$ 14.00; Napa 1½–2 hrs/US$ 15.00. **Travis/Solano Airporter** (☎ (707) 437-4611) operates to Vallejo, Fairfield and Travis Air Force Base at 0000, 0545, 0715, 0845ⓐ, 1100, 1300, 1545, 1730ⓐ, 1900, 2105. Journey times/fares: Vallejo 1¾–2 hrs/US$ 12.00; Fairfield 2–2¼ hrs/ US$ 15.00.
Connecting services also possible by taking **SFO Airporter** or **Samtrans** bus to downtown San Francisco, or **Samtrans** bus to Daly City (see under downtown San Francisco for details), then transferring to **BART (Bay Area Rapid Transit)** (☎ 788-2278) train to Oakland and all stations on the Richmond, Concord and Fremont lines.

To East Bay (South) area (services depart from the blue column, lower level of all terminals): **FUN Connexion** (☎ (415) 791-7160) operates to Fremont/Union City/Newark at 0700ⓐ,

0800ⓒ, 0900ⓐ, 1100ⓐ, 1300, 1600ⓐ, 1700ⓒ, 1800ⓐ, 200▮ 2200. Journey time 50 mins; fare US$ 15.00. **San Ramo▮ Valley Airporter Express** (☎ (415) 484-4044) operates ▮ Castro Valley, Alamo, Danville, San Ramon, Dublin an▮ Pleasanton at 0630ⓐ, 0645ⓒ, 0830, 1000, 1200, 1330ⓒ 1400ⓒ, 1500ⓐ, 1630ⓒ, 1645ⓒ, 1815, 1945ⓒ, 2030ⓒ, 2115ⓒ 2215ⓒ, 2245ⓐ. Journey times: Castro Valley 35 mins, Alam▮ Danville/San Ramon 50 mins, Dublin/Pleasanton 1 hr 15 min▮ fare US$ 17.00. **United Shuttle Systems** (☎ (800) 243-660▮ operates to Dublin, Livermore, Tracy, Manteca, Modesto an▮ Turlock at 0800, 1350 and 2120. Journey times/fares: Dubl▮ 50 mins/US$ 13.00; Tracy 1½ hrs/US$ 21.00; Modesto 2 hr▮ US$ 23.00.
Connecting services also possible by taking **SFO Airporter** ▮ **Samtrans** bus to downtown San Francisco, or **Samtrans** bu▮ to Daly City (see under downtown San Francisco for details▮ then transferring to **BART (Bay Area Rapid Transit)** (☎ 78▮ 2278) train to Oakland and all stations to Fremont.

To South Bay area: Greyhound (☎ (415) 877-0366) operate▮ from the lower level of Terminal C to Los Gatos and San▮ Cruz at 1055, 1910ⓧ; to San Jose, Gilroy, Salinas, Fort O▮ and Monterey at 0650 (San Jose only), 0840, 1055 (Ft. O▮ and Monterey only), 1250, 1525, 1910ⓧ. Journey times/fare▮ Santa Cruz 2–2¼ hrs/US$ 13.50; San Jose 1–2 hrs/US$ 10.0▮ Salinas 2 hrs 20 mins – 4 hrs 50 mins/US$ 16.70; Montere▮ 2¾–4¼ hrs/US$ 18.85. **Samtrans** (☎ (415) 761-7000/(41▮ 367-1500) services depart from the upper level between th▮ South and International Terminals, and the upper level of th▮ North Terminal. Route **7F** (express) operates to San Mate▮ Belmont, San Carlos, Redwood City and Palo Alto at 002▮ 0125, 0606ⓒ, 0655, 0725ⓒ, 0755, then every 30 mins un▮ 1755, 1824, 1851, 1925, 2025, 2125, 2225, 2325. Journe▮ times: San Mateo 13 mins; San Carlos 23 mins; Palo Alto ▮ mins. Rout **7B** (local) operates to Burlingame, San Mate▮ Belmont, San Carlos and Redwood City at 0006, 0106, 0536ⓒ 0606, 0636ⓐ, 0710, then every 30 mins until 1840, 1907, 193▮ 2006, 2106, 2206, 2306. Journey times: San Mateo 21 mir▮ San Carlos 41 mins; Redwood City 46 mins. **Santa Cr▮ Airporter** (☎ (800) 223-4142) services depart from the blu▮ column, lower level of all terminals, for San Jose, Scotts Valle▮ Santa Cruz, Soquel/Capitola, Aptos and Watsonville at 003▮ 0630⚡ (not Watsonville), 0800ⓐ, 1000 and hourly until 220▮ Journey times/fares: San Jose 45–60 mins/US$ 20.00; San▮ Cruz 2 hrs/US$25.00; Watsonville 3 hrs/US$35.

To all destinations: Taxi information displays are located ▮ the yellow column, lower level of all terminals. Taxis a▮ available to all destinations in the Bay Area – uniformed ta▮ dispatchers are on duty 0600–0200 to assist passenger▮ Metered rates apply to all destinations except for a 'Share-th▮ Fare' fixed rate (US$ 24.00 per taxi – minimum two person▮ a maximum of 3 destinations) arrangement to downtown S▮ Francisco.

SEATTLE

Seattle-Tacoma International Airport,
PO Box 68727, Seattle, WA 98168-0727, USA

Situation: 13 miles/21 km from Seattle
Airport Code: SEA
Time Zone: GMT-8 (GMT-7 Apr–Sept)
Telephone Number: (206) 433-4645
Telefax number: (206) 439-7725

AIRPORT & TOURIST INFORMATION

Airport information general numbers ☎ 431-4444 or toll-free 1-800-544-1965. Visitor information booth located in centre of baggage claim area, open 0930–1930, ☎ 433-5217. There is a separate booth for ground transport information located outside the north end of the baggage reclaim area, open 0700–0200, ☎ 431-5906 or Button 46 at one of the courtesy phones in the baggage reclaim area.

BANKS & BUREAUX DE CHANGE

Foreign exchange and other travel services can be obtained ▮ the booths in the centre of the Main Terminal (open 060▮ 2130) and in the North and South Satellites (open for m▮ flights). Automatic cash dispensers are located in the centre ▮ the Main Terminal (**Seafirst** and **US Bank**), near the south e▮ of the baggage reclaim level (**Security Pacific**) and near t▮ centre of the baggage claim (**American Express**).

FACILITIES FOR DISABLED TRAVELLERS

Restrooms throughout the airport, as well as adapted telepho▮ booths, mailboxes and elevator panels. TDD phones for t▮ deaf. Disabled parking at south of main terminal, and ext▮ wide spaces on each floor of main garage. Transit buses, tax▮ and hire cars available with wheelchair lifts.

LOST PROPERTY & LEFT LUGGAGE

Lost property facility is on mezzanine level of Main Termin▮ ☎ 433-5312. Baggage storage is available under escalator ne▮

arousel 12 in baggage claim area. Lockers are situated at beginning of Concourses A, B, C and D and satellite transit system levels of North and South satellites.

CATERING FACILITIES
ain terminal offers a variety of bars and eateries, including **Fresh Express** 24-hour cafeteria and the **Carvery** restaurant centre of terminal), open 0700–2200.

SHOPS & DUTY-FREE FACILITIES
ift shops and duty-free shops in Main Terminal and satellites nd at concourses Other facilities include bookshop, flower ands and barber shop.

AIRLINE REPRESENTATION
here is one international terminal from which the following rlines depart: **Air Canada, Air San Juan, Alaska Airlines, merica West Airlines, American Airlines, British Airways, ontinental Airlines, Delta Air Lines, Harbor Airlines, awaiian Airlines, Horizon Air, Japan Airlines, Northwest irlines, Scandinavian Airlines, Thai Airways, Time Air, rans World Airlines, United Airlines, United Express, SAir.**

PUBLIC TRANSPORT
Within the Airport: Satellite Transit System connects the ain Terminal and the North and South Satellites. South loop ops on Concourse B; North loop stops on Concourse C; a uttle connects the two loops. Trains run every 2 mins.

downtown Seattle: **Seattle Transit** (☎ 553-3000) Metro uses **174/184/194** operate from outside the south end of the aggage reclaim area to downtown Seattle at 0018, 0048, 248, 0403, 0504ⓐ, 0519ⓐ, 0538ⓐ, 0549ⓐ, 0608ⓐ, 0619ⓒ,

0623ⓐ, 0628ⓐ, 0649ⓐ, 0705†, then about every 30 mins (30–60 mins on †) until 2348ⓒ, 2353ⓐ. Journey time 30 mins (**184/194**) / 45 mins (**174**); fare US$ 1.00 (US$ 1.50 at peak times). **Grayline Express** (☎ 626-6088) operate to most downtown hotels 0500–0030 every 30 mins. Journey time 30 mins; fare US$ 7.00. **Shuttle Express** (☎ 622-1424) operates 24 hours per day approx. every 2 hours. Journey time 30 mins; fare US$ 14.00 (1 person); US$ 7.00 per additional passenger.

To Seattle Suburbs: Seattle Transit (☎ 553-3000) Metro Bus **340** operates from outside the south end of the baggage reclaim area to Burien, Southcenter, Renton, Bellevue and Aurora Village. Call for times and fares. **Shuttle Express** (☎ 622-1424) operates shared ride door-to-door service to Auburn, Bellevue, Bothell, Everett, Federal Way, Fife, Kent, Kirkland, Lakewood, Mercer Island, Puyallup, Redmond, Renton, Stilacom and Woodinville; call for times and fares.

To Tacoma: Shuttle Express (☎ 622-1424) operates shared ride door-to-door service to Tacoma; call for times and fares. **Seattle Transit** (☎ 553-3000) Metro Buses **174/194** operate from outside the south end of the Baggage Reclaim area to Federal Way Transit Center for connection with **Pierce Transit** (☎ 593-4500) buses **500/501** (approx. 0600–2330 every 30–60 mins ⓐ; approx. 0750–2340 about hourly ⓖ; 0835 and about every 2 hours until 2245, 2340 ⓖ) to Tacoma.

To other destinations: Greyhound (☎ 624-3456) operate services from the airport which connect with state- and nationwide services. Call for details.

To all destinations: Taxis available at all doors from baggage reclaim area and centre doors at ticketing level. ☎ 246-9999, 431-5906 and 431-5904, or use kerbside phones at baggage reclaim level. Fare to downtown Seattle approx. US$25.00.

TORONTO

Toronto - Lester B. Pearson International Airport, PO Box 6003, Toronto AMF, Ontario, L5P 1B5, Canada

Situation: 25 km/15 miles west of Toronto
Airport Code: YTO-YYZ
Time Zone: GMT-5 (GMT-4 Apr–Sept)
Telephone Number: (416) 676-3506
Flight enquiries: Terminals 1 & 2 (416) 247-7678 (0800-2300); Terminal 3 (416) 612-5100 (0700-2400)
Telefax number: (416) 676-3555

AIRPORT & TOURIST INFORMATION
tourist information but general information available at formation counters and on the phone numbers given under ight enquiries'

BANKS & BUREAUX DE CHANGE
rminals 1 and 2: **Royal Bank of Canada**. rminal 3: **Canadian Imperial Bank of Commerce**. eneral hours of opening are 0530–2300.

FACILITIES FOR DISABLED TRAVELLERS
ones for the hard-of-hearing at information counters; lifts and ets/washrooms are accessible to handicapped persons in eelchairs; moving walkways; etc.

LOST PROPERTY & LEFT LUGGAGE
st property details not available. Left luggage facilities at rminals 1 and 2 are under the control of **Travellers Support rvices**; at Terminal 3 by individual airlines.

CATERING FACILITIES
staurant in Terminal 3 is open 1200–2300, elsewhere 1200–00. Main cafeterias open 24 hours daily. Coffee shops, snack rs, refreshment kiosks open as traffic demands. Three bars Terminal 1, two in Terminal 2.

POST OFFICE
Post office in the cargo building area: open 0800–1745ⓐ.

SHOPS & DUTY-FREE FACILITIES
Bookshop, gift shops, chemists, general shops, etc. are open 0530–2200. At Terminal 3 fashion goods and accessories, foodstuffs, executive gifts, toys and games, books and newspapers, confectionery, tableware, batteries and Canadian souvenirs are on sale as well as duty-free items, and there is a Harrods shop. Duty-free facilities – including the sale of wines, spirits and gifts – at all terminals are usually open 0530–2300.

AIRLINE REPRESENTATION
Terminal 1: **Aeroflot, Aerolineas Argentinas, American Trans Air, Air Niagara, Alitalia, Business Express, BWIA International, Carnival Airlines, Comair, Delta, Inter Canadien (Intair), Nationair Canada, Northwest, Olympic, Sterling, TAESA, TAP Air Portugal, United Airlines, USAir, Varig.**
Terminal 2: **Air Canada** (handling agent), **Air India, Air Jamaica, Air Ontario, Cubana, El Al, Finnair, First Air, Guyana Airways, Iberia, JAT, Korean Airlines, LOT Polish Airlines, PIA, Singapore Airlines, Swissair, Thai International, Viasa.**
Terminal 3: **Air China, Air France, Air New Zealan**d, **American Airlines, British Airways, Canadian International Airlines** (main handling agent) and **Canadian Partners, Condor German Airlines, Japan Airlines, KLM, Lufthansa, Pem-Air, Qantas, SATS.**
Main ground handling agents are **Air Canada, Canadian Airlines** and **Hudson General**.

PUBLIC TRANSPORT
Within the Airport: A free shuttle bus connects all terminals.
To downtown Toronto (direct link): **Gray Coach Lines** (☎ 351-3311) operates from all airport terminals to various hotels in downtown area and to Toronto Bus Terminal. From Airport Terminal 3 (calls 5 mins later at Terminal 1; 10 mins later at Terminal 2) 0650 and every 30 mins until 0020. Journey time to Bus Terminal 35 mins; fare C$ 10.75. Connecting services also possible – see under 'Suburbs' for details.

To Toronto Suburbs: *Gray Coach Lines* (☎ 351-3311) operates from all airport terminals to various *TTC* (*Toronto Transit Commission* – ☎ 393-INFO) subway stations for onward connections (subway operates 0600✻/0900⑦–0130; flat fare C$ 1.30). Service connects with Spadina Subway at Yorkdale (for NW suburbs, downtown Toronto and Union Station), and at York Mills (for northern suburbs). Bus departs Terminal 2 (calls 5 mins later at Terminal 1; 10 mins later at Terminal 3) 0635, 0710 then every 40 mins until 0030. Journey times/fares: to Yorkdale 25 mins/C$ 6.50; to York Mills 35 mins/ C$ 7.50. Alternative service connects with Bloor-Danforth Subway at Islington (for western suburbs, downtown Toronto and eastern suburbs). Bus departs Terminal 3 (calls 5 mins later at Terminal 1; 10 mins later at Terminal 2) 0620 and every 40 mins until 0020. Journey time 30 mins; fare C$ 6.00. *TTC* operate Malton Bus *58A* from Terminal 2 to Lawrence West Station (for onward connection by *TTC* Spadina Subway to NW suburbs, downtown Toronto and Union Station). Bus service from Airport 0623 and about every 30 mins (more frequent in rush hours) until 0100 on ⑥; 0545⑦, 0550⑥, then every 15–40 mins until 0932; then hourly until 2332, 0015, 0040 on ©. Journey time about 35 mins; fare C$ 2.70. *Mississauga*

Transit (☎ 279-5800) bus **7** operates from Terminal 2 Mississauga Square One at 0621 and about every 30 mins (' mins in rush hours) until 2317 on ⑥; 0816 and every 30 mi until 1916 on ⑥; no service on ⑦; journey time 45 mins; fare C 1.40. Also to Mississauga Westwood Mall 0638 and abo every 30 mins (15 mins in rush hours) until 2235 on ⑥; 07: and every 30 mins until 1932 on ⑥; no service on ⑦; journe time 20 mins; fare C$ 1.40. *TTC* bus *58B* operates fro Terminal 3 to Mississauga Westwood Mall at about 053(0550, 0630, then about every 25-30 mins until 0138 on ⑥; service on ©. Journey time about 15 mins; fare C$ 1.4 *–Thls trip operates from Terminals 1 and 2; **not** Terminal

To other destinations: *GO (Government of Ontario Tran:* – ☎ 630-3933*)* and *VIA Rail* (☎ 366-8411) operate rail servic from Union Station to other locations in Ontario and beyor various long-distance bus services operate from Toronto B Terminal. See the Tables Section of this book for detai'

To all destinations: Taxi to downtown Toronto takes betwee 30 and 60 mins; fare C$ 28.00 to destinations south of Dund; Street and C$ 30.00 north of Dundas Street.

VANCOUVER

Vancouver International Airport, PO Box 23750, Richmond, Vancouver, British Columbia, V7B 1Y7, Canada

Situation: 13 km/8 miles south-west of Vancouver
Airport Code: YVR
Time Zone: GMT-8 (GMT-7 Apr–Oct)
Telephone Number: (604) 276-6208
Telefax number: (604) 276-7755, 270-0610

AIRPORT & TOURIST INFORMATION
Tourist information available 0630–2400 on ☎276-6101.

BANKS & BUREAUX DE CHANGE
Bank of America/Canada foreign currency exchange faciliies open 0630–2200. *Bank of America/Canada*, *Bank of Montreal* and *Royal Bank of Canada* 24-hour automatic cash dispensers are available.

FACILITIES FOR DISABLED TRAVELLERS
Washrooms/toilets, telephones, water fountains, ramps and lifts are all accessible to wheelchairs. Electrocars operated by the airlines.

LOST PROPERTY & LEFT LUGGAGE
Lost and Found office on level 1 opens 0800–2000 ☎ 276-6104. Luggage storage facilities open 0500–0030

CATERING FACILITIES
Level 1: *Happy Landing Lounge.*
Level 2: *Gourmet Grill and Bar.*
Level 3: *Jolly Chef* (cafeteria), *Sea Island Dining Room and Lounge.*
Snack food and beverage services are available at the gate areas. Restaurants are generally open 0600–2000, bars 1000–0200 and coffee shops/snack bars 24 hours daily.

POST OFFICE
On Level 3; open 0900–1600.

SHOPS & DUTY-FREE FACILITIES
General shops sell flowers, confectionery and food, photographic goods, books and newspapers, gifts and souvenirs and toys; there is also a hairdressers, chemists and florists. Duty-free shops sell wines and spirits, perfume and cosmetics, jewellery, leather goods, etc.

AIRLINE REPRESENTATION
Main Terminal – Level 2: *AirBC* (USA flights), *Air Cana;* (USA flights) *Alaskan Airlines*, *American Airlines. America; Transair, Canadian Airlines* (USA flights), *Continental, De Airlines, Great American Airways, Horizon Airline Transcontinental, United Airlines.*
Main Terminal – Level 3: *Aerocancun, Air 2000, AirE* (domestic flights), *Air Canada* (domestic and internatior flights), *Air China, Air New Zealand, British Airway Canada 3000, Canadian Airlines* (domestic and internationa *China Airlines, Cathay Pacific, First Air, Japan Airline KLM, Korean Airlines, LOT Polish Airlines, Lufthans Nationair, Qantas, Singapore Airlines, Time Air,*
Courtesy buses runs between the two terminals.
Main ground handling agents are Air Canada and Canadi International.

PUBLIC TRANSPORT
To downtown Vancouver (direct link): *Perimiter Airp Express* (☎ 273-9023) operates from Level 2 to downto' Vancouver hotels, SkyTrain Rapid Transit stations, the SeaB Terminal and *BC Transit* Bus Terminal, at 0000, 0030, 06 and every 15 mins until 2230, 2300, 2330. Journey time abc 30 mins; fare C$ 8.25. *BC Transit* (☎ 261-5100) buses ser the entire downtown area, but there is no direct service fr the Airport. Connections possible by taking bus **100** from Le' 3 (operates 0607⑥, 0708⑥, 0717† and about every 15-30 mi ⑥, 30 mins ⑥, hourly †, until 1917, then hourly until 0017), th for downtown (Granville) and Hastings (for Waterfront a SeaBus Terminal) transfer to bus **20** (frequent service) at 7(Ave; for *VIA Rail* Station and Stration St. Bus Terminal trans to bus **3** (frequent service) at Main. Journey times (includi transfer) about 45 mins; fare (including transfer) C$ 1.35 (; 2.00 at ⑥ peak times).

To Vancouver suburbs: *BC Transit* (☎ 261-5100) oper; bus **100** (see above for details) to Marine Drive, 22nd ; Skytrain Station and New Westminster (for eastern and ; suburbs). Also bus **404/405** from Level 3 (combined servi every 15–30 mins) to Richmond and to Ladner Exchan; North Shore suburbs accessed by bus transfer in downto' Vancouver or by *BC Transit* SeaBus Ferry (see **Table 31** For North Vancouver *BC Rail* Station (nearest bus stop Marine Drive/Pemberton; about 1 km distant) transfer c either be made downtown (Granville/Georgia) to bus **240** (eve 15–30 mins), or from SeaBus Ferry at Lonsdale Quay to b **239** (every 15–30 mins).

To other destinations: To Horseshoe Bay Ferry Terminal *BC Ferries* service to Nanaimo (see **Table 31**): trans downtown to *BC Transit* (☎ 261-5100) bus **250** (every 15– mins), or **257** (express – every 2 hours (30 mins ⑥ peaks); late evening service). To Tsawwassen Ferry Terminal for ▶

WASHINGTON: DULLES INTERNATIONAL

ashington-Dulles International Airport, PO Box
7045, Washington, DC 20041, USA

tuation: 42 km/26 miles west of Washington
rport Code: WATS-IAD
me Zone: GMT–5 (–4 Apr–Sept)
lephone Number: (703) 471-4322
elefax number: (703) 661-6517

IRPORT & TOURIST INFORMATION
reign Visitors Information Desk is located just outside the
ernational Arrivals area and is open 1000 to 1900 daily; ☎
1-6732/6743.

ANKS & BUREAUX DE CHANGE
vran Bank situated on the lower level of the Main Terminal is
en 0900–1300 and 1500–1700 Mon.–Fri. Foreign currency
change facilities are available 0700 to 2100 daily. Automatic
sh dispensers and change machines are available 24 hours
ily.

ACILITIES FOR DISABLED
RAVELLERS
heelchairs and escorts are available in the Main Terminal and
accessing the Midfield Concourses. Skycap assistance
rvice is available ☎ 661-8150/1. Accessible restroom/toilet
d telephone facilities in all terminals. Lifts at east and west
ds of the Main Terminal.

OST PROPERTY & LEFT LUGGAGE
st and found articles are handled by the Airport Police ☎
1-4114. Left luggage lockers in secured area of the Main
rminal are available 24 hours per day.

ATERING FACILITIES
e Diplomat Restaurant opens 1100–2100 daily; International
fe 0700–2000. There is a 24-hour snack bar and other bars,
ing lounges and snack bars open at various hours.

OST OFFICE
e post office in the Gateway Building (on the East-West
rvice road) opens 0900 to 1700 Mon.–Fri. and 0900–1200

Sat. There is a 24-hour self-service postal facility at the lower
level (West end) of the Main Terminal. Postboxes and postage
stamp machines are located in all airport terminals.

SHOPS & DUTY-FREE FACILITIES
Books, newspapers, confectionery, gifts, flowers, souvenirs and
American speciality goods are available. Duty-free shops can
be found at the upper level of the Main Terminal and are open
daily from 0700 to 2300. There is also a hairdressers.

AIRLINE REPRESENTATION
Northwest, USAir and American commuter airlines have desks
at the Main Terminal; all other airlines use the Midfield
Concourses.

PUBLIC TRANSPORT
Within the Airport: The Midfield and Main terminals are
connected by a courtesy Mobile Lounge service which operates
as required.

To National Airport: *The Metropolitan Washington Airports
Authority* operate the *Washington Flyer Bus and Van
Service* (☎ (703) 685-1400) between Dulles and National
Airports. Daily from Dulles (Main Terminal) hourly 0500–2300;
from National (all terminals) hourly 0600–2300, journey time 45
mins.; fare US$ 14.00.

To Downtown Washington: *Washington Flyer* (☎ (703)
685-1400) operate daily from the Main Terminal to the
Downtown Air Terminal (16th and K Streets, NW) 0520 and
every 30 mins. until 2150. Connecting loop services are
available to the main downtown hotels. *Washington Flyer*
also operate to West Falls Church Metrorail Station for onward
connection by Metrorail to Downtown and Washington Suburbs.
From the Main Terminal 0600–2230 every 20-30 mins.Ⓐ; 0800–
2230 every 30 mins.Ⓒ; 1030, 1130, 1230, 1330 and every 30
mins. until 2230Ⓞ.

To Bethesda: *Washington Flyer* (☎ (703) 685-1400) operate
an express service to Bethesda Terminal (10215 Fernwood
Road) and onward to Bethesda hotels. Departs Main Terminal
0500 and hourly to 2200; journey 40 mins.; fare US$ 17.00.

To all destinations: Taxis are located on the East and West
ramps on the arrivals level. Dispatchers are on duty 24 hours
per day. Fare to Downtown Washington approx. US$ 40.00

WASHINGTON: NATIONAL

ashington-National Airport, Washington, DC
0001, USA

tuation: 7 km/4 miles south of Washington
rport Code: WATS-DCA
me Zone: GMT–5 (–4 Apr–Sept)
lephone Number: (703) 685-8000
lefax number: (703) 521-6329

RPORT & TOURIST INFORMATION
ormation available through the airport Traveler's Aid desks in
Main and Interim Terminals.

ANKS & BUREAUX DE CHANGE
st American Bank of Virginia on the upper level of the Main
rminal is open 0900 to 1400 Mon.–Thurs., 0900–1900 Fri.
d 0900–1200 Sat. Automatic cash dispensers are available.

ACILITIES FOR DISABLED
RAVELLERS
eelchairs and escorts are available to assist disabled
sons within the airport's terminals and assistance is
ilable through the Skycap Office – ☎ 979-5070. Lifts are

available in both terminals. There is a Handicapped Courtesy
Van Service for use between the terminal buildings, the
Metrorail Station and public car parks.

LOST PROPERTY & LEFT LUGGAGE
Lost and found items are handled by the airport police station
at the Main Terminal – ☎ 685-8035. Left luggage lockers are
situated behind security check-points and are usually available
(depending on location) between 0630 and 2200

CATERING FACILITIES
Full catering facilities at the Vie de France Restaurant in the
Main Terminal, generally open 0600–2300. Other dining
lounges and snack bars are available through the terminal
buildings and include the Deli Market, Food Court and Cafe/Bar
situated in the Interim Terminal.

POST OFFICE
Post office in the Main Terminal is open 0830 to 1700 Mon.–
Fri. and 0830 to 1200 on Sat.

SHOPS & DUTY-FREE FACILITIES
Goods available include: books and newspapers, confectionery,
gifts, American speciality goods, etc. No duty-free shops at the
airport; duty-free goods are available at the Downtown Airports
Terminal duty-free shop in Washington.

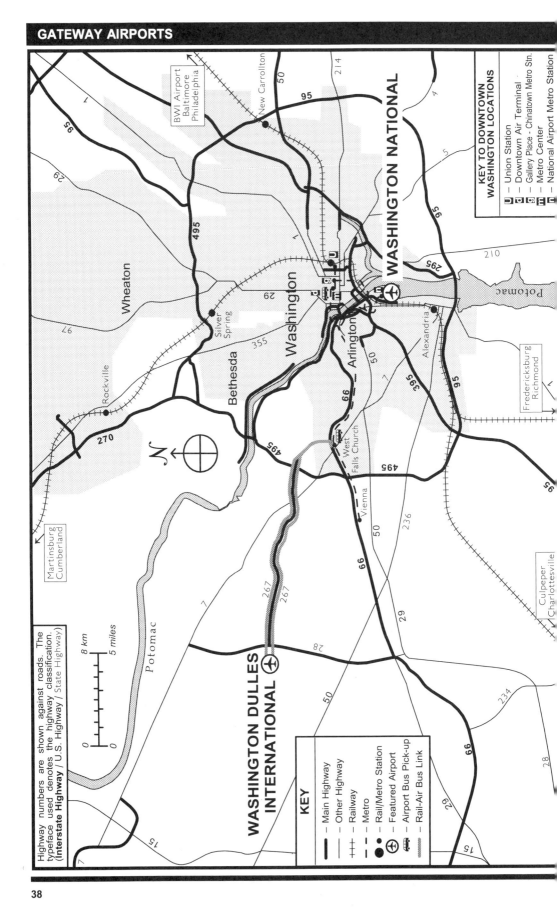

AIRLINE REPRESENTATION

Washington National is served by major American international and domestic/commuter airlines. The Main Terminal is used by all airlines with the exception of Delta, Delta Connection/Business Express and USAir, which use the Interim Terminal.

TAXIS & LIMOUSINES

Journey time by taxi to city centre is about 15–20 mins. fare approx. US$ 10. Approx. limousine fare is US$ 35. Taxis also serve suburban Maryland and Virginia.

PUBLIC TRANSPORT

Within the Airport: Courtesy shuttle buses run frequently between all terminals and the Metrorail station.

To Dulles International Airport: *The Metropolitan Washington Airports Authority* operate the *Washington Flyer Bus and Van Service* (☎ (703) 685-1400) between National and Dulles Airports. Daily from National (all terminals) hourly 0600–2300; from Dulles (Main Terminal) hourly 0500–2300; journey time 45 mins.; fare US$ 14.00.

To Downtown Washington: *Washington Flyer* (☎ (703) 685-1400) operate daily from the all terminals to the Downtown Air Terminal (16th and K Streets, NW) 0625 and every 30 mins. until 2125. Connecting loop services are available to the main downtown hotels. The *Metrorail* (☎ (202) 637-2437) station is located opposite the Main Terminal and is within walking distance of all terminals, or a courtesy shuttle bus is available. *Metrorail* trains operate frequent services to downtown Washington and to the suburbs 0530–2400Ⓐ; 0800–2400Ⓢ; 1000–2400Ⓢ; journey approx. 15 mins; fare US$ 1.20 peak periods, US$ 1.00 other times.

To Washington suburbs: by *Metrorail* (see above); *Metrobus* (☎ (703) 685-1400) operate to areas not served by *Metrorail* from a stop at the base of the *Metrorail* station.

To other destinations: *Groome Transportation* (call ☎ (202) 587-7629 for details) operate bus services to Fredicksburg and Richmond.

To all destinations: Washington DC, Maryland and Northern Virginia taxicabs are available at the exits of each terminal. Dispatchers are available to assist passengers.

CITY INFORMATION

This section contains details of urban and suburban transport in some of the major cities of North America, together with notes on how to get to locations in the surrounding area. It should be used in conjunction with the Timetable Section of the Guide.

BOSTON

GENERAL INFORMATION

A large port on the North-east seaboard of the USA. Founded in 1630 and famous for its association with the early Pilgrims, Boston is one of the oldest cities in the USA and therefore has a much deeper sense of history than most. Due to its early beginnings, the historical centre is quite compact by American standards, and much of the central area can be explored on foot. The political capital of Massachusetts, it is also often regarded as the area capital of the whole of New England.

GETTING AROUND

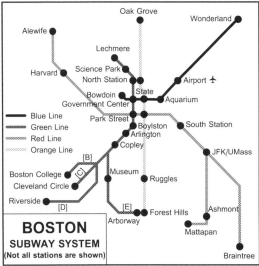

BOSTON SUBWAY SYSTEM
(Not all stations are shown)

Metropolitan Boston: *Massachusetts Bay Transportation Authority (MBTA)* (popularly referred to as the 'T') operates a comprehensive bus and subway network which covers the whole area. Fares range from US$ 0.85 to 1.50 (zone system); system-wide passes are available at US$ 5.00 (1-day), 9.00 (3-days) or 18.00 (7-days). These also offer discounts on popular attractions. Obtainable from Greater Boston Convention & Visitors Bureau Information Center at Boston Common; details of other sales outlets and information on routes and schedules available on ☎(617) 722-3200.

Boston Suburbs: *MBTA* commuter rail services cover many of the suburbs and a number of towns in Eastern Massachusetts.

Surrounding area: Plymouth and the Cape Cod area are served by *Plymouth and Brockton Street Railway* buses to North Plymouth, Hyannis *(for The Steamship Authority ferries to Nantucket)* and Provincetown, and by *Bonanza Bus Lines* to

Wood's Hole *(for The Steamship Authority ferries to Martha's Vineyard)*. In the Rhode Island area Providence can be reached by *MBTA*, by *AMTRAK* (services continue to New London and along the coast via New Haven and Stamford to New York and beyond) and by *Bonanza Bus Lines* (service also to Newport). In Central and Western Massachusetts Worcester and Springfield are served by *AMTRAK* (services continue to Albany and Chicago), *Greyhound Lines* (services continue to Albany, Buffalo and Cleveland) and by *Peter Pan Bus Lines* (services continue to Albany). **Gardner** and **Fitchburg** are served by *MBTA*. In Northern Massachusetts Lowell, Lawrence, Haverhill, Ipswich and Rockport are all on the *MBTA* network. In New Hampshire, Vermont and Maine, **Manchester** and **Concord** are served by *Vermont Transit* (services continue to White River Junction, Barre, Montpelier, Burlington and Montréal) and *Concord Trailways* (services continue to Littleton *(for Mt. Washington Cog Railway)*, Laconia, Conway and Berlin). **Portsmouth** is served by *C&J Trailways* (service continues to Dover), and by *Concord Trailways* and *Greyhound Lines* (services continue to Portland and Bangor).

MAIN TRANSPORT CENTRES

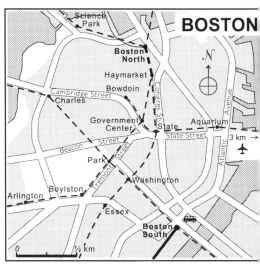

Logan International Airport (3 km E): Major gateway for many international flights; also domestic flights to most US cities. See 'Gateway Airports' section of this guide for details.

South Station (Red Line subway to Boston South): The *AMTRAK* terminus in Boston, and boarding point for North East Corridor trains to New York, Philadelphia and Washington, and for services to Springfield

Albany and Chicago. **MBTA** commuter rail services on the Attleboro, Framingham, Franklin and Providence lines also leave from here.

orth Station (Green/Orange Lines to Boston North): **MBTA** terminus for commuter rail services on the Fitchburg, Gardner, Haverhill, Ipswich, Lawrence, Lowell, Lynn and Rockport lines.

ack Bay Station (Orange Line to Back Bay): **AMTRAK** services from/to South Station pick up and set down here but cannot be used for local journeys between South and Back Bay or v.v. **MBTA** services from/to South Station also call here; these **can** be used for local journeys. See under 'South Station' for details of **AMTRAK/MBTA** services.

reyhound Bus Terminal (720 Atlantic Ave. – adjacent to South Station) (Red Line to Boston South): The Greyhound ticket office is located in the **AMTRAK** area of South Station. **For services of Greyhound Lines and Vermont Transit Lines.**

eter Pan Bus Terminal (555 Atlantic Avenue) (Red Line to Boston South): For services of **C & J Trailways**, **Concord Trailways**, **Peter Pan Trailways**, and **Plymouth & Brockton Street Railway**.

onanza Bus Terminal (145 Dartmouth Street – adjacent to Back Bay Station) (Orange Line to Back Bay). For services of **Bonanza Bus Lines**.

USEFUL TELEPHONE NUMBERS

Emergencies (Ambulance/Fire/Police)	**911**
Traveler's Aid Society.	(617) 542-7286
Thomas Cook Currency Services . .	(617) 426-0016
Boston Visitor Information Center . .	(617) 536-4100
Connecticut Dept. of Economic Dev.	(203) 258-4200
Maine Office of Tourism.	1-800-533-9595
Massachusetts Travel & Tourism . .	(617) 727-3201
New Hampshire Vacation Travel . .	(603) 271-2343
Rhode Island Tourism Division . . .	(401) 277-2601
State of Vermont Travel Division . .	(802) 828-3236
AMTRAK	(617) 482-3660
Bonanza Bus Lines.	(401) 331-7500
C&J Trailways.	(603) 742-5111
Concord Trailways	(603) 228-3300
Greyhound Lines.	(617) 423-5810
MBTA	(617) 722-3200
Peter Pan Bus Lines	(413) 781-2900
Plymouth & Brockton Street Railway	(617) 746-0378
The Steamship Authority	(508) 540-2022
Vermont Transit	(802) 864-6811

CHICAGO

ENERAL INFORMATION

he Heart of the Midwest' and 'The City on the Lake' are two descriptions often applied to Chicago. As the largest city in the Midwest and with a 29-mile frontage (much of it with parks and beaches) on Lake Michigan, these descriptions are well deserved (as is, at times, that other well-known attribute – 'The Windy City'!). Chicago is also the home of the busiest airport in the USA and of the tallest skyscrapers in the world. In 1994 it will be the venue of the opening ceremonies and games of the FIFA World Cup Football championships. Finding your way around is relatively easy due to the numerical grid system of streets which originates at the intersection of State and Madison Streets.

ETTING AROUND

etropolitan Chicago: Chicago Transportation Authority (CTA) operate the Rapid Transit System which comprises both the elevated ('L') and subway rail lines, (confusingly often both referred to as 'The Subway' but the recent change from calling the lines by cumbersome end-destination names to a simpler colour-code system should ease this) and buses (routes **1-204**) which cover the whole of the downtown area and the inner suburbs. Flat fares apply, with a system of upgrades to change a bus to a rail ticket, add a transfer (valid 2 hours), or pay an express surcharge (certain bus routes and Purple Line). The basic bus fare may be paid to the driver or purchased in advance as tokens (minimum 10) from banks, currency exchanges, certain supermarkets and from bus garages. Transfer tickets are required to change from bus to Rapid Transit and v.v., and also to change in the Downtown area between the 'L' and subway lines. To speed up the system, some Rapid Transit lines (Blue, Brown and Red Lines) operate a 'skip-stop' system 0600-1900 Mon-Fri., whereby alternate trains, designated 'A' or 'B', stop only at stations similarly designated. The stopping pattern is displayed at the station and on the trains, but the route name on train signs does **not** change to correspond with the direction of travel, so ensure you check the platform indicators. The Green Line is expected to close for approximately 2 years for repairs.

Chicago Suburbs: Pace operate suburban buses (Routes **208** and above); **CTA** monthly passes and transfers are available on these services. Buses can be flagged down at intersections since most bus stops are not marked. **Metropolitan Rail (METRA)** operates commuter trains from various downtown stations to the suburbs and beyond, and to locations in northwestern Indiana.

Surrounding area: In Northwestern Indiana, **Hammond**, **Gary** and **Michigan City** are served by **METRA** in association with the **Northern Indiana Commuter Transportation District ("The South Shore Line")** trains (service continues to South Bend); bus services are provided by **American Trailways**, by **Greyhound Lines** (services continue to Grand Rapids, to Indianapolis and Cincinnati), by **Indian Trails** (service continues to Kalamazoo, Flint and Bay City), and by **Southeastern Trailways** (services continue to Indianapolis and Cincinnati). In Northern Illinois, **Kankakee** is served by **AMTRAK** and **Greyhound Lines** (both services continue to Champaign, Memphis and New Orleans); **Joliet** is served by *METRA*, by *AMTRAK* (service continues to St. Louis, Kansas City, Albuquerque and Los Angeles) and by *Greyhound Lines* (service continues to Bloomington, Springfield and St. Louis); **Peoria** is served by *Blue Star Coaches*; **Aurora** is served by *METRA* and by *Greyhound Lines* (service continues to Moline, Davenport, Des Moines, Omaha, Denver and Salt Lake City); **Geneva**, **Harvard** and **Fox Lake** are served by *METRA*, and **Elgin** is served by *METRA* and by *Greyhound Lines* (service continues to Rockford, Beloit and Madison). In Wisconsin, **Kenosha** is served by *METRA*; **Milwaukee** by *AMTRAK* (service continues to La Crosse and

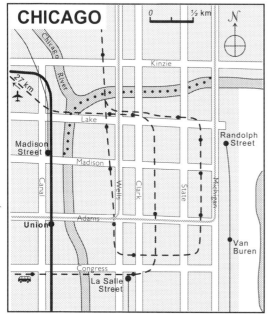

Minneapolis-St. Paul), and by *Greyhound Lines.*

MAIN TRANSPORT CENTRES

O'Hare International Airport (28 km NW): Major gateway for many international flights; also domestic flights to many US cities. See 'Gateway Airports' section of this guide for details.

Midway Airport (15 km SW) (Orange Line to Midway): Domestic flights to major US cities. Serves *America West Airlines*, *Cayman Airways*, *Delta Comair Airlines*, *Northwest Airlines*, *Southwest Airlines*, *TWA*, *United Airlines*, *USAir*.

Union Station (Buses 1, 60, 125, 151, 156, 157 *AMTRAK's* main station in Chicago and with 50 or so arrivals/departures per day, the hub of the AMTRAK system. Places served direct include Grand Rapids, Port Huron, Detroit, Cleveland, Boston, New York, Pittsburgh, Philadelphia, Memphis, New Orleans, St Louis, Dallas, Houston, San Antonio, El Paso, Tucson, Phoenix, Los Angeles, Kansas City, Albuquerque, Flagstaff, Pasadena, Denver, Salt Lake City, Reno, Sacramento, Oakland, Portland, Seattle, Minneapolis-St. Paul and Milwaukee. *METRA* Commuter Rail services to Fox Lake, Elgin and Aurora, plus a few Mon-Fri. evening peak journeys to Orland Park and Joliet also depart from here.

Randolph Street Station (Buses 3, 4, 60; Blue and Purple lines to Randolph/Wabash — one-block away): *METRA* Commuter Rail services to University Park and *NICD* "The South Shore Line" to Hammond, Gary, Michigan City and South Bend.

La Salle Street Station (Blue Line to La Salle/Congress): *METRA* Commuter Rail services to Joliet.

Madison Street Station: (Buses 20, 56, 131, 157) *METRA* Commuter Rail to Kenosha, Harvard and Geneva.

Greyhound Bus Terminal (630 West Harrison Street) (Bus 60; Blue Line to Clinton/Congress — one block away): For services of *American Trailways*, *Blue Star Coaches*, *Greyhound Lines*, *Indian Trails* and *Southeastern Trailways*.

USEFUL TELEPHONE NUMBERS

Emergencies (Police) 911
Traveler's Aid (O'Hare) . . . . . . (312) 686-7556
Thomas Cook Currency Services . . (312) 993-7544
Chicago Convention & Tourism Bureau (312) 567-8500
Chicago Office of Tourism . . . . . (312) 744-2400
Illinois Bureau of Tourism 1-800-223-0121

American Trailways . . . . (317) 635-4000
AMTRAK . . . . (312) 558-1075
Blue Star Coaches . . . . (309) 674-5133
Chicago Transit Authority (CTA) . . (312) 836-7000
Greyhound Lines . . . . (312) 781-2900
Indian Trails . . . . (517) 725-5100
METRA Commuter Rail . . . . . . (312) 836-7000
Midway Airport . . . . (312) 767-0500
NICD ("The South Shore Line") . . 1-800-356-2079
Pace Suburban Buses . . . . . . (312) 836-7000
Southeastern Trailways . . . . . (312) 951-6800

LOS ANGELES

GENERAL INFORMATION

It is easy to underestimate distances in Los Angeles. With an urban area of over 100 kilometres from east to west and some 70 km from north to south, Greater Los Angeles is huge. Not, as can be imagined, a city easily explored on foot. In fact, many Angelenos, as the locals are called, wouldn't dream of exploring **anywhere** on foot, in their city of boulevards and freeways dedicated to King Automobile. In recent years, however, the situation has begun to change. A slow, creeping paralysis, where commuter journeys by car can take up to 2 hours (and one then has the problem of finding somewhere to park it) has forced Angelenos into looking afresh at ways of getting around their city. The abrupt medium- to long-term closure of several freeways damaged by the 1994 earthquake will probably accelerate this process. The public transport system in Los Angeles, while acceptable in a such a car-minded city, would be considered hopelessly inadequate anywhere else.

Although the suburbs have a comprehensive bus network, services are not very frequent when compared to suburban services elsewhere. Metro construction is in its infancy, with just two lines open, and an extension and third line being built.

GETTING AROUND

Downtown Los Angeles: *Southern California Rapid Transit District (RTD)* operate a comprehensive bus and, as yet, limited metro system. The 35-km Blue Line Metro runs from 7th St. Metro Center to Long Beach, an hour's journey away; the first 7 kms of the Red Line (opened in 1993) currently operates from Union Station to Westlake/MacArthur Park; extensions to Wilshire/Vermont and Hollywood/Vine are under construction. The two lines connect at 7th St. Metro Center. A new 32-km metro (the Green Line) is due to open in 1995. Bus lines numbered below **100** are local services covering the downtown area.

Los Angeles Suburbs: *Metrolink* operate commuter rail services Mon-Fri. to the northwestern, eastern and southern suburbs. *RTD* buses cover the suburbs with bus lines numbered **100** and above, and which are arranged as follows: the **100s** are local East-West services, the **200s** local North-South services, the **300s** are limited stop, the **400s** and **500s** are express services and the **600s** are special event services.

Surrounding area: Northwards along the coast **Oxnard** and **Santa Barbara** are served by *AMTRAK* (service continues to San Luis Obispo, Oakland, Portland and Seattle) and by *Greyhound Lines* (also serving Malibu Beach and Ventura, and continuing to San Jose and San Francisco). In Inland California, **Bakersfield** (for *AMTRAK* trains to Fresno, Merced, Stockton and Oakland) is served by *AMTRAK* thruway buses which connect with the trains at Bakersfield, and by *Greyhound Lines* (services continue to Fresno, Merced, Stockton, Oakland, San Francisco and Sacramento). **Mojave** is served by *Greyhound Lines* (service continues to Bishop and Reno). **San Bernardino** and **Riverside** are served Mon–Fri. by *Metrolink*, and daily by *AMTRAK* (service continues to Barstow, Las Vegas and Salt Lake City) and by *Greyhound Lines* (services continue to Barstow, Las Vegas, Flagstaff, Albuquerque and Oklahoma City). Southwards along the coast, **Oceanside** and **San Diego** can be reached by *AMTRAK.*

MAIN TRANSPORT CENTRES

Los Angeles International Airport (24 km SW): Often referred to by its international designator code

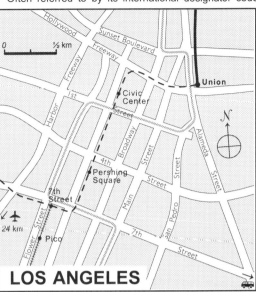

LOS ANGELES

of LAX. Major gateway of many international and domestic flights. See under 'Gateway Airports' section of this guide for more details.

Union Station (Blue Line Metro to Union Station): All *AMTRAK* trains depart from here; also the pick-up point for *AMTRAK* thruway buses to Bakersfield. All *Metrolink* trains also call here (service Mon-Fri. only).

Greyhound Bus Terminal (1716 East 7th St.) (Bus 60, 61, 360): For services of *Greyhound Lines*.

USEFUL TELEPHONE NUMBERS

Emergencies (Ambulance/Fire/Police)	**911**
Thomas Cook Currency Services . .	(213) 624-4221
Anaheim Visitor & Convention Bureau	(714) 999 8999
California Office of Tourism	1-800 862 2543
Greater Los Angeles Visitor Center .	(213) 689-8822
AMTRAK	1-800-USA-RAIL
Greyhound Lines.	(213) 629-8401
Metrolink	1-800-371-LINK
RTD	(213) 626-4455

MIAMI

GENERAL INFORMATION

A large city, port and resort on Florida's East Coast at the southern end of the 100-km conurbation which stretches from West Palm Beach to South Miami. The warm Florida climate attracts not only many holidaymakers, but also a number of former residents of northern US cities who have made Miami their home; as a result the Miami area is one of the fastest-growing in the USA.

GETTING AROUND

Metropolitan Miami: *Metro-Dade Transit* operate a comprehensive bus network throughout Dade County,

which embraces the whole of Metropolitan Miami. A 33-km elevated rapid transit metro connects the north-west and south-west suburbs via the downtown area; in the downtown area itself, an elevated 3-km 'people mover' connects with the metro at Government Center Station. These three constituents are referred to as Metrobus, Metrorail and Metromover respectively. A flat-fare system operates, with a transfer arrangement (transfers must be purchased at the start of the first journey) for changing from bus to bus, bus to rail or v.v., or mover to rail (rail to mover is free).

Miami suburbs: *Metro-Date Transit* buses and trains

serve the inner suburbs. Buses reach Miami Beach and Key Biscayne by causeways; these services employ route letters rather than the more usual numbers found elsewhere in Miami. *Tri-Rail* connects Miami International Airport with the northern suburbs at Metrorail and Golden Glades stations; the downtown area can be reached by changing to *Metrorail* at Metrorail Station.

Surrounding Area: Southward from Miami via **Homestead**, the remarkable trip along the causeways and bridges of the Florida Keys all the way to **Key West** is made by *Greyhound Lines*. To the west, the Everglades are crossed by *Greyhound Lines* en route to **Fort Myers** (service continues to St. Petersburg and Tampa). To the north, Fort Lauderdale and West Palm Beach are served by *Tri-Rail* and by *AMTRAK* (services continue to Orlando,

Jacksonville, Richmond, Washington and beyond), and by *Greyhound Lines* (services continue to Orlando, Tallahassee, New Orleans, Jacksonville, Richmond and New York).

MAIN TRANSPORT CENTRES

Miami International Airport (10 km W): Major International and domestic gateway; for full details see under 'Gateway Airports' section of this guide.

Miami AMTRAK Station (Metrorail to TriRail Station - one block; Bus L to AMTRAK Station): *AMTRAK's* most southerly station, about 12 km from Downtown Miami. Departure point for trains to Jacksonville, Charleston, Richmond, Washington, Philadelphia and New York; also to New Orleans, Houston, El Paso, Phoenix and Los Angeles.

Miami Airport Station: The southern terminus of *TriRail*; trains depart from here to Golden Glades, Fort Lauderdale, Boca Raton and West Palm Beach. The station is actually some 15 blocks from the Airport; TriRail operate a free shuttle bus between the station and the airport.

Greyhound Bus Terminal (700 Biscayne Blvd, Miami Bayside – Downtown location; open daily 0630-1800 only) (Metromover to College/Bayside – 2 blocks): Serves *Greyhound Lines*.

Greyhound Bus Terminal (4111 N.W. 27th St., Miami West – 11 km from Downtown Miami; open 24 hours) (Bus 7; TriRail ShuttleBus): Serves *Greyhound Lines*.

USEFUL TELEPHONE NUMBERS

Emergencies	**911**
Thomas Cook Currency Services . .	(305) 381-9252
Florida Division of Tourism	(904) 487-1462
AMTRAK	1-800-USA-RAIL
Greyhound Lines (Miami Bayside) .	(305) 374-6160
Greyhound Lines (Miami West) . . .	(305) 871-1810
Metro-Dade Transit	(305) 638-6700

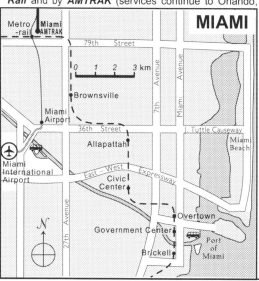

MIAMI

MONTRÉAL

GENERAL INFORMATION

Set on a series of islands in the midst of the St. Lawrence River, Montréal is the second-largest French-speaking city in the world. It has a cosmopolitan flavour, with a unique culture and ambience ranging from French village to glittering metropolis.

GETTING AROUND

Metropolitan Montréal: The *Société de transport de la Communauté urbaine de Montréal* (mercifully abbreviated to *STCUM*) operates a metro system which serves mainly the Downtown area and inner suburbs, a comprehensive network of buses which covers the whole of Metropolitan Montréal, and two commuter rail services which serve the western and northwestern suburbs.

Montréal suburbs: To the north and west across the Rivière-des-Prairies (Montréal North Shore), urban transport is provided by *Société de transport de Laval (STL)*. STCUM commuter rail services reach Dorval, Île-Perrot, Dorion, Hudson and Rigaud in the

west, and stations in Western Laval en route to Deux-Montagnes in the north west. To the south and east across the St. Lawrence (Montréal South Shore), urban transport is provided by *Société de transport de la Rive-Sud de Montréal (STRSM)*. Yellow Line 4 of the *STCUM* metro crosses the St. Lawrence to connect with *STRSM* buses at Longueuil.

Surrounding area: To the south west, **Cornwall** is served by *VIA Rail* and by *Voyageur Colonial* buses (both services continue to Kingston, Belleville, Oshawa and Toronto). To the west, **Ottawa** can be reached by *VIA Rail* and by *Voyageur Colonial*. To the north west, **St. Jérome** and **Ste. Agathe** are served by *Autobus Auger N-O* (service continues to Mont Laurier, Grand Remous, Val d'Or and Noranda-Rouyn). To the north east, **Shawinigan** is reached by *VIA Rail* (services continue to Chambord and Jonquière, and to La Tuque, Senneterre and Cochrane); **Trois Rivières** by *Orléans Express* buses (service continues to Québec) and **St. Hyacinthe** and **Drummondville** by *VIA Rail* (services continue to Québec, and to Lévis, Rivière du Loup,

Mont Joli, Gaspé, Moncton, Amherst, Truro and Halifax). To the east, **Sherbrooke** is served by *VIA Rail* (service continues to Saint John, Moncton, Amherst, Truro and Halifax), and by *Autobus Auger Estrie* and *Autobus Bernier Lemay*. To the south east, **Newport** is served by *Autobus Viens*. To the south, **Burlington** is served by *AMTRAK* trains to Essex Junction (service continues to White River, New London, New Haven and New York), and by *Greyhound Lines*; and **Plattsburg** by *AMTRAK* and by *Greyhound Lines* (both services continue to Albany and New York).

MAIN TRANSPORT CENTRES

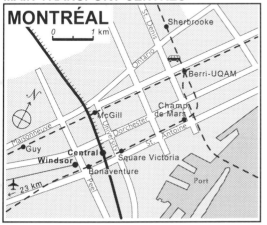

Montréal International Airport (Mirabel): Main gateway for international flights other than from North America. See 'Gateway Airports' section of this guide for details.

Montréal International Airport (Dorval) (Autocar Connaisseur/Gray Line bus)**:** For flights within Canada and to USA.

Central Station (Orange Line 2 Métro to Bonaventure)**:** All *VIA Rail* and *AMTRAK* services leave from here; also *STCUM* trains on the Deux-Montagnes line.

Windsor Station (Orange Line 2 Métro to Bonaventure)**:** For *STCUM* trains on the Rigaud Line.

Voyageur Bus Terminal (505 de Maisonneuve Blvd. East) (Green Line 1, Orange Line 2 or Yellow Line 4 Métro to Berri-UQAM)**:** For services of *Greyhound Lines* and *Voyageur Colonial*.

USEFUL TELEPHONE NUMBERS

Emergencies	**911**
Thomas Cook Currency Exchange .	(514) 397-4029
Greater Montréal Tourism Bureau. .	(514)·873-2015
Tourisme Québec	(514) 873-2015
AMTRAK	1-800-426-8725
Autobus Auger Estrie	(514) 691-1654
Autobus Auger N-O	(514) 691-1654
Autobus Bernier Lemay	(514) 546-2490
Autobus Viens.	(514) 293-3129
Autocar Connoisseur/Gray Line. . .	(514) 934-1222
Dorval Airport	(514) 633-3105
Greyhound Lines.	(514) 842-2281
Orléans Express	(514) 847-4020
VIA Rail	(514) 871-1331
Voyageur Bus Terminal	(514) 842-2281

NEW YORK

GENERAL INFORMATION

New York, New York. The Big Apple. Broadway. Yellow cabs. Steaming hydrants. "Walk/Don't Walk" signs. Everything you've seen on the films, but for real. And with one of the most comprehensive public transport systems in the world, it's very easy to get around. The *Metropolitan Transit Authority (MTA)* is the co-ordinating body for the main transport agencies which operate in and around New York:- *New York City Transit Authority (TA)* (subway system, buses in New York City, and Staten Island Rapid Transit); *Long Island Rail Road (LIRR)* (trains from New York City to Long Island destinations); *Metro-North Commuter Railroad* (trains from New York City on the Hudson, Harlem and New Haven lines, and from Hoboken on the Port Jervis and Pascack Valley lines); *Metropolitan Suburban Bus Authority (MSBA)* (buses linking western Long Island with *LIRR* stations and with the subway).

GETTING AROUND

Metropolitan New York: Comprised of the boroughs of Bronx, Brooklyn, Manhattan, Queens and Staten Island. All are served by *TA* buses, which carry a prefix (Bx, B, M, Q, S) in front of the route number according to the borough they primarily serve. Staten Island has its own self-contained *TA* Rapid Transit;

the other 4 boroughs are all served by *TA* subway. The subway system is one of the most intensive in the world, with 25 lines, each designated either by a number or letter. However, most lines are operated as part of a larger group, and run on group tracks in Manhattan, only separating into branches at the outer ends of the lines, so it's not as complicated as it seems. Various patterns of service operate, with local, skip-stop, express, peak-hour or night-only services. Subway maps are available free-of-charge at token booths (or you can write for a copy to: Customer Information, 130 Livingston St., Brooklyn, NY 11201). In Manhattan, platform signs for "Uptown" refer to northbound trains and "Downtown" to southbound trains. A flat-fare system (currently $1.25) operates on both the subway and the buses. For the subway this must be exchanged for a token at the token booth on entry to the system, or a 'Ten Pak' can be purchased. These save time if you are using the system a lot and they are also available from various other locations, including some tourist attractions or even McDonalds restaurants. You can transfer to another subway line at designated stations without extra charge. Buses accept either tokens or coins (exact change only); free transfers to intersecting bus routes are permitted (ask the driver for a transfer ticket when you board the first bus), but are only valid for 1 hour and for onward (not return) journeys.

New York suburbs: In New Jersey, **Newark** (for *New Jersey Transit (NJ Transit)* rail and bus services to southern and western New Jersey suburbs) is served by *Port Authority Trans-Hudson Corporation (PATH)*, *NJ Transit* and *AMTRAK* trains (only certain *AMTRAK* trains may be used for local journeys from New York to Newark or v.v.; see timetables for details), and by *Greyhound Lines* buses; **Jersey City** and **Hoboken** (for *NJ Transit* rail and bus services to central and western New Jersey suburbs; also *Metro-North/NJ Transit* trains on the Port Jervis and Pascack Valley lines) is served by *PATH*. In New York State, the northern suburbs of New York city are served by *Metro-North* trains; the eastern suburbs by *LIRR* trains and by *MSBA* buses.

Surrounding area: Southwards along the coast, **Atlantic City** can be reached by *AMTRAK*, and by *Greyhound Lines* and *NJ Transit* buses. New Jersey is comprehensively served by *NJ Transit* buses and trains. In Pennsylvania, **Philadelphia** is served by *AMTRAK* (services continue to Baltimore, Washington, Richmond, Charlotte, Jacksonville, Tampa and Miami, and to Harrisburg, Pittsburgh and Chicago); **Bethlehem** and **Allentown** by *Trans-Bridge Lines*, and **Scranton** by *Greyhound Lines* (services continue to Binghamton, Rochester and Buffalo). For destinations in upstate New York, **Albany**, **Syracuse**, **Rochester** and **Buffalo** are all reached by *AMTRAK* (services continue to Cleveland, Toledo and Chicago, to Niagara Falls and Toronto, and to Plattsburgh and Montréal), by *Greyhound Lines* (services continue to Cleveland, and to Plattsburg and Montréal) and by *Adirondack Trailways*. In Connecticut and Massachusetts, **Danbury** and **Waterbury** are both reached by branches of *Metro-North*; **Hartford** and **Springfield** by *AMTRAK* and by *Greyhound Lines*; **Stamford**, **Bridgeport** and **New Haven** by *Metro-North* and by *AMTRAK* (service continues to New London, Providence and Boston)

MAIN TRANSPORT CENTRES

John F. Kennedy International Airport (24 km SE in Queens); **La Guardia Airport** (13 km NE in Queens); **Newark International Airport** (28 km SW in Newark NJ): All 3 airports serve New York with both international and domestic flights; for details see the 'Gateway Airports' section of this guide.

Pennsylvania Station (Midtown Manhattan) (Subways 1, 2, 3, 9, A, C, E to Penn Station, or B, D, F, N, Q, R to 34th St; within walking distance of Port Authority Bus Station): Usually abbreviated to 'Penn', Pennsylvania is the arrival/departure point for all *AMTRAK* services, and also for Manhattan services of *NJ Transit* and *LIRR*.

Grand Central Terminal (Midtown Manhattan) (Subways 4, 5, 6, 7, S to Grand Central): Rather less 'Grand' these days than in its heyday, Grand Central Terminal is now confined to handling the commuter services of *Metro-North* on the Hudson, Harlem and New Haven lines to the northern New York suburbs and to Connecticut.

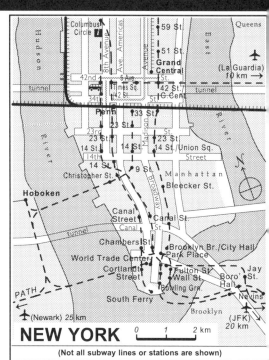

NEW YORK

0   1   2 km

(Not all subway lines or stations are shown)

33rd Street PATH Station (Midtown Manhattan) (Subways B, D, F, N, Q, R to 34th St. offer nearby access. Subway stations 33rd St. on subways 4, 5, 6 and 34th St. on 1, 2, 3, 9 are a good walk away (34th St. on A, C, E is further still) but all these are connected to 33rd Street PATH station by bus M34): Midtown Manhattan terminus (trains also call at 23rd, 14th, 9th and Christopher Streets) for *PATH* trains to Hoboken and Jersey City.

World Trade Center (Lower Manhattan) (Subway E to World Trade Center; 1, 9 and N, R to Cortland Street; 2, 3 to Park Place): Lower Manhattan terminus for *PATH* trains to Hoboken, Jersey City and Newark

Flatbush Avenue (Downtown Brooklyn) (Subways 2, 3, 4, 5, D, Q to Atlantic Ave.; B, M, N, R to Pacific St.) Main western terminus for *LIRR* trains to various Long Island destinations.

Jamaica (Queens) (LIRR from Penn; subways E, J, Z) The 'Clapham Junction' of the *LIRR* system (all lines except Flushing call here) and probably the best place to head for if your Long Island destination does not have a direct or convenient service from Penn

Hoboken (NJ) (PATH train from 33rd St.; PATH train or Hoboken Ferry from World Trade Center/Battery Park): For *PATH* trains to Jersey City and Newark; *NJ Transit* trains to various destinations throughout New Jersey; *NJ Transit/Metro-North* trains on the Port Jervis and Pascack Valley lines to destinations in New Jersey and New York State.

Port Authority Bus Terminal (Midtown Manhattan) (Subways A, C, E to 42nd St; 1, 2, 3, 7, 9, N, R, S to Times Square; within walking distance of Penn Station): Main bus station in New York, serving *Adirondack Trailways*, *Bonanza Bus Lines*, *Capitol Trailways*, *Carey Transportation*, *Greyhound Lines*, *Martz Trailways*, *NJ Transit*, *Short Line*

Susquehanna Trailways, *Trans-Bridge Bus Lines*, *Vermont Transit*.

George Washington Bridge Bus Station (Upper Manhattan) (Subway A to 175th St; 1, 9 to 181st St.)**:** Serves **NJ Transit**; also commuter buses to Upstate New York counties.

USEFUL TELEPHONE NUMBERS

Emergencies	**911**
Thomas Cook Currency Services . .	(212) 757-6915
New York Convention & Visitors Bureau	(212) 397-8222
Adirondack Trailways	1-800-858-8555
AMTRAK	1-800-872-7245
Bonanza Bus Lines.	1-800-556-3815
Capitol Trailways.	1-800-858-8555
Carey Transportation	(718) 632-0500
Greyhound Lines.	(212) 971-6361
Long Island Rail Road	(718) 217-LIRR
Martz Trailways	(212) 868-5973
Metro-North Commuter Railroad . .	(212) 532-4900
New Jersey Transit.	(201) 762-5100
PATH	1-800-234-7284
Short Line	(212) 736-4700
Susquehanna Trailways.	1-800-858-8555
Trans-Bridge Bus Lines	(215) 868-6001
Vermont Transit	(212) 971-6361

ORLANDO

GENERAL INFORMATION

Situated in sunny Central Florida, Orlando is the home of Walt Disney World, famed for its Epcot Centre and Magic Kingdom. To many people the two are synonymous, but splendid though it is, there is far more to Orlando than Disneyworld; even before Micky Mouse, Donald Duck, Goofy et al arrived in 1971, Orlando already had several theme parks as part of its quest to become Fun Capital of the World, and today boasts so many attractions that it would need a stay of several weeks to do justice to them all. Because today's Orlando has developed over the last 30 years or so, it is a very spacious city, designed for the car (although notwithstanding this, it can become surprisingly congested during the rush hours), and many of the larger attractions are several miles out of town. Local public transport is currently undergoing major administrative re-organisation together with an expansion programme; this has already resulted in a new co-ordinated operating company **(LYNX)**. The operation is so far limited mainly to buses which cover the downtown area and inner suburbs; to emphasise the new company these operate on 'links' rather than the more usual routes or lines. The recent re-organisation has resulted in a number of changes to the link network; these could still be ongoing, so check with **LYNX** for current information when you arrive. While transport is available to most of the out-of-town attractions, this often tends to be operated by shuttle buses provided by (or on behalf of) the attractions themselves, or by private companies. These shuttle buses generally run on a 'when-and-where-required' basis rather than to a fixed schedule, and we suggest that you contact the organisation concerned or the Orlando/Orange County Convention and Visitors Bureau for details of them.

GETTING AROUND

Metropolitan Orlando: **LYNX** operate a network of buses throughout the downtown area and inner suburbs. A flat-fare (currently $0.75) system is in operation; a transfer ($0.10) must be purchased to change from one bus to another. This transfer is free if using a book of 10 or 20 tickets.

Orlando suburbs: **Sanford** is reached by **LYNX** bus **39**, which visits the northern suburbs en route; **Kissimmee** is served by **LYNX** bus **4**.

Surrounding area (for specific attractions see notes above)**:** **Daytona Beach** is reached by **Greyhound Lines** buses (service continues to Jacksonville); **Cocoa** *(for Cape Canaveral and Port Canaveral),* **Melbourne** and **Fort Pierce** by **Greyhound Lines** (service continues to West Palm Beach, Fort Lauderdale and Miami); **Kissimmee** and **Sebring** by **AMTRAK** (service continues to Okeechobee, West Palm Beach, Fort Lauderdale and Miami); **Lakeland** and **Tampa** *(for Clearwater and St. Petersburg) by* **AMTRAK**; **Ocala** by **Greyhound Lines** (service continues to Gainesville, Tallahassee, Pensacola, Mobile and New Orleans).

MAIN TRANSPORT CENTRES

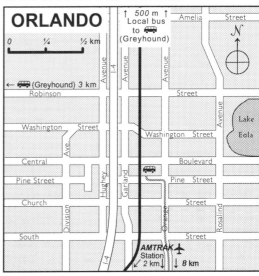

Orlando International Airport: Major national and international gateway; see 'Gateway Airports' section of this guide for details.

AMTRAK Station (Bus 34 to Sligh Boulevard)**:** About 2 km south of Downtown area. For all **AMTRAK** services.

Greyhound Bus Station (555 N. Magruder Blvd.) About 3 km west of Downtown area (Bus 30 from Colonial Drive)**:** Serves **Greyhound Lines**.

LYNX Downtown Bus Terminal (between Central Blvd. and Pine Street)**:** For **LYNX** local services.

USEFUL TELEPHONE NUMBERS

Emergencies	**911**
Thomas Cook Currency Services . .	(407) 351-4334
Orlando/Orange County Visitors Bureau	(407) 363-5800
Florida Division of Tourism	(904) 487-146?
AMTRAK	1-800-USA-RAI?
Greyhound Lines.	(407) 292-342?
LYNX	(407) 841-824?

PHILADELPHIA

GENERAL INFORMATION

Located almost half way between New York and Washington, Philadelphia is often overlooked by overseas visitors as a holiday destination. Yet this fifth-largest city and one-time capital of the USA has much to offer, both historically and culturally. One of the oldest US cities, the historic area situated near the waterfront of the Delaware River is relatively compact and is easily explored on foot. The Downtown area is known as Center City Philadelphia.

GETTING AROUND

Metropolitan Philadelphia: The *Southeastern Pennsylvania Transportation Authority (SEPTA)* operates a comprehensive system of buses and trams (streetcars) throughout the city, plus two subway lines, subway-surface lines and a suburban rail network. A flat-fare (currently $ 1.50 – exact fare only) applies on most routes; reduced-rate tokens and passes are available. The *Port Authority Transit Corporation of Pennsylvania and New Jersey (PATCO)* operates a suburban line which calls at several Center City stations and which can be used between these.

Philadelphia suburbs: *SEPTA* commuter rail services operate to suburbs and nearby towns in Pennsylvania and also to Wilmington in Delaware and to Trenton in New Jersey. The *PATCO* Hi-Speed Line crosses the Delaware River to serve the southeastern suburbs in New Jersey, including Camden (*for connecting New Jersey Transit (NJ Transit) bus services to other destinations in Southern New Jersey*), Collingswood and Lindenwold.

Surrounding area: Within Pennsylvania, **Lancaster** and **Harrisburg** are served by *AMTRAK*, and by *Greyhound Lines* buses (service operates via York and Gettysburg); **Pottstown** and **Reading** by *Carl R. Bieber Tourways* buses, and **Allentown** and **Bethlehem** by *Capitol Trailways* buses. In New Jersey, **Trenton** is reached by *AMTRAK* (service continues to Princeton, Newark, New York and Boston) and by *SEPTA* trains (*connecting NJ Transit trains to Princeton, Newark and New York, and buses to various destinations in Central New Jersey*); **Atlantic City** by *Greyhound Lines* and *NJ Transit* buses. In Delaware, **Wilmington** is reached by *AMTRAK* (services continue to Baltimore, Washington, Richmond, Charleston, Jacksonville, Tampa and Miami, to Atlanta and New Orleans, and to Cincinnati, Indianapolis and Chicago), and by *SEPTA* trains.

MAIN TRANSPORT CENTRES

Philadelphia International Airport (12 km SW): Gateway for a number of International and domestic flights. See the 'Gateway Airports' section of this guide for details.

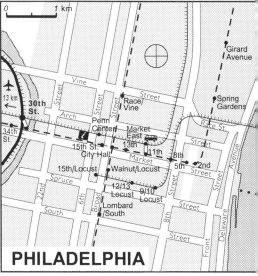

PHILADELPHIA

30th Street Station (Market-Frankford Subway o Subway-Surface Line to 30th St.): All *AMTRA?* services leave from here, as do all the Regional Ra lines of *SEPTA*.

Penn Center (Suburban) Station (Market-Frankfor? Subway or Subway-Surface Line to 15th St.; Broa? Street Subway to City Hall): Alternative departur? point for all *SEPTA* Regional Rail lines.

Market East Station (Market-Frankford Subway to 11t? Street): Alternative departure point for all *SEPT?* Regional Rail lines.

Market Street Station (Market-Frankford Subway t? 8th St.): For *PATCO* trains to Camden an? Lindenwold. These can also be boarded at 15-16th S? or 12-13th St. (both a couple of blocks from Walnut Locust on the Broad Street Subway) or from 9-10th S?

Greyhound Bus Terminal: (1001 Filbert Stree? (Regional Rail lines to Market East; Market-Frankfor? Subway to 11th St.): For services of *Carl R. Biebe? Tourways*, *Greyhound Lines* and *NJ Transit*.

Capitol Trailways Bus Terminal (55 N. 11th St? (Regional Rail lines to Market East; Market-Frankfor? Subway to 11th St.): For services of *Capito? Trailways* and *Peter Pan Trailways*.

USEFUL TELEPHONE NUMBERS

Emergencies (Police, Fire, Ambulance) . . .	**91?**
Thomas Cook Currency Services . .	(215) 563-554?
Traveler's Aid	(215) 546-057?
Visitor Information	(215) 636-166?
AMTRAK	(215) 824-160?
Capitol Trailways.	1-800-444-287?
Greyhound Bus Terminal	(215) 931-400?
PATCO	(215) 922-460?
SEPTA.	(215) 580-780?

SAN DIEGO

GENERAL INFORMATION

Birthplace of California, San Diego is the second-largest city in the state and sixth-largest in the USA. Yet unlike Los Angeles, 190 km to the north, it doesn't have the feel of a large city. The Downtown area is relatively compact, the airport is only 5 km from the centre, and it has a laid-back feel to it, perhaps due in part to its proximity to Mexico, only some 30 km to the south (if you intend to visit Mexico, non-US citizens need a multiple-entry visa as well as a passport). The climate is ideal year-round, the beaches are superb, there's plenty of history; in short, San Diego is an ideal holiday destination.

GETTING AROUND

Metropolitan San Diego: The area is served by seven public transit operators who work together through two agencies (the Metropolitan Transit Development Board [MTDB] in the south of the county, and North County Transit District [NCTD] in the north). Between them, these operators and agencies provide one co-ordinated operation, the **Metropolitan Transit System (MTS)**. *MTS* operates a comprehensive network of bus routes, and also the San Diego Trolley light rail system which comprises two lines, both of which serve the downtown area (known in San Diego as Centre City). Flat-fare arrangements apply on local and express buses; the Trolley fare depends on distance travelled. Transfers between vehicles, and between one mode of transport and another are available at a small supplement.

San Diego suburbs: All suburbs are served by the *MTS* network of local and express buses (express service numbers end in '0', so they are easily identified). Additionally in the north, Del Mar is on the *AMTRAK* rail line to Los Angeles; in the east the San Diego Trolley reaches as far as El Cajon Transit Center, and in the south it runs to San Ysidro on the Mexican border.

Surrounding area: Northwards along the coast, **Oceanside** and **Los Angeles** are reached by *AMTRAK* trains. To the east, **Calexico** *(for buses across the border to Mexicali, from where onward bus and rail services further into Mexico are available)* is served by *Greyhound Lines* buses (service continues to Yuma and Phoenix). To the south, **San Ysidro** trolley station is only 100 metres from the frontier; from here (see comments regarding documentation above) it is but a few minutes walk or short taxi ride into downtown Tijuana *(from where onward bus services further into Mexico are available)*.

MAIN TRANSPORT CENTRES

San Diego International Airport (Lindbergh Field) (5km NW) (Bus 2 to/from Broadway)**:** Gateway for a number of domestic and international flights.

AMTRAK Station (Trolley to Santa Fe Depot)**:** For all *AMTRAK* services to Del Mar, Oceanside and Los Angeles.

Greyhound Bus Station (Trolley to Civic Center)**:** For all *Greyhound Lines* services.

USEFUL TELEPHONE NUMBERS

Emergencies	**911**
Thomas Cook Currency Services	(619) 235-0900
Del Mar Chamber of Commerce	(619) 755-4844
Oceanside Chamber of Commerce	(619) 722-1534
San Diego Visitors Bureau	(619) 232-3101
San Ysidro Chamber of Commerce	(619) 428-1281
AMTRAK	1-800-USA-RAIL
Greyhound Lines	(619) 239-8082
Metropolitan Transit System (MTS)	(619) 233-3004

SAN FRANCISCO

GENERAL INFORMATION

San Francisco. A city full of character, with its famous Golden Gate Bridge and its cable cars. Surrounded on three sides by water, San Francisco has a temperate climate, which is probably just as well if you intend to do much exploring on foot, as parts of the city are incredibly hilly. So much so, in fact, that motorists must, *by law*, turn their wheels into the kerb when parking on hills. Fortunately for non-motorists and non-mountaineers, there is an excellent public transport system. It was the hills (or grades, as they are known in North America) that spawned the first San Francisco public transport system in 1873 – the cable car network. This reached its heyday in the early part of this century with 8 lines and over 175 km of track, but in later years the system was gradually allowed to fall into disrepair (a process assisted from time to time by earthquakes). Nowadays, after a restoration programme in the early 1980s, 3 cable car lines remain with about 18 km of track. Over the years they have been joined by ferries, buses, a metro-streetcar system which operates underground in Downtown and on the streets in the suburbs, and a futuristic rapid transit network. Together, these networks serve the whole of the Bay Area of Greater San Francisco.

GETTING AROUND

Metropolitan San Francisco: *San Francisco Municipal Railway* (usually abbreviated to *'San Francisco Muni'* or just *'Muni'*) operates a 5-line metro (light-rail) system which connects the downtown area (where it runs underground) with the western and southwestern suburbs. This is supplemented throughout the city by a comprehensive network of buses, and additionally in the downtown area by the cable cars, which, although now a also tourist attraction, are still used by some members of the local population for the purpose for which they were originally intended – as a means of public transport. The Metro lines are identified by letter (J, K, L, M, N), buses by route numbers supplemented by colour-coded destination signs (black and white = local service, green and white = limited-stop, red and white = express), and the cable cars by route name of the streets on which the line operates. A flat-fare system applies which allows one free transfer to a second vehicle for an onward journey – fares are currently $1.00 for metro and local buses, $1.50 for express buses and $3.00 for cable cars. Various duration passes ('passports') are available, starting at $6.00 for a one-day passport; these are valid on all Muni scheduled services. The *Bay Area Rapid Transit (BART)* has 8 stations in San Francisco and many more in the suburbs (see below); fares depend on distance travelled.

San Francisco Suburbs: The inner suburbs are served by *Muni* metro and buses. To the north, **Sausalito** and **Larkspur** are reached by *Golden Gate Transit* ferries and buses; **Tiburon** by *Red & White Fleet* ferries; **Mill Valley** by *Golden Gate Transit* buses which also serve **San Raphael** together with *Greyhound Lines*. Across the Bay, **Richmond, El Cerrito, Berkeley, Oakland, Hayward** and **Fremont** are all reached by *BART* trains and by *Alameda-Contra Costa Transit District (AC Transit)* buses. To the south, **Daly City** is the western terminus of *BART* and is also served by *Muni* and *San Mateo County Transit District (SamTrans)* buses; **Pacifica** by *SamTrans* buses; **South San Francisco, San Bruno, Burlinghame, San Mateo, San Carlos** and **Redwood City** by *Southern Pacific Passenger Rail Line (CalTrain)* and by *SamTrans* buses; **Menlo Park** and **Palo Alto** by *CalTrain* and by *SamTrans* and *Santa Clara County Transit* buses; **Mountain View** by *CalTrain* and *Santa Clara County Transit* buses.

Surrounding area: To the north, **Petaluma** and **Santa Rosa** are served by *Golden Gate Transit* and *Greyhound Lines* buses (service continues to Ukiah, Willits, Eureka and Portland); **Napa** is reached by *Greyhound Lines*, as is **Vallejo** (services continue to Redding, Eugene and Portland, and to Sacramento and Reno); **Sacramento** by *AMTRAK** (services continue to Redding, Eugene, Portland and Seattle and to Reno and Salt Lake City). To the east, **Concord** is served by *BART*; **Stockton** by *AMTRAK* (service continues to Merced *(for Yosemite Transportation Service buses to Yosemite Park)* Fresno *(for Gray Line buses to Yosemite Park)* and Bakersfield). To the south, **Santa Cruz** and **Monterey** are reached by *Greyhound Lines*; **Salinas** by *AMTRAK* and by *Greyhound Lines* (both services continue to San Luis Obispo, Santa Barbara and Los Angeles); **San Jose** by *CalTrain*, by *AMTRAK** and *Greyhound Lines* (both services continue to Salinas, San Luis Obispo, Santa Barbara and Los Angeles and by *Santa Clara County Transit* buses.

* – AMTRAK services depart from Emeryville Station in Oakland (see below).

MAIN TRANSPORT CENTRES

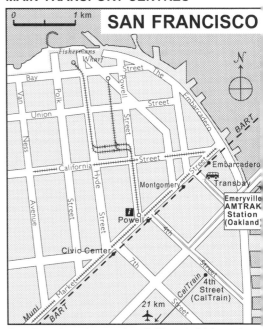

SAN FRANCISCO

San Francisco International Airport: Major gateway for both international and domestic flights; see 'Gateway Airports' section of this guide for details.

AMTRAK Station (Oakland Emeryville) (AMTRAK shuttle bus from Transbay Terminal)**:** For all *AMTRAK* services.

AMTRAK Station (San Jose) (CalTrain to San Jose) For *AMTRAK* services to Salinas, San Luis Obispo, Santa Barbara and Los Angeles.

AMTRAK Station (Richmond) (BART to Richmond) For *AMTRAK* services to Sacramento, Redding, Eugene and Portland, and to Merced, Fresno and Bakersfield.

CalTrain Station (Muni bus 30, 32, 38, 42, 45, 76)**:** For *CalTrain* services to the southern suburbs, San Mateo, Redwood City, Palo Alto and San Jose *(for AMTRAK services to Salinas, San Luis Obispo, San Barbara and Los Angeles).*

Ferry Terminal (Muni bus 2, 7, 8, 9, 14, 21, 31; a few blocks from BART/Muni Embarcadero Metro Station): For **Golden Gate Transit** ferries to Larkspur and Sausalito, and **Red & White** ferries to Tiburon and Vallejo.

Transbay Terminal (Muni bus 5, 6, 12, 14, 15, 42, 76; one block from BART/Muni Embarcadero Metro Station): For **Golden Gate Transit** buses to northern suburbs, **SamTrans** buses to southern suburbs, **Greyhound Lines** buses to all destinations and shuttle bus to **AMTRAK** Oakland Emeryville Station.

USEFUL TELEPHONE NUMBERS

Emergencies	**911**
Traveler's Aid Society	(415) 255-2252

Thomas Cook Currency Services . .	(415) 362-6271
San Francisco Visitors Bureau . . .	(415) 391-2000
AC Transit	(415) 839-2882
AMTRAK	1-800-872-7245
BART	(415) 788-BART
CalTrain	(415) 495-4546
Golden Gate Transit	(415) 332-6600
Gray Line	(415) 558-9400
Greyhound Lines	(415) 558-6789
Red & White Fleet Ferries	1-800-229-2784
SamTrans	(415) 761-7000
San Francisco Municipal Railway (Muni)	(415) 673-MUNI
Santa Clara County Transit	(415) 965-3100
Yosemite Transportation Service . .	(209) 372-4611

TORONTO

GENERAL INFORMATION

Named Toronto *("place of meeting")* by the Huron Indians, this largest city in Canada is located on the northwest shore of Lake Ontario, a situation which tempers the severity of the Canadian winter and results in one of the mildest climates in the country. Fast-growing Toronto has become one of the most ethnically diverse cities of the world, a fact borne out by the bewildering choice of cuisine among the 5000-or-so restaurants. The fabulous view from the CN Tower, whether by day or by night, will reveal Toronto as a gleaming, modern city. Rather less obvious from this vantage point are the pockets of Toronto's 200-year history, nestling among – and dwarfed by – the surrounding skyscrapers. Although a large city, much of Downtown Toronto can be explored on foot, both on the surface and in the world's largest subterranean complex (with more than 1000 shops) located under the Financial District. The city has an efficient public transport system, with a network of subways, buses, and trams (streetcars) and a suburban rail system.

GETTING AROUND

Metropolitan Toronto: Comprises the municipalities of Toronto, Etobicoke, Scarborough, York, North York and East York. Throughout the six municipalities the *Toronto Transit Commission (TTC)* operates a comprehensive bus and tram network and two subway lines, plus the Scarborough Rapid Transit and the Harbourfront LRT. A flat-fare system using a ticket, token, pass, transfer or exact change applies within the Metropolitan Area; special fares may be charged on routes which run beyond its boundaries. Transfers are free but must be purchased when you pay your fare. *Government of Ontario (GO)* operate suburban rail and bus services designed primarily to serve communities beyond the Metropolitan Area, but some of these may be used for journeys within it. The *GO* Lakeshore Line operates a frequent all-day service from Burlington in the west to Whitby in the east; the other *GO* rail lines and extended Lakeshore services to Hamilton and Oshawa operate mainly in peak hours only and are replaced by buses outside these periods.

Toronto suburbs: To the west, **Mississauga** is served by *GO* buses and trains, and by *Mississauga Transit* buses; **Oakville**, **Burlington**, **Hamilton** and **Milton**, are all reached by *GO* buses and trains, as are **Aldershot** (the *VIA Rail* station and major transit centre serving Burlington and Hamilton), **Brampton** and **Georgetown** (all additionally served by *VIA Rail*) and **Guelph** (also served by *VIA Rail* and by *Gray Coach Lines*). To the north, **Bradford**, **Barrie**, **Richmond Hill** and **Stouffville** are reached by *GO* buses and trains, as is **Markham**, which is also served by **Markham Transit**. To the east, *GO* buses and trains serve **Pickering**, **Whitby** and **Oshawa**.

Surrounding Area: To the south around the Lake, **St. Catharines** and **Niagara Falls** can be reached by *VIA Rail* (service continues to Buffalo and New York) and by *Gray Coach Lines* (service continues to Buffalo). To the west, **Woodstock** and **London** are reached by *VIA Rail* (services continue to Windsor and to Sarnia), and by *Greyhound Lines of Canada* (service continues to Chatham, Windsor and Detroit); **Kitchener** by *VIA Rail* (service contines to **Stratford** *(for **Sherwood Transportation** buses to Goderich)* and to **London** and **Windsor**). To the north, **Owen Sound** is served by *Gray Coach Lines* and by *Penetang Midland Coach Lines*; **Washago** by *VIA Rail* (service continues to Parry Sound, Sudbury, Capreol, Sioux Lookout, Winnipeg, Saskatoon, Edmonton and Vancouver) and by *Ontario Northland* buses and trains (both services continue to North Bay; rail goes onward to Cochrane). To the east, **Peterborough** is served by *Voyageur Colonial* buses (services continue to Pembroke, and to Havelock and Ottawa); **Belleville** by *VIA Rail* (services continue to Kingston, Ottawa, Cornwall and Montréal) and by *Voyageur Colonial* buses (service continues to Kingston, Cornwall and Montréal).

MAIN TRANSPORT CENTRES

Toronto – Lester B. Pearson International Airport: Major gateway for international and national flights. See 'Gateway Airports' section of this guide for details.

Union Station (Yonge-University-Spadina Subway to Union Station): Main station of Toronto; departure point for all *VIA Rail* and *Ontario Northland* rail services, and hub of the *GO* Rail System. The *TTC*

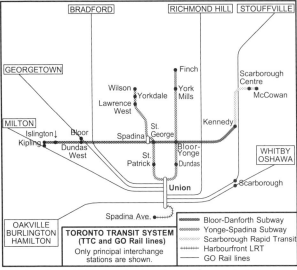

BRADFORD | RICHMOND HILL | STOUFFVILLE

GEORGETOWN

Finch

Scarborough
Centre

Wilson
Yorkdale

York
Mills

McCowan

Lawrence
West

MILTON

Kennedy

Islington
Kipling

Bloor
Dundas
West

Spadina

St.
George

St.
Patrick

Bloor-
Yonge
Dundas

WHITBY
OSHAWA

Scarborough

Union

Spadina Ave.

OAKVILLE
BURLINGTON
HAMILTON

TORONTO TRANSIT SYSTEM
(TTC and GO Rail lines)
Only principal interchange
stations are shown.

Bloor-Danforth Subway
Yonge-Spadina Subway
Scarborough Rapid Transit
Harbourfront LRT
GO Rail lines

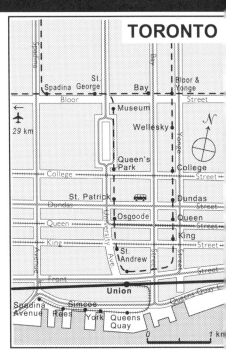

TORONTO

Harbourfront LRT also leaves from here, and *GO* buses which replace trains depart from outside the station in Front Street.

Metro Toronto Coach Terminal (610 Bay Street) (Yonge-University-Spadina Subway to Dundas or St. Patrick – 1-2 blocks; across street from Penetang-Midland Terminal): Serves *Greyhound Lines of Canada*, *Ontario Northland* buses, *Voyageur Colonial,* and *Hamilton GO Bus.*

Penetang Midland Terminal (627 Bay Street) (Yonge-University-Spadina Subway to Dundas or St. Patrick – 1-2 blocks; across street from Metro Toronto Terminal): Serves *Penetang Midland Coach Lines.*

Kipling (Bloor-Danforth Subway to Kipling): Transfer point from subway to *GO* trains on the Milton Line.

Islington (Bloor-Danforth Subway to Islington): For *Gray Coach Airport Express Bus,* and for connections with *Mississauga Transit* services.

Lawrence West (Yonge-University-Spadina Subway to Lawrence West): For *TTC* bus *58A* to Lester B. Pearson Airport.

Yorkdale (Yonge-University-Spadina Subway to Yorkdale): For *Gray Coach Airport Express Bus* and *Hamilton*, *Milton*, *Northwest*, *North* and *East GO Bus* services.

York Mills (Yonge-University-Spadina Subway to York Mills): For *Gray Coach Airport Express Bus* and *Hamilton*, *Milton*, *Northwest* and *East GO Bus* services.

Finch (Yonge-University-Spadina Subway to Finch): For *North Yonge*, *Bayview* and *North GO Bus* services, and connections with *Markham Transit* services.

Kennedy (Bloor-Danforth Subway to Kennedy Transfer point from subway to *TTC* Scarborou Rapid Transit.

Scarborough Centre (Bloor-Danforth Subway Kennedy; then Scarborough RT to Scarborou Centre): For *North* and *North East GO Bus* service

USEFUL TELEPHONE NUMBERS

Emergencies	9
Thomas Cook Currency Services . .	(416) 363-480
Ontario Ministry of Tourism	(416) 314-09
Toronto Visitors Association (MTCVA)	(416) 203-250
Tourism Canada	(613) 954-39
GO Transit	(416) 665-00
Gray Coach Lines	(416) 393-79
Greyhound Lines of Canada	(416) 594-03
Markham Transit	(416) 475-48
Metro Toronto Coach Terminal . . .	(416) 393-79
Mississauga Transit	(416) 279-58
Ontario Northland	(705) 472-45
Penetang Midland Coach Lines . . .	(416) 364-65
Sherwood Transportation	(519) 524-20
Toronto Transit Commission (TTC) .	(416) 393 46
VIA Rail	(416) 366-84
Voyageur Colonial	(514) 843-42

VANCOUVER

GENERAL INFORMATION

Located in the southwestern corner of British Columbia about 40 kilometres from the US border, Vancouver is set in breathtaking natural surroundings between the Rocky Mountains and the sea. A modern yet interesting city, it is also an ideal base for exploring the surrounding area, both the mountainous hinterland and the many islands, including the large Vancouver Island across the Strait of Georgia. Although Vancouver is an extensive city, it has a comprehensive regional transit system which makes getting about easy.

GETTING AROUND

Metropolitan Vancouver: The *Vancouver Regional Transit System* of *BC Transit* operate a network of buses and trolleys, plus the SkyTrain Rapid Transit (underground in the downtown area and elevated in the suburbs) and the SeaBus ferry to North Vancouver. A zonal fare system applies during Mon–Fri. peak hours; outside these times a flat-fare system is in operation. Fares are currently CA$ 1.50 for travel within one zone, CA$ 2.25 for two zones and CA$ 3.00 for three zones; off-peak CA$ 1.50 for any distance. Transfers are free, but must be obtained when you board the first vehicle. A day pass is available (currently CA$ 4.50). Fares, transfers and passes are valid on all methods of transport and for interchange between them.

Vancouver suburbs: North across the Burrard Inlet, **Horseshoe Bay** *(for BC Ferries to Nanaimo, Bowen Island and Langdale)* and **West Vancouver** are served by *BC Transit* buses, as is **North Vancouver** which is reached additionally by *BC Transit* seabus. In the east, *BC Transit* buses reach Burnaby, Port Moody and Coquitlam. In the south east, *BC Transit* SkyTrain and buses serve **New Westminster** and **Surrey**; the bus services also extend to **Langley, White Rock** and **Delta.** In the south, **Richmond, Ladner** and **Tsawwassen** *(for BC Ferries to Swartz Bay, Nanaimo and the southern Gulf Islands)* are all reached by *BC Transit* buses.

Surrounding area: Northwards along the coast, **Powell River** is reached by *Maverick Coach Lines*; inland, **Squamish** and **Whistler** by *BC Rail* (service continues to Lillooet, Williams Lake, Quesnel and Prince George). To the east, **Port Coquitlam** and **Chilliwack** are served by *VIA Rail* (service continues to Kamloops, Jasper, Edmonton, Saskatoon, Winnipeg and Toronto), and **Hope** is served by

Greyhound Lines of Canada (services continue to Kamloops, Revelstoke, Lake Louise and Calgary, and to Penticton and Kelowna). To the south, **Bellingham** and **Seattle** are reached by *Greyhound Lines of Canada*, *Quick Shuttle* (Seattle only) and *Trailways Northwest*. To the south and west across the Strait of Georgia, **Victoria** can be reached by *BC Ferries* Tsawwassen – Swartz Bay service (*BC Transit* and *Pacific Coach Lines* provide bus connections between ferry terminals and downtown areas), or direct by *Greyhound Lines of Canada* bus-ferry service. The southern **Gulf Islands** are served by *BC Ferries* from Tsawwassen. **Nanaimo** can be reached by *BC Ferries* services from Tsawwassen and Horseshoe Bay, or direct by *Greyhound Lines of Canada* bus-ferry service.

MAIN TRANSPORT CENTRES

VANCOUVER

Vancouver International Airport: Major international and domestic gateway. See 'Gateway Airports' section of this guide for details.

Pacific Central Station (SkyTrain to Science World-Main Street; bus 3 or 8; adjacent to bus terminal): Western terminus of the *VIA Rail* system and departure point for all *VIA Rail* services.

North Vancouver Station (Special BC Transit bus from Stadium SkyTrain Station (also picks up along Georgia), or from North Vancouver SeaBus Terminal): Departure point for all *BC Rail* trains.

Bus Terminal (SkyTrain to Science World-Main Street; bus 3 or 8; adjacent to Pacific Central Station): Serves *Greyhound Lines of Canada*, *Maverick Coach Lines*, *Pacific Coach Lines, Quick Shuttle* and *Trailways Northwest*.

SeaBus Terminal (SkyTrain or bus 1 or 50 to Waterfront): For *BC Transit* SeaBus ferry to North Vancouver (Lonsdale Quay).

Horseshoe Bay (BC Transit bus 250 or 257 or Maverick Coach Lines from Georgia): For *BC Ferries* to Nanaimo, Bowen Island and Langdale.

Tsawwassen (Direct by Pacific Coach Lines from Cambie, or by BC Transit bus 601 from Howe to Ladner Exchange, then BC Transit bus 404 (summer only) or 640): For *BC Ferries* to Swartz Bay, Nanaimo and the southern Gulf Islands.

USEFUL TELEPHONE NUMBERS

Emergencies	**911**
Thomas Cook Currency Services . .	(604) 687-6111
Discover British Columbia	(604) 663-6000
Tourism Assoc. of Southwestern B.C.	(604) 739-9011
Tourism Victoria	(604) 382-2127
Vancouver Travel Info Centre. . . .	(604) 683-2000
BC Ferries	(604) 669-1211
BC Rail.	(604) 984-5246
BC Transit (Vancouver)	(604) 261-510(
BC Transit (Victoria)	(604) 382-616
Bus Terminal	(604) 662-757;
Greyhound Lines of Canada	(604) 662-322;
Maverick Coach Lines	(604) 662-805
Pacific Coach Lines	(604) 662-757;
Quick Shuttle	(604) 244-374·
Trailways Northwest	(604) 662-757·
VIA Rail	(604) 669 305;

WASHINGTON

GENERAL INFORMATION

The American custom of appending state names to their cities has some validity here, as Washington shares its name with the State of Washington on the other side of the country. For this reason, Americans invariably refer to their capital city, situated in its own federal district (District of Columbia), as 'Washington DC'. The overwhelming impression of Washington for most first-time visitors is one of space. Although it contains some of the largest buildings in the country, including, of course, the White House, the Capitol and the vast Pentagon, these are separated by wide avenues and parklands which keeps everything in perspective. One result of this spaciousness is that it is easy to underestimate distances; 'a few blocks' may not sound very far, but it does rather depend on the size of the blocks. However, it is relatively easy to find your way around, as Washington is laid out on a grid pattern. Streets which run north-south are numbered, and streets which run east-west are lettered; the numbers/letters rise as you progress away from the Capitol, which is the hub of the system. This principle applies equally to the house or building numbering system and can result in up to four apparently identical addresses, so it's important to identify in which quadrant (NW, NE, SW, SE) the required address is situated. Streets which run diagonally are all 'avenues' and are named after states.

GETTING AROUND

Metropolitan Washington: The *Washington Metropolitan Area Transit Authority (WMATA)* operates a comprehensive network of subways (Metrorail) and buses (Metrobus) throughout the District of Columbia and into neighbouring states. Th collective name of the system is 'Metro'. The Metrora network is modern (the first section was opened i 1976) and now comprises 5 lines (Red, Orange, Blu Green and Yellow); the system is still being expandec Metrorail stations are easily identified by a brow column with a large 'M' at the top; underneath this is stripe (or stripes) in the colour(s) of the line(s) servir the station. Fares vary according to the distanc travelled and the time of day; they are higher in th peak periods (0530-0930 and 1500-1900 Mon–Fri than at other times. A farecard must be purchased c arrival at the station; this electronically records th amount paid. The farecard must be inserted into gate on both entry and exit; the fare for the journe will be automatically deducted as you exit. If there any remaining credit when you leave the system, th farecard will be returned to you; otherwise th machine retains it, and, in the event of an insufficie amount on the farecard to meet the cost of th journey just made, you will be instructed to go th 'Addfare' machine to pay the shortfall. If you intend continue your journey by Metrobus, you should buy transfer on entering the Metrorail system. This mu be presented to the driver on boarding the bu together with any additional transfer fees. Metrobi services run throughout DC; bus schedules are c ordinated with those of Metrorail. A flat-fare syste (currently US$ 1.00) applies for journeys wholly with DC; supplements apply during peak periods and f journeys which cross into Maryland or Virgini Transfers to another Metrobus service are free ar are valid 2 hours; however, transfers are **not** availab from Metrobus to Metrorail.

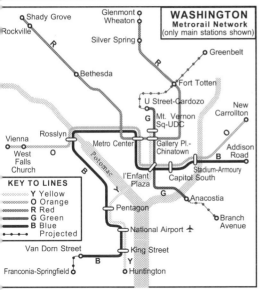

WASHINGTON
Metrorail Network
(only main stations shown)

Shady Grove
Rockville
Glenmont
Wheaton
Silver Spring
Greenbelt
Bethesda
Fort Totten
U Street-Cardozo
Mt. Vernon
Sq-UDC
New
Carrollton
Vienna
Rosslyn
Metro Center
Gallery Pl.-
Chinatown
Addison
Road
West
Falls
Church
l'Enfant
Plaza
Stadium-Armoury
Capitol South
Anacostia
Pentagon
Branch
Avenue
National Airport
Van Dorn Street
King Street
Franconia-Springfield
Huntington

KEY TO LINES
- Y Yellow
- O Orange
- R Red
- G Green
- B Blue
- Projected

Washington suburbs: *WMATA* Metro services extend into the suburbs; additionally the northwestern, northern and northeastern suburbs are served by *Maryland Department of Transportation (MARC)* trains; the northwestern and northern suburbs also have their own bus network provided by *Montgomery County Transit*, operating under the name of *Ride On*. Some southern and southwestern suburbs can be reached by *Virginia Railway Express*. Buses are provided throughout the southern, southwestern and western suburbs by *Fairfax Connector*, and individual transit systems in Alexandria by *DASH* and in Fairfax City by *CUE*.

Surrounding area: To the south, **Fredericksburg** is reached by *Virginia Railway Express* and by *AMTRAK* (not all AMTRAK services can be used for journeys between Washington and Fredericksburg – see timetables); **Richmond** by *AMTRAK* (services continue to Charleston, Jacksonville and Miami, and also to Williamsburg and Newport News), and by *Greyhound Lines* buses (services continue to Atlanta). To the south west, **Culpeper** and

Charlottesville are both served by *AMTRAK* (services continue to Atlanta and New Orleans, and to Charleston (WV), Cincinnati and Chicago); **Charlottesville** is also served by *Greyhound Lines* (services continue to Roanoke, Knoxville, Nashville and Memphis). To the north west, **Brunswick** and **Martinsburg** are reached by *MARC* and by *AMTRAK* trains (service continues to Pittsburgh, Cleveland and Chicago), and **Hagerstown** by *Greyhound Lines* (service continues to Pittsburgh, Cleveland and Chicago). To the north east, **Baltimore**, **Wilmington** and **Philadelphia** are all on *AMTRAK's* North East Corridor (service continues to Newark, New York and Boston); **Baltimore** can also be reached by *MARC*. To the east, **Annapolis**, Lewes *(for Cape May – Lewes Ferry service to Cape May)*, **Rehoboth Beach** and **Ocean City** can be accessed by *Carolina Trailways* buses.

MAIN TRANSPORT CENTRES

Washington Dulles International Airport (42km W): Major gateway for international flights – see 'Gateway Airports' section of this guide for details.

Washington National Airport (7km S): Major hub for domestic flights with connections to most US cities – see 'Gateway Airports' section of this guide for details.

Baltimore-Washington International Airport (48km NE) (MARC or AMTRAK train to BWI Airport): For some international and a number of domestic flights.

Union Station (Red line metro to Union Station): Restored to its former glory, and now also a major shopping centre, Union Station is **the** rail station of Washington. All *AMTRAK*, *MARC*, and *Virginia Railway Express* services arrive and depart here.

Greyhound Terminal (1st and L Sts – Red line metro to Union Station, then 1 km walk): For services of *Capitol Trailways*, *Carolina Trailways* and *Greyhound Lines*.

Peter Pan Terminal (1st and L Sts – Red line metro to Union Station, then 1 km walk): For services of *Peter Pan Trailways*.

USEFUL TELEPHONE NUMBERS

Emergencies	**911**
Thomas Cook Currency Services	(202) 371-9219
Maryland Office of Tourist Development	(301) 333-6611
Virginia Division of Tourism	(804) 786-2051
Washington Visitor Information Center	(202) 789-7038
Washington DC Visitors Association	(202) 789-7000
AMTRAK	(202) 484-7540
Baltimore-Washington Airport	(410) 859-7100
Capitol Trailways	(202) 289-5154
Carolina Trailways	(202) 289-5154
CUE	(202) 385-7859
DASH	(202) 370-3274
Fairfax Connector	(202) 339-7200
Greyhound Lines	(301) 565-2662
MARC	(301) 694-2065
Montgomery County Transit (Ride On)	(202) 217-7433
Peter Pan Trailways	(202) 371-2111
WMATA (Metrobus/Metrorail)	(202) 637-7000

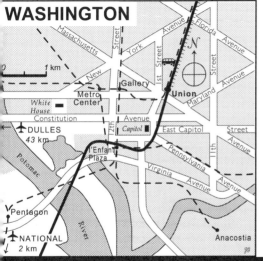

WASHINGTON

Massachusetts
Florida
York
Gallery
Metro
Center
Union
White
House
Constitution
Avenue
DULLES
43 km
Capitol
East Capitol
Street
l'Enfant
Plaza
Pennsylvania
Virginia
Avenue
Pentagon
River
NATIONAL
2 km
Anacostia

UPDATE NOTES TO TIMETABLES

The notes below summarise the latest timetable situation with regard to various operators as we went to press. However, the world of schedules and timetables is a volatile one; transport operators reserve the right to change schedules according to demand and circumstances 'at any time', so even a 'current' or 'valid' timetable is subject to alteration. We would advise you to plan your trip in reasonable detail, using the timetable section of this guide in conjunction with the notes below, but to build a degree of flexibility into your plans so that they can be altered without too much disruption in the event of timetable changes. How much a 'degree' of flexibility amounts to rather depends on the frequency of the service; a 15-minute interval service which changes into 20-minute intervals is hardly likely to be noticeable, whereas a once-weekly service which suddenly starts operating one day earlier is likely to throw your whole trip into confusion. Follow the golden rule; **always** check with the operator in advance, especially for the less frequent services, and for journeys undertaken after October 1994 (when many operators are expected to introduce new winter schedules).

Timings should also be double-checked on journeys which involve entering or leaving the following areas: Alberta, Eastern Québec, Saskatchewan and Western Ontario in Canada, and Arizona and Indiana in the USA. This is because, unlike the rest of Canada and the USA, these regions do not observe Daylight Saving Time, and results in an apparent discrepancy of one hour in these areas when the clock changes occur in April and October. Journeys made entirely outside these areas are generally unaffected; those wholly within them are also unlikely to change unless they make connections with services from neighbouring areas. Timetables introduced during the current season take these time differences into account, but those which commenced before the clock change occurred and which cross the time-zone boundary will invariably be one hour out for part of the journey.

We generally show a fares summary in each table; this is not comprehensive, and is featured as a guide only, to help you plan your budget. The schedules we receive from operators and other sources frequently do not include fares information and we may have to obtain this from alternative sources. As a result, our fares information may not always be completely up-to-date and you are advised to be prepared for possible changes to the fares we show.

The **AMTRAK** services in the timetables are based on **AMTRAK's** summer 1994 schedules and should, therefore, be those in operation throughout the summer. However, frequent changes in Federal funding policies have resulted in **AMTRAK** having to change schedules at short notice in the recent past, and it is rumoured that there could be a mid-term 'unscheduled' change during the validity of the current timetable, resulting in the introduction of new schedules. So follow the golden rule of 'Check-before-you-go', particularly if your journey is later in the summer. As we went to press, sources were suggesting that **AMTRAK** intend to introduce a passenger service between Seattle and Vancouver before October 1994, but until (and if) this proves correct, passengers will have to rely on bus travel between these points. There were also unconfirmed reports that **AMTRAK** intends to prohibit smoking on all of its daylight services; again, no official notification has been received about whether (or when) this regulation is to become effective, so our advice to smokers is 'Check-before-you-light-up!'

Most **VIA Rail** services we show are based on current (spring 1994) schedules. The steady decline of **VIA Rail** appears to be halting at last; indeed, a number of services from summer '93 which could have been expected to be withdrawn for the winter season were retained. Another optimistic sign is that **VIA Rail** have begun tailoring their timetables to suit passengers' needs; for example, the once-train-per-day service on Vancouver Island between Victoria and Courtney now runs at various times on different days of the week, rather than the fixed daily ake-it-or-leave-it schedule previously operated. It is to be hoped that this new customer-driven policy will result in more taking it and less leaving it... Other recent minor improvements would suggest that *VIA Rail* services for summer '94 will be as good as, if not better than, the current spring services we show. However, this could mean changes (even if for the better), so do check before embarking on a journey.

Recent rail schedule changes made by suburban operators *MBTA* in the Boston area, *SEPTA* in the Philadelphia area, *MARC* in the Washington DC area, and *Metrolink* in the Los Angeles area are included in our timetables, and (hopefully) suggest that these will remain reasonably static for a while. In general, details of services we show for other rail operators are the latest we have received, and should be checked with operators.

On the buses, many services of *Greyhound Lines* have altered recently (our timetables incorporate these), but this does not necessarily mean that no more changes are forthcoming. *Greyhound Lines* have adopted a policy of not publishing advance timetables; rather you are requested to enquire (inquire, in North American English) about each trip before you book it. This policy is not very helpful to those resident outside North America trying to plan a holiday (nor, incidentally, to timetable publishers!), and it can only be hoped that should *Greyhound Lines* find themselves overwhelmed with enquiries (or even inquiries), they may review this policy. So our advice, as always, is check, enquire or inquire before your journey.

Our timetables for *Capitol Trailways*, *Carolina Trailways*, *Delta Bus Co.*, *Indian Trails*, *North Star Lines*, *TNM&O Coaches* and *White Pine Transit* were current as of press date and, hopefully, will remain valid for some time. In the case of other US operators, we show the latest information at our disposal, and our usual advice applies.

Details of the latest schedules from *Greyhound Lines of Canada* arrived just as we went to press. We have included them in the timetables, but from past experience we would expect minor revisions to come into effect on about 26 June, so check with the operator before making a specific journey after that date.

Of other Canadian bus operators, our timetables reflect new schedules received from *AJ Bus*, *Arctic Frontier Carrier*, *CN*, *Saskatchewan Transportation* and *Trentway-Wagar Inc*. Timetables shown for other operators are based on the latest information we have received, but are, of course, subject to alteration.

In general, the information we show on ferry services is subject to confirmation and we would advise checking with the operator before your journey in all cases.

AVOIDING CONFUSION . . .

'Nations divided by a common language', it was once said. Perhaps a slight exaggeration, but differences do exist on either side of the 'Pond'. In general, we will leave you to explore this linguistic minefield yourself (it can be fun, but dictionaries are available for the faint-hearted); however, we list below a few North American transport-related terms which British English speakers may find confusing.

Alternate. Means 'alternative', **not** 'every other' (= 'every other' or 'every second').
Holiday. Means 'Bank' or 'Public' holiday, **not** 'annual' or 'school' holiday (= 'vacation').
Pavement. Means 'road surface', **not** an area reserved for pedestrians (= 'sidewalk').

DATES AND TIMES
The North American order of showing dates is month-day-year, not day-month-year as in Europe. So 5-11-94 should be read as May 11, **not** Nov. 5.
Most operators show times in 12-hour clock format (with p.m. times in **bold** typeface); in Canada the 24-hour system may also be encountered.

THOMAS COOK PUBLICATIONS

EUROPEAN TIMETABLE

The only comprehensive monthly guide to the rail services throughout Europe.

OVERSEAS TIMETABLE

Brings together in one book surface travel timetables for virtually all countries outside Europe. Published bi-monthly.

AIRPORTS GUIDE – EUROPE

A useful compact guide to the 76 major airports in Europe for the business or leisure traveller.

EUROPEAN RAIL TRAVELLER'S PHRASEBOOK

The first of its kind to cater for rail travellers – includes vocabulary specific to rail travel as well as for general situations. Over 350 phrases translated into 9 European languages. Pocket-sized – 288 pages.

GREEK ISLAND HOPPING 1994

The fourth edition of the unique Thomas Cook Guide to making the most of an island-hopping holiday. Practical advice and honest descriptions.

NEW! NORTH AMERICAN RAIL & BUS GUIDE

An essential handbook for budget travellers in the USA and Canada – and for those who do not want to fly between each point on their trip.

NEW! ON THE RAILS AROUND EUROPE

A revolutionary new guide for the leisure traveller in Europe. Specially designed to help rail pass holders make the most of a touring holiday by train. A comprehensive planning aid and an invaluable travelling companion.

NEW! NEW RAIL MAP OF EUROPE

Not just an update of the famous Rail Map of Europe, but a new map, researched from scratch by Thomas Cook and created in four colours by leading UK cartographers.

VISITOR'S RAIL MAP OF GREAT BRITAIN & IRELAND

A map for the rail tourist featuring all principal passenger railways with InterCity and express routes and stations clearly distinguished. Plus tourist information for sights within reach of major stations.

These titles are obtainable in the UK from:

Thomas Cook Publishing
PO Box 227
Thorpe Wood
PETERBOROUGH
PE3 6SB

☎ (0733) 505821/268943

In the USA they can be obtained from:

Forsyth Travel Library, Inc.
9154 West 57th Street
PO Box 2975
Dept. TCT
SHAWNEE MISSION
Kansas 66201

☎ 1-800-"FORSYTH"
(dial 800-367-7984)
Kansas orders call
☎ (913) 384-3440

THOMAS COOK TRAVELLERS*

A series of 192-page compact (192mm x 130mm) guides, each fully illustrated in colour and with completely new research and mapping. Created for the holidaymaker of the 1990s. Titles available:

The Algarve

Amsterdam

Belgium

Boston & New England

California

Cyprus

Eastern Caribbean

Egypt

Florence & Tuscany

Florida

Ireland

Kenya

London

Malta

Munich & Bavaria

New York

Paris

Prague

Singapore & Malaysia

Sydney & New South Wales

Thailand

Turkey

Vancouver & British Columbia

Vienna

*Thomas Cook Travellers are published in the USA as **'PASSPORTS ILLUSTRATED GUIDES FROM THOMAS COOK'** and are available from bookstores.

HOW TO USE THE TIMETABLES

1. To find the service required, refer either to the index of place names or to the index map of the area concerned (see 'Contents' for page numbers). The numbers of the tables appear along the lines to which they refer. Rail services are denoted by a thick (main railway) or thin (secondary railway) solid black line with table numbers in **BOLD** type, bus services by a grey line and table numbers in GREY, and shipping services by a dotted black line and table numbers in NORMAL type. See the 'Key to maps and town plans' on page 61.

2. All timings are given in the twenty-four hour clock format. The hours are numbered consecutively from 1 to 24, starting from midnight. A train or bus arriving or departing at 1.10 p.m. is shown as 13.10; at 5.15 p.m. as 17.15; at 9.30 p.m. as 21.30, and so on. The figures "2400" indicate a service arriving at midnight, but a departure at that hour is shown as "0000". Arrivals and departures at any time between midnight and 1.00 a.m. are expressed by "0001" to "0059".

3. One list of places serves, in many of the tables, for both directions. In these cases the times on the left of the names are to be read downwards, but those on the right must be read upwards, from bottom to top. Most tables have small arrows above the place names or by the times to indicate in which direction the times should be read.

4. Places on branch lines or routes are printed slightly to the right as compared with those of the primary line/route and those of connecting lines/routes appear in italics. When a table number (e.g. **101**) is added, see that table for full details of the service on the connecting line or route, including train or trip numbers. Table numbers appearing against other place names indicate another table covering the same journey.

5. In rail tables, the classes of accommodation are usually printed at the head of each train thus: C, P, S, 1, etc. Details of these classes are shown under the individual country introductions for Canada and the USA. This heading denotes the accommodation available in the class concerned; more details of special accommodation and through cars is shown by footnotes. The classes shown may not apply to the trains over connecting lines, for which see the tables indicated.

6. Various categories of sleeping accommodation are available on Via Rail and Amtrak services; details can be found in the 'Train and Bus Accommodation' section.

7. Other indications at the head of the train columns refer to the train category and the train number; supplements are charged for travel on certain trains and in superior accommodation. These categories are explained at the head of the first table of the country concerned.

8. A list of the standard symbols used to denote days of running, sleeping and restaurant cars, etc., appears on page 61. All other notes (for example those giving dates of running for seasonal trains) are explained at the table concerned. All services run daily unless otherwise stated.

9. All timings throughout the Timetable are given in Local Time unless otherwise stated. Both Canada and the USA have a number of time zones; furthermore, most (but not all) states and territories adopt Daylight Saving Time throughout the summer months. Details can be found in the 'Country Information' section; time zone boundaries are shown on the map on page 62.

10. The services shown are liable to alteration, and travellers are therefore recommended to compare these tables with the local tables at the stations before commencing each journey. Every care has been taken to render the timetable correct in accordance with the latest advices received, but changes are constantly being made by the administrations concerned, and the publishers cannot hold themselves responsible for the consequences of either changes or inaccuracies. The inclusion of a fare does not imply that Thomas Cook can supply tickets at the rate shown, or at all.

SPECIMEN TABLE

HEADINGS: Each table has a heading showing the table number, the main service covered, the type of transport used (symbols page 61) and the operator code(s) (in *italics*) – see footnote.

FARES: Fares are given from the fares basepoint in the table (shown as 0 or 0.00). This is normally the first town in the table, but can occasionally be the last, or even at a mid-point, in which cases the fares should be read upwards or in both directions from the basepoint. The fares are for basic accommodation in the class shown (see introduction at the beginning of each country's entry), and are shown in local currencies whenever possible (for conversion rates see the COUNTRY INFORMATION pages) and are generally one-way fares. In a few cases, round-trip fares are shown (indicated by RT). Fares are for direct services and usually do not include stopovers. Readers are reminded that these fares are for guidance only; in some cases different operators on the same route have different fare scales – in these cases we have shown the highest fares we have received for the class.

KILOMETRES: Kilometres are normally shown from the first town in the table (shown as 0) and are via the most direct route.

TOWNS: For each table we have selected the towns to be shown and the omission of a town does not automatically mean that the town is not served by the services shown. The main towns are shown in **bold**. Towns with more than one station/terminus have the relevant station after their names. Towns whose station serves other places of note have these places shown in brackets and *italics*. Indented towns are served by branch routes. Towns in *italics* only have services connecting with the main service shown. Full service will be shown in the table indicated (**9999**) in bold.

Symbols and letters against town names are explained in the footnotes. Times shown against town names are normally departure times (d., a. = arrival time); certain services may arrive at stations some time before the departure times shown.

Information shown above the list of towns refers to all services in the table.

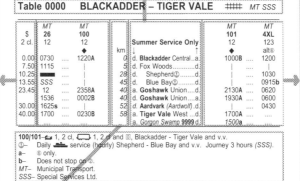

Table 0000   BLACKADDER – TIGER VALE   ⌗⌗⌗⌗ *MT SSS*

	MT 26	MT 100			MT 101	MT 4XL
$ 2 cl.	12	12	Summer Service Only	◆	12	123 alt®
km	↓		↑		◆	
0.00	0730	1220A	0 d. **Blackadder** Central..a.	↑	1000B	1200
7.50	1115	....	5 d. Fox Woods............d.			....
10.25	....	....	28 d. Shepherd①.......d.			1030
13.55	SSS	....	45 d. Blue Bay⑥........d.			0915b
23.45	12	2358A	40 a. **Goshawk** Union....d.		2130A	0620
	1536	0002B	40 a. **Goshawk** Union....a.		1930A	0600
30.00	1625s	....	52 d. **Aardvark** (Aardwolf).d.			0430
40.00	1700	0230B	58 a. **Tiger Vale** West ...d.		1700A	....
			a. *Gorgon Swamp* **9999** d.		*1500a*	

100/101–🚃 1, 2 cl, 🍽, 1, 2 🍽 and Ⓕ, Blackadder - Tiger Vale and v.v.
①– Daily 🚌 service (hourly) Shepherd - Blue Bay and v.v. Journey 3 hours *(SSS)*.
a– ⑥ only.
b– Does not stop on ②.
MT– Municipal Transport.
SSS– Special Services Ltd.

FOOTNOTES: Footnotes explain non-standard letters and symbols used in the tables and **should always be referred to**.

Standard footnotes (e.g. 's' in this example) are shown on page 61 and are not repeated in individual tables; always therefore check page 61 if a symbol or letter does not have an explanation in the footnotes to a table.

SERVICES AND TIMES: Each service is headed by the operator code (in tables with more than one operator) in *italics* and the train or service number (where known) in **bold**. Other symbols indicate accommodation and dining facilities available (see introduction at the beginning of each country's entry) and days of running (see page 61). Fuller details of services indicated with black diamonds ◆ can be found in the footnotes (listed by train/service number). Non-standard symbols and letters are explained in the footnotes. Times are shown in the 24-hour clock system throughout the book (see page 59, and also the conversion table below) and are normally in local times (see the COUNTRY INFORMATION section).

Where two services are shown in the same column and are separated by a thick black line ▬▬ the services are totally independent of one another and no through facility is available.

Times in *italics* are connecting services; passengers must change en route.

Condensed bold CAPITAL letters against service times indicate duration of travel: A = First day, B = Second day etc.

Services operate daily unless otherwise qualified by a number or letter in a circle (see page 61). These symbols may be further combined, for example: alt ⑥ = Operates on alternate Saturdays; Ex ⑤ = Daily except Fridays; ①–④ = Daily Mondays to Thursdays.

Symbols in the tables are explained in the footnotes or on page 61.

In tables with a central list of town names, times should be read **down** on the left and **up** on the right, as indicated by the small arrows above the departure and arrival columns.

CONVERSION TABLES
Read centre unit columns as either metric or Imperial measure

Kilometres – Miles

1 Kilometre = 0.6214 Miles
1 Mile = 1.609 Kilometres

Km	Unit	Miles	Km	Unit	Miles
1.61	1	0.62	160.93	100	62.14
3.22	2	1.24	321.86	200	124.27
4.83	3	1.86	482.79	300	186.41
6.44	4	2.49	643.72	400	248.45
8.05	5	3.11	804.65	500	310.69
9.66	6	3.73	965.58	600	372.82
11.27	7	4.35	1126.51	700	434.96
12.87	8	4.97	1287.44	800	497.10
14.48	9	5.59	1448.37	900	599.23
16.09	10	6.21	1609.30	1000	621.37
32.22	20	12.74	3218.60	2000	1242.74
48.28	30	18.64	4827.90	3000	1864.11
64.37	40	24.85	6437.20	4000	2485.48
80.47	50	31.07	8046.50	5000	3106.86
96.56	60	37.28	9655.80	6000	3728.23
112.66	70	43.50	11265.10	7000	4349.60
128.74	80	49.71	12874.40	8000	4970.96
144.84	90	55.92	14483.70	9000	5992.33

Celsius – Fahrenheit

1 Deg. Celsius = 1.8 Deg. Fahrenheit
1 Deg.Fahrenheit = 0.55 Deg. Celsius

°C	Unit	°F	°C	Unit	°F
-40	-40	-40	10	50	122
-37	-35	-31	13	55	131
-34	-30	-22	15	60	140
-31	-25	-13	18	65	149
-29	-20	-4	21	70	158
-26	-15	5	24	75	167
-23	-10	14	26	80	176
-20	-5	23	29	85	185
-18	0	32	32	90	194
-15	5	41	35	95	203
-12	10	50	37	100	212
-10	15	59	40	105	221
-7	20	68	43	110	230
-4	25	77	46	115	239
-1	30	86	48	120	248
2	35	95	51	125	257
4	40	104	54	130	266
7	45	113	57	135	275

N.B. When using the *formula* for converting *into* Fahrenheit, add 32 at end of calculation. When converting *from* Fahrenheit, subtract 32 at start of calculation. (The figures in the table take this calculation into account).

24-hour Clock

All timings in this book are shown in the 24-hour clock format.

This system is explained in note 2 of 'how to use the Timetable' (page 59).

The standard time in any particular zone can be found in the COUNTRY INFORMATION section under Canada or the USA. Standard Time Zones are also shown on the 'Principal Routes Map' on page 62.

EXPLANATION OF SIGNS USED IN THE TIMETABLES

Railway	⌗⌗⌗⌗	Daily except Saturdays	⑧
Bus	🚌	Mondays	①
Taxi	🚕	Tuesdays	②
Ferry/Ship	⛴	Wednesdays	③
Tram	🚋	Thursdays	④
Mountain railway		Fridays	⑤
Cablecar		Saturdays	⑥
Through car		Sundays	⑦
Sleeping car		Saturdays, Sundays and holidays	ⓒ
Couchettes		Sundays and holidays	†
Restaurant car	✕	Calls by request	r
Buffet car	⊗	Calls to set down only	s
Light Refreshment	⍭	Calls to take up only	u
Observation car	⏢OB	Train/bus does not stop	⏐
Dome-car	Ⓓ	Runs when required	¶
Car-carrier	🚗	No fixed schedules	◑
Air-conditioned	‡	Service temporarily suspended	Σ
Railcar	🚗	Subject to confirmation	▲
Reservation obligatory	Ⓡ	Information not available at press date	❖
Some, or all, of the services shown in	♿	Supplement payable	⊡
this table offer special facilities for the		Alternate days only	●
carriage of disabled passengers		International bus journey	♣
Frontier point	▦	See footnote (by number)	◆
Daily except Sundays and holidays	✕	See footnote	P,Q,b,◇, etc.
Mondays to Fridays only, except holidays	Ⓐ	Train or bus number	1, 103, 81EE etc.

KEY TO SYMBOLS USED IN MAPS AND TOWN PLANS

▬▬▬	Main railway	⠶⠶⠶⠶	Bus route	🚡	Cablecar
⊥⊥⊥⊥	(electrified)	• • • • •	Ship/ferry service	🚠	Mountain railway
────	Secondary railway	— · —	Frontier	🚌	Bus station
⊥⊥⊥⊥	(electrified)	●	Station (main line)	○	Town/city
⊥⊥⊥⊥	Tramway	●	Station (local/metro)	𝒊	Information point
─ ─ ─	Metro	⊃	Station (interchange)		

CALENDAR
(For days of the week see above)

1994

JANUARY						
①	②	③	④	⑤	⑥	⑦
..	..	..	..	..	1	2
	4	5	6	7	8	9
	11	12	13	14	15	16
	18	19	20	21	22	23
	25	26	27	28	29	30
	..	..	..	..	..	..

FEBRUARY						
①	②	③	④	⑤	⑥	⑦
..	1	2	3	4	5	6
7	8	9	10	11	12	13
14	15	16	17	18	19	20
21	22	23	24	25	26	27
28	..	..	..	..	..	..

MARCH						
①	②	③	④	⑤	⑥	⑦
..	1	2	3	4	5	6
7	8	9	10	11	12	13
14	15	16	17	18	19	20
21	22	23	24	25	26	27
28	29	30	31	..	..	..

APRIL						
①	②	③	④	⑤	⑥	⑦
..	..	..	..	1	2	3
4	5	6	7	8	9	10
11	12	13	14	15	16	17
18	19	20	21	22	23	24
25	26	27	28	29	30	..

MAY						
①	②	③	④	⑤	⑥	⑦
..	..	..	..	..	..	1
2	3	4	5	6	7	8
9	10	11	12	13	14	15
16	17	18	19	20	21	22
23	24	25	26	27	28	29
30	31	..	..	..	..	..

JUNE						
①	②	③	④	⑤	⑥	⑦
..	..	1	2	3	4	5
6	7	8	9	10	11	12
13	14	15	16	17	18	19
20	21	22	23	24	25	26
27	28	29	30	..	..	..

JULY						
①	②	③	④	⑤	⑥	⑦
..	..	..	..	1	2	3
	5	6	7	8	9	10
	12	13	14	15	16	17
	19	20	21	22	23	24
	26	27	28	29	30	31

AUGUST						
①	②	③	④	⑤	⑥	⑦
1	2	3	4	5	6	7
8	9	10	11	12	13	14
15	16	17	18	19	20	21
22	23	24	25	26	27	28
29	30	31	..	..	..	..

SEPTEMBER						
①	②	③	④	⑤	⑥	⑦
..	..	1	2	3	4	
5	6	7	8	9	10	11
12	13	14	15	16	17	18
19	20	21	22	23	24	25
26	27	28	29	30	..	..

OCTOBER						
①	②	③	④	⑤	⑥	⑦
..	..	..	..	..	1	2
3	4	5	6	7	8	9
10	11	12	13	14	15	16
17	18	19	20	21	22	23
24	25	26	27	28	29	30
31	..	..	..	..	..	..

NOVEMBER						
①	②	③	④	⑤	⑥	⑦
..	1	2	3	4	5	6
7	8	9	10	11	12	13
14	15	16	17	18	19	20
21	22	23	24	25	26	27
28	29	30	..	..	..	..

DECEMBER						
①	②	③	④	⑤	⑥	⑦
..	..	..	1	2	3	4
5	6	7	8	9	10	11
12	13	14	15	16	17	18
19	20	21	22	23	24	25
26	27	28	29	30	31	..

1995

JANUARY						
①	②	③	④	⑤	⑥	⑦
..	..	..	..	..	..	1
	4	5	6	7	8	
	11	12	13	14	15	
	17	18	19	20	21	22
	24	25	26	27	28	29
	31					

FEBRUARY						
①	②	③	④	⑤	⑥	⑦
..	..	1	2	3	4	5
	7	8	9	10	11	12
13	14	15	16	17	18	19
20	21	22	23	24	25	26
27	28	..	..	..	..	..

MARCH						
①	②	③	④	⑤	⑥	⑦
..	..	1	2	3	4	5
6	7	8	9	10	11	12
13	14	15	16	17	18	19
20	21	22	23	24	25	26
27	28	29	30	31	..	..

APRIL						
①	②	③	④	⑤	⑥	⑦
..	..	..	..	..	1	2
3	4	5	6	7	8	9
10	11	12	13	14	15	16
17	18	19	20	21	22	23
24	25	26	27	28	29	30

MAY						
①	②	③	④	⑤	⑥	⑦
1	2	3	4	5	6	7
8	9	10	11	12	13	14
15	16	17	18	19	20	21
22	23	24	25	26	27	28
29	30	31	..	..	..	..

JUNE						
①	②	③	④	⑤	⑥	⑦
..	..	..	1	2	3	4
5	6	7	8	9	10	11
12	13	14	15	16	17	18
19	20	21	22	23	24	25
26	27	28	29	30	..	..

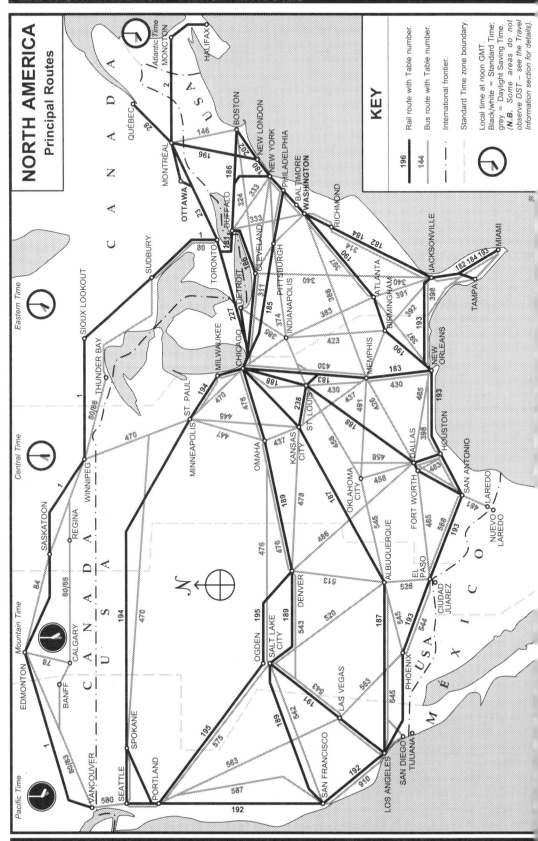

NORTH AMERICA
Principal Routes

KEY

— 196 — Rail route with Table number.

--- 144 --- Bus route with Table number.

–·–·– International frontier.

······· Standard Time zone boundary.

Local time at noon GMT.
Black/white = Standard Time;
grey = Daylight Saving Time.
(*N.B.* Some areas do not
observe DST – see the Travel
Information section for details).

CANADA

Rail services in Canada are operated mainly by VIA RAIL. A basic one-class structure is provided, with a standard fare allowing travel in ordinary seats. A range of 'additional' accommodation is provided (parlour [club] cars on certain day trains, sleeping accomodation on overnight and long-distance trains), for which supplementary charges are payable. Sleeping cars will be shown as S. Children of 2 but under 12 years pay half the basic fare but full accommodation charges; children of 12 and over must pay full fare. One child, under 2 years, not occupying a separate seat or unit of accommodation, may travel free with each passenger of 18 years or over. Excellent bus services operate throughout the country, except in the far North; many services are fully air-conditioned and most of the operators have through booking arrangements allowing tickets to be purchased in advance.

In this timetable, trains conveying coaches will be shown as C class, whilst those offering club cars (VIA 1 Service, which includes complimentary meals) will be shown as P.

Table 1 — CANADIAN ‖‖‖ VIA
SUMMARY TABLE

1	arr	dep		arr	dep		
1	....	1245	Toronto Union 18	2050	....	↑	D
↓	2000	2015	Capreol 10	1310	1325	↑	D
↓	1055	1110	Sioux Lookout 10	1952	2007	↑	C
↓	1730	1830	Winnipeg 10	1245	1345	↑	C
↓	0305	0325	Saskatoon 6	0350	0410	↑	C
↓	0830	0900	Edmonton 6	2010	2040	↑	B
↓	0830	....	Vancouver 6	....	2000	2	A

④⑥: ⟵‡, ◻, ⟐ and ✕ Vancouver(2)-Toronto. ⃟.
①⑥: ⟵‡, ⟐ and ✕ Toronto(1)-Vancouver. ⃟.
– Dome car. ‡–Air-conditioned. ⟵–Sleeping car. ⟐–Seating car.
– Reservation obligatory. ①–Mondays.
① Tuesdays. ④–Thursdays.
⑥ Saturdays. ✕–Restaurant car.
A– VIA Rail. ☏ Toronto 366 8411.

Table 2 — ATLANTIC ‖‖‖ VIA
SUMMARY TABLE

12	arr	dep		arr	dep		
12	....	1845	Montréal Central 27	0845	....	↑	B
↓	0836	0846	Saint John 27	2027	2037	↑	A
↓	1040	1100	Moncton 27	1823	1843	↑	A
↓	1351	1351	Truro 27	1539	1539	↑	A
↓	1520	....	Halifax 27	....	1400	11	A

①⑥: ⟵‡, ⟐, and ✕ Halifax(11/12)-Montréal and v.v. ⃟.
– Dome car. ‡–Air-conditioned. ⟵–Sleeping car. ⟐–Seating car.
– Reservation obligatory. ⟐–Seating car.
– Mondays. ④–Thursdays.
– Saturdays. ✕–Restaurant car.
A– VIA Rail. ☏ Montréal 871 1331.

Table 3 — VANCOUVER ISLAND ‖‖‖ VIA

CA $ C cl.	199 C‡ ◆⑤	199 C‡ ①④⑦	199 C‡ ◆⑤	299 C‡ ◆⑦	km ↓		198 C‡ ◆⑤	198 C‡ ◆⑤	198 C‡ ◆ ①④⑦	198 C‡ ◆⑦
0.00	0745	0815	1200	1800	0	d.Victoria..........a.	1325	1700	1745	2140
16.00	1020	1100	1435	2035	117	d.Nanaimo.........d.	1102	1437	1522	1917
30.00	1210	1250	1625	2225	225	a.Courtenay ......d.	0900	1235	1315	1715

8/9– MALAHAT.
– Air-conditioned.
A– VIA Rail. ☏ Winnipeg 949 1830.

Table 6 — PRINCE RUPERT - WINNIPEG ‖‖‖ BCT VIA

CA $ C cl.	6 S‡C‡ ◻◆ ②⑤⑦	2 S‡C‡ ◻◆ ①④⑥✕		km ↓	VIA	1 S‡C‡ ◻◆ ③⑤⑦	5 S‡C‡ ◻◆ ③⑤⑦
35.00	....	1130	....	0	d.Prince Rupert...a.	✕	1540
41.00	....	1350	....	95	d.Terrace (Kitimat)d.		1311
46.00	....	1606	....	181	d.New Hazelton...d.		1050
52.00	....	1755	....	227	d.Smithers ....d.		0935
64.00	....	2130r	....	373	d.Fort Fraser ...d.		0527r
45.00	....	0005	....		a.}Prince George VIA {d.		0300
	....	0035	....	467	{d.		0230
	....	....	2000	÷846	d. Vancouver § ...a.	0830		
					d. New Westminster §.d.			
00.00	....	....	2055	÷818	d. Port Coquitlam d.	0710	
39.00	....	....	2220	÷755	d. Chilliwack ...d.	0514	
				÷412	d. Kamloops CP ..d.			
44.00	....	....	0501	÷438	d. Kamloops North .d.	2305	
55.00	....	0900	1455	721	d.Jasper.........d.	1530	2010
55.00	....	....	1712	991	d.Edson..........d.	1205	
	....	....	2010		a.}Edmonton {d.	0900	
82.00	....	....	2040	1099	{d.	0830	
96.00	....	....	2303	1302	d.Wainwright ....d.	0610	
00.00	....	....	0225	1528	d.Biggar...........d.	0446	
	....	....	0350		a.}Saskatoon {d.	0325	
55.00	....	....	0410	1618	{d.	0305	
00.00	....	....	0519	1718	d.Watrous........d.	0150	
00.00	....	....	0734	1926	d.Melville.........d.	2342	
00.00	....	....	1028	2070	d.Brandon North ..d.	2040	
00.00	....	....	1136	2288	d.Portage la Prairie d.	1928	
00.00	....	....	1245	2378	a.Winnipeg ....d.	1830	

– CANADIAN–see Table 1.
– SKEENA–⟵‡, ◻, ⟐ and ✕.
– Km ex Jasper.
Local ‖‖‖ service (BCT) (C cl. only) operates Vancouver-New Westminster and v.v., from Vancouver Main Street: 0555④/0655④/0855† and frequent to 0120; from New Westminster: 0520④/0620④/0820† and frequent to 0045.
§ Km ex Vancouver.
T– BC Transit (Skytrain). ☏ Vancouver 604 264 5000.
– VIA Rail. ☏ Winnipeg 949 1830.

Table 4 — PRINCE GEORGE - VANCOUVER ‖‖‖ BCR

CA $ C cl.	2 C‡ ◆P ▼	2 C‡◻ ◆Q ▼	km ↓		1 C‡ ◆R ▼	1 C‡◻ ◆S ▼
91.00	....	0715	0	d.Prince George BCR a.	....	2030
78.00	....	0905	125	d.Quesnel........d.	....	1841
63.50	....	1050	239	d.Williams Lake...d.	....	1700
55.00	....	1220	327	d.Exeter Ω.......d.	....	1526
	....	1334r		d.Clinton.........d.	....	1409r
35.50	....	1520 1520	491	d.Lillooet.........d.	1250 1250	
28.00	....	1632 1632	546	d.D'Arcy.........d.	1116 1116	
20.50	....	1727 1727	592	d.Pemberton.....d.	1018 1018	
16.00	....	1810r 1810r	623	d.Whistler........d.	0934r 0934r	
10.00	....	1915 1915	680	d.Squamish ⊠...d.	0822 0822	
0.00	....	2035 2035	744	a.North Vancouver ⊠ d.	0700 0700	

1/2– CARIBOO–⟵ C‡ cl. Vancouver(1/2)-Lillooet and v.v.; conveys on days in note S; ⟵ C‡ cl. and ✕ Vancouver(1/2)-Prince George, returning on days in note Q.
P– ②③⑤⑦ to June 13 and from Sept. 18.
Q– ①④⑥ (daily June 14-Sept. 17).
R– ①②④⑥ to June 13 and from Sept. 18.
S– ③⑤⑦ (daily June 14-Sept. 17).
i– Calls by request. ⟐–Facilities for the disabled.
– Self-propelled train/railcar. ‡–Air-conditioned. ◻–Reservation obligatory.
Ω– For 100 Mile House. ①–Mondays. ②–Tuesdays. ③–Wednesdays.
④– Thursdays. ⑤–Fridays. ⑥–Saturdays. ⑦–Sundays.
– ROYAL HUDSON steam train (⚙) operates daily ex①② North Vancouver-Squamish and v.v. from early June to mid Sept.
▼– ✕ and ♀ service is available only to holders of reserved seats, at supplements varying from $11.50 to $45.50.
BCR– BC Rail. ☏ Vancouver 604 984 5246.

Table 7 — VANCOUVER - SEATTLE ‖‖‖ NRPC

US $ C cl.			km ↓		↑		
	....	....	0	d.Vancouver........a.	....		
	....	....		d.Bellingham ......d.	....		
	....	....		d.Everett ....d.	....		
0.00	....	....		a.Seattle............d.	....		

NRPC– National Railroad Passenger Corporation (AMTRAK). ☏ Los Angeles 213 624 0171.

Table 8 — WINNIPEG - CHURCHILL ‖‖‖ VIA

CA $ C cl.	295 C ①	295 C ⑦	693 S‡C‡ ⓪④⑦	km ↓		692 S‡C‡ ◻ ②④⑥	294 C ⑥	294 C ③
0.00	....	2155	0	d.Winnipeg .... a.	0800			
16.00	....	2310	88	d.Portage la Prairie .d.	0650			
44.94	....	0150	283	d.Dauphin.........d.	0420			
68.48	....	0510	484	d.Canora..........d.	0055			
74.90	....	0651r	586	d.Reserve.........d.	2303r			
80.25	....	0740	635	d.Hudson Bay....d.	2225			
97.37	....	0935	777	a.}The Pas {d.	2020			
	....	1050		{a.	1905			
116.63	....	1343r	949	d.Ponton.........d.	1606r			
121.98	....	0830	1445	997	d.Wabowden.....d.	1520	1605	
131.64	....	1010	1557	1074	d.Thicket Portage .d.	1345	1433	
134.82	....		1920	1135	d.Thompson ......d.	1140		
153.01	1000	1500	0125	1302	d.Gillam φ........d.	0510	1000	1635
175.48	....	1735	0820	1597	a.Churchill ....d.	2100		0900

92/93– HUDSON BAY–⟵‡, ⟐ and ✕.
φ– Nelson River.
VIA– VIA Rail. ☏ Winnipeg 949 1830.

Table 10 — WINNIPEG - CAPREOL ‖‖‖ VIA

CA $ C cl	2 S‡C‡ ◻◆ ①③⑤✕			km ↓		1 S‡C‡ ◻◆ ②④⑥✕		↑
0.00	1345	....	....	0	d.Winnipeg..........a.	....	1730	
33.00	1618	....	....	183	d.Minaki...........d.	....	1452	
36.00	1645	....	....	217	d.Redditt...........d.	....	1430	
38.00	1702r	....	....	223	d.Farlane..........d.	....	1409r	
49.00	1811	....	....	290	d.Red Lake Road ..d.	....	1300	
65.00	2007	....	....	405	d.Sioux Lookout ...d.	....	1110	
79.00	2126	....	....	465	d.Savant Lake .....d.	....	0934	
95.00	0011	....	....	629	d.Armstrong.......d.	....	0900	
117.00	0217	....	....	809	d.Nakina...........d.	....	0623	
139.00	0556	....	....	1020	d.Hornepayne.....d.	....	0340	
145.00	0647	....	....	1083	d.Oba ....d.	....	0209	
161.00	0911	....	....	1258	d.Foleyet ....d.	....	2355	
184.00	1310	....	....	1498	a.Capreol.........d.	....	2015	
221.00	2050	....	....	1958	a.Toronto 20.......d.	....	1245	

1/2– CANADIAN–see Table 1.
VIA– VIA Rail. ☏ Winnipeg 949 1830.

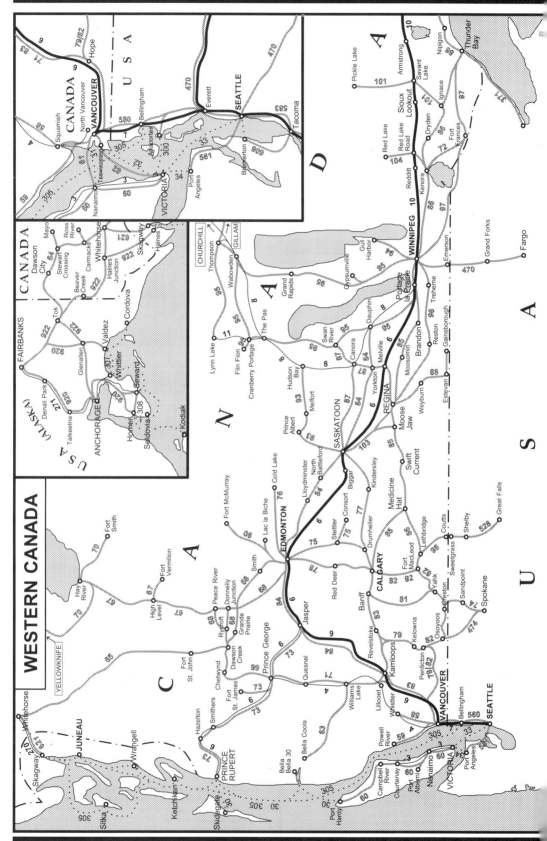

Table 11 — THE PAS - LYNN LAKE ### VIA

CA $ C cl.	291 C ①③⑤		km	↓	↑	290 C ②④⑥	
0.00	....	1100	....	0	d.The Pas.........a.		1735	....
16.00	....	1235	....	89	d.Cranberry Portage a.		1604	....
18.00	....	1300r	....	115	d.Optic Lake.........d.		1524r	....
24.00	....	1355	....	157	d.Sherridon.........d.		1439	....
51.00	....	2115	....	389	a.Lynn Lake.........d.		0730	....

VIA– VIA Rail. ☎Winnipeg 949 1830.

Table 12 — HEARST - SAULT STE. MARIE ### ACR

CA $ C cl.	2 C‡ Q ①⑥⑦	4 C‡ T ✕	2 C‡ P ex②		km	↓	↑	3 C‡ T ⑦	1 C‡ Q ✕	1 C‡ P ex①
73.10	0800	....	0815	....	0	d.Hearst.........a.		1820	1915	....
60.50	0918	....	1000	....	82	d.Oba.........d.		1645	1744	....
53.85	0955	....	1037	....	126	d.Mosher.........d.		1602	1658	....
48.15	1029	....	1121	....	162	d.Franz.........d.		1527	1614	....
40.75	1135	....	1225	....	211	d.Hawk Junction..d.		1430	1520	....
29.90	1259	....	1350	....	282	d.Eton.........d.		1259	1350	....
28.15	1311	1330	1410	....	292	d.Canyon.........d.	1130	1238	1330	....
10.00	1700	1700	1810	....	475	a.Sault Ste. Maried.	0800	0900	0930	....

■– May 17-Oct. 12: 🚍 Sault(1/2)-Hearst and v.v.; conveys on ③-⑦: ✕ Sault(1/2)-Eton and v.v.

◆– Oct. 13-May 16: 🚍 Sault(1/2)-Hearst and v.v.; conveys on ⑥⑦ Jan. 2-March 20: ✕ Sault(1/2)-Eton and v.v.

✕– June 8-Oct. 12.

ACR– Algoma Central Railway. ☎Sault Ste. Marie 254 4331.

Table 13 — WHITE RIVER - SUDBURY ### VIA

CA $ C cl.	186 🚍 C‡ ③⑤⑦		km	↓	↑	185 🚍 C‡ ②④⑥	
0.00	....	0930	....	0	d.White River.....a.		1800	....
14.00	....	1105	....	49	d.Franz.........d.		1635	....
26.00	....	1400	....	130	d.Chapleau.........d.		1430	....
58.00	....	1900	....	301	a.Sudbury.........d.		0940	....

VIA– VIA Rail. ☎Winnipeg 949 1830.

Table 14 — TIMMINS/COCHRANE ### ON

CA $ C cl.	423 C‡ ⒝R ✕	421 C‡ T	421 C‡ ①③⑤	121 C‡ ⒝⑧ ③		km	↓ d.Toronto 18......d.	↑	122 C‡ ⒝◆ ⑧	622 C‡ S	620 C‡ Q	624 C‡ ⒝R ✕
	....	....	....	1200	367			1835				
0.00	....	....	....	1650	0	d.North Bay ON ..a.		1350				
62.86	....	....	1855	146	d.Cobalt.........d.		1145					
93.06	....	....	1910	161	d.New Liskeard.....d.		1130					
93.06	....	....	1945	205	d.Englehart.........d.		1100					
103.15	....	....	2020	255	d.Swastika.........d.		1020					
108.12	....	....	2125		d.Matheson.........d.		0920					
123.26	....	....	2255a	417	a. Timmins.........d.		0800a					
128.61	0830	1010	1040	2150	386	d.Cochrane.........d.		0850	1430	1945	2120
131.29	1250	1545	1615			a. Moosonee.....d.		0900	1430	1715	
△77.04	....	....		2315a	594	a.Kapuskasing.....d.		0715a				
147.39	....	....		0030a	695	a.Hearst.........d.		0600a				

121/2– NORTHLANDER—🚍 and ✕ Toronto(121/2)-Cochrane and v.v.

Q– ⑤ June 26-Sept. 6.
R– POLAR BEAR EXPRESS–Daily ex ⑤ June 26-Sept. 6.
S– ②④⑥ (also ⑤ June 26-Sept. 6). T–②④ June 26-Sept. 6.
a– Connection by 🚍. ⚘–RT fare ex Cochrane.
ON– Ontario Northland. ☎ North Bay 472 4500.

Table 16 — TORONTO - GUELPH - LONDON ### GO VIA

CA $ C cl.	VIA 85 C‡ ◆✕	VIA 685 C‡ ◆†	VIA 689 C‡ ◆†	GO 841 C‡ Ⓐ	GO 843 C‡ Ⓐ	GO 845 C‡ Ⓐ	GO 847 C‡ Ⓐ	VIA 89 C‡ ◆✕		km	↓	↑	GO 840 C‡ Ⓐ	GO 842 C‡ Ⓐ	GO 844 C‡ Ⓐ	GO 846 C‡ Ⓐ	VIA 84 C‡ ◆	VIA 88 C‡ ◆✕	VIA 688 C‡ ◆†
0.00	....	0750	1200	1630	1630	1655	1720	1745	1845	....	0	d.Toronto Union ....a.	0723	0748	0813	....	0838	....	1035	....	2106	2326
△9.00	....	0827	1233	1700	1712	1737	1802	1827	1915	....	34	d.Brampton.........d.	0643	0708	0733	....	0758	....	1006	....	2026	2245
△9.00	....	0839	1245	1711	1728	1753	1818	1843	1926	....	47	d.Georgetown.....d.	0629	0654	0719	....	0744	....	0955	....	2016	2234
△15.00	....	0903	1310	1733	1815a		1905a		1948	....	79	d.Guelph.........d.	0535a		0625a		....	....	0929	....	1950	2209
17.00	....	0934	1333	1757					2017	....	101	d.Kitchener.........d.					....	....	0907	....	1927	2147
23.00	....	1002	1402	1827					2047	....	143	d.Stratford.........d.					....	....	0839	....	1859	2117
34.00	....	1050	1450	1915					2135	....	195	a.London.........d.					....	....	0752	....	1815	2030

84/89/689–HURON—🚍 and ✕ Sarnia(84/89/689)-Toronto and v.v. 85/88/685/688–see Table 17. a–By 🚍. ⒝–GO fares are $4.35, 5.75 and 8.55. GO–Government of Ontario Transit. ☎Toronto 630 3933. VIA–VIA Rail. ☎Toronto 366 8411.

Table 17 — TORONTO - LONDON - WINDSOR/BUFFALO ### GO NRPC VIA

CA $ C cl.		km	VIA 85 C‡ ◆ ✕	VIA 71 P‡C‡ ◆	VIA 97 C‡ ◆	VIA 685 C‡ ◆ †	VIA 73 P‡C‡ ◆	VIA 75 P‡C‡ ◆	VIA 689 P‡C‡ ◆	VIA 973 C‡ Ⓐ	VIA 81 P‡C‡◆ ✕	VIA 77 P‡C‡ ◆	VIA 977 C‡ Ⓐ	GO 925 C‡ Ⓐ	GO 95 🚍 S‡C‡ ⑥⑦ ◆	NRPC 62 C‡ ◆	VIA 89 C‡ ✕⚘		VIA 79 P‡C‡ ◆ ✕
0.00	Toronto Union ∃ d.	0	....	0750	....	0840	0930	....	1200	....	1235	1615	1630	1637	1715	1715	1719	1743	1745	....	1845	....	1920
Ⓐ8.00	Oakville ∃.........d.	34	....	....	....	0902	0952	....	....	....	1258	1638		1706		1745	1820	1810	....	....	....	1944
Ⓐ12.00	Aldershot.........d.	56	....	....	....	0917	1007	....	....	....	1313		1731	1752	1752	1810	1846	1824	....	....	....	2000
19.00	Brantford.........d.	96	....	....	a	0952	....	....	a	....	1348	1724	a		1824	1824		....	a	....	2035
23.00	Woodstock.........d.	139	....	....	....	1020	....	....	....	....	1416				1851	1851		....	....	....	2104
34.00	London.........d.	185	....	1100	....	1105	....	....	1500	....	1450	1823	1925		1919	1929		....	2145	....	2150
Ⓐ7.00	Sarnia 🚊 a..a.	280	....	1205	....	....	....	....	1602	....		2034						....	2254	....	
57.00	Chatham.........d.	290	....	....	....	1211	....	....	....	....	1555	1930		2038				....	....	....	2256
57.00	Windsor ....a.	360	....	....	....	1258	....	....	....	....	1643	2020		2125				....	....	....	2345
10.00	Hamilton CN ...d.	63	....	....	....	....	....	....	....	....			1744		1823	1859		....	....	....	
19.00	St. Catharines ..d.	114	....	....	....	1059	....	....	....	....						1916		....	....	....	
19.00	N. Falls Canada 🚊 d.	133	....	....	....	1130	....	....	....	....						1943	2045	....	....	....	
21.00	N. Falls USA 🚊 d.	153	....	....	....	1305	....	....	....	....							2310	....	....	....	
Ⓐ15.25	Buffalo Depew a.	192	....	....	....	1352	....	....	....	....							2357	....	....	....	
Ⓐ96.00	New York 215 ..a.	879	....	....	....	2140	....	....	....	....							0745	....	....	....	

		GO 960 C‡ Ⓐ	GO 962 C‡ Ⓐ	GO 964 C‡ Ⓐ	VIA 90 C‡◆ ①–⑤	VIA 80 ◆✕ ✕	VIA 70 C‡✕ ✕	NRPC 65 S‡C‡ ⑥⑦	VIA 92 C‡ ◆†	VIA 84 C‡ ◆	VIA 670 C‡ ◆†	VIA 72 P‡C‡ ◆	VIA 74 P‡C‡◆ ①⑤⑦		VIA 76 P‡C‡ ◆	NRPC 63 C‡ ◆	VIA 88 C‡ ◆✕	VIA 78 P‡C‡ ◆	VIA 688 C‡ ◆†
New York 215 ....d.	↓	....	....	....	....	....	....	2230b	....	....	....	....	....		....	0715	....	....	....
Buffalo Depew ....d.		....	....	....	....	....	....	0550	✕	....	....	....	....		....	1502	....	....	....
Niagara Falls USA 🚊.d.		....	....	....	....	....	....	0700		....	....	....	....		....	1600	....	....	....
N. Falls Canada 🚊 ..d.		....	....	....	....	....	0635	0715	0830	....	....	....	....		....	1715	....	....	....
St. Catharines ....d.		....	....	....	....	....	0656		0852	....	....	....	....		....	1737	....	....	....
Hamilton CN .....d.		....	0621	0641	0701	....	....			....	....	....	....		....	....	....	....	....
Windsor ....d.		....	....	....	....	0600	....			0700	....	0955	1130		1435		1815	....	
Chatham ....d.		....	....	....	....	0648	....			0750	....	1044	1219		1523		1900	....	
Sarnia 🚊 ....d.		....	....	....	....	....	....			0635	....				1710		1925		
London ....d.		....	....	....	0633	0757	....			0752	0859	1153	1325		1631		1815	2006	2030
Woodstock ....d.		....	....	....	0700	0831	....			0930	....	1224					2042		
Brantford ....d.		....	....	....	0728	0900	....		a	0958	....	1252	1419		1724		2112	a	
Aldershot ....d.		....	0634	0654	0714	0745	....	0932	0943	1031	....	1326			1758	1830	2147		
Oakville ∃ ....d.		....	0700	0720	0740	0759	....	0946	0957	1045	....	1341	1504		1812	1845	2203		
Toronto Union ∃ a.		....	0727	0743	0803	0825	0832	1012	1021	1035	1111	1403	1529		1838	1914	2056	2227	2316

62–NIAGARA RAINBOW—🚍‡, 🚍 and ♀ Niagara Falls(62)-New York. 63–MAPLE LEAF—🚍 and ✕ New York(63)-Niagara Falls(98)-Toronto. 65–NIAGARA RAINBOW—🚍‡, 🚍 and ♀ New York(65)-Niagara Falls. 70–TRILLIUM. 71–TRILLIUM—🚍‡ and ♀ (✕ on ⑧). 72–POINTE PELÉE. 73–POINTE PELÉE—🚍‡ and ♀ (✕ on ⑧). 75–ERIE. 76–ERIE—🚍‡ and ♀ (✕ on ⑧). 77–ST. CLAIR. 78–MOHAWK—🚍‡ and ♀ (✕ on ⑧). 79–MOHAWK. 80/81–FOREST CITY. 84–HURON. 85–INTERNATIONAL—🚍‡ and ✕ Toronto(85)-Sarnia(365)-Chicago. 88–INTERNATIONAL—🚍‡ and ✕ Chicago(364)-Sarnia(88)-Toronto. 89–HURON. 90/92/95–GENERAL BROCK. 97–MAPLE LEAF—🚍 and ✕ Toronto(97)-Niagara Falls(64)-New York. 670–TRILLIUM. 685–INTERNATIONAL—🚍‡ and ✕ Toronto(685)-Sarnia(367)-Chicago. 688–INTERNATIONAL—🚍‡ and ✕ Chicago(366)-Sarnia(688)-Toronto. 689–HURON. a–Via Stratford. b–⑨⑩. ∃–Local trains (GO, C ■ only) operate Toronto-Oakville and v.v., from Toronto: 0013, 0623⑩, 0643⑥, 0703⑩, 0708⑩, 0743①, 0843⑤, 0943, 1043, 1243, 1343, 1443, 1543, 1643⑦, 1643, 1702⑩, 1719⑦, 1725⑩, 1743, 1755⑥, 1823⑩, 1843, 1943, 2043, 2143, 2243; from Oakville: 0610⑩, 0630⑩, 0700⑩, 0710⑩, 0720⑩, 0730⑤, 0740⑩, 0750⑩, 0815⑩, 0830⑤, 0930, 1030, 1130, 1230, 1330, 1430, 1530, 1630, 1704⑩, 1730⑥, 1752⑩, 1830, 1930, 2030, 2130, 2230, 2330. △–US$. ⒶGO fares are $4.00, 5.45 and 6.60. GO–Government of Ontario Transit. ☎Toronto 630 3933. NRPC–National Railroad Passenger Corporation (AMTRAK). ☎New York 736 4545. VIA–VIA Rail. ☎Toronto 366 8411.

Check update notes to timetables and with operator before starting your journey

Table 18 — CAPREOL/NORTH BAY - TORONTO #### GO ON VIA

CA $ C cl.	GO 830 C‡ Ⓐ	GO 832 C‡ Ⓐ			GO 834 C‡ Ⓐ	GO 836 C‡ Ⓐ	ON 122 C‡◆ ⑧	VIA 2 S‡C‡⑧ ◆②④⑦		km ↓		↑	ON 121 C‡◆ ⑧	VIA 1 S‡C‡⑧ ◆②④⑥	GO 831 C‡ Ⓐ	GO 833 C‡ Ⓐ		GO 835 C‡ Ⓐ	GO 837 C‡ Ⓐ
63.13	....	....	....	....	....	....	....	1325		460	d.**Capreol**..............a.		....	2000	....	....		....	....
63.13	....	....	....	....	....	....	....	1356		426	d.Sudbury Junction.......d.		....	1925	....	....		....	....
41.73	....	....	....	....	....	....	....	1634		257	d.Parry Sound............d.		....	1627	....	....		....	....
33.00	....	....	....	....	....	....	1400	✕		367	d. **North Bay** ON.....a.		1640	✕	....	....		....	....
25.00	....	....	....	....	....	....	1553			235	d. Huntsville............d.		1447		....	....		....	....
25.00	....	....	....	....	....	....	1634			180	d. Gravenhurst..........d.		1402		....	....		....	....
24.61	....	....	....	....	....	....	1653	1817		159	d.Washago..............d.		1343	1452	....	....		....	....
17.12	....	....	....	....	....	....		1907		101	d.Barrie................d.			1406	....	....		....	....
2.95	0650	....	0710	....	0745	0810	....			34	d. Richmond Hill......a.				1711	1744		1811	1921
0.00	0728	....	0748	....	0823	0848	1835	2050		0	a.**Toronto** Union......a.		1200	1245	1630	1703		1730	1840

1/2– CANADIAN–see Table **1**.
121/2– NORTHLANDER–🚲 and Ⓧ Toronto(**121/2**)-Cochrane and v.v.
GO– Government of Ontario Transit. ☎Toronto 630 3933.
ON– Ontario Northland. ☎ North Bay 472 4500.
VIA– VIA Rail. ☎ Toronto 366 8411.

Table 22 — OTTAWA - MONTRÉAL #### STCUM VIA

CA $ C cl.	30 P‡C‡ ◆ ⒶⓍ	630 C‡ ◆③ Ⓢ Ⓧ	32 P‡C‡ ◆ Ⓐ		34 P‡C‡ ◆⑧ Ⓧb	36 P‡C‡ ◆ a	km ↓	VIA	↑	31 P‡C‡ ◆ 🏃a	33 P‡C‡ ◆ d		35 P‡C‡ ◆ ⑤Ⓧ	37 P‡C‡ ◆ a
32.00	0655	....	0800	1000	1440	1730	0	d.**Ottawa** Union..........a.		0859	1239		1642	1947
16.00	0745r	....	0858r	1054r	1532r	1824r	87	d.Alexandria ....d.		0816r	1143r		1549r	1854r
12.00	0813r	....	0920r	1115r	1559c		124	d.Coteau ....d.			1122r			1825e
π	0838	....	0944	1139	1623	1915	167	d.Dorval πð...........d.		0712	1057		1457	1802
		....					188	a. **Montréal** Windsor ð..a.						
0.00	0858	....	1005	1159	1643	1934	187	a.**Montréal** Central π....d.		0655	1040		1440	1745

30/31–VILLE MARIE. 32/33–GATINEAU. 34/35–VANIER. 36/37–LAURIER. 630–VILLE MARIE. a–Conveys Ⓧ (🍴 on ⑥). b–Conveys Ⓧ (🍴 on †). c–Calls on ⑤ only. Note applies. d–Conveys Ⓧ (🍴 on ⑥). e–Calls on ⑦ only. Note u applies. π–Local traffic not carried. ð–Local services (STCUM) operate Montréal Windsor-Dorval and v.v. **From Montré.** Windsor: 0715⑥, 0747Ⓐ, 1000Ⓐ, 1200⑥, 1220Ⓐ, 1330†, 1500⑥, 1538Ⓐ, 1640Ⓐ, 1700🏃, 1715†, 1718Ⓐ, 1725Ⓐ, 1745Ⓐ, 1830Ⓐ, 2000Ⓐ, 2100†, 2200Ⓐ, 2310Ⓐ; **from Dorval:** 0639⑥, 0711.. 0732Ⓐ, 0746Ⓐ, 0758Ⓐ, 0821Ⓐ, 0840Ⓐ, 0852Ⓐ, 0931Ⓐ, 1141Ⓐ, 1256†, 1331Ⓐ, 1504Ⓐ, 1631Ⓐ, 1641†, 1738Ⓐ, 1809Ⓐ, 1856⑥, 2026†, 2132Ⓐ. STCUM–Société de Transport de Communauté urbaine de Montréal. ☎Montréal 288 6287. VIA–VIA Rail. ☎ Montréal 871 1331.

Table 23 — TORONTO - MONTRÉAL #### GO VIA

CA $ C cl.		km	VIA 52 P‡C‡ ⑧ 🏃Ⓧ	VIA 40 P‡C‡ ⑧◆ 🏃Ⓧ	VIA 56 P‡C‡ ◆⑧ Ⓧ	VIA 42 P‡C‡ ⑧◆ Ⓧ	VIA 60 P‡C‡ ⑧◆ Ⓧ		VIA 44 P‡C‡ ◆Ⓧ ex②⑥	VIA 64 P‡C‡ ⑧◆ 🏃Ⓧ		VIA 66 P‡C‡ ◆ ⑥Ⓧ	VIA 46 P‡C‡ ⑧◆ Ⓧ	GO 978 C‡ Ⓐ	VIA 68 P‡C‡ ◆ Ⓧ
0.00	**Toronto** Union Φ⊿ d.	0	....	....	0800	0900	1000	1100	1200	....	1500	1545	....	1700	1730	1733	1800
§3.60	Guildwood Φ⊿...d.	20	....	....	0816	0916	1015	1116	1218	....	1516	1601	....		1747	1800	1821
§14.00	Oshawa...........d.	51	....	....	0833		1133	1235		....			....		1807	1824	
31.00	Belleville........d.	182	....	....	0940			1243	1345	....	1629		....		1916		
49.00	Kingston.........d.	254	....	....	1017	1101	1200	1320	1427	....	1706	1747	....		1956		2013
52.00	Brockville........d.	335	....	....	1055	1141		1359	1511	....	1746		....		2035		2056
72.00	**Ottawa** Union ..a.	446	....	....		1301		1512		....	1903		....		2148		
62.00	Cornwall ....d.	428	....	....	1139		1319		1601	....			....				2146
79.00	Dorval Φ..........d.	521	....	....	1224		1405		1649	....		1946	....	2036			2231
79.00	**Montréal** Central Φ ..a.	539	....	....	1243		1427		1713	....		2007	....	2059			2251

			GO 953 C‡ Ⓐ	VIA 41 P‡C‡ ◆⑧ Ⓧ		VIA 641 P‡C‡ ⑥Ⓧ 🏃Ⓧ	VIA 53 P‡C‡ ◆⑧ 🏃Ⓧ	VIA 57 P‡C‡ ◆⑧ Ⓧ	VIA 43 P‡C‡ ⑧◆ Ⓧ		VIA 61 P‡C‡ ⑧Ⓧ		VIA 45 P‡C‡ ◆⑧ 🏃Ⓧ	VIA 65 P‡C‡ ◆⑧ Ⓧ	VIA 67 P‡C‡ ⑧◆ Ⓧ	VIA 47 P‡C‡ ⑧◆ Ⓧ	VIA 69 P‡C‡ ⑧◆ Ⓧ
Montréal Central Φ..d.			....	....	....	0715	1000	....	....	....	1215	....	....	1545	1700	....	1800
Dorval Φ.................d.			....	....	....	0733	1021	....	....	....	1233	....	....	1603	1718	....	1818
Cornwall...............d.			....	....	....	0817	1110	....	....	....		....	....	1648		....	1910
Ottawa Union ....d.			....	0600	....	0740		1130	....	....	1535	....	1740			....	
Brockville..............d.			....	0708	....	0850	1200	1247	....	....	1645	....	1855			....	1957
Kingston...............d.			....	0747	....	0928	0937	1245	1330	....	1725	1807	1935			....	2037
Belleville...............d.			....	0823	....	1004		1326		....	1507a	1801	1907		2008b	....	2114
Oshawa................d.			0717		....		1116	1438		....						....	2226
Guildwood Φ⊿ ....d.			0739	0942	....	1124	1132	1455	1523	....	1622	1924	1953		2124	....	2242
Toronto Union Φ⊿...a.			0803	1002	....	1144	1152	1515	1542	....	1944	2014	2059	2142	....	2259

40/41– CAPITAL. 42/3–LAKESHORE. 44/5– RIDEAU. 46/7–SIMCOE. 52/53–YORK. 56/57–LA SALLE. 60/61–MERIDIAN. 64/65–RENAISSANCE. 66/67–METROPOLIS. 68/69–BONAVENTURE.
641– CAPITAL. a–Calls on ⑦ only. b–Calls on ② only.
Φ– Local traffic Toronto-Guildwood and Montréal-Dorval or v.v. not carried on VIA trains.
§– Fare by GO to Guildwood; GO fare to Oshawa: 5.35.
⊿– GO trains operate Toronto-Guildwood and v.v.; **from Toronto:** 0013, 0613🏃, 0631Φ, 0658Φ, 0713🏃, 0813🏃, 0913, 1013, 1113, 1213, 1313, 1413, 1513, 1549Φc, 161 1633Ⓐ, 1650Φc, 1703Ⓐ, 1713, 1733Ⓐ, 1747Ⓐ, 1813, 1913, 2013, 2113, 2213, 231 **from Guildwood:** 0611Ⓐ, 0631Ⓐ, 0651Ⓐ, 0711Ⓐ, 0713Ⓐ, 0739Ⓐ, 0753Ⓐ, 0813 0823Ⓐ, 0833Ⓐ, 0912Ⓐ, 0913Ⓐ, 1013, 1113, 1213, 1313, 1413, 1513, 1612Ⓐ, 1613 1640Ⓐ, 1713Ⓒ, 1721Ⓐ, 1752Ⓐ, 1812Ⓐ, 1813Ⓒ, 1832Ⓐ, 1912Ⓐ, 1913Ⓒ, 2012 2013Ⓒ, 2113, 2213, 2313.
GO– Government of Ontario Transit. ☎ Toronto 630 3933.
VIA– VIA Rail. ☎Toronto 366 8411.

Table 24 — MONTRÉAL - JONQUIÈRE/COCHRANE #### VIA

CA $ C cl.		601 C‡ ①③⑤ ◆🍴	603 S‡C‡ ◆ ①③	803 C‡ ④ ◆	605 S‡C‡ ②④ ⑤	805 C‡ ⑥	km ↓		↑	806 C‡ ⑦	606 S‡C‡ ◆ ⑦	804 C‡ ②④	604 S‡C‡ ◆ ②④		600 C‡ ②④ ◆🍴	602 C‡ ⑦ ◆🍴
0.00	....	1420	....	2000	....	2000	0	d.**Montréal** Central.......a.		....	0610	....	1105		1935	2155
22.00	....	1649	....	2246	....	2246	156	d.Shawinigan............d.		....	0355	....	0850		1724	1944
28.00	....	1739	....	2337	....	2337	203	d.Hervey................d.		....	0302	....	0757		1634	1854
30.00	....	1835r	....		....		237	d.Rivière à Pierre ......d.		....		....			1542	1802
41.00	....	2013	....		....		325	d.Lac Édouard..........d.		....		....			1404	1624
53.00	....	2205	....		....		430	d.Chambord ....d.		....		....			1210	1430
54.00	....	2310	....		....		496	a.**Jonquière**...........d.		....		....			1105	1325
38.00	....		....	0110	....	0110	283	d. La Tuque............d.		....	0145	....	0640			
51.00	....		....	0338	....	0338	402	d. Sanmaur............d.		....	2316	....	0411			
57.00	....		....	0505	....	0505	481	d. Parent..............d.		....	2156	....	0251			
65.00	....		....	0605	....	0605	547	d. Clova...............d.		....	2049	....	0144			
83.00	....		0850	0945	0850	0905	703	d. **Senneterre** ....d.		1755	1810	2250	2305			
91.00	....		....	1055	....	1014	772	d. Amos................d.		1641		2136				
97.00	....		....	1140	....	1126	817	d. Taschereau..........d.		1555		2050				
116.00	....		....		....	1515	999	a. **Cochrane** ....d.		1145						

600/1/2–SAGUENAY. 603-6–ABITIBI–🚲 ‡, 🚲 and 🍴. VIA–VIA Rail. ☎Montréal 871 1331.

Table 25 — TORONTO - STOUFFVILLE ╫╫╫ GO

CA $ C cl.	862 C‡ ⑥	864 C‡ ⑥	km	↓	863 C‡ ⑥	865 C‡ ⑥
0.00	1720	1803	0	d.Toronto Union ..a.	0727	0811
4.90	1821	1904	46	a.Stouffville.........d.	0628	0712

O– Government of Ontario Transit. ☎ Toronto 630 3933.

Table 26 — SEPT ÎLES - SCHEFFERVILLE ╫╫╫ QNSL

CA $ C cl.	C S ④	C ①		km	↓ ↑	C S ④	C ②
0.00	0800	....	1900	0	d.Sept Îles..........a.	1915	2000
9.90	1515	....	0030	361	a.Ross Bay Junctiond.	1205	1300
9.90	....	....	0230	420	a. Labrador City ..d.	1030	1200
4.70	1915	....	....	576	a.Schefferville........d.	0800	....

🚌 🚃 and Ɏ.
🚌 🚃 and Ɏ Sept Îles-Schefferville and v.v.; 🚃 and 🚃 Sept Îles-Labrador City and v.v.
Lower fares are charged for Indians.
QNSL– Québec, North Shore and Labrador Railway. ☎ Sept Iles 968 7539.

Table 27 — MARITIME PROVINCES ╫╫╫ VIA

CA $ C cl.	12 S‡C‡ 🚃◆	14 S‡C‡ 🚃◆	16 S‡C‡ 🚃◆		km	↓ ↑	17 S‡C‡ 🚃◆	15 S‡C‡	15 S‡C‡
	①④⑥✕	③⑤⑦	①④⑥				①④⑥	③⑤⑦	①④⑥✕
0.00	1845	1900	1900	....	0	d.Montréal Central a.	0815	0815	0845
	1900u	1915u	1915u	....	6	d.St. Lambert ......d.	0751s	....	0751s0832s
9.00	1932	1946	1946	....	53	d.St. Hyacinthe....d.	0720	0720	0756
4.00	....	2019	2019	101	d.Drummondville ..d.	0647	0647	
2.00	....	2150	2150	....	246	d.Charny ....d.	0521	0521	
2.00	....	2235	2235	....	259	d.Lévis ....d.	0459	0459	
7.00	....	2323	2323	....	317	d.Montmagny ......d.	0359	0359	
0.00	....	0038	0038	....	401	d.Rivière du Loup..d.	0245	0245	
3.00	....	0111	0111	....	487	d.Trois Pistoles ..d.	0210	0210	
5.00	....	0205	0205	....	549	d.Rimouski ....d.	0104	0104	
9.00	....	0241	0241	....	578	d.Mont Joli ......d.	0041	0041	
0.00	....	0444	0450	....	727	d.Matapédia ......d.	2234	2234	
0.00	....	....	0945	....	989	d. Percé ....d.	1735		
3.00	....	....	1100	....	1052	a. Gaspé ....d.	1620		
5.00	....	0633	....		748	d.Campbellton ....d.		2304	
5.00	....	0858	....		920	d.Newcastle ....d.		2017	
7.00	2021				119	d. Richmond .....d.			0710
3.00	2105				151	d. Sherbrooke ...d.			0622
0.00	2311				283	d. Mégantic 🚃...d.			0412
7.00	0231				471	d. Brownville Junctiond.			0037
2.00	0458				616	d. Vanceboro 🚃d.			2152
3.00	0636				626	d. McAdam ......d.			2237
3.00	0721				690	d. Fredericton Junction d.			2134
5.00	0836				761	a.} Saint John {d.			2037
	0846					d.} {a.			2027
0.00	0940				833	d. Sussex ....d.			1934
6.00	1040	1040			906	a.}Moncton {d.		1843	1843
	1100	1100				d.} {a.		1823	1823
2.00	1210	1210			983	d.Amherst ....d.		1719	1719
7.00	1351	1351			1107	d.Truro ....d.		1539	1539
4.00	1520	1520			1210	a.Halifax ....d.		1400	1400

◆12– ATLANTIC–see Table 2.
◆15– OCEAN–🚃‡, 🚃 and ✕.
◆17– CHALEUR–🚃‡, 🚃 and ✕.
A– VIA Rail. ☎ Montréal 871 1331.

Table 28 — MONTRÉAL - QUÉBEC ╫╫╫ VIA

CA $	20 P‡C‡ ◆	620 C‡ ◆	22 P‡C‡ ◆		24 P‡C‡ ◆	26 C‡ ◆	12 P‡C‡	14/16 P‡C‡
	④⑥	⑥Ɏ	⑦		⑥Ⓧ	Ⓧ	①④⑥Ɏ	ex⑥②✕
0.00	Montréal Central..d.	0700	0820	1320	....	1600	1800	1845	1900
7.00	St. Lambert ......d.	6		0832		1612		1900u	1915u
	St. Hyacinthe......d.	53	0738	0858		1835	1932	1946
1.00	Drummondville ....d.	100	0802	0923	1421	1701	1900	2019
	Charny ....d.	246		1534		2150
3.00	Ste. Foy ....a.	250	0920	1039	1544	1824	2026
0.00	Québec Palais ....a.	272	0942	1107	1609	1850	2055

	15/17 S‡C‡ ◆	11	21 P‡C‡ ◆	621 C‡ ◆		23 P‡C‡ ◆		25 P‡C‡ ◆	27 P‡C‡ ◆
	ex⑥✕②⑤⑦✕	④⑥	⑥Ɏ	Ⓧ		Ⓧ		④⑥	Ⓧ
Québec Palais ..d.			0635	0800		1020	....	1400	1735
Ste. Foy ..d.			0654	0819		1039		1419	1754
Charny ..d.		0521				1046			
Drummondville ..d.		0647	0817	0937		1159		1541	1916
St. Hyacinthe ..d.		0720	0756			1224			1942
St. Lambert ..a.		0751s	0832s			1249		1628	2007
Montréal Central ..a.		0815	0845	0921	1046	1302		1649	2029

◆17– ATLANTIC/OCEAN/CHALEUR–see Table 27.
◆21– CHAMPLAIN.
◆23– CITADELLE.
◆25– CHAUDIÈRE.
◆27– FRONTENAC.   620/1–CHAMPLAIN.
A– VIA Rail. ☎ Montréal 871 1331.

Table 30 — ▲ PORT HARDY - PRINCE RUPERT ▲ 🚢 BCF

CA $			km	V ⑥	W ⑥	V ③⑤⑦	X ⑥	X ③⑦	Y ①	V ●	X ①
0.00	Port Hardy (Bear Cove).d.		0	1600	....	....	....	....	....	0730	....
33.00	Bella Bella ....d.		220	2215	....	....	....	....	....	1300a	....
50.00	Prince Rupert ... {a.		480	0900	....	....	....	....	....	2230	....
0.00	{d.			....	1200	1200	....	1200	2100	....	2300
12.00	Skidegate ....a.		630	....	1800	1800	....	1800	0600	....	0600

	↓			Y	V	X	V		X	W
Skidegate ....d.				....	1000	1100	....	2300	2300	2300
Prince Rupert .... {a.				....	1700	1100	....	0700	0735	0735
{d.	0735		1000							
Bella Bella ....d.	1700a		2345							
Port Hardy(BearCove).a.	2230		0800							

V– Oct. 13-May 29.   W–July 1-Aug. 31.
X– June 1-Sept. 30.   Y–June 1-Sept. 30.
a– Calls at Bella Bella about once each week.
BCF– BC Ferries. ☎ Victoria ❖.

Table 31 — NANAIMO 🚢 BCF

■ service Nanaimo-Horseshoe Bay and v.v. Journey: 1½ hours. Fare: CA $: 4.50.
From Nanaimo (Departure Bay): June 25-Sept. 8: ❖; Sept. 9-June 24: 0700, 0900, 1100, 1300, 1500, 1700, 1900, 2100.
From Horseshoe Bay: June 25-Sept. 8: ❖; Sept. 9-June 24: 0700, 0900, 1100, 1300, 1500, 1700, 1900, 2100.
■ service Nanaimo-Tsawwassen and v.v. 55 km. Journey: 2 hours. Fare: CA $: 5.00.
From Nanaimo (Departure Bay): June 25-Sept. 8: ❖; Sept. 9-June 24: 0530, 0800, 1030, 1300, 1530, 1800, 2030, 2300.
From Tsawwassen: June 25-Sept. 8: ❖; Sept. 9-June 24: 0530, 0800, 1030, 1300, 1530, 1800, 2030, 2300.
BCF– BC Ferries. ☎❖.

Table 31a — VANCOUVER 🚢 VRTS

■ service Vancouver-North Vancouver and v.v. 2 km. Journey: 10 mins. Fare: CA $: 0.75.
From Vancouver Granville Waterfront: 0017ex①, 0047ex①, 0632⑥/0647⑥/0847† and every 15 mins. (every 30 mins. on †, early ⑥ and all evenings) to 2317, 2347✕.
From North Vancouver Lonsdale Quay: 0003ex①, 0033ex①, 0618⑥/0633⑥/0833† and every 15 mins. (every 30 mins. on †, early ⑥ and all evenings) to 2303, 2333✕.
VRTS– Vancouver Regional Transit System (SeaBus). ☎ Vancouver 604 264 5000.

Table 32 — TSAWWASSEN 🚢 BCF

■ service Swartz Bay-Tsawwassen and v.v. 39 km. Journey: 1½ hours. Fare: CA $: 4.50.
From Swartz Bay: Mar. 22-Sept. 8: ❖; Sept. 9-Nov. 15: 0700 and hourly to 1900, 2000⑤⑦, 2100, 2200⑤⑦; Nov. 16-Jan. 3µ: 0700, 0800ex⑦, 0900, 1000ex⑦, 1100, 1200ex⑥, 1300, 1400ex⑥, 1500, 1600ex⑥, 1700, 1800ex⑥, 1900, 2100; Jan. 4-Mar. 21: 0700, 0800ex⑦, 0900, 1100, 1200⑤⑦, 1300, 1400⑤⑦, 1500, 1600⑤⑦, 1700, 1800⑤⑦, 1900, 2100.
From Tsawwassen: Mar. 22-Sept. 8: ❖; Sept. 8-Nov. 15: 0700 and hourly to 1900, 2000⑤⑦, 2100, 2200⑤⑦; Nov. 16-Jan. 3µ: 0700, 0800ex⑦, 0900, 1000ex⑦, 1100, 1200ex⑥, 1300, 1400ex⑥, 1500, 1600ex⑥, 1700, 1800ex⑥, 1900, 2100; Jan. 4-Mar. 21: 0700, 0900, 1000ex⑦, 1100, 1200⑤⑦, 1300, 1400⑤⑦, 1500, 1600⑤⑦, 1700, 1800④⑤⑦, 1900, 2100.
µ– Special services operate during the Christmas/New Year holiday period.
BCF– BC Ferries. ☎❖.

Table 33 — VICTORIA - SEATTLE 🚢 BCSL IJ

US $	IJ	BCSL S	BCSL T	IJ	km	↓ ↑	IJ	BCSL S	BCSL U	IJ
69.00	....	....	....	1700	0	d.Vancouver........a.	....	....	....	1615
45.00	....	....	1845		120	a.} Victoria {d.	....	....	....	1430
	....	0930	1600	1730	1930		d.} {a.	....	0845	1230	1445	1345
0.00	1115	2045	2215	2115	250	a.Seattle ....d.	0700	0800	1000	1200

S– June 10-Sept. 17. Fare: US $:29.00.
T– May 13-Dec. 21 and Jan. 26-Mar. 31. Fare: US $:18.00-29.00.
U– May 13-Dec. 22 and Jan. 27-Mar. 31. Fare: US $: 18.00-29.00.
BCSL– British Columbia Stena Line. ☎ Victoria 604 388 7397.   IJ–Island Jetfoil. ☎❖.

Table 34 — VICTORIA - PORT ANGELES 🚢 BBT

US $		km	U	R			T	Q	V
0.00	Victoria..............d.	0	0620	1030	....		1500	1600	1930
6.25	Port Angeles.......a.	40	0755	1205	....		1635	1735	2105

		P		V	Q		V		S
Port Angeles..........d.		0820		1245	1400		1715		2130
Victoria...................a.		0955		1420	1535		1850		2305

P– Jan. 1-22; Feb. 10-Dec. 31.   Q– May 19-Oct. 18; Oct. 6-Nov. 30.
R– Mar. 10-Nov. 30.   S–June 2-Sept. 20.
T– Jan. 1-22; Feb. 10-Mar. 9; May 19-Oct. 5; Dec. 1-31.
U– June 3-Sept. 21.   V–May 19-Oct. 5.
BBT– Black Ball Transport Inc. ☎ Bellevue 206 622 2222.

Table 35 — NIAGARA FALLS 🚢 MM

Regular 🚢 cruises to the foot of the falls, from both US and Canadian sides, May to end of October. Every 15 mins. Duration 30 mins. Fare: CA $: 8.65. Hooded raincoats provided.
From Niagara Falls (USA): Spring/Autumn (Fall) 1000-1700④/1800©; Summer 0915-1930 (2000 in peak season).
From Niagara Falls (Canada): Spring/Autumn (Fall) 0945-1645④/1745©; Summer 0900-1915 (1945 in peak season).
MM– Maid of the Mist Cruises. ☎ Niagara Falls (Canada) 416 358 5781.

Table 36   PELEE ISLAND   PIT

service Pelee Island-Leamington/Kingsville and v.v. 25 km. Journey 1½ hours. Fare: CA $: 5.00.

June 24-Sept. 6т.

From Leamington: 1230, 1600, 2100.
From Kingsville: 0830, 1745.
From Pelee Island (to Leamington): 1030 1415, 1930.
From Pelee Island (to Kingsville): 0700, 1615.

service Pelee Island-Sandusky and v.v. 37 km. Journey 2 hours. Fare: CA $: 9.00.

June 20-Sept. 5.

From Pelee Island: 0530⑥, 1015, 1800.
From Sandusky: 0800, 1315, 2100⑥.

т–   Reduced sailings operate March-June and Sept.-Dec.
PIT–   Pelee Island Transportation. ☎Pelee Island 519 724 2115.

Table 37   WOLFE ISLAND   HT MTC

(MTC) service Kingston-Wolfe Island and v.v. 5 km. Journey: 25 mins. Free ferry.
Subject to alteration during ice conditions.

From Kingston: 0040, 0200, 0615, 0715, 0830, 0930, 1030a, 1100b, 1130a, 1230, 1400, 1500, 1600, 1700, 1800, 1920, 2040, 2200, 2320.
From Wolfe Island: 0000, 0120, 0545, 0645, 0800, 0900, 1000a, 1015b, 1100a, 1145b, 1200a, 1315, 1430, 1530, 1630, 1730, 1840, 2000, 2120, 2240.

(HT) service Cape Vincent-Wolfe Island and v.v. 🚗 11 km. Journey: 10 mins. Fare: CA $: 1.00.

May 12-Oct. 22 only.

From Cape Vincent: 0815, 0930, 1030, 1130, 1230, 1400, 1500, 1600, 1700, 1800, 1930c.
From Wolfe Island: 0800, 0915, 1015, 1115, 1215, 1315, 1445, 1545, 1645, 1740, 1900c.
a–May 12-Oct. 22.   b–Oct. 23-May 11.   c–Daily May 12-Sept. 23; ⑤⑥⑦ Sept. 24-Oct. 22.
HT–Horne Transportation. ☎Wolfe Island 613 385 2291.   MTC–Ministry of Transportation & Communications. ☎Wolfe Island 613 544 2231.

Table 38   ST. LAWRENCE FERRIES   STQ

service Lévis-Québec and v.v. 2 km. Journey: 10 mins. Fare: CA $: 1.00. ♿.
From Lévis: 0315, 0600, 0700 and every 30 mins. to 1800, then hourly to 0200.
From Québec: 0345, 0630, 0730 and every 30 mins. to 1830, then hourly to 0230.
service Montmagny-Île aux Grues and v.v. 4 km. Journey: 25 mins. Free ferry.
From Montmagny and Île aux Grues: Apr. 1-Nov. 30: 1-3 sailings daily (times variable).
service Tadoussac-Baie Ste. Catherine and v.v. 1 km. Journey: 8 mins. Free Ferry. ♿.
From Tadoussac and Baie Ste. Catherine: Hourly (night service). Every 20-40 mins. (day service).
service Matane-Baie Comeau and v.v. 62 km. Journey: 2½ hours. Fare: CA $: 7.50. ♿.
From Matane: Mar. 23-May 28 and Sept. 3: 1400ex⑦, 1500②. May 29-Sept. 15: 1100①⑤, 1400⑥⑦, 1700①–⑤, 2000⑥. Jan. 4-Mar.31: 0800⑥, 1400①⑤, 1500⑦.
From Baie Comeau: Mar. 23-May 28 and Sept. 3: 1700ex⑦, 1800⑦. May 29-Sept. 15: 1400①⑤, 1700⑥⑦, 2000①–⑤, 2300⑥. Jan. 4-Mar. 31: 1700①⑤⑥, 1800⑦.
service Matane-Godbout and v.v. 55 km. Journey: 2½ hours. Fare: CA $: 7.50. ♿.
From Matane: Mar. 23-May 28 and Sept. 16-Jan. 3: 0800ex⑦, 0900⑦. May 29-Sept. 15: 0500①–⑤, 0800⑥⑦, 1100②③④. Jan. 4-Mar. 31: 0800①⑤⑥.
From Godbout: Mar. 23-May 28 and Sept. 16-Jan. 3: 1100ex⑦, 1200⑦. May 29-Sept. 15: 0800①–⑤, 1100⑥⑦, 1400②③④. Jan. 4-Mar. 31: 1100①⑤, 1700②③④.
STQ– Société des Traversiers du Québec. ☎✢.

Table 39   ▲ ST. LAWRENCE RIVER ▲   SLCL

3-night (c) HERITAGE WATERWAY cruise from Kingston to Montréal and v.v. calling at 1000 Islands Retreat, Upper Canada Village and Côteau Landing downstream; Côte Ste. Catherines, Upper Canada Village and Rockport/Brockville upstream. 296 km. Fares from US $: 562.
From Kingston: Sept. 4, 10, 16; Oct. 2, 5.
From Montréal: Sept. 7, 13, 19; Oct. 5, 8.
5-night (c) CANADIAN CONNECTION cruise from Kingston to Québec and v.v. calling at 1000 Islands Retreat, Upper Canada Village, Côteau Landing, Montréal and Trois Rivières downstream; Québec City, Trois Rivières, Côte Ste. Catherines and Upper Canada Village and Brockville upstream. 520 km. Fares from US $: 935.
From Kingston: Oct. 14.
From Québec: Oct. 19.
5-night (c) CANADA'S CAPITAL cruise from Kingston to Ottawa and v.v. calling at 1000 Islands Retreat, Upper Canada Village, Côteau Landing, Montréal and Montebello downstream; Montebello, Ste. Anne de Bellevue, Côte Ste. Catherines, Upper Canada village and Rockport/Brockville upstream. ✢ km. Fares from US $: 935.
From Kingston: Sept. 22.
From Ottawa: Sept. 27.
7-night (v) SAGUENAY FJORD EXPEDITIONS cruise from Kingston to Montréal and v.v. calling at Brockville, Cornwall, Trois Rivières, La Malbaie, Saguenay Cove and Québec City. ✢ km. Fares from US $: 1512.
From Kingston: Sept. 11 and alt ⑧ to Oct. 9.
From Montréal: Sept. 4 and alt ⑧ to Oct. 16.
SLCL– St. Lawrence Cruise Lines Inc. (c–Canadian Empress, v–Victorian Empress). ☎ Kingston 613 549 8091.

Table 40   RIMOUSKI - BLANC SABLON   LN

CA $			km	↓ April 8-Dec. 8 ↑		
Ꙅ						
0.00	....	1900②	0	d.**Rimouski** ....a.	....	1030①	....
	....	1400③	215	d.Sept Îles ....a.	....	2330⑦	....
	....	0700④	385	d.Havre St. Pierre d.	....	1015⑦	....
73.00	....	1600④	506	d.Natashquan ....d.	....	0300⑦	....
80.00	....	1930④	548	d.Kegaska ....d.	....	2245⑥	....
121.00	....	2130⑤	918	a.**Blanc Sablon** ....d.	....	0001⑥	....

Ꙅ–   Basic fare only (berth and meals extra).
LN–   Logistec Navigation Co. ☎✢.

Table 41   BLANC SABLON - ST. BARBE   N

service Blanc Sablon-St. Barbe and v.v. 31 km. Journey: 1½ hours. Fare: CA $: 7
From Blanc Sablon: 0630①–④and⑧◇, ①③△, ②④◇. 0800⑤△. 0830③⑧◇, daily♡. 0845②④◇△. 1015⑦◇△. 1100②④△, ②④◇. 1115②④⊡. 1230⑤◇△◇. 1315②④⊡. 1445⑦◇△◇. 1530①③△. 1700⑤◇△◇.
From St. Barbe: 0630②④and⑧◇, ①③△, ②④◇. 0845①–④and⑧◇, ①③△, ②④◇. 1015④△. 1100②④△ ③⑧◇, daily♡. 1230⑦◇△◇. 1315③③△. 1330②④, ②④◇. 1430daily⊡. 1445⑤◇△. 1530②④⊡. 1700⑦◇△◇. 1915⑤◇◇.

⊙–May 1-June 30.   △–July 1-Aug. 31.   ◇–Sept. 1-Oct. 31.   ♡–Nov. 1-Dec. 13 and D 21-end of Season (except Dec. 25, 26 and Jan. 1).   ⚓–Dec. 14-20.
NCL– Northern Cruiser Ltd. (m.v. Northern Princess). ☎ 418 461 2056.

Table 42   RIVIÈRE DU LOUP - ST. SIMÉON   TR

service Rivière du Loup-St. Siméon and v.v. 26 km. Crossing: 65 mins. (1½ hours trips marked **d**). Fare: CA $: 8.25.

No service Jan. 5-Apr. 15.

From Rivière du Loup: 0700c, 0800ab, 0830e, 1015c, 1100d, 1115b, 1200a, 13⁻ 1345c, 1445b, 1500d, 1600a, 1700c, 1800b, 1830d, 2000b.
From St. Siméon: 0830c, 0915d, 0930ab, 1000e, 1200c, 1300d, 1400a, 1500e, 153⁻ 1630b, 1645d, 1730a, 1830c, 1930b, 2115c.
a–Apr. 16-May 31 (except May 15, 18); Sept. 8-Nov. 28 (except Oct. 9, 12).   b–May 15, June 14-July 4; Aug. 16-Sept 7; Oct. 9, 12).   c–July 5-Aug. 15.   d–July 10-Aug. 7.   e– Nov. 29-Jan. 4.
TRLS– Traverse Rivière du Loup-St. Siméon Ltée. ☎418 862 9545. Fax: 418 862 5382.

Table 43   PRINCE EDWARD ISLAND   N

service Borden-Cape Tormentine and v.v. 14 km. Journey: 45-60 mins. Fare: CA 6.50.
From Borden and Cape Tormentine: 12-18 sailings daily.
MA–   Marine Atlantic/Marine Atlantique. ☎902 794 5700. Fax: 902 564 7480.

Table 44   TROIS PISTOLES - ESCOUMINS   T

service Trois Pistoles-Les Escoumins and v.v. 30 km. Journey: 1½ hours. Fare: C 6.00.

May 1-Oct. 14 ♂.

From Trois Pistoles and Les Escoumins: 1-3 sailings daily. Sailing times vary accordir tides.
♂–Season extended if necessary.   TPE–Traverse Trois Pistoles-Les Escoumins. ☎•

Table 45   SYDNEY - ARGENTIA   N

CA$	P		Q		km	↓ June 2–Oct 23 ↑		
	②⑤		②⑤				③⑤	
0.00	0700	....	1600	....	0	d.North Sydney...a.	....	2230	....
45.00	2130	....	0630	....	426	a.Argentia ....d.	....	0900	....

P–   June 19-Sept. 4.
Q–   June 2–16 and Sept. 8–Oct. 23.
MA–   Marine Atlantic/Marine Atlantique. ☎ 902 794 5700. Fax: 902 564 7480.

Table 46   HALIFAX - ST. PIERRE   A

cargo/passenger service Halifax-St. Pierre and v.v. 400 km. Journey: 30 hours. F CA$: 75.00.

Summer service.

From Halifax: 1600②.
From St. Pierre: 2359⑦.

Winter service.

From Halifax and St. Pierre: Sailings every 10 days.
APD–   Armement Paturel-Dagort. ☎ •✢.

Table 47   YARMOUTH - PORTLAND

US$	P		km		Q
0.00	1000	....	0	d.**Yarmouth** ....a. ↑	....	0900	....
*55.00	2000	....	298	a.**Portland** ....d.	....	2100	....

P–May 7-Oct. 25: daily except May 7, 11, 13, 15, 18, 20, 27; June 3, 10, 17; Sept. 9, 16, 30; Oct. 7, 14, 16, 19, 21, 23.   Q–May 4-June 22 and Sept. 26-Oct. 22: daily except May 12, 14, 17, 19, 26; June 2, 9, 16; Sept. 8, 15, 22, 29; Oct. 6, 13, 15, 18, 20, 22, 25.
*–US$75.00 June 19-Sept 22.   PF–Prince of Fundy Cruises. ☎Portland 207 775 561

Table 48   YARMOUTH - BAR HARBOR   N

♧CA$	Q		P	R	No Service Mar. 1–Apr. 11		R	Q	S	F
	②④⑦		②④⑦		km	↑		①③⑤	②④⑦	②④
0.00	0800	....	1500 1630	....	0	d.**Yarmouth** ....a.	....	1500 1530 1530 06		
♤30.00	1330	....	2030 2130	....	153	a.**Bar Harbor** ....d.	....	0800 0800 0800 23		

P–   Jan. 1-Feb. 29, Apr. 12-May 15 and Oct. 18-Dec. 31.   Q–Sept. 14–Oct. 17.
R–   June 26-Sept. 13.   S–May 16–June 25.
♤–   CA$ 45.00 June 1-Sept. 30.
♧–   Fare payable in US$ ex Bar Harbor.
MA–   Marine Atlantic/Marine Atlantique. ☎902 794 5700.

Table 49   GRAND MANAN

service Black's Harbour-North Head and v.v. 38 km. Journey: 1½hours. Fare (ro trip-payable at North Head only): CA$: 8.00.

Jan. 2-Apr. 3, May 15-June 25, Sept. 8-Dec. 31.

From Black's Harbour: 0930, 1330, 1730.
From North Head: 0730, 1130, 1530.

Apr. 4-May 14.

From Black's Harbour: 0900ex③④⑤, 0930③④⑤, 1300③④⑤, 1330ex③④⑤, 1700③ 1730ex③④⑤.
From North Head: 0700ex③④⑤, 0730③④⑤, 1100③④⑤, 1130ex③④⑤, 1500③④⑤, 1530ex③ 1900③④⑤.

June 26-Sept. 7.

From Black's Harbour: 0730☼, 0930, 1200☼, 1400, 1600, 1800.
From North Head: 0730, 0930☼, 1200, 1400☼, 1600, 1800.

CT–   Coastal Transport. ☎Grand Manan 506 636 3922.

Table 50 — SAINT JOHN - DIGBY 🚢 MA

🚢 service Saint John-Digby and v.v. *69 km.* Journey: 2½-3hrs. Fare: CA$: 15.00/20.00.

Jan. 1–June 20, Sept. 13–Oct. 8 and Oct. 13–Dec. 31
ᵐ Saint John: 0001②–⑥, 1000.
ᵐ Digby: 0500②–⑥, 1430.

June 21–Sept. 12
ᵐ Saint John: 0030✕, 0930, 1645.
ᵐ Digby: 0500✕, 1300, 2015.

Oct. 9–12
ᵐ Saint John: 0001⑥, 0030①⑤, 1000, 1645①⑤.
ᵐ Digby: 0500✕, 1300①⑤, 1430⑥, 2015①⑤.
— Marine Atlantic/Marine Atlantique. ☎ Saint John 902 794 7500. Fax: 902 564 7480.

Table 51 — SYDNEY - PORT AUX BASQUES 🚢 MA

CA$		↓	km	P ④⑦	Q ③⑧	R	S	Q ②⑤	T ③⑧	Q ③④⑥⑦	U
.00	North Sydney......d.		0	0100	0130	0900	1130	1330	1600	1600	2330
.00	Port aux Basques..a.		174	0700	0700	1500	1900	1900	2130	2200	0700

		Q ②⑤	T ex②⑤	S	Q ⑦	T ②⑤	Q ③⑧	P ex②⑤	S
rt aux Basques....d.		0800	0900	0900	1130	....	1600	1600	2000	2330	2330
rth Sydney..........a.		1230	1330	1400	1800	....	2030	2130	0030	0500	0600

June 2-Oct. 24.   **Q**–June 14-Sept. 12.   **R**–Daily ex③⑧ June 2-13 and Sept. 13-Oct. 24;
P–Port aux Basques and v.v.   *425 km.* Fare: CA$: 0.125 per mile (minimum CA$ 5.70).
June 14-Sept. 12.   **S**–Jan. 4-June 1 and Oct. 25-Dec. 24.   **T**–June 2-13 and Sept. 13-
.. 24.   **U**–Daily Jan. 1-June 1 and Oct. 25-Dec.31; ex②⑤ June 2-13 and Sept. 13-Oct. 24;
② June 2-13 and Sept. 13-Oct. 24.
② June 14-Sept. 12.   **MA**–Marine Atlantic/Marine Atlantique. ☎ 902 794 7500. Fax: 902
4 7480.

Table 52 — NEWFOUNDLAND SOUTH COAST 🚢 MA

🚢 service Terrenceville-English Harbour West-Harbour Breton-Galtois-Ramea-Burgeo-
ᵐ Terrenceville to Port aux Basques: Jan. 5-Apr. 29 and Nov. 30-Dec. 17: 2100③⑥,
May 2-June 17 and Sept. 10-Nov. 27: 0800①, Dec. 19-Jan. 4: 0900①③, 2100⑤;
to Burgeo: May 2-June 17 and Sept. 10-Nov. 27: 0800④, June 18-Sept. 9: 0800①④⑥.
ᵐ Port aux Basques to Terrenceville: Jan. 5-Apr. 29 and Nov. 30-Dec. 17: 0900②⑤,
May 2-June 17 and Sept. 10-Nov. 27: 0800③, Dec. 19-Jan. 4: 0900①③⑤;
to Harbour Breton: May 2-June 17 and Sept. 10-Nov. 27: 0800⑦.
ᵐ Hermitage: June 18-Sept. 9: 0800④⑥.
ᵐ Harbour Breton to Terrenceville: May 2-June 17 and Sept. 10-Nov. 27: 0800⑦.
ᵐ Burgeo to Port aux Basques: May 2-June 17 and Sept. 10-Nov. 27: 0800⑤;
to Terrenceville: June 18-Sept. 9: 0800②⑤⑦.
ᵐ Hermitage to Port aux Basques: June 18-Sept. 9: 0800②⑤⑦.
— Marine Atlantic. ☎❖.

Table 53 — LABRADOR COAST 🚢 MA

CA$				km	Direct Service **June 15-Sept. 7** ↑			
		①	④		↓	②		⑥
.00		1000A	....	1900A	....	0	d.Lewisporte ......a.	1300C	....	....	0030C
			1800B	....	508	d.Cartwright ....d.	1500B	....		
		1930A	....	0600C	....	821	a.Goose Bay ......d.	2359A	....	....	1600A

🚢 stopping service Lewisporte-St. Anthony-Battle Harbour-Port Hope Simpson-Black
Tickle-Spotted Islands-Domino-Indian Tickle-Cartwright-Rigolet-Goose Bay-Makkovik-
Hopedale-Davis Inlet-Nain and v.v. Ⓕ. *2133 km.*

June 21-Nov. 14 only.
ᵐ Lewisporte: ❖.
— Marine Atlantic/Marine Atlantique. ☎ 902 794 7500. Fax: 902 564 7480.

Table 54 — MADELEINE ISLANDS 🚢 CTMA

🚢 service Souris-Cap-aux-Meules and v.v. *70 km.* Journey: 5 hours. Fare: CA$: 24.20.

Apr. 1-June 15 and Sept. 14-30
ᵐ Souris: 1400ex①.
ᵐ Cap-aux-Meules: 0800ex①.

June 16-Sept. 13
ᵐ Souris: 0200③, 1400ex②.
ᵐ Cap-aux-Meules: 0800ex②, 2000②.

Oct. 1-Nov. 30
ᵐ Souris: 0800③, 1000②, 1400③⑥⑦.
ᵐ Cap-aux-Meules: 0800ex②⑤.

Dec. 1-Jan. 23
ᵐ Souris: 0800②(Jan. only)④⑥, 1000②(Dec. only).
ᵐ Cap-aux-Meules: 0800①③⑤.

🚢 Cargo/passenger service Montréal-Cap-aux-Meules and v.v. *1200 km.* Journey: 2
days. Fare: CA$. 302.00.

▲ **Apr. 1-Jan. 9** ▲
ᵐ Montréal: ②.
ᵐ Cap-aux-Meules: 0800⑤.
CTMA–CTMA Traversier. ☎❖.

Table 55 — FORTUNE - ST. PIERRE 🚢 ABF

A$	X	②⑤⑦	②⑦	⑤	km	↓	↑	②⑤⑦	X	⑤
.00	1430	....	....	....	37	d.Fortune ....a.	....	1355	....
.00		0915	1745	1815	15	d.Miquelon ....d.	0855	1725		1755
.00	1555	1010	1840	1910	0	a.St. Pierre ....d.	0800	1630	1330	1700

①③⑤⑥ June 16-29 and Sept. 4-25; daily June 30-Sept. 3.
⬅ Armement Borotra Frères. ☎ St. Pierre 412078.

Table 56 — DARTMOUTH - HALIFAX 🚢 DFC

🚢 service Dartmouth-Halifax and v.v. *1 km.* Journey: 15 mins. Fare: CA$: 0.25.
ᵐ Dartmouth: 0630✕ and frequent to 2330✕. (Also † June 5-Sept. 25).
ᵐ Halifax: 0645✕ and frequent to 2345✕. (Also † June 5-Sept. 25).
✲ Dartmouth Ferry Commission. ☎: ❖.

Table 57 — TORONTO - NORTH BAY 🚆 ON

CA$	799	711	731	783	km	↓		738	722	772	790
0.00	0030	0900	1430	1900	0	d.Toronto ....a.		0715	1300	1545	2230
	0200	1035	1600	2030	58	d.Barrie ....d.		0545	1130	1415	2100
	0235	1115	1635	2105	90	d.Orillia ....d.		0500	1045	1330	2020
	0255	1135		2120	115	d.Washago ....d.			1025		1955
	0310	1155	1705	2140	180	d.Gravenhurst .....d.		0410	0945	1250	1915
	0400	1315	1800	2250	235	d.Huntsville...........d.		0326	0845	1205	1815
	0545	1500	1930	0030	367	a.North Bay..........d.		0200	0700	1045	1630

ON– Ontario Northland. ☎ North Bay 705 472 4500.

Table 58 — PEMBERTON 🚆 MCL

CA$	25	27	31	37	km	↓	↑	22	26	30	36
0.00	0800	1100	1400	1900	0	d.Vancouver........d.		1100	1600	1900	2145
6.75	0910	1210	1510	2010	65	d.Squamish ....d.		0945	1445	1745	2035
13.00	1025	1325	1625	2130	121	d.Whistler ....d.		0830	1330	1630	1915
16.75	1110	....	1710	2210	152	a.Pemberton ....d.		0730	1250	....	1835

MCL– Maverick Coach Lines. ☎ Vancouver 604 255 1171.

Table 59 — POWELL RIVER 🚆 MCL

CA$	1		5		km	↓	↑	4	6	
0.00	0830	....	....	1830	0	d.Vancouver........a.		1345	2145	....
	0930u	....	....	1925u	10	d.Horseshoe Bay..d.		1300s	2100s	....
15.90	1100	....	....	2100	60	d.Sechelt ....d.		1135	1930	....
24.75	1340	....	....	2340	150	a.Powell River......d.		0815	1630	....

MCL–Maverick Coach Lines. ☎ Vancouver 604 255 1171.

Table 60 VICTORIA - NANAIMO - CAMPBELL RIVER

ICL

CA$	4		18	6	8	10		12	14		16	km		5		7	3		9	11	13	15		17
	⑥										⑤⑦		↓ ↑							⑥		⑤⑦		
0.00	0620	....	....	0800	1145	1345	....	1645	1915	....	2115	0	d.**Victoria**...a.	1010	....	1320	1505	....	1720	....	1915	2055	....	2300
14.70	0820	....	....	1015	1410	1620	....	1915	2105	....	2300	124	a.Nanaimo...d.	0745	....	1100	1300	....	1505	....	1650	1900	....	2100
14.70	|	0900	....	1100	|	|	1700	....	|	2115	....	124	d. Nanaimo...a.	....	1025	|	1215	1420	....	....	|	....	2015	|
25.20	|	1025	....	1230	|	|	1830	....	|	2240	....	211	a. Port Alberni...d.	....	0845	|	1045	1250	....	....	|	....	1850	|
14.70	0900	....	....	1100	1500	1700a	....	....	2115	....	....	124	d.Nanaimo...a.	....	....	1005	....	....	....	1405	1605	....	....	2005
29.40	1050	....	....	1250	1650	1850a	....	....	2250	....	....	234	d.Courtenay...d.	....	....	0805	....	....	....	1205	1405	....	....	1805
33.60	1150	....	....	1345	1745	1945a	....	....	2345	....	....	280	a. **Campbell River** ...d.	....	....	0715	....	....	....	1115	1315	....	....	1715
	....	....	1215	....	....	....	....	....	....	....	....		d. **Campbell River** ...a.	....	....	....	....	....	....	....	1220	....	....	....
72.45	....	....	1630	....	....	....	....	....	....	....	....	360	a.Port Hardy...d.	....	....	....	....	....	....	....	0845	....	....	....

a– ex②③.

ICL– Island Coach Lines. ☎ Victoria 604 388 5248.

Table 61 VANCOUVER LOCAL SERVICES

CCS MCL PFC VRTS

Local services operate in the Vancouver area as follows:

Abbotsford *(CCS)* (*65* km, CA $: ❖). From Vancouver: 0745Ⓐ, 0900Ⓐ, 0930Ⓒ, 1030Ⓐ, 1135Ⓒ, 1330, 1530Ⓐ, 1540Ⓐ, 1630Ⓐ, 1640Ⓐ, 1650Ⓒ, 1730Ⓐ, 1800Ⓒ, 2130, 2245Ⓒ, 2300Ⓐ, returning at 0455Ⓐ, 0525Ⓐ, 0540Ⓐ, 0555Ⓐ, 0610Ⓐ, 0630Ⓐ, 0725Ⓒ, 0930, 1100Ⓒ, 1115Ⓐ, 1130Ⓐ, 1330Ⓐ, 1400Ⓒ, 1530Ⓐ, 1800, 2015Ⓒ, 2030Ⓐ. Journey: 1½ hours.

Burnaby *(VRTS)* (*12* km, CA $: 1.25 [1.75 at peaks]). From Vancouver: 0600⚒/0700† and frequent to 2330, returning at 0530⚒/0630† and frequent to 2300. Journey: 45 mins.

Chilliwack *(CCS)* (*89* km, CA $: ❖). From Vancouver: 0900Ⓐ, 0930Ⓒ, 1030Ⓐ, 1135Ⓒ, 1330, 1540Ⓐ, 1630Ⓐ, 1640Ⓐ, 1650Ⓒ, 1730Ⓐ, 2130, 2245Ⓒ, 2300Ⓐ, returning at 0500Ⓐ, 0520Ⓐ, 0530Ⓐ, 0555Ⓐ, 0640Ⓒ, 0845, 1010Ⓒ, 1030Ⓐ, 1245Ⓐ, 1310Ⓒ, 1445Ⓐ, 1710, 1930Ⓒ, 1945Ⓐ. Journey: 2 hours.

Coquitlam *(VRTS)* (❖ km, CA $: ❖). From Vancouver: 0600⚒/0800† and frequent (hourly on †) to 2300, returning at 0700⚒/0900† and frequent (hourly on †) to 2359. Journey: 1 hour.

Departure Bay *(MCL)* (❖ km, CA $: ❖). From Vancouver: 0600, 0800, 1000, 1200, 1400, 1600, 1800, 2000, returning at 0700, 0900, 1100, 1300, 1500, 1700, 1900, 2100. Journey: 2½ hours.

Horseshoe Bay *(VRTS)* (*10* km, CA $: 1.35 [2.75 at peaks]). From Vancouver: 0605⚒/0705† and about every 30 mins. to 2305†/0010②-⑦, returning at 0558Ⓐ/0703⑥/0803† and about every 30 mins. to 0005. Journey: 45 mins.

Ladner *(VRTS)* (*17* km, CA $: 1.35 [2.75 at peak periods]). From Vancouver: 0507Ⓐ/0638⑥/0641† and about every 30 mins. to 0143, returning at 0530⚒/0700† and about every 30 mins. to 2330. Journey: 45 mins.

Maple Ridge (❖ km, CA $: ❖). From Vancouver: ❖, returning at ❖. Journey: ❖.

Nanaimo *(MCL)* (*96* km, CA $: 13.25). From Vancouver: 0600, 0800, 1000, 1200, 1400, 1600, 1800, 2000, returning at 0630, 0830, 1030, 1230, 1430, 1630, 1830, 2030. Journey: 3 hours.

New Westminster *(VRTS)* (*10* km, CA $: 1.25[1.75 at peaks]). From Vancouver: 0600⚒/0700† and frequent to 2330, returning at 0530⚒/0630† and frequent to 2400. Journey: 50 mins.

North Vancouver *(VRTS)* (*6* km, CA $: 1.25 [1.75 at peaks]). From Vancouver: 0605⚒/0705† and frequent (every 30 mins. on Ⓒ) to 0110, returning at 0547⚒/0636† and frequent (every 30 mins. on Ⓒ) to 0036. Journey: 40 mins.

Pitt Meadows *(CCS)* (❖ km, CA $: ❖). From Vancouver: 1400Ⓒ, 1600Ⓐ, 1635Ⓐ, 1705Ⓐ, 1800Ⓒ, 1805Ⓐ, returning at 0610Ⓐ, 0640Ⓐ, 0710Ⓐ, 1245Ⓒ. Journey: 1¼ hours.

Port Coquitlam *(VRTS)* (❖ km, CA $: ❖). From Vancouver: 0700⚒/0900† and frequent (hourly on †) to 2230, returning at 0630⚒/0830† and frequent (hourly on †) to 2200. Journey: 1 hour. Also by *CCS* from Vancouver at 0900Ⓐ, 1300Ⓐ, 1400Ⓒ, 1600Ⓐ, 1635Ⓐ, 1705Ⓐ, 1800Ⓒ, 1805Ⓐ, returning at 0620Ⓐ, 0650Ⓐ, 0720Ⓐ, 1155Ⓐ, 1255Ⓒ, 1655Ⓒ. Journey: 1 hour.

Port Moody *(VRTS)* (❖ km, CA $: 1.25 [1.75 at peaks]). From Vancouver: 0600⚒/0700† and freque (hourly on †) to 2330, returning at 0530⚒/0630† and frequent (hourly on †) to 2300. Journey: 30 mir

Richmond *(VRTS)* (*5* km, CA $: 1.25 [1.75 at peaks]). From Vancouver: 0600 and frequent (every mins. on Ⓒ) to 2300, returning at 0530 and frequent (every 30 mins. on Ⓒ) to 2230. Journey: 35 mir

Surrey *(VRTS)* (*14* km, CA $: 1.25 [1.75 at peaks]). From New Westminster Skytrain ◇: 0050①, 0055ex 0559Ⓐ, *0628Ⓐ*, *0642⑥*, 0659Ⓐ, 0726⑦, 0728⑥, 0729Ⓐ, 0757⑥, 0758Ⓐ, 0825⑥, 0826⑦, 0827Ⓐ, 0855 0857Ⓐ and about every 30 mins. to 2255, 2325⚒, 2355, returning at 0053ex①, 0542Ⓐ, 0550Ⓐ, 0611 0612⑥, 0619Ⓐ, 0641Ⓐ, 0649Ⓐ, 0654⑥, 0657⑦, 0719Ⓐ, 0727⑥, 0749⚒, 0819⚒, 0849⚒, 0855⑦ a about every 30 mins. to 1920⚒, 1922⑦, 1950⚒, 1952⑦, 2050⚒, 2052⑦, 2150⚒, 2152⑦, 2250 2256⑦, 2353⚒, 2356⑦. Journey: 40 mins.

Tsawwassen *(VRTS)* (*20* km, CA $: 1.35 [2.75 at peaks]). From Vancouver: *0507Ⓐ/0638⑥/0641†* a about hourly to *0143*, returning at *0757* and about hourly to *2307*. Journey: 55 mins.

Victoria *(PFC)* (*84* km, CA $: 20.75). From Vancouver: 0545, 0645〒, 0745, 0845〒. 0945, 1045〒, 11 1245〒, 1345, 1445〒, 1545, 1645〒, 1745, 1845〒, 1945. Journey: 3½ hours.

West Vancouver *(VRTS)* (*7* km, CA $: 1.25 [1.75 at peaks]). From Vancouver: 0605⚒/0705† and ab every 30 mins. to 2305†/0010②-⑦, returning at 0611Ⓐ/0717⑥/0818† and about every 30 mins. to 00 Journey: 30 mins.

◇– Continue by different bus, or by SkyTrain to downtown Vancouver.
〒– July 1-Sept. 1.
CCS– Cascade Charter Service. ☎ Sardis 604 795 7443. Fax 604 795 4433.
MCL– Maverick Coach Lines. ☎ Vancouver 604 255 1171.
PFC– Pacific Coach Lines. ☎ Vancouver 662 4275.
VRTS– Vancouver Regional Transit System. ☎ Vancouver 604 264 5000.

Table 62 VICTORIA LOCAL SERVICES

PFC VRT

Local services operate in the Victoria area as follows:

Esquimalt *(VRT)* (❖ km, CA $: 1.25). From Victoria: 0002, 0600Ⓐ/0720⑥/0805† and frequent (about every 40 mins. on †) to 1922, 1942Ⓐ, 2002, 2042, 2122, 2202, 2242, 2322, returning at 0017, 0614Ⓐ/0703⑥/0823† and frequent (about every 40 mins on †) to 1903Ⓒ, 1904Ⓐ, 1924Ⓐ, 1943⑥, 1944Ⓐ, 1948†, 2000Ⓐ, 2023, 2103, 2143, 2223, 2303, 2343. Journey: 15 mins.

Saanich *(VRT)* (❖ km, CA $: 2.50). From Victoria: 0519Ⓐ, 0530⑥, 0554Ⓐ, 0624Ⓐ, 0659Ⓐ, 0700†, 0703⑥, 0759Ⓐ, 0800†, 0803⑥, 0856Ⓐ, 0900Ⓒ, 0956Ⓐ, 1000Ⓒ, 1056Ⓐ, 1100Ⓒ, 1205Ⓐ, 1208Ⓒ, 1301Ⓐ, 1308Ⓒ, 1401Ⓐ, 1408Ⓒ, 1501Ⓐ, 1505⑥, 1507†, 1555Ⓐ, 1605⑥, 1607†, 1625Ⓐ, 1655Ⓐ, 1705⑥, 1707†, 1740Ⓐ, 1805⑥, 1810Ⓐ, 1817†, 1917, 2017, 2117, 2217, 2300, 2330, returning at 0012, 0635Ⓐ, 0705Ⓐ, 0720⑥, 0745Ⓐ, 0759†, 0820⚒, 0859†, 0920⚒, 0959†, 1020⚒, 1059†, 1120⚒, 1159†, 1220⚒, 1320†, 1332⑥, 1338Ⓐ, 1420†, 1432⑥, 1438Ⓐ, 1520†, 1532⑥, 1538Ⓐ, 1620†, 1632⑥, 1638Ⓐ, 1720†, 1732⑥, 1738Ⓐ, 1820†, 1832⑥, 1838Ⓐ, 1917, 2017, 2117, 2217, 2312. Journey: 1¼ hours.

Swartz Bay *(VRT)* (❖ km, CA $: 3.75). From Victoria: 0530⑥, 0545Ⓐ, 0641Ⓐ, 0642†, 0646⑥, 0742Ⓑ, 0746⑥, 0840Ⓐ, 0842†, 0846⑥, 0940, 1040, 1138⚒, 1140†, 1237⑥, 1238Ⓐ, 1240†, 1338⚒, 1340†, 1438⚒, 1440†, 1538⚒, 1540†, 1600Ⓐ, 1630Ⓐ, 1638⑥, 1640†, 1700Ⓐ, 1715⚒, 1740, 1817†, 1840⚒, 1917, 2017, 2117, 2217, 2300, 2330, returning at 0549Ⓐ, 0619Ⓐ, 0630⑥, 0647Ⓐ, 0654⑥, 0717 0754⚒, 0755†, 0854Ⓐ, 0855†, 0954Ⓐ, 0955†, 1054Ⓐ, 1055†, 1154Ⓐ, 1155†, 1254Ⓐ, 1255†, 1354 1355†, 1454Ⓐ, 455†, 1554Ⓐ, 1555†, 1654Ⓐ, 1655†, 1755†, 1756Ⓐ, 1855, 1955, 2055, 2155. Journe 1¼ hours.

Vancouver *(PFC)* (*84* km, CA $: 20.75). From Victoria: 0600, 0700η, 0800, 0900η, 1000, 1100η, 12 1300η, 1400, 1500η, 1600, 1700η, 1800, 1900η, 2000. Journey: 3½ hours.

η– July 1- Sept. 1.
PFC– Pacific Coach Lines. ☎ Vancouver 662 7575.
VRT– Victoria Regional Transit System. ☎ Victoria 382 6161.

Table 63 BELLA COOLA - WILLIAMS LAKE

CPT

CA$					km					
		②⑤				↓ ↑		①④		
0.00	....	0900	....	....	0	d.**Bella Coola**...a.	....	1800	....	....
60.00	....	1700	....	....	484	a.**Williams Lake**..d.	....	0930	....	....

CPT– Central Pacific Transit. ☎ Williams Lake 604 392 5461.

Table 64 DAWSON CITY

MT NOR NWS

CA $		NOR	NWS				NWS		NOR	
		202							**205**	
		P	②⑤		km	↓ ↑	②⑤		P	
0.00	....	0900	0930	....	0	d.**Whitehorse**...a.	2245	....	2315	...
24.61	....	1115	1150	....	180	d.Carmacks...d.	2030	....	2115	...
59.92	....	|	1545	....	❖	a. Ross River...d.	1630	....	|	....
47.00	....	1320	....	....	345	a.Stewart Crossing...d.	....	....	1830	...
66.00	....	1600	....	....	560	a.**Dawson City**...d.	....	....	1600	...
CA $		P		P	km	*MT*		P	P	
0.00	....	1335	....	1905	0	d.Stewart Crossing...a.	....	1310	1800	...
15.00	....	1410	....	2030	60	a.**Mayo**...d.	....	1230	1730	...
CA $					km					
0.00	....	....	....	....	0	d.**Dawson City**...a.	....	....	....	...
25.00	....	....	....	....	130	d.Action Jackson 🏨..d.	....	....	....	...
55.00	....	....	....	....	275	a.**Tok**...d.	....	....	....	...

P– ③⑤ Jan. 1-May 31 and Sept. 1-Dec. 31; ①③⑤ June 1-Aug. 31.
MT– Mayo Taxi. ☎ Mayo 996 2240.
NOR– Norline Coaches (Yukon) Ltd. ☎ Whitehorse 668 3355.
NWS– North West Stage Lines. ☎ Whitehorse 403 668 7240.

Table 65 WHITEHORSE - DAWSON CREEK

GLC

CA $	522	522	524	522	km		521	523	521	401
	②④⑥	③⑤⑦	ex⑦	②④⑥			ex⑦	ex⑦	②④⑥	
	Q	Q	R	Q		↓ ↑	Q	R	Q	
0.00	1201	....	1201	....	0	d.**Whitehorse**...a.	....	0515	0515	....
18.75	1430	....	1430	....	182	d.Teslin...d.	....	0330	0330	....
45.15	1815	....	1815	....	451	d.Watson Lake...d.	....	2345	2345	....
83.70	r	....	r	....		d.Summit Lake...d.	....	1650	1650	....
98.40	0220	0235	0235	0830	982	d.Fort Nelson...d.	1410	1430	1430	....
137.75	....	0845	0745	1430	1374	d.Fort St. John...d.	1000	0900	....	1730
145.35	....	0945	0845	1530	1450	a.**Dawson Creek**.d.	0900	0800	....	1620

Q– Sept. 8-June 26.
R– June 27-Sept. 7.
GLC—Greyhound Lines of Canada. ☎ Dawson Creek 604 782 4275.

Table 66 MEDICINE HAT - LETHBRIDGE

GLC

CA $	1150	1152	1158	1140	km	↓ ↑	1147	1579	1157	
17.85	0515	....	1345	....	0	d.**Medicine Hat**...a.	....	1250	2105	....
0.00	0820	1400	1630	1745		d.**Lethbridge**...d.	0730	1020	1840	....
5.40	0900	1445	1715	1830		a.Fort MacLeod...d.	0645	....	1740	....

GLC– Greyhound Lines of Canada. Tel.: Lethbridge 403 327 1551.

Table 67 HAY RIVER - PEACE RIVER

GLC NBS

CA $	GLC	NBS						NBS	GLC	
	808	**2**						**1**	**807**	
	ex①	⚒			km	↓ ↑		⚒	ex⑦	
64.90	0830	....	....	....	0	d.**Hay River**...a.	....	....	1545	...
60.35	0900	....	....	....	45	d.Enterprise...d.	....	....	1515	...
39.15	1115	....	....	....		d.Meander River...d.	....	....	1300	...
31.90	1230a	1215	....	....	318	d.High Level...d.	....	1030	1215b	...
♡8.56	|	1315	....	....	400	a. Fort Vermilion .d.	....	0900	|	..
0.00	1600	....	....	....	629	a.**Peace River**...d.	....	....	0745	...

a– Arr 1201.
b– Arr 1130.
♡– Fare ex High Level.
GLC– Greyhound Lines of Canada. Tel.: Calgary 403 265 9111.
NBS– Norline Bus Service. Tel.: La Crete 403 928 3995.

Check update notes to timetables and with operator before starting your journey

Table 68 EDMONTON - DAWSON CREEK GLC

CA $	401	117	505	101	103	501	801 ⑧		703	km	494	704	702	502	118	202	602	604 ⑦	506 ex⑦	802
0.00		0830	1130		1830	1800	2345	2345		0	d.Edmonton ....a.		0535	0530		1245	1405	1940	1945		2245
16.35				2030						162	d.Athabasca ....d.										
21.75				2130						239	d.Smith ....d.										
25.95			1500	2230					0310	240	d.Slave Lake ....d.			0225		0950					
20.40	1130				2110	0220				348	d.Whitecourt ....d.			0330		1115	1720	1730			2050
37.70	1330		1835		2310	0430				425	d.Valley View ....d.			0110		0845	1450	1500	1815	1835	
37.70		1730		s					0533	425	d.Donnelly Junction ...d.					0657					1730
44.10		1835		0115			0630		0730	491	a.Peace River ....d.	2130	2215			0600					1630
44.10		■■■							0905	577	d.Fairview ....d.	2010	■■■								
44.10									1005	632	d.Rycroft ....d.	1930									
44.10	1510	207	1945	509	0035	0610			1100	462	d.Grande Prairie ......d.	1815	510	2345		208	0730	1325	1335	1705	
57.45	1545	1605		1030		0700				581	d.Dawson Creek ......d.		1555	2030		0605			1021	1010	
67.95		1725		1155						676	d.Chetwynd ....d.		1440			0450					
77.10		2225		1710						998	a.Prince George ......d.		0930			0001					

‖LC– Greyhound Lines of Canada. Tel.: Edmonton 403 421 4211.

Table 69 ELLIOT LAKE AJB

CA $	23	25	27		394	km	22	26	28
0.00		0930	1610	2130	d.Serpent River ...a.	0	0910	1410	2130
3.88		1000	1630	2200	a.Elliot Lake ....d.	32	0845	1350	2045

AJB– A J Bus Lines Ltd. Tel.: Elliot Lake 705 848 3013.

Table 70 YELLOWKNIFE - HAY RIVER AFC

CA $	1▽ ex⑦	1 ex⑦		394	km	2 ex⑦	2▽ ex⑦
40.00		0055		d.Yellowknife ......a.	0		2250
30.00		0220		d.Rae ....d.	73		2130
17.00		0515		d.Fort Providence ...d.	285		1845
3.00		0740		d.Enterprise ....d.	425		1705
0.00		0010	1030	d.Hay River ....d.	470	0845	1630
			1935	a.Fort Smith ....d.	752	0540	

▽– Service liable to disruption April-May and October-December when icing conditions on Mackenzie River prevent normal operation.
AFC– Arctic Frontier Carriers. Tel.: Yellowknife 403 873 4437.

Table 71 PRINCE GEORGE - VANCOUVER GLC

CA $	1251	1253	1255		494	km	1252	1254	1256
0.00	0800	1745	2300	d.Prince George ...a.	0	2030	0540	0830
❖	0950	1935	0030	d.Quesnel ....d.	❖	1840	0405	0650
❖	1200	2130	0215	d.Williams Lake .....d.	❖	1645	0220	0520
❖	1410	2345	0430	d.Clinton ....d.	❖	1430	0005	0305
❖	1515	0020	0515	d.Cache Creek ......d.	❖	1355	2330	0240
❖	1750	s	0805	d.Hope ....d.	❖	1030	2030	2300
❖	s	s	s	d.Chilliwack ....d.	❖	s		
❖	s	s	s	d.New Westminster .d.	❖	0830	1830	2110
❖	1950	0645	1035	a.Vancouver ....d.	❖	0800	1800	2045

GLC– Greyhound Lines of Canada. Tel.: Vancouver 604 662 3222.

Table 72 KENORA - FORT FRANCES XL

CA $	23 ex③		692	km	24 ex①
0.00	1030		d.Kenora ....a.	0	1810
	1305		d.Emo ....d.	188	1545
	1335		a.Fort Frances .....d.	224	1515

XL– Excel Coach Lines. Tel.: Kenora 807 468 6667.

Table 73 PRINCE RUPERT GLC

CA $	1529	511	1531	209		394	km	512	1630	210	1632
0.00			2200			d.Edmonton ....a.	0				1015
❖			0250			d.Jasper ....d.	❖				0505
	1245					d.Valemount ....d.		1040			
❖	1625	2315	0630	0900		d.Prince George ....d.	❖	0615	0700	2150	2300
❖		0035	1020			d.Vanderhoof ....d.	❖	0500		2035	
						a. Fort St.James .d.					
❖		0240	1250			d.Burns Lake ....d.	❖	0305		1850	
		r	r			d.Broman Lake .....d.		r		r	
❖		0500	1510			d.Smithers ....d.	❖	0115		1615	
❖		0550	1600			d.New Hazelton .....d.	❖	0005		1510	
❖		0800	1755			d.Terrace ....d.	❖	2225		1320	
❖		0950	1940			a.Prince Rupert .....d.	❖	2030		1115	

GLC–Greyhound Lines of Canada. Tel.: Prince George 604 564 5454.

Table 74 CRESTON - SPOKANE

US $		394	km
25.00		d.Creston ▦ ....a.	245
21.00		d.Bonners Ferry ....d.	195
14.00		d.Sandpoint ....d.	135
		d. St. Maries ....a.	
7.00		d.Coeur d'Alene ....d.	57
0.00		a.Spokane ....d.	0

Table 75 EDMONTON - CONSORT FBL GLC

CA $	GLC 153 ⑥⑦	GLC 155 ex⑥⑦	FBL 157		494	km	FBL 158 ex⑦	GLC 154 ex⑦	FBL 158 ⑦	GLC 154 ⑦
0.00	1800	1815		d.Edmonton ....a.	0	1100a		1550	
5.95	2000	2000		d.Camrose ....d.	95	0950		1415	
12.40	2125	2125	2135	d.Stettler ....d.	211	0800	0805	1225	1230
21.80			2340	a.Consort ....d.	360	0600		1020	
18.60	2255	2255		a.Drumheller ....d.	315	0645		1100	

a– Arr. 1135 on ①.
FBL– Ferguson Bus Lines. Tel.: Edmonton 403 421 4211.
GLC– Greyhound Lines of Canada. Tel.: Edmonton 403 421 4211.

Table 76 EDMONTON - COLD LAKE GLC

CA $	177 ⑦	135 ex⑦	139		394	km	138/140 ex⑦	178	136 ⑦
0.00	1130	1130	1815	d.Edmonton ....a.	0	1120	1720	2230
	1310	1335	2000	d.Smoky Lake ......d.	110	0945	1545	2045
	1415	1455	2125	d.St. Paul ....d.	203	0825	1435	1920
	1550	1645	2330	a.Cold Lake ....d.	330	0630	1300	1730

GLC– Greyhound Lines of Canada. Tel.: Edmonton 403 421 4211.

Table 76a ROCKY MOUNT - RED DEER GLC

CA $	162 ex⑦	164		394	km	163	161 ⑧
0.00	0710	1800		d.Rocky Mountain House a.	0	1635	2220
	0830	1925		a.Red Deer ....d.		1500	2050

GLC– Greyhound Lines of Canada. Tel.: Edmonton 403 421 4211.

Table 77 CALGARY - SASKATOON FBL GLC SAS

CA $	SAS 31 ex⑦	GLC 1164	FBL 1166	GLC 1166		494	km	FBL 1161 ex⑦⑦	SAS 107	SAS 32	SAS 105
0.00		0745	1730	2245	d.Calgary ....d.	0	1155	2125b		0620b
8.20		0940	1940	0035	d.Drumheller ....d.	142	0955	1930b		0435b
13.10		1040	2055	0135	d.Hanna ....d.	220	0845	1830b		0340b
30.70			1410a	0405a	d.Kindersley ....d.	426		1515		0110
35.00	1035		1515a	0500a	d.Rosetown ....d.	518	1415	1930		0005
41.90	1210		1640a	0630a	a.Saskatoon ....d.	634	1245	1800		2245

a–SAS. b–GLC. FBL–Ferguson Bus Lines. Tel.: Calgary 403 265 9111. GLC– Greyhound Lines of Canada. Tel.: Calgary 403 265 9111. SAS–Saskatchewan Transportation Co. Tel.: Saskatoon 306 664 5700.

Table 78 EDMONTON - CALGARY GLC RA

394		GLC 1111	GLC 1117	RA 8	GLC 1195	GLC 1105	GLC 1189	GLC 2001	GLC 149	GLC 1181	RA 10	GLC 1113	GLC 1107	GLC 1191	GLC 1177	GLC 1185	RA 12	GLC 1179	GLC 1109	RA 14	GLC 1193		GLC 2003	GLC 1187
CA $	km					ex⑦		⑦																
0.00	0	Edmonton ....d.	0001	0800	0800	0930	1000	1100	1100	1200	1215	1300	1300	1400	1500	1600	1635	1700	1730	1800	1800	1900		1900	2000
∝	5	South Edmonton ...d.	0015	0810	0815	0945	1015	1115	1110	1215	1225	1315	1300	1315	1415	1515	1615	1640	1715	1745	1800	1815		1915	2015
4.30	69	Wetaskiwin ....d.	0120				1055				1210				1510						1900				
14.00	156	Red Deer ....d.	0240	0955	1000	0955	1225		1300		1415	1500	1700		1700		1900	2030	2000					2100	2200
23.00	303	Calgary ....a.	0535	1235	1130	1140		1320	1445		1520	1545	1645	1730	1840	1920	1945	2040		2130	2120			2245	2345

94		GLC 1112	GLC 1120	GLC 1118	RA 7	GLC 146/8/156	GLC 1114	GLC 1194	GLC 1106	GLC 1188	RA 9	GLC 1116	GLC 1108	GLC 1190	GLC 1178	GLC 1182	RA 11	GLC 1180	GLC 1110	GLC 1192	RA 13	GLC 1196	GLC 148	GLC 1186
					ex⑦					⑤⑦⑥⑥				⑧							⑦			
Calgary ....d.		0135	0700		0800		0900	1000	1100	1200	1215	1300		1400	1500	1600	1630	1700	1745	1800	1900		2000	
Red Deer ....d.		0355	0840	0845	0945		1045		1400	1505	1700		1700		1845	2040		1945	2100		2225		rs	
Wetaskiwin ......d.		0530	1015	1025		1525									1835						2225			
South Edmonton ...a.		0640	1025	1115	1120	1135	1230	1630	1500	1535	1640	2035	1715	1850	1930	2020	2105	2115	2230	2310	2310			
Edmonton ....a.		0655	1040	1130	1130	1145	1245	1315	1650	1515	1545	1655	2055	1730	1905	1915	1945	2045	2120	2130	2245		2320	2325

–Local fares not available. ⑥–Runs on ① (instead of ⑦) on holiday weekends. GLC–Greyhound Lines of Canada. Tel.: Calgary 403 265 9111. RA–Red Arrow Deluxe Services. Tel.: Edmonton 403 468 6360.

Table 79 — VANCOUVER - VERNON - KAMLOOPS — GLC

CA $	4	450	1264	38	3012	1268	32	1266	3016	36	3008	km	494	19	35	3009	1265	33	39	3017	1267	21	1263	43
0.00	0030	....	....	0800	0800	....	1230	....	*1330*	*1800*	*1800*	0	d.**Vancouver**......a.	....	1305	*1540*	....	1540	1925	*1950*	....	2305	....	0540
	0050			0830	0830		1255		*1400*	*1830*	*1830*	20	d.New Westminster...d.		s	s		s	s	s		s		s
												116	d.Chilliwack.........d.			*1420*		1420						s
	0250		1010	1020				1555	2015	2020		174	d.Hope.............d.		s	1330		1345	s	1745		s		0330
	0420		1140			1600							d.Merritt..........d.			1130				1545				s
				1250				1810		2215			d.Princeton........d.			1130				1545				s
				1350				1910		2305			d.Keremeos.........d.			1000				1430				
		0600	*0830*	1435	*1500*	*1700*		1955		2350			d.Penticton........d.	0910		0915	*1135*			1345	*1515*		2125	
					1510								d. Okanagan Falls..d.			*r*				1315				
					1600								d. Osoyoos.........d.			0715				1230				
					1640								a. Rock Creek......d.							1140				
	0730	0710	1000	1415	*1615*	1630	1740		1825		2340		d.**Kelowna**........d.	0750	0800	*0800*	1015	1030	1400	1215	1330	1800	2005	0015
	0820		1055	1505		1725	*1950*	1920			0015		d.**Vernon**.........d.	0705		0930				1235		1625	1910	*2110*
						2050	2025						d. Salmon Arm......d.	0555				1130						*2000*
			1245				1900	2215					d.**Kamloops**.......d.			0750		1000				1720		
			1345					2315					a.Cache Creek......d.			0515						1510		
	1030			1710			*2220*						a. Revelstoke......d.	0425								1410		*1830*
	1730			0015			*0520*						a. *Calgary 83*.....d.	2330								0845		*1300*

GLC– Greyhound Lines of Canada. Tel.: Vancouver 604 662 3222.

Table 80 — TORONTO - WINNIPEG - VANCOUVER — GLC
SUMMARY TABLE

CA $						km	494 SUMMARY TABLE						
0.00	....	0100A	....	1300A	1700A	0	d.**Toronto**........a.	....	0550C	....	1515D	....	1745D
40.40	....	0600A		1830A	2215A	397	a.}Sudbury........{d.	....	0050C	....	1000D	....	1245D
	....	0715A		1915A	2315A		d.}	....	2340B	....	0845D	....	1135C
80.00	....	0650B		1825B	2255B	2137	a.}Winnipeg.......{d.	....	2200A	....	0730C	....	1030C
	....	0730B	1400A	1900B	2345B		d.}	....	2115A	....	0545C	....	0905C 1735B
	....	1500B	2150A	0125C	0555C	2721	a.}Regina.........{d.	....	1145A	....	2045B	....	0055C 1735B
	....	1525B	2220A	0140C	0640C		d.}	....	1125A	....	1945B	....	2345B 0630B
	....	0130C	0810B	1130C	1730C	3505	a.}Calgary........{d.	....	0045A	....	0815B	....	1330B 2000A
	....	0145C		1215C	1830C		d.}	....	....	....	0520B	....	1045B
	....	1555C		0015D	0800D	4590	a.**Vancouver**.......d.	....	....	....	1330A	....	2045A

GLC– Greyhound Lines of Canada. Tel.: Calgary 403 265 9111.

Table 81 — CALGARY - BANFF - CRANBROOK — GLC

CA $		1155	km	494	1676	
0.00	....	1830	0	d.**Calgary**..........a.	1720	....
14.28	....	2035	127	d.**Banff**............d.	1545	
28.68	....	2230		d.Radium Hot Springs.d.	1350	
43.82	....	0030		d.Kimberley.........d.	1135	
47.08	....	0100		a.**Cranbrook**.......d.	1100	

GLC– Greyhound Lines of Canada. Tel.: Calgary 403 265 9111.

Table 81a — EDMONTON - SWAN HILLS — GLC

CA $		127 ex⑦	127 ⑦	km	494	128 ex⑦	128 ⑦
0.00	....	1815	2015	0	d.**Edmonton**........a.	1040	1945
	....	1935	2145		d.Westlock.........d.	0900	1805
	....	2015	2225		d.Barrhead.........d.	0830	1725
	....	2130	2330		a.**Swan Hills**.....d.	0715	1600

GLC– Greyhound Lines of Canada. Tel.: Edmonton 403 421 4211.

Table 82 — CALGARY - VANCOUVER — GLC SB

CA $	1575	1683	1375	1681	km	494 GLC	1680	1476	1676	1156
0.00	0645	2130			0	d.**Calgary**..........a.		0830	1720	1940
17.80	0935	0005			75	d.Fort MacLeod....a.		0545		1650
34.30	1250	0250			340	d.Fernie...........d.		0320		1420
37.35	1310	0310r				d.Elko.............d.	r			1350
44.00	1425	0430			441	d.Cranbrook........d.	0205	1100	1300
50.45	1415	0415			595	d.Yahk.............d.	2345	0825	
54.60	1505	0510			645	d.Creston..........d.	2315	0750	
63.00	1700	0700				d.Salmo............d.	2140	0640	
67.00	1750	0750				d.Nelson...........d.	2050	0515	
	1800a	0800a				d. Trail...........a.	2030a	0500a	
69.90	1840	0835				d.Castlegar........d.	2000	0430	
69.90	2030	1020				d.Grand Forks......d.	1830	0255	
69.90	2105	1055			790	d.Greenwood........d.	1710	0220	
	2135	2135	1135	1140		d.Rock Creek.......d.	1640	1645	0155	
69.90		2225		1230		d.Osoyoos..........d.	1600			
69.90		2325		1335		d. Penticton.......d.	1450			
69.90	2320	0055	1320	1615		a. Kelowna........d.	1215	1445	0001	
81.20						d.Princeton........d.				
87.00						d.Hope.............d.				
87.00						d.Chilliwack.......d.				
87.00						a.**Vancouver**.......d.				

a– Connection by SB.
GLC– Greyhound Lines of Canada. Tel.: Calgary 403 265 9111.
SB– Dewdney Coach Lines Ltd. Tel.: Trail 604 368 5555.

Table 83 — VANCOUVER - KAMLOOPS - CALGARY — GLC

CA $	62	38	2	14	6	64	1256	4	20	1267	km	494	3	61	21	63	5	1266	1253	11	9	19
0.00	0800	0800	1330	....	....	1800	2045	2045	0030	....	0	d.**Vancouver**........a.	1555	....	1940	2305	0015	....	....	0645	0800	1245	....
	0830	0830	1400			1830	2110	2110	0050		20	d.New Westminster....d.	s		s	s				s	s	s	
		s				s					116	d.Chilliwack........d.	1345							s	s	
15.55	1010	1010	1545			2015	2300	2300	0250		174	d.Hope..............d.	1310	s	2115	2215				s	0505	1040
	1135		1715			2145						d.Merritt...........d.	1125							s	0900	
35.25	1315		1915			2320	0140	0120		0800	1000	449	d.**Kamloops**........d.	1025	1515		2005		2150	0200	0235	0800	
42.60	1435		2050	2050		0050				0945	1125		d.Salmon Arm........d.	0815	1325	1820	2000	2025			0105	0555	0055
52.90	1615	1740	2230	2230		0220	0415		1040	1145	665	d.**Revelstoke**......d.	0645	1155	1410	1655	1830			2335	0430	0425
67.75	1930	2045	0140	0140		0520	0740		1400	1455		d.**Golden**..........d.	0505	1035	1315	1540	1705			2225	0315	0320
77.70		2150	0250	0250		0635				1605		898	d.Lake Louise.......d.	s		1120		1535			2115	0155	0155
86.45		2240	0345	0345		0740			1605	1700		958	d.**Banff**...........d.	0315	0840	1030		1445			2025	0105	0105
87.00	2235	0015	0520	0520		0935	1045		1730	1835		1085	a.**Calgary**.........d.	0145	0700	0845	1215	1300			1830	2330	0330

GLC– Greyhound Lines of Canada. Tel.: Calgary 403 265 9111.

Table 84 VANCOUVER - EDMONTON - WINNIPEG

GLC SAS

A $	GLC 1828	SAS 14 ex⑤⑦	GLC 1428	GLC 1632	GLC 76 🅁	GLC 1826 🅁	GLC 1834 ②④⑥	GLC 1830 ex⑦	GLC 1172	GLC 1628	GLC 1628	km	494 ↓ ↑	GLC 1531	GLC 75 🅁	GLC 71 🅁	SAS 13/701	GLC 1527	GLC 1733 ①③⑤	GLC 1725 ⑧	GLC 1729 🅁	GLC 1327	GLC 1171
.00	....	....	1330	....	....	1830	....	....	....	0030	....	0	d.**Vancouver**................a.	....	....	1230	....	2300	....	....	....	0955	....
	....	....	1400u	....	....	1900u	....	....	....	0050u	....	20	d.New Westminster......d.	....	....	s	....	s	....	....	....	s	....
.50	....	....	│	....	....	│	....	....	....	│	....	116	d.Chilliwack..................d.	....	....	│	....	│	....	....	....	s	....
.55	....	....	1545	....	....	2100	....	....	....	0300	....	174	d.Hope.........................d.	....	....	s	....	2100	....	....	....	0755	....
.25	....	....	1915	....	....	0005	....	....	....	0630	....	449	d.Kamloops..................d.	....	....	0800	....	1810	....	....	....	0510	....
.65	....	....	2330	....	....	0415	....	....	....	1045	....		d.Valemount.................d.	....	....	│	....	1240	....	....	....	0040	....
.10	....	....	0205	0505	....	0650	....	....	....	1400	....		d.Jasper.......................d.	0245	....	0300	....	1210	....	....	....	0015	....
.15	....	....	0315	0605	....	0750	....	....	....	1500	....		d.Hinton........................d.	0150	....	│	....	1040	....	....	....	2310	....
.40	....	....	0410	0730	....	0920	....	....	....	1610	....		d.Edson........................d.	0030	....	│	....	0940	....	....	....	2210	....
).00	....	....	0635	1015	....	1135	....	....	....	1845	....		a. **Edmonton**............d.	2200	....	2315	....	0700	....	....	....	1930	....
.00	....	....	0800	....	1250	1250	....	....	1815	....	2330		d. **Edmonton**............a.	....	2250	▬	....	0510	....	....	1255	1905	1915
.45	....	....	0915	....	│	1405	....	....	1945	....	0050		d.Vegreville..................d.	....	│	....	....	0355	....	....	1135	│	1800
.55	....	....	1150	....	│	1615	....	....	2200	....	0305		d.Lloydminster..............d.	....	2000	....	....	0205	....	....	0940	│	1600
	....	....	│	....	1530	│	....	....	│	....	│		d. Wainwright............d.	....	│	....	....	│	....	....	│	1640	│
.45	....	1015	1340	....	1745	1745	....	....	2330	....	0445		d.North Battleford.........d.	....	1806	....	1930	0006	....	....	0740	1410	1400
.40	....	1230	1515	....	1925	1920	....	....	....	....	0620		a. Saskatoon.............d.	....	1630	....	1715	2230	....	....	0600	1220	....
	....	....	1700a	....	....	2005	....	....	....	....	0710		d. Saskatoon.............a.	....	....	GLC	....	2140	....	....	0515	1150b	....
	....	....	1950a	....	....	2225	....	....	....	....	0950		d.Wynyard....................d.	....	....	**1727**	....	1920	....	....	0300	0915b	....
.75	1315	....	2140a	....	....	0010	....	0445	....	....	1245		d.Yorkton......................d.	....	....	1645	....	1705	....	0115	0130	0715b	....
.40	│	....	....	....	....	│	....	0800	....	....	1610		d.Dauphin.....................d.	....	....	│	....	1425	....	0001	│	....	....
	1549	....	....	....	....	0220	0730	│	....	....	│		d. Russell.....................d.	....	....	1615	....	│	2310	│	0050	....	....
).55	1804	....	....	....	....	0355	0925	│	....	....	│		d. Minnedosa..............d.	....	....	1405	....	│	2110	│	2308	....	....
2.90	│	....	....	....	....	0415	1005	1015	....	....	1845		d.Neepawa...................d.	....	....	│	....	1220	2045	2155	2245	....	....
1.05	2059	....	....	....	....	0515	1115	1120	....	....	2000		d.Portage la Prairie......d.	....	....	1125	....	1030	1910	2020	2110	....	....
7.00	2210	....	....	....	....	0645	1245	1245	....	....	2115		a.**Winnipeg**..................d.	....	....	1000	....	0915	1800	1900	2000	....	....

⑧. b–Ex ⑦. *GLC*–Greyhound Lines of Canada. Tel.: Edmonton 403 421 4211. *SAS*–Saskatchewan Transportation Co. Tel.: Saskatoon 306 664 5700.

Table 85 CALGARY - WINNIPEG

GLC SAS

$	SAS 36 ③-⑥	GLC 12	GLC 1828	SAS 34 ③-⑥	SAS 361 ξ	GLC 2	SAS 78 ⑧	GLC 64 🅁	GLC 42 ex⑦	GLC 10	km	494 ↓ ↑	SAS 55 Ⓐ	SAS 351 ξ	GLC 3	GLC 1727	SAS 51 ⑧	SAS 33 ②-⑤	SAS 35 ②-⑤	GLC 5	GLC 41 ⑧	GLC 63 🅁	GLC 11
00	....	0045	....	....	....	0815	....	1330	....	2000	0	d.**Calgary**..............a.	....	....	0130	....	....	....	....	0810	....	1130	1730
	....	0225	....	....	....	1010	....	│	....	2155		d.Bassano..............d.	....	....	2330	....	....	....	....	0610	....	0935	1530
	....	0255	....	....	....	1100	....	1540	....	2245		d.Brooks ....d.	....	....	2300	....	....	....	....	0540	....	0905	1500
	....	0430	....	....	....	1300	....	1730	....	0030	306	d.Medicine Hat........d.	....	....	2145	....	....	....	....	0425	....	0745	1350
	....	0545	....	....	....	1410	....	1845	....	0145		d.Maple Creek.........d.	....	....	2020	....	....	....	....	0300	....	0605	1205
	....	0800	....	....	....	1630	....	2050	....	0340	533	d.Swift Current.........d.	....	....	1850	....	....	....	....	0135	....	0440	1020
	0945	1025	....	1140	1840	1850	2030	2250	....	0535	713	d.Moose Jaw...........d.	0825	1055	1620	....	1825	1840	1900	2310	....	s	0730
	1045	1145	....	1235	1935	2045	2125	0005	....	0730	784	d.**Regina**...............d.	0730	1000	1525	....	1730	1745	1800	2220	....	0140	0640
	....	1245	....	....	....	s	....	│	....	0830	853	d.Indian Head.........d.	....	....	1405	....	....	....	....	2100	....	│	r
	....	1445	....	....	....	2315	....	│	....	1010		d.Whitewood...........d.	....	....	1245	....	....	....	....	1940	....	│	0356
	....	1520	....	....	....	2345	....	│	....	1045	1007	d.Moosomin............d.	....	....	1140	....	....	....	....	1850	....	│	0324
	....	1715	....	....	....	0145	....	0425	....	1240	1163	d.Virden ....d.	....	....	1150	....	....	....	....	1900	....	2320	0340
	....	1845	1925	....	....	0300	....	0615	0730	1430	1252	d.Brandon ....d.	....	....	1045	1255	....	....	....	1750	2125	2215	0240
	....	│	2059	....	....	s	....	0750	│	1555	1282	d.Portage la Prairie..d.	....	....	0840	1125	....	....	....	1525	1940	│	0055
50	....	2115	2210	....	....	0545	....	0905	1025	1735	1368	a.**Winnipeg**............d.	....	....	0730	1000	....	....	....	1400	1830	1900	2345

Runs on † (ex on ⑦ of holiday weekends). *GLC*–Greyhound Lines of Canada. Tel.: Calgary 403 265 9111. *SAS*–Saskatchewan Transportation Co. Tel.: Saskatoon 306 664 5700.

Table 86 TORONTO - WINNIPEG

GLC

A $	3	1077 ⑦	47 ex③⑦	7	49 ③	47 ⑦	63 🅁	1079 ex⑦	11	km	494 ↓ ↑	12	1080	2 🅁	64 🅁	50	48 ex③	48 ③
.00	0100	....	....	....	....	....	1300	....	1700	0	d.**Toronto**....................a.	0550	....	1515	1745	....	....	....
.40	0715	....	....	1300	....	....	1915	....	2315	397	d.Sudbury.....................a.	2340	....	0845	1135	1645	....	....
	0820	....	....	1405	....	....	2017	....	0015		d.Espanola...................d.	2245	....	0755	1023	1532	....	....
	0912	....	....	1457	....	....	2107	....	s		d.Serpent River............d.	2140	....	r	0928	1436	....	....
.80	1230	....	....	1735	....	....	2355	....	0315	710	d.Sault Ste. Marie ....d.	1920	....	0430	0715	1215	....	....
	1530	....	....	....	....	....	s	....	0605		d.Wawa.........................d.	1550	....	0135	0340	....	....	....
.00	1632	....	....	....	....	....	0400	....	0717	1038	d.White River ....d.	1407	....	0030	0235	....	....	....
	1820	....	....	....	....	....	0505	....	0916		d.Marathon...................d.	1255	....	2320	│	....	....	....
	1955	....	....	....	....	....	r	....	1045		d.Schreiber...................d.	1120	....	2145	│	....	....	....
.00	2105	2120	....	....	....	....	s	1105	1155	1318	d.Nipigon.......................d.	1010	2015	2035	2300	....	....	....
.00	2320	2250	....	....	....	....	1005	1235	1415	1427	d.Thunder Bay ....d.	0840	1845	1905	2135	....	....	....
	0050	....	....	....	....	....	r	....	1605		d.Upsala........................d.	0545	....	1620	1900	....	....	....
	0115	....	....	....	....	....	1210	....	1630		d.Ignace........................d.	0335	....	1355	1635	....	....	....
.00	0240	....	0700	....	0700	1310	1350	....	1830	1790	d.Dryden........................d.	0225	....	1240	1525	....	2315	2345
.00	0420	....	0850	....	0850	1455	1535	....	2025	1926	d.Kenora........................d.	0035	....	1025	1325	....	2130	2200
.00	0650	....	1115	....	1205	1725	1825	....	2255	2137	a.**Winnipeg**..................d.	2200	....	0730	1030	....	1830	1830

C– Greyhound Lines of Canada. Tel.: Winnipeg 204 783 8840.

Table 87 SASKATOON - YORKTON

SAS

A $	62	94	60 ②④⑥⑦	72 ①③⑤	km	394 ↓ ↑	71 ①③⑤	59 ②④⑥⑦	95	61
.00	0800	....	1730	1730	0	d.**Saskatoon**........a.	1215	1215	....	2215
.40	0925	....	1910	1920	112	d.Humboldt...........d.	1032	1032	....	2050
❖	│	0845	....	│	~243	d. **Regina**............a.	│	....	2130	│
❖	│	1035	....	│	~93	d. Melville............d.	│	....	1930	│
❖	│	1145	....	│	~49	d. Yorkton ....d.	│	....	1855	│
.60	1230	1235	....	2225	296	d.Canora ....d.	0715	....	1745	1745
.10	1310	│	....	....	339	a.**Yorkton** ....d.	....	....	│	1700
.60	....	1445	....	....	431	a. Swan River...d.	....	....	1530	....

\- Km ex Canora.
S– Saskatchewan Transportation Co. Tel.: Saskatoon 306 664 5700.

Table 88 REGINA - GAINSBOROUGH

SAS

CA $	902 ①⑥⑦	90 ②-⑤	92 ⑧	km	394 ↓ ↑	93 ex⑦	903 ①⑥⑦	91 ②-⑤
0.00	1115	1115	1730	0	d.**Regina**..............a.	1205	1715	2145
8.20	1305	1305	1930	117	d.Weyburn............d.	1030	1545	2015
12.50	1410	1435	2040	204	d.Estevan.............d.	0915	1430	1900
19.40	....	1630	....	323	a.**Gainsborough**..d.	....	....	1700

SAS– Saskatchewan Transportation Co. Tel.: Regina 306 787 3346.

Table 89 MATAGAMI

NOR

CA $	1	3 ⑧	5	km	293 ↓ ↑	2	4 ⑧	6
0.00	0630	1530	2245	0	d.**Val d'Or**...........a.	0920	2345	0040
	0725	1705	2340	70	d.Amos.................d.	0800	2250	2345
	....	1945	....	288	a.**Matagami**.........d.	....	2030	....

NOR– Autobus Norouest Inc. Tel.: Rouyn Noranda 819 762 0735.

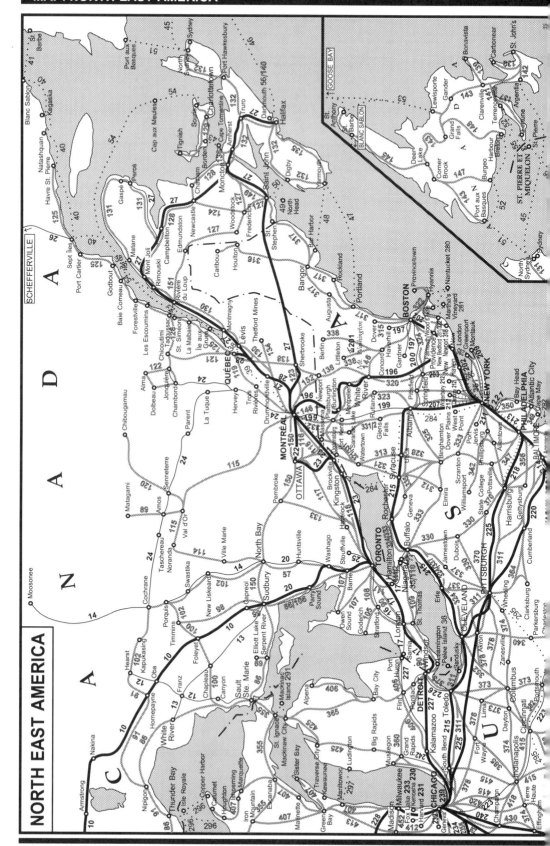

Table 90 — EDMONTON - FORT McMURRAY 🚌 GLC RA

CA $	GLC 181	GLC 133	RA 18	GLC 105	GLC 105	RA 20	GLC 129	GLC 119	GLC 131	494	km
	ex⑦Ⓡ	Ⓑ⑦	⑦	Ⓡ			⑧Ⓡ	⑥Ⓡ	ex⑧⑦	↓	0
0.00	0001	0730	0815	0945	1300	1730	1730	1730	1830	d.Edmonton ....a.	0
				1110					1947	d.Thorhild ....d.	
10.25		0905	1000	1205		1900			2045	d.Boyle ....d.	
	0140				1445		1915		r	d.Athabasca ....d.	
		0940		1225	1530		1940	2000	2109	d.Grassland ....d.	
				1300					2150	a. Lac la Biche ....a.	
15.60		1010	1100		1600	2015	2010	2035		d.Wandering River ....d.	
30.00	0520	1230	1330	....	1815	2230	2215	2245	....	a.Fort McMurray ....d.	440

494	GLC 132	GLC 130	RA 19	GLC 132	GLC 106	RA 17	GLC 134
	ex⑦⑦	Ⓡ		⑦	Ⓡ		Ⓡ
↓ ....↑	1145	1225	1330	1650	1700	2230	2245
	1015			1528		2030	
	0920	1025	1130	1435			
				1500		2100	
	0835	0955		1415	1425	1915	2025
	0800			1330			
		0910	1015		1340	1915	1940
	....	0700	0815	....	1130	1715	1730

GLC– Greyhound Lines of Canada. Tel.: Edmonton 403 421 4211.
RA– Red Arrow Deluxe Services. Tel.: Edmonton 403 468 6360.

Table 90a — TORONTO - DETROIT 🚌 GLC

CA $	2111	91	2151	367	2163	2117	2135/7	361	97	2145	2141	494	km
	Ⓡ	Ⓡ	Ⓡ	Ⓡ	Ⓡ			Ⓡ	Ⓡ		ex⑦	↓	0
0.00	0830	1030	1030	1230	1315	1430	1700b	1830	2030	2315	0100	d.**Toronto** ....a.	0
							1730a					d. Mississauga ....d.	
		1050										d. Oakville ....d.	
		1105					1745a						
		1140	1350		1820					0015	0200	d.Hamilton ....d.	
		1220	1425		1900					0050	0235	d.Brantford ....d.	
		1305	1505		1950							d.Woodstock ....d.	
	1105	1250	1415	1510	1730	1730	2045	2105	2250	0215	0350	d.**London** ....d.	
										0340		a. Port Huron 🚉 ......d.	
	1235	....	1555	1910				2235				d.Chatham ....d.	
	1254	....	1618	1933				s				d.Tilbury ....d.	
	1345	....	1700	1725	2055	1945		2335			0620	a.Windsor 🚉 ....d.	
	1410	....	1755	....	2015			0005			0650	a.**Detroit** ....d.	

364	2146	92	2164	366	2126	2120	2152	2124	368	2112	494
ex⑦			Ⓡ		Ⓡ		Ⓡ		Ⓡ	Ⓡ	↑
0600	0830	1050	1400	1335	1545	1815	1950	2035	2050	2350	d.**Toronto** ....a.
											d. Mississauga ....d.
											d. Oakville ....d.
s	0715		1305				1715		1935	2250	d.Hamilton ....d.
s	0635		1230				1640		1900	2215	d.Brantford ....d.
			1150						1810	2135	d.Woodstock ....d.
0310	0530	0830	1100	1100	1330	1530	1730	1715	1830	2045	d.**London** ....d.
	0345										a. Port Huron 🚉 ......d.
			0855		1130	1340				1850	d.Chatham ....d.
			0825		1050					1823	d.Tilbury ....d.
0055		0645	0815	1010	1230			1540	1740		a.Windsor 🚉 ....d.
0030		0745	0940	1205				1515	1715		a.**Detroit** ....d.

—⑤† only. b–1650 ex ⑤†. GLC–Greyhound Lines of Canada. ☎ Toronto 416 393 7911.

Table 90b — LONDON - WINDSOR 🚌 GLC

CA $	2163	km		2164
0.00	1730	0	d.**London**............a.	1030
	1910		d.Chatham ....d.	0855
	1933		d.Tilbury ....d.	0825
	2000		d.Leamington ......d.	0750
	2017		d.Kingsville ....d.	0730
	2055		a.**Windsor**............d.	0645

GLC– Greyhound Lines of Canada. Tel.: Toronto 416 393 7911.

Table 91 — HEARST - THUNDER BAY (GLC)

CA $	1079 ex⑦		1077 ⑦	km	494			1080
0.00	0600	....	1615	0	d.Hearst............a.	....	....	0120
	0625	....	1640	55	d.Calstock..........d.	....	....	0055
❖	0645r	....	1700r		d.Hornepayne.......d.	....	....	0035r
❖	0820	....	1835		d.Longlac...........d.	....	....	2300
❖	0850	....	1905		d.Geraldton ....d.	....	....	2230
❖	1005	....	2020		d.Beardmore ....d.	....	....	2130
❖	1105	....	2120		d.Nipigon ....d.	....	....	2015
❖	1235	....	2250		a.ThunderBay (PA)..d.			1845

GLC– Greyhound Lines of Canada. ☎ Thunder Bay 807 345 2194.

Table 92 — CALGARY - LETHBRIDGE (GLC)

CA $	394	km	1147	1575	1151	1579	1141	1157	1145	1375
0.00	Calgary................↓	0	....	0645	0700	....	1345	1500	1815	2130
10.00	Fort MacLeod......d.	167	0645	0920		0925		1740		2345
13.00	Lethbridge ....a.	219	0730		0950	1010	1635	1825	2130	

394			1476	1198	1150	1152	1158	1156	1140	1144
Lethbridge.........d.	↓		....	0745	0820	1400	1630	....	1745	2145
Fort MacLeod......d.			0600		0910	1445	1715	1730	1830	2230
Calgary............a.			0830	1050	1150	1720		1940	2115	

GLC– Greyhound Lines of Canada. ☎ Calgary 403 265 9111.

Table 93 — SASKATOON - HUDSON BAY (SAS)

CA S	29	63	65 ②~⑤	3	km	394		64	4	30
0.00	0830	1400	1800	1800	0	d.Saskatoon..........a.	....	1135	1550	1950
3.10	r	r		1823	30	d.Warman...........d.	....	1112	r	r
9.10					147	d.St. Louis..........d.				
9.10	1020	1550	1940	2005	160	a.Prince Albert....d.	....	0930	1400	1800

CA S	9011 ③	83 ①③⑤	901 ②④	9 ①⑤⑥	km	394	82 ③⑤	10 ②④⑥⑤	1012 ③	1011 ⑦
0.00	1830		1730	1830	0	d. Saskatoon......a.	....	1055b	1055	2115
3.90		2015	2015		31	d.Prince Albert....a.	0955			
8.20	2150	2135	2150	2150	112	d.Melfort ....d.	0840	0845	0945	1830
10.00	2225		2225	2225	151	d.Tisdale ....d.		0805	0805	1750
16.80	2355		0025	0025	266	a.Hudson Bay ....d.	....	0600	0630	1500

b–1145 on ⑥. SAS–Saskatchewan Transportation Co. ☎Saskatoon 306 664 5700.

Table 94 — WINNIPEG - RIVERTON (GG)

CA $	025 ✗	025 †	km	394		026 ✗	026 †
0.00	....	1800	2030	0	d.Winnipeg..........a.	1000	1940
2.25	....	1840	2110	33	d.Selkirk...........d.	0920	1900
6.30	....	1910	2135		d.Matlock...........d.	0845	1825
9.15	....	1920	2145		a.Winnipeg Beach d.	0830	1810
12.10	....	1935	2200	89	a.Gimli.............d.	0810	1750
17.10	....	2030	2230	129	a.Riverton..........d.	0720	1700

GG– Grey Goose Bus Lines. ☎ Winnipeg 204 786 8891.

Table 95 — WINNIPEG - THOMPSON (GG)

CA $	045	091/031	041	035 ex⑦	037	099 ③	033	047	033 ⑧	043 ⑧	km	394	046	044	048	034 ex①⑦	039	032 ⑥	100	036	038	084 ex⑦	042
0.00	....	1030	1130	1201	1730	1800	2030			2200	0	d.Winnipeg..........a.	....	0705	....	0755	1440	1625	1840	2040	2045	....	2200
28.20		1720								0315	448	d.Grand Rapids........d.		0155									1635
5.25		1145		1310			2135				88	d. Portage la Prairie...d.				0650		1515		1930			
20.00		1535		1645	2145		0050				328	d. Dauphin ....d.				0405	1030	1145		1630	1630		
30.85		1740		1855			0300				505	d. Swan River ....d.				0200		0915		1350			
43.95			2150			0135	0600				744	d. The Pas ....d.					2315		1100	1050			
50.65			2250				0710				864	d. Cranberry Portage ..d.					2200			0935			
52.30			2330			0745	0630				895	a. Flin Flon ....d.			2225	2115				0900			
58.85		1935				0925		0510			⇌650	d.Ponton............d.					2350	1935					1425
58.85		2005				1000		0545			⇌710	d.Wabowden.........d.					2315	1840					1345
58.85		2115				1110	1730	0700			⇌820	d.Thompson.........d.	2100	2200	1730							1200	1230
Ⓡ19.85	0815	1315									⇌1190	a.Lynn Lake ....d.	1600										
Ⓡ20.25						2110					⇌1365	a. Gillam ....d.										0800	

a–30 mins. later on ⑥. ⇌–Via Grand Rapids. Ⓡ–Fare ex Thompson. GG–Grey Goose Bus Lines. ☎ Winnipeg 204 786 8891.

Table 96 — WINNIPEG - REGINA (GLC)

CA $	3021 ex⑦	3041 ex⑥⑦	km	394		3042 ex①⑦	3022 ex①⑦	3020 ⑦
0.00	....	1745	0	d.Winnipeg..........a.		1220	1815	
7.75	....	2005	132	d.Treherne..........d.		1020	1615	
	2200	2200		d. Brandon...........d.	0800	0815	1415	
13.90		2240	259	d.Souris............d.	0720			
17.95		2325	328	d.Reston............d.	0630			
18.55			375	d.Redvers...........d.				
23.60			486	d.Stoughton.........d.				
				d.Fillmore..........d.				
35.05			626	a.Regina............d.				

GLC– Greyhound Lines of Canada. ☎ Winnipeg 204 783 8840.

Table 97 — WINNIPEG - THUNDER BAY (GG)

CA $	053 Ⓐ	053 †	055 ♣	051 ♣	km	494		052 ♣	056 †	054 ♣	052 ✗
0.00	....		1000	1800	0	d.Winnipeg..........a.	1510	1840		1225
					260	d.Baudette ⊞.......d.				
23.90	0730	1000	1540	2330	372	d.Fort Frances......d.	1000	1320	2200	0715
❖	1040	1310	1845		d.Atikokan..........d.		1220	2105		
39.00			s		722	a.Thunder Bay ≫ d.		s		
39.00	1325	1555	2125		724	a.Thunder Bay N.∅ d.		0930	1800	

∅–Port Arthur. ≫–Fort William. GG–Grey Goose Bus Lines. ☎Winnipeg 204 786 8891.

Table 98 — LETHBRIDGE - SWEETGRASS (GLC)

CA $	1151 ♣	km	494			1152
0.00	....	1000	0	d.Lethbridge........a.	....	1330
6.35	....	1120	109	d.Coutts ⊞.........d.	....	1210
10.90	....	1125	111	a.Sweetgrass 528 d.	....	1152

GLC– Greyhound Lines of Canada. ☎ Lethbridge 403 327 1551.

Table 99 492 — CAPREOL - SUDBURY (NWB)

service Capreol-Sudbury and v.v. 35 km. Journey: 1 hour. Fare: CA $: ❖.

From Capreol: 0645Ⓐ, 0750✗, 1000✗, 1200†, 1230✗, 1530✗, 1645✗, 1730✗, 1930✗, 2200†, 2215✗.

From Sudbury: 0800Ⓐ, 0850✗, 1115✗, 1315†, 1430✗, 1640✗, 1735✗, 1830✗, 2115✗, 2315.

NWB– Northway Bus Lines. ☎ Capreol 705 858 1341.

Table 100 — TIMMINS - SAULT STE MARIE (ON)

CA $	25 ②⑤	9 ①④⑥	km	394		10 ①④⑥	28 ②⑤
0.00	....	1945	0	d.Timmins ....a.	....	1135	....
❖	....	2110	113	d.Foleyet...........d.	....	1010	....
❖	....	2215	209	d.Chapleau..........d.	....	0850	....
❖	....	2355	338	d.Hawk Junction...d.	....	0720	....
❖	0900	0015	344	d.Wawa.............d.	....	0700	2005
❖	1150		573	a.Sault Ste. Marie.d.			1715

ON– Ontario Northland. ☎North Bay 705 472 4500.

Table 101 — PICKLE LAKE (LL)

CA $	km	492	
0.00 ❖	0	d.Ignace............a.	❖
❖		d.Valora............d.	❖
❖		d.Savant Lake ......d.	❖
❖		d.Central Patricia..d.	❖
❖		a.Pickle Lake ......d.	❖

LL– L&L Transportation. ☎Ignace ❖.

Table 102 — TORONTO - HEARST (ON)

CA $	1 ⑧	37	3	12	km	394		11	4	38 ⑧	2
0.00	0030	....	0930	1300	0	d.Toronto 57.......a.	1830	2230	....	0715
26.00	0615	1615				d.North Bay ....d.	1545	....		0140
			1840			d. Sudbury ....d.	1250			
39.00	0805	1805			146	d.Cobalt............d.	1355			2355
39.00	0830	1830			161	d.New Liskeard......d.	1330			2330
43.00	0905	1905			205	d.Englehart.........d.	1250			2250
❖	0955	1955			251	d.Kirkland Lake ....d.	1205			2205
46.00	1005	2005			255	d.Swastika ....d.	1150			2150
53.00	1100	2100			363	d.Matheson ....d.	1100			2100
57.00	1215	2245	2240		417	a.Timmins ....d.	0850	1005		2005
❖	1150	2140			344	a. Iroquois Falls ...d.	1005			2015
58.00	1225	2215	2215		386	a. Cochrane ....d.	0930	0840		1940
69.00	1420	2340	0050		594	a.Kapuskasing.......d.	0640	0715		1740
≤48.75	1530	0050	0200		695	a.Hearst ....d.	0530	0600		1630

≤– Fare ex North Bay.
ON– Ontario Northland. ☎North Bay 705 472 4500.

Table 103 — SASKATOON - REGINA (SAS)

CA $	52 Ⓐ	36 ③~⑧	56 ③~⑧	34	54 ζ	361	2 ⑧	78	km	394		77 Ⓐ	771 Ⓒ	55 ζ	351	53	1	51 ⑧	33 ②~⑤	35 ②~⑤
0.00	0700	....	0800	....	1330	....	1730	1730	0	d.Saskatoon.............a.		1005	1035	1140	....	1630	....	2035	2140	....
14.30	....	0945	....	1140	....	1840	....	2030	233	d.Moose Jaw...........d.		....	0835	1055				1835	1840	1900
15.10	1005	1045	1110	1235	1635	1935	2035	2125	306	a.Regina..............d.		0700	0730	0730	1000	1330	1730	1730	1745	1800

ζ–Runs on † (ex on ⑦ of holiday weekends). SAS–Saskatchewan Transportation Co. ☎Regina 306 787 3346.

Table 104 — RED LAKE 🚌 XL

CA $	3					4	
				km	↓		↑
0.00	....	1030	....	0	d.**Kenora**............a.	....	1800
❖	....	1140	....	95	d.Vermilion Bay ....d.	....	1650
❖				❖	d.Red Lake Road .d.		
❖	....	1305	....	198	d.Ear Falls............d.	....	1530
❖	....	1400	....	270	a.**Red Lake**.......d.	....	1430

XL– Excel Coach Lines. ☎ Kenora 807 468 6667.

Table 105 — GODERICH - STRATFORD 🚌 ST

🚌 service Goderich-Stratford and v.v. 72 km. Journey: 1¼ hours. Fare: CA $: 7.30
From Goderich: 0750⚡, 1700P.
From Stratford: 1900.
P– Runs on † (ex on ⑦ of holiday weekend).
ST– Sherwood Transportation. ☎ Goderich 519 524 2092.

Table 106 — SUDBURY - PARRY SOUND - TORONTO 🚌 GLC ON

CA $	ON 16		GLC 2 Ⓡ	GLC 64 Ⓡ	ON 32		ON 40	GLC 12			GLC 3		ON 21 Ⓡ	GLC 63	ON 23		ON 49	GLC 11 Ⓡ		
						km	↓		↑										
0.00	....	0630	1000	1230	1300	....	1700	0050	0	d.**Sudbury**............a.	0600	....	1615	1830	1830	....	2230	2215	....	....
	....	0755			1425					d.Pointe au Baril.......d.		....		1700		....	r		....	....
16.25	....	0830			1500	....	1900		165	d.Parry Sound ....d.		....	1405		1620	....	2020		....	....
29.55	....	1030			1800	....	2045		302	d.Barrie ....d.		....	1230		1430	....	1830		....	....
34.50	....	1200	1515	1745	1830	....	2215	0550	397	a.**Toronto**.......d.	0100	....	1100	1300	1300	....	1700	1700	....	....

GLC–Greyhound Lines of Canada. ☎ Toronto 416 393 7911. ON–Ontario Northland. ☎ North Bay 705 472 4500.

Table 107 — OWEN SOUND - TORONTO 🚌 GLC PMCL

CA $	PMCL 1O	GLC 5605 ex⑦	PMCL 9C ex⑦	GLC 5505 ⑦	GLC 5611 ⑦	PMCL 5O ex⑦	PMCL 15XO ⑦	GLC 5517 ex⑦	GLC 5635 ⑦	GLC 5523 ⑦			PMCL 20C ex⑦	GLC 5620 ex⑦	GLC 5504 ex⑦	GLC 5510 ⑦	GLC 5640 ⑦	PMCL 10SO		PMCL 8O ex⑦	GLC 5650 ⑦	GLC 5522 ⑦	PMCL 36FO
											km	↓	↑										
0.00	....	0815	0900	1015	1230	1300	1515	1600	1630	1800	1900	0	d.**Toronto**............a.	1005	1050	1240	1525	1655	1715	....	1950	2055	2125	2340
9.85	....	0955		1150		1700				1815	2030	98	d.Barrie ....d.					1545		....	1820			2210
					1415								d. Guelph............d.			1110	1410			....			2010	
16.00	....	1115		1315		1825	1825			1935		173	d.Collingwood ....d.	0640					1430	....	1640			2045
9.20	....		1035		1435				1935			73	d. Orangeville ....d.		0915			1520		....		1920		
11.90	....		1059		1459				1959			96	d. Shelburne ....d.		0846			1451		....		1856		
20.15	....	1220	1220		1640	1620	1930	1930	2040	2120	2255	≪194	a.**Owen Sound** ....d.		0725	0825	1125	1330	1330	....	1530	1735	1725	1940

≪–Km via Collingwood. GLC–Greyhound Lines of Canada. ☎ Toronto 416 393 7911. PMCL–Penetang Midland Coach Lines. ☎ Midland 705 526 0161.

Table 108 — TORONTO - GUELPH - LONDON 🚌 CHHO GLC

CA $	2K ⚡	3K	6K	8K		CHHO		1K ⚡	4K	5K	7K
					km	↓	↑				
0.00	....	....	....	....	0	d.**Toronto** ≫......a.	....	....	....	....	....
8.95	....	....	....	....	80	d.Guelph ≫ ......d.	....	....	....	....	....
11.05	0850	1205	1505	1755	100	d.Kitchener ≫ ......d.	1000	1240	1700	1900	
	0920	1235	1535	1825		d.New Hamburg ...d.	0935	1220	1630	1845	
	0930	1245	1545	1835		d.Shakespeare ....d.	0925	1210	1620	1835	
15.05	0950	1305	1605	1855	140	d.Stratford ....d.	0910	1155	1605	1815	
	1005	1320	1620	1915		d.St. Marys.......d.	0855				
16.50	1045	1405	1705	2005	195	a.**London**............d.	0800	1100	1520	1715	

≫– 🚌 service (GLC) Toronto-Kitchener and v.v. Journey: 2 hours. From Toronto at 0550ex⑥⑦, 0730ex⑦, 0930, 1130, 1300, 1445, 1530, 1615ex⑥⑦, 1630⑤, 1645ex⑥⑦, 1700, 1730ex⑥⑦, 1815⑤⑦, 1830, 1900⑤⑦, 2030, 2130, returning at 0550ex⑥⑦, 0610ex⑥⑦, 0630ex⑥⑦, 0730ex⑦, 0830ex⑦, 0900⑦, 0930⑦, 1030, 1130, 1300, 1430, 1530, 1600⑤, 1640, 1730, 1800⑤⑦, 1930, 2200; 🚌 service (GLC) Toronto-Guelph and v.v. Journey: 1½ hours. From Toronto at 0550ex⑦, 0730ex⑦, 0930, 1130ex⑦, 1230⑦, 1300, 1445, 1615ex⑥⑦, 1630ex⑦, 1700, 1730ex⑥⑦, 1830, 1900⑦, 2030, 2330, returning at 0545ex⑥⑦, 0630ex⑥⑦, 0645ex⑥⑦, 0710ex⑦, 0810ex⑦, 0910⑦, 1010ex⑦, 1110ex⑦, 1210, 1340, 1410⑦, 1610, 1715, 1810, 2010, 2240.

CHHO–Cha-Co Trails. ☎ Chatham 519 681 2861. GLC–Greyhound Lines of Canada. ☎ Toronto 416 393 7911.

Table 109 — BUFFALO - LONDON 🚌 CHHO GLC

US $	CHHO 3A ⚡	GLC♦ 2103 ②					CHHO 2A ⚡	GLC♦ 2104 ①
					km	↓	↑	
0.00	....	0745	....	....	0	d.**Buffalo**............a.	....	1635
6.00	....	0820	....	....	40	d.Niagara Falls USA ⬛..d.	....	1600
6.00	....	0840	....	....	47	d.N. Falls Canada ⬛ ..d.	....	1540
6.40	....	0910	....	....	68	d.Welland ....d.	....	1510
18.90	0930	1222	....	....	258	d.St. Thomas.......d.	0840	1150
26.00	1015	1255	....	....		a.**London**............d.	0800	1115

CHHO–Cha-Co Trails. ☎ Chatham 519 681 2861.
GLC– Greyhound Lines of Canada. ☎ London 519 434 3245.

Table 110 — NIAGARA FALLS 🚌 CCL GLC NF

🚌 service (GLC) links Niagara Falls (Canada) with Buffalo, St. Catharines and Toronto. See Table **111**.
🚌 service (CCL) links Niagara Falls (Canada) with Buffalo, St. Catharines, Hamilton (Table **112**) and Kitchener (6-7 daily).
🚌 service (NF) links Niagara Falls (USA) with Buffalo. See Table **377**.
CCL– Canada Coach Lines. ☎ Mount Hope 416 527 2100.
GCL– Gray Coach Lines. ☎ Toronto 416 973 7911.
NF– Niagara Frontier Transit Metro. ☎ Buffalo 285 9319.

Table 111 — TORONTO - BUFFALO 🚌 GLC

CA $	2015	1017	1025	302	1041	1049	1061	1059	1079	2083	1091			1010 ⑥⑦♣	1006	1014 ⚡	2016 ♣	2020 ♣	305	1048	1054	2060 ♣	1066 ♣	1078 ♣
				♣		♣	♣	♣	♣	♣	♣	km	↓ ↑											
0.00	0745	0815	1000	1030	1400	1600	1700	1800	2000	2100	2330	0	d.**Toronto** Ω............a.	0700	0750	0900	0905	1035	1315	1740	1910	2000	2130	2350
			1025		1425							44	d.Mississauga ....d.				s			s	s		s	
12.20		0940	1135		1540	1740	1835	1940	2120		0055	107	d.Burlington Ω............d.		s	0730				1600	1730		2000	2230
13.55		1000	1155		1605	1800	1900	2005	2145		0115	120	d.St. Catharines ⊗ Ω....d.		0705	s	s			1535	1705		1935	2205
16.00	1005			1245	1705		2005		2245	2315	0215	153	d.Niagara Falls Canada ⊗Ω⬛..d.	s										
16.00				1310								❖	d.**Buffalo** ⊗............a.	0405	0405		0620	0800	1100	1420	....	1745	....	2100
													a.Buffalo International Airport.d.	....	....	....	....	1040	....	....	....	....	....	....

⊗– Intermediate traffic not carried between St. Catharines and Buffalo.
Ω– Additional trips Toronto-Niagara Falls at 1200, 1900⑤⑦, returning at 0535④, 0905, 1135, 1335, 1835⑤⑦, 2035⑨⑦.
GLC– Greyhound Lines of Canada. ☎ Toronto 416 393 7911.

Table 112 — HAMILTON - BUFFALO 🚌 TRW

CA $	100A Ⓐ	101A ♣	102A ♣		103A ♣	104A ⑤	105A ♣	109A †	108A ⑤	106A ♣	107A ♣			107B Ⓐ	100B ⚡♣	101B ♣	102B ♣	103B ♣	104B ⑤	105B ♣	111B †	109B ♣	106B ♣	108B
												km	↓ ↑											
0.00	0630	0805a	1010	....	1200	1415	1615	1715	1730	1815	2030	0	d.**Hamilton**............a.	0815	1000	1135	1340	1555	1800	1930	2055	2235	....
6.20	0745	0910	1110	....	1315	1515	1735	1810	1820	1935	2140	59	d.St. Catharines ....d.	0655	0845	1040	1230	1450	1645	1835	1930	1955	2140
8.50	0810	0935	1155	....	1340	1540	1815	1825	1845	2000	2205	72	d.Niagara Falls Canada ⬛ .d.	0625	0820	1010	1200	1420	1615	1810	1900	1930	2115	0015
12.35	....	1035	1255	....		1915					2255	105	a.**Buffalo**............d.	....	0620		1045			1715			2010	2325
14.55												112	a.Buffalo International Airport.d.											

⚡–⚡ only. TRW–Trentway-Wagar Inc. ☎ Peterborough 705 748 6411.

Check update notes to timetables and with operator before starting your journey

Table 114 — NORANDA - NORTH BAY 🚌 NOR

CA $	1 ⑧			km	↓	↑		4 ⑧
0.00	....	0825	....	0	d.Noranda Rouyn a.		....	2030
15.65	....	1010	....	138	d.Ville Marie ....d.		....	1840
31.00	....	1235	....	301	a.North Bay ....d.		....	1600

NOR– Autobus Norouest Inc. Tel.: Rouyn Noranda 819 762 0735.

Table 115 — NORANDA - MONTRÉAL 🚌 ANO

CA $	81E	83E	813E	87E ex⑥⑦	km	↓	↑	810E	82E ex⑥⑦	84E	88EE
0.00	0730	1300	1700	2200	0	d.Noranda Rouyn a.		1435	1705	2255	0800
11.65	0930	1505	1835	2355	108	d.Val d'Or............d.		1300	1535	2125	0630
34.65	1300	1830		0320	365	d.Grand Remous..d.		1210	1800		0310
38.15	1325	1855		0345	400	d.Mont Laurier......d.		1100	1655		0150
51.05		2035s		0530s	540	d.Ste. Agathe........d.		0900	1510		0025
55.40		2050s		0600s	585	d.St. Jérome........d.		0820			r
60.95	1615	2205		0700	640	a.Montréal...........d.		0730	1400		2315

ANO– Autobus Auger N-O inc. 🚌 Chateauguay 514 691 1654.

Table 116 — MONTRÉAL - OTTAWA 🚌 VCL

CA $	102	29	222	33		km	↓	↑	28	219	32	107
0.00	0820	0815		1810		0	d.Montréal...........a.		1215	....	2210	2215
		0939		1934			d.Lachute.........d.		1048	....	2042		
16.00	1020	1020	1605	2015		104	d.Hawkesbury....d.		1020	1325	2015	2015
		1212		2207			a.Hull................d.		0816		1811		
29.85	1220	1230	1715	2225		215	a.Ottawa...........d.		0800	1215	1755	1815

VCL– Voyageur Colonial Ltd. Tel.: Montréal 514 842 2281.

Table 117 — OTTAWA - TORONTO 🚌 VCL

CA $	235	201	121	203	205	107 ⑤⑦	209	211	213	115 ⑤⑦	231	km	↓	↑	118	120	204	206	108	210	224	212	114	220 ⑤⑦	228
0.00	0005	0700	0845	0930	1130	1215	1430	1630	1800	1820	2000	0	d.Ottawa...............a.		0525	1550	1435	1625	1855	1925	2045	2135	2335	2335	0140
		1255				1600				2135		245	d.Havelock..........d.			1135						2025			
37.55		1350				1650				2225		286	d.Peterborough....d.		0205	1055			1505			1945			
46.95	0545	1205	1435	1625	1900	1925	2135	2305	0020	0135		428	a.Toronto ....d.		0020	0810	0930	1130	1430	1430	1630	1720	1830	2000

VCL– Voyageur Colonial Ltd. 🚌 Ottawa 613 238 5900.

Table 118 — MONTRÉAL - TORONTO 🚌 VCL

CA $	179	265 P	239 P	267 P	245	269 P	251	183	257 ⑤⑦	253	263	km	↓	↑	170	266 P	242	268 P	234	176	270 P	250	256 ⑤⑦	252	264
0.00	0630	0830	0830	1030	1030	1400	1400		1530	1730	0005	0	d.Montréal...........a.		1435	1530	1555	1830	1845	....	2045	2120	2220	0055	0715
	0645											23	d.Dorval.............d.												
17.00	0845		1005		1205		1535			1905	0120	130	d.Cornwall..........d.		1220		1415		1705			1940		2315	0535
	1015											✣	d.Prescott...........d.		1030					1955a					
	1042											226	d.Brockville.........d.		0934				1615s	1932a		1850s		2225s	
33.90	1330		1225		1430		1800	1800	2135	0400	308	d.Kingston ....d.		0810		1235		1525	1700		1800		2135	0355
	1515						1936		2220s	0445s	388	d.Belleville...........d.		....				1520						0145s
	1652						2116						d.Port Hope........d.		....				1331						
56.00	1845	1500	1530	1700	1735	2030	2105	2310	2200	0050	0715	587	a.Toronto ....d.		0900	0900	1200	1200	1115	1415	1415	1600	1800	1800	0015

P–June 30-Sept. 8 and Dec. 22-Jan. 3.   a–⑤⑦ only.   b–⑤ only.   VCL–Voyageur Colonial Ltd. 🚌 Montréal 514 843 4231.

Table 119 — MONTRÉAL - QUÉBEC 🚌 OEX

CA $	169 ex⑦	201 ⑦	51	233		251	171 ⑦	235		11	km	↓	↑	30 ex⑦	202		52	230		204	234	166	236
0.00	0555	0730	1000	1300	....	1530	1740	1900	....	2200	0	d.Montréal ∧ ....a.		0835	1155		1415		....	1805	2005	2150	2220	....
18.00		1010	1155	1500		1735		2045		0005	150	d.Trois Rivières ....d.		0630	1010		1230	1329		1620	1735		2035	
		1128				1853						d.Portneuf...........d.			1212						1912		
32.00	0950	1239		1655		2004	2130				270	a.Québec ∧ ....d.			1100					1530	1800	1800	

∧– Additional (non-stop, journey 3 hours) trips from Montréal: 0100⑤⑥⑦, 0600 and hourly to 2100, 2300; from Québec: 0600ex⑦, 0700 and hourly to 2100, 2300.
OEX– Orleans Express Inc. 🚌 Montréal 514 847 4020.

Table 120 — CHIBOUGAMAU 🚌 MES

CA $	2J			km	↓	↑	1J	
0.00	....	0920	....	0	d.Chibougamau ..a.		2205	....
39.05	....	1420	....	348	d.Senneterre........d.		1700	....
44.85	....	1520	....	420	a.Val d'Or.........d.		1605	....

MES– Autobus Messier Chibougamau Inc. 🚌 Chateauguay 514 691 1654.

Table 121 — QUÉBEC - JONQUIÈRE 🚌 ICR

CA $	1	3	5	9		km	↓	↑	2	4	6	14/16/24 ◇
0.00	1030	1230	1430	1830		0	d.Québec...........a.		0925	1225	1625	2225
22.45	1254	1454	1654	2054		195	d.Laterrière.........d.		0701	1001	1401	2001
22.45	1310	1510	1710	2110		211	a.Chicoutimi........d.		0645	0945	1345	1945
22.45	1330	1530	1730	2130		222	a.Arvida.............d.		0620	0920	1320	1920
22.45	1340	1540	1740	2140		229	a.Jonquière.........d.		0605	0905	1305	1905

◇–1 hour earlier on ⑤⑦.   ICR–Intercar. Tel.: Jonquière 418 547 2167.

Table 122 — DOLBEAU/ALMA 🚌 AJ AL

CA $	AJ 251 ex⑦	AL 100 ex⑦	AL 102	AJ 253	AL 104 ⑥⑦	AJ 104	AJ 255 P ⑥		km	↓	↑	AL 101 ex⑦		AL 103	AJ 254 ex⑦	AJ 105 Q	AL 105	AJ 256
0.00	0730	0810	1210	1235	....	1710	1715		0	d.Chicoutimi...........a.		1030		1450	1510	....	1930	2020
✣	0745	0820	1220	1250	....	1720	1730		✣	d.Arvida.................d.		1015		1435	1455	....	1915	2005
✣	0800	0835	1235	1305	....	1735	1745		✣	d.Jonquière............d.		1005		1425	1445	....	1905	1955
✣		0915	1315		1815	1825			✣	d. Alma ....d.		0925		1345		1815	1825	
8.55	0910			1420	....		1900		✣	d.Chambord............d.				1330			1850	
16.55	1055			1600	....	1940	2045		✣	a.Dolbeau..............d.				1200	1700		1710	

P–⑤ Sept. 1-Apr. 30.   Q–⑦ Sept. 1-Apr. 30.   AJ–Autocars Jasmin. 🚌 Jonquière 547 2167.   AL–Autobus Laterrière. 🚌 Chicoutimi 549 2463.

Table 123 — MONTRÉAL - SHERBROOKE 🚌 AQC LEM

🚌 service Montréal-Sherbrooke and v.v. 159 km. Journey: 2½-3 hours. Fare: CA $: 16.95.
From Montréal: AQC at 0645ex⑥⑦, 0730ex⑦, 0900, 1000⑥, 1100, 1300, 1305, 1500, 1600, 1700, 1800⑤⑦, 1830, 1900⑤⑦, 2000, 2100, 2330; LEM at 0945⑥, 1225⑤, 1500⑦, 1610①-④, 1710⑤.
From Sherbrooke: AQC at 0600ex⑦, 0800, 0845, 1000, 1100, 1255, 1300, 1500, 1600, 1700, 1730, 1800⑤⑦, 1900⑦, 2000, 2045⑤⑦, 2230; LEM at 0800①-④, 1200⑦, 1300⑥, 1750⑤⑦.
AQC– Autobus Auger Estrie Inc. 🚌 Chateauguay 514 691 1654.   LEM–Autobus Bernier Lemay Inc. Tel.: Acton Vale 514 546 2490.

Table 124 — FREDERICTON - NEWCASTLE 🚌 SMT

A208-

CA $	32			km	↓	↑	33	
0.00	....	1230	....	0	d.Fredericton ......a.		1805	....
	....	1440	....	175	a.Newcastle.........d.		1550	....

SMT– SMT (Eastern) Ltd. 🚌 Moncton 506 859 5100.

KNOW THE LATEST?

For last-minute amendments and updates, see the update notes on pages 56–57.

Table 125 — QUÉBEC - SEPT ÎLES 🚌 ICR LIT

CA $		LIT 1 ⑥	LIT 1 ⑥	ICR 1 ④	LIT 1 ④	ICR 3 ⑤	ICR 5 ⑦	ICR 7 ex⑤⑦	ICR 11
	km ↓								
0.00 Québec ....d.	0	....	....	0920	....	1300	1430	1500	1830
4.60 La Malbaie ....d.	143	....	....	1210	....	1455	1635	1710	2110
7.75 St. Siméon ....d.	177	....	....	1242	....				2140
3.15 Tadoussac ....d.	215	....	....	1345	....				2235
Les Escoumins ....d.	259	....	....	1428	....				2311
2.95 Forestville ....d.	313	....	....	1515	....	1735			0000
6.60 Baie Comeau ....d.	417	1300	....	1705	1730	1850			0129
5.50 Godbout ....d.	467	1345	....		1815				
17.25 Port Cartier ....d.	579	1545	....		2015				
22.55 Sept Îles ....d.	634	1630	1700		2110				
Magpie ....d.			1905						
39.80 Mingan ....d.	814		1940						
44.10 Havre St. Pierre ...d.	849		2010						

	ICR 2 ex⑦	ICR 4 ④	LIT 1 ⑥	LIT 6 ⑦	ICR 8 ④	LIT 1 ⑤	LIT 1 ⑤	ICR 10 ⑤	ICR 12 ⑤
↓									
Havre St. Pierre ...d.					0800				
Mingan ....d.					0830				
Magpie ....d.					0910				
Sept Îles ....d.			0800		1100	1230			
Port Cartier ....d.			0845			1330			
Godbout ....d.			1040			1515			
Baie Comeau ....d.		0800	1140	1215		1610			1930
Forestville ....d.		0940		1347					2055
Les Escoumins .....d.		1025		1433					2135
Tadoussac ....d.		1110		1514					2205
St. Siméon ....d.		1200		1600					2250
La Malbaie ....d.	0740	1320		1720	1720			2025	2330
Québec ....a.	0955	1535		1935	1935			2235	0120

$ — Fare ex Baie Comeau. *ICR*–Intercar. Tel.: Jonquière 418 547 2167.
T– Autobus du Littoral. ☎Sept Îles 962 2126.

Table 126 — CHICOUTIMI - TADOUSSAC 🚌 ATT

🚌 service Chicoutimi-Tadoussac and v.v. *140* km. Journey 1³/₄ hours. Fare CA $: ❖.
From Chicoutimi: 1120.   From Tadoussac: 1520.

ATT –Autobus Tremblay & Tremblay. Tel.: Chicoutimi 549 2463.

Table 130 — MONTRÉAL - RIMOUSKI 🚌 OEX

CA $	3	227	31		33	37	243		km ↓		150	160	132		66	136		130
									0	d.Montréal ....d.						2035		0610
	....	0930			....	2230	....			d. Québec ....a.	1030	1430	1325		1725			
	1045		1300		1600	0100			259	d.Lévis ....d.	0950	1350				1755		0220
8.10	1125	1210			1640	0135			314	d.Montmagny ....d.	0910	1305				1635		0050
2.15	1315	1315			1730	0205	0215		449	d.Rivière du Loup ...d.	0725	1100	1105		1505	1505		0013
9.00	1420	1450	1520		2010	0355	0355		❖	d.Trois Pistoles .....d.	0648	0951				1423		0013
❖					2046				559	a.Rimouski ....d.	0600	0855	0930		1335	1335		2325
2.05		1610	1640		2140	0515	0515											

OEX–Orléans Express Inc. Tel.: Montréal 514 847 4000.

Table 131 — RIMOUSKI - GASPÉ 🚌 OEX SMT

CA $	143	39			129	127	111		km ↓	OEX ↑		32	70	236		34	230
0.00	0600	0615	....	....	1720	1720	1730		0	d.Rimouski ....a.	....	0844	1235	1245	....	2250	2255
	0633	0646	....	....		1757			32	d.Mont Joli ....d.	....	0810	1156	1215	....	2218	2225
	0743		....	....	1830	1905			94	d. Matane ....d.	....	0710		1115	....		2125
	0857		....	....		2019			182	a. Ste. Anne des Monts d.				0955			2005
		0903							192	d.Matapédia ....d.						2001	
		1050a							213	a. Campbellton ......d.						1845a	
		1425				0035			471	a.Percé ....d.			0535			1445	
	1255	1515			2340	0125			391	a.Gaspé ....d.			0445	0640		1350	1605

–SMT..   OEX–Orléans Express Inc. Tel.: Montréal 514 847 4000.   *SMT*–SMT (Eastern) Ltd. Tel.: Moncton 506 859 5100.

Table 132 — HALIFAX - SYDNEY/YARMOUTH 🚌 ALL

CA $	53	37	47L	63L	41L	61L	35	55	45	75	55		21		km ↓	↑	56 ①-③	56 ✗	36		22	72	46	64L	42L	38	22A		54	76 ⑧
0.00	0800	0800	0815	1300	1300	1330	1415	1645		1730			1815		0	d.Halifax ......a.		1105	1110		1235	1445		1715	1800	1945	2150		2150	0010
6.75	0955		0935		1415	1450	1830	1840	1845	1845					93	d.Truro ....d.	0915	0920			1335	1420	1605	1655					2010	2305
1.00	1100				1605			1935	2001						156	d.New Glasgow ..d.	0755				1230		1510						1855	2215
4.75	1220			1600	1720			2030	2045						214	d.Antigonish ...d.	0700				1140		1420						1800	2130
3.75	1335				1820			2125							277	d.Port Hawkesbury .d.					1025								1625	2030
3.50				1835	2056			2325							428	d.North Sydney ..d.					0755		1125							1825
5.50	1550			1900	2130			2345							450	a.Sydney ....d.					0730		1100						1415	1800
5.50		1120		1605			2125								225	a. Amherst ......d.							1135		1455					
5.00		0915					1533						1915		69	d. Windsor ......d.			0945		1140				1830	2055				
4.00		1016					1639						2005		111	d. Kentville .....d.			0840		1050				1737	2005				
4.50		1240											2135		211	d. Annapolis Royal..d.					0910				1508	1825				
3.75		1323											2210		245	d. Digby ....d.					0840				1425	1755				
9.25													0005		352	a. Yarmouth .....d.					0645				1600					

LL– Acadian Lines. Tel.: Halifax 902 453 0353.

Table 127 — MONCTON - EDMUNDSTON 🚌 SMT

CA $	30	32			km ↓	↑	31	33
0.00	1020	1630	....	....	0	d.Saint John ....a.	1240	2000
9.75	1200	1810	....	....	108	a.Fredericton ....d.	1100	1820

CA $	23	25			km ↓	↑	20	22
0.00	....	1045	1745	....	0	d.Moncton ....a.	1300	1715
7.00	....	1155	....	....	76	d.Sussex ....d.		1615
16.75	....	1415	2005	....	194	d.Fredericton ....d.	1050	1430
26.25	....	1540	2130	....	300	d.Woodstock ....d.	0920	1240
28.00	....	1725	....	....	423	d.Grand Falls ....d.		1050
32.00	....	1820	2340	....	487	a.Edmundston ....d.	0700	1000

SMT– SMT (Eastern) Ltd. ☎ Moncton 506 859 5100.

Table 128 — CAMPBELLTON - MONCTON 🚌 SMT

CA $	30	41			km ↓	↑	40	33
0.00	....	1215			0	d.Campbellton ....a.	1825	....
❖	....	1415			❖	d.Bathurst ....d.	1640	....
16.75	1450				182	d. Newcastle ....d.		1545
17.25	1505	1520			188	d.Chatham ....d.	1530	1530
25.00	....	1725			346	a.Moncton ....d.	1305	

SMT–SMT (Eastern) Ltd. Tel.: Moncton 506 859 5100.

Table 129 — PRINCE EDWARD ISLAND 🚌 IT

CA $		ex③⑦	Y	km ↓	↑	P ex③⑦	W ex③⑦	Y	
14.40		....	1425	104	d. New Glasgow ......a.	....	1400		
7.00	0730	....		80	d. Souris ....d.			1935	
0.00	0845	1600	1730	0	d Charlottetown ......d.	1015	1115	1045	1800
8.15		1720		71	d.Summerside ....d.	0905	1005		
12.00		1900		153	a.Tignish ....d.	0700	0800		

P–May 29-Oct. 28.   *W*–Oct. 30-May 26.   *Y*–May 29-Oct. 9.   *IT*–Island Transit. Tel.: Charlottetown 902 368 5100.

Table 133 — TORONTO - PEMBROKE 🚌 VCL

CA $	126		km ↓	↑	127 ex⑦	129 ⑦
0.00	....	1245	0	d.Toronto ....a.	1545	2010
	....	1345	64	d.Oshawa ....d.		1913
17.50	....	1515	88	d.Peterborough....d.	1350	1800
19.50	....	2005	410	a.Pembroke ....d.	0840	1300

VCL– Voyageur Colonial Ltd. Tel.: Ottawa 613 238 5900.

Table 134 — THETFORD MINES 🚌 DRU

🚌 service Montréal-St. Hyacinthe-Drummondville-Victoriaville-Thetford Mines and v.v. ❖ km. Journey 3½ hours. Fare CA $: ❖.
From Montréal: 1010, 1715ex⑦, 1815⑤, 2010⑦.
From Thetford Mines: 0715, 1630ex⑦, 1830⑦.

DRU–Autobus Drummondville Ltée. Tel.: Drummondville 477 2111.

Table 135 — HALIFAX - YARMOUTH 🚌 MKB

CA $	12	4B ✗	4 ⑤	4A ✗		km ↓	↑	1 ✗	1A ✗	13 ①	19 ⑦
0.00	0900	1745	1745	1745		0	d.Halifax ....a.	0815	1115	1415	1945
5.50	0935			1840		52	d.Hubbards............d.	0735	1020	1335	1905
7.00	0955			1855		71	d.Chester ....d.		1005		
9.50	1015			1920		97	d.Mahone Bay ....d.	0715	0940	1315	1845
10.00	1030			1935		107	d.Lunenburg ....d.		0925		
11.00	1110	1910	1915	1955		129	d.Bridgewater.........d.	0700	0900	1305	1830
15.00	1150		2000			177	d.Liverpool............d.		1215	1730	
20.50	1300		2045			241	d.Shelburne ....d.		1115	1630	
21.50	1340					281	d.Barrington Passage..d.		1025	1540	
26.00	1455					355	a.Yarmouth ....d.		0915	1430	

MKB–Mackenzie Bus Line. Tel.: Bridgewater 902 543 2491.

Table 136 — CHARLOTTETOWN 🚌 SMT

CA$	50 ⑤⑦	52		km ↓		↑	51	53 ⑥⑦
0.00	0745	1230	....	0	d.**Charlottetown**........a.		1745	2115
5.00	0850	1335	....	60	d.Summerside....d.		1650	2020
7.25	0910	1355	....	84	d.Borden........d.		1630	2000
10.00			....	100	d.Cape Tormentine...d.			
12.00	1110		....	152	a. Amherst ....d.			
17.00	1220	1630	....	218	a.**Moncton**........d.		1400	1745

SMT– SMT (Eastern) Ltd. ☎ Moncton 506 859 5100.

Table 137 — FORTUNE 🚌 SPM

CA$	W 🚫			km ↓		↑	W 🚫
0.00	0800	....	....	0	d.**St. John's**........a.		1730
❖	1230	....	....	247	a.**Fortune**........d.		1300

W– June 28-Sept. 2.
SPM– SPM Tours. Tel.: St. John's 709 722 3892.

Table 138 — QUÉBEC - WHITE RIVER 🚌 AQC VT

US$	VT 9096	AQC 2 ex⑦	AQC 12		km ↓		↑	AQC 1	AQC 13	VT 9093 ex⑦
80.45	....	0750	1815	....	0	d.**Québec** ◇ ....a.		1145	2200	....
50.00	....	1117	2207	....	228	d.**Sherbrooke** ◇....a.d.		0750	1820	....
41.00	0735	....	....	....	311	d.Newport........d.				1940
36.00	0845	....	....	....	387	d.St. Johnsbury ....d.				1830
26.00	1025	....	....	....	495	d.**White River Junction**...d.				1700

◇– Additional trips from Québec: 1335, 1630⑤, 1745⑤, 2030†, returning from Sherbrooke at 1320, 1630⑦.
AQC– Autobus Auger Inc. ☎ Chateauguay 514 691 1654.
VT– Vermont Transit. Tel.: Burlington 802 864 6811.

Table 139 — ST. JOHN'S - BONAVISTA 🚌 CL NH

CA$		NH	CL		km ↓		↑	CL ex⑦	NH	CL ⑦
❖	....	❖	1700	....	0	d.**St. John's**........a.		1145	1545	....
❖	....	....	1805	....	84	d.Whitbourne Junction d.		1020	1420	....
0.00	....	2000	2015	....	185	d.Clarenville ....d.		0830	0930	1230
4.00	....	2125		....	242	d.Trinity ....d.			0825	
7.00	....	2215	2215	....	328	d.**Bonavista**........d.		0600	0730	1000
	....			....	129	a. Carbonear........d.				

CL–Clarenville Transportation. Tel.: Clarenville 463 2492. *NH*–Newhook's Bus Service.
Tel.: Argentia ❖.

Table 140 — DARTMOUTH 🚌 MT

🚌 service (route **11**) Halifax-Dartmouth and v.v. 3 km. Journey: 15 mins. Fare: CA$:
1.00.
From Halifax: 0600☼/0645† and frequent to 0001①/0030ex①.
From Dartmouth: 0608☼/0653† and frequent to 0016①/0021⑦/0023ex①⑦.

MT– Metro Transit. Tel.: Halifax 421 6600.

Table 141 — TERRENCEVILLE 🚌

CA$				km ↓		↑		
0.00	....	❖	....	0	d.**Terrenceville** ....a.		❖	....
❖	....	❖	....		a.**St. John's**........d.		❖	....

Table 142 — ARGENTIA 🚌 NH

CA$	☼	†	⑦		km ↓		↑		†	
0.00	0800	1400	....	1830	0	d.**Argentia** ....a.		1115	1915	
❖	0845	1445	....	1915		a.**Whitbourne** ....d.		1020	1820	

NH– Newhook's Bus Service. Tel.: Argentia ❖.

Table 143 — NEWFOUNDLAND ♿ 🚌 CN

CA$	519 ④⑤⑦	503		km ↓		↑	504	522 P
0.00	1730	0800	....	0	d.**St. John's**........a.		2205	....
12.50	1845	0915	....	84	d.Whitbourne Junction d.		2100	....
24.25	2015	1045	....	187	d.Clarenville ....d.		1930	....
37.25	2215	1300	....	331	d.**Gander Airport**....d.		1725	....
44.25	2310		....	392	d.Lewisporte ....d.			....
44.25	2350	1410	....	414	d.Bishop's Falls ....d.		1550	....
46.00	0005	1440	....	428	d.Grand Falls ....d.		1535	....
47.25		1500	....	457	d.Badger ....d.		1500	....
60.75		1720	....	639	d.Deer Lake ....d.		1240	....
64.25		1825	....	687	d.Corner Brook ....d.		1200	1730
≤22.50		1930	....	761	d.Stephenville........d.		1030	1625
79.75		2205	....	904	a.**Port aux Basques**....d.		0800	1400

P–Runs on † (except on ⑦ of holiday weekends). ○–Windsor. ≤–Fare ex Port aux
Basques. *CN*–CN Roadcruiser. Tel.: St. John's 709 737 5912.

Table 145 — ST. ANTHONY - CORNER BROOK 🚌 VE

CA$		②④⑦			km ↓		↑	①③⑤	
0.00	....	1100	....	0	d.**St. Anthony** ....a.		0000	....
❖	....	1140	....		d.St. Barbe ....d.		2135	....
❖	....	1610	....	285	d.Deer Lake ....d.		1650	....
❖	....		....	333	a.**Corner Brook** ....d.			....

VE– Viking Express. Tel.: St Barbe 877 2314.

Table 146 — MONTRÉAL - BOSTON 🚌 GL VT

US$	VT 9424	VT 9124	VT 9098 ⑧	VT 9128		km ↓		↑	VT 9127 ex⑦	VT 9129 ♣	VT 9321	VT 9523
0.00		0730b		0945b		0	d.**Montréal** ....a.		1830b			
13.00						118	d.St. Albans 🚉 ....d.		1620b			
19.00	0820	1310	1430	1715		170	d.Burlington ....d.		0700	1510	1915	2330
24.00	0915	1235	1525	1810		231	d.Montpelier ....d.		0605	1410	1820	2235
25.00				1830		242	d.Barre ....d.		0545			
33.00	1040	1400	1700	1945		330	d.White River Junction d.		0445	1300	1710	2130
41.00			1825			418	d.Concord ....d.					
43.00	1215	1520	1850	2110		446	d.Manchester ....d.		0220	1105	1505	1940
50.00			1920			474	d.Nashua ....d.					1915
50.00						508	d.Lowell ....d.					
53.00	1320	1630	2015	2105		560	a.**Boston** ....d.		0115	1000	1400	1815
53.00	1345					567	a.Boston Airport ≪....d.					

b–GL. ≪–Logan Airport. *GL*–Greyhound Lines. Tel.: Dallas 214 744 6500. *VT*–
Vermont Transit. Tel.: Burlington 802 862 9671.

Table 147 — BURGEO 🚌 DBS

CA$		☼			km ↓		↑	☼	
0.00	....	0800	....	0	d.**Burgeo** ....a.		1800	....
25.00	....	1100	....	211	a.**Corner Brook** ....d.		1500	....

DBS– Devins/Vineys Bus Services. Tel.: Burgeo ❖.

Table 148 — HARBOUR BRETON 🚌 HBS

CA$		①③⑤			km ↓		↑	①③⑤	
0.00	....	0800	....	0	d.**Harbour Breton** ....a.		1900	....
25.00	....	1100	....		a.**Grand Falls** ....d.		1600	....

HBS– Hickeys Bus Service. Tel.: Harbour Breton ❖.

Table 149 — SAINT JOHN - AMHERST 🚌 SMT

CA $	10	12		km ↓		↑	11	13
0.00	1030	1515	....	0	d.**Saint John** ....a.		1525	2005
	1135	1620	....	69	d.Sussex ....d.		1425	1905
	1345	1800	....	146	d.Moncton ....d.		1315	1755
	1445	1900	....	215	a.**Amherst** ....d.		1130	1615

SMT– SMT (Eastern) Ltd. ☎ Moncton 506 859 5100.

Table 150 — SUDBURY - OTTAWA - MONTRÉAL 🚌 GLC VCL

CA $	VCL 104 ex⑦	VCL 106 ⑦	GLC 2768	VCL 222 ⑤⑦	GLC 2762	GLC 2764	GLC 2782		km			VCL 127	GLC 2777	VCL 103	VCL 207	VCL 113 ⑤⑦	VCL 119	VCL 121 ⑤
0.00			0930	....	1340	1830	....	0001	0	d.**Sudbury** ....a.		0645a	....	1220	....	1805a	1900a	....
			1140b	....	1630b	2020	....	0145b	124	d.North Bay ....d.		0500a	....	1030	....	1610a	1720a	2350
63.96	0810	1240	1455b	2010	2010b		....	0450b	341	d.Pembroke ....d.		0145	....	1230	....	1410	1835	2000 2045
	1045	1515	1715b	2220	2220b		....	0650b	502	a.**Ottawa** ≠ ....d.		2345	....	1000	....	1200 1630	1725 1825	....
83.30			2020b		0155b		....	1020b	700	a.**Montréal** ≠ ....d.		2100	....	0700	....	0900		

a–GLC. *b*–VCL. ≠–Local VCL services operate between Montréal and Ottawa throughout the day, from Montréal at 0001, 0600⑥, 0700 and hourly to 2200, returning at 0600☼, 0700 and
hourly to 2200, 2330. *GLC*–Greyhound Lines of Canada. Tel.: Winnipeg 204 783 8840. *VCL*–Voyageur Colonial. Tel.: Ottawa 613 238 5900.

Table 151 — EDMUNDSTON 🚌 SMT

CA $	20	24	26		km			21	23	25
0.00	0410	1530	2015		0	d.**Rivière du Loup** a.		1050	1950	0030
	0545	1820	2305		125	a.**Edmundston** ....d.		0850	1750	2355

SMT– SMT (Eastern) Ltd. Tel.: Moncton 506 859 5100.

Table 152 — MONTRÉAL - NEWPORT 🚌 AVI

CA $	1 ♠⑥	13	5/7	9		km ↓		↑	2 ♠⑥	6	14 ♣	8
0.00	1020	1100	1810	2115		0	d.**Montréal** ....a.		0920	1705	1705	2015
	1230	1310	2020	2325		131	d.Knowlton ....d.		0710	1455	1455	1805
	1255	1335	2045a			159	d.Mansonville ....d.			1430	1430	1740
	1302					165	d.Highwater 🚉 ....d.			1423		
	1335					187	a.**Newport** ....d.			1350		

a– ⑤ only.
AVI– Autobus Viens Inc. Tel.: Farnham 514 293 3129.

THOMAS COOK TRAVELLERS

This series of 192-page compact (192mm x 130mm) guides, each fully illustrated in colour and with completely new research and mapping, has been created for the holidaymaker of the 1990s by Thomas Cook Publishing and leading guidebook publishers AA Publishing..

Features include:

★ Facts at your fingertips ★ Background information on history, politics and culture ★ Descriptions of major sights plus snippets about lesser known places ★ A 'get-away-from-it-all' section ★ A street-by-street shopping and entertainment guide ★ An A-Z help list packed with practical information ★ Tips on 'finding your feet' ★ Up to 10 city walks or excursions with full-colour maps ★ Superb value for money – £10-worth for only £6.99!

These books contain not only a conventional guide to the sights of the cities and countries, but everything the traveller needs to know, and are presented in a way that is accessible, concise and innovative. The series reflects on every page Thomas Cook's depth of expertise on the destinations and on the subjects that are of most interest and concern to today's travellers.

Titles in the series (☆ denotes new title for 1994):

☐ ALGARVE   ☐ AMSTERDAM   ☆ BELGIUM   ☆ BOSTON & NEW ENGLAND   ☐ CALIFORNIA   ☐ CYPRUS
☆ EASTERN CARIBBEAN   ☆ EGYPT   ☆ FLORENCE & TUSCANY   ☐ FLORIDA   ☆ IRELAND
☆ KENYA   ☐ LONDON   ☆ MALTA   ☆ MUNICH & BAVARIA   ☐ NEW YORK   ☐ PARIS   ☆ PRAGUE
☆ SINGAPORE & MALAYSIA   ☐ SYDNEY & NEW SOUTH WALES   ☐ THAILAND   ☆ TURKEY
☐ VANCOUVER & BRITISH COLUMBIA   ☐ VIENNA

Available at £6.99 each from all good UK high-street bookshops or from many Thomas Cook outlets in the UK.

Also obtainable by post at £7.99 (UK), £9.50 (Europe), £10.70 (overseas air mail) from Thomas Cook Publishing (TPO/FA), P.O. Box 227, Thorpe Wood, PETERBOROUGH PE3 6SB, UK.
☎ (0733) 505821/268943. Fax: (0733) 267052.

UNITED STATES OF AMERICA

Rail services in the USA are provided mainly by the National Railroad Passenger Corporation, trading as AMTRAK. Suburban services, in general, are *not* operated by AMTRAK, and on common sections of route, fares are usually different and tickets are not interavailable. AMTRAK trains offer one basic class of accommodation - coach class, shown as 'C' in the following tables. Supplements are payable for superior accommodation, such as overnight sleeping accommodation or club car (parlor car) seats, which are shown as 'S' or 'P' in the tables. Some trains convey 'Slumbercoaches' (high-density sleeping cars) and these are shown as ◄ in the tables. Metroliners, high-speed trains operating generally between New York and Washington, charge higher basic fares, and a further supplement is payable for travel by 'Metroclub'. A few trains, on selected routes, include 'Custom Class' - a high quality coach class for which a small premium is paid. Where available this will be shown as '1' class. Children of under 2 years travel free; those of 2 but under 12 years pay 50% of basic coach fare (but full accommodation charges); those of 12 and over pay full fare. Children below 12 years are not generally permitted to travel unaccompanied, whilst those who are must pay full fare. A network of excellent bus services, usually air-conditioned, operates throughout the country.

Table 180 — NIGHT OWL — ####### NRPC
SUMMARY TABLE

	arr	dep		arr	dep		
A	67	....	2220	Boston South 202	0839	....	↑	B
A	↓	2319	2319	Providence 202	0738	0738	↑	B
A	↓	0128	0143	New Haven 202	0454	0518	↑	B
B	↓	0316	0345	New York Penn. Stn. 202	0217	0315	↑	B
B	↓	0524	0542	Philadelphia 30th Street 213	0024	0031	↑	B
B	↓	0711	0711	Baltimore Penn. Stn 213	2258	2258	↑	A
B	↓	0755	....	Washington Union 213	....	2210	66	A

ex ⑤⑥+🍴▮🚻, 🚻 and 🖭 Washington(66/67)-Boston and v.v.
▮🚻 Washington(866/7)-New York and v.v. See Table 213 for full details.
+–   For weekend service, see Trains 76/77 on Tables 202 and 213.
NRPC–National Railroad Passenger Corporation (AMTRAK). Tel.: New York 212 582 6875.

Table 182 — SILVER METEOR — ####### NRPC
SUMMARY TABLE

	arr	dep		arr	dep		
A	87	....	1830	New York Penn. Stn. 222	1125	....	↑	B
A	↓	2037u	2037u	Philadelphia 30th Street 222	0913s	0933s	↑	B
A	↓	2209u	2209u	Baltimore Penn. Stn. 222	0740s	0740s	↑	B
A	↓	2255u	2325u	Washington Union 222	0615s	0615s	↑	B
B	↓	0125	0135	Richmond 222	0404	0415	↑	B
B	↓	0804	0804	Charleston 222	2103	2103	↑	A
B	↓	0951	1001	Savannah 222	1917	1927	↑	A
B	↓	1223	1318	Jacksonville 222	1618	1703	↑	A
B	↓	1623	1623	Orlando 222	1316	1316	↑	A
B	↓	1807	1825	Tampa 222	1100	1130	88	A
B	↓	1855	....	St. Petersburg 222 ▼	....	1030	↑	A
B	97	↓	1258	Jacksonville 222	1624	....	↑	A
B	↓	1442	1442	Ocala 222	1416	1416	↑	A
B	↓	1852	1852	West Palm Beach 222	1004	1004	↑	A
B	↓	1947	1947	Fort Lauderdale 222	0906	0906	↑	A
B	↓	2055		Miami 222	....	0830	98	A

Daily: 🍴▮ and 🖭 New York(87/88)-Tampa and v.v.▮.
🍴▮ and 🖭 and 🖭 New York(87/88)-Jacksonville(97/98)-Miami and v.v. ▮.
🍴 Jacksonville(87/88)-Tampa and v.v.
▼–   Connection by 🚌.
NRPC–National Railroad Passenger Corporation (AMTRAK). Tel.: New York 212 582 6875.

Table 181 — MAPLE LEAF — ####### NRPC VIA
SUMMARY TABLE

	arr	dep		arr	dep		
A	97	....	0930	Toronto Union 17	1914	....	↑	A
A	↓	1124	1130	Niagara Falls Canada 17 🚻	1610	1715	↑	A
A	64	1305	1305	Niagara Falls USA 215 🚻	1600	1600	98	A
A	↓	1352	1352	Buffalo Depew 215	1502	1502	↑	A
A	↓	1840	1905	Albany Rensselaer 207	0950	1015	↑	A
A	↓	2140	....	New York Penn. Stn. 207	....	0715	63	A

Daily: 🖭 and 🖭 Toronto(97)-Niagara Falls(64)-New York.
🖭 and 🖭 New York(63)-Niagara Falls(98)-Toronto.
NRPC–National Railroad Passenger Corporation (AMTRAK). Tel.: New York 212 582 6875.
VIA–   VIA Rail. Tel.: Toronto 366 8411.

U.S.A. BY RAIL

From New York to the Pacific, from the Mexican border to polar bear country, more people each year are experiencing North America by train. There's no better way to see the sights, meet new people, and broaden your horizons – all for an amazingly low price.

Obtainable by post at £12.90 (U.K.), £13.50 (Europe), £15.30 (overseas air mail) from Thomas Cook Publishing (TPO/FA), P.O. Box 227, PETERBOROUGH PE3 6SB, U.K.

☎(0733) 505821/268943.
Fax: (0733) 267052.

Table 183 — CITY OF NEW ORLEANS
SUMMARY TABLE

	arr	dep		arr	dep	
A	59	1950	Chicago Union **240**...............	0903	.... ↑	B
A	↓ 2227	2227	Champaign Urbana **240**	0615	0615 ↑	B
B	↓ 0125	0145	Carbondale **240**...............	0253	0313 ↑	B
B	↓ 0612	0627	Memphis **240**...............	2213	2228 ↑	A
B	↓ 1030	1030	Jackson **240**...............	1821	1821 ↑	A
B	↓ 1418	....	New Orleans **240**...............	....	1440 58	A

Daily: 🛏‡, 🛏‡, 🍽 and ⊗ New Orleans(**58/59**)-Chicago and v.v.🚭.
NRPC–National Railroad Passenger Corporation (AMTRAK). Tel.: Chicago 312 558 1075.

Table 184 — SILVER STAR
SUMMARY TABLE

	arr	dep		arr	dep	
A	81	0942	New York Penn. Stn. **222**...............	2006	.... ↑	B
A	↓ 1130u	1137u	Philadelphia 30th Street **222**	1755s	1810s ↑	B
A	↓ 1311u	1311u	Baltimore Penn. Stn. **222**	1618s	1618s ↑	B
B	↓ 1412u	1445u	Washington Union **222**	1445s	1540s ↑	B
A	↓ 1650	1705	Richmond **222**...............	1225	1240 ↑	B
A	↓ 2042	2042	Raleigh **222**...............	0855	0855 ↑	B
B	↓ 0033	0033	Columbia **222**...............	0455	0455 ↑	B
B	↓ 0255	0305	Savannah **222**...............	0219	0229 ↑	B
B	↓ 0523	0538	Jacksonville **222**...............	2350	2359 ↑	A
B	↓ 0845	0845	Orlando **222**...............	2038	2038 ↑	A
B	↓ 0903	0903	Kissimmee **222**...............	1957	2000 ↑	A
B	↓ 1107	1115	Tampa **222**...............	1750	1822 82	A
B	↓ 1145	....	St. Petersburg **222** ◇	....	1720 ↑	A
B	91	0903	Kissimmee **222**...............	1958	.... ↑	A
B	↓ 1224	1224	West Palm Beach **222**	1655	1655 ↑	A
B	↓ 1317	1317	Fort Lauderdale **222**	1600	1600 ↑	A
B	↓ 1400	....	Miami **222**...............	....	1525 92	A

Daily: 🛏‡, 🍽 and ⊗ New York(**81/82**)-Kissimmee(**91/92**)-Miami and v.v.🚭.
🛏‡, 🛏‡, 🍽 and 🍽 New York(**81/82**)-Tampa and v.v.🚭.
◇– By 🚌.
NRPC–National Railroad Passenger Corporation (AMTRAK). Tel.: New York 212 582 6875.

Table 185 — BROADWAY LIMITED
SUMMARY TABLE

	arr	dep		arr	dep	
A	41	1245	New York Penn. Stn. **218**...............	1750	.... ↑	B
A	↓ 1431u	1457u	Philadelphia 30th Street **218**	1529s	1529s ↑	B
A	↓ 1655	1710	Harrisburg **218**...............	1315	1325 ↑	B
A	↓ 2242	2302	Pittsburgh **225**...............	0725	0740 ↑	B
B	↓ 0232	0232	Akron **225**...............	0325	0325 ↑	B
B	↓ 0814	....	Chicago Union **225**...............	....	2015 40	A

Daily: 🛏‡, 🍴‡, 🚌 and 🍽 Chicago(**40/41**)-New York and v.v.🚭.
NRPC–National Railroad Passenger Corporation (AMTRAK). Tel.: New York 212 582 6875.

Table 186 — LAKE SHORE LIMITED
SUMMARY TABLE

	arr	dep		arr	dep	
A	49	1910	New York Penn. Stn. **207**...............	1449	.... ↑	B
A	↓ 2153	....	Albany Rensselaer **207**	....	1150 48	B
A	449	1620	Boston South **200**...............	1650	.... ↑	B
A	↓ 1835	1845	Springfield **200**...............	1420	1430 ↑	B
A	↓ 2115	....	Albany Rensselaer **200**	....	1200 448	B
A	49	2223	Albany Rensselaer **215**	1117	.... ↑	B
B	↓ 0321	0351	Buffalo Depew **215**	0602	0617 ↑	B
B	↓ 0656	0706	Cleveland **215**...............	0251	0301 ↑	B
B	↓ 0909	0934	Toledo **215**...............	0026	0049 ↑	B
B	↓ 1258	....	Chicago Union **215**...............	....	1915 48	A

Daily: 🛏‡, 🚌 and 🍽 Chicago(**48/49**)-New York and v.v.🚭.
🛏‡, 🍴‡ and 🚌 Chicago(**48/49**)-Albany(**448/9**)-Boston and v.v.🚭.
⊗ Albany(**448/9**)-Boston and v.v.
NRPC–National Railroad Passenger Corporation (AMTRAK). Tel.: New York 212 582 6875.

Table 187 — SOUTHWEST CHIEF
SUMMARY TABLE

	arr	dep		arr	dep	
A	3	1700	Chicago Union **236**...............	1525	.... ↑	C
B	↓ 0045	0105	Kansas City **236**...............	0645	0705 ↑	C
B	↓ 0227	0227	Topeka **236**...............	0443	0443 ↑	C
B	↓ 1655	1715	Albuquerque **248**...............	1255	1315 ↑	B
B	↓ 2115	2115	Flagstaff **248**...............	0625	0625 ↑	B
C	↓ 0715	0715	Fullerton **248**...............	2050	2050 ↑	A
C	↓ 0815	....	Los Angeles **248**...............	....	2015 4	A

Daily: 🛏‡, entertainment car (‡), 🚌 and 🍽 Chicago(**3/4**)-Los Angeles and v.v.🚭.
NRPC–National Railroad Passenger Corporation (AMTRAK). Tel.: Chicago 312 558 1075.

Table 188 — THE TEXAS EAGLE ♿
SUMMARY TABLE

	arr	dep		arr	dep	
A	21	1745	Chicago Union **238**...............	1335	.... ↑	D
A/B	↓ 2330	0015	St Louis **238**...............	0655	0735 ↑	D
B	↓ 0723	0723	Little Rock **243**...............	2337	2337 ↑	C
B	↓ 1424	....	Dallas **243**...............	....	1605 22	C
B	521	1515	Dallas **243**...............	1505	.... ↑	C
B	↓ 2200	....	Houston **243**...............	....	0825 522	C
B	21	1449	Dallas **243**...............	1600	.... ↑	C
B	↓ 1612	1632	Fort Worth **243**...............	1410	1430 ↑	C
B	↓ 1912	1912	Temple **243**...............	1130	1130 ↑	C
B	↓ 2107	2107	Austin **243**...............	0935	0935 ↑	C
B/C	↓ 2340	0255	San Antonio **243**...............	0525	0705 22	C
C	↓ 1325	1345	El Paso **244**...............	1640	1700 ↑	D
C	↓ 1755	1755	Tucson **258**...............	0935	0935 ↑	B
C	↓ 2140	2140	Phoenix **258**...............	0708	0708 ↑	B
D	↓ 0048	0048	Yuma **258**...............	0258	0258 ↑	B
D	↓ 0615	....	Los Angeles **258**...............	....	2230 2	A

Runs daily from Chicago to St Louis and v.v.; ①③⑥ (②⑤⑦ from Chicago) from St Louis to Los
Angeles; ②③⑦ from Los Angeles (②④⑦ from San Antonio) to St Louis and Chicago.
①③⑥: ⊗ Dallas(**521**)-Houston
①③④⑥: 🚌 and 🍽 Chicago(**21**)-St Louis.
②④⑦: 🛏‡ and 🚌 Houston(**522**)-Dallas(**22**)-Chicago.
⊗ Houston(**522**)-Dallas.
🍽 San Antonio(**22**)-Chicago.
🍽 San Antonio(**1**)-Los Angeles.
②④⑥⑦: 🍽 St Louis(**22**)-Chicago.
②⑤⑦: 🛏‡, entertainment car (‡) and 🚌 Chicago(**21**)-San Antonio(**1**)-Los Angeles.🚭.
🛏‡, entertainment car (‡) and 🚌 Los Angeles(**2**)-San Antonio(**22**)-Chicago.🚭.
🛏‡ and 🚌 Chicago(**21**)-Dallas(**521**)-Houston.
🍽 Chicago(**21**)-San Antonio. 🍽 Los Angeles(**2**)-San Antonio.
NRPC–National Railroad Passenger Corporation (AMTRAK). Tel.: Chicago 312 558 1075.

Table 189 — CALIFORNIA ZEPHYR ♿
SUMMARY TABLE

	arr	dep		arr	dep	
A	5	1505	Chicago Union **235**...............	1615	.... ↑	C
A	↓ 2335	2359	Omaha **235**...............	0625	0650 ↑	C
B	↓ 0102	0112	Lincoln **245**...............	0515	0525 ↑	C
B	↓ 0810	0910	Denver Union **245**...............	1940	2100 ↑	C
B/C	↓ 2331	0030	Salt Lake City **250**	0345	0505 ↑	A
C	↓ 0936	0936	Reno **250**...............	1640	1640 ↑	A
C	↓ 1430	1435	Sacramento **250**...............	1212	1217 ↑	A
C	↓ 1650	....	Emeryville (Oakland) **250** ℘	....	1010 6	A

Daily: 🛏‡, entertainment car (‡), 🚌 and 🍽 Chicago(**5/6**)-Oakland and v.v.🚭.
🛏‡ and 🚌 Chicago(**5/6**)-Salt Lake City(**35/36**)-Los Angeles and v.v.🚭.
②⑤⑦: 🛏‡ and 🚌 Chicago(**5**)-Denver(**25**)-Seattle.🚭.
①③⑥: 🛏‡ and 🚌 Seattle(**26**)-Denver(**6**)-Chicago.🚭.
℘– Emeryville will open at a date to be announced. Prior to opening trains will continue to
call at the Oakland Wood Street Station.
NRPC–National Railroad Passenger Corporation (AMTRAK). Tel.: Chicago 312 558 1075.

Table 190 — THE CRESCENT
SUMMARY TABLE

	arr	dep		arr	dep	
A	19	1342	New York Penn. Stn. **223**...............	1435	.... ↑	B
A	↓ 1402u	1402u	Newark...............	1411s	1411s ↑	B
A	↓ 1538u	1538u	Philadelphia 30th Street	1227s	1227s ↑	B
A	↓ 1709u	1709u	Baltimore Penn. Stn.	1050s	1050s ↑	B
A	↓ 1810u	1850	Washington Union **223**	0928	0928s ↑	B
A	↓ 2105	2105	Charlottesville Union **223**	0648	0648 ↑	B
A	↓ 2225	2225	Lynchburg **223**...............	0533	0533 ↑	B
B	↓ 0048	0113	Greensboro **223**...............	0255	0315 ↑	A
B	↓ 0258	0258	Charlotte **223**...............	0104	0104 ↑	A
B	↓ 0520	0535	Greenville **223**...............	2240	2255 ↑	A
B	↓ 0830	0845	Atlanta **223**...............	1920	1945 ↑	A
B	↓ 1148	1203	Birmingham **223**...............	1350	1420 ↑	A
B	↓ 1510	1515	Meridian **223**...............	1100	1105 ↑	A
B	↓ 1928	....	New Orleans **223**...............	....	0705 20	A

Daily: 🛏‡, 🚌 and 🍽 New York(**19/20**)-New Orleans and v.v.🚭.
🍴‡ New York(**19/20**)-Atlanta and v.v.
🚌 and 🍽 New York(**19/20**)-Birmingham(**519/520**)-Mobile and v.v.🚭.
NRPC–National Railroad Passenger Corporation (AMTRAK). Tel.: New York 212 585 6875.

Table 191 — THE DESERT WIND ♿
SUMMARY TABLE

	arr	dep		arr	dep	
A	35	0040	Salt Lake City **256**...............	0330	.... ↑	B
A	↓ 0745	0800	Las Vegas **256**...............	1745	1800 ↑	A
A	↓ 1515	....	Los Angeles **256**...............	....	1055 36	A

Daily: 🛏‡, entertainment car (‡), 🚌 and 🍽 Salt Lake City(**35/36**)-Los Angeles and v.v.🚭
🛏‡ and 🚌 Chicago(**5/6**)-Salt Lake City(**35/36**)-Los Angeles and v.v.🚭.
NRPC–National RR Passenger Corporation (AMTRAK). Tel.: Los Angeles 213 624 0171.

Table 192 — COAST STARLIGHT ♿
SUMMARY TABLE

	arr	dep		arr	dep	
A	11	0940	Seattle **264**...............	2010	.... ↑	B
A	↓ 1350	1415	Portland **264**...............	1530	1555 ↑	B
B	↓ 0550	0550	Sacramento **266**...............	2359	2359 ↑	B
B	↓ 0750	0755	Emeryville (Oakland) **266** ℘	2118	2123 ↑	B
B	↓ 0935	0935	San Jose **265**...............	2005	2005 ↑	B
B	↓ 1700	1700	Santa Barbara **265**	1225	1225 ↑	B
B	↓ 2010	....	Los Angeles **265**...............	....	0955 14	A

Daily: 🛏‡, entertainment car (‡), 🚌 and 🍽 Seattle(**11/14**)-Los Angeles and v.v.🚭.
℘– Emeryville will open at a date to be announced. Prior to opening trains will continue
call at the Oakland Wood Street Station.
NRPC–National RR Passenger Corporation (AMTRAK). Tel.: Los Angeles 213 624 0171.

Table 193   SUNSET LIMITED ⑤   ╫╫ NRPC
SUMMARY TABLE

arr	dep		arr	dep		
1	....	1230	Miami 222....................	2250	....	↑ D
↓ 2055	2120	Jacksonville 244...............	1405	1425	↑ D
↓ 1100	1320	New Orleans 244...............	1935	2240	↑ C
↓ 2140	2140	Houston 244...................	1055	1055	↑ C
↓ 0225	0255	San Antonio 244...............	0525	0610	↑ C
↓ 1325	1345	El Paso 244...................	1640	1700	↑ C
↓ 1755	1755	Tucson 258....................	0935	0935	↑ B
↓ 2140	2140	Phoenix 258..................	0708	0708	↑ B
↓ 0048	0048	Yuma 258.....................	0258	0258	↑ B
↓ 0615	....	Los Angeles 258..............	....	2230	2 A

②⑤⑦: ◻╫, entertainment car (‡), ◻◻ and ✕ Miami(1)-Los Angeles.◻.
②, entertainment car (‡), ◻◻ and ✕ Los Angeles(2)-Miami.◻.
NRPC–National Railroad Passenger Corporation (AMTRAK). Tel.: Los Angeles 213 624 0171.

Table 194   EMPIRE BUILDER ⑤   ╫╫ NRPC
SUMMARY TABLE

arr	dep		arr	dep		
7	....	1515	Chicago Union 228.............	1534	....	↑ C
↓ 1651u	1651u	Milwaukee 228................	1356s	1356s	↑ C
↓ 2340	2359	Minneapolis/St. Paul 228......	0650	0720	↑ C
↓ 0443	0443	Fargo 241....................	0128	0128	↑ C
↓ 1600	1600	Havre 241....................	1225	1225	↑ B
↓ 0150	0215	Spokane 241..................	0005	0040	↑ B
↓ 1025	....	Seattle 260..................	....	1650	8 A
↓ 27	....	0225	Spokane 260..................	2330	....	↑ A
↓ 0955	....	Portland 260.................	....	1625	28 A

Daily: ◻╫, ◻◻ and ✕ Chicago(7/8)-Seattle and v.v.◻.
◻╫, entertainment car (‡) and ◻◻ Chicago(7/8)-Spokane(27/28)-Portland and v.v.◻.
Ⓧ Spokane(27/28)-Portland and v.v.
NRPC–National Railroad Passenger Corporation (AMTRAK). Tel: Chicago 312 558 1075.

Table 195   THE PIONEER ⑤   ╫╫ NRPC
SUMMARY TABLE

arr	dep		arr	dep		
A 25	....	0945	Denver 255....................	1745	....	↑ B
A	2057	2117	Ogden 255....................	0607	0627	↑ B
B	0345	0345	Boise 255....................	2315	2315	↑ A
B	1345	1440	Portland 255..................	1125	1140	↑ A
B	1835	....	Seattle 264..................	....	0730	26 A

①③⑥ from Denver and Seattle.
②⑤⑦: ◻╫, ◻◻ and ✕ Chicago(5)-Denver(25)-Seattle.◻.
②③⑥: ◻╫ and ✕ Seattle(26)-Denver(6)-Chicago.◻.
NRPC–National Railroad Passenger Corporation (AMTRAK). Tel.: Chicago 312 558 1075.

Table 196   NEW HAVEN - MONTRÉAL   ╫╫ NRPC

US$ C cl.	470 C‡	60 S‡C‡					61 S‡C‡	473 C‡
		◆▽			km ↓	↑	◆	◆▽
0.00	1130	2045	....	....	0 d.New York 202.......a.	....	0755	1621
21.00	1318	2240u	....	....	d.New Haven..........a.	....	0550s	1413
26.50		2340	....	....	d.New London.........a.	....	0445		
	1445		....	....	a. Springfield........d.	....		1250
37.00		0240	....	....	d.Amherst...........d.	....	0115	
40.00	1640a	0325	....	....	d.Brattleboro........d.	....	0025	1020a
46.00	1710a	0400	....	....	d.Bellows Falls......d.	....	2350	0950a
		0425	....	....	d.Claremont.........d.	....	2320	
54.00	1755a	0510	....	....	d.White River Junction d.	....	2250	0855a
64.00	1925a	0625	....	....	d.Montpelier.........d.	....	2115	0745a
66.00	2015a	0715	....	....	d.Essex Junction ◇ ..d.	....	2030	0655a
70.00		0755	....	....	d.St. Albans ▦......d.	....	2000	
72.00		1045	....	....	a.Montréal Central....d.	....	1720	

60/61–MONTREALER–◻╫, ◻◻ and Ⓧ Washington(136/137)-New York(60/61)-Montréal and v.v. 470–See Table 202. 473–See Table 202. a–Connction by ⟷ ◇–Burlington. NRPC–National Railroad Passenger Corporation (AMTRAK). Tel.: New York 212 582 6875.

Table 197   BOSTON LOCAL RAIL SERVICE   ╫╫ MBTA

Local ╫╫ services (C‡ only) operate in the Boston area as follows:

Attleboro (✢ km, US$: 3.75). From Boston South: 0535⑩, 0645⑩, 0650⑩, 0755⑩, 0825⑩, 0940⑩, 0945⑩, 1045⑩, 1220⑩, 1245⑩, 1415⑩, 1445⑩, 1545⑩, 1635⑩, 1645⑩, 1705⑩, 1735⑩, 1820⑩, 1845, 2020⑩, 2045⑩, 2145⑩, 2300⑩, 2359⑩, returning at 0113②-⑥, 0547⑩, 0632⑩, 0655⑩, 0709⑩, 0730⑩, 0756⑩, 0827⑩, 0855✗⑩, 1000⑩, 1055⑩, 1145⑩, 1255⑩, 1403⑩, 1455⑩, 1550⑩, 1655⑩, 1700⑩, 1813⑩, 1855⑩, 2000⑩, 2055⑩, 2148⑩, 2235⑩. Journey: 45 mins.
Fitchburg (81 km, US$: 4.75). From Boston North: 0010②-⑥, 0830⑩, 0850⑩, 0935⑩, 1120✗, 1200✗, 1320⑩, 1530⑩, 1650⑩, 1720⑩, 1730⑩, 1815⑩, 2045⑩, 2135†, 2230⑩, 2300⑩, returning at 0545⑩, 0630⑩, 0640⑩, 0655⑩, 0715⑩, 0750†, 0920⑩, 1029⑩, 1115⑩, 1124⑩, 1130†, 1305⑩, 1415†, 1445⑩, 1505⑩, 1725†, 1735⑩, 1905⑩, 2230⑩. Journey: 1½ hours.
Framingham (34 km, US$: 3.25). From Boston South: 0500⑩, 0520⑩, 0600⑩, 0650⑩, 0735⑩, 0800⑩, 0905⑩, 1030⑩, 1105⑩, 1235⑩, 1255⑩, 1430⑩, 1440⑩, 1630, 1700⑩, 1730⑩, 1805⑩, 1830⑩, 1855⑩, 2020⑩, 2030⑩, 2135⑩, 2300⑩, 2305⑩, returning at 0000⑩, 00052-⑥, 0615⑩, 0700✗, 0730⑩, 0800⑩, 0835⑩, 0900⑩, 1000⑩, 1130⑩, 1205⑩, 1330⑩, 1440, 1545, 1730, 1840⑩, 1930⑩, 2020⑩, 2120⑩, 2130⑩. Journey: 50 mins.
Franklin (✢ km, US$: 3.50). From Boston South: 0350⑩, 0400⑩, 0720⑩, 0750⑩, 0910⑩, 0920⑩, 1015⑩, 1050⑩, 1245⑩, 1320⑩, 1445⑩, 1520⑩, 1600⑩, 1700⑩, 1710⑩, 1740⑩, 1815⑩, 1920⑩, 1925⑩, 2045⑩, 2120⑩, 2220⑩, 2300⑩, 2359⑩, returning at 0522⑩, 0552⑩, 0622⑩, 0642✗, 0717⑩, 0752⑩, 0842⑩, 0913⑩, 1022⑩, 1042⑩, 1142⑩, 1211⑩, 1407⑩, 1442⑩, 1608⑩, 1642⑩, 1732⑩, 1842⑩, 1937⑩, 2042⑩, 2047⑩, 2228⑩, 2242⑩, 2342⑩. Journey: 50 mins.
Haverhill (53 km, US$: 3.75). From Boston North: 0655⑩, 0750⑩, 0845⑩, 0850⑩, 1145⑩, 1320⑩, 1445⑩, 1520⑩, 1630⑩, 1715⑩, 1745⑩, 1815⑩, 2020⑩, 2045⑩, 2330⑩, 2359⑩, returning at 0535⑩, 0608⑩, 0632⑩, 0700⑩, 0715⑩, 0715⑩, 0820⑩, 1015⑩, 1023⑩, 1315⑩, 1453⑩, 1615⑩, 1810⑩, 1915⑩, 2215⑩. Journey: 65 mins.
Ipswich (US$: 3.50). From Boston North: 0645⑩, 0815⑩, 0940⑩, 1115⑩, 1130⑩, 1315⑩, 1330⑩, 1515⑩, 1630⑩, 1710⑩, 1735⑩, 1830⑩, 1845⑩, 2120⑩, 2200⑩, 2240⑩, returning at 0602⑩, 0652⑩, 0720⑩, 0752⑩, 0900⑩, 0948⑩, 1100⑩, 1118⑩, 1300⑩, 1318⑩, 1500✗, 1627⑩, 1735⑩, 2038✗, 2230⑩. Journey: 1 hour.
Lawrence (42 km, US$: 3.50). From Boston North: 0655⑩, 0750⑩, 0845⑩, 0850⑩, 1145⑩, 1320⑩, 1445⑩, 1520⑩, 1630⑩, 1715⑩, 1745⑩, 1815⑩, 2020⑩, 2045⑩, 2330⑩, returning at 0546⑩, 0619⑩, 0643⑩, 0711⑩, 0720⑩, 0726⑩, 0831⑩, 1026⑩, 1034⑩, 1326⑩, 1504⑩, 1626⑩, 1821⑩.

Lowell (52 km, US$: 3.50). From Boston North: 0550⑩, 0635⑩, 0725⑩, 0800⑩, 0805⑩, 0910⑩, 1000⑩, 1010⑩, 1110⑩, 1200⑩, 1210⑩, 1310⑩, 1400⑩, 1410⑩, 1510⑩, 1600⑩, 1610⑩, 1640⑩, 1710⑩, 1745⑩, 1800⑩, 1815⑩, 1930⑩, 2000⑩, 2030⑩, 2140⑩, 2240⑩, 2300⑩, 2359⑩, returning at 0535⑩, 0615⑩, 0650⑩, 0700⑩, 0720⑩, 0750⑩, 0825⑩, 0900⑩, 0907⑩, 1007⑩, 1100⑩, 1107⑩, 1207⑩, 1300⑩, 1307⑩, 1407⑩, 1500⑩, 1507⑩, 1610⑩, 1700⑩, 1710⑩, 1745⑩, 1815⑩, 1900⑩, 1915⑩, 2030⑩, 2100⑩, 2130⑩, 2230⑩. Journey: 45 mins.
Lynn (✢ km, US$: 2.25). From Boston North: 0645⑩, 0720⑩, 0745⑩, 0815⑩, 0830⑩, 0940⑩, 1015, 1115⑩, 1130⑩, 1215, 1315⑩, 1330⑩, 1415, 1515⑩, 1600⑩, 1630✗, 1710⑩, 1730⑩, 1735⑩, 1805⑩, 1830⑩, 1845⑩, 2000⑩, 2030⑩, 2120⑩, 2200⑩, 2240⑩, 2330⑩, 2359⑩, returning at 0559⑩, 0632⑩, 0701⑩, 0723⑩, 0748⑩, 0752⑩, 0822⑩, 0847⑩, 0930⑩, 0955✗, 1018⑩, 1048, 1130⑩, 1148⑩, 1248, 1330⑩, 1348⑩, 1448, 1530✗, 1658⑩, 1803⑩, 1823⑩, 2018⑩, 2032⑩, 2108✗, 2248⑩, 2313⑩. Journey: 25 mins.
Providence (69 km, US$5.50). From Boston South: 0650⑩, 1635⑩, 1705⑩, 1735⑩, 1820⑩, returning at 0613⑩, 0651⑩, 0711⑩, 0811⑩, 1755⑩. Journey: 1¼ hours.
Rockport (✢ km, US$: 4.00). From Boston North: 0745⑩, 0830, 1015, 1215, 1415, 1600⑩, 1700⑩, 1725⑩, 1730⑩, 1805⑩, 2000⑩, 2040⑩, 2330⑩, 2359⑩, returning at 0511⑩, 0611⑩, 0653⑩, 0700⑩, 0722⑩, 0907⑩, 1000, 1200, 1400, 1544⑩, 1715⑩, 1734⑩, 1930⑩, 1943⑩, 2200⑩, 2224⑩. Journey: 1¼ hours.
Salem (✢ km, US$: 2.50). From Boston North: 0645⑩, 0720⑩, 0745⑩, 0815⑩, 0830, 0940⑩, 1015, 1130⑩, 1215, 1315⑩, 1330⑩, 1415, 1515⑩, 1600⑩, 1630✗, 1710⑩, 1725✗, 1730⑩, 1735⑩, 1805⑩, 1830⑩, 1845⑩, 2000⑩, 2030⑩, 2120⑩, 2200⑩, 2240⑩, 2330⑩, 2359⑩, returning at 0549⑩, 0622⑩, 0651⑩, 0731⑩, 0734⑩, 0738⑩, 0741⑩, 0803⑩, 0812⑩, 0831⑩, 0920⑩, 0945⑩, 1008⑩, 1038, 1120⑩, 1138⑩, 1238, 1320⑩, 1338, 1438, 1520✗, 1620⑩, 1648⑩, 1753⑩, 1755⑩, 1813⑩, 2008⑩, 2022⑩, 2058✗, 2238⑩, 2303⑩. Journey: 35 mins.

MBTA–Massachusetts Bay Transportation Authority. Tel.: Boston 722 3200.

Table 198   HYANNIS - PROVIDENCE   ╫╫ NRPC

US$ C cl.	235 P‡C‡			234 P‡C‡		
		▦◆			▦◆	
		⑦▽	July 1-Sept. 11 only		⑨▽	
		km ↓			↑	
0.00	....	....	1515	0 d.Hyannis........a.	....	....	2245
✢	....	....	1543	24 d.Sandwich.......d.	....	....	2205
✢	....	....	1600	36 d.Buzzard's Bay...d.	....	....	2151
✢	....	....	1610r	46 d.Wareham.......d.	....	....	2137r
✢	....	....	1755	122 d.Providence.......d.	....	....	2003
	....	....	1942s	304 d.New Haven 202 d.	....	....	1801u
	....	....	2035s	354 d.Stamford 202....d.	....	....	1703u
	....	....	2127	426 a.New York Penn. Stn.d.	....	....	1617

34/5– THE CAPE CODDER.
NRPC–National Railroad Passenger Corporation (AMTRAK). Tel.: New York 212 582 6875.

Table 200   BOSTON - ALBANY   ╫╫ NRPC

US$ C cl.	469 C‡	475 C‡	449 S‡C‡			448 S‡C‡	470 C‡	476 C‡
			◆			◆	◆	
			▽	▦Ⓧ	km ↓	↑	▽	▽
0.00	....	0635	1225	1620	0 d.Boston South ....a.	1650	1715	2330
	....	0639u	1229u	1624u	2 d.Boston Back Bay ..a.	1639s	1709s	2324s
7.25	....	0708u	1258u	1653u	34 d.Framingham......d.	1602s	1632s	2247s
0.50	....	0735	1325	1720	71 d.Worcester.........d.	1535	1605	2220
9.00	....	0853	1453	1845	158 d.Springfield.......d.	1430	1500	2115
3.50	....	....	....	2000	239 d.Pittsfield.........d.	1305	....	....
7.00	....	....	....	2115	321 a.Albany Rensselaer.d.	1200	....	....
3.00	....	....	1258	1544	a.Chicago 215.......d.	1915	....	....

8/9–LAKE SHORE LIMITED–see Table 186.
9-476–see Table 202.
NRPC–National Railroad Passenger Corporation (AMTRAK). Tel.: Boston 617 482 3660.

Table 199   ALBANY - MONTRÉAL   ╫╫ NRPC

US$ C cl.	245 1‡C‡	69 C‡	71 C‡	269 1‡C‡			68 C‡	260 1‡C‡
		▦◆					◆	▦◆
	⑥⑦	✗↑	†	⑤	km ↓	↑		⑥⑦
0.00	0745	0815	1050	1645	0 d.New York 207 ...a.	....	2020	2240
40.00	1005	1115	1350	1910	229 d.Albany Rensselaer .a.	....	1715	2005
45.00		1140	1415	1935	258 d.Schenectady 215 d.	....	1640	
45.00	1105	1203	1438	2005	288 d.Saratoga Springs d.	....	1553	1915
49.00		1223	1458		320 d.Fort Edward ★..d.	....	1533	
54.00		1244	1519		355 d.Whitehall.........d.	....	1511	
58.00		1351	1626		436 d.Westport.........d.	....	1404	
65.00		1426a	1701a		479 d.Port Kent.........d.	....	1329a	
65.00		1451	1726		500 d.Plattsburgh ....d.	....	1316	
67.00		1528	1803		538 d.Rouses Point ▦.d.	....	1247	
67.00		1731	2006		617 a.Montréal Central d.	....	1025	

68-71– ADIRONDACK–◻◻ and Ⓧ Montréal(68/69/71)-New York and v.v.
245– THE TRAVERS–⑥⑦ July 23-Aug. 28: ◻◻◻ and ▽ New York(245)-Saratoga Springs.
246– JIM DANDY–⑧ July 4-Sept. 5: ◻◻◻ and ▽ Saratoga Springs(246)-New York.
269– SPA EXPRESS–⑤ July 1-Sept. 2: ◻◻◻ and ▽ New York(269)-Saratoga Springs.
a– May 19-Oct. 16 only. Note r applies. ★–Glens Falls.
NRPC–National Railroad Passenger Corporation (AMTRAK). Tel.: New York 212 582 6875.

Table 201   MOUNT WASHINGTON   ⚙ MWCR

Cog railway service (steam operated) from Base Station to summit of Mount Washington. 5 km. Journey: R.T.: 2 hours. Fare: US $: R. T.: 32.00.
Departures from Base Station for summit and return: **May 29-June 25:** 0900 and hourly to 3 hours before sunset; operates in accordance with demand, and as track maintenance permits. **June 26-Sept. 6:** 0800 and hourly to 3 hours before sunset. **Sept. 7-Oct. 11:** 1000 and as required to 3 hours before sunset.

MWCR–Mount Washington Cog Railway. ☎ Bretton Woods 603 846 5404.

Table 202 — BOSTON - NEW YORK

CDT NRPC

US$ C cl.	NRPC ↓	km	205 P‡C‡	61 S‡C‡	141 C‡	143 C‡	653 C‡	151 P‡C‡	469 C‡	155 P‡C‡	169 P‡C‡	153 P‡C‡	171 P‡C‡	173 P‡C‡	475 C‡	175 P‡C‡	177 C‡	179 C‡	157 P‡C‡	235 P‡C‡	167 C‡	193 C‡	77 S‡C‡	67 S‡C‡
0.00	**Boston** South ....d.	0	....	....	....	....	....	0600	0635	0710	0725	0905	0925	1125	1225	1325	1530	1630	1640	....	1740	1901	2130	2220
	Boston Back Bay ....d.	2	....	....	....	....	....	0605u	0639u	0715u	0731u	0910u	0931u	1131u	1229u	1331u	1536u	1636u	1645u	....	1746u	1906u	2138u	2226u
	Route 128 ....d.		....	....	....	....	....	0617u		0727	0744	0922u	0944	1145		1344	1551	1649	1657u	....	1759u	1918u	2151	2239
13.00	Providence ....d.	69	....	....	....	....	....	0645		0754	0814	0949	1014	1215		1415	1622	1722	1724f	1755	1829	1948	2228	2319
	Kingston ....d.	140	....	....	....	....	....				0839		1039	1241			1653				1920	2017	2258	2345
	Westerly ....d.		....	....	....	....	....				0856						1715					2035	2323	0002
	Mystic ....d.	169	....	....	....	....	....				0907											2047		
25.50	**New London** ....d.	169	....	0445	....	....	....	0741	b	0853	0921		1121	1326	b	1521	1738	1826	1823		1935	2102	2346	0026
	Old Saybrook ⊠ ....d.		....	....	....	....	....				0941		1143			1542	1758	1846			1955	2127	0008	0047
35.00	New London ⊠..........d.	251	0550	0608s	0707	0732	0825	0843	1037	0952	1037	1142	1236	1437	1640	1640	1847	1937	1925	1949s	2047	2214	0104	0143
35.00	Bridgeport ....d.	218	0611				0851		1102		1102			1500	1704	1704					2237			
35.00	Stamford ....d.	301	0636	0656s	0758	0827	0917		1130		1130		1325	1526	1730	1730	1935	2023	2013	2035s	2135	2306	0157	0230
45.00	New Rochelle ....d.	314	0657		0822	0848	0939						1346	1550				2044				2327		
45.00	**New York** Penn. Stn. a.	373	0734	0755	0856	0917	1007	1014	1219	1124	1219	1315	1421	1621	1817	1817	2025	2110	2103	2127	2224	2354	0258	0316
61.00	Philadelphia 30th Street 213..d.	519	0915	1007	1053	1117		1407		1407		1607	1803	2007	2007	2216	2309		0010		0200	0537	0524	
92.00	Washington Union 213 a.	735	1059	1214	1250	1315		1613		1613		1820	2015	2215	2215	0024	0110		0227		....	0805	0755	

	NRPC ↓	66 S‡C‡	76 S‡C‡	12 C‡	198 C‡	190 C‡	170 C‡	470 C‡	154 P‡C‡	172 P‡C‡	174 P‡C‡	234 P‡C‡	156 P‡C‡	176 P‡C‡	476 C‡	142 C‡	178 P‡C‡	228 P‡C‡	222 P‡C‡	60 S‡C‡	654 C‡
	Washington Union 213 d.	2210c	2210e	0300	....	....	0735	0735	....	0935	....	1135	....	1335	1335	1435	1535	1630	1700	1635	....
	Philadelphia 30th Street 213 .d.	0031	0102	0509	0735	0735	0931	0931	1132	1333		1539	1539	1638	1731	1810	1835	1837		
	New York Penn. Stn..a.	0315	0415	0701	0930	0930	1130	1130	1242	1335	1525	1617	1655	1744	1744	1833	1925	1950	2045	2250
	New Rochelle ....d.						1159	1159		1404		1554				1902	1953	2018	2048		2320
	Stamford ....d.	0405	0521	0749	1020	1020	1223	1223	1425		1619	1703u		1840	1840		2014	2038	2107	2138u	2340
	Bridgeport ....d.			0815			1047	1047		1452				1905	1905	1948		2104	2133		0005
	New Haven ....d.	0518	0634	0900	1130	1130	1334	1318	1414	1544	1721	1801u	1834	1946	1940	2013	2117	2131	2206	2240u	0130
	Old Saybrook ⊠ ....d.	0556	0711		1211	1211	1413		1626		1818			2029			2155				
	New London ....d.	0617	0732	1001	1233	1233	1434	b	1647					2050	b		2216		2300a	2340	
	Mystic ....d.	0633	0747		1246	1246			1700								2230				
	Westerly ....d.	0645	0758		1257	1257			1729		1839						2242				
	Kingston ....d.	0703	0814		1314	1314					1856			2125			2258				
	Providence ....d.	0738	0848	1106	1340	1340	1539		1607	1757	1937	2003	2023g	2155			2328		2358a		
	Route 128 ....d.	0814s	0925s		1140s	1409s	1409s		1614		1638s	1830	2010		2049s	2224s		2359s		0026s	
	Boston Back Bay ....d.	0829s	0942s	1154s	1423s	1423s			1626s	1709s		1650s	1845s		2020s		2100s	2239s	2324s		0016s
	Boston South ....a.	0839	0953	1204	1433	1433	1635	1715	1655	1853		2028			2108	2247	2330		0026		0056d

Table 203 — SPRINGFIELD - NEW HAVEN

NRP

US$ C cl.	↓	km	141 C‡	143 C‡	653 C‡		469 C‡	471 C‡			473 C‡	475 C‡			477 C‡	479 C‡		467 C‡	
0.00	**Springfield** ....d.	0	....	0528	0600	0650	....	0853	1052	....	1250	1453	....	....	1655	1755	....	1906	....
6.00	Windsor Locks ....d.	22	....	0550	0622	0711	....	0913	1111	....	1308	1512	....	....	1714	1814	....	1925	....
9.00	Hartford ....d.	41	....	0609	0641	0728	....	0927	1125	....	1321	1525	....	....	1729	1830	....	1938	....
11.00	Berlin ....d.	58	....	0622	0654	0740	....	0940	1138	....	1332	1536	....	....	1740	1841	....	1950	....
13.00	Meriden ....d.	70	....	0633	0705	0751	....	0948	1146	....	1340	1547	....	....	1749	1849	....	2001	....
16.00	**New Haven**..............a.	100	....	0658	0730	0818	....	1014	1212	....	1413	1624	....	....	1817	1920	....	2029	....

	↓	412 C‡	490 C‡	498 C‡		470 C‡	472 C‡	474 C‡		476 C‡	142 C‡		654 C‡
	New Haven............d.	0850	1121	1121	....	1318	1527	1712	....	1940	2023	....	0041
	Meriden ....d.	0919	1150	1150	....	1346	1555	1741	....	2009	2053	....	0109
	Berlin ....d.	0928	1159	1159	....	1355	1605	1754	....	2018	2105	....	0119
	Hartford ....d.	0943	1212	1212	....	1409	1619	1807	....	2031	2121	....	0135
	Windsor Locks ....d.	0956	1228	1228	....	1422	1635	1822	....	2041	2139	....	0151
	Springfield ....a.	1021	1249	1249	....	1500	1700	1848	....	2115	2203	....	0216

NOTES for Tables 202 and 203

12– FAST MAIL—🚃 and ♀ Washington(12)-Boston; 🚃 Washington(12)-New Haven(412)-Springfield.
60/61– MONTREALER–see Table 196.
66/67– NIGHT OWL–see Table 180.
76/77– WEEKEND NIGHT OWL–🚃‡, 🚃, and ♀ Washington(76/77)-Boston and v.v.
141– BANKERS–🚃 and ♀ Springfield(141)-Washington.
142– BANKERS–🚃 and ♀ Washington(142)-Springfield.
143– THE NUTMEG STATE–🚃 and ♀ Springfield(143)-Washington.
151-7 NEW ENGLAND EXPRESS.
167– NARRAGANSETT–🚃 and ♀ Boston(167)-Washington; 🚃 Springfield(467)-New Haven(167)-Washington.
169– MAYFLOWER–🚃 and ♀ Boston(169)-Washington.
170– YANKEE CLIPPER–🚃 and ♀ Washington(170)-Boston.
171– MINUTE MAN–🚃 and ♀ Washington(171)-Boston; 🚃 Springfield(471)-New Haven(171)-Washington.
172– PATRIOT–🚃 and ♀ Washington(172)-Boston; 🚃 Washington(172)-New Haven(472)-Springfield.
173– YANKEE CLIPPER–🚃 and ♀ Boston(173)-Washington; 🚃 Springfield(473)-Washington.
174– MAYFLOWER–🚃 and ♀ Washington(174)-Boston; 🚃 Springfield(174)-New Haven(474)-Springfield.
175– PATRIOT–🚃 and ♀ Boston(175)-Washington.
176– SENATOR–🚃 and ♀ Washington(176)-Boston.
177– SENATOR–🚃 and ♀ Boston(177)-Washington; 🚃 Springfield(477)-New Haven(177)-Washington.
178– MERCHANTS LIMITED–🚃 and ♀ Washington(178)-Boston.
179– MERCHANTS LIMITED–🚃 and ♀ Boston(179)-Washington; 🚃 Springfield(479)-New Haven(179)-Washington.
190– BENJAMIN FRANKLIN–🚃 Philadelphia(190)-Boston; 🚃 Philadelphia(190)-New Haven(490)-Springfield; ♀ New York(190)-Boston.
193– BENJAMIN FRANKLIN–🚃 Boston(193)-Philadelphia; ♀ Boston(193)-New York.
198– BENJAMIN FRANKLIN–🚃 Philadelphia(198)-Boston; 🚃 Philadelphia(198)-New Haven(498)-Springfield; ♀ New York(198)-Boston.
205– METROLINER–🚃 and ♀ New Haven(205)-Washington. Runs as Tr. 161 between New Haven and New York, with no supplement for local passengers.
222– METROLINER–🚃 and ♀ Washington(222)-New Haven (Boston on ⑤). Runs as train 162 between New York and Boston with no supplement for local passengers.
228– METROLINER–🚃 and ♀ Washington(228)-New Haven.
234– THE CAPE CODDER–⑥ July 1-Sept. 11: 🚃 and ♀ New York(234)-Hyannis.
235– THE CAPE CODDER–⑦ July 1-Sept. 11: 🚃 and ♀ Hyannis(235)-New York.
412– FAST MAIL–🚃 Washington(12)-New Haven(412)-Springfield.

467– NARRAGANSETT–🚃 Springfield(467)-New Haven(167)-Washington.
469– CONNECTICUT YANKEE–🚃 and ♀ Springfield(469)-Washington.
470– CONNECTICUT YANKEE–🚃 and ♀ Washington(470)-Boston.
471– MINUTE MAN–🚃 Springfield-New Haven(171)-Washington.
472– PATRIOT–🚃 Washington(172)-New Haven(472)-Springfield.
473– YANKEE CLIPPER–🚃 Springfield(473)-New Haven(173)-Washington.
474– MAYFLOWER–🚃 Washington(174)-New Haven(474)-Springfield.
475– BAY STATE–🚃 and ♀ Boston(475)-Springfield-New Haven(175)-Washington.
476– BAY STATE–🚃 and ♀ Washington(476)-Boston.
477– SENATOR–🚃 Springfield(477)-New Haven(177)-Washington.
479– MERCHANTS LIMITED–🚃 Springfield(479)-New Haven(179)-Washington.
490– BENJAMIN FRANKLIN–🚃 Philadelphia(190)-New Haven(490)-Springfield.
498– BENJAMIN FRANKLIN–🚃 Philadelphia(198)-New Haven(498)-Springfield.
653– ATLANTIC CITY EXPRESS–🚃 and ♀ Springfield(653)-Atlantic City.
654– ATLANTIC CITY EXPRESS–🚃 and ♀ Atlantic City(654)-Springfield.
a– ⑤ only.
b– Via Springfield.
c– ex ⑤⑥.
d– ⑥ only.
e– ⑤⑥ only.
f– Does not stop when tr. 235 runs. Note u applies.
g– Deos not stop when tr. 234 runs.
⊠– Local CDT #### service (C cl. only) New Haven-Old Saybrook and v.v. **From New Haven** at: 0700④, 0810④, 1520④, 1615④, 1705④, 1730④, 1811④, 1916④, 2016④, 2059④, returning at 0448④, 0550④, 0648④, 0725④, 0750④, 0858④, 1640④, 1718④.
CDT– Connecticut Department of Transportation. Tel.: New Haven 203 777 7433.
NRPC–National Railroad Passenger Corporation (AMTRAK). Tel.: New York 212 582 6875.

Table 207 NEW YORK - POUGHKEEPSIE - ALBANY

NRPC

US $ C cl.		km	63	245	69	71	281	253	283	257	285	259	269	265	269	267	49	271	65	277
			C‡	1‡C‡	C‡	C‡	1‡C‡	1‡C‡	C‡	1‡C‡	1‡C‡	1‡C‡	1‡C‡	1‡C‡	1‡C‡	1‡C‡	S‡C‡	1‡C‡	S‡C‡	1‡C‡
	↓			⑥⑦				Ⓑ		Ⓐ	⑦	Ⓐ	⑤	ex⑤⑦	⑤	⑦		Ⓑ	⑤⑥	⑦
0.00	**New York** Penn. Stn. d.	0	0715	0745	0815	1050	1150	1255	1425	1550	1645	1645	1645	1738	1738	1825	1910	2035	2230	2345
5.25	Yonkers d.	24	0739u	|	0840u	1114u	1213u	|	1449u	1613u	|	|	|	1801u	1801u	1848u	|	2058u	|	|
6.75	Croton Harmon d.	54	0800u	0827u	0900u	1134u	1233u	|	1510u	1633u	|	|	|	1821u	1821u	1908u	1955u	2118u	|	0028u
1.75	Poughkeepsie d.	118	0840u	|	0943u	1214u	1312u	|	1550u	1712u	|	|	|	1859u	1859u	1947u	2042u	2157u	|	0107u
	Rhinecliff ⌒ d.		0855	|	0958	1229	1327	1425	1605	1727	1815	1815	1815	1915	1915	2002	|	2212	0002	0122
30.00	Hudson d.	184	0918	|	1020	1251	1348	1446	1628	1748	1836	1836	1836	1936	1936	2023	2123	2233	0025	0143
40.00	**Albany Rensselaer** d.	229	0950	1000	1050	1325	1420	1515	1700	1820	1905	1905	1905	2008	2008	2055	2153	2305	0055	0215

	62	242	246	248	250	252	284	48	256	282	286	264	68	64	270	260	288
	S‡C‡	1‡C‡	1‡C‡	1‡C‡	1‡C‡	1‡C‡	C‡	S‡C‡	1‡C‡	1‡C‡	1‡C‡	1‡C‡	1‡C‡	C‡	1‡C‡	1‡C‡	1‡C‡
↓	①⑦		Ⓐ			†			⑦	†		Ⓑ			⑦	⑦	†
Albany Rensselaer d.	0510	0620	0702	0745	0910	0910	1015	1150	1255	1350	1445	1610	1745	1905	2015	2015	2050
Hudson d.	0534	0644	|	0807	0932	0932	1037	1220s	1317	1412	1509	1632	1809	1929	2037	2037	2112
Rhinecliff ⌒ d.	0557	0707	|	0828	0953	0953	1058	|	1338	1433	1532	1653	1831	1951	2058	2058	2133
Poughkeepsie d.	|	|	|	0843s	1008s	1008s	1113s	1305s	|	1448s	1547s	1708s	1846s	2006s	|	|	2149s
Croton Harmon d.	|	0758	|	0922s	1048s	1048s	1152s	1350s	|	1527s	1627s	1747s	1926s	2046s	|	2150s	2227s
Yonkers d.	|	|	|	0942s	|	|	1212s	|	|	1547s	1647s	1809s	1946s	2106s	|	|	2247s
New York Penn. Stn. a.	0745	0848	0917	1015	1140	1140	1250	1449	1520	1625	1720	1840	2020	2140	2240	2240	2320

3/49– LAKE SHORE LIMITED–see Table **186**.
2– NIAGARA RAINBOW–‡, and Niagara Falls (Canada)(**62**)-New York.
3/64– THE MAPLE LEAF–see Table **181**.
5– NIAGARA RAINBOW–‡, and New York(**65**)-Niagara Falls (Canada).
8– ADIRONDACK– and Montréal(**68**)-New York.
9– ADIRONDACK– and New York(**69**)-Montréal.
1– ADIRONDACK– and New York(**71**)-Montréal.
42– HUDSON HIGHLANDER.
45– THE TRAVERS–⑥⑦ July 23-Aug. 28: and New York(**245**)-Saratoga Springs.
46– THE STORM KING– and Schenectady(**246**)-New York.
48– BEAR MOUNTAIN. **250**–KNICKERBOCKER.
52– ELECTRIC CITY EXPRESS– and Schenectady(**250**)-New York.
53– SPUYTEN DUYVIL. **256/7**–PALISADES.
59– BEAR MOUNTAIN–Runs on Ⓐ (ex ⑤ July 1-Sept. 2): and New York(**259**)-Schenectady.
60– JIM DANDY–⑥⑦ July 4-Sept. 5: and Saratoga Springs(**260**)-New York.
264– HENDRICK HUDSON.
265– CATSKILL. **267**–THE HALF MOON.
269– SPA EXPRESS–⑤ July 1-Sept. 2: and New York(**269**)-Saratoga Springs.
270– CATSKILL–⑦ to July 3 and from Sept. 6.
271– PATROON.
277– SLEEPY HOLLOW.
281– MOHAWK– and New York(**281**)-Niagara Falls.
282– EMPIRE STATE EPXRESS– and Niagara Falls(**282**)-New York.
283– EMPIRE STATE EXPRESS– and New York(**283**)-Niagara Falls.
284 MOHAWK and Niagara Falls(**284**)-New York.
285– WATER LEVEL EXPRESS– and New York(**285**)-Niagara Falls.
286– EMPIRE STATE EXPRESS– and Niagara Falls(**286**)-New York.
288– WATER LEVEL EXPRESS– and Niagara Falls(**288**)-New York.
289– CATSKILL– and New York(**289**)-Syracuse.
⌒– Kingston.
NRPC–National Railroad Passenger Corporation (AMTRAK). Tel.: New York 212 582 6875.

Table 209 NEW YORK - MONTAUK

LIRR

US$ C cl.		km	8700	2702	8702	2704	8706	2732	2706	8710	2710	2712	2734	2716	2736	8738	2738	2720	8712	8740	2740	8742
			C‡	C‡	C‡	C‡	C‡	C‡	C‡	C‡	P‡C‡	C‡	C‡	C‡	C‡	C‡	C‡	C‡	C‡	C‡	C‡	C‡
	↓		Ⓒ	Ⓐ	Ⓒ	Ⓐ	Ⓒ	Ⓐ	Ⓐ	Ⓒ	⑤	Ⓐ	Ⓐ	Ⓐ	Ⓐ	Ⓒ	Ⓐ	Ⓐ	Ⓒ	Ⓒ	Ⓐ	Ⓒ
0.00	**New York** Penn. Stn. d.	0	*0038*	*0036*	*0758*	*0749*	*1006*	*1031*	*1202*	*1153*	*1601*	*1619*	*1710*	*1751*	*1830*	*1908*	*1930*	*2031*	*2043*	*2208*	*2229*	*2310*
1.00	Speonk d.	117	0236	0241	1000	0942	1200	1229	1355	1346	|	1830	1923	1955	2034	2119	2135	2232	2250	0027	0035	0106
4.00	Southampton d.	146	0314	0315	1036	1014	1236	....	1426	1424	1759	1905	....	2028	....	....	....	2308	2324	....	....	....
4.00	East Hampton d.	164	0330	0331	1054	1030	1254	....	1442	1442	1817	1923	....	2044	....	....	....	2332	2340	....	....	....
4.00	**Montauk** a.	188	0356	0357	1121	1057	1321	....	....	1509	1838	1950	....	2111	....	....	....	2357	0006	....	....	....

	2701	2731	2733	8731	2737	8733	2703	2739	8701	8735	8737	2707	2741	8739	2709	8705	8741	8707	8711	2745	2747	2711
	C‡	C‡	C‡	C‡	C‡	C‡	C‡	C‡	C‡	C‡	C‡	C‡	C‡	C‡	C‡	C‡	C‡	C‡	C‡	C‡	C‡	C‡
↓	Ⓐ	Ⓐ	Ⓐ	Ⓒ	Ⓐ	Ⓒ	Ⓐ	Ⓐ	Ⓒ	Ⓒ	Ⓒ	Ⓐ	Ⓐ	Ⓒ	Ⓐ	Ⓒ	Ⓒ	Ⓒ	Ⓒ	Ⓐ	Ⓐ	Ⓐ
Montauk d.	0051	....	....	....	....	....	0538	....	0655	....	....	1125	....	....	....	1530	....	1702	1930	....	....	2236
East Hampton d.	0117	....	....	....	....	....	0603	....	0721	....	....	1151	....	....	1515	1557	....	1729	1957	....	....	2302
Southampton d.	0133	....	....	....	....	....	0619	....	0736	....	....	1207	....	....	1531	1615	....	1748	2016	....	....	2325
Speonk d.	0209	0430	0505	0513	0610	0637	0651	0727	0810	1013	1213	1242	1405	1407	1611	1653	1745	1826	2055	2103	2202	2356
New York Penn. Stn a.	*0409*	*0644*	*0657*	*0727*	*0823*	*0838*	*0840*	*0938*	*1010*	*1209*	*1409*	*1425*	*1612*	*1609*	*1820*	*1849*	*1934*	*2017*	*2240*	*2308*	*0016*	*0206*

LIRR– Long Island Railroad. Tel.: Jamaica 718 990 7400.

Table 211 NEW YORK - PORT JERVIS

MNCR PATH

US$ C cl.	71/81	51	1751	55	57	59	61	75/85	63	1163	km	↓ MNCR ↑	48	50	52	54	70/80	56	1752	58	74/84	1118	76
	C‡	C‡	C‡	C‡	C‡	C‡	C‡	C‡	C‡	C‡			C‡	C‡	C‡	C‡	C‡	C‡	C‡	C‡	C‡	C‡	C‡
	Ⓒ	Ⓐ	⑥	Ⓐ	Ⓐ	Ⓐ	Ⓐ	Ⓒ	Ⓐ	Ⓐ			Ⓐ	Ⓐ	Ⓐ	Ⓐ	Ⓒ	Ⓐ	⑥	Ⓐ	Ⓒ	Ⓐ	⑥
0.00	0907	0935	1245	1545	1645	1742	1823	1840	1905	2115	0	d.**Hoboken** ◇ a.	0653	0736	0819	0855	0950	1058	1455	1604	1930	2326	2345
5.00	0937	1010	1322	1629	1715	|	|	1918	1945	2155	34	d.Ridgewood d.	|	|	|	0823	0913	1019	1415	1519	1900	2246	2315
5.50	0949	1030	1345	1649	1737	1831	1906	1938	2006	2216	55	d.Suffern d.	0610	0650	0729	0803	0855	1002	1356	1502	1848	2230	2303
8.75	1042	1124	*1445*	1744	1833	1926	1959	2033	2059	*2314*	106	d.Middletown d.	0516	0555	0633	0712	0801	0908	*1247*	1408	1754	*2117*	2209
0.75	1114	1156	*1517*	1816	1905	1958	2031	2105	2131	*2346*	140	a.**Port Jervis** d.	0443	0523	0601	0642	0729	0835	*1215*	1335	1722	*2044*	2137

◇–*PATH* runs frequent service (C cl. only) linking Hoboken with 33rd Street and Broadway, Jersey City and Newark 24 hours each day (every 30 mins. at night). *MNCR*–Metro-North Commuter Railroad/New Jersey Transit. Tel.: New York 800 638 7646/Newark 201 762 5100. *PATH*–Port Authority Trans Hudson Corporation. Jersey City 201 659 8823.

Table 212 NEW YORK LOCAL RAIL SERVICE

CDT LIRR MNCR MTA NYCTA PATH

Local services (C‡ only) operate in the New York area as follows:

Ansonia *(CDT)* (*174* km, US $: 12.25). From New York Grand Central: *0602Ⓐ*, *0807Ⓒ*, *0907Ⓐ*, *1207*, *1607Ⓒ*, *1622Ⓐ*, *1830Ⓐ*, *2107*, returning at *0659Ⓐ*, *0743Ⓒ*, *0941Ⓐ*, *1143Ⓒ*, *1241Ⓐ*, *1541Ⓐ*, *1543Ⓒ*, *1921Ⓐ*, *1943Ⓒ*, *2143Ⓐ*. Journey: 2 hours.

Babylon *(LIRR)* (*61* km, US $: 7.75). From New York Penn Stn.: 0009, 0036Ⓐ, 0038Ⓒ, 0140Ⓒ, 0146Ⓐ, 0242Ⓒ, 0313Ⓐ, 0454Ⓐ, 0510Ⓒ, 0610Ⓒ, 0636Ⓐ, 0708Ⓒ, 0710Ⓐ, 0731Ⓐ, 0735Ⓒ, 0749Ⓐ and frequent (about hourly on Ⓒ) to 2108Ⓒ, 2109Ⓐ, 2134Ⓐ, 2139Ⓒ, 2207Ⓐ, 2208Ⓒ, 2229Ⓐ, 2238Ⓐ, 2306Ⓐ, 2310Ⓒ, 2331Ⓐ, 2338Ⓒ, 2339Ⓐ, returning at 0055, 0103, 0139Ⓐ, 0153Ⓒ, 0313Ⓐ, 0339Ⓐ, 0350Ⓒ, 0439Ⓐ, 0450Ⓒ, 0502Ⓐ, *0519Ⓐ*, 0520Ⓒ, 0541Ⓐ, 0550Ⓒ, 0556Ⓐ, 0609Ⓐ, 0612Ⓐ, *0615Ⓐ*, 0618Ⓒ, 0620Ⓒ and frequent (about hourly on Ⓒ) to 2009Ⓐ, 2037Ⓒ, 2039Ⓐ, 2050Ⓒ, 2109Ⓐ, 2137Ⓒ, 2139Ⓐ, 2150Ⓒ, 2203Ⓐ, 2209Ⓐ, 2235Ⓒ, 2239Ⓐ, 2241Ⓒ, 2309Ⓐ, 2339. Journey: 1¼ hours.

Brewster *(MNCR)* (*83* km, US $: 9.25). From New York Grand Central: 0030, 0130, 0600, 0713, 0744Ⓐ, 0747⑥, 0847 and hourly to 1447, 1547Ⓒ, 1548⑤, 1552Ⓐ, 1615Ⓐ, 1639Ⓐ, 1647Ⓒ, 1657Ⓐ, 1717Ⓐ, 1722Ⓐ, 1739Ⓐ, 1747Ⓒ, 1803Ⓐ, 1806Ⓐ, 1829Ⓐ, 1832Ⓐ, 1847Ⓒ, 1858Ⓐ, 1922Ⓐ, 1947Ⓒ, 1950Ⓐ, 2047, 2147, 2247, 2347, returning at 0511Ⓐ, 0545⑥, 0549Ⓐ, 0612Ⓐ, 0641Ⓐ, 0711, 0718Ⓐ, 0726Ⓐ, 0747Ⓐ, 0809Ⓐ, 0811Ⓒ, 0842Ⓐ, 0911 and hourly to 1511, 1611Ⓒ, 1613Ⓐ, 1643Ⓐ, 1711Ⓒ, 1713Ⓐ, 1811Ⓒ, 1813Ⓐ, 1900†, 1911, 2011, 2111, 2316. Journey: 1½ hours.

Bridgeport *(CDT)* (*155* km, US $: 11.25). From New York Grand Central: 0035, 0130, 0540Ⓒ, 0602Ⓐ, 0705Ⓐ, 0807 and hourly to 1407, 1502⑤, 1507, 1537**P**, 1602Ⓐ, 1607, 1622Ⓐ, 1635Ⓐ, 1637**Q**, 1641Ⓐ, 1645Ⓐ, 1702Ⓐ, 1707Ⓒ, 1713Ⓐ, 1718Ⓐ, 1735Ⓐ, 1737**Q**, 1739Ⓐ, 1804Ⓐ, 1807Ⓒ, 1830Ⓐ, 1837**Q**, 1906Ⓐ, 1907Ⓒ, 1937**P**, 2007, 2107, 2207, 2320, returning at 0516Ⓐ, 0548Ⓐ, 0606Ⓐ, 0619Ⓒ, 0621Ⓐ, 0650Ⓐ, 0709Ⓐ, 0719⑥, 0723Ⓐ, 0735Ⓐ, 0750Ⓐ, 0756Ⓐ, 0806**Q**, 0808Ⓐ, 0816Ⓐ, 0819Ⓒ, 0827Ⓐ, 0906**Q**, 0913Ⓐ, 0919Ⓒ, 1006**Q**, 1019, 1106**Q**, 1119, 1206**Q**, 1219, 1319, 1419, 1519, 1616Ⓐ, 1619Ⓒ, 1719 and hourly to 2219, 2344. Journey: 1¼ hours.

Croton Harmon *(MNCR)* (*54* km, US $: 6.75). From New York Grand Central: 0020, 0120, 0620, 0720, 0748Ⓐ, 0755Ⓒ, 0820, 0855Ⓒ, 0858Ⓐ, 0920, 0955Ⓒ, 1020, 1055, 1120, 1158Ⓒ, 1220 and frequent to 2020, 2055, 2120, 2201, 2220, 2315, 2320, returning at 0501Ⓐ, 0531Ⓐ, 0536Ⓒ, 0547Ⓐ, 0558Ⓐ, 0620Ⓐ, 0629Ⓐ, 0633Ⓐ, 0636Ⓒ, 0654Ⓐ, 0702Ⓐ, 0707Ⓐ, 0720Ⓒ, 0721Ⓐ, 0724Ⓐ and frequent to 1114, 1136, 1214Ⓒ, 1236, 1320, 1336, 1420Ⓒ, 1436 and frequent to 2036, 2114Ⓒ, 2136, 2220Ⓒ, 2231Ⓐ, 2236Ⓐ, 2346. Journey: 1 hour.

Danbury *(CDT)* (*104* km, US $: 10.75). From New York Grand Central: *0807*, *1107Ⓒ*, *1207Ⓐ*, *1407Ⓒ*, *1507Ⓐ*, 1659Ⓐ, *1707Ⓒ*, 1737Ⓐ, 1807Ⓐ, *1906Ⓐ*, *2007*, *2207Ⓐ*, *2320Ⓒ*, returning at 0538Ⓐ, 0621Ⓐ, 0652Ⓐ, *0731Ⓐ*, *0744Ⓒ*, *1044*, *1344Ⓒ*, *1444Ⓐ*, *1644Ⓒ*, *1710Ⓐ*, *1944Ⓒ*, *2012Ⓐ*, *2209Ⓐ*, *2309Ⓒ*. Journey: 1 hour 50 mins.

Derby Shelton *(CDT)* (*171* km, US $: 12.25). From New York Grand Central: *0602Ⓐ*, *0807Ⓒ*, *0907Ⓐ*, *1207*, *1607Ⓒ*, *1622Ⓐ*, *1830Ⓐ*, *2107*, returning at *0703Ⓐ*, *0747Ⓒ*, *0945Ⓐ*, *1147Ⓒ*, *1245Ⓐ*, *1545Ⓐ*, *1547Ⓒ*, *1925Ⓐ*, *1947Ⓒ*, *2147Ⓐ*. Journey: 2 hours.

Dover Plains *(MNCR)* (*124* km, US $: 11.75). From New York Grand Central: *0600Ⓒ*, *0713Ⓐ*, *0847*, *1047*, *1247*, *1447Ⓐ*, *1547Ⓒ*, 1717Ⓐ, *1747Ⓒ*, *1803Ⓐ*, *1947Ⓒ*, *1950Ⓐ*, *2147Ⓐ*, returning at *0531Ⓐ*, *0632Ⓒ*, 0633Ⓐ, *0803Ⓐ*, *0832Ⓒ*, *0932Ⓐ*, *1032Ⓐ*, *1132Ⓒ*, *1332*, *1532Ⓒ*, *1534Ⓐ*, *1700Ⓐ*, *1822⑥*, 1822†, *2032*, *2229*. Journey: 2 hours.

Flushing *(LIRR)* (❖ km, US $: 5.75). From New York Penn Stn.: 0019Ⓐ, 0020Ⓒ, 0119Ⓐ, 0120Ⓒ, 0319Ⓐ, 0350Ⓒ, 0520Ⓒ, 0529Ⓐ, 0620Ⓒ, 0631Ⓐ, 0701Ⓐ, 0720Ⓒ, 0753Ⓐ, 0820Ⓒ, 0823Ⓐ, 0850Ⓐ, 0919Ⓐ, 0920Ⓒ, 1019Ⓐ, 1020Ⓒ, 1119Ⓐ, 1120Ⓒ, 1219Ⓐ, 1220Ⓒ, 1319Ⓐ, 1320Ⓒ, 1419Ⓐ, 1420Ⓒ, 1519Ⓐ, 1520Ⓒ, 1549Ⓐ, 1620Ⓒ, 1625Ⓐ, 1649Ⓐ, 1720Ⓒ, 1729Ⓐ, 1756Ⓐ, 1814Ⓐ, 1820Ⓒ, 1850Ⓐ, 1919Ⓐ, 1920Ⓒ, 1949Ⓐ, 2019Ⓐ, 2020Ⓒ, 2049Ⓐ, 2119Ⓐ, 2120Ⓒ, 2149Ⓐ, 2219Ⓐ, 2220Ⓒ, 2249Ⓐ, 2319Ⓐ, 2320Ⓒ, 2349Ⓐ, returning from Flushing Main Street at 0005, 0105, 0202Ⓒ, 0205Ⓐ, 0342Ⓒ, 0405Ⓐ, 0536Ⓐ, 0602Ⓐ, 0605Ⓒ, 0649Ⓐ, 0700Ⓐ, 0705Ⓒ, 0727Ⓐ, 0805Ⓒ, 0812Ⓐ, 0839Ⓐ, 0852Ⓐ, 0905Ⓒ, 0915Ⓐ, 0943Ⓐ, 1005, 1047Ⓐ, 1105Ⓒ, 1147Ⓐ, 1205Ⓒ, 1247Ⓐ, 1305Ⓒ, 1347Ⓐ, 1405Ⓒ, 1447Ⓐ, 1505Ⓒ, 1547Ⓐ, 1605Ⓒ, 1632Ⓐ, 1702Ⓐ, 1705Ⓒ, 1726Ⓐ, 1757Ⓐ, 1805Ⓒ, 1836Ⓐ, 1843Ⓐ, 1858Ⓐ, 1905Ⓒ, 1935Ⓐ, 2005, 2035Ⓐ, 2105, 2135Ⓐ, 2205, 2235Ⓐ, 2305. Journey: 20 mins. Also, by *MTA/NYCTA* from New York Times Square: 0005 and frequent (every 30 mins. at night) to 2350, returning from Flushing Main Street at 0012 and frequent (every 30 mins. at night) to 2352. Journey: 40 mins.

Freeport ◇ *(LIRR)* (❖ km, US $: 6.50). From New York Penn Stn.: 0009, 0036Ⓐ, 0038Ⓒ, 0140Ⓒ, 0146Ⓐ, 0242Ⓒ, 0313Ⓐ, 0454Ⓐ, 0510Ⓒ, 0610Ⓒ, 0636Ⓐ, 0708Ⓒ, 0710Ⓐ, 0731Ⓐ, 0735Ⓒ, 0749Ⓐ and frequent to 2107Ⓐ, 2108Ⓒ, 2134Ⓐ, 2139Ⓒ, 2207Ⓐ, 2208Ⓒ, 2229Ⓐ, 2238Ⓐ, 2306Ⓐ, 2310Ⓒ, 2331Ⓐ, 2338Ⓒ, 2339Ⓐ, returning at 0008, 0123, 0208Ⓐ, 0220Ⓒ, 0330Ⓐ, 0408Ⓐ, 0419Ⓒ, 0508Ⓐ, 0519Ⓒ, 0529Ⓐ, *0547Ⓐ*, 0549Ⓒ, 0610Ⓐ, 0619Ⓒ, 0626Ⓐ and frequent to 2200Ⓒ, 2008Ⓐ, 2019Ⓒ, 2038Ⓐ, 2050Ⓒ, 2108Ⓐ,

2119©, 2138®, 2150©, 2208®, 2219©, 2238®, 2308®, 2310©, 2338®. Journey: 45 mins.
Glen Cove (LIRR) (✥ km, US $: 6.50). From New York Penn Stn.: 0036®, 0038©, 0735©, 0739®, 0841®, 0930©, 1022®, 1134©, 1143®, 1258®, 1334©, 1422®, 1531®, 1533©, 1619®, 1654®, 1733, 1808®, 1828©, 1835®, 1934©, 1939®, 2043®, 2126©, 2139®, 2245®, 2316®, returning at 0526®, 0558®, 0627©, 0642®, 0722®, 0727©, 0750®, 0830®, 0927©, 0938®, 1045®, 1127©, 1210®, 1327©, 1332®, 1452®, 1527©, 1615®, 1627©, 1727®, 1805®, 1845®, 1927©, 2015®, 2027©, 2144®, 2227©, 2315®. Journey: 1¼ hours.
Hempstead (LIRR) (✥ km, US $: 5.75). From New York Penn Stn.: 0036®, 0038©, 0140©, 0146®, 0300©, 0334®, 0530©, 0539®, 0617©, 0655®, 0735©, 0739®, 0841, 0937®, 0939©, 1039®, 1040©, 1134©, 1137®, 1237®, 1238©, 1334®, 1339®, 1432®, 1433®, 1533©, 1534®, 1632®, 1633©, 1643®, 1707®, 1717®, 1733©, 1738®, 1751®, 1808®, 1830©, 1839®, 1905®, 1934®, 1939®, 2036®, 2043®, 2139®, 2238®, 2245©, 2331®, 2339®, returning at 0001, 0115, 0201®, 0212©, 0407®, 0411©, 0501®, 0541©, 0602®, 0633©, 0638®, 0658®, 0714®, 0723©, 0724©, 0736©, 0803®, 0808©, 0820®, 0839®, 0842©, 0903®, 0941©, 1002®, 1041©, 1041®, 1101®, 1151©, 1201®, 1241©, 1301©, 1341©, 1401®, 1441©, 1500®, 1541©, 1600®, 1641©, 1653®, 1741®, 1745©, 1820®, 1843©, 1909®, 1947©, 2000®, 2041®, 2110®, 2148©, 2201®, 2208©, 2301®, 2302©. Journey: 50 mins.
Hoboken (PATH) (4 km, US $: ✥). From New York 33rd Street: 0012, 0042, 0112 and every 30 mins. to 0612, 0630®, 0640®, 0642©, 0650®, 0700®, 0710®, 0715® and frequent to 2310®, 2316®, 2327®, 2342, returning at 0026 and every 30 mins. to 0556, 0610®, 0623®, 0626®, 0633®, 0643®, 0653®, 0658®, 0703®, 0713®, 0723®, 0728©, 0729® and frequent to 2254®, 2259®, 2311®, 2325®, 2326®, 2358. Journey: 14 mins.
Jamaica (LIRR) (18 km, US $: 4.25). From New York Penn Stn.: 0000®, 0001®, 0009, 0015, 0036®, 0038©, 0059®, 0105©, 0107®, 0114®, 0115®, 0140©, 0146®, 0242©, 0246®, 0300®, 0306®, 0313®, 0316®, 0334®, 0454®, 0510®, 0511©, 0514®, 0530©, 0539® and frequent to 2306®, 2310®, 2314, 2316®, 2317®, 2331®, 2338®, 2339®, returning at 0000, 0007, 0017®, 0023©, 0033, 0047, 0107, 0117, 0148, 0206©, 0207®, 0209®, 0215®, 0233®, 0244®, 0350®, 0430®, 0433®, 0435®, 0436©, 0443®, 0511®, 0533®, 0543©, 0551® and frequent to 2301®, 2307, 2316®, 2327®, 2333®, 2334©. Also, by MTA/NYCTA from New York Times Square: 0005 and frequent (every 30 mins. at night) to 2350, returning from Jamaica 179 Street at 0010 and frequent (every 30 mins. at night) to 2355; or from New York 42nd Street at 0007 and frequent (every 30 mins. at night) to 2352, returning from Jamaica Center at 0000 and frequent (every 30 mins. at night) to 2345. Journey: 40 mins.
Jersey City (PATH) (5 km, US $: ✥). From New York World Trade Center: 0027®, 0030©, 0100 and every 30 mins. to 0600®/0700® and frequent to 2342©, 2357®, returning at 0010 and every 30 mins. to 0540 and frequent to 2340®, 2345©. Journey: 11 mins.
Milford (CDT) (✥ km, US $: 8.00). From New York Grand Central: 0035, 0130, 0540©, 0602®, 0705®, 0807 and hourly to 1407, 1502®, 1507, 1537**P**, 1602®, 1637**Q**, 1645®, 1702®, 1707®, 1713®, 1718®, 1735®, 1737**Q**, 1739®, 1804®, 1807®, 1830®, 1837**Q**, 1906®, 1907®, 1937**P**, 2007, 2107, 2207, 2320, returning at 0504®, 0536®, 0554®, 0609, 0638®, 0657®, 0709®, 0711®, 0723®, 0738®, 0756**P**, 0804®, 0809®, 0815®, 0856**Q**, 0901®, 0909®, 0956**Q**, 1009, 1056**Q**, 1109, 1156**Q**, 1209, 1309, 1409, 1509, 1606®, 1609®, 1709 and hourly to 2209, 2334. Journey: 1½ hours.
Mount Vernon (CDT/MNCR) (✥ km, US $: 5.25). From New York Grand Central to Mount Vernon: 0040, 0130, 0535©, 0540©, 0640, 0710® and about every 30 mins. (hourly on ©) to 2240, 2310©, 2340, returning at 0101, 0535®, 0605®, 0633®, 0636®, 0654®, 0717®, 0732®, 0736® and about every 30 mins. (hourly on ©) to 2006®, 2036, 2136, 2236, 2336®, 2346®. Also from New York Grand Central to Mount Vernon West: 0030, 0130, 0600, 0630®, 0653®, 0713®, 0730®, 0731® and about every 30 mins. (hourly on ©) to 2203®, 2230, 2303®, 2330, returning at 0022, 0521®, 0553®, 0554©, 0622®, 0639®, 0656®, 0657®, 0706®, 0721®, 0722® and about every 30 mins. (hourly on ©) to 1854®, 1922©, 1924®, 2022, 2122, 2222, 2322. Journey: 25-30 mins.
New Haven (CDT) (116 km, US $: 9.75). From New York Grand Central: 0035, 0130, 0540©, 0602®, 0705®, 0807 and hourly to 1407, 1502®, 1507, 1537**P**, 1602®, 1622®, 1635®, 1637**Q**, 1645®, 1702®, 1707®, 1713®, 1718®, 1735®, 1737**Q**, 1739®, 1804®, 1807®, 1830®, 1837**Q**, 1906®, 1907®, 1937**P**, 2007, 2107, 2207, 2320, returning at 0035®, 0525®, 0543®, 0558, 0627®, 0646®, 0658®, 0700®, 0712®, 0727®, 0745**P**, 0753®, 0758®, 0804®, 0845**Q**, 0850®, 0858®, 0945**Q**, 0958, 1045**Q**, 1058, 1158, 1258, 1358, 1458, 1555®, 1558®, 1658 and hourly to 2158, 2323. Journey: 1³⁄₄ hours.
New Rochelle (CDT) (53 km, US $: 5.25). From New York Grand Central: 0040, 0130, 0535©, 0540©, 0604, 0710®, 0740®, 0742®, 0810®, 0840, 0910®, 0940, 1010®, 1040, 1110®, 1140, 1210®, 1240, 1310®, 1340, 1410®, 1440, 1510**P**, 1540, 1609®, 1610**Q**, 1629®, 1640®, 1654®, 1710®, 1716®, 1720®, 1733®, 1739®, 1740©, 1801®, 1810®, 1819®, 1840, 1915®, 1940, 2010®, 2040, 2110®, 2140, 2210®, 2240, 2310®, 2340, returning at 0054, 0529®, 0559®, 0627®, 0629®, 0648®, 0711®, 0726®, 0729®, 0741®, 0756®, 0759®, 0816®, 0829®, 0839®, 0854®, 0859®, 0906®, 0926®, 0929®, 0955®, 1029®, 1034®, 1059®, 1129, 1159®, 1229, 1259®, 1329, 1359®, 1429, 1459®, 1529, 1559®, 1629, 1651®, 1659®, 1725®, 1729®, 1734®, 1804®, 1829®, 1834®, 1904®, 1929®, 1934®, 1959®, 2029, 2129, 2229, 2334®, 2339®. Journey: 35 mins.
North White Plains (MNCR) (✥ km, US S$: 6.00). From New York Grand Central: 0030, 0130, 0600, 0630®, 0653®, 0713®, 0730®, 0731®, 0744®, 0747®, 0757®, 0830, 0847, 0903®, 0930, 0947 and frequent (twice hourly on ©) to 2103®, 2136, 2147, 2236, 2247, 2330, 2347, returning at 0500®, 0530®, 0531®, 0555®, 0601®, 0617®, 0627®, 0628®, 0633®, 0633®, 0643®, 0652®, 0659®, 0701®, 0705®, 0717®, 0729®, 0734®, 0754®, 0759®, 0801®, 0823®, 0829®, 0831®, 0854®, 0859®, 0900®, 0925®, 0928® 0954 and frequent (twice-hourly on ©) to 1959, 2054, 2059, 2154, 2159, 2259, 2359. Journey: 50 mins.
Oyster Bay (LIRR) (✥ km, US $: 6.50). From New York Penn. Stn.: 0036®, 0038©, 0735©, 0739®, 0841®, 0930©, 1022®, 1134©, 1143®, 1258®, 1334©, 1422®, 1531®, 1533©, 1619®, 1654®, 1733, 1808®, 1828©, 1835®, 1934©, 1939®, 2043®, 2126®, 2134®, 2245®, 2316®, returning at 0513®, 0545®, 0614®, 0629®, 0706®, 0714®, 0723®, 0739®, 0815®, 0914®, 0924®, 1031®, 1114©, 1156®, 1314®, 1318®, 1438®, 1514®, 1602®, 1614®, 1714®, 1752®, 1832®, 1914®, 2002®, 2014®, 2231®, 2302®. Journey: 1¼ hours.
Passaic (NJT) (✥ km, US $: 2.80). From Hoboken: 0035ex⑦, 0605®, 0640®, 0713®, 0741®, 0830®, 0840®, 1110®, 1135®, 1335®, 1445®, 1540®, 1545®, 1615®, 1715®, 1720®, 1741®, 1807®, 1840®, 1935®, 2035®, 2215®, 2320®, returning at 0559®, 0701®, 0733®, 0754®, 0804®, 0824®, 0852®, 0914®, 1012®, 1055®, 1222®, 1439®, 1539®, 1639®, 1700®, 1729®, 1854®, 1929®, 2245®. Journey: 25 mins.
Patchogue (LIRR) (90 km, US $: 9.75). From New York Penn Stn: 0036®, 0038©, 0749®, 0758®, 1006®, 1031®, 1153®, 1202®, 1219®, 1619®, 1710®, 1751®, 1830®, 1908®, 1930®, 2031®, 2043®, 2208®, 2229®, 2310®, returning at 0027®®, 0238®, 0458®, 0535®, 0542®, 0639®, 0706®, 0716®, 0756®, 0839®, 1037®, 1237®, 1306®, 1434®, 1436®, 1635®, 1718®, 1807®, 1849®, 2118®, 2131®, 2229®. Journey: 1½ hours.
Paterson (NJT) (26 km, US $: 3.60). From Hoboken: 0035, 0605®, 0640®, 0713®, 0741®, 0807®, 0840®, 1110®, 1135®, 1335®, 1445®, 1540®, 1545®, 1615®, 1715®, 1720®, 1741®, 1807®, 1840®, 1935®, 1945®, 2035®, 2215®, 2320®, returning at 0544®, 0650®, 0722®, 0745®, 0753®, 0843®, 0905®, 1002®, 1045®, 1212®, 1429®, 1529®, 1629®, 1650®, 1729®, 1845®, 1920®, 2235®, 2256®. Journey: 35 mins.
Port Washington (LIRR) (✥ km, US $: 6.50). From New York Penn Stn.: 0036®, 0038©, 0200®, 0119®, 0120®, 0319®, 0350®, 0520©, 0529®, 0620®, 0631®, 0720®, 0753®, 0820®, 0823®, 0850®, 0919®, 0920®, 1019®, 1020®, 1119®, 1120®, 1219®, 1220®, 1319®, 1320®, 1419®, 1420®, 1519®, 1520®, 1549®, 1620®, 1622®, 1646®, 1703®, 1711®, 1720®, 1726®, 1744®, 1811®, 1820®, 1827®, 1850®, 1919®, 1920®, 1949®, 2019®, 2020®, 2049®, 2119®, 2120®, 2149®, 2219®, 2220®, 2249®, 2319®, 2320®, 2349®, returning at 0039, 0136®, 0139®, 0316®, 0339®, 0509®, 0536®, 0539®, 0622®, 0631®, 0639®, 0645®, 0720®, 0736®, 0739®, 0747®, 0806®, 0817®, 0839®, 0845®, 0911®, 0939, 1021®, 1039®, 1121®, 1139®, 1221®, 1239®, 1321®, 1339®, 1421®, 1439®, 1521®, 1539®, 1606®, 1636®, 1639®, 1700®, 1723®, 1739®, 1824®, 1839®, 1909®, 1939, 2009®, 2039, 2109®, 2139, 2209®, 2239, 2339. Journey: 45 mins.
Poughkeepsie (MNCR) (118 km, US $: 11.75). From New York Grand Central: 0020, 0120, 0620®, 0748®, 0755®, 0855®, 0858®, 0955®, 1055®, 1055®, 1158®, 1255, 1355®, 1358®, 1455®, 1458®, 1555®, 1557®, 1649®, 1655®, 1712®, 1744®, 1758®, 1818®, 1847®, 1855®, 1917®, 1948®, 1955®, 2055, 2201®, 2201®, 2315, returning at 0445®, 0531®, 0604®, 0619®, 0625®, 0649®, 0657®, 0719®, 0729®, 0815®, 0819®, 0919, 1119, 1119®, 1219, 1319®, 1419, 1519, 1619, 1719, 1819, 1919®, 1919®, 2019®, 2035®, 2119®, 2130®, 2245. Journey: 1 hour 50 mins.

Rockville Centre (LIRR) (✥ km, US $: 6.50). From New York Penn Stn: 0009, 0036®, 0038©, 0140©, 0146®, 0242©, 0313®, 0454®, 0510®, 0610®, 0636® and frequent to 2207®, 2208©, 2238®, 2306®, 2310©, 2338®, 2339®, returning at 0014, 0130, 0214®, 0226®, 0414®, 0425®, 0514®, 0525®, 0535®, 0553®, 0555®, 0617®, 0625®, 0633®, 0647®, 0652®, 0655® and frequent to 2214®, 2225®, 2244®, 2314®, 2316®, 2344®. Journey: 40 mins.
Rye (CDT) (✥ km, US $: 6.25). From New York Grand Central: 0040, 0130, 0535©, 0540©, 0640, 0710®, 0740®, 0742®, 0810®, 0840, 0910®, 0940, 1010®, 1040, 1110®, 1140, 1210®, 1240, 1310®, 1341®, 1410®, 1440, 1510**P**, 1540, 1607®, 1610**Q**, 1622®, 1640®, 1645®, 1710®, 1713®, 1729®, 1739®, 1740©, 1755®, 1810®, 1815®, 1837®, 1840, 1909®, 1915®, 1940, 2010®, 2040, 2110®, 2140, 2210®, 2240, 2310®, 2340, returning at 0041, 0516®, 0546®, 0614®, 0616®, 0635®, 0652®, 0713®, 0716©, 0725®, 0746®, 0759®, 0816®, 0821®, 0846⑧, 0859®, 0916®, 0928®, 0942®, 1006**Q**, 1016, 1046®, 1106**Q**, 1116, 1146®, 1206**Q**, 1216, 1246®, 1316, 1346®, 1416, 1446®, 1516®, 1616, 1638®, 1646®, 1716®, 1721®, 1751®, 1816®, 1821®, 1851®, 1916®, 1921®, 1946®, 2016, 2116, 2216, 2310®, 2326®. Journey: 45 mins.
South Norwalk (CDT) (✥ km, US $: 8.50). From New York Grand Central: 0035, 0130, 0535©, 0602®, 0705®, 0807 and hourly to 1507, 1537**Q**, 1605®, 1607, 1635®, 1637**Q**, 1641®, 1645®, 1659®, 1707®, 1713®, 1723®, 1737**P**, 1739®, 1744®, 1750®, 1807, 1834®, 1837**Q**, 1906®, 1907®, 1909®, 1937**P**, 2007, 2107, 2207, 2320, returning at 0005, 0539®, 0611®, 0631®, 0641®, 0645®, 0651®, 0709®, 0714®, 0722®, 0734®, 0741®, 0744®, 0759®, 0817®, 0828®, 0840®, 0851®, 0940®, 0941®, 0946®, 1014, 1040, 1140, 1240, 1340, 1440, 1540, 1639®, 1640®, 1740®, 1742®, 1840®, 1842®, 1940, 2040, 2140, 2240, 2301®. Journey: 1 hour.
Stamford (CDT) (66 km, US $: 6.00). From New York Grand Central: 0035, 0040, 0130, 0535©, 0540©, 0602®, 0640 and frequent to 2107, 2110®, 2140, 2207, 2210®, 2240, 2310®, 2320, 2340, returning at 0018, 0025, 0500®, 0530®, 0558®, 0600®, 0619®, 0625®, 0638®, 0643®, 0651®, 0655 and frequent to 2100, 2153, 2200, 2253, 2305®, 2310®. Journey: 50-65 mins.
Tarrytown (MNCR) (✥ km, US $: 5.00). From New York Grand Central: 0020, 0120, 0620, 0720, 0748®, 0755®, 0820®, 0855®, 0858®, 0920, 0955®, 1020, 1055, 1120, 1158®, 1220, 1255, 1320, 1355®, 1358®, 1420, 1455®, 1458®, 1520, 1545®, 1555®, 1620, 1642®, 1655®, 1652®, 1704®, 1720®, 1732®, 1736®, 1753®, 1758®, 1818®, 1820, 1850®, 1855, 1917®, 1920, 1948®, 1953®, 1955®, 2020, 2055, 2120, 2201, 2220, 2315, 2320, returning at 0514, 0542®, 0600®, 0601®, 0609®, 0634®, 0643®, 0649®, 0708®, 0718®, 0726®, 0731®, 0746®, 0753®, 0820®, 0826®, 0834®, 0849®, 0856®, 0903®, 0949, 1026, 1049, 1126, 1149, 1226®, 1249, 1331, 1349, 1431®, 1449, 1526, 1549, 1626, 1649, 1726®, 1728®, 1744®, 1749®, 1826, 1849, 1926®, 1949, 2026®, 2031®, 2049, 2126®, 2149, 2231®, 2244®, 2249®, 2359. Journey: 50 mins.
Valley Stream (LIRR) (✥ km, US $: 5.75). From New York Penn Station: 0000®, 0001®, 0009, 0059®, 0105®, 0107®, 0140©, 0242®, 0300®, 0313®, 0510®, 0511®, 0539®, 0548®, 0610®, 0636® and frequent to 2207®, 2208®, 2229®, 2306®, 2314®, 2316®, returning at 0005®, 0011©, 0035, 0100, 0155®, 0159®, 0202®, 0334®, 0414®, 0520®, 0527©, 0539®, 0555®, 0627®, 0633®, 0649® and frequent to 2227®, 2235®, 2251®, 2254®, 2304®, 2351. Journey: 35 mins.
Waterbury (CDT) (200 km, US $: 12.75). From New York Grand Central: 0602®, 0807®, 0907®, 1207®, 1607®, 1622®, 1830®, 2107, returning at 0634®, 0717®, 0916®, 1117®, 1216®, 1516®, 1517®, 1856®, 1917®, 2118®. Journey: 2¼ hours.
White Plains (MNCR) (✥ km, US S$: 4.50). From New York Grand Central: 0030, 0100, 0600, 0630®, 0653®, 0713®, 0730®, 0731®, 0744®, 0747®, 0757®, 0830, 0847, 0903®, 0930, 0947 and frequent (twice-hourly on ©) to 2103®, 2130, 2147, 2203®, 2230, 2247, 2330, 2347, returning at 0500®, 0503®, 0533®, 0535®, 0558®, 0604®, 0620®, 0630®, 0631®, 0636®, 0637®, 0646®, 0655®, 0700®, 0703®, 0708®, 0720®, 0723®, 0733®, 0738®, 0744®, 0757®, 0803®, 0805®, 0808®, 0827®, 0830®, 0833®, 0834®, 0856®, 0857®, 0903®, 0904®, 0928®, 0932®, 0957 and frequent (twice-hourly on ©) to 2003, 2057, 2103, 2157, 2203, 2303. Journey: 45 mins.
Yonkers (MNCR) (24 km, US $: 5.25). From New York Grand Central: 0020, 0120, 0620, 0720, 0748®, 0755®, 0820®, 0858®, 0920, 0955®, 1020, 1055, 1120, 1158®, 1220, 1255, 1320, 1355®, 1358®, 1420, 1455®, 1458®, 1520, 1545®, 1555®, 1620, 1642®, 1655®, 1652®, 1704®, 1720®, 1736®, 1758, 1820, 1850®, 1855, 1917®, 1920, 1948®, 1953®, 1955®, 2020, 2055, 2120, 2201, 2220, 2315, 2320, returning at 0020, 0120, 0620, 0709, 0712, 0722®, 0738®, 0741®, 0752®, 0804®, 0807®, 0818®, 0835®, 0837®, 0907®, 0917®, 0937®, 0942®, 1007, 1107, 1137, 1207, 1237®, 1307, 1341, 1407, 1441®, 1507, 1537, 1607, 1637, 1707, 1737®, 1739®, 1802®, 1807®, 1837, 1907, 1939®, 2007, 2037®, 2041®, 2107, 2137, 2207, 2241®, 2302®, 2307®. Journey: 35 mins.

Table 213 NEW YORK - PHILADELPHIA - WASHINGTON

MARC NJT NRPC SEP

US $ C cl.	NRPC ↓	km	201 P‡C‡ [R]P 🍷⊡Ⓐ	101 P‡C‡ [R]P 🍷⊡Ⓐ	79 C‡ ◆	203 P‡C‡ [R]P 🍷⊡Ⓐ	103 P‡C‡ [R]P 🍷⊡Ⓐ	89 C‡ ◆	207 P‡C‡ [R]P 🍷⊡⑥	43 C‡ ◆	205 P‡C‡ [R]◆ ⊡Ⓐ	209 P‡C‡ [R]P 🍷⊡Ⓒ	61 S‡C‡ ◆	107 P‡C‡ [R]P 🍷⊡Ⓐ	141 C‡ ◆ Ⓐ	51 S‡C‡ [R]◆ ③⑤⑦	143 C‡ ◆ Ⓒ	109 P‡C‡ [R]P 🍷⊡Ⓐ	669 C‡ ◆ Ⓐ	653 C‡ [R]◆	135 C‡ ◆ 🍷Ⓒ	111 P‡C‡ [R]P 🍷⊡Ⓐ	95 C‡ ◆[R] Ⓐ	181 C‡ ◆ 🍷	113 P‡C‡ [R]P 🍷⊡Ⓐ
	Boston **202** ....d.	0	....	....	....	....	....	....	....	....	....	....	....	....	....	....	....	....	....	....	....	....	....	....	....
0.00	**New York** Penn. Stn. Ω d.	373	0520	0600	0620	0640	0715	0723	0730	0745	0800	0830	0831	0900	0920	0930	0940	1000	....	1030	1040	1100	1125	1140	1200
8.00	Newark Ω ....d.	389	0533u	0613u	0634u	0654u	0728u	0740u	0743u	0759u	0813	0843u	0850	0913u	0935	0943u	0958u	1013u	....	1045u	1056	1113u	1140u	1153u	1213u
17.00	New Brunswick Ω d.	426	|	|	0656	|	|	|	|	0824	|	|	|	|	|	|	|	|	....	|	|	|	|	|	|
22.00	Princeton Junction ★Ω.d.	451	0606	0645	0711	|	|	|	|	0838	|	|	|	|	1010	1024u	1033	|	....	|	1130	|	|	|	|
25.00	Trenton ◇Ω ....d.	467	0614	0654	0721	|	|	0824	|	0851	|	|	0928	|	1020	|	1043	|	....	1128	1139	|	1224u	1233	|
30.00	North Philadelphia ◇ .d.	512	|	|	0748	|	|	|	|	0913	|	|	|	|	|	|	|	|	....	|	|	|	|	|	|
30.00	**Philadelphia** 30th Str.◇ .d.	519	0646	0724	0800	0753	0830	0859	0845	0920	0915	0945	1007	1015	1053	1100u	1117	1111	1150	|	1210	1210	1300	1313	1311
37.00	Wilmington ....d.	569	0705	0746	0825	|	0851	0923	0907	....	0937	1007	1027	1037	1116	1121	1139	1133	1214	a	1233	1232	1324	1337	1333
59.00	**Baltimore** Penn. Stn. d.	670	0753	0831	0917	0857	0938	1025	0950	....	1021	1051	1127	1121	1203	1214	1230	1218	1308	....	1319	1318	1421	1426	1418
59.00	BWI Airport ....d.	687	|	|	0929	|	|	|	|	....	|	|	|	|	1215	|	1243	|	|	....	1334	|	|	|	|
64.00	New Carrollton ...a.	716	|	0855s	0946	|	|	1050	1014s	....	|	1121s	1159s	|	1235s	1249	1259s	|	|	....	1350s	|	1445	1453	1442s
64.00	**Washington** Union a.	735	0824	0906	1005	0929	1011	1105	1030	....	1059	1133	1214	1157	1250	1303	1315	1255	1350	....	1405	1355	1505	1509	1455

↓	211 P‡C‡ [R]P 🍷⊡†	643 C‡ ◆ Ⓐ	469 P‡C‡ ◆	169 P‡C‡ ◆	115 P‡C‡ [R]P 🍷⊡Ⓐ		183 C‡ ◆ Ⓒ🍷	99 C‡ ◆	117 P‡C‡ [R]P 🍷⊡Ⓐ	215 P‡C‡ [R]P 🍷⊡⑦	171 P‡C‡ ◆	119 P‡C‡ [R]P 🍷⊡Ⓐ	217 P‡C‡ [R]P 🍷⊡⑦	647 C‡ ◆ †	85 C‡ ◆	121 P‡C‡ [R]P 🍷⊡Ⓐ	223 P‡C‡ [R]P 🍷⊡Ⓐ	219 P‡C‡ [R]P 🍷⊡⑦	662 C‡ [R]◆ Ⓑ	173 P‡C‡ ◆	623 C‡ Ⓐ	123 P‡C‡ [R]P 🍷⊡Ⓐ	641 C‡ ◆ Ⓐ	627 C‡ Ⓐ	221 P‡C‡ [R]P 🍷⊡Ⓒ
Boston **202**..............d.	....	....	0635	0725	....	....	....	....	....	....	0925	....	....	....	....	....	....	....	....	1125	....	....	....	....	....
New York Penn. Stn. Ω .d.	1230	1235	1240	1240	1300	....	1335	1340	1400	1430	1440	1500	1530	1535	1540	1600	1630	1630	....	1640	1645	1700	1708	1713	1730
Newark Ω ....d.	1243u	1250u	1255	1255	1313u	....	1349u	1355u	1413u	1443u	1455	1513u	1543u	1551	1554	1613u	|	1643u	....	1655	1659	1713u	1723u	1729	1743u
New Brunswick Ω.....d.	|	|	|	|	|	....	|	|	|	|	|	|	|	|	|	|	|	|	....	|	|	|	|	|	|
Princeton Junction ★Ω.d.	|	|	|	|	|	....	|	|	|	|	|	|	|	|	|	|	|	|	....	|	1735	|	|	1811	|
Trenton ◇Ω ....d.	|	|	1335	1335	|	....	1426	1435u	|	|	1535	|	|	|	1632	|	|	|	....	1730	1753	|	|	1823	|
North Philadelphia ◇ .d.	|	1343	|	|	|	....	|	|	|	|	|	|	|	1646	|	|	|	|	....	|	1824	|	1822	1902	|
Philadelphia 30th Str. ◇d.	1341	1350	1412	1412	1411	....	1457	1515	1511	1547	1615	1611	1641	1654	1713	1709	|	1746	1741	1808	1840	1816	c	1912	1843
Wilmington ....d.	1403	....	1438	1438	1433	....	1522	1538	1533	1609	1636	1633	1703	....	1734	1731	|	1808	1804	1828	....	1838	....	....	1905
Baltimore Penn. Stn..d.	1448	....	1529	1529	1518	....	1611	1626	1618	1655	1731	1720	1749	....	1822	1817	1839s	1852	1901	1927	....	1922	....	....	1951
BWI Airport ....d.	|	....	1545	1545	|	....	|	|	|	|	1744	|	1800	....	1834	1828	|	|	1914	1942	....	|	....	....	2002
New Carrollton ....a.	1512s	....	1559s	1559s	1542s	....	1643s	1656s	1642s	1720s	1803	1743s	1817s	....	1854	1845s	1903s	1918s	1931	2001s	....	1948s	....	....	2018s
Washington Union ..a.	1527	....	1613	1613	1555	....	1656	1705	1655	1732	1820	1759	1828	....	1908	1859	1914	1929	1949	2015	....	1959	....	....	2029

↓	187 C‡ ◆ 🍷	645 C‡ ◆ Ⓒ	629 C‡ Ⓐ	125 P‡C‡ [R]P 🍷⊡Ⓐ	633 C‡ Ⓐ	649 C‡ ◆ Ⓐ	225 P‡C‡ [R]P 🍷⊡⑦	475 C‡ ◆	175 P‡C‡ ◆	127 P‡C‡ [R]P 🍷⊡Ⓐ#	139 C‡ ◆ 🍷⑤	664 C‡ [R]◆	227 P‡C‡ [R]P 🍷⊡†	189 C‡ ◆ 🍷⑦	129 P‡C‡ [R]P🍷⊡ ①②③④	177 P‡C‡ ◆	179 C‡ ◆ Ⓐ	639 C‡ †	668 C‡ [R]◆ ⑥	167 C‡ ◆ Ⓒ	193 C‡ ◆	77 S‡C‡ ◆ ⑥⑦	877 S‡ ◆ ⑥⑦	867 S‡ ◆ Ⓐ	67 S‡C‡ ◆ Ⓐ
Boston **202**..............d.	....	....	....	....	....	....	....	1225	1325	....	....	....	....	....	....	1530	1630	....	....	1740	1901	2138f	....	....	2210g
New York Penn. Stn. Ω.d.	1735	1740	1740	1800	1803	1829	1830	1840	1840	1900	1925	....	1930	1940	2000	2045	2140	2140	....	2245	0030	0335	0335	0345	0345
Newark Ω..................d.	1751u	1755u	1756	1813u	1817	1843	1843u	1855	1855	1913u	|	....	1943u	1955	2013u	2101	2156	2157u	....	2302	0045	0410	0410	0405	0405
New Brunswick Ω.....d.	|	|	|	|	|	|	|	|	|	|	|	....	|	|	|	|	|	|	....	|	|	|	|	|	|
Princeton Junction ★Ω.d.	|	|	1834	|	1852	|	|	|	|	|	|	....	|	|	|	|	|	|	....	|	|	|	|	|	|
Trenton ◇Ω ....d.	|	1832	1850	|	1907	|	|	1936	1936	|	|	....	|	2035	|	2142	2236	2236	....	2341	0129	0503	0503	0454	0454
North Philadelphia ◇ .d.	|	1856	1923s	|	1939s	1933s	|	|	|	|	|	....	|	|	|	|	|	|	....	|	|	|	|	|	|
Philadelphia 30th Str.◇ d.	1857	1906	1936	1913	1952	1945	1945	2017	2017	2015	|	2036	2042	2109	2115	2216	2309	2307	2335s	0017	0200	0554	0554	0542	0542
Wilmington ....d.	1919	....	....	1935	....	....	2007	2041	2041	2037	|	2058	2104	2131	2137	2237	2330	....	|	0041	....	0620	0620	0608	0608
Baltimore Penn. Stn..d.	2010	....	....	2021	....	....	2050	2130	2130	2120	2150s	2158	2148	2221	2222	2333	0026	....	0051s	0135	....	0717	0717	0711	0711
BWI Airport ....d.	|	....	....	2032	....	....	|	2141	2141	|	|	2217	|	|	|	2347	|	....	0106s	0152	....	0734	0734	0725	0725
New Carrollton ....a.	2040s	....	....	2048s	....	....	2115s	2200	2200	2145s	2215s	2237	2215s	2249s	2247s	0008s	0054s	....	0127s	0211s	....	0750	0750	0743	0743
Washington Union ..a.	2055	....	....	2059	....	....	2126	2215	2215	2156	2230	2250	2227	2305	2259	0024	0110	....	0147	0227	....	0805	0805	0755	0755

US $	401 C‡ Ⓐ	503 C‡ Ⓐ	405 C‡ Ⓐ	507 C‡ ⒶQ	409 C‡ Ⓐ	511 C‡ ⒶR	421 C‡ Ⓐ	423 C‡ Ⓐ🍷	427 C‡ Ⓐ	429 C‡ Ⓐ🍷	435 C‡ Ⓐ⊠	km	*MARC* ↓ ↑	400 C‡ Ⓐ	402 C‡ Ⓐ	404 C‡ Ⓐ	406 C‡ Ⓐ	408 C‡ Ⓐ🍷	414 C‡ Ⓐ🍷	520 C‡ ⒶS	424 C‡ Ⓐ	526 C‡ ⒶT	430 C‡ Ⓐ	436 C‡ Ⓐ▼
5.25	0520	0550	0615	0640	0650	0722	1053	1145	1350	1450	1755	0	d.**Baltimore** Penn. Stn. a.	0732	0836	0925	1040	1125	1427	1655	1743	1809	1846	2111
4.50	0536	0609	0633	0658	0702	0739	1107	1202	1407	1507	1811	17	d.BWI Airport................d.	0714	0814	0907	1018	1102	1405	1638	1718	1750	1826	2053
3.00	0559	0636	0659	|	0728	|	1129	1228	1433	1533	1834	46	d.New Carrollton ....d.	0652	0752	0838	0953	1038	1343	|	1653	|	1801	2031
0.00	0612	0649	0712	0730	0741	0809	1142	1245	1450	1550	1847	65	a.**Washington** Union ...d.	0639	0739	0825	0940	1025	1330	1615	1640	1715	1748	2018

43– PENNSYLVANIAN–[C] and 🍷 New York(**43**)-Pittsburgh.
51– CARDINAL–🛏‡, ▬‡, [C] and ⊗ New York(**51**)-Chicago (Table **223**).
61– MONTREALER–🛏‡, [C] and ⊗ Montréal(**61**)-Washington.
67– NIGHT OWL–🛏‡, [C] and 🍷 Boston(**67**)-Washington.
77– WEEKEND NIGHT OWL–🛏‡, [C] and 🍷 Boston(**77**)-Washington.
79– CAROLINIAN–[C] and 🍷 New York(**79**)-Charlotte.
85– CHESAPEAKE–[C] and 🍷 New York(**85**)-Washington (Richmond on Ⓒ).
89– PALMETTO–[C] and 🍷 New York(**89**)-Jacksonville.
95– OLD DOMINION–[C] and 🍷 New York(**95**)-Newport News.
99– VIRGINIAN–[C] and 🍷 New York(**99**)-Richmond (Newport News on ⑤⑥⑦).
135– POTOMAC. **139**–CAPITOL HILL EXPRESS.
141– BANKERS–[C] and 🍷 Springfield(**141**)-Washington.
143– THE NUTMEG STATE–[C] and 🍷 Springfield(**143**)-Washington.
167– NARRAGANSETT–[C] and 🍷 Boston(**167**)-Washington; [C] Springfield(**467**)-New Haven(**167**)-Washington.
169– MAYFLOWER–[PC] and 🍷 Boston(**169**)-Washington.
171– MINUTE MAN–[PC] and 🍷 Boston(**171**)-Washington; [C] Springfield(**471**)-New Haven(**171**)-Washington.
173– YANKEE CLIPPER–[PC] and 🍷 Boston(**173**)-Washington; [C] Springfield(**473**)-New Haven(**173**)-Washington.
175– PATRIOT–[PC] and 🍷 Boston(**175**)-Washington.
177– SENATOR–[PC] and 🍷 Boston(**177**)-Washington; [C] and 🍷 Springfield(**477**)-New Haven(**177**)-Washington.
179– MERCHANTS LIMITED–[C] and 🍷 Boston(**179**)-Washington; [C] Springfield(**479**)-New Haven(**179**)-Washington.
181– CONGRESSIONAL. **183**–FORT McHENRY. **187**–INDEPENDENCE.
189– EMBASSY.
193– BENJAMIN FRANKLIN–[C] Boston(**193**)-Philadelphia.
205– METROLINER–[PC] and 🍷 New Haven(**205**)-Washington.
469– CONNECTICUT YANKEE–[C] and 🍷 Boston(**469**)-Washington.
475– THE BAY STATE–[C] and 🍷 Boston(**475**)-Washington.
641– KEYSTONE STATE EXPRESS–[C] and 🍷 New York(**641**)-Harrisburg.
643– KEYSTONE–[C] and 🍷 New York(**643**)-Harrisburg.
645– SUSQUEHANNA–[C] and 🍷 New York(**645**)-Harrisburg.
647/9–KEYSTONE–[C] and 🍷 New York(**647/9**)-Harrisburg.
653– ATLANTIC CITY EXPRESS–[C] and 🍷 Springfield(**653**)-Atlantic City.
662– ATLANTIC CITY EXPRESS–[C] and 🍷 Atlantic City(**662**)-Washington (Richmond on Ⓐ).
664– ATLANTIC CITY EXPRESS–[C] and 🍷 Atlantic City(**664**)-Washington (Richmond on Ⓒ).
668– ATLANTIC CITY EXPRESS–[C] and 🍷 Atlantic City(**668**)-Washington.
669– CAPITAL CITY.
867– EXECUTIVE SLEEPER–🛏‡ and 🍷 New York(**867**)-Washington. 🛏 may be boarded from 2130.
877– EXECUTIVE SLEEPER–🛏‡ and 🍷 New York(**877**)-Washington. 🛏 may be boarded from 2130.
P– METROLINER. **Q**–THE FREE STATE EXPRESS. **R**–THE MORNING EXECUTIVE.
S– THE MARYLAND EXPRESS. **T**–THE AFTERNOON EXECUTIVE.
a– To Atlantic City. **c**–To Harrisburg.
f– ⑤⑥ only. **g**–ex ⑤⑥. #–No service on ⑤ July 1-Sept. 9.
◇– Local #### service (*SEP*), C cl. only, West Trenton-Bethayres-Jenkintown-Philadelphia 30th Street (Journey 1 hour), **from West Trenton** at: 0552Ⓐ, 0621Ⓐ, 0636Ⓐ, 0652Ⓐ, 0706Ⓐ, 0721Ⓐ, 0737Ⓐ, 0742⑥, 0750Ⓐ, 0842Ⓒ, 0843Ⓐ, 0942Ⓒ, 0943Ⓐ, 1042Ⓒ, 1043Ⓐ, 1142Ⓒ, 1143Ⓐ, 1242Ⓒ, 1243Ⓐ, 1342Ⓒ, 1343Ⓐ, 1442Ⓒ, 1443Ⓐ, 1542Ⓒ, 1559Ⓐ, 1642Ⓒ, 1655Ⓐ, 1725Ⓐ, 1742⑥, 1800Ⓐ, 1842⑥, 1858Ⓐ, 2000Ⓐ, 2047Ⓐ, 2147Ⓐ, 2257Ⓐ; also Trenton-North Philadelphia-Philadelphia 30th Street (Journey 50 minutes), **from Trenton** at: 0010①⑦, 0544Ⓐ, 0616Ⓐ, 0636Ⓐ, 0657Ⓐ, 0658Ⓒ, 0715Ⓐ, 0731Ⓐ, 0801Ⓒ, 0804Ⓐ, 0836Ⓐ, 0901Ⓒ, 0936Ⓐ, 0958Ⓒ, 1030Ⓐ, 1058Ⓒ, 1133Ⓐ, 1158Ⓒ, 1232Ⓐ, 1258Ⓒ, 1330Ⓐ, 1358Ⓒ, 1432Ⓐ, 1458Ⓒ, 1541Ⓐ, 1601Ⓒ, 1637Ⓐ, 1658Ⓒ, 1708Ⓐ, 1752Ⓐ, 1758Ⓒ, 1824Ⓐ, 1858Ⓒ, 1902Ⓐ, 1934Ⓐ, 1958Ⓒ, 2025Ⓐ, 2058Ⓒ, 2136Ⓐ, 2158Ⓒ, 2225Ⓐ, 2258Ⓒ, 2346Ⓐ.
★– Local #### service (*NJT*), C cl. only, Princeton Junction-Princeton at 0027②-⑥, 0039①⑦, 0051②-⑥, 0555Ⓐ, 0632Ⓒ, 0711Ⓐ, 0729Ⓐ, 0739Ⓒ, 0801Ⓐ, 0821Ⓐ, 0849Ⓒ, 0847Ⓐ, 0915Ⓐ, 0939Ⓒ, 0945Ⓐ, 1015Ⓐ, 1045Ⓐ, 1032Ⓒ, 1108Ⓐ, 1140Ⓒ, 1211Ⓐ, 1234Ⓒ, 1245Ⓐ, 1311Ⓐ, 1339Ⓒ, 1346Ⓐ, 1409Ⓐ, 1436Ⓒ, 1445Ⓐ, 1516Ⓐ, 1539Ⓐ, 1540Ⓒ, 1621Ⓐ, 1640Ⓒ, 1647Ⓐ, 1712Ⓐ, 1734Ⓒ, 1745Ⓐ, 1818Ⓐ, 1832Ⓒ, 1846Ⓐ, 1906Ⓐ, 1924Ⓐ, 1935Ⓒ, 1946Ⓐ, 2020Ⓐ, 2032Ⓒ, 2050Ⓐ, 2120Ⓐ, 2139Ⓒ, 2145Ⓐ, 2208Ⓐ, 2237Ⓒ, 2239Ⓐ, 2329Ⓐ, 2340Ⓒ.
Ω– Local #### service (*NJT*), C cl. only, New York-Newark-New Brunswick-Princeton Junction-Trenton at 0040, 0140, 0439Ⓐ, 0509Ⓒ, 0550Ⓐ, 0632Ⓒ, 0642Ⓐ, 0716Ⓐ, 0738Ⓐ, 0742Ⓒ, 0809Ⓐ, 0829Ⓐ, 0832Ⓒ, 0902Ⓐ, 0925Ⓒ, 0934Ⓐ, 1002Ⓐ, 1027Ⓒ, 1034Ⓐ, 1104Ⓐ, 1127Ⓒ, 1137Ⓐ, 1204Ⓐ, 1232Ⓒ, 1237Ⓐ, 1302Ⓐ, 1329Ⓒ, 1337Ⓐ, 1407Ⓐ, 1432Ⓒ, 1430Ⓐ, 1510Ⓐ, 1525Ⓒ, 1544Ⓐ, 1608Ⓐ, 1625Ⓒ, 1633Ⓐ, 1703Ⓐ, 1724Ⓐ, 1725Ⓒ, *1736*Ⓐ, 1738Ⓐ, 1810Ⓐ, *1822*Ⓐ, 1825Ⓒ, 1835Ⓐ, *1852*♂, 1910Ⓐ, 1925Ⓒ, 1940Ⓐ, 2010Ⓐ, 2032Ⓒ, 2039Ⓐ, 2104Ⓐ, 2130Ⓒ, 2135Ⓐ, 2225Ⓐ, 2232Ⓒ, 2325Ⓐ, 2332Ⓒ, 2340Ⓐ.
⊠– Additional trips: 0757Ⓐ, 0900Ⓐ, 0953Ⓐ, 1253Ⓐ, 1555Ⓐ, 1655Ⓐ, 2025Ⓐ.
▼– Additional trips: 1140Ⓐ, 1235Ⓐ, 1445Ⓐ, 1545Ⓐ, 1810Ⓐ, 1849Ⓐ, 2148Ⓐ.
♂– Runs on Ⓐ (ex ⑤ May 28-Sept. 3).

MARC–Maryland Department of Transportation. Tel.: Washington 202 906 3104. *NJT*–New Jersey Transit. Tel.: Newark 201 762 5100. *NRPC*–National Railroad Passenger Corporation (AMTRAK). Tel: New York 212 582 6875. *SEP*–Southeastern Pennsylvania Transportation Authority. Tel.: Philadelphia 580 7800.

Table 213–contd WASHINGTON - PHILADELPHIA - NEW YORK

╫╫╫ *NJT NRPC SEP*

US$ C cl.	*NRPC* ↓	km	12	620	624	626	134	100	628	190	198	200	202	640	180	102	130	204	642	104	170	470	106	661	182
			C‡	C‡	C‡	C‡	C‡	P‡C‡	C‡	C‡	C‡	P‡C‡	P‡C‡	C‡	C‡	P‡C‡	C‡	P‡C‡	C‡	P‡C‡	P‡C‡	C‡	P‡C‡	C‡	C‡
			◆	Ⓐ	Ⓐ	ex①⑦	◆	ⓇP	Ⓐ	◆	◆	ⓇP	ⓇP	◆	◆	ⓇP	◆	ⓇP	◆	ⓇP	◆	◆	ⓇP	◆Ⓡ	◆
							🍷①	🍷⊡Ⓐ		Ⓐ	Ⓒ	🍷⊡Ⓐ	🍷⊡Ⓐ	Ⓐ	🍷Ⓐ	🍷⊡Ⓐ	🍷Ⓒ	🍷⊡⑥		🍷⊡Ⓐ			🍷⊡Ⓐ	⑥	
0.00	**Washington** Union ...d.	0	0300	....	....	....	0445	0545	....	....	....	0610	0650	....	0620	0700	0640	0730	....	0800	0735	0735	0900	0825	0835
★6.00	New Carrollton ....d.	16	|	....	....	....	0455	0554u	....	....	....	0619u	0659u	....	0630u	0709u	0650u	0739u	....	0809u	0745	0745	0909u	0836u	0844
★10.00	BWI Airport ....d.	48	|	....	....	....	0510	0608	....	....	....	0633	|	....	0645	0723	0705	|	....	|	|	|	|	|	0903
★12.00	**Baltimore** Penn. Stn. d.	65	0331	....	....	....	0525	0622	....	....	....	0647	|	....	0658	0737	0718	0803	....	0833	0809	0809	0933	0908u	0916
31.00	Wilmington ....d.	175	0429	....	....	0625	0625	0707	....	....	....	0732	|	....	0753	0820	0815	0851	....	0917	0904	0904	1017	|	1006
40.00	**Philadelphia** 30th Street Ω d.	216	0509	0540	0620	0650	0650	0730	0705	0735	0735	0755	|	c	0824	0843	0843	0911	0915	0938	0931	0931	1038	1027u	1042
40.00	North Philadelphia Ω .d.	223	|	0550u	0631	0658	0658	|	0715	0743	0745	|	|	0808	|	|	|	|	|	|	|	|	|	....	|
47.00	Trenton Ω ⊠..............d.	268	|	0614	0702	|	|	|	0748	|	0809	|	|	0831	0853	|	0915	|	|	|	1007	1007	|	....	1113
50.00	Princeton Junction◇⊠d.	283	|	0629	0712	|	|	|	0801	|	0817	|	|	0842	|	|	|	|	|	|	|	|	|	....	|
62.00	New Brunswick ⊠.....d.	309	|	|	0729	|	|	|	0817	|	|	|	|	|	|	|	|	|	|	|	|	|	|	....	|
64.00	Newark ⊠.................d.	345	0624	0709	0753	0750s	0750s	0829s	0839	0834	0850	0855s	|	0915	0934s	0944s	0956	1013s	1022s	1039s	1047	1047	1139s	....	1155
64.00	**New York** Penn. Stn ⊠ .a.	361	0641	0727	0810	0807	0807	0844	0857	0853	0904	0910	0925	0930	0950	0959	1015	1029	1040	1055	1110	1110	1155	....	1210
98.00	*Boston South* **202** .....a.	735	1204	....	....	....	....	....	....	1433	1433	....	....	....	....	....	....	....	....	....	1635	1715	....	....	....

↓	663	667	206	108	172	110	86	646	112	174	208	94	114	184	116	176	476	210			118	142	214	120	665
	C‡	C‡	P‡C‡	P‡C‡	P‡C‡	P‡C‡	C‡	C‡	P‡C‡	P‡C‡	P‡C‡	C‡	P‡C‡	C‡	P‡C‡	P‡C‡	C‡	P‡C‡			P‡C‡	C‡	P‡C‡	P‡C‡	C‡
	Ⓡ◆	◆Ⓡ	ⓇP	ⓇP	◆	ⓇP	◆	◆	ⓇP	◆	ⓇP	◆	ⓇP	◆	ⓇP	◆	◆	ⓇP			ⓇP	◆	ⓇP	ⓇP	◆
	Ⓐ	Ⓒ	🍷⊡Ⓒ	🍷⊡Ⓐ		🍷⊡Ⓐ	Ⓒ	Ⓑ	🍷⊡Ⓐ		🍷⊡⑦	Ⓡ	🍷⊡Ⓐ	🍷†	🍷⊡Ⓐ			🍷⊡⑦			🍷⊡Ⓐ		🍷⊡⑦	🍷⊡Ⓐ	ⓇⒷ
Washington Union .....d.	0845	0900	0930	1000	0935	1100	1035	....	1200	1135	1230	1210	1300	1235	1400	1335	1335	1430	....	....	1500	1435	1530	1600	1520
New Carrollton ....d.	0856	0911	0939u	1009u	0946	|	1046	....	1209u	1145	1239u	1222	|	1246	|	1345	1345	1439u	....	....	|	1445	1539u	1609u	1531u
BWI Airport ....d.	0915	0930	|	|	1002	|	|	....	|	1159	|	|	|	1301	|	1401	1401	|	....	....	|	1500	|	|	1550
Baltimore Penn. Stn...d.	0936	0946	1003	1033	1015	1130	1110	....	1233	1213	1303	1246	1330	1314	1430	1414	1414	1503	....	....	1530	1513	1603	1633	1606
Wilmington ....d.	1028	1038	1048	1119	1107	1216	1204	....	1320	1306	1349	1338	1416	1405	1517	1506	1506	1549	....	....	1616	1602	1648	1718	1658
Philadelphia 30th Street Ωd.	1052	1102	1108	1139	1132	1236	1240	1315	1340	1333	1410	1405	1436	1432	1537	1539	1539	1609	....	....	1636	1638	1708	1738	1721
North Philadelphia Ω ...d.	....	....	|	|	|	|	|	|	|	|	|	|	|	|	|	|	|	|	....	....	|	|	|	|	....
Trenton Ω ⊠...............d.	....	....	|	|	1203	|	1311	|	|	1401	|	1437s	|	1501	|	1613	1613	|	....	....	|	1711	|	|	....
Princeton Junction◇⊠d.	....	....	|	|	1216	|	|	|	|	|	|	|	|	|	|	|	|	|	....	....	|	|	|	|	....
New Brunswick ⊠.......d.	....	....	|	|	|	|	|	|	|	|	|	|	|	|	|	|	|	|	....	....	|	|	|	|	....
Newark ⊠...................d.	....	....	1212s	1241s	1253	1340s	1353s	1418s	1441s	1449	1510u	1514s	1540s	1542s	1640s	1655	1655	1714s	....	....	1741s	1751	1813s	1843s	....
New York Penn. Stn. ⊠.a.	....	....	1228	1255	1316	1355	1410	1438	1455	1505	1525	1530	1555	1557	1655	1715	1715	1730	....	....	1759	1808	1829	1859	....
Boston South **202** ....a.	....	....	....	....	1853	....	....	....	....	2028	....	....	....	....	....	2247	2330	....	....	....	....	....	....	....	....

↓	42	178	220	216	228	222		60	218	124	188	224	44	126	80	654	226	128	96	90	66	866	76	876	670
	C‡	C‡	P‡C‡	P‡C‡	P‡C‡	P‡C‡		S‡C‡	P‡C‡	P‡C‡	C‡	P‡C‡	C‡	P‡C‡	C‡	C‡	P‡C‡	P‡C‡	C‡	C‡	S‡C‡	S‡C‡	S‡C‡	S‡C‡	C‡
	◆	◆	ⓇP	ⓇP	Ⓡ◆	Ⓡ◆		◆	ⓇP	ⓇP	◆	ⓇP	◆	ⓇP	◆	Ⓡ◆	ⓇP	ⓇPℜ	◆	◆	◆	◆	◆	◆	◆
	⚒		🍷⊡Ⓐ	🍷⊡⑥	⊡⑦	⊡Ⓐ			🍷⊡⑦	🍷⊡Ⓐ	🍷	🍷⊡⑦	†	🍷⊡Ⓐ			🍷⊡⑦	🍷⊡Ⓐ			ex⑤⑥	ex⑤⑥	⑤⑥	⑤⑥	ex①⑦
Washington Union .....d.	....	1535	1630	1630	1630	1700	....	1635	1730	1800	1735	1830	....	1900	1840	....	1930	2000	1940	2040	2210	2210	2210	2210	0010
New Carrollton ....d.	....	1545	|	1639u	1639u	|	....	1647	1739u	1809u	1745	1839u	....	1909u	1850	....	1939u	2009u	1951	2051	2220	2220	2220	2220	|
BWI Airport ....d.	....	|	|	|	|	|	....	|	|	|	1801	|	....	|	1905	....	|	|	2006	|	2239	2239	2239	2239	0040
Baltimore Penn. Stn...d.	....	1610	|	1703	1703	1730	....	1711	1803	1833	1814	1903	....	1933	1918	....	2003	2033	2020	2116	2258	2258	2258	2258	0055s
Wilmington ....d.	....	1705	|	1749	1749	1814	....	1805	1848	1918	1910	1948	....	2018	2007	....	2048	2118	2122	2211	0001	0001	0001	0001	|
Philadelphia 30th Street Ωd.	1722	1731	1800	1810	1810	1835	....	1837	1908	1938	1942	2008	2015	2038	2033	a	2108	2138	2149	2238	0031	0031	0102	0102	0220
North Philadelphia Ω ...d.	1730	|	|	|	|	|	....	|	|	|	|	|	2023	|	|	|	|	|	|	|	|	|	|	|	....
Trenton Ω ⊠...............d.	1751	1801	1826	|	|	|	....	1914	|	|	2014	|	2047	|	2110	2139	|	|	2218	2310	0110	0110	0145	0145	....
Princeton Junction◇⊠d.	|	1810	1835	|	|	|	....	1922	|	|	|	|	|	|	2121	|	|	|	|	|	|	|	|	|	....
New Brunswick ⊠.......d.	|	1822	|	|	|	|	....	|	|	|	2030	|	|	|	|	|	|	|	|	|	|	|	|	|	....
Newark ⊠...................d.	1827s	1848	1910s	1914	1914	1939	....	2000	2014s	2044s	2058	2111s	2128s	2140s	2201	2216	2215s	2241s	2301s	2352s	0156	0156	0237	0237	....
New York Penn. Stn. ⊠.a.	1850	1905	1929	1927	1927	1957	....	2018	2030	2100	2120	2128	2145	2157	2220	2230	2230	2258	2317	0010	0217	0217	0306	0306	....
Boston South **202** ....a.	....	0026	....	....	....	0056b	....	....	....	....	....	....	....	....	....	....	....	....	....	....	0839	....	0953	....	....

12– FAST MAIL–🚃 and 🍷 Washington(**12**)-Boston; 🚃 Washington(**12**)-New Haven(**412**)-Springfield.
42– PENNSYLVANIAN–🚃 and 🍷 Pittsburgh(**42**)-New York.
44– PENNSYLVANIAN–🚃 and 🍷 Pittsburgh(**44**)-New York.
60– MONTREALER–🛏‡, 🚃 and ⊗ Washington(**60**)-Montréal.
66– NIGHT OWL–🛏‡, 🚃 and 🍷 Washington(**66**)-Boston.
76– WEEKEND NIGHT OWL–🛏‡, 🚃 and 🍷 Washington(**76**)-Boston.
80– CAROLINIAN–🚃 and 🍷 Charlotte(**80**)-New York.
86– THE VIRGINIAN–🚃 and 🍷 Richmond (Washington on †)(**86**)-New York.
90– PALMETTO–🚃 and 🍷 Jacksonville(**90**)-New York.
94– OLD DOMINION–🚃 and 🍷 Newport News(**94**)-New York.
96– TIDEWATER–🚃 and 🍷 Washington (Newport News on ⑤⑦ [④⑤⑦ May 26-Sept. 7])(**96**)-New York.
130– CENTRAL PARK.
134– FIRST STATE.
142– BANKERS–🚃 and 🍷 Washington(**140**)-Springfield.
170– YANKEE CLIPPER–🚃P and 🍷 Washington(**170**)-Boston.
172– PATRIOT–🚃P and 🍷 Washington(**172**)-Boston; 🚃 Washington(**172**)-New Haven(**472**)-Springfield.
174– MAYFLOWER–🚃P and 🍷 Washington(**174**)-Boston; 🚃 Washington(**174**)-New Haven(**474**)-Springfield.
176– SENATOR–🚃P and 🍷 Washington(**176**)-Boston.
178– MERCHANTS LIMITED–🚃P and 🍷 Washington(**178**)-Boston.
180– INDEPENDENCE.
182– THE NEW YORKER.
184– POTOMAC.
188– CONGRESSIONAL.
190– BENJAMIN FRANKLIN–🚃 Philadelphia(**190**)-Boston; 🚃 Philadelphia(**190**)-New Haven(**490**)-Springfield.
198– BENJAMIN FRANKLIN–🚃 Philadelphia(**198**)-Boston; 🚃 Philadelphia(**198**)-New Haven(**498**)-Springfield.
222– METROLINER–🚃P and 🍷 Washington(**222**)-New Haven (Boston on ⑤).
228– METROLINER–🚃P and 🍷 Washington(**222**)-New Haven.
470– CONNECTICUT YANKEE–🚃 and 🍷 Washington(**470**)-Boston.
476– BAY STATE–🚃 and 🍷 Washington(**476**)-Boston.
640– KEYSTONE STATE EXPRESS–🚃 and 🍷 Harrisburg(**640**)-New York.
642– KEYSTONE–🚃 (also 🍷 on ⑥⑦) Harrisburg(**642**)-New York.
646– KEYSTONE–🚃 Harrisburg(**646**)-New York.
654– ATLANTIC CITY EXPRESS–🚃 and 🍷 Atlantic City(**654**)-Springfield.
661– ATLANTIC CITY EXPRESS–🚃 and 🍷 Washington(**661**)-Atlantic City.
663– ATLANTIC CITY EXPRESS–🚃 and 🍷 Richmond(**663**)-Atlantic City.
665– ATLANTIC CITY EXPRESS–🚃 and 🍷 Washington(**665**)-Atlantic City.
667– ATLANTIC CITY EXPRESS–🚃 and 🍷 Richmond(**667**)-Atlantic City.
866– EXECUTIVE SLEEPER–🛏‡ and 🍷 Washington(**866**)-New York. Passengers may remain in 🛏 until 0800.
876– EXECUTIVE SLEEPER–🛏‡ and 🍷 Washington(**876**)-New York. Passengers may remain in 🛏 until 0800.
P– METROLINER. **a**–From Atlantic City. **b**–⑥ only.
c– From Harrisburg.
ℜ– No service on ⑤ July 1-Sept. 9.
◇– Local ╫╫╫ service (*NJT*), C cl. only, Princeton-Princeton Junction at 0546Ⓐ, 0604Ⓐ, 0617Ⓒ, 0622Ⓐ, 0644Ⓐ, 0702Ⓐ, 0717Ⓒ, 0722Ⓐ, 0741Ⓐ, 0812Ⓐ, 0817Ⓒ, 0830Ⓐ, 0859Ⓐ, 0917Ⓒ, 0925Ⓐ, 0954Ⓐ, 1017Ⓒ, 1025Ⓐ, 1054Ⓐ, 1117Ⓒ, 1157Ⓐ, 1217Ⓒ, 1231Ⓐ, 1257Ⓐ, 1317Ⓒ, 1332Ⓐ, 1355Ⓐ, 1417Ⓒ, 1431Ⓐ, 1500Ⓐ, 1517Ⓒ, 1525Ⓐ, 1603Ⓐ, 1617Ⓒ, 1634Ⓐ, 1658Ⓐ, 1717Ⓒ, 1731Ⓐ, 1759Ⓐ, 1817Ⓒ, 1827Ⓐ, 1855Ⓐ, 1915Ⓐ, 1917Ⓒ, 2005Ⓐ, 2017Ⓒ, 2030Ⓐ, 2100, 2129Ⓐ, 2154Ⓐ, 2217Ⓒ, 2305Ⓐ, 2317Ⓒ, 2359Ⓐ.
★– *MDT* fares are cheaper.
Ω– Local ╫╫╫ service (*SEP*), C cl. only, Philadelphia-Jenkintown-Bethayres-West Trenton (Journey 1 hour), **from Philadelphia 30th Street** at: 0528Ⓐ, 0620Ⓐ, 0715Ⓐ, 0810⑥, 0812Ⓐ, 0910⑥, 0914Ⓐ, 1010, 1110, 1210, 1310, 1410, 1510, 1550Ⓐ, 1610Ⓒ, 1620Ⓐ, 1640Ⓐ, 1650Ⓐ, 1709Ⓐ, 1710Ⓒ, 1712Ⓐ, 1742Ⓐ, 1810Ⓒ, 1823Ⓐ, 1910⑥, 1912Ⓐ, 2014Ⓐ, 2114Ⓐ, 2214Ⓐ, 2314Ⓐ, also Philadelphia 30th Street-North Philadelphia-Trenton (Journey 50 minutes) at: 0004②-⑥, 0504Ⓐ, 0524Ⓐ, 0621Ⓒ, 0637Ⓐ, 0713Ⓐ, 0721Ⓒ, 0807Ⓐ, 0821Ⓒ, 0906Ⓐ, 0921Ⓒ, 1004Ⓐ, 1016Ⓒ, 1104Ⓐ, 1121Ⓒ, 1204Ⓐ, 1216Ⓒ, 1304Ⓐ, 1321Ⓒ, 1404Ⓐ, 1421Ⓒ, 1504Ⓐ, 1516Ⓒ, 1604Ⓐ, 1616Ⓒ, 1631Ⓐ, 1654Ⓐ, 1716Ⓐ, 1721Ⓒ, 1740Ⓐ, 1754Ⓐ, 1815Ⓒ, 1826Ⓐ, 1904Ⓐ, 1916Ⓒ, 2004Ⓐ, 2016Ⓒ, 2104Ⓐ, 2116Ⓒ, 2204Ⓐ, 2216Ⓒ, 2304Ⓐ, 2321Ⓒ.
⊠– Local ╫╫╫ service (*NJT*), C cl. only, Trenton-Princeton Junction-New Brunswick-Newark-New York at 0330Ⓐ, 0530Ⓒ, 0525Ⓐ, 0550Ⓐ, *0605*Ⓐ, 0617Ⓒ, 0620Ⓐ, 0630Ⓐ, 0649Ⓐ, 0711Ⓐ, 0717Ⓒ, 0718Ⓐ, 0740Ⓐ, 0817Ⓒ, 0818Ⓐ, 0900Ⓐ, 0917Ⓒ, 0930Ⓐ, 1000Ⓐ, 1017Ⓒ, 1030Ⓐ, 1110Ⓐ, 1117Ⓒ, 1130Ⓐ, 1210Ⓐ, 1217Ⓒ, 1240Ⓐ, 1310Ⓐ, 1317Ⓒ, 1340Ⓐ, 1410Ⓐ, 1417Ⓒ, 1440Ⓐ, 1510Ⓐ, 1517Ⓒ, 1540Ⓐ, 1605Ⓐ, 1617Ⓒ, 1640Ⓐ, 1710Ⓐ, 1717Ⓒ, 1740Ⓐ, 1805Ⓐ, 1817Ⓒ, 1835Ⓐ, 1855Ⓐ, 1920Ⓒ, 1930Ⓐ, 2005Ⓐ, 2017Ⓒ, 2035Ⓐ, 2100Ⓒ, 2105Ⓐ, 2145Ⓐ, 2205Ⓐ, 2217Ⓒ, 2305Ⓐ, 2317Ⓒ, 2359Ⓐ.
NJT– New Jersey Transit. Tel.: Newark 201 762 5100.
NRPC–National Railroad Passenger Corporation (AMTRAK). Tel.: New York 212 582 6875.
SEP– Southeastern Pennsylvania Transportation Authority. Tel.: Philadelphia 580 7800.

Table 214 BALTIMORE - WASHINGTON

╫╫╫ *MARC*

US$ C cl.		241	243	245	247	249	251		253	255	257	km	↓ ↑		240	242	244	246		248	250	252	254	256
		C‡	C‡	C‡	C‡	C‡	C‡		C‡	C‡	C‡				C‡	C‡	C‡	C‡		C‡	C‡	C‡	C‡	C‡
		Ⓐ	Ⓐ	Ⓐ	Ⓐ	Ⓐ	Ⓐ		Ⓐ	Ⓐ	Ⓐ				Ⓐ	Ⓐ	Ⓐ	Ⓐ		Ⓐ	Ⓐ	Ⓐ	Ⓐ	Ⓐ
5.25	....	0535	0630	0705	0805	1100	1550	....	1650	1750	1835	0	d.**Baltimore** Camden ....a.	....	0749	0825	0930	1235	....	1736	1820	1912	2009	2105
3.75	....	0607	0706	0739	0836	1131	1619	....	1720	1820	1907	31	d.Laurel ....d.	....	0715	0745	0855	1156	....	1657	1739	1831	1932	2026
0.00	....	0637	0740	0814	0906	1210	1650	....	1750	1850	1940	60	a.**Washington** Union ....d.	....	0650	0720	0830	1130	....	1630	1710	1800	1905	2000

MARC–Maryland Department of Transportation. Tel.: Washington 202 906 3104.

88 **Check update notes to timetables and with operator before starting your journey**

Table 215 — ALBANY - BUFFALO - CLEVELAND - CHICAGO

NRPC

US $ C cl.	29 S‡C‡	63 C‡	69 C‡	71 C‡		281 1‡C‡	283 1‡C‡	285 1‡C‡	259 1‡C‡	269 1‡C‡	289 1‡C‡	49⊠ S‡C‡	65 S‡C‡		km	
	◆											◆⊠	◆⊠†			
0.00		0715	0815	1050		1150	1425	1645	1645	1645	1738	1910	2230		0	d.New York 207 ....a.
◇36.00												1620				d. Boston 200 ....a.
40.00		1015	1115	1415		1440	1725	1910s	1915	1915	2047	2049	0120		229	d.Albany Rensselaer a.
45.00		1037	1140	1415		1502	1747	1942	1935	1935	2047	2248			258	d.Schenectady 199 ...d.
57.00		1100				1520	1805	2000			2105				286	d.Amsterdam..........d.
59.00		1156				1616	1901	2056			2201	0004			382	d.Utica...............d.
69.00		1209				1629	1914	2109			2214				404	d.Rome...............d.
69.00		1253				1713	1958	2153			2255	0057	0340		459	d.Syracuse...........d.
79.00		1411				1831	2116	2311				0222	0458		597	d.Rochester..........d.
82.00		1502				1922	2207	0007				0351	0550		693	d.Buffalo Depew......d.
82.00		1514				1934	2219	0019				0605			706	d. Buffalo Exchange Street d.
82.00		1600				2020	2305	0105				0700			745	a. Niagara Falls USA ⊠ d.
96.00		1914										1021			879	a. Toronto 17 ....d.
94.00											0523				843	d.Erie...............d.
94.00	0322										0706		0429		995	d.Cleveland Lakefront d.
94.00	0354										0739		0301		1036	d.Elyria (Lorain) ....d.
	0519										0909		0213		1167	d.Toledo Central Union { a.
101.00	0545										0934		0049			{ d.
113.00	0650										1036		2230		1382	d.Elkhart ....d.
114.00	0718										1101		1903		1409	d.South Bend ....d.
124.00	0817s										1204s		1839		1509	d.Hammond NRPC....d.
124.00	0910										1258		1737u		1544	a.Chicago Union......d.

US $ C cl.	30 S‡C‡	246 1‡C‡	252 1‡C‡	284 1‡C‡	48⊠ S‡C‡		282 1‡C‡	286 1‡C‡	68 C‡	64 C‡	288 C‡		62 S‡C‡
	◆				◆†◆⊠								◆⊠†
0.00		0917	1140	1250	1740		1625	1720	2020	2140	2320		0745
36.00				1650									
40.00		0655	0905	1030	1117		1330	1420	1715	1840	2010		0440
45.00		0630	0840	0935	1045		1305	1355	1640	1815	2010		
57.00			0916		1244		1149	1241	1756	1949			
59.00			0821	0925			1135	1225	1645	1840			
69.00		0805		1131				1616	1811			0220
69.00		0736	0840		1106		1156	1616	1811				0220
79.00		0605	0715		1025		1445	1640					0050
82.00		0512	0617		0842		0932	1352	1547				2357
82.00		0500			0830		0920	1340	1535				2345
82.00		0425			0755		0845	1305	1500				2310
96.00								0930					1745
94.00					0429								
94.00	0024				0301								
94.00	2347				0213								
	2230				0049								
101.00	2215				0026								
113.00	1903				2117								
114.00	1839				2050								
124.00	1737u				1944u								
124.00	1710				1915								

29/30– CAPITOL LIMITED–▟⊿‡, ⊠↧, ▭ and ✕ Washington(29/30)-Chicago and v.v.
48/49– LAKESHORE LIMITED–see Table 186.
62– NIAGARA RAINBOW–▟◆, ▭, and ♀ Niagara Falls (Canada)(62)-New York.
63/64– MAPLE LEAF–▭ and ⊗ New York(63/64)-Niagara Falls(98/97)-Toronto and v.v.
65– NIAGARA RAINBOW–▭‡ and ♀ New York(65)-Niagara Falls (Canada).
68/69/71–ADIRONDACK–▭ and ⊗ Montréal(68/69/71)-New York and v.v.
246– STORM KING–▭ and ♀ Schenectady(246)-New York.
252– ELECTRIC CITY EXPRESS–▭ and ♀ Schenectady(250)-New York.
259– BEAR MOUNTAIN–▭ and ♀ New York(259)-Schenectady.
269– SPA EXPRESS–⑤ July 1-Sept. 2: ▭ and ♀ New York(269)-Saratoga Springs.
281– MOHAWK–▭ and ♀ New York(281)-Niagara Falls.

282– EMPIRE STATE EXPRESS–▭ and ♀ Niagara Falls(282)-New York.
283– EMPIRE STATE EXPRESS–▭ and ♀ New York(283)-Niagara Falls.
284– MOHAWK–▭ and ♀ Niagara Falls(284)-New York.
285– WATER LEVEL EXPRESS–▭ and ♀ New York(285)-Niagara Falls.
286– EMPIRE STATE EXPRESS–▭ and ♀ Niagara Falls(286)-New York.
288– WATER LEVEL EXPRESS–▭ and ♀ Niagara Falls(288)-New York.
289– CATSKILL–▭ and ♀ New York(289)-Syracuse.
◇– Fare ex Albany.
♀– No service on ⑤ July 1-Sept. 2.
NRPC–National Railroad Passenger Corporation (AMTRAK). Tel: New York 212 582 6875.

Table 218 — PHILADELPHIA - HARRISBURG

NRPC SEP

US $ C cl.	NRPC	km	601 C‡ ⓐ	603 C‡ ⓐ	605 C‡ ⓑ		43 C‡	607 C‡ ⓐ	609 C‡ ⓒ	643 C‡	41⊠ S‡C‡ ◆✕	615 C‡		647 C‡ ◆†		617 C‡ ⓐ		641 C‡ ◆ⓐ	645 C‡ ◆ⓐ	649 C‡ ◆ⓒ	696 C‡ ◆	621 C‡
	New York 213 ....d.			0345a	0620		0745	0920	1040	1235	1245	1440		1535		1540		1708	1740	1829	1840	2045
0.00	Philadelphia 30th Street ◇.d.	0	0530	0628	0820		0941	1115	1245	1415	1457u	1630		1715		1735		1930	2005	2045	2245	
6.00	Paoli ....d.	32	0600	0658	0850		1010	1143	1313	1445	1530u	1658		1745		1802		1900	1958	2115	2315	
8.00	Downingtown......d.	48	0617	0715	0904		1024	1157	1327	1501		1717		1759		1820		1914	2016	2049	2129	2332
11.00	Lancaster ....d.	109	0655	0751	0940		1058	1232	1404	1537	1615u	1755		1835		1858		1947	2052	2125	2205	0009
15.00	Middletown........d.	151	0724					1432r	1603		1824					1927			2122		2232r	0036r
18.00	Harrisburg.......a.	166	0739	0831	1020		1133	1313	1446	1618	1655u	1839		1917		1943		2028	2135	2207	2247	0051

US $ C cl.		600 C‡ ⓐ	640 C‡ ⓐ	642 C‡ ⓐ		693 C‡ ◆ⓒ	606 C‡ ⓐ		646 C‡ ◆ⓐ	610 C‡	40⊠ S‡C‡ ◆✕		612 C‡		42 S‡ ◆✕	614 C‡ ⅄	616 C‡ ⅄	44 C‡ ◆†		618 C‡ ⓐ	622 C‡ †
Harrisburg...........d.		0535	0605	0646		0800	0810		1100	1100	1325s		1355		1507	1620	1720	1757		1948	2015
Middletown..........d.		0547r		0658		0812r	0822r									1732				2000r	2027r
Lancaster ....d.		0616	0644	0729		0841	0848		1141	1141	1405s		1435		1545	1700	1803	1835		2030	2057
Downingtown........d.		0653	0714	0804		0916	0920		1216	1218			1506		1617	1733	1840	1907		2105	2130
Paoli ....d.		0713	0731	0820		0930	0932		1230	1230	1451s		1520		1631	1747	1857	1921		2121	2144
Philadelphia 30th Street ◇ a.		0739		0848		0956	0959		1256	1256	1529s		1548		1659	1815	1923	1950		2149	2210
New York 213 ....a.		0910	0930	1040		1210	1210		1438	1505	1750		1808		1850	2018	2120	2145		0010	0010

40/41– BROADWAY LIMITED–see Table 185.
42-44– PENNSYLVANIAN–▭ and ♀ Pittsburgh(42/44/43)-New York and v.v.
640/1– KEYSTONE STATE EXPRESS–▭ and ♀ Harrisburg(640/1)-New York and v.v.
642– KEYSTONE–▭ (also ♀ on ⓒ) Harrisburg(642)-New York.
643– KEYSTONE–▭ New York(643)-Harrisburg.
645– SUSQUEHANNA–▭ and ♀ New York(645)-Harrisburg.
646/7/9–KEYSTONE–▭ Harrisburg(646/7/9)-New York and v.v.
693/6–ATLANTIC CITY EXPRESS–▭ and ♀ Harrisburg(693/6)-Atlantic City and v.v.
◇– Local ▦ service (SEP), C cl. only, from Philadelphia 30th Street at: 0004⑦, 0019②-⑦, 0619⑥, 0649⑥, 0719⑥, 0732⑥, 0749⅄, 0819⑥, 0822⑥, 0849⅄, 0919, 0949⅄, 1019, 1049⅄, 1119, 1149⅄, 1219, 1249⅄, 1319, 1349⅄, 1419, 1449⅄,

1519, 1549⅄, 1612⑥, 1619ⓒ, 1639ⓒ, 1649ⓒ, 1654⑥, 1700⑥, 1713⑥, 1719, 1740ⓒ, 1743⑥, 1749⑥, 1810⑥, 1813ⓒ, 1818⑥, 1819†, 1849⅄, 1908†, 1919⑥, 1935ⓒ, 1949⑥, 2019⑥, 2049⅄, 2119ⓒ, 2149⑥, 2219⑥, 2249⑥, 2319ⓒ; from Paoli at 0529⑥, 0552ⓒ, 0619ⓒ, 0643ⓒ, 0655ⓒ, 0704⅄, 0718ⓒ, 0723ⓒ, 0734ⓒ, 0737ⓒ, 0742ⓒ, 0758ⓒ, 0804ⓒ, 0807ⓒ, 0831ⓒ, 0841ⓒ, 0901ⓒ, 0904ⓒ, 0934ⓒ, 0937ⓒ, 1004⅄, 1034, 1104⅄, 1134, 1204⅄, 1234, 1304⅄, 1334, 1404⅄, 1434, 1501⑥, 1504⑥, 1531⑥, 1534ⓒ, 1559⑥, 1604⑥, 1625⑥, 1634ⓒ, 1701ⓒ, 1725†, 1734⑥, 1736⑥, 1804ⓒ, 1830ⓒ, 1834ⓒ, 1904ⓒ, 1934ⓒ, 2004ⓒ, 2034ⓒ, 2104ⓒ, 2134ⓒ, 2144†, 2204ⓒ, 2234ⓒ, 2304ⓒ.
NRPC–National Railroad Passenger Corporation (AMTRAK). Tel.: Philadelphia 215 824 1600.
SEP– Southeastern Pennsylvania Transportation Authority. Tel.: Philadelphia 580 7800.

Table 219 — PHILADELPHIA - ATLANTIC CITY

NJT NRPC PAT

US $ C cl.		km	PAT 4603 C	NJT 4505 C‡	NJT 4407 C‡ ⓐ	NJT 4607 C‡ ⓐ	NJT 4409 C‡ ⓒ	NJT 4609 C‡	NJT 4611 C‡	NRPC 693 C‡R ◆⊠ⓒ	NRPC 661 C‡R ◆⊠ⓐ	NRPC 663 C‡R ◆⊠ⓐ	NRPC 667 C‡R ◆⊠ⓐ	NRPC 653 C‡R	NJT 4513 C‡	NJT 4615 C‡	NJT 4417 C‡ ⓐ	NJT 4619 C‡R	NRPC 665 C‡R ◆⊠	NRPC 685 C‡R ◆⊠ ♀	NJT 4521 C‡	NJT 4523 C‡	NRPC 4625 C‡	NJT 4527 C‡
28.00	New York 213 ...d.									1030														
40.00	Washington 213 ...d.									0825	0845	0900						1520						
15.00	Philadelphia 30th Street ⊠ .d.	0		0453		0652		0744	0954	1012	1031u	1104		1343		1643	1728	1728			2023			
Ω5.00	Philadelphia 15/16 Locust d.		★	★	★	★	★	★	★						★	★	★	★			★	★		★
Ω5.00	Camden Broadway d.		★	★	★	★	★	★	★						★	★	★	★			★	★		★
Ω3.00	Lindenwold ⊠ ℳ.d.	35	★	0526	0612	0723	0726	0812	0820	1027	1047u		1237	1416	1602	1723	1804u	1804u	1814	2016	2055	2227	
Ω1.85	Egg Harbor.......d.			0558	0649	0758	0758	0852	1059		1309	1449	1637	1748		1851	2048	2133	2259					
0.00	Atlantic City ......a.	109		0624	0715	0825	0918	0918	1125	1135	1145	1218	1225	1305	1335	1515	1707	1814	1851	1851	1921	2118	2200	2329

			PAT 4600 C	NJT 4502 C‡	NJT 4604 C‡ ⓐ	NJT 4404 C‡ ⓐ	NJT 4606 C‡ ⓐ	NJT 4406 C‡ ⓒ	NJT 4608 C‡	NJT 4510 C‡	NRPC 4612 C‡R ◆⊠	NJT 4414 C‡R ◆⊠	NRPC 662 C‡R ◆⊠ⓐ	NRPC 682 C‡R ◆⊠ⓐ	NJT 4516 C‡	NJT 4618 C‡	NJT 4520 C‡	NRPC 696 C‡R ◆⊠		NRPC 664 C‡R ◆⊠ⓐ	NRPC 654 C‡R	NJT 4522 C‡		NRPC 668 C‡R ◆⊠	NJT 4624 C‡
Atlantic City ......d.				0045	0442	0618	0618	0706	0706	0843	0941	1331	1440	1612	1612	1632	1739	1846	1908		1915	1950	2043		2215	2254
Egg Harbor........d.				0103	0500	0636	0636	0727	0727	0905	0959	1349	1502			1650	1801	1904					2101			2312
Lindenwold ⊠ ℳ..d.			★	0135	0532	0708	0711	0800	0804	0937	1032	1421	1538			1722	1836	1936	1948s		1958s		2133		2257s	2343
Camden Broadway ..a.			★	★	★	★	★	★	★	★					★	★	★			★		★		★	★
Philadelphia 15/16 Locust a.			★	★	★	★	★	★	★	★					★	★	★			★		★		★	★
Philadelphia 30th Street ⊠ a.				0215		0748		0836		1016		1501		1732	1732		1918		2024		2034			2335s	0018
Washington 213 ...a.												1949								2250					0147
New York 213 ......a.																			2230						

653/4– ▭ and ♀ Springfield(653/4)-Atlantic City and v.v.
661– ▭ and ♀ Washington(661)-Atlantic City.
662– ▭ and ♀ Atlantic City(662)-Richmond (Washington on †).
663– ▭ and ♀ Richmond(663)-Atlantic City.
664– ▭ and ♀ Atlantic City(664)-Washington.
665/6– ▭ and ♀ Washington(665/6)-Atlantic City and v.v.
667– ▭ and ♀ Richmond(667)-Atlantic City.
696– ▭ and ♀ Atlantic City(696)-Harrisburg.

R– ATLANTIC CITY EXPRESS.
ℳℛ– At a date to be announced during 1994, AMTRAK trains will stop calling at Lindenwold, and will start using a new station at Cherry Hill. Further information not yet available.
⊠– Local traffic not carried on NRPC trains. Ω–NJT/PAT fares.
NJT– New Jersey Transit. Tel.: Newark 201 762 5100.
NRPC–National Railroad Passenger Corporation (AMTRAK). Tel.: Philadelphia 215 824 1600.
PAT– Port Authority Transit - PATCO. Tel.: Philadelphia 215 922 4600.
★–Journey: 25 mins. Frequent service 24 hours, daily.
693– ▭ and ♀ Harrisburg(693)-Atlantic City.

Check update notes to timetables and with operator before starting your journey

Table 220 — WASHINGTON - PITTSBURGH - CLEVELAND #### MARC NRPC

US$ C cl	MARC 271 C‡ Ⓐ	MARC 273 C‡ Ⓐ	MARC 275 C‡ Ⓐ	NRPC 29 S‡C‡ Ⓐ	MARC 277 C‡ Ⓐ	MARC 279 C‡ Ⓐ	MARC 281 C‡ ♥Ⓐ		MARC 283 C‡ Ⓐ	MARC 285 C‡ Ⓐ	MARC 287 C‡ Ⓐ	km ↓		MARC 270 C‡ ♥Ⓐ	MARC 272 C‡ Ⓐ	MARC 274 C‡ ♥Ⓐ		MARC 276 C‡ ♥Ⓐ	MARC 278 C‡ Ⓐ	MARC 280 C‡ Ⓐ	MARC 282 C‡ Ⓐ	NRPC 30 S‡C‡ Ⓐ	MARC 284 C‡ ♥Ⓐ	MARC 286 C‡ Ⓐ
0.00	0845	1300	1615	1640	1655	1710	1730	....	1805	1850	1955	0 d.**Washington** Union ....a.	↑	0638	0705	0725		0740	0810	0830	0920	1107	1610	1830
3.00	0858	1313	1628		1709	1725	1745	....	1820	1905	2010	11 d.Silver Spring ....d.		0621	0644	0705		0724	0750	0811	0903		1553	1813r
3.00	0904	1318r	1634		1731	1750		....	1826	1911	2015r	18 d.Kensington ....d.		0615	0636			0717	0744		0857		1546	1807r
Ⓖ5.00	0911	1327	1643	1702	1721	1740	1800	....	1835	1920	2024	28 d.Rockville ....d.		0606	0627	0653		0708	0734	0759	0848	1025	1538	1758r
3.75	0918	1335	1653		1748	1807		....	1843	1929	2032	34 d.Gaithersburg ....d.		0557	0619	0643		0659	0725	0750	0841		1531	1751r
6.00	0956	1420	1737		1801	1834	1850	....	1929	2012	2112	79 d.Brunswick ....d.		0515	0540	0605		0620	0640	0712	0800		1500	1710
★13.00	....	....	....	1744	1811		1900	....			2021	89 d.Harper's Ferry ......d.				0555				0702		0943		
Ω19.00	....	....	....	1806	1840		1929	....			2050	119 d.**Martinsburg** ....d.				0530				0635		0921		
31.00	....	....	....	1941				....				236 d.Cumberland ....d.										0756		
51.00	....	....	....	2156				....				386 d.Connellsville ....d.										0521		
64.00	....	....	....	2352				....				480 a.}**Pittsburgh** ....{d.										0355		
	....	....	....	2359				....				d.										0340		
81.00	....	....	....	0152				....				616 d.Alliance ⊠..............d.										0147		
82.00	....	....	....	0322				....				704 a.**Cleveland** ....d.										0024		
89.00	....	....	....	0519				....				872 a.Toledo 215 ....d.										2230		
118.00	....	....	....	0910				....				1280 a.Chicago 215 ....d.										1710		

29/30–CAPITOL LIMITED–🛏‡, ⫫‡, ⊡ and ✕ Washington(**29/30**)-Chicago and v.v.   **274/277**–BLUE RIDGE.   **276/281**–THE METROPOLITAN SPECIAL.   Ⓖ–MARC fare: $3.75.   ★–MARC fare: $6.75.   Ω–MARC fare: $7.50.   ⊠–for Canton.   MARC–Maryland Department of Transportation. Tel.: Washington 202 906 3104.   NRPC–National Railroad Passenger Corporation (AMTRAK). Tel.: Washington 202 484 7540.

Table 221 — NEW YORK - BAY HEAD #### NJT

Local #### service (C cl. only) New York Penn. Stn.-Newark-Matawan-Long Branch-Asbury Park-Point Pleasant Beach-Bay Head and v.v. 108 km. Journey: 1³/₄-2 hours. Fare: US$ 9.60.
From New York Penn. Stn.: (change at Newark or Long Branch on all services) 0037†, 0137Ⓓ, 0637Ⓓ, 0707Ⓐ, 0829Ⓐ, 0837Ⓒ, 0941Ⓓ, 1037Ⓒ, 1143Ⓓ, 1237Ⓒ, 1243⌢, 1407Ⓐ, 1437Ⓒ, 1535▽, 1552Ⓓ, 1611Ⓐ, 1637Ⓒ, 1642Ⓐ, 1703Ⓓ, 1721Ⓐ, 1732Ⓐ, 1742Ⓑ, 1810Ⓐ, 1837Ⓒ, 1852⌢, 1907Ⓑ, 2007Ⓐ, 2037Ⓒ, 2112Ⓐ, 2230Ⓐ, 2332Ⓓ, 2337Ⓒ.
From Bay Head: (change at Long Branch or Newark on all services) 0454Ⓐ, 0506Ⓒ, 0516Ⓐ, 0549Ⓐ, 0606Ⓓ, 0617Ⓐ, 0649Ⓐ, 0706Ⓒ, 0717Ⓐ, 0748Ⓐ, 0849Ⓐ, 0906Ⓓ, 1006Ⓐ, 1106Ⓒ, 1206Ⓐ, 1306Ⓒ, 1453Ⓓ, 1506Ⓒ, 1600Ⓐ, 1635∝, 1700Ⓐ, 1706Ⓐ, 1806Ⓒ, 1906Ⓒ, 1908Ⓐ, 2008Ⓐ, 2106Ⓒ, 2145Ⓐ, 2259Ⓓ, 2319Ⓒ.

Through #### service (C cl. only) Hoboken-Newark-Matawan-Long Branch-Asbury Park-Point Pleasant Beach-Bay Head and v.v. ❖ km. Journey: 1³/₄ hours. Fare: US $: 7.35.
From Hoboken: 0833Ⓐ, 1412Ⓐ, 1644Ⓐ, 1709Ⓓ, 1737Ⓐ, 1814Ⓐ, 1855Ⓓ.
From Bay Head: 0516Ⓐ, 0549Ⓐ, 0617Ⓐ, 0649Ⓐ, 0849Ⓐ, 1453Ⓐ, 1635∝.

⌢–Ⓢ May 28-Sept. 3. ▽–Ⓐ May 28-July 2. ∝–Ⓖ May 30-July 4. NJT–New Jersey Transit. Tel.: Newark 201 762 5100.

Table 222 — WASHINGTON - JACKSONVILLE - TAMPA/MIAMI #### NRPC TR VRE

US $ C cl	93 C‡ ♦	83 C‡ ♦	79 C: ♦	89 C: ♦	73 C‡ ♦	91 S‡C‡ ♦⊞	81 S‡C‡ ♦⊞	53 S‡C‡ ♦⊞	95 C‡ ♦	99 C‡ ♦	85 C‡ ♦	662 C‡ Ⓒ⊞	664 C‡ Ⓒ⊞	87 C‡ ♦	97 S‡C‡ ♦		NRPC	98 S‡C: ♦	88 S‡C: ♦	663 C: Ⓒ	667 C: Ⓒ	86 C: ♦	52 S‡C‡ ♦✕	1 C‡ ♦	94 C‡ ♦	92 C: ♦	82 C: ♦	80 C: ♦	96 C: ♦	90 C‡ ♦	84 C‡ ♦	78 C‡ ♦
64.00	....	....	0620	0723	....	0942	0942	....	1125	1340	1540	....	....	1830	1830	0	d.o.New York 213 .....a.	1125	1125	....	....	1410	....	....	1530	2006	2006	2220	2317	0010	....
34.00	....	....	0800	0859	....	1137u	1137u	....	1300	1515	1713	1144	2036	2037u	2037u	246	d.Philadelphia 213 ...a.	0913Ⓐ	0913s	1059	1104	1233	....	....	1405	1755s	1755s	2033	2149	2238	....
0.00	0900	....	1040	1135	....	1445u	1445u	....	1530	1735	1935	2010	2310	2325u	2325u	361	d.**Washington** Union ..a.	0615s	0615s	0825	0840	1005	....	....	1142	1445s	1445s	1740	1900	1940	2130
5.00	0917	....	1055	1152	....	1502	1502	....	1547	1752	1952	2027	2327	2342	2342	361	d.Alexandria ⊠........a.	0549	0549	0759	0814	0939	....	....	1116	1419	1419	1710	1834	1914	2104
	....	....	....	....	....			1530								396	d. Lorton ....a.							0900							
9.00	0944r	....	1121r	1218r	....				1614r	1819r	2018r	2053r	2353r			417	d.Quantico ⊠ ....d.			0734r	0749r	0914r			1051r			1644r	1809r	1849r	2039r
11.00	1002r	....	1139r	1236r	....	1550u	1550u	....	1632r	1837r	2036r	2111r	0011r			448	d.Fredericksburg ⊠ .d.			0715r	0730r	0855r			1032r	1331r	1331r	1625r	1750r	1830r	2020r
21.00	1108	1155	1250	1350	....	1705	1705	....	1740	1945	2135	2210	0110	0135	0135	521	d.**Richmond** ....a.	0415	0415	0625	0640	0805	....	....	0942	1240	1240	1535	1700	1740	0007
28.00	1215	1300			....			....	1845	2050b						625	a. Williamsburg Boundary Street d.								0818				1538		1808 2253
35.00	1250	1332			....			....	1917	2127b						668	a. **Newport News** ....d.								0755				1515		1745 2230
21.00	....	....	1324	1424	....	1737	1737	....						0208	0208	583	d.Petersburg ⊠ ....d.	0312	0312			74			1141	1141	1437		1635		
40.00	....	....	1449	1554	....	1900	1900	....						0331	0331	739	d.Rocky Mount ⊠ ....d.	0142	0142			C‡			1016	1016	1317		1515		
41.00	....	....	1506	1613	....			....								765	d.Wilson ....d.					♦			1226		1451				
45.00	....	....	1628		....	2042	2042	....								805	d. Raleigh ....d.					ℜ			0855	0855	1155				
49.00	....	....	1705		....			....									d. Durham .....d.					ℜ			1105						
58.00	....	....	1833		....			....									d. Greensboro .d.					ℜ			0944						
75.00	....	....	....		....	2231	2231	....									d. Hamlet ....d.								0658	0658					
87.00	....	....	....		....	0033	0033	....								1133	d. Columbia ....d.								0455	0455					
71.00	....	....	1716		....			....				0456	0456			884	d.Fayetteville ....d.	0017	0017										1349		
80.00	....	....	1803		....			....								969	d.Dillon ....d.												1300		
82.00	....	....	1856		....			....				0629	0629			1018	d.Florence ....d.	2256	2256										1230		
104.00	....	....	2016		....			....			2	0804	0804			1170	d.**Charleston** ....d.	2103	2103										1049		
104.00	....	....	....		....			....			S‡C‡	0851	0851			1256	d.Yemassee ....d.	2013	2013										1001		
115.00	....	....	2213		....	0305	0305	....			♦⊞	0901	1001			1333	d.Savannah ....d.	1927	1927						0229	0229			0920		
130.00	....	....	0038		....	0523	0523	....				1223	1223			1572	a.**Jacksonville** ...{d.	1703	1703						2359	2359			0700		
	....	....	....		....	0538	0538	....				1425	1318	1258			d.	1624	1618						2350	2350					
148.00	....	....	....		0900	0749	0749	0900				1635	1534			1797	d. Sanford ......d.			1356				1530	1805	2116	2116				
150.00	....	....	....		....	0815	0815	....				1700	1556			1823	d. Winter Park ...d.			1332				1742	2053	2053					
150.00	....	....	....		....	0845	0845	....				1730	1623			1831	d. Orlando ◇.....d.			1316				1728	2038	2038					
152.00	....	....	....		....	0903	0903	....				1747	1643			1872	d. Kissimmee ....d.			1245				1700	2000	2000					
153.00	....	....	....		....	1018		....					1724			1930	d. Lakeland ......d.			1203					1854						
153.00	....	....	....		....	1107		....					1807			1978	a. **Tampa** ....d.			1130					1822						
153.00	....	....	....		....	1150		....					1900			2032	a. Clearwater ...d.			1025					1715						
153.00	....	....	....		....	1145		....					1855			2053	a. St. Petersburg ..d.			1030					1720						
140.00	....	....	....		....			....				1357				1688	d.Waldo ⊠ ....d.	1459													
145.00	....	....	....		....			....				1442				1761	d.Ocala ⊠ ....d.	1416													
148.00	....	....	....		....			....				1511				1811	d.Wildwood ....d.	1342													
153.00	....	....	1016		....			....				1842	1639			1907	d.Winter Haven ....d.	1214							1612	1855					
153.00	....	....	1054		....			....				1920	1720			1973	d.Sebring ⊠ ....d.	1134							1533	1816					
153.00	....	....	....		....			....				1955	1755				d.Okeechobee ......d.	1057							1458						
157.00	....	....	1224		....			....				2055	1852			2138	d.West Palm Beach ⊛.d.	1005							1405	1655					
161.00	....	....	1317		....			....				2148	1947			2207	d.Fort Lauderdale ★.d.	0906							1300	1600					
	....	....	....		....			....									d.**Miami** Metrorail ★.d.														
161.00	....	....	1400		....			....				2250	2055			2241	a.**Miami** AMTRAK ...d.	0830							1230	1525					
	....	....	....		....			....									a.Miami International Airport ★ d.														

1/2– SUNSET LIMITED–see Table **193**.
52/53– AUTO TRAIN–🛏‡, ⫫‡, cinema car, ⊗, ⊡ and ⊡.
73/74– PIEDMONT.
79/80– CAROLINIAN–⊡ and ♀ New York(**79/80**)-Charlotte and v.v.
81/82– SILVER STAR–see Table **184**.
83– TIDEWATER.
84– TIDEWATER–Ⓕ May 1-Sept. 3.
85– CHESAPEAKE–⊡ and ♀ New York(**85**)-Richmond.
86– THE VIRGINIAN–⊡ and ♀ Richmond(**86**)-New York.
87/88– SILVER METEOR–see Table **182**.
89/90– PALMETTO–⊡ and ♀ New York(**89/90**)-Jacksonville and v.v.
91/92– SILVER STAR–see Table **184**.
93– TIDEWATER–Ⓢ to May 25; Ⓖ⑤Ⓢ May 26-Sept. 4; Ⓢ from Sept. 4.
94/95– OLD DOMINION–⊡ and ♀ Newport News(**94/95**)-New York and v.v.
96– TIDEWATER–Ⓓ to May 25 and from Sept. 4; Ⓖ⑤Ⓢ May 26-Sept. 7; ⊡ and ♀ Newport News(**96**)-New York.
97/98– SILVER METEOR–see Table **182**.
99– THE VIRGINIAN–⊡ and ♀ New York(**99**)-Richmond (Newport News on Ⓢ⑥⑦).
662/3/4/7–ATLANTIC CITY EXPRESS–⊡ and ♀ Atlantic City(**662/3/4/7**)-Richmond and v.v.
a– To Alexandria only.
b– Ⓢ⑥⑦ only.

c– By 🚌 .
◇– For Disney World.
★– Local service (TR🚇) operates West Palm Beach-Fort Lauderdale-Miami Metrorail-Miami International Airport and v.v.; Journey time 1¼ hours end to end:
From West Palm Beach: 0449Ⓓ, 0545Ⓓ, 0550Ⓓ, 0645Ⓓ, 0745Ⓓ, 0755Ⓓ, 0800†, 0903Ⓓ, 1002Ⓓ, 1006Ⓓ, 1144Ⓓ, 1159Ⓓ, 1300†, 1416Ⓓ, 1417Ⓓ, 1532Ⓓ, 1555†, 1617Ⓓ, 1632Ⓓ, 1732Ⓓ, 1820Ⓓ, 1832Ⓓ, 1835†, 1932Ⓓ, 2030Ⓓ, 2032Ⓓ, 2230Ⓓ, 2232Ⓓ.
From Miami International Airport: 0447Ⓓ, 0547Ⓓ, 0550Ⓓ, 0647Ⓓ, 0747Ⓓ, 0755Ⓓ, 0800†, 0853Ⓓ, 0908Ⓓ, 1002†, 1106Ⓓ, 1200Ⓓ, 1215Ⓓ, 1300Ⓓ, 1415Ⓓ, 1417Ⓓ, 1535Ⓓ, 1555†, 1612Ⓓ, 1635Ⓓ, 1735Ⓓ, 1820Ⓓ, 1835Ⓓ, 1935Ⓓ, 2033Ⓓ, 2035Ⓓ, 2235Ⓓ, 2308Ⓓ.
⊠– Local service (VRE) operates Washington-Alexandria-Quantico-Fredericksburg and v.v. **From Washington** Union: 1615Ⓓ, 1625Ⓓa, 1715Ⓓ, 1725Ⓓa, 1745Ⓓ, 1755Ⓓa, 1820Ⓓa, 1830Ⓓ; **from Fredericksburg:** 0529Ⓓ, 0629Ⓓ, 0659Ⓓ, 0729Ⓓ; **from Alexandria:** 0614Ⓓ, 0624Ⓓ, 0714Ⓓ, 0724Ⓓ, 0744Ⓓ, 0754Ⓓ, 0814Ⓓ, 0824Ⓓ.
ℜ– Train not yet in operation.
NRPC–National Railroad Passenger Corporation (AMTRAK). Tel.: Washington 202 484 7540.
TR– Tri-Rail. Tel.: Miami 305 728 8445.
VRE– Virginia Railway Express. Tel.: Washington 703 497 7777.

Table 223 NEW ORLEANS/CHICAGO

NRPC

US $ C cl.	79 C‡ ♦ Ⓡ	51 S‡C‡ ♦Ⓡ ③⑤⑦	19 S‡C‡ ♦Ⓡ ✕	519 S‡C‡ ♦ 🍷	km	↓ ↑	520 S‡C‡ ♦ 🍷	20 S‡C‡ ♦Ⓡ ✕	80 C‡ ♦ Ⓡ	50 S‡C‡ ♦Ⓡ ②④⑥
64.00	0620	0930	1342	....	*0*	d.*New York* **213** ...a.	....	1435	2220	2310
0.00	1040	1345	1850	....	*361*	d.**Washington** Union a.	....	0928	1740	1905
5.00	1055	1404	1907	....	*375*	d.Alexandria ....d.	....	0858	1710	1832
13.00	|	1514	2012**r**	....	*470*	d.Culpeper............d.	....	0738**r**	|	1715
	|	*1420***b**	|	....		d. Richmond ...a.	....	|	|	*1745***b**
22.00	|	1620	2105	....	*542*	d.Charlottesville....d.	....	0648	|	1611
35.00	**a**	|	2225	....	*639*	d.Lynchburg ....d.	....	0533	**a**	|
50.00	|	|	2333	....	*741*	d.Danville ....d.	....	0415	|	|
58.00	1833	|	0113	....	*818*	d.Greensboro ....d.	....	0315	0944	|
62.00	1847	|	0126**r**	....	*843*	d.High Point ....d.	....	0237**r**	0922	|
68.00	1926	|	0208	....	*899*	d.Salisbury ....d.	....	0155	0844	|
75.00	2020	|	0258	....	*966*	d.Charlotte ....d.	....	0104	0800	|
79.00	▬	|	0328**r**	....	*1004*	d.Gastonia............d.	....	0032**r**	....	|
88.00	....	|	0430	....	*1090*	d.Spartanburg ......d.	....	2332	....	|
91.00	....	|	0535	....	*1140*	d.Greenville *SC* ....d.	....	2255	....	|
112.00	....	|	0730	....	*1302*	d.Gainesville.........d.	....	2038	....	|
119.00	....	|	0830	....	*1381*	a. **Atlanta** .... d.	....	1945	....	|
	....	|	0845	....		d. **Atlanta** .... a.	....	1920	....	|
132.00	....	|	1005	....	*1544*	d.Anniston ....d.	....	1550	....	|
140.00	....	|	1203	1223	*1647*	d.Birmingham ....d.	1330	1420	....	|
143.00	....	|	|	1421		d. Montgomery..d.	1108	|	....	|
154.00	....	|	|	1505		d. Greenville *AL* d.	1026	|	....	|
155.00	....	|	|	1808		a. **Mobile** ....d.	0755	|	....	|
147.00	....	|	1313	....	*1736*	d.Tuscaloosa ....d.	▬	1240	....	|
158.00	....	|	1515	....	*1892*	d.Meridian ....d.	....	1105	....	|
160.00	....	|	1614**r**	....	*1986*	d.Laurel ....d.	....	0952**r**	....	|
167.00	....	|	1645	....	*2029*	d.Hattiesburg........d.	....	0921	....	|
180.00	....	|	1928	....	*2218*	a.**New Orleans** ....d.	....	0705	....	|
28.00	....	1718	▬	....	*248*	d. Staunton ....d.	....	▬	....	1512
38.00	....	1828	....	....	*339*	d. Clifton Forge ...d.	....	....	....	1401
47.00	....	1917	....	....	*394*	d. White Sulphur Springs d.	....	....	....	1306
75.00	....	2250	....	....	*622*	d. Charleston ......d.	....	....	....	0955
82.00	....	2348	....	....	*704*	d. Huntington ......d.	....	....	....	0837
83.00	**315**	0008	**317**	....	*721*	d. Catlettsburg ....d.	**316**	**318**	....	0816
86.00	1‡C‡	0110	1‡C‡	....	*778*	d. South Portsmouth d.	1‡C‡	1‡C‡	....	0708
92.00	♦🍷	0355	♦🍷	....	*965*	d. **Cincinnati** ......d.	♦🍷	♦🍷	....	0500
98.00	②③⑤⑦	0445	①④⑥	....	*1008*	d. Hamilton..........d.	①②④⑥	③⑤⑦	....	0340
102.00	0645	0645	0955	....	*1167*	d. **Indianapolis** ...d.	1900	2220	....	2359
106.00	0748	0751	1058	....	*1242*	d. Crawfordsville .d.	1739	2059	....	2239
108.00	0820	0824	1130	....	*1285*	d. Lafayette ....d.	1709	2029	....	2208
118.00	1115	1125	1425	....	*1479*	a. **Chicago** Union.d.	1430	1750	....	1940

19/20–CRESCENT–see Table **190**. **50/51**–CARDINAL–🛏‡, 🛏‡, 🚃 and ⊗ Chicago(**50/51**)-New York and v.v. **79/80**–CAROLINIAN–🚃 and 🍷 New York(**79/80**)-Charlotte and v.v. **315-8**–HOOSIER STATE. **519/20**–GULF BREEZE–see Table **190**. **a**–via Raleigh. **b**–Connection by 🚌. *NRPC*–National Railroad Passenger Corporation (AMTRAK).

Table 224 PHILADELPHIA AIRPORT

SEP

Local #### service (C cl. only) Philadelphia-Philadelphia Airport and v.v. *13* km. Journey: 20 mins. Fare: US $: 6.00.

From Philadelphia 30th Street: 0534 and every 30 mins. to 2334.

From Philadelphia Airport: 0010, 0610 and every 30 mins to 2340.

SEP– Southeastern Pennsylvania Transportation Authority.

Table 225 HARRISBURG - CHICAGO

NRPC

US $ C cl.	43 C‡ ♦		41 S‡C‡ ♦Ⓡ ✕	29 S‡C‡ ♦Ⓡ	km	↓ ↑	30 S‡C‡ ♦Ⓡ	40 S‡C‡ ♦Ⓡ ✕	42 C‡ ♦ ⚒	44 C‡ ♦ †
0.00	0745	....	1245	....	*0*	d.*New York* **213** ...a.	....	1750	1850	2145
30.00	0941	....	1457**u**	....	*145*	d.*Philadelphia* **218** a.	....	1529**s**	1659	1950
44.00	1141	....	1710**u**	....	*310*	d.**Harrisburg**........a.	....	1315	1507	1757
82.00	1418	....	1945	....	*521*	d.Altoona..............d.	....	1026	1218	1513
88.00	1519	....	2049	....	*584*	d.Johnstown ....d.	....	0919	1117	1412
88.00	1659	....	2242	....	*710*	a. **Pittsburgh** .... d.	....	0740	0940	1235
	....	....	2302	2359		d. **Pittsburgh** .... a.	0340	0725	....	....
90.00	....	....	0127	|	*832*	d.Youngstown ......d.	|	0430	....	....
90.00	....	....	0232	**a**	*920*	d.Akron ....d.	**a**	0325	....	....
97.00	....	....	0424	|	*1080*	d.Fostoria ....d.	|	0125	....	....
102.00	....	....	0509	|	*1232*	d.Garrett...............d.	|	2254	....	....
105.00	....	....	0552	|	*1312*	d.Nappanee..........d.	|	2202	....	....
124.00	....	....	0714**s**	0817**s**	*1440*	d.Hammond NRPC d.	1737**u**	2042**u**	....	....
124.00	....	....	0814	0910	*1465*	a.**Chicago** Union..d.	1710	2015	....	....

29/30–CAPITOL LIMITED–🛏‡, 🄳‡, 🚃 and ✕ Washington(**29/30**)-Chicago and v.v. **40/41**–BROADWAY LIMITED–see Table **185**. **42-44**–PENNSYLVANIAN–🚃 and 🍷 Pittsburgh(**42/44/43**)-New York and v.v. **a**–Via Cleveland (Table **220**). *NRPC*–National Railroad Passenger Corporation (AMTRAK).

Table 226 UNIVERSITY PARK

MR

service Chicago-University Park and v.v. *55* km. Journey: 1¼ hours. Fare: US $: 4.10.

From Chicago Randolph Street: 0050, 0515⚒, 0530†, 0630†, 0635⚒, 0753⚒, 0830Ⓑ, 0930⚒, 1030, 1130⚒, 1230, 1330⚒, 1430, 1520⚒, 1538⚒, 1608⚒, 1630†, 1632Ⓐ, 1638⑥, 1647Ⓐ, 1702Ⓐ, 1708Ⓐ, 1717Ⓐ, 1737Ⓐ, 1738⑥, 1808⚒, 1830†, 1838⚒, 1925⚒, 2020⚒, 2030†, 2120⚒, 2220⚒, 2230†, 2320⚒.

From University Park: 0420⚒, 0445†, 0515⚒, 0550⚒, 0634Ⓐ, 0640Ⓐ, 0644⑥, 0645†, 0655Ⓐ, 0710Ⓐ, 0714⑥, 0725Ⓐ, 0744⑥, 0745Ⓑ, 0751Ⓐ, 0801Ⓐ, 0826⑥, 0856⚒, 0945†, 0956⚒, 1056⚒, 1145†, 1156⚒, 1256⚒, 1354†, 1356⚒, 1456⚒, 1545†, 1556⚒, 1640⚒, 1740⚒, 1745†, 1838⚒, 1939⚒, 1945†, 2038⚒, 2138⚒, 2145†, 2238⚒, 2338⚒, 2345†.

MR– Metropolitan Rail.

Table 227 CHICAGO - DETROIT/PORT HURON

NRPC

US $ C cl.	350 1‡C‡ ♦ 🍷	364 C‡ ♦ ⚒			366 C‡ ♦ †		352 1‡C‡ ♦	30 S‡C‡ ♦Ⓡ ✕	354 1‡C‡ ♦ 🍷	48 S‡C‡ ♦Ⓡ ✕		km	↓ ↑	29 S‡C‡ ♦Ⓡ ✕	351 1‡C‡ ♦ 🍷	49 S‡C‡ ♦Ⓡ ✕	353 1‡C‡ ♦			365 C‡ ♦ ⚒	355 1‡C‡ ♦🍷		367 C‡ ♦ †	
0.00	0700	0820	....	....	1050	....	1525	1710	1815	1915	....	*0*	d.**Chicago** Union..........a.	0910	1135	1258	1645	....	....	1835	2145	....	2240	....
4.00	0726	0846	....	....	1116	....	1551	1737**u**	1841	1944**u**	....	*25*	d.Hammond NRPC.......a.	0817**s**	1058	1204**s**	1601	....	....	1756	2105	....	2201	....
13.00	|	|	....	....	|	....	|	|	1917	|	....	*34*	d.Michigan City............d.	|	1018	|	|	....	....	|	|	....	|	....
18.00	0939	1100	....	....	1326	....	1809	|	2051	|	....	*141*	d.Niles.........................d.	|	1037	|	1553	....	....	1748	2057	....	2151	....
26.50	1036	1152	....	....	1418	....	1903	|	2146	|	....	*221*	d.Kalamazoo ....d.	|	0945	|	1503	....	....	1658	2007	....	2058	....
29.00	1103	1228	....	....	1458	....	1933	|	2215	|	....	*258*	d.Battle Creek ....d.	|	0917	|	1433	....	....	1630	1939	....	2030	....
40.00	|	1327	....	....	1602	....	|	|	|	|	....	*335*	d. East Lansing ....d.	|	|	|	|	....	....	1515	|	....	1915	....
50.00	|	1357	....	....	1632	....	|	|	|	|	....	*382*	d. Durand....................d.	|	|	|	|	....	....	1445	|	....	1845	....
50.00	|	1424	....	....	1659	....	|	|	|	|	....	*409*	d. Flint.........................d.	|	|	|	|	....	....	1423	|	....	1823	....
57.00	|	1605	....	....	1825	....	|	|	|	|	....	*513*	d. **Port Huron** 🏛 ....d.	|	|	|	|	....	....	1315	|	....	1715	....
59.00	|	1625	....	....	1845	....	|	|	|	|	....	*518*	a. Sarnia 🏛..................d.	|	|	|	|	....	....	1210	|	....	1605	....
95.00	|	2106	....	....	2326	....	|	|	|	|	....	*796*	a. *Toronto* **17** ....d.	|	|	|	|	....	....	0750	|	....	1200	....
29.00	1148	....	....	....	....	....	2025	|	2303	|	....	*331*	d.Jackson......................d.	|	0827	|	1341	....	....	....	1849	....	....	....
29.00	1226	....	....	....	....	....	2104	|	2342	|	....	*390*	d.Ann Arbor...................d.	|	0751	|	1306	....	....	....	1814	....	....	....
29.00	1259**s**	....	....	....	....	....	2139**s**	|	0015**s**	|	....	*439*	d.Dearborn ....d.	|	0717**u**	|	1232**u**	....	....	....	1741**u**	....	....	....
29.00	1324	....	....	....	....	....	2204	|	0040	|	....	*450*	a. Detroit Woodward Avenue d.	|	0647	|	1200	....	....	....	1713	....	....	....
	1328	....	....	....	....	....	2215	|	0045	|	....		d. Detroit Woodward Avenue a.	|	0645	|	1150	....	....	....	1710	....	....	....
30.00	1420	....	....	....	....	....	|	|	0137	|	....		a. Pontiac ....d.	|	0605	|	|	....	....	....	1630	....	....	....
55.00	....	....	....	....	....	....	2355	2215	....	0026	....	*542*	a.Toledo Central Union d.	0545	....	0934	1010	....	....	....	....	....	....	....

29/30–CAPITOL IMITED–see Table **220**. **48/49**–LAKESHORE LIMITED–see Table **186**. **350/1**–WOLVERINE. **352/3**–LAKE CITIES–🚃 Chicago(**352/3**)-Toledo and v.v.; 🍷 Chicago(**352/3**)-Detroit and v.v. **354/5**–TWILIGHT LIMITED. **364**–INTERNATIONAL–🚃 and ⊗ Chicago(**364**)-Sarnia(**88**)-Toronto. **365**–INTERNATIONAL–🚃 and ⊗ Toronto(**85**)-Sarnia(**365**)-Chicago. **366**–INTERNATIONAL–🚃 and ⊗ Chicago(**366**)-Sarnia(**688**)-Toronto. **367**–INTERNATIONAL–🚃 and ⊗ Toronto(**685**)-Sarnia(**367**)-Chicago. *NRPC*–National Railroad Passenger Corporation (AMTRAK).

Table 228 MINNEAPOLIS - CHICAGO

NRPC

US $ C cl.	330 C‡ ♦ ⚒		332 C‡ ♦		334 C‡ ♦	336 C‡ ♦	8 S‡C‡ ♦Ⓡ ✕	338 C‡ ♦		340 C‡ ♦	342 C‡ ♦	km	↓ ↑	331 C‡ ♦ ⚒	333 C‡ ♦	335 C‡ ♦	337 C‡ ♦	7 S‡C‡ ♦Ⓡ ✕		339 C‡ ♦		341 C‡ ♦		343 C‡ ♦
72.00	....	....	....	....	....	....	0720	....	....	....	....	*0*	d.St. Paul/Minneapoliss Midway .a.	....	....	....	....	2340	....	....	....	....	....	....
72.00	....	....	....	....	....	....	0826	....	....	....	....	*76*	d.Red Wing ....d.	....	....	....	....	2203	....	....	....	....	....	....
60.00	....	....	....	....	....	....	0930	....	....	....	....	*177*	d.Winona......................d.	....	....	....	....	2055	....	....	....	....	....	....
56.00	....	....	....	....	....	....	1005	....	....	....	....	*221*	d.La Crosse..................d.	....	....	....	....	2020	....	....	....	....	....	....
53.00	....	....	....	....	....	....	1045	....	....	....	....	*287*	d.Tomah........................d.	....	....	....	....	1933	....	....	....	....	....	....
41.00	....	....	....	....	....	....	1124	....	....	....	....	*359*	d.Wisconsin Dells ....d.	....	....	....	....	1854	....	....	....	....	....	....
37.00	....	....	....	....	....	....	1143	....	....	....	....	*386*	d.Portage ....d.	....	....	....	....	1835	....	....	....	....	....	....
26.50	....	....	....	....	....	....	1213	....	....	....	....	*432*	d.Columbus ....d.	....	....	....	....	1804	....	....	....	....	....	....
16.00	0620	....	0800	....	1035	1235	1356**s**	1505	....	1740	2040	*536*	d.**Milwaukee** ....d.	0957	1202	1405	1637	1651**u**	....	1845	....	2007	....	0032
15.00	0644	....	0824	....	1059	1259	|	1529	....	1804	2104	*574*	d.Sturtevant (Racine) ...d.	0926	1131	1334	1606	|	....	1813	....	1936	....	0001
5.00	0725	....	0902	....	1137	1337	1458**s**	1607	....	1842	2142	*645*	d.Glenview ◇............ d.	0848	1053	1256	1528	1539**u**	....	1732	....	1858	....	2323
0.00	0757	....	0932	....	1207	1407	1534	1637	....	1912	2212	*673*	a.**Chicago** Union..........d.	0825	1030	1233	1505	1515	....	1708	....	1835	....	2300

7/8–EMPIRE BUILDER–see Table **194**. **330-343**–HIAWATHA. ◇–Local passengers not carried Glenview-Chicago or v.v. unless connecting at Chicago with other *NRPC* trains. *NRPC*–National Railroad Passenger Corporation (AMTRAK).

Table 229 — CHICAGO LOCAL RAIL SERVICE #### CTA MR

Local #### services (C‡ only) operate in the Chicago area as follows:
Evanston (MR) (19 km, US $. 2.55). From Chicago Madison Street: 0035, 0624④, 0635⑤, 0650④, 0709④, 0725④, 0800④, 0835⑤, 1035, 1135④, 1235, 1335④, 1435, 1535④, 1615④, 1630④, 1635, 1710④, 1715④, 1721④, 1735④, 1800④, 1831④, 1835④, 1935⑤, 2035④, 2135⑤, 2235, 2335④, returning from Evanston Davis Street at 0045②-⑥, 0549⑤, 0619④, 0651④, 0700④, 0713④, 0719④, 0739④, 0745④, 0753④, 0759④, 0800④, 0810④, 0835④, 0857④, 0900④, 0929④, 1000, 1100⑤, 1150†, 1300, 1400④, 1500④, 1600④, 1700, 1732④, 1800④, 1806④, 1900④, 2000, 2100④, 2200④, 2300†.

2330⑤; also by CTA from Chicago Van Buren: 0500⑤/0700† and frequent to 2359, returning frtom Evanston Davis Street at 0430⑤/0630† and frequent to 2330. Journey: 25 mins.
Skokie (CTA) (❖ km, US $: ❖). From Chicago Van Buren: 0500⑤/0700† and frequent to 2359, returning from Skokie Dempster at ❖. Journey: 25 mins.

CTA– Chicago Transit Authority.
MR– Metropolitan Rail.

Table 230 — CHICAGO - KENOSHA #### MR

US $		km	301 C‡		305 C‡⑤		311 C‡④	315 C‡⑤		317 C‡⑧	801 C‡⑥	319 C‡④	803 C‡†	321 C‡⑤		323 C‡④	325 C‡⑤	805 C‡†	327 C‡④	329 C‡④	
0.00	Chicago Madison Street..d.	0	0035	....	0635	....	0725	0835	....	1035	1035	1135	1235	1235	....	1335	1435	1535	1615	....	
3.30	Ravinia Park ◇ ..d.	36		....		....			....				1320		....			1520		....	
4.45	Waukegan.........d.	58	0150	....	0751	....	0842	0950	....	1150	1150	1250	1350	1350	....	1450	1550	1550	1650	1715	....
5.60	Kenosha.........a.	84	0215	....	0810	....			....		1215			1415	....			1615		1737	....

		807 C‡⑥	333 C‡④		335 C‡④		337 C‡④	339 C‡④			343 C‡⑧	809 C‡⑥	345 C‡④	347 C‡④		349 C‡④	351 C‡⑤	353 C‡⑤		355 C‡④		357 C‡⑤		359 C‡		361 C‡④
Chicago Madison Street d.		1635	1635	....	1707	....	1710	1715	....		1735	1735	1745	1800	....	1831	1835	1935	,....	2035	....	2135	....	2235	....	2335
Ravinia Park ◇ ....d.		1720		....		....			....			1820		1850	....		1920	2020	....	2120	....	2220	....	2320	....	0020
Waukegan..............d.		1750	1745	....	1804	....	1815	1820	....		1845	1850	1900	1920	....	1928	1950	2050	....	2150	....	2250	....	2350	....	0050
Kenosha..............a.		1815		....	1828	....		1839	....		1908	1915			....	1950			....		....	2315	....		....	

		300 C‡⑤	302 C‡④	304 C‡④	800 C‡⑥	306 C‡④			310 C‡④		314 C‡④	316 C‡④	802 C‡⑥		318 C‡④		322 C‡④			324 C‡④	326 C‡⑤	804 C‡⑥	
Kenosha..............d.					0549	0555	....		0620			0655	0649	....			0715	....			0754		....
Waukegan..............d.			0500	0530	0558	0610	0617	....	0641		0710	0715	0710	....	0720		0737	....		0747	0815	0810	....
Ravinia Park ◇ ....d.								....						....				....					....
Chicago Madison Street a.		....	0615	0645	0715	0725	0735	....	0800		0815	0824	0825	....	0834		0840	....		0900	0915	0925	....

		330 C‡	332 C‡⑤	810 C‡††		334 C‡		336 C‡④	338 C‡④		340 C‡④	342 C‡		346 C‡④		350 C‡④	352 C‡④	812 C‡⑥	354 C‡⑤	356 C‡④	816 C‡††	814 C‡⑥	358 C‡④	360 C‡④
Kenosha..............d.		0849									1449						1749		1849			2220		2335
Waukegan..............d.		0910		1010	1055		1210		1310	1410		1510	1610		1710		1810	1910	1910	2010	2110	2210	2240	2240	2335
Ravinia Park ◇ ....d.												1638b		1738		1838	1938	1938a		2238	2308	2308	0023
Chicago Madison Street a.		1025		1125	1215		1325		1425	1525		1625	1725		1825		1925	2025	2025	2125	2225	2325	2355	2355	0110

a– ⑥ only.
b– © only.
◇– June 23-Sept. 3 only, for concerts/meetings only.
MR– Metropolitan Rail.

Table 231 — CHICAGO - HARVARD #### MR

US $		km	601 C‡	603 C‡④	605 C‡④	607 C‡④	609 C‡④	701 C‡⑥		611 C‡④	613 C‡⑤	705 C‡†	615 C‡⑤		617 C‡	707 C‡⑥	619 C‡④		621 C‡④	709 C‡©	711 C‡④	623 C‡④	625 C‡④	713 C‡⑥
0.00	Chicago Madison Street..d.	0	0030	0555	0630	0713	0730	0830	....	0900	1030	1030	1130	....	1230	1310	1330	....	1430	1430	1530	1530	1610	1630
3.30	Arlington Park ...d.	30	0119	0645	0719	0758	0819	0919	....	0949	1119	1119	1219	....	1319	1353	1419	....	1519	1519	1619	1622	1705	1719
4.10	Barrington ....d.	52	0133	0657	0733	0812	0833	0933	....	1003	1133	1133	1233	....	1333	1407	1433	....	1533	1533	1633	1636	1719	1733
6.40	Harvard ....a.	101	0218				0918	1018	....		1218	1318		....		1453	1518	....		1618		1720	1805	....
5.60	McHenry ....a.	83		0722					....	1845				....				....						

		715 C‡†	627 C‡④	629 C‡④	631 C‡④	633 C‡④	717 C‡⑥	635 C‡④	637 C‡④	639 C‡④	641 C‡④	643 C‡④	645 C‡④	647 C‡④	649 C‡④	651 C‡④	653 C‡④	719 C‡⑥	655 C‡④	657 C‡④		659 C‡④		661 C‡④		663 C‡⑧
Chicago Madison Street d.		1630	1639	1645	1648	1658	1705	1706	1712	1716	1720	1723	1733	1746	1802	1820	1830	1830	1930	2030	....	2130	....	2230	....	2330
Arlington Park ....d.		1719	1727			1736	1754	1753		1750	1800	1819	1813	1842		1911	1906	1919	2019	2119	....	2219	....	2319	....	0019
Barrington ....d.		1733	1741	1727	1754	1750	1808	1807	1817		1813	1836	1829	1856	1847	1925	1920	1933	2033	2133	....	2233	....	2333	....	0033
Harvard ....a.		1818								1844			1915			2005	2018		2218	2318	....					
McHenry ....a.				1800							1845															

		662 C‡②-⑥	602 C‡④	604 C‡④	606 C‡④	608 C‡④	610 C‡④	612 C‡④	700 C‡⑥	614 C‡④	618 C‡④	620 C‡④	702 C‡⑥	622 C‡④	704 C‡⑥	624 C‡④	626 C‡④	628 C‡④	706 C‡⑥	630 C‡④	632 C‡④	634 C‡④	708 C‡⑥	710 C‡④	636 C‡④	714 C‡††
McHenry ....d.						0553							0654								0736		0730			
Harvard ....d.						0548					0622	0621						0659	0708				0735	0735	0835
Barrington ....d.		0012	0507	0537	0557	0618	0634	0627	0636	0638	....	0711	0707	0724	0716	0715	0727	0742	0743	0754	0804	0747	0756	0816	0836	0916
Arlington Park ....d.		0024	0519	0549	0609	0632	0643	0641	0648	0652	0711		0722		0728	0729	0740	0756	0755		0801	0808	0828	0828	0928
Chicago Madison Street a.		0108	0612	0642	0703	0714	0719	0735	0740	0740	0753	0800	0805	0815	0820	0824	0830	0835	0840	0840	0851	0853	0900	0920	0920	1020

		638 C‡⑤	640 C‡④	716 C‡⑥	718 C‡©	642 C‡④	644 C‡⑤	720 C‡††		646 C‡⑤		648 C‡④		650 C‡④		652 C‡④	654 C‡④	656 C‡⑥		722 C‡††		658 C‡⑤		660 C‡
McHenry ....d.									....		....		....		....				....		....		....	
Harvard ....d.			0935		1035			1235	....	1335	....		....		....	1635		1735	....	1835	....		....	2035
Barrington ....d.		0916	1016	1116	1116	1116	1216	1316	....	1416	....	1516	....	1616	....	1716	1805	1816	....	1916	....	2016	....	2116
Arlington Park ....d.		0928	1028	1028	1128	1128	1228	1328	....	1428	....	1528	....	1628	....	1728	1816	1828	....	1928	....	2028	....	2128
Chicago Madison Street a.		1020	1120	1120	1220	1220	1320	1420	....	1520	....	1620	....	1720	....	1820	1857	1920	....	2020	....	2120	....	2220

MR– Metropolitan Rail.

Table 232 — CHICAGO - GENEVA #### MR

service Chicago-West Chicago-Geneva and v.v. 75 km. Journey: 1-1¼ hours. Fare: US $: 4.45‡.
From Chicago Madison Street: 0040②-⑦, 0620④, 0650④, 0740④, 0840⑤, 0940⑦, 1040⑤, 1240, 1440⑤, 1540⑥, 1614④, 1640⑥, 1704④, 1717④, 1730④, 1740④, 1810④, 1840⑤, 1940④, 2040, 2140④, 2240⑤, 2340④.
From Geneva: 0500④, 0541⑤, 0605④, 0609④, 0637④, 0654④, 0705④, 0725④, 0740④, 0805⑤, 0905④, 1005⑤, 1205⑤, 1405, 1605⑤, 1705④, 1805⑤, 1905⑦, 2005④, 2105④, 2205.

service (1.435m.) Chicago-Orland Park and v.v. ❖ km. Journey: 1 hour. Fare: US $: 3.30‡.
From Chicago Union: 1630④, 1657④, 1730④, 1845④.
From Orland Park 143rd Street: 0533④, 0630④, 0705④, 0738④.
MR– Metropolitan Rail.

Table 233 — CHICAGO - FOX LAKE/ELGIN #### MR

service C‡ cl. Chicago-Fox Lake and v.v. 81 km. Journey: 1½ hours. US $: C cl.: 5.25; Chicago-Elgin and v.v. ❖ km. Journey: 1¼ hours. Fare: US $: 4.45.
From Chicago Union: 0025, 0705④, 0835, 1035, 1235, 1435⑤, 1535④, 1620④, 1645⑤, 1710④, 1725④, 1730④, 1735④, 1748④, 1845④, 1935, 2035④, 2135⑤, 2205④.
From Fox Lake: 0450④, 0520⑤, 0550④, 0612④, 0620④, 0632④, 0642, 0655④, 0701④, 0721④, 0842, 1042, 1242⑤, 1442, 1605④, 1642④, 1915, 2205.
From Chicago Union: 0030, 0545④, 0625⑤, 0640④, 0715④, 0815④, 0840④, 0940④, 1040⑤, 1240, 1340⑤, 1440⑤, 1540④, 1625④, 1640④, 1650④, 1705④, 1717④, 1740④, 1805④, 1840, 1940④, 2040, 2140④, 2240④.
From Elgin: 0425④, 0500④, 0505④, 0536④, 0556④, 0605④, 0625④, 0658④, 0705©, 0727④, 0742④, 0805④, 0830④, 0905④, 0935④, 1005④, 1105, 1205④, 1405, 1505④, 1600④, 1705, 1815④, 1905⑤, 1935④, 2035④, 2135.
MR– Metropolitan Rail.

Table 234 — CHICAGO - AURORA #### MR

service Chicago-Downers Grove-Naperville-Aurora and v.v. 62 km. Journey: 1 hour. Fare: US $: C cl.: 4.45‡.
From Chicago Union: 0030②-⑥, 0620④, 0740④, 0845④, 0930④, 1030④, 1130©, 1230⑤, 1330, 1430⑤, 1520④, 1530©, 1555④, 1628④, 1630④, 1700④, 1716④, 1728④, 1730©, 1732④, 1740④, 1810④, 1820④, 1830④, 1850④, 1930④, 2030, 2130④, 2230④, 2330.
From Aurora: 0452④, 0535④, 0542④, 0602⑤, 0620④, 0640④, 0642④, 0700④, 0702†, 0720④, 0722④, 0740④, 0802⑤, 0902, 0922⑤, 1102©, 1202④, 1302©, 1402④, 1502, 1600④, 1645④, 1702④, 1802, 1902④, 2102, 2202④, 2240④.
MR– Metropolitan Rail.

Table 235 CHICAGO - OMAHA   ╫ NRPC

US $ C cl.	5 S‡C‡ ◆▣ ✕	347 C‡ ◆		km	↓		348 C‡ ◆ ☲	346 C‡ ◆ ☲	6 S‡C‡ ◆▣ ☲
0.00	....	1505	1755	0	d.Chicago Union...a.		1035	1150	1615
	....	1540u	1832u	41	d.Naperville.........d.		0940s	1055s	1454s
23.00	....	1650	1941	211	d.Princeton.........d.		0831	0946	1345
30.00	....		2004	211	d.Kewanee.........d.		0808	0923	
37.00	....	1744	2036	261	d.Galesburg S. Seminary Str.d.		0740	0855	1255
37.00	....		2116	326	a. Macomb...d.		0700	0815	
45.00	....		2203	424	a. Quincy...........d.		0612	0727	
51.00	....	1837		330	d.Burlington.......d.				1200
64.00	....	1947		450	d.Ottumwa.........d.				1038
87.00	....	2146		632	a.Creston.........d.				0847
100.00	....	2335		798	a.Omaha.........d.				0650
163.00	....	0810		1664	a.Denver 245.....d.				2100
211.00	....	2331		2582	a.Salt Lake City 250 d.				0505
262.00	....	1650		3895	a.Emeryville☲250☲.d.				1010

5/6–CALIFORNIA ZEPHYR–see Table 189. 346-8–ILLINOIS ZEPHYR. ☲–Oakland.
☲–Emeryville will open at a date to be announced. Prior to opening trains will continue to call at the Oakland Wood Street Station.   NRPC–National Railroad Passenger Corporation (AMTRAK).

Table 236 CHICAGO - KANSAS CITY   ╫ NRPC

US $ C cl.	3 S‡C‡ ◆▣ ✕			km	↓		4 S‡C‡ ◆▣ ✕	
0.00	....	1700	....	0	d.Chicago Union...a.	....	1525	....
9.75	....	1755	....	60	d.Joliet Union.......d.	....	1329	....
27.00	....	1916	....	209	d.Chillicothe.........d.	....	1157	....
30.00	....	1959	....	285	d.Galesburg North Broad Street d.	....	1110	....
52.00	....	2050	....	377	d.Fort Madison.......d.	....	1020	....
69.00	....	0045	....	725	a.Kansas City.....d.	....	0705	....
207.00	....	1655	....	2174	a.Albuquerque 248 d.	....	1315	....
253.00	....	0815	....	3604	a.Los Angeles 248 d.	....	2015	....

3/4– SOUTHWEST CHIEF–see Table 187.
NRPC–National Railroad Passenger Corporation (AMTRAK).

Table 237 CHICAGO - JOLIET ╫ MR

╫ service (C‡ cl. only) Chicago-Joliet and v.v. 60 km. Journey: 1¼ hours. Fare: US $: C cl.: 4.45.
From Chicago Union: 1650④, 1725④.
From Chicago La Salle Street: 0030ex⑥, 0657④, 0745④, 0830, 0930④, 1030, 1130④, 1230, 1330④, 1430, 1545④, 1610④, 1630©, 1635④, 1710④, 1720④, 1730⑥, 1740④, 1815④, 1840, 1940④, 2045, 2145④, 2255.
From Joliet Union to Chicago Union: 0625④, 0705④.
From Joliet Union to Chicago La Salle Street: 0504④, 0533④, 0550④, 0604©, 0612④, 0632④, 0648④, 0704④, 0719④, 0724⑥, 0737④, 0824, 0924④, 1024, 1124④, 1224, 1324④, 1424, 1524④, 1624, 1717④, 1818④, 1824©, 1918④, 2024©, 2124④, 2224✕.
MR– Metropolitan Rail.

Table 238 CHICAGO - ST. LOUIS   ╫ NRPC

US $ C cl.				km			301 C‡ ◆ ☲	311 1‡C‡ ◆ ☲	303 1‡C‡ ◆ ☲		305 1‡C‡ ◆ ☲	3 S‡C‡ ◆▣ ✕	21 S‡C‡ ◆ ✕	321 1‡C‡ ①③④⑥
0.00		Chicago Union ....d.		0				0820	1030		1530	1700	1745	1745
9.75		Joliet Union........d.		60				0910	1120		1620	1755	1840	1840
15.50		Pontiac............d.		148				1003			1711		1932	1932
20.50		Bloomington.......d.		204				1030	1240		1740	a	2005	2005
25.00		Lincoln............d.		252				1059	1310		1813		2040	2040
31.00		Springfield.........d.		298				1150	1345		1850		2117	2117
38.00		Carlinville.........d.		360					1425		1930			
40.50		Alton..............d.		414					1455		2000		2227	2227
★14.50		Centralia 240 .....d.		◇ 103			0430b							
44.50		St. Louis........{a.		457			0600b	1600		2105		2330	2330
		{d.					0810	1630						
★4.25		Kirkwood..........d.		480			0835	1655						
★21.50		Jefferson City.......d.		658			1030	1855						
★30.00		Sedalia............d.		760			1141	2001						
★37.50		Kansas City ......a.		912			1340	2200			0045			

				300 1‡C‡ ◆ ☲	302 1‡C‡ ◆ ☲	322 C‡ ◆ ☲ ②④⑥⑦	22 S‡C‡ ◆ ✕ ①③⑤	4 S‡C‡ ◆▣ ✕	312 1‡C‡ ◆ ☲	304 1‡C‡ ◆ ☲			306 C‡ ◆ ☲
	Kansas City ....d.							0705		0815	....		1635
	Sedalia...............d.									1005	....		1825
	Jefferson City ....d.									1116	....		1936
	Kirkwood..............d.									1306	....		2126
	St. Louis ....{a.									1345	....		2205
	{d.			0430	0555	0735	0735			1415	....		2220b
	Centralia 240 ....a.										....		2350b
	Alton ....d.			0520	0645	0823	0823			1505	....		
	Carlinville ....d.			0550	0715					1535	....		
	Springfield ....d.			0635	0800	0943	0943		1500	1618	....		
	Lincoln ....d.			0705	0830	1013	1013		1528	1648	....		
	Bloomington ....d.			0738	0903	1100	1100	a	1600	1723	....		
	Pontiac ....d.			0806	0931				1627		....		
	Joliet Union ....d.			0858	1023	1215	1215	1329	1725	1843	....		
	Chicago Union ....a.			1000	1125	1335	1335	1525	1830	2008			

3/4– SOUTHWEST CHIEF–see Table 187.
21/22– THE TEXAS EAGLE–see Table 188.
300/2/5–THE STATE HOUSE.
301– KANSAS CITY MULE.
303/4– ANN RUTLEDGE.
306– ST. LOUIS MULE.
311/2– THE LOOP.
321/2– THE TEXAS EAGLE.
a– Via Galesburg (Table 236).
b– Connection by ⎯.
◇– Km west of St. Louis.
★– Fare ex St. Louis.
NRPC–National Railroad Passenger Corporation (AMTRAK).

Table 239 CHICAGO - MICHIGAN CITY - SOUTH BEND ╫ NICD

US $ C cl.		101/601 C‡ ©	505 C‡ ④	7 C‡ ©	507 C‡ ④	107 C‡ ©	509 C‡ ④	109 C‡ ④	511 C‡ ④	111 C‡ ④	113 C‡ ④	513 C‡ ④	115 C‡ ④	117 C‡ ④	19 C‡ ④	119 C‡ ④	219 C‡ ④	121 C‡ ④	515 C‡ ④	23 C‡ ④	517 C‡ ④	123 C‡ ④	619 C‡ ©	125 C‡ ④
0.00	Chicago Randolph Street d.	0	0045	0800	0845	1000	1015	1159	1225	1400	1425	1558	1600	1625	1656	1710	1728	1732	1758	1800	1858	2000	2015	2200	2215
3.65	Hammond CSSB d.	34	0125	0840	0920	1040	1055	1240	1305	1440	1505	1638	1640	1705	1737	1754	1808	1813	1838	1840	1938	2040	2051	2240	2251
4.45	Gary CSSB ....d.	50	0141	0856	0936	1056	1111	1256	1321	1456	1521	1654	1656	1722	1755	1812	1821	1830	1855	1856	1955	2056	2107	2256	2307
6.30	Michigan City 11th Street d.	90	0220	0935	1015	1135	1150	1335	1400	1535	1600	1733	1735	1801	1835	1845	1900	....	1933	1935	2033	2135	2145	2335	2345
8.65	South Bend ....a.	141		1020	1100	1220		1420		1620		1820		1927			....	2020	2115	2220				

		102 C‡ ④	104 C‡ ④	600 C‡ ④	106 C‡ ④	108 C‡ ④	10 C‡ ©	110 C‡ ④	210 C‡ ④	502 C‡ ©	12 C‡ ④	504 C‡ ④	212 C‡ ④	114 C‡ ④	506 C‡ ④	214 C‡ ④	16 C‡ ④	508 C‡ ④	116 C‡ ④	510 C‡ ©	216 C‡ ©	118 C‡ ©	512 C‡ ©	514 C‡ ©	20 C‡ ©	516 C‡ ©
	South Bend............d.					0545			0640	0805	0840			1040		1201	1240		1440			1640	1840	1938	2040
	Michigan City 11th Street d.	0407	0502	0525	0558	0610	0630	0702		0725	0850	0925		1034	1125		1246	1325	1404	1440	1525		1645	1725	1925	2023	2125
	Gary CSSB ....d.	0445	0542	0604	0638	0650	0709	0742	0757	0804	0929	1004	1012	1114	1204	1223	1325	1404	1520	1604	1635	1725	1804	2004	2104	2204
	Hammond CSSB ....d.	0502	0559	0620	0655	0710	0723	0746	0815	0820	0945	1020	1030	1130	1220	1240	1342	1420	1537	1620	1652	1742	1820	2020	2121	2220
	Chicago Randolph Street ..a.	0540	0638	0700	0735	0747	0805	0836	0852	0900	1020	1055	1100	1210	1300	1320	1422	1500	1615	1700	1732	1822	1900	2100	2158	2300

NICD–Northern Indiana Commuter Transportation District ("The South Shore Line").

Table 240 CHICAGO - NEW ORLEANS ╫ NRPC

US $ C cl.	391 C‡ ◆ ☲	59 S‡C‡ ◆▣ ✕		km	↓		58 S‡C‡ ◆▣ ✕	392 C‡ ◆ ☲
0.00	1600	1950	....	0	d.Chicago Union...a.	....	0903	2130
11.00	1710	2110	....	92	d.Kankakee.........d.	....	0721	1956
21.00	1829	2227	....	208	d.Champaign Urbana d.	....	0615	1852
33.00	1933	2330	....	323	d.Effingham.........d.	....	0453	1737
43.00	2021	0021	....	408	d.Centralia.........d.	....	0404	1653
48.50	2130	0145	....	498	d.Carbondale.......d.	....	0313	1600
74.00		0411	....	725	d.Newbern ▶.....d.	....	0005	
83.00		0627	....	850	d.Memphis.........d.	....	2228	
104.00		0907	....	1097	d.Durant............d.	....	1921	
112.00		0939	....	1154	d.Canton...........d.	....	1850	
116.00		1030	....	1191	d.Jackson..........d.	....	1821	
125.00		1156	....	1316	d.McComb.........d.	....	1634	
133.00		1253	....	1400	d.Hammond........d.	....	1538	
136.00		1418	....	1486	a.New Orleans.....d.	....	1440	

58/59– CITY OF NEW ORLEANS–see Table 183.
391/2– ILLINI.
▶– For Dyersburg.
NRPC–National Railroad Passenger Corporation (AMTRAK).

Table 241 MINNEAPOLIS - SPOKANE   ╫ NRPC

US $ C cl.	7 S‡C‡ ◆✕ ▣		km	↓		8 S‡C‡ ◆✕ ▣
0.00		1515	0	d.Chicago 228 ....a.	....	1534
64.00	....	2359	673	d.Minneapolis/St.Paul Midway a.	....	0650
83.00	....	0140	785	d.St. Cloud......d.	....	0425
107.00	....	0443	1069	d.Fargo..........d.	....	0128
121.00	....	0603	1194	d.Grand Forks....d.	....	0008
131.00	....	0725	1337	d.Devils Lake ....d.	....	2245
136.00	....	0950	1528	d.Minot..........d.	....	2030
151.00	....	1154	1720	d.Williston.......d.	....	1815
184.00	....	1414	2077	d.Malta..........d.	....	1335
202.00	....	1600	2218	d.Havre..........d.	....	1225
215.00	....	1738	2386	d.Shelby.........d.	....	1039
227.00	....	1905a	2501	d.Glacier Park....d.	....	0910a
238.00	....	2140	2628	d.Whitefish......d.	....	0650
245.00	....	0018	2927	d.Sandpoint......d.	....	0155
245.00	....	0150	3034	a.Spokane.......d.	....	0040
245.00	....	1025	3671	a.Seattle 260.....d.	....	1650

7/8– EMPIRE BUILDER–see Table 194.
a– May 8-Oct. 11.
NRPC–National Railroad Passenger Corporation (AMTRAK).

Check update notes to timetables and with operator before starting your journey

Table 242 — CHICAGO - GRAND RAPIDS #### NRPC

US $ C cl.	370 1‡C‡ ◆ ☖		371 1‡C‡ ◆ ☖		
		km	↓		↑
0.00	 1730	0	d.**Chicago** Union..a.	1035	....
3.50	 1754	25	d.Hammond NRPC d.	0952	....
❖	 2011	140	d.Benton Harbor ◇d.	0934	....
31.50	 2123	241	d.Holland.............d.	0823	....
33.50	 2220	282	a.**Grand Rapids** ..d.	0745	....

370/1– PERE MARQUETTE.
◇– Benton Harbor (*St. Joseph*).
NRPC–National Railroad Passenger Corporation (AMTRAK).

Table 243 — ST. LOUIS - SAN ANTONIO & #### NRPC

US $ C cl.	21 S‡C‡ ◆☖ ①③⑤	521 S‡C‡ ◆☖ ①③⑤			522 S‡C‡ ◆☖◆☖ ②④⑦	22 S‡C‡ ◆☖ ②④⑦
			km	↓		↑
	.... 1745a		0	d.Chicago 237......a.	 1335	
0.00	 0015		457	d.**St. Louis**..........a.	 0655	
32.50	 0403		717	d.Poplar Bluff......d.	 0244	
45.00	 0457		813	d.Walnut Ridge......d.	 0135	
63.00	 0723		1007	d.Little Rock........d.	2337	....
	 0829		1127	d.Arkadelphia........d.	2202	....
87.00	 1004		1240	d.Texarkana........d.	2047	....
93.00	 1119		1347	d.Marshall..........d.	1918	....
93.00	 1149		1384	d.Longview..........d.	1846	....
115.00	 1449	1515	1588	d.**Dallas**..........d.	1505 1605	....
❖	|	1645	1658	d. Corsicana......d.	1225	
❖	|	2200	1995	a. **Houston** Union d.	0825	|
115.00	 1632		1638	d.**Fort Worth**......d.	 1430	
131.00	 1912		1844	d.Temple............d.	 1130	
138.00	 2012		1906	d.Taylor............d.	 1025	
143.00	 2107		1962	d.Austin............d.	 0935	
144.00	 2147		2011	d.San Marcos......d.	 0845	
157.00	 2340		2090	a.**San Antonio**......d.	 0705	

21/22/521/2–THE TEXAS EAGLE–see Table **188**. a–②⑤⑦.
NRPC–National Railroad Passenger Corporation (AMTRAK).

Table 244 — JACKSONVILLE - EL PASO & #### NRPC

US $ C cl.	1☖ S‡C‡ ◆☖ ②⑤⑦		2☖ S‡C‡ ◆☖ ①③⑥	
		km	↓	↑
	 2120	996	d.**Jacksonville**.....a.	 1405
	 0055	727	d.Tallahassee........d.	 0955
	 0430	399	d.Pensacola........d.	 0410
	 0730	234	d.Mobile............d.	 0140
0.00	 1100	0	a.⎫**New Orleans**⎧d.	 2240
	 1320		d.⎭............⎩a.	 1935
24.00	 1602	202	d.New Iberia........d.	 1558
25.00	 1628	237	d.Lafayette........d.	 1533
45.00	 1752	352	d.Lake Charles......d.	 1406
50.00	 1915	451	d.Beaumont........d.	 1242
64.00	 2140	583	d.**Houston** Union..d.	 1055
90.00	 0255	922	d.San Antonio......d.	 0610
127.00	 0557	1194	d.Del Rio............d.	 0142
161.00	 1030	1544	d.Alpine............d.	 2134
185.00	 1325	1895	a.**El Paso**............d.	 1700
230.00	 2140	2590	a.Phoenix **258**......d.	 0708
230.00	 0615	3271	a.Los Angeles**258** d.	.... 2230a

1/2– SUNSET LIMITED–see Table **193**. Also conveys cars of THE TEXAS EAGLE, Table **188**.
a– ②⑤⑦.
NRPC–National Railroad Passenger Corporation (AMTRAK).

Table 245 — OMAHA - DENVER & #### NRPC

US $ C cl.	5 S‡C‡ ◆ ☖✕		6 S‡C‡ ◆ ☖✕
		km	↓ ↑
0.00	 1505	0	d.Chicago **235**......a. 1615 ....
98.00	 2359	798	d.**Omaha**............a. 0625 ....
100.00	 0112	886	d.Lincoln............d. 0525 ....
118.00	 0245	1042	d.Hastings..........d. 0347 ....
139.00	 0446	1254	d.McCook..........d. 0147 ....
163.00	 0607	1538	d.Fort Morgan......d. 2215 ....
163.00	 0810	1664	d.**Denver**............d. 2100 ....
201.00	 2331	2582	a.Salt Lake City **250** d. 0505 ....

5/6– CALIFORNIA ZEPHYR–see Table **189**.
NRPC–National Railroad Passenger Corporation (AMTRAK).

Table 247 — GRAND CANYON #### GCR

R.T. US $ C cl.	1C P		1C P
		km	↓ ↑
0.00	0930	0	d.**Williams** ....a. 1730 ....
47.00	1145	103	a.**Grand Canyon** ..d. 1515 ....

P– ⑤⑥⑦ Feb. 1-28; ex①② Mar. 1-20; daily Mar. 23-Oct. 30; ⑤⑥⑦ Nov. 1-31; ⑥⑦ Dec. 1-18; daily Dec. 26-Jan. 1.
GCR– Grand Canyon Railroad.

Table 248 — KANSAS CITY - LOS ANGELES & #### NRPC

US $ C cl.	3 S‡C‡ ◆ ☖ ✕	35 S‡C‡ ◆ ☖ ✕			36 S‡C‡ ◆ ☖ ✕	4 S‡C‡ ◆ ☖ ✕
			km	↓		↑
0.00	 1700		0	d.Chicago **236**......a.	1525	....
69.00	 0105		725	d.**Kansas City** ......a.	0645	....
90.00	 0202		789	d.Lawrence..........d.	0508	....
91.00	 0227		831	d.Topeka............d.	0443	....
100.00	 0327		930	d.Emporia..........d.	0343	....
108.00	 0455		1047	d.Newton............d.	0238	....
114.00	 0528		1100	d.Hutchinson......d.	0139	....
136.00	 0704		1294	d.Dodge City......d.	2359	....
139.00	 0743		1374	d.Garden City......d.	2322	....
153.00	 0754		1535	d.Lamar............d.	2111	....
163.00	 0935		1619	d.La Junta..........d.	2030	....
179.00	 1047		1751	d.Trinidad..........d.	1838	....
179.00	 1149		1787	d.Raton............d.	1737	....
194.00	 1330		1964	d.Las Vegas........d.	1555	....
207.00	 1510		2067	d.Lamy............d.	1417	....
207.00	 1715		2174	d.**Albuquerque** ..d.	1315	....
238.00	 1935		2433	d.Gallup............d.	1000	....
245.00	 2013		2638	d.Winslow..........d.	0725	....
245.00	 2115		2732	d.**Flagstaff**........d.	0625	....
253.00	 0016		3011	d.Kingman..........d.	0330	....
253.00	 0143		3106	d.Needles..........d.	0210	....
253.00	 0425	1120	3378	d.Barstow..........d.	1430	2335 ....
	....	1155		d.Victorville......d.	1350	....
253.00	 0615	1300	3509	d.San Bernardino ..d.	1233	2148 ....
253.00	 0715	1413s		d.Fullerton..........d.	1130u	2050 ....
253.00	 0815	1515	3604	a.**Los Angeles**......d.	1055	2015 ....

3/4– SOUTHWEST CHIEF–see Table **187**.
35/36– THE DESERT WIND–see Table **191**.
NRPC–National Railroad Passenger Corporation (AMTRAK).

Table 250 — DENVER - SAN FRANCISCO & #### DRG NRPC

US $ C cl.	NRPC 721 C‡ ◆	DRG 1 C‡ ◆ ✕	NRPC 5 S‡C‡ P ☖			DRG 2 C‡ P ◆ ✕	NRPC 6 S‡C‡ ◆ ☖	NRPC 726 C‡ ◆
				km	↓			↑
0.00	....	....	1505	0	d.Chicago **235**......a.		1615	....
163.00	....	0730	0910	1664	d.**Denver** Union......d.	1830	1940	....
191.00	....	1000	1105	1763	d.Winter Park......d.	1600	1655	....
191.00	....		1135	1784	d.Granby ....d.		1630	....
201.00	....		1450	1961	d.Glenwood Springs d.		1320	....
201.00	....		1650	2106	d.Grand Junction..d.		1135	....
201.00	....		1955	2401	d.Helper............d.		0800	....
201.00	....		2200	2510	d.Provo............d.		0555	....
201.00	....		2331	2582	a.⎫**Salt Lake City**⎧d.		0505	....
	....		0030	2582	d.⎭............⎩a.		0345	....
262.00	....		0343	2976	d.Elko............d.		2158	....
262.00	....		0550	3229	d.Winnemucca ....d.		1955	....
262.00	....		0925	3504	d.Sparks............d.		1715	....
262.00	....		0936	3511	d.Reno............d.		1640	....
262.00	....		1029	3566	d.Truckee..........d.		1545	....
262.00	....		1237	3672	d.Colfax............d.		1334	....
	0645		1343		d.Roseville........d.		1244	2105
262.00	0712		1435	3757	a.**Sacramento**......d.		1217	2025
262.00	0905		1650	3895	a.Emeryville ☖ **262**..d.		1010	1830
262.00	0930b		1705b	3907	a.**San Francisco**..d.		0935b	1800b

5/6– CALIFORNIA ZEPHYR–see Table **189**.
721/6– CAPITOL–🚌 and ☖ Roseville(**721/726**)–San Jose and v.v.
P– ⑥⑦ Jan. 1-Mar. 31; 🚌 and ☖.
b– Connection by 🚌. ☖–Oakland.
DRG– Denver and Rio Grande Western Railroad.
NRPC–National Railroad Passenger Corporation (AMTRAK).

Table 251 — PIKE'S PEAK 🚋 MPP

R.T. US $			C Q	C R	C T	C T	C R	C T	C T	C Q
		km								
0.00	Manitou Ω ....d.	0	0800	0920	1040	1200	1320	1440	1600	1720
			0915	1035	1155	1315	1435	1555	1715	1835
◇	Summit (Pike's Peak) ⎰a.	14	1000	1120	1240	1400	1520	1640	1800	1920
	⎱d.									
17.00	Manitou Ω ....a.	28	1110	1230	1350	1510	1630	1750	1910	2030

Q– June 1-Aug. 31.
R– May 1-Oct. 31.
T– June 1-Aug. 31, also, if required, May 15-31 and Sept. 1-Oct. 31.
◇– Round trip fares only; all services operate subject to weather conditions. Passengers should be at Manitou station 30 mins. before scheduled departure; advance reservations advised. Services will not operate if there are less than 20 passengers.
Ω– Manitou is 10 km from Colorado Springs.
MPP– Manitou and Pike's Peak Railway.

Table 252 — DURANGO - SILVERTON #### DSRR

R.T. US $ C cl.	SJE C♈ T	1 Ca♈ S	2 PC♈ U&	3 C♈ V	km		SJE C♈ T	1 Ca♈ S	2 PC♈ U&	3 C♈ V
0.00	0730	0830	0930	1015	0	d.**Durango** ....a.	1600	1725	1825	1855
37.15	1045	1145	1245	1330	81	a.**Silverton**..........d.	1245	1400	1500	1545

OW fares sold only if space is available at time of departure.
S– May 2-Sept. 27.
T– June 22-Aug. 16.
U– May 23-Oct. 25.
V– June 8-Aug. 23.
a– Conveys 🚌 and & May 2-22.
DSRR–Durango and Silverton Railroad.

Table 253 — LOS ANGELES - SAN DIEGO   ##### MTL NRPC

J6 $ NRPC	CNRPC	NRPC	NRPC	NRPC	NHPC	NRPC	MTL		NRPC	NRPC											
C cl.	568	570	572	590	774	576	578	780	582		584	786										
	‡‡C‡	‡‡C‡	‡‡C‡	‡‡C‡	‡‡C‡	‡‡C‡	C‡	‡‡C‡	C‡		‡‡C‡	‡‡C‡										
	◆ ♀R	♀R	♀R	◎♀R	◆	♀R	♀R	◆	◆◎		♀R	♀R	km	↓								
0.00	0450	0640	0840	0940	1045	1245	1440	1645	1740	....	1845	2100	....	0	d.Los Angeles .... a.							
			0857				1457		1757	....		2117	....		d.Commerce .... d.							
5.25	0525	0717	0918	1015	1120	1320	1518	1720	1818	....	1920	2138	....	40	d.Fullerton .... d.							
7.00	0534	0726	0928	1025	1130	1330	1528	1730	1827	....	1930	2147	....	47	d.Anaheim (Disneyland) d.							
8.00	0543	0734	0938	1035	1140	1339	1538	1740	1836	....	1940	2156	....	57	d.Santa Ana .... d.							
	0556	0747			1352	1551	1754	1850		....	1953	2207	....		d.San Juan Capistrano d.							
	0618	0803	1002	1057	1204	1405	1603	1807	1912	....	2006	2218	....		d.Oceanside .... d.							
		1015								....			139		d.San Clemente .... d.							
4.50	0651	0833	1035	1130	1235	1435	1634	1839		....	2038	2252	....	139	d.Oceanside .... d.							
8.00	0715	0850	1053	1150	1253	1453	1651	1857		....	2054	2310	....	167	d.Del Mar .... d.							
1.50	0759	0937	1138	1238	1340	1542	1738	1943		....	2140	2355	....	205	a.San Diego .... d.							

MTL	NRPC	CNRPC	NRPC	CNRPC	NRPC	CNRPC	NRPC	CNRPC	NRPC	CNRPC	NRPC	CNRPC	NRPC	NRPC	CNRPC
569	571	767	773	575	777	579	581	783	593					585	587
C‡	‡‡C‡	‡‡C‡	‡‡C‡	‡‡C‡	‡‡C‡	‡‡C‡	‡‡C‡	‡‡C‡	‡‡C‡					‡‡C‡	‡‡C‡
◆◎	◎♀R	◆◎	◆◎	♀R	◆	♀R	♀R	◆	◎♀R					♀R	♀R
0725	0800	0855	0918	1145	1347	1545	1749	1950	2045	....	....	2148	2355		
0702	0731						1720						2327		
0644	0714	0808	0834	1100	1303	1501	1703	1859	2000	....	2103	2310		
0635	0706	0758	0824	1050	1253	1452	1653	1850	1951	....	2054	2300		
0626	0657	0748	0814	1040	1243	1443	1644	1841	1942	....	2045	2250		
0613	0645	0736	0801		1231	1431	1632	1828	1929	....	2033	2239		
0600	0631	0723	0747	1017	1217	1417	1618	1814	1915	....	2019	2227		
							1604							
0558	0653	0715	0944	1144	1344	1544	1739	1842	....	1944	2153		
0540	0635	0655	0925	1125	1325	1525	1720	1820	....	1925	2135		
0505	0600	0620	0850	1050	1250	1450	1645	1745	....	1850	2100		

67/773/7/786–SAN DIEGAN–◆♀☻ and ♀ San Diego(767/773/7/786)–Santa Barbara.   774/780/6–SAN DIEGAN–◆♀☻ and ♀ Santa Barbara(774/780/6)–San Diego.   R–SAN DIEGAN.   MTL–Metrolink (Southern California Regional Rail Authority).   NRPC–
National Railroad Passenger Corporation (AMTRAK).

Table 254 — ANTONITO - CHAMA   ##### CTSR

R.T. US $	C	C		June 11-Oct. 14	C	C	
C cl.	♀	♀	↑		♀	♀	↑
0.00	....	1000	....	0	d.Antonito .... a.	....	1700	....
◎27.00	....	1315	....	61	a.}Osier ✕......{d.	....	1415	....
	....	1330	....		a.}Osier ✕......{a.	....	1300	....
◎41.50	....	1630	....	103	a.Chama .... d.	....	1030	....

◎– Special inclusive round-trip facilities are available, one way by #####, one way by 🚌 and intermediately.
CTSR–Cumbres and Toltec Scenic Railroad.

Table 255 — DENVER - PORTLAND 🚻   ##### NRPC

US $	25			26	
C cl.	S‡C‡			S‡C‡	
	▣✕◆			▣✕◆	
	①③⑤	km	↓	↑	①③⑥
0.00	....	0945	0	d.Denver Union.... a.	1745
	....	1150		d.Cheyenne ◇ ....d.	1425
	....	1250		d.Laramie ....d.	1330
	....	1440		d.Rawlins ....d.	1143
	....	1620		d.Rock Springs....d.	1003
	....	2117		d.Ogden ....d.	0627
	....	2355		d.Pocatello ....d.	0305
	....	0131		d.Shoshone ....d.	0125
	....	0345		d.Boise ....d.	2315
	....	0444		d.Nampa (Caldwell)d.	2240
	....	0614		d.Baker ....d.	1852
	....	0719		d.La Grande ....d.	1752
	....	0948		d.Pendleton ....d.	1537
	....	1155		d.The Dalles.......d.	1322
	....	1345		a.Portland ....d.	1140
	....	1835		a.Seattle 264....d.	0730

25/26– PIONEER–see Table 195.
◇– Borie.
NRPC–National Railroad Passenger Corporation (AMTRAK).

Table 256 — SALT LAKE CITY - LOS ANGELES 🚻   ##### NRPC

US $	3	35			36	4
C cl.	S‡C‡	S‡C‡			S‡C‡	S‡C‡
	◆▣	◆▣			◆▣	◆▣
		✕	km	↓	↑	✕	✕
0.00	....	0040	....	0	d.Salt Lake City .. a.	0330	....
41.00	....	0347	....	333	d.Milford (Cedar City) d.	2330	....
	....	0450	....		d.Caliente ....d.	2030	....
77.00	....	0800	....	724	d.Las Vegas ....d.	1800	....
09.00	0425	1120	....	1020	d.Barstow ....d.	1430	2335
		1155	....		d.Victorville.........d.	1350	
16.00	0615	1300	....	1152	d.San Bernardino ..d.	1233	2148
16.00	0715	1413s	....	1227	d.Fullerton ....d.	1130u	2050
16.00	0815	1515	....	1247	a.Los Angeles....d.	1055	2015

3/4– SOUTHWEST CHIEF–see Table 187.
35/36– THE DESERT WIND–see Table 191.
NRPC–National Railroad Passenger Corporation (AMTRAK).

Table 257 — PALM SPRINGS   🚠 MSJ

🚠 service Palm Springs-Mount San Jacinto and v.v. 4 km. Journey: 15 mins. Fare: R.T. US $:13.95.
From Palm Springs: 0800◎/1000④-2100 (2000 Nov.-Apr.).Ω.
From Mount San Jacinto: 0830◎/1030④-2130 (2030 Nov.-Apr.).Ω.
Ω– No service Aug. 7-18.
MSJ– Palm Springs Aerial Tramway.

Table 258 — EL PASO - LOS ANGELES 🚻   ##### NRPC

US $	1▣			2▣	
C cl.	S‡C‡			S‡C‡	
	◆✕			◆✕	
	②④⑦	km	↓	↑	②⑤⑦
0.00	1320a	0	d.New Orleans 244 d.	1935
29.50	1345	1895	d.El Paso.........a.	1640
	1600	2134	d.Lordsburg........d.	1349
	1655	2304	d.Benson...........d.	1053
60.00	1755	2395	d.Tucson...........d.	0935
70.00	2140	2590	d.Phoenix.........d.	0708
91.00	0048	2869	d.Yuma............d.	0258
110.00	0239	3065	d.Indio............d.	0109
122.00	0436	3220	d.Pomona..........d.	2314
122.00	0615	3271	a.Los Angeles....d.	2230

1/2– SUNSET LIMITED–see Tables 188 and 193.   a–①③⑥.
NRPC–National Railroad Passenger Corporation (AMTRAK).

Table 259 — WINE TRAIN   ##### NVR

R.T. US $	C⊗	C✕	C✕	C✕		
C cl.	◎	☐	◎	②-⑥	km	↓
0.00	0855	1130	1800	1830	0	d.Napa	Passengers board about 30 mins. earlier
						d.St. Helena...........	Passengers remain on train
70.00	1130	1430	2100	2130		a.Napa	Leave train on arrival

☐–Runs 1 hour later on ◎.   NVR–Napa Valley Railroad.

Table 260 — SPOKANE - SEATTLE 🚻   ##### NRPC

US $	7▣	27▣			8▣	28▣
C cl.	S‡C‡	S‡C‡			S‡C‡	S‡C‡
	◆✕	◆⊗	km	↓	↑	◆✕	◆⊗
	1515	1515	0	d.Chicago 241.....a.	1534	1534
	2359	2359	673	d.Minneapolis/St Paul a.	0650	0650
0.00	0215	0225	3034	d.Spokane.........a.	0005	2330
30.50	0530		3268	d.Wenatchee.......d.	2053	
51.00	0830		3412	d.Everett..........d.	1745	
58.00	1025		3671	a.Seattle ....d.	1650	
24.00		0515	3528	d. Pasco............d.		2038
58.00		0910	3627	d. Vancouver........d.		1647
58.00		0955	3643	a. Portland ....d.		1625

7/8/27/28–EMPIRE BUILDER–see Table 194.
NRPC–National Railroad Passenger Corporation (AMTRAK).

Table 261 — TIJUANA   🚃 SDT

🚃 service San Diego-San Ysidro 🚃 (for Tijuana) and v.v. 16 km. Journey: 45 mins. Fare: US $: 2.25.
From San Diego: 0445 and frequent (every 30 mins. evenings) to 0015.
From San Ysidro: 0502 and frequent (every 30 mins. evenings) to 0102.
SDT– San Diego Trolley.

Table 262 SAN JOSE - OAKLAND - BAKERSFIELD/SACRAMENTO #### NRPC

US $ C cl.	702 C‡	722 C‡	6 S‡C‡	708 C‡		704 C‡	724 C‡	710 C‡	726 C‡	14 S‡C‡		km		11 S‡C‡	721 C‡	711 C‡		723 C‡		5 S‡C‡	703 C‡	725 C‡	709 C‡	705 C‡
	....	0635					1235		1710	2005	....	71	d.San Jose...............a.	0935	1040			1540			2120			
	0700	0730	0935	1035		1305	1330	1655	1800	2020	....	0	d. San Francisco Transbay★ a.	0830	0930	1138		1430		1720	1740	2010	2138	0105
0.00	0725	0755	1010	1100		1330	1355	1725	1830	2123	....	0	d.Emeryville ℋ............a.	0750	0905	1110		1405		1650	1715	1945	2110	0040
3.75	0739	0808	1021	1114		1344	1408	1739	1843	2138	....	27	d.Richmond.................d.	0735	0853	1040		1353		1610	1649	1933	2041	0014
6.00	0811	0839	1053	1146		1416	1439	1811	1914	2211	....	46	d.Martinez.................d.	0705	0824	1009		1324		1541s	1618	1904	2010	2344
	....	0859	1115				1459		1934		....	74	d. Suisun Fairfield ▶ d.		0802			1302		1519s	1842			
	....	0925	1143				1525		2000	2301	....	117	d. Davis...................d.	0610	0736			1236		1455s	1816			
	....	1000	1212				1600		2022	2339	....	138	a. Sacramento.........d.	0550	0715			1215		1435	1755			
13.50	0912	....	....	1245		1515	....	1915		....	....	125	d.Stockton.................d.	....	....	0907				1520		1912	2245	
18.50	0937	....	....	1310		1542	....	1940		....	....	166	d.Riverbank (Modesto).d.	....	....	0839				1448		1844	2214	
25.00	1017	....	....	1350		1622	....	2020		....	....	230	d.Merced...................d.	....	....	0800				1410		1805	2135	
32.00	1115	....	....	1450		1720	....	2120		....	....	323	d.Fresno...................d.	....	....	0705				1312		1707	2040	
37.50	1148	....	....	1523		1753	....	2153		....	....	362	d.Hanford..................d.	....	....	0630				1237		1633	2003	
49.50	1320	....	....	1655		1925	....	2320		....	....	501	a.Bakersfield............d.	....	....	0515				1120		1515	1845	
	1550	....	....	1925		2155	....	0200		....	....	686	a.Los Angeles ★.........d.	....	....	0200				0840		1235	1555	

5/6– CALIFORNIA ZEPHYR–see Table 189.
11/14– COAST STARLIGHT–see Table 192.
702-11–SAN JOAQUIN.
721/726–CAPITOL–🚌 and ♀ Roseville(721/726)–San Jose and v.v.
720/2-5–CAPITOL.
★– Connection by 🚌.
▶– For Travis Air Force Base.
ℋ– Oakland.
NRPC–National Railroad Passenger Corporation (AMTRAK).

Table 263 LOS ANGELES LOCAL RAIL SERVICE #### MTL SCRTD

Local #### services (SCRTD are 🚌 services) (C‡ cl. only) operate in the Los Angeles area as follows:
Burbank (MTL) (✧ km, US $: 3.50). From Los Angeles Union: 0626Ⓐ, 0700Ⓐ, 0743Ⓐ, 0810Ⓐ, 0840Ⓐ, 1020Ⓐ, 1305Ⓐ, 1315Ⓐ, 1615Ⓐ, 1625Ⓐ, 1700Ⓐ, 1732Ⓐ, 1740Ⓐ, 1823Ⓐ, 1831Ⓐ, 2040Ⓐ, returning at 0554Ⓐ, 0602Ⓐ, 0642Ⓐ, 0654Ⓐ, 0733Ⓐ, 0805Ⓐ, 0812Ⓐ, 0927Ⓐ, 1141Ⓐ, 1454Ⓐ, 1537Ⓐ, 1647Ⓐ, 1701Ⓐ, 1751Ⓐ, 2007Ⓐ. Journey: 25 mins.
Claremont (MTL) (✧ km, US $: 5.50). From Los Angeles Union: 0605Ⓐ, 0900Ⓐ, 1023Ⓐ, 1233Ⓐ, 1525Ⓐ, 1635Ⓐ, 1723Ⓐ, 1745Ⓐ, 1820Ⓐ, 1906Ⓐ, 2036Ⓐ, returning at 0507Ⓐ, 0605Ⓐ, 0633Ⓐ, 0713Ⓐ, 0738Ⓐ, 0801Ⓐ, 1045Ⓐ, 1133Ⓐ, 1417Ⓐ, 1622Ⓐ, 1923Ⓐ. Journey: 50 mins.
Covina (MTL) (✧ km, US $: 4.50). From Los Angeles Union: 0900Ⓐ, 1233Ⓐ, 1525Ⓐ, 1635Ⓐ, 1723Ⓐ, 1745Ⓐ, 1820Ⓐ, 1906Ⓐ, 2036Ⓐ, returning at 0520Ⓐ, 0618Ⓐ, 0646Ⓐ, 0726Ⓐ, 0751Ⓐ, 0814Ⓐ, 1058Ⓐ, 1146Ⓐ, 1430Ⓐ, 1635Ⓐ. Journey: 40 mins.
El Monte (MTL) (25 km, US $: 4.50). From Los Angeles Union: 0605Ⓐ, 0900Ⓐ, 1023Ⓐ, 1233Ⓐ, 1525Ⓐ, 1635Ⓐ, 1723Ⓐ, 1745Ⓐ, 1820Ⓐ, 1906Ⓐ, 2036Ⓐ, returning at 0533Ⓐ, 0631Ⓐ, 0659Ⓐ, 0739Ⓐ, 0804Ⓐ, 0827Ⓐ, 1111Ⓐ, 1159Ⓐ, 1443Ⓐ, 1652Ⓐ, 1950Ⓐ. Journey: 25 mins.
Glendale (MTL) (9 km, US $: 3.50). From Los Angeles Union: 0626Ⓐ, 0700Ⓐ, 0743Ⓐ, 0810Ⓐ, 0840Ⓐ, 1020Ⓐ, 1305Ⓐ, 1315Ⓐ, 1615Ⓐ, 1625Ⓐ, 1700Ⓐ, 1732Ⓐ, 1740Ⓐ, 1823Ⓐ, 1831Ⓐ, 2040Ⓐ, returning at 0601Ⓐ, 0609Ⓐ, 0649Ⓐ, 0701Ⓐ, 0740Ⓐ, 0812Ⓐ, 0819Ⓐ, 0934Ⓐ, 1148Ⓐ, 1501Ⓐ, 1544Ⓐ, 1654Ⓐ, 1708Ⓐ, 1758Ⓐ, 2014Ⓐ. Journey: 15 mins.
Long Beach (SCRTD) (35 km, US $: 1.50). From Los Angeles 7th Street: 0500 and frequent to 2240, returning from Long Beach Mall at 0500 and frequent to 2120. Journey: 1 hour.
Pomona (MTL) (✧ km, US $: 5.50). From Los Angeles Union: 0605Ⓐ, 0900Ⓐ, 1023Ⓐ, 1233Ⓐ, 1525Ⓐ, 1635Ⓐ, 1723Ⓐ, 1745Ⓐ, 1820Ⓐ, 1906Ⓐ, 2036Ⓐ, returning at 0510Ⓐ, 0608Ⓐ, 0636Ⓐ, 0716Ⓐ, 0741Ⓐ, 0804Ⓐ, 1048Ⓐ, 1136Ⓐ, 1420Ⓐ, 1625Ⓐ, 1926Ⓐ. Journey: 50 mins.
Rialto (MTL) (✧ km, US $: 7.50). From Los Angeles Union: 0900Ⓐ, 1233Ⓐ, 1635Ⓐ, 1723Ⓐ, 1745Ⓐ, 1906Ⓐ, 2036Ⓐ, returning at 0443Ⓐ, 0541Ⓐ, 0609Ⓐ, 0649Ⓐ, 0714Ⓐ, 1020Ⓐ, 1352Ⓐ. Journey: 1¼ hours.
Riverside (MTL) (✧ km, US $: 7.50). From Los Angeles Union: 1303Ⓐ, 1620Ⓐ, 1730Ⓐ, 1823Ⓐ, returning at 0510Ⓐ, 0620Ⓐ, 0720Ⓐ, 1430Ⓐ. Journey: 1¼ hours.
San Bernardino (MTL) (95 km, US $: 7.50). From Los Angeles Union: 1635Ⓐ, 1723Ⓐ, 1745Ⓐ, returning at 0532Ⓐ, 0600Ⓐ, 0640Ⓐ. Journey: 1½ hours.
Santa Clarita (MTL) (✧ km, US $: 5.50). From Los Angeles Union: 0626Ⓐ, 0743Ⓐ, 1315Ⓐ, 1615Ⓐ,
Simi Valley (MTL) (✧ km, US $: 5.50). From Los Angeles Union: 1305Ⓐ, 1625Ⓐ, 1700Ⓐ, 1740Ⓐ, 1823Ⓐ, returning at 0528Ⓐ, 0608Ⓐ, 0659Ⓐ, 0738Ⓐ, 1503Ⓐ. Journey: 70 mins.
1732Ⓐ, 1831Ⓐ, 2040Ⓐ, returning at 0522Ⓐ, 0622Ⓐ, 0733Ⓐ, 0855Ⓐ, 1422Ⓐ, 1719Ⓐ, 1935Ⓐ. Journey: 50 mins.

MTL–Metrolink (Southern California Regional Rail Authority). SCRTD–Los Angeles County Metropolitan Transportation Authority.

Table 264 SEATTLE - PORTLAND & #### NRPC

US $ C cl.	26 S‡C‡	11 C‡	793 C‡	797 C‡		km		796 C‡	25 S‡C‡	14 C‡	792 C‡
	◆①③⑤	◆	◆🅱	◆				◆	◆②④⑦	◆🅱	◆🅱
	🍴	🍴	🍴	♀				🍴	🍴	🍴	🍴
0.00	0730	0940	1130	1730		0	d.Seattle King Street..a.	1130	1835	2010	2155
7.00	0824	1037	1220	1820		64	d.Tacoma.............d.	1024	1733	1902	2049
11.50	0906	1124	1302	1902		121	d.Olympia............d.	0938	1647	1813	2003
13.50	0928	1148	1323	1923		151	d.Centralia..........d.	0918	1626	1750	1943
17.00	1013	1235	1407	2007		217	d.Kelso Longview .d.	0835	1542	1702	1900
24.50	1054	1319	1445	2045		280	d.Vancouver.........d.	0756	1502	1619	1821
24.50	1125	1350	1525	2125		294	a.Portland...........d.	0735	1440	1555	1800
136.00	1745	....	....	....		1738	a. Denver 255 ....d.	....	0945	....	....
117.00	....	0750	....	....		1482	a.Emeryville ℋ266 ᴣ d.	....	....	2123	....
157.00	....	0955	....	....		2233	a.Los Angeles 265d.	....	....	1955	....

11/14–COAST STARLIGHT–see Table 192. 25/26–PIONEER–see Table 195. 792/3–NORTHWEST TALGO. 796/7–MOUNT RAINIER. ℋ–Oakland. ᴣ–Emeryville will open at a date to be announced. Prior to opening trains will continue to call at the Oakland Wood Street Station. NRPC–National Railroad Passenger Corporation (AMTRAK).

Table 265 SAN FRANCISCO - LOS ANGELES & #### NRPC

US $ C cl.	774 1‡C‡	780 1‡C‡	11 S‡C‡	786 1‡C‡		km		767 1‡C‡	773 1‡C‡	14 S‡C‡	777 1‡C‡	783 1‡C‡
	◆	◆	◆🅱	◆				Ⓒ	Ⓐ	🍴	◆	◆
			🍴									
	....	....	0940	....		0	d.Seattle 264.........a.	....	....	2010	....	....
	....	....	1415	....		294	d.Portland 266........a.	....	....	1530	....	....
	....	....	0730	....		1471	d.San Francisco Transbay ᐳᐳ..a.	....	....	2125	....	....
0.00	....	....	0755	....		1482	d.Emeryville ℋ262....a.	....	....	2118	....	....
13.00	....	....	0935	....		1553	d.San Jose...........a.	....	....	2005	....	....
24.50	....	....	1101	....		1660	d.Salinas............d.	....	....	1805	....	....
48.50	....	....	1430	....		1876	d.San Luis Obispo...d.	....	....	1515	....	....
65.00	0745	1345	1700	1750		2068	d.Santa Barbara.....d.	1150	1215	1225	1635	2245
65.00	0835	1435	1750	1840		2127	d.Oxnard.............d.	1049	1114	1126	1533	2144
66.00	0956	1601	1925s	2006		2224	d.Glendale...........d.	0930	0955	1013	1414	2025
66.00	1025	1625	2010	2040		2233	a.Los Angeles.......d.	0915	0940	0955	1400	2010

11/14– COAST STARLIGHT–see Table 192. ℋ–Oakland. ᐳᐳ–Connection by 🚌.
767/773/7/783–SAN DIEGAN–🚌 and ♀ San Diego(767/773/7/783)–Santa Barbara. NRPC–National Railroad Passenger Corporation (AMTRAK).
774/780/6–SAN DIEGAN–🚌 and ♀ Santa Barbara(774/780/6)–San Diego.

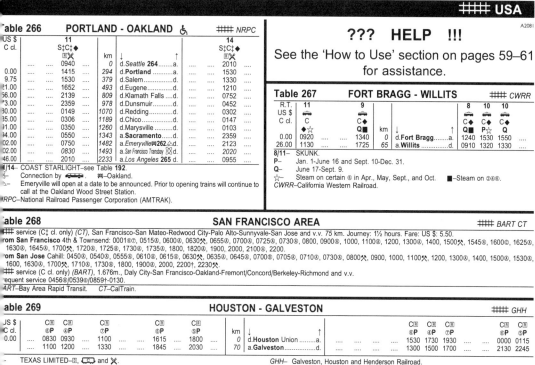

Table 266 — PORTLAND - OAKLAND ### NRPC

A208I

US $	11		km	↓		14	
C cl.	S‡C‡◆					S‡C‡◆	
	⊞✕					⊞✕	
0.00	....	0940	0	d.Seattle 264 .....a.	....	2010	....
10.00	....	1415	294	d.Portland ....a.	....	1530	....
9.75	....	1530	379	d.Salem ....d.	....	1330	....
21.00	....	1652	493	d.Eugene ....d.	....	1210	....
56.00	....	2139	809	d.Klamath Falls ....d.	....	0752	....
73.00	....	2359	978	d.Dunsmuir ....d.	....	0452	....
80.00	....	0149	1070	d.Redding ....d.	....	0302	....
85.00	....	0306	1189	d.Chico ....d.	....	0147	....
91.00	....	0350	1260	d.Marysville ....d.	....	0103	....
94.00	....	0550	1343	a.Sacramento ......d.	....	2359	....
102.00	....	0750	1482	a.Emeryville⬛262△d.	....	2123	....
102.00	....	0830	1493	a.San Francisco Transbay ⊠.d.	....	2020	....
146.00	....	2010	2233	a.Los Angeles 265 d.	....	0955	....

1/14– COAST STARLIGHT–see Table 192.
⬛– Connection by 🚌. 🚌–Oakland.
△– Emeryville will open at a date to be announced. Prior to opening trains will continue to call at the Oakland Wood Street Station.
NRPC–National Railroad Passenger Corporation (AMTRAK).

??? HELP !!!

See the 'How to Use' section on pages 59–61 for assistance.

Table 267 — FORT BRAGG - WILLITS ### CWRR

R.T.	11		9			km	↓	↑	8	10	10	
US $	🚃		🚃						🚃	🚃	🚃	
C cl.	C		C◆						C◆	C◆	C◆	
			Q■						Q■	P☆	Q	
0.00	0920	....	1340	....		0	d.Fort Bragg........a.		1240	1530	1550	....
26.00	1130	....	1725	....		65	a.Willits ....d.		0910	1320	1330	....

8/11– SKUNK.
P– Jan. 1-June 16 and Sept. 10-Dec. 31.
Q– June 17-Sept. 9.
☆– Steam on certain ⑥ in Apr., May, Sept., and Oct. ■–Steam on ②④⑥.
CWRR–California Western Railroad.

Table 268 — SAN FRANCISCO AREA ### BART CT

service (C‡ cl. only) (CT), San Francisco-San Mateo-Redwood City-Palo Alto-Sunnyvale-San Jose and v.v. 75 km. Journey: 1½ hours. Fare: US $: 5.50.
From San Francisco 4th & Townsend: 0001⑥⑦, 0515⑤, 0600⑤, 0630✕, 0655⑤, 0700⑤, 0725⑤, 0730⑤, 0800, 0900⑤, 1000, 1100⑤, 1200, 1300⑤, 1400, 1500✕, 1600©, 1625⑤, 1630⑤, 1645⑤, 1700✕, 1720⑤, 1725⑤, 1730⑤, 1735⑤, 1800, 1820⑤, 1900, 2000, 2100⑤, 2200.
From San Jose Cahill: 0450⑤, 0540⑤, 0555⑤, 0610⑤, 0615⑤, 0630✕, 0635⑤, 0645⑤, 0700⑤, 0705⑤, 0710⑤, 0730⑤, 0800✕, 0900, 1000, 1100✕, 1200, 1300⑤, 1400, 1500⑤, 1530⑤, 1600, 1630⑤, 1700✕, 1710⑤, 1730⑤, 1800, 1900⑤, 2000, 2200†, 2230✕.
service (C cl. only) (BART), 1.676m., Daly City-San Francisco-Oakland-Fremont/Concord/Berkeley-Richmond and v.v.
Frequent service 0456④/0539⑥/0859†-0130.
BART–Bay Area Rapid Transit. CT–CalTrain.

Table 269 — HOUSTON - GALVESTON ### GHH

US $	C⑥	C⑥	C⑥		C⑥	C⑥	km	↓	↑	C⑥	C⑥	C⑥		C⑥	C⑥
C cl.	⑥P	④P	⑦P		⑥P	⑤P				⑥P	④P	⑦P		⑥P	⑤P
0.00	0830	0930	1100		1615	1800	0	d.Houston Union ....a.		1530	1730	1930		0000	0115
	1100	1200	1330		1845	2030	70	a.Galveston................d.		1300	1500	1700		2130	2245

–– TEXAS LIMITED–⊞, ⫟ and ✕.
GHH– Galveston, Houston and Henderson Railroad.

Table 270 — SKAGWAY - WHITEHORSE ### WPY

US $	1	99	5		km	↓ May 15-Sept. 22 ↑	2	100	6	
C cl.	C	C⑥	C⑥				C⑥	C⑥	C	
	◇	★					★		◇	
0.00	0810	0845	1245	1315	0	d.Skagway..........a.	1145	1200	1615	1815
3.50		1000		1450	44	a.White Pass 🚊.....d.	1020		1500	
1.50	1000		1430		62	a.Fraser............d.	....	1020	....	1630
7.00			1515b		88	a. Bennett ....d.				1545c
9.00			1830a		179	a.Whitehorse......d.	....	0815a	....	....

–– Connection by 🚌.
–– Connection by 🚌 (⊞) for hikers using Chilkoot Trail to/from Lake Bennett.
–– Connection by 🚌 (⊞) for hikers using Chilkoot Trail to/from Lake Bennett. Note ★ applies.
b– May 18-Sept. 22.
c– June 15-Sept. 22.
WPY– White Pass & Yukon Route.

Table 271 — ANCHORAGE - FAIRBANKS ### ARR

US $	4	10	2	4		km	↓	↑	3	9	1	3
C cl.	C‡R	C‡S	C‡	C‡R					C‡R	C‡S	C‡	C‡R
	③⑥	⑥	R⑦	⑦					③⑥	⑦	R⑦	⑦
0.00	0630	0830	0830	1201		0	d.Anchorage ....a.		1630	2000	2030	2200
14.00	0750	0950	0950	1320		74	d.Wasilla ....d.		1440	1718r	1800	2010
31.50	0930	1121	1120	1500		180	d.Talkeetna.........d.		1300	1559	1630	1830
44.00	1050	1310r		1620		267	d.Hurricane...........d.		1140	1405r		1720
68.00	....	1512r	1615	....		377	d.Denali Park ....d.		....	1205r	1230	....
	....	1559r		....		393	d.Healy...............d.		....	1120r		....
	....	1714r	1800	....		478	d.Nenana ....d.		....	1003r	1000	....
122.00	....	1900	2030	....		572	a.Fairbanks..........d.		....	0830	0830	....

R– May 18-Sept. 19.
S– Sept. 20-May 17.
ARR– Alaska Railroad.

Table 272 — ANCHORAGE - WHITTIER ### ARR

US $	C‡Ⓣ	🚗	C	C	C	C	C	C	C	km	↓	↑	C	C	C	C	C	C	C	C	C‡Ⓣ
cl.C		🚗	VW	U⑥	U⑤⑦	VW	U⑤⑦	VW	VW				C	C	C	C		C	C	C	
XW	T	XW									d.Anchorage ....a.		XW	XW	U⑥	VW		U⑤⑦	U⑤⑦	VW	T
	....	0645	....	1145a	....	....	....	....	....	0	d.Anchorage ....a.		....	....	....	1730a	....	....	....	....	2200
0.00	0800		1045		1330	1415	1520	1700	1820 1900	2130	82	d.Portage ⓖ ....d.		0700	1000	1230	1355	1600	....	1750	1830	2010 2100	
3.00	0830		1115		1400	1455	1600	1735	1900 1930	2200	101	a.Whittier ⓖ ....d.		0630	0930	1200	1315	1530	....	1710	1900	1930 2000	
11.00		1100									210	a. Seward ....d.										1800

May 21-Sept. 5 and ⑥⑦ Sept. 10-25.
Sept. 21-May 9. V–May 10-Sept. 20.
⫟ and 🚗
Ex ②③ May 10-Sept. 20.

a– Connection by 🚌. ◇–Fare ex Portage. ★–Fare ex Anchorage.
ⓖ– Additional trips, from Portage (U③ only, ⫟ only): 0700, 0900, 1935, 2145, returning at 0600, 0800, 1830, 2030.
ARR– Alaska Railroad.

Advertisement
A4214

THOMAS COOK OVERSEAS TIMETABLE

Probably the most adventurous timetable ever published, the Thomas Cook Overseas Timetable brings together in one book surface travel timetables for virtually every country outside Europe. It contains much information not readily available in any other form.

Published every two months. Obtainable at £7.90 from Thomas Cook UK Retail Shops, or by post at £9.10 (UK), £11.20 (Europe) or £12.40 (overseas air mail) from Thomas Cook Publishing, (TPO/FA) P.O. Box 227, PETERBOROUGH PE3 6SB, U.K.

☎ (0733) 505821/268943. Fax: (0733) 267052.

A4135e

TRAVEL THE WORLD WITH THOMAS COOK PUBLICATIONS

EUROPEAN TIMETABLE – *Every month* ● **OVERSEAS TIMETABLE** – *Every 2 months*

AIRPORTS GUIDE – EUROPE ● **ON THE RAILS AROUND EUROPE**

GUIDE TO GREEK ISLAND HOPPING ● **EUROPEAN RAIL TRAVELLERS PHRASEBOOK**

NORTH AMERICAN RAIL & BUS GUIDE

THOMAS COOK TRAVELLERS – *WORLDWIDE GUIDEBOOK SERIES*

VISITOR'S RAIL MAP OF BRITAIN AND IRELAND ● **NEW RAIL MAP OF EUROPE**

All regularly revised and updated.
Available from Thomas Cook Publishing.

Table 280 — NANTUCKET ISLAND 🚢 TS

🚢 service Hyannis–Nantucket Island and v.v.. ❖km. Journey: 2¼ hours. Fare: US$ 9.75.
Service Mar. 19–Nov. 4
From Hyannis: 0745a, 0915, 1320b, 1445, 1850, 2015b. **From Nantucket Island**: 0630, 1030a, 1200, 1605b, 1730, 2130bc.

a–May 21–Sept. 17 and Oct. 10–12. b–May 21–Sept. 17 and Oct. 9–12. c–Operates to Wood's Hole (not Hyannis) on Sept. 12. ₵–Facilities available except on trips marked a/b
TSA–The Steamship Authority (Wood's Hole, Martha's Vineyard and Nantucket Steamship Authority). ☎ Wood's Hole (508) 540-2022.

Table 281 — MARTHA'S VINEYARD 🚢 CIE TS

🚢 (WHV) service Wood's Hole–Vineyard Haven and v.v. ❖ km.
Journey: 45 mins. Fare: US$: 4.00/4.50. ₵ facilities available on some trips.
From Wood's Hole: 5-14 sailings daily throughout the year.
From Vineyard Haven: 5-14 sailings daily throughout the year.

🚢 (WHV) service Wood's Hole–Oak Bluffs and v.v. ❖ km. Journey: 45 mins.
Fare: US$: 4.00/4.50. ₵. **Operates May 21–Nov. 4 only.**
From Wood's Hole: 0945, 1215, 1445, 1715.
From Oak Bluffs: 1100, 1330, 1600, 1830.

🚢 (CIE) service New Bedford-Vineyard Haven and v.v. 36 km. Journey: 1½ hours.
Fare: US$: 8.50.
May 14-June 18 (except May 25) and Sept. 14-Oct. 11 (except Sept. 16).
From New Bedford: 0900, 1300⑤-⑦, 1700⑤-⑦, 2100⑤.
From Vineyard Haven: 1100⑤-⑦, 1500⑤-⑦, 1600①-④, 1845⑤-⑦, 2245⑤.

May 25, June 19-Sept. 13 and Oct. 12.
From New Bedford: 0900, 1300, 1700, 2100⑤.
From Vineyard Haven: 1100, 1500, 1845, 2245⑤.

CIE– Cape Island Express Lines (m.v. Schamonchi). ☎ (508) 997-1688.
TSA–The Steamship Authority (Wood's Hole, Martha's Vineyard and Nantucket Steamship Authority). ☎ Wood's Hole (508) 540-2022.

Table 282 — SHELTER ISLAND 🚢 NF

🚢 service Greenport-Shelter Island and v.v. 1 km. Journey: 10 mins. Fare: US$: 0.50.
From Greenport: 0600 and frequent to 0000.
From Shelter Island: 0540 and frequent to 2345.

NF– North Ferry.

Table 283 — CHAMPLAIN FERRIES 🚢 LCTC

🚢 service Burlington-Port Kent and v.v. ❖ km. Journey: 1 hour. Fare: US$: 3.00.
From Burlington: 8-10 journeys daily, May 16-Oct. 19.
From Port Kent: 8-10 journeys daily, May 16-Oct. 19.
Other, local 🚢 services operate Charlotte-Essex (May 16-Jan. 4) and Grand Isle-Plattsburgh (all year) and v.v.

LCTC–Lake Champlain Transport Co.

Table 284 — ERIE CANAL 🚢 ACCL

🚢 (ACCLc/m/s) SAGUENAY cruise: Warren - via New York Harbor, Hudson River, Erie Canal, Lake Ontario - Clayton - Upper Canada Village - Montréal - via Saguenay Fjord - Québec - 🚌➜ to Warren or v.v.. ❖ km. Duration (RT) 12 days. Fares (RT) from US$ 1190. Sold on RT basis Warren-Warren only.
From Warren (by 🚢, returning by 🚌➜): 1500 Sept. 5.
From Warren (by 🚌➜, returning by 🚢): 0715 Sept. 3, 10, 17.

🚢 (ACCLc/m/s) FALL FOLIAGE cruise: Warren - via New York Harbor, Hudson River - West Point - Kingston - via Erie Canal, Lake Ontario - Clayton - Upper Canada Village - Montréal - Québec - 🚌➜ to Warren or v.v.. ❖ km. Duration (RT) 12 days. Fares (RT) from US$ 1190. Sold on RT basis Warren-Warren only.
From Warren (by 🚢, returning by 🚌➜): 1500 Sept. 19, 26; Oct. 3.
From Warren (by 🚌➜, returning by 🚢): 0715 Oct. 1, 8, 15.

ACCL–American Canadian Caribbean Line. ☎ Warren 401 247 0955 Fax: 401 245 8303. (c–Caribbean Prince, m–Mayan Prince, s–New Shoreham II).

Table 285 — LONG ISLAND 🚢 BPJ CSF

🚢 (BPJ) service Bridgeport-Port Jefferson and v.v. ❖ km. Journey: 1½ hours. Fare: US$ 10.00 (US$8.00 off-peak).
From Bridgeport: 0730⊛, 0900, 1030, 1200, 1330, 1500, 1630a, 1645b, 1800a, 1830, 1930a, 2000b, 2100ac, 2130b, 2245†c.
From Port Jefferson: 0600⊛, 0730, 0900, 1030, 1200, 1330, 1500, 1630a, 1645b, 1800, 1830b, 1930ac, 2000b, 2130†c.

🚢 (CSF) service New London-Orient Point ★ and v.v. ❖ km. Journey: 1½ hours. Fa ❖.
From New London and Orient Point: 4-12 sailings daily.

a– ①-④. b–⑤-†. c–Operates May 1-Oct. 12 only.
★– For Greenport.
BPJ– Bridgeport & Port Jefferson Steamboat Co. ☎ Port Jefferson (516) 473-0286.
CSF– Cross Sound Ferry Services Inc. ☎ New York (516) 323 23525.

Table 286 — NEW YORK 🚢 CL H

Regular 🚢 tours (CL) round Manhattan Island and surrounding areas Mar. 6–Dec. 27. ❖ km. Journey: 3 hours (day cruises)/2 hours (Harbor Lights cruise). Fare: US$ 16.00.
From New York W. 42nd Street Pier: 2-11 sailings daily (no sailings Nov. 26 or Dec. 25)
Local 🚢 service (HF) Hoboken-New York City and v.v. 3 km. Journey: 8 mins. Fare: US$ 2.00.
From Hoboken Ferry Terminal: 0650④/1000© and frequent to 2150©/2250④. φ.
From New York Battery Park: 0700⑤/1020© and frequent to 2200©/2300④. φ.
φ–On ©, service extends from Battery Park to/from Statue of Liberty until 1845. CL–Circle Line. ☎ New York (212) 563 3200. HF–Hoboken Ferry.

Table 287 — FISHERS ISLAND 🚢 FIF

🚢 service New London-Fishers Island and v.v. 11 km. Journey: 45 mins. Fare: US$: 3. (US$ 4.50 on certain early morning, late afternoon and evening sailings).
Apr. 28-Oct. 29.
From New London and Fishers Island: 4-9 sailings daily.

FIF– Fishers Island Ferry District. ☎ Fishers Island 516 788 7463.

Table 288 — BLOCK ISLAND 🚢 INC NNC

🚢 (INC) service Galilee (Point Judith)-Block Island and v.v. 40 km. Journey: 1 hour 10 mins. Fare: US$: 6.60.
From Galilee: 1100 (up to 8 additional sailings during peak periods).
From Block Island: 1400⊛, 1500† (up to 8 additional sailings during peak periods).
🚢 (NNC) service New London-Block Island and v.v. 105 km. Journey: 2 hours. Fare: US$: 13.50.
Operates June 12-Sept. 12 only.
From New London: 0900, 1915⑤.
From Block Island: 1630.

INC– Interstate Navigation Company. ☎ Galilee 401 789 3502.
NNC– Nelseco Navigation Company. ☎ New London 203 442 7891.

Table 289 — PHILADELPHIA - CAMDEN 🚢 RB

🚢 ferry service Philadelphia-Camden and v.v. 1 km. Journey: 10 mins. Fare: US$ 2.
From Philadelphia Penn's Landing: 0815④/0915© and every 30 mins. to 1745ζ/1945ω/2015ω/2115∂/2345σ.
From Camden Aquarium: 0800④/0900© and every 30 mins. to 1730ζ/1930φ/2000ω/2100ω/2330σ.

ζ– ④ in winter. φ–© in winter.
ω– ①②④ in summer.
∂– ③⑤ in summer.
σ– ⑥ in summer.
RB– Riverbus Inc.

Table 291 — MACKINAC ISLAND

(AT) service Mackinaw City-Mackinac island and v.v. *11* km. Journey: 35 mins. Fare: US$: 7.00.
From **Mackinaw City**: 5-23 sailings daily May 8-Oct. 22.
From **Mackinac Island**: 5-23 sailings daily May 8-Oct. 22.
No winter sailings.

(SMIF) service Mackinaw City and St. Ignace-Mackinac Island and v.v. *11* km. Journey: 16 mins. Fare: (RT) US$: 9.00. &.
From **Mackinaw City**: 5-31 sailings daily May 1-Oct. 31.
From **St. Ignace**: 5-27 sailings daily May 1-Oct. 31.

(AT) service Mackinac Island-St. Ignace and v.v. *10* km. Journey: 30 mins. Fare: US$: 7.00.
From **Mackinac Island**: 6-23 sailings daily May 8-Oct. 30.
From **St. Ignace**: 6-23 sailings daily May 8-Oct. 30.
Reduced service operates in winter.

From **Mackinac Island** to Mackinaw City: 5-31 sailings daily May 1-Oct. 31.
From **Mackinac Island** to St. Ignace: 5-27 sailings daily May 1-Oct 31.

T– Arnold Transit.

SMIF–Shepler's Mackinac Island Ferry. ☎Mackinaw City 616 436 5023.

Table 292 — CAPE MAY - LEWES

local service Cape May-Lewes and v.v. *27* km. Journey: 1¼ hours. Fare: US$: 4.50 (foot passenger).
From **Cape May**Ⓔ: 0620, 0820P, 0940, 1040Q, 1140R, 1300, 1400Q, 1500R, 1620, 1820P, 1940.
From **Lewes**Ⓔ: 0800, 1000P, 1120, 1220Q, 1320R, 1440, 1540Q, 1640R, 1800, 2000P, 2120.
- May 20-Oct. 10.
- June 17-Sept. 19.
- Mar. 25-Nov. 28.
- Additional sailings may operate at peak times.

MLF– Cape May-Lewes Ferry. ☎Cape May 609 886 2718.

Table 293 — OCRACOKE ISLAND

service Cedar Island-Okracoke and v.v. *35* km. Journey: 2¼ hours. Fare: US$: 1.00 (passenger).

Apr. 15-Oct. 31
From **Cedar Island**: 0700, 0815. 0930, 1200, 1315, 1500, 1800, 2030.
From **Ocracoke**: 0700, 0930, 1045, 1200, 1500, 1615, 1800, 2030.

Nov. 1-Apr. 14
From **Cedar Island**: 0700, 1300.
From **Ocracoke**: 1000, 1500.

service Swan Quarter-Ocracoke and v.v. *50* km. Journey: 2½ hours. Fare: US$: 1.00 (passenger).

From **Swan Quarter**: 0930, 1600.

From **Ocracoke**: 0630, 1230.

CDT–North Carolina Department of Transportation. ☎Ocracoke 919 928 3841.

Table 294 — HAWAIIAN ISLANDS

Local services link Kauai (Kapaa), Oahu (Honolulu), Molokai (Kepuhi), Lanai (Kaumalapau), Maui (Wailuku) and Hawaii (Hilo), with regular tours and excursions throughout the year. Few services operate as real "transport", and most trips will take you back where you started after your visits have finished.

There are no scheduled sailings between the Hawaiian Islands and mainland USA any longer.

Table 295 — MISSISSIPPI RIVERBOATS (No winter services)

Cruises, often using sternwheel steamers, are operated out of many ports on the Mississippi, and there are occasional trips by *ACL* and *DQS* which operate over longer distances, taking anything from 3 to 10 days for the complete voyage. The major ports served are New Orleans, Baton Rouge, St. Francisville, Natchez, Vicksburg, Greenville, Memphis, Cairo, St Louis, Hannibal, Burlington, Davenport, Dubuque, La Crosse and St. Paul. There are also local cruises, with occasional long-distance services, on the Cumberland River between Cairo, Paducah and Nashville, on the Tennessee River between Cairo, Paducah, Florence, Decatur and Chattanooga, and on the Ohio between Cairo, Paducah, Evansville, Louisville, Cincinnati, Huntington and Pittsburgh.

CL– American Cruise Lines *(New Orleans)*.   *DQS*–Delta Queen Steamboat Co. *(Delta Queen, Mississippi Queen &)*.

Table 296 — ISLE ROYALE

(IRNP) service Houghton-Rock Harbor and v.v. *118* km. Journey: 6 hours. Fare: US$: 30.00.
June 2-Sept. 12
From **Houghton**: 0900②⑤.
From **Rock Harbor**: 0900③⑥.

(IRFS) service Copper Harbor-Rock Harbor and v.v. *90* km. Journey: 4½ hours. Fare: US$: 28.00.
May 11-June 10 and Sept. 5-30
From **Copper Harbor**: 0800①⑤.
From **Rock Harbor**: 1400①⑤.
June 11-Sept. 4
From **Copper Harbor**: 0800 (ex③④ June 11-July 31; ex⑦ June 11-30).
From **Rock Harbor**: 1530 (ex③④ June 11-July 31; ex⑦ June 11-30).

(GPIR) service Grand Portage-Windigo and v.v. *35* km. Journey: 3 hours. Fare: US$: 25.00.
June 11-Sept. 5
From **Grand Portage**: 0930★.
From **Windigo**: 1400.

(GPIR) service Grand Portage-Windigo-Rock Harbor and v.v. *125* km. Journey: 6 hours. Fare: US$: 35.00.
May 7-Oct. 31
From **Grand Portage**: 0930★③⑥; also ① May 30-Sept. 5.
From **Rock Harbor**: 0700④⑦; also ② May 31-Sept. 6.

Times from Grand Portage are in **Central Time**; all other times shown are in **Eastern Time.**
R–Grand Portage-Isle Royale Transportation Lines. ☎Duluth 218 728 1237.   *IRFS*–Isle Royale Ferry Service. ☎Copper Harbor 906 289 4437 (summer), 906 482 4950 (winter).   *IRNP*– Royale National Park. ☎Houghton 906 482 0984.

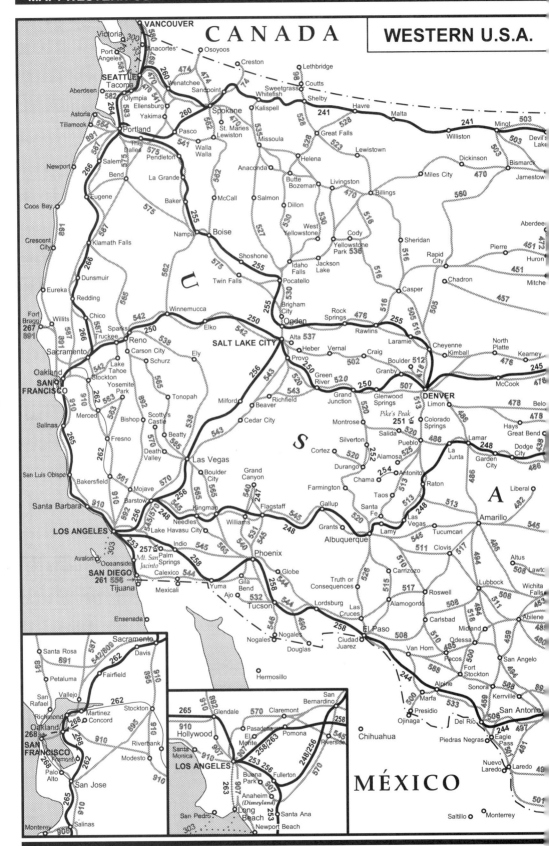

WESTERN U.S.A.

For key to map symbols see page 61

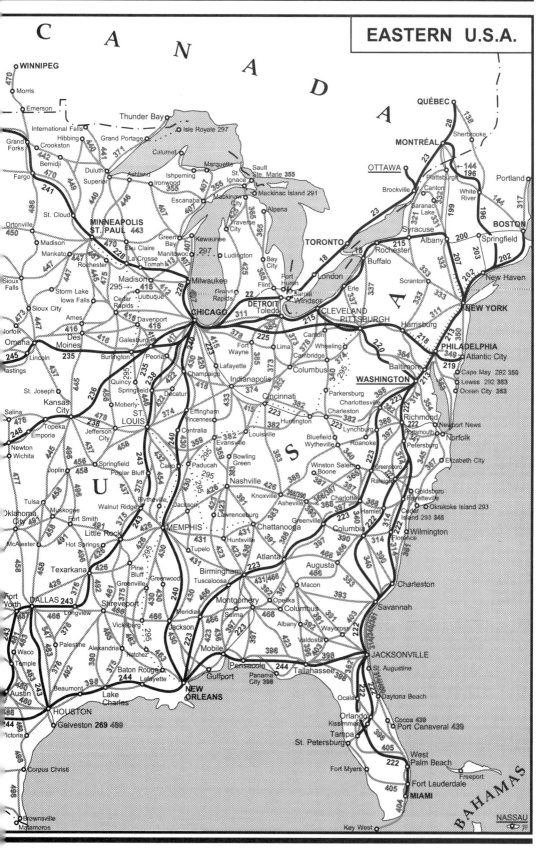

EASTERN U.S.A.

A2C

Table 297   LAKE MICHIGAN FERRIES ♿   🚢 MWF

US$	T	V	S		km		R	T	V	
			Ⓐ						Ⓐ	
0.00	0930	....	0930	2130	0	d.**Ludington** ....a.	0730	1930	1930	....
25.00	1230	....	1230	0030	40	a.**Manitowoc**...........d.	0230	1430	1430	....

R– June 10-Sept. 8.
S– June 9-Sept. 7.
T– June 9-Sept. 8.
V– Sept. 9-June 7. ▲.
MWF–Michigan-Wisconsin Ferry.

Table 298   SEATTLE - BREMERTON   🚢 WSF

Frequent 🚢 service Seattle-Bremerton and v.v. 40 km. Journey: 1 hour. Fare: (R.T.) US$: 3.30.

WSF–Washington State Ferries.

MYSTIFIED
by all the symbols?
See page 61 for an explanation!

Table 300   ANACORTES - SIDNEY   🚢 WSF

US$					km	↓	↑			
0.00	0845	....	....	....	0	d.**Anacortes**...........a.	....	1520	....	....
6.05	1140	....	....	....	93	a.**Sidney** ....d.	....	1201	....	....

WSF–Washington State Ferries.

Table 303   SANTA CATALINA ISLAND   🚢 CC CE CP CPS S..

🚢 service (CE) San Pedro-Avalon/Two Harbors and v.v. 35 km. Journey: 1½ hours. Fare: US$ 17.25.
    From San Pedro: 0700a, 0800⑥t, 0900⑥⑦a, 1100a, 1100①③⑤bt, 1400⑦t, 1430⑥⑦a, 1600ex⑥a, 1830⑥t, 1900⑤a.
    From Avalon/Two Harbors: 0900a, 1000⑥t, 1100⑥⑦a, 1245②④⑦a, 1245①③⑤av, 1345①③⑤t, 1600⑦t, 1630⑥⑦a, 1800ex⑤a, 2030⑥t, 2100⑤a.
🚢 service (CC) Long Beach-Avalon/Two Harbors and v.v. 35/57 km. Journey: 2/2½ hours. Fare: US$ 17.75.
    From Long Beach to Avalon: 0800A, 0900, 1100B, 1130C, 1245A, 1330D, 1345E, 1445F, 1700B, 1730G, 1830A, 1930H. **From Long Beach** to Two Harbors: 0900J, 1100B, 1130D, 1930H. **From Avalon** to Long Beach: 1030A, 1115K, 1215L, 1315B, 1400C, 1600M, 1700N, 1930A, 1945G, 2045Q, 2145H. **From Two Harbors** to Long Beach: 1230J, 1515C, 1645D, 2300H.
🚢 service (CE) Long Beach-Avalon and v.v. 35 km. Journey: 1 hour. Fare: US$ 17.75.
    From Long Beach: 0700⑥, 0900, 1000⑥, 1200⑦, 1330, 1530⑦, 1645, 1945⑤.   **From Avalon:** 0830⑥, 1030, 1130⑥, 1330⑦, 1500, 1700⑦, 1815, 2115⑤.
🚢 service (CPS) Newport Beach-Avalon and v.v. 35 km. Journey: 1¼ hours. Fare: US$ 32.50. Operates Mar. 3-Nov. 27.
    From Newport Beach: 0900.   **From Avalon:** 1630.
🚢 service (CP) San Diego-Avalon and v.v. 140 km. Journey: ❖. Fare (RT): US$ 49.00.
    From San Diego: ❖.   **From Avalon:** ❖.
🚢 service (SJC) San Diego-Avalon and v.v. 140 km. Journey: ❖. Fare (RT): US$ 49.00.
    From San Diego: ❖.   **From Avalon:** ❖.

A–⑥⑦ June 25-Sept. 6; ⑧ Sept. 7-Oct. 3. B–①–⑤ June 25-Sept. 6. C–⑦ Sept. 7-Oct. 25. D–Ex⑥ June 25-Sept. 6. E–Nov. 22-June 24. F–⑥ June 25-Sept. 6; ex⑥ Sept. 7-Oct. 3; da Oct. 4-Nov. 21. G–⑦ Sept. 7-Oct. 3. H–⑤ Sept. 7-Nov. 21. J–⑥ June 25-Sept. 6; ①③⑤ Sept. 7-Nov. 21. K–Daily Nov. 22-June 24). L–⑦ Sept. 7-Oct. 3. ⑥⑦ Oct. 4-Nov. 21. Nov. 22-June 24; ⑥⑦ June 25-Sept. 6; ⑦ Sept. 7-Oct. 3. N–June 25-Nov. 21. Q–June 25-Sept. 6. a–To/from Avalon. b–Via Avalon. t–To/from Two Harbors. v–Via Two Harbors. CC–Catalina Cruise Flyer). ♿. ☎ 714 673 5245. SJC–SeaJet Cruise Lines. ☎ 619 696 0088. CE–Catalina Express. ☎ 310 519 1212. Fax: 310 548 7389. CP–Catalina Pacifica. ☎ 619 224 7688. Fax: 619 224 7561. CPS–Catalina Passenger Service (Catal. ☎ 213 253 9800.

Table 305   BELLINGHAM/PRINCE RUPERT - ALASKA   🚢 AM

Regular 🚢 services are operated throughout the year from Bellingham and Prince Rupert to Alaskan ports and v.v.. Days of operation for summer 1993 are shown below (A = day 1, B = da 2, etc); a reduced service operates in winter. Timings vary according to tides and should be checked with operator.

US$		km	Pa	Pb	Pc	Pd	Pe	Pf	Pg	Ph	Pi	Pj	Pk	Pl	Pm	Pn	Po	Pp	Pq	Pr	Ps	Pt	Pu	Pv	Pw
	Bellingham..............d.	0	A	A	A																				
0.00	**Prince Rupert**..........d.	900			C	A	A	A	A	A															
	Stewart/Hyder.........d.										A	A													
32.00	Ketchikan ....d.	1200	C	C	C	A	A	A	A	A	B	A	A	A											
46.00	Hollis ....d.	1170				A	B					A	B	A											
50.00	Wrangell ....d.	1300	C	C	C			A	B	B															
62.00	Petersburg ....d.	1350	C	D	D			B	B	B			B	A	A	A									
74.00	Kake.......................d.	1450												A	A	A	A								
80.00	Sitka ....d.	1650		D						B					A	A	A	A	A	A					
98.00	Juneau/Auke Bay .....d.	1600	D	E	D			B	B	C				B	A	B	B	B	B	B	A	B	A	A
112.00	Haines.....................d.	1750	D	E	D			B	B	C							B				B		B	A	A
118.00	**Skagway**................a.	1770	D	E	D			B	B	C						B			B				A	A

		Qa	Qb	Qc	Qd	Qe	Qf	Qg	Qh	Qi	Qj	Qk	Ql	Qm	Qn	Qo	Qp	Qq	Qr	Qs	Qt	Qu	Qv	Qw	Qx
Skagway................d.		A	A	A	A	A	A	A	A	A	B	A	A	A	A	A	A								
Haines...................d.		A	A	A	A	A	A	A	A	B	B	A	A	A	A	B	A								
Juneau/Auke Bay....d.		A	A	A	B	A	B	B	B	B	B	A	A	B	B	A	A	A	A						
Sitka ....d.			B	B		A			B			B	A	B	B	B	B		A	B					
Kake.......................d.			C	C													B	B	B						
Petersburg ....d.			C		B	B	B	B	C	B	B	B	C	C				B	C						
Hollis ....d.					B	B	B	B	C	B	B	B	C	C	C					C	A	A	A	A	
Ketchikan ....d.			B		B	B	B	C	C	B	B	C	C	C				C		C	A	B	A	A	
Stewart/Hyder.........d.																						B		B	
Prince Rupert.........d.				C	C	C	C	C	D		D	D	E	E									B		A
Bellingham..............a.																									

Pa–⑤ Apr. 30-Sept. 24. Pb–② June 1-Sept. 7. Pc–Sept. 14. Pd–③ May 19-Sept. 22; ④ May 6-13. Pe–May 9. Pf–② May 4-24; ④ June 3-Sept. 9; Sept. 23; ⑧ June 5-Sept. 25. P Aug. 10; ⑦ June 6-Sept. 26. Ph–② June 4; Aug. 3; Aug. 17-Sept. 28; ⑧ May 7-21. Pi–⑤ May 21-June 25; July 9-Sept. 24. Pj–July 2. Pk–① May 3-Sept. 27; ② May 4-28; ③ Ma 12; Sept. 29; ④ May 20-Sept. 30; ⑤ May 7-14; ⑥ May 8-Sept. 25; ⑦ May 16-Sept. 26. Pl–May 1; ② May 19-Sept. 29; ④ May 8-Sept. 25. Pm–May 1. Pn–④ Aug. 12, 26; Sept. 9-23. Po– June 3-24; Aug. 5; Aug. 19; Sept. 2, 30. Pp–④ May 6-27. Pq–① May 3-31. Pr–① June 7-Sept. 27. Ps–⑤ May 8-Aug. 7; Aug. 21-Sept. 25. Pt–July 1. Pu–Aug. 11. Pv–Jul Aug. 12, 16. Pw–June 14.

Qa–June 14 ◇; July 5; Aug. 12, 16; Sept. 6. Qb–⑥ May 7-14, 21◇,28. Qc–July 6◇; Aug. 10; ② Aug. 24-Sept. 28. Qd–May 31⬦; ② June 1-29; July 13-Aug. 3; Aug. 17. Qe–④ June 3- 24; May 8-22; Aug. 5; ⑦ May 9-23. Qf–② June 14; Aug. 3; July 1, 29; Aug. 12-Sept. 30. Qg–June 3, 17; July 1, 29; Aug. 9-Sept. 30. Qh–③ May 5-26; ⑤ June 4; Sept; 24; ⑦ June 6-July Aug. 1-Sept. 26. Qi–July 25. Qj–June 7, 21-28; July 5-12; Aug. 9; Sept. 6. Qk–④ Sept. 11. Ql–June 15; July 6; Sept. 7. Qm–Aug. 23, 30. Qn–① May 3-24; June 7, 21- July 12-Aug. 9; Sept. 13-27. Qo–Aug. 15. Qp–Aug. 15. Qq–June 4-Sept. 24. Qr–June 13⬦; ② May 2-June 6; June 20; July 4-Aug. 8; Aug. 22-Sept. 26. Qs–③ May 5- Qt–Apr. 30. Qu–② May 3-Sept. 27; ④ May 4-Sept. 21; ④ May 5-Sept. 29; ④ May 7-14; ⑥ May 8-Sept.25; ⑦ May 16-Sept. 26. Qv–⑤ May 7-14; July 25. Qw–⑤ May Sept. 30. Qx–May 9, 18; ② June 1-Sept. 21; ③ May 5-12. Qy–May 30.

◇–Arrives/calls Juneau 1 day later. ⬦–Calls Haines 1 day earlier. ⬦–Arrives Kake 1 day earlier.
AMH–Alaska Marine Highway. ☎ Juneau (907) 465-3941. Fax: (907) 277 4829.

Table 307   WHITTIER - VALDEZ - CORDOVA   🚢 A

US$	P	Q	R	S	T	U		km	↓ May 1-Sept. 23 ↑	Q	V	W	X	Y	Z	
0.00	....	....	0900	....	1445	1445	1445 1445	0	d. **Whittier** ....a.	0730	1400	1400	1330	....	....	....
56.00	....	0845	1800		2130	2345	0030	130	d. **Valdez**................d.		0715	0715		1430	1845	....
56.00	....	1430		2145		0530	0615	325	a. **Cordova**..............d.	0030	0030	....	0630	....	1300	....

P–May 2, 5, 7. Q–May 8. R–May 9; ①⑥ May 10-Sept. 23. S–④⑥ May 10-Sept. 23. T–④⑦ May 10-Sept. 23. U–May 10-Sept. 23. V–②④⑥ May 10-Sept. 23. W–⑦ May 9-Sept. X–①⑤ May 10-Sept. 23. Y–May 4. Z–May 1, 6.
AMH–Alaska Marine Highway. ☎ Juneau (907) 465-3941. Fax: (907) 277 4829.

Table 308 — KODIAK - HOMER - SELDOVIA — AMH RT

(AMH) service Kodiak - Homer - Seldovia and v.v. 200 km. Journey 15-16 hours. Fare US$ 50.00. Timings vary and should be checked with operator.

From Kodiak: May 2h, 4, 8v, 9h, 11, 12, 22v, 23h, 25h, 29v, 30h, 31h; June 1, 5v, 6h, 8, 12v, 13h, 15, 16, 26v, 27h, 29; July 3v, 4h, 6, 10v, 11h, 13, 17v, 18h, 20, 21, 31v; Aug. 1h, 3, 7v, 8h, 10, 14v, 15h, 17, 19, 28v, 29h, 31; Sept. 4v, 5h, 7, 11v, 12h, 14, 15, 25v, 26h, 28.

From Seldovia: May 2, 3h, 4v, 9, 10h, 11, 13, 23, 24hv, 30, 31h; June 2hv, 6, 7h, 8v, 13, 14h, 15, 17, 27, 28h, 29v; July 4, 5h, 6v, 11, 12h, 13v, 18, 19h, 20, 22; Aug. 1, 2h, 3v, 8, 9h, 10v, 15, 16h, 17, 19, 29, 30h, 31v; Sept. 5, 6h, 7v, 12, 13h, 14, 16, 26, 27h, 28v.

(RT) service Homer - Seldovia and v.v. 30 km. Journey ✧. Fare US$ 20.00▲. **Service operates June 20-Sept. 1▲.**

From Homer: 1900▲. **From Seldovia:** 0700▲.

●–Commences from/continues to Seward.   h–Terminates at/commences from Homer, **not** Seldovia.   v–Commences from/continues to Valdez.
AMH–Alaska Marine Highway. ☎ Juneau (907) 465-3941. Fax: (907) 277 4829.   RT–Rainbow Tours. ☎ Homer (907) 235-7272.

Table 309 — ALEUTIAN ISLANDS — AMH

service Kodiak - Chignik - Sand Point - King Cove - Cold Bay - Unalaska and v.v. 930 km. Journey 56 hours. Fare US$ 200.00.

From Kodiak: 0800 May 14; June 18; July 24; Aug. 20; Sept. 17.   **From Unalaska:** 2000 May 16; June 20; July 26; Aug. 22; Sept. 19.

AMH–Alaska Marine Highway. ☎ Juneau (907) 465-3941. Fax: (907) 277 4829.

Table 310 — NEW YORK LOCAL SERVICES — HTL IBS

Local services operate in the New York area as follows:
Bayonne (✧ km, US $: ✧). From New York: ✧, returning at ✧. Journey: ✧.
Englewood (✧ km, US $: ✧). From New York: ✧, returning at ✧. Journey: ✧.
Levittown (✧ km, US $: ✧). From New York: ✧, returning at ✧. Journey: ✧.
North Bergen (✧ km,, US $: ✧). From New York: ✧, returning at ✧. Journey: ✧.
Paramus (HTL) (✧ km, US $: ✧). From New York: 0715, 0815, 0910, 1045, 1315, 1510, 1935⑩, 2245,
    returning at 0706⑩, 1043, 1300, 1458, 1639, 1855, 2027, 2230, 2323⑦; also by IBS from New York at
    0845, 1115, 1145⑤, 1815⑩, returning at 1000, 1230, 1630, 1830⑩. Journey: 30 mins.

Union City (✧ km, US $: ✧). From New York: ✧, returning at ✧. Journey: ✧.
West New York (✧ km, US $: ✧). From New York: ✧, returning at ✧. Journey: ✧.

HTL– The Short Line.   IBS– International Bus Services Inc.

Table 311 — NEW YORK/WASHINGTON - CHICAGO — CPB GL PPB

US $	km	GL 4441	GI 1323	GL 1379	GL 1601	GL 4439	GL 4469	GL 4693	PPB 1329	GL 401	GL 1371	CPB 4459	GL 201	GL 4431	GL 1319	PPB 403	GL 4445	CPB 203	GL 1375 ⑤	GL 4475	GL 4447	CPB 1377	GL 205	GL 1321
0.00	**New York** ......d.	0	....	2115	2045	0001	....	0015	0500	....	0730	0700	0800	0845	....	1330	1300	....	1315	1530	1400	....	1700	1725	1730
	Newark ....d.		....	2145	2120		....				....	0740	0835		....	1405					1745			1810
19.00	Philadelphia ......d.	149	....		2355		....	0300	0730		0945a	1020		....	1515a					1700	2025		
22.00	King of Prussia ......d.	✧					....	0815			1025a	1100		1110		1555a		1545		1750			1950	
	Easton ......d.	✧									0955												
18.00	Bethlehem ......d.	✧									1020												
19.00	Allentown ......d.	✧									1040												
32.00	Harrisburg ......d.	✧			0215			0520	1030		1245a	1310	1225	1340			1750a		1815		2000		2250	2210
	DuBois ......d.		....	0320																			
✧	**Washington** ......d.	✧	2145				0115			0645			GL 1317	1100		1400				1900			
✧	Silver Spring ......d.											1130			1430							
✧	Hagerstown ......d.	✧	2335					0835				⑤⑦	1315		1615							
67.00	**Pittsburgh** ......d.	618	0400		0615		0700	1045	1655	1245	1655a	1750		1545	1830		2200a	2130		2335	0005	0045	0250
✧	Youngstown ......d.	✧	0540						1430					2015								
73.00	Warren ......d.	✧		GL			GL	GL			GL						GL	GL				
✧	Akron ......d.	✧		4415			4401	1325			4449			2115			4411	4413				
82.00	**Cleveland** ......d.	811	0720	0800	0815	1000	0930	1230	1230	1700		1700	1845	2220	0045		2359	0045	0400		0315		0400
82.00	Sandusky ......d.	✧			0940				1355	1825		1825										
✧	Toledo ......d.	✧			1105				1520	1950		1950					0300	0620				0620
92.00	**Detroit** ......a.	1067			1225			1545				2105					0410	0730				
✧	Elkhart ......d.	✧							1820	2250												0920
✧	South Bend ......d.	✧							1855	2325												1000
✧	Gary ......d.	✧							1905													
98.00	Hammond ......d.	✧							1925													
98.00	**Chicago** ......a.	1344			1315		1530			2015	0005			0005		0600						1040

	GL 1318	CPB 404	GL 4404	GL 4412	GL 4440	GL 1368	GL 1320	GL 4444	GL 4414	GL 1370	GL 4446	GL 1322	GL 4436	GL 1324	CPB 202	GL 1326	GL 3200	GL 4448	GL 4416	GL 1374	CPB 402	GL 4456	GL 1376	GL 1328	GL 208
Chicago ......d.	0200	....	....	....	....	0645	....	....	....	1300	....	1615	....	1730	....	....	....	....	....	....	2230	....	
Hammond ......d.						0740						1710											
Gary ......d.						0800						1730											
South Bend ......d.						1015						1945							0140				
Elkhart ......d.						1050						2020											
Detroit ......d.			0815				1240	1545			1915				2200								
Toledo ......d.	0755		0935				1355	1715			2045	2320			2315								
Sandusky ......d.			1045				1515	1500	1835														
Cleveland ......d.	1045		1100	1210	1300		1730	1630	2000		2045	2130	2310	0130		0200		0200	0125			0800	
Akron ......d.												2140											
Warren ......d.			GL				1855																
Youngstown ......d.	1220		1366	1440			1945				2305												
Pittsburgh ......d.			1230	1430	1400	1730	1730	2200			2330	0030				0515		0515	0800		0900	1201	
Hagerstown ......d.			1900		2140											0920					1550	
Silver Spring ......d.					2255s											1055						
Washington ......a.	1435		2050		2325	0300			0530							1125	CPB				1725	
DuBois ......d.															0535		204					
Harrisburg ......d.		1645		1845		2210						0600		0715		0950	1000	1210	1400	1400		1500	
Allentown ......d.																		1545				
Bethlehem ......d.																		1605				
Easton ......d.																		1630				
King of Prussia ......d.		1840		2030								0835		0900		1225	1145	1410		1545		1750	
Philadelphia ......a.		1915		2110		0015			0535					0940		1225	1445		1625			
Newark ......a.	2035s			2340								1120	1159		1505		1745	1915			
New York ......a.	2105	2125b		0015		0235			0620		0700		1055	1150	1230		1450	1540	1540b	1815	1950	2005	

–CPB.   b–PPB.   CPB–Capitol Trailways.   GL–Greyhound Lines.   PPB–Peter Pan Trailways.

Table 312 — SYRACUSE - ELMIRA — ETW

US$	900	904 ✕	902 ⑦	km			903 ⑥	901 ⑥	
0.00	....	1240	1820	2015	0	d.**Syracuse** ......a.	0920	1750	....
	....	1325	1905	2100		d.Cortland ......d.	0835	1705	....
	....	1405	1945	2140		d.Ithaca ......d.	0755	1625	....
	....	1500	2040	2235		a.**Elmira** ......d.	0700	1530	....

ETW–Empire Trailways.

Table 313 — OGDENSBURG - UTICA — NETV

US$				km				
0.00	....	....	....	0	d.**Ogdensburg** ......a.		....	....
3.40	....	1000	....	83	d.Watertown ......d.		1725	....
	....	1045	....		d.Carthage ......d.		1640	....
	....	1225	....		a.**Utica** ......d.		1500	....

NETV– NorthEastern TransVan.

Table 314 — NEW YORK - FLORIDA — CCC GL SES

US $		km	GL 1047	SES 142		GL 1015	CCC 509	CCC 507	SES 138	CCC 517	SES 120		GL 1003		GL 1043		GL 1017	GL 1005	GL 1007	SES 132	GL 1011	GL 1045 ⑥		SES 134	CCC 503
0.00	New York ....d.	0	....	....	....	....	....	....	....	....	....		1400		....		1800	2130						....	....
37.00	Washington ......d.		....	....		....	....	....	....	....	....				....									....	....
53.00	Richmond..........d.	❖	0930			1030	1300	1600		1830			2130		0105		0120		0410		0410	0410			0630
56.00	Petersburg.........d.	❖	1010			1110	1340		1910										0445					0710
	Henderson.........d.					1245	1520		2045										0620						0850
	Rocky Mount ......d.	1240												0330						0645				
73.00	Raleigh ....d.	❖				1400	1645		2200										0740				1000
77.00	Fayetteville........d.	❖		1550		1605	1805	2015b	2015	2345b	0145		0145				0515	0815	0815	1000			1150	1205b
85.00	Florence ....d.	❖		1815		1830			2210		0315							1015	1000	1315			1400	1415b
92.00	North Charleston d.	❖	2115			2045									1145					1530	1530			
92.00	Sumter.............d.	❖							2300		0405							1105	1045				1445	1505b
92.00	Columbia .....a.	❖		2000					2359		0500								1145				1545	
98.00	Orangeburg ....d.	❖																						1635b
104.00	Savannah ....d.	❖	0020			0100b							0645		1500			1510					1925b
	Brunswick.........d.	❖	0230												1715		1100s	1630					2045b
118.00	Jacksonville......a.	❖	0345			0320b		0630b					0915		1830		1230	1800					2215b
142.00	Miami..............a.	❖				1110b							1705				2010						
131.00	Orlando............a.	❖																	1730				
131.00	Tampa ....a.	❖																	1955				

1016	1046			GL 205	GL 1018	SES 143	GL	SES				GL 1012	GL 1044	GL 1002	SES 139	GL	SES		GL 1014	GL 516			GL 1024	SES 133	GL 506	CCC 502	GL 500	SES 131	GL 1048 ⑦
Tampa ....d.				....	....	....	....	....				....	....	....	....				....	....			....	....	....	....	....	....	....
Orlando ....d.														1330															
Miami.................d.				....	....	....	....	....				....	....	....	....				....	....			1330		1900				
Jacksonville.......d.				0315		0730						1415							1345	1715			2130		0015	0315			
Brunswick..........d.						0900													1515										
Savannah ....d.				0615		1100									1845				1715	2015			0020						
Orangeburg ....d.						1315																							
	Columbia ....d.				1345		1715								2100									0400			0900		
	Sumter...............d.				1445	1815									2155												0955		
North Charleston ......d.	0915	0915											1615					2015								0615		
Florence ....d.	1201			1545	1605	1930								2300	2245						0530				1045		
Fayetteville.........d.	1530			1745	1845	2145					2300		2345	0045	0115	0115a			0525	0715	0745a	0745	1045a	1230	
Raleigh................d.	1705				2035																0930				
Rocky Mount ....d.		1750							0025												1055			1500	
Henderson...........d.	1830				2130																				
Petersburg..........a.	2005	1950			2305														0835		1230	as		1700	
Richmond.............a.	2045	2030			2345									0230	0245			0445	0445a		0915		1115a	1310	1430a		1740
Washington ....a.												1020		0945												
New York ....a.																	1220								

a–CCC.   b–GL.   CCC–Carolina Trailways.   GL–Greyhound Lines.   SES–Southeastern Stages.

Table 315 — DOVER - BOSTON — CJR

service Dover-Portsmouth-Logan Airport/Boston and v.v. *112 km. Journey: 1¼ hours.*
Fare: US $: ❖.
From Dover to Boston and Logan: 0425④, 0525, 0540④, 0610, 0640④, 0700④, 0740, 0840, 0940, 1040, 1140, 1310, 1510, 1640, 1840.
From Logan: 0715, 0815, 1015, 1115, 1245, 1415, 1515, 1615, 1700④, 1715©, 1815④, 1915, 2115; **from Boston:** 0800, 0900, 1100, 1200, 1330, 1500, 1600, 1630④, 1715, 1730④, 1800, 1900④, 2000, 2200.
CJR– C&J Trailways.

Table 316 — CARIBOU - BANGOR — CJT

US $	2		km			1
❖	....	0645	....	0	d.**Caribou** ....a.	....	2200
❖	....	0710	....	25	d.Presque Isle ....d.	....	2135
❖	....	0825	....	193	d.Houlton...............d.	....	2035
❖	....	1005	....	❖	d.Lincoln................d.	....	1840
0.00	....	1130	....	390	a.**Bangor** ....d.	....	1700

CJT– Cyr Bus Line.

Table 317 — BANGOR - PORTLAND - BOSTON — CLI GL PPB SMT STC VT

US $	CLI 51	VT 9639	VT 9623		CLI 55	CLI 9625	VT 9631	CLI 59A	VT 9627	STC 11 ▲ ⑦	CLI 9683 ⑨⑦	VT 15 ⑨⑦		km			VT 9624		CLI 12 ▲	STC 9626	VT 52	CLI 9628		VT 56	CLI 56A ③	CLI 9622	CLI 9644/82	VT	CLI 9646	SMT 14 ⑧†
❖												1540		❖	d.**Saint John** ....↑															143■
❖												1740		❖	d.St. Stephen ⚑....a.														123■
❖							0930							❖	d.Calais ⚑.............a.			1930											
❖							1000							❖	d. Machias ....a.			1815											
❖										1225				❖	d. Bar Harbor ....a.														
❖														❖	d. Ellsworth ....d.			1635											
0.00		0600		0715	0715	0810	1115	1300	1315	1340	1515	1500	1930	0	d.**Bangor** ....d.	1230	1415	1600	1725	1800		1830		2215	2115	2155f	2230		0830■
11.00		0705				0915			1440					99	d.Waterville...........d.	1130			1625						s	sf			
13.00		0735				0945			1515					132	d.Augusta..............d.	1055			1550						1945				
20.00		0825							1605	1645				181	d.Lewiston.............d.	1010									1910	sf			
8.00				0810				CLI 1410					VT	34	d. Belfast..............d.				1700				2115						
12.00				0855				59	1455				9641	95	d. Rockland ....d.				1615				2030						
21.00	0645			1035	1030				1445	1635				184	d. Brunswick ....d.			1505	1435			1845	1850		2005				CLI■
24.00	0730	0815	0930		0930	1130	1130	1330	1545	1530	1715	1710	1730 1740 0615	246	d.**Portland**...........d.	0920	1201	1430	1400	1515	1615	1815	1815	1820	1940	2015	2230	221	
26.00														275	d.Biddeford..........d.														
32.00		0920					1235				1805		0715	322	d.Portsmouth........d.	0805			1310				1705	1820		2125			
❖							1310				1840		0745	361	d.Newburyport.......d.	0735			1235				1635			2050			
39.00		0925	1040	1140		1125	1335	1525	1745	1725	1940	1925	1940 0845	424	d.**Boston**............d.	0645	1000		1145	1201	1315	1415	1615		1545	1700	1815	2000	201
❖		1430c	1545a	1710a		1830c	1935a	2030c	2300a	2230c		0100a	0045c 0100a 1345a	794	a.New York ....d.	0015a	0330c		0630a	0615d	0800a	0830c		0900a	1201a	1030c	1500a	141	

a– GL.
c– PPB.
d– ex ⑦.
e– ex ②③.
f– ⑨⑦ only.
CLI– Concord Trailways.

GL– Greyhound Lines.
PPB– Peter Pan Trailways.
SMT– SMT (Eastern) Ltd.
STC– St. Croix Bus Service.
VT– Vermont Transit.

Table 318 — BOSTON - NEWPORT — BZ

US $	371 ✵	351	355	357 ④	359 ④		361 ④	363	365	367 †		km			350 ④	352 ✵	354 ④	356		358		362	364	366	368 †
0.00	0800	1000	1400	1600	1700	....	1730	1800	2000	2200		0	d.**Boston** ◇ ....a.		0725	0745	0835	0940	....	1140	....	1540	1740	1940	2140
8.95	0900	1100	1500	1700	1800	....	1830	1900	2100	2300		66	a.Fall River...........d.		0620	0640	0730	0840	....	1040	....	1440	1640	1840	2040
12.20	0935	1135	1535	1735		....		1935	2135	2335		95	a.**Newport**...........d.			0600		0800	....	1000	....	1400	1600	1800	2000

◇– Service also operates Boston-Providence and v.v. *70 km. Journey: 1 hour. Fare: US $: 7.00.* **From Boston:** 0015, 0630①⑥, 0650, 0730✵, 0800†, 0900✵, 1000, 1100, 1201, 130 1400, 1500, 1600, 1700, 1800, 1900, 2000, 2100, 2300. **From Providence:** 0520①⑥, 0600, 0715✵, 0830, 0930 and hourly to 2130, 2315.
BZ– Bonanza Bus Lines.

Table 320 — WHITE RIVER - NEW YORK 🚌 GL VT

US$	VT 123	VT 127	VT 129	VT 133 ⑨⑦	km		GL 122	GL 124	GL 128	GL 134
1.00	0715	1040	1400	1700	0	d.White River Junction .a.	1235b	1605b	2045b	0050b
	0820	1130	1455			d.Bellows Falls ...a.	1125b	1455b	1935b	2350b
	0935	1205	1535	1810		d.Brattleboro ...a.	1050b	1420b	1855b	2255b
	1005	1235	1605	1840		d.Greenfield ...a.	1015b	1345b	1825b	2225b
	1035s	1305	1635s	1910s		d.Northampton ...a.	0950b	1315b	1800b	2200b
	1115a	1400a	1710a	1935a		d.Springfield ...a.	0925b	1250b	1735b	2140b
	1201a	1450a	1815a	2010a		d.Hartford ...a.	0830	1115	1620	2100
	1305a	1555a	1930a			d.New Haven ...a.	0720	1000	1435	
	1335a	1625a	2000a			d.Bridgeport ...a.	0645		1400	
	1410a	1700a	2030a			d.Stamford ...a.			1325	
	1525a	1825a	2155a	2300a		a.New York ...d.	0515	0730	1201	1800

GL. b–VT. GL–Greyhound Lines. VT–Vermont Transit.

Table 321 — SYRACUSE - PLATTSBURGH 🚌 ADT GL

US$	ADT 119	GL 4154	GL 4156	km		GL 4151	GL 4157	ADT 106B
0.00	....	0745	1800	0	d.Syracuse ...a.	1220	....	1610
8.00	....	0840	1855	55	d.Pulaski ...d.	1125	....	1515
11.00	....	0905	1920	84	d.Adams ...d.	1100	....	1455
13.00	....	0945	1955	113	d.Watertown ...d.	1035	....	1425
21.00	....	1040	2050	173	d.Gouverneur ...d.	0925	....	1310
24.00	0830	1115	2125	210	d.Canton ...d.	0850	....	1235 2015
25.00	0855	1150	2150	228	d.Potsdam ...d.	0830	....	1215 2000
	....				d. Ogdensburg ...a.			
30.00	0925	....	2220	259	d. Massena ...d.	0800	....	1930
32.00	1015			294	d.Malone ...d.		....	1845
40.00				387	a.Plattsburgh ...d.			

ADT–Adirondack Trailways GL–Greyhound Lines.

Table 322 — CAPE COD 🚌 BZ PLB

US$	501 ex⑤	505	507	509	511 Ⓐ	513	515	517	519	521	km		500 ex⑤	502	504	508	510	512	514	516	518	520
0.00	0800	....	1000	1201	1400	1515	1615	1715	1815	2000	2200	0	d.Boston ★ ...a.	0655	0730	0825	0940	1205	1340	1605	1655	1835	 2105
❖	0925	....	1125	1325	1525	1640	1740	1840	1940	2135	2335	106	d.Falmouth ...d.	0530	0600	0700	0810	1040	1210	1440	1530	1710	 1940
.25	0935	....	1135	1335	1535	1650	1750	1850	1950	2145	2345	120	a.Wood's Hole ...d.	....	0645	0800	1030	1030	1200	1430	1520	1700	 1930

US$	400	402	BZ	401	403	km		BZ	801	1803 ⑥	1809 ©	809 Ⓐ
0.00	....	1201 1815	0	d.Springfield ...a.	1210 1755							
	....	1340 1955	146	a.Providence ...d.	1030 1615							

US$	800	810	km		PLB	801	1803 ⑥	1809 ©	809 Ⓐ
0.00	0650 1430	0	d.Provincetown ...a.	1245	1345	1920	1920	
	0830 1630	82	d.Hyannis ...d.	1115	1215	1745	1745	
	1015 1820		a.Boston ...d.	0915	1015	1515	1545	

US$	200	202	204	206	208	212	214	216 ex⑤	216 ⑤	km		BZ	201	203	205	207	209	211	213 Ⓐ	215
0.00	0545	....	0900	1145 1345 1545		1745	2000	2200	2200	0	d.Providence ...a.	0720	0830	....	1030 1230 1430	1730	1835	....	1930
.95	0610	....	0925	1210 1410 1610		1810	2025	2225	2225	26	d.Fall River ...d.	0655	0800	....	1000 1201 1400	1650	1810	....	1900
.00	0630	....	0046	1230 1430 1630		1830	2046	2246	2246	50	d.New Bedford ...d.	0630	0735	....	0935 1135 1335	1625		....	1835
.15	....	1050	1335	1535 1735		1935	2145	2345	2345	127	a.Hyannis ...d.	....	0630	0830	1030 1230	1520		....	1730

🚌 service (PLB) Boston ★-North Plymouth-Hyannis and v.v. 113 km. Journey: 1¾-2 hours. Fare: US$: 5.70.
om Boston: 0730④, 0815⑤, 0915④, 1015⑤, 1115, 1215④, 1315, 1415, 1510④, 1515⑤, 1530④, 1545④, 1600④, 1615©, 1620④, 1630④, 1645④, 1655④, 1710④, 1715©, 1720④, 1740④, 1800④, 1815, 1835©, 1915, 2015®, 2115, 2340.
om Hyannis: 0430④, 0450④, 0515④, 0525④, 0530④, 0535④, 0545④, 0555④, 0605④, 0615④, 0630④, 0640④, 0700④, 0720④, 0730©, 0750④, 0830, 0930, 1030, 1130④, 1230, 1330④, 1430, 1530, 1630, 1830©, 1930④, 2030©.
–Certain trips operate to/from Logan Airport. BZ–Bonanza Bus Lines. PLB–Plymouth and Brockton Street Railway.

Table 323 — NEW YORK - RUTLAND 🚌 BZ GL VT

US$	VT 9047	BZ 750	VT 9043	VT 9045	BZ 752	BZ 754	BZ 728 ⑤	km		BZ 751	BZ 753	VT 9042	BZ 711	VT 9044	BZ 755	VT 9046
0.00		0600d 0845a	1130d 1315d	1415		1715	1930	0	d.New York ...a.	1225	1440	1530d	1745	1820d	2050b	0105d
4.30		0635d	1205d 1350d			1845	2055	30	d.Ridgewood ...d.			1445d		1735d		0030f
1.45		1030			1545	1845	2055	134	d. Danbury ...d.	1100	1315		1620		1915	2115
3.20		1325			1815	2115	2325	250	d. Pittsfield ...d.	0830	1045		1330		1645	
9.95	0910			1435 1645				263	d.Albany ...d.	....	1145			1530		2115
2.05	r			r r				271	d.Troy ...d.	s			s			s
3.75	1015 1420			1545 1750		2200		313	d.Bennington ...d.		0930 1040		1420	1530		2005
7.90	1201			1720 1920				406	d.Rutland ...d.		0930		1300			1840
7.70	1355			1920 2105				512	d.Burlington ...d.		0735		1045			1630
❖								660	a. Plattsburgh ...d.							

0845 on ①-④. b–2050 on ①-④. c–VT. d–GL. e–⑤⑦ only. f–⑤⑦ only. Note s applies. BZ–Bonanza Bus Lines. GL–Greyhound Lines. VT–Vermont Transit.

Table 324 — BOSTON - ALBANY - CLEVELAND 🚌 ADT BZ ETW GL LFL PPB

	km	GL 4266	LFL 13	GL 4185	ADT 500A	GL 4181	ADT 502	ADT 510	GL 4268	GL 4179	PPB 31	GL 401	ADT 524	ADT 512 ⑤⑦	PPB 33	GL 4171	ADT 506	PPB 35	GL 403	ADT 514	ADT 518	GL 4177	ADT 508	GL 4175
Boston ⊠ ...d.	0	....								0715	0800	1000g			1200	1201		1500				1600		2015
Worcester ⊠ ...d.	71									0825	0905					1310						1710		2125
Springfield ⊠ ...d.	188									0935	1015	1215			1410			1715 1815				1820		1930
Pittsfield ...d.										1125	1320				1520			1825 1925				1930		
New York ...d.		2330			0600	0700	0845	0945	0900	1000d		1300			1315	1300			1745 1930	1830	2215		2100
Albany ...d.				0810	0905	1010				1230	1300d 1415	1430	1600	1620	1620	1640	1925	2020	2100		2135		0020
Schenectady ...d.				0835	0935	1035				1300	1325d				1650	1705					2125		2200s
Utica ...d.				1005	1110	1215				1440	1505d				1825	1850					2255		2335s
Syracuse ...d.		0445		0900	1120c	1300	1330	1350c	1535	1625	1625c				1745c	1920c		2000	2000c		0010	0030c 0100	0300c 0325
Rochester ...d.				1055	1310c	1500		1540c		1820	1820c				1925c	2105c		2155	2145c		0210c	0250 0440c	0520
Buffalo ...d.		0725		1130	1320	1445c	1700		1710c	1815	2015	2000c			2055c	2230c		0001	2320c		0340c	0500 0605c	0730
Erie ...d.				1330	1500	1720e	1905			2210									0700			0930
Ashtabula ...d.																						1020
Cleveland ...a.				1525	1640	1920e	2045			2350									0850			1120

	GL 4182	GL 4265	ETW 614	ETW 618	ETW 622	BZ 400	GL 4176	ETW 600 ⑤	ADT 515	PPB 32	GL 4188	BZ 402	ETW 4267 ⑤⑦	GL 602	PPB 34	ETW 604	PPB 505	GL 4186	ETW 620 ⑤⑦	GL 4269	ETW 606	GL 4275	ETW 608	GL 4184 P	LFL 10
eveland ...d.	1815				0045							0330						0715				1045	1215e 1315		1615
htabula ...d.	1915																	0815							
ie ...d.	2010																	0915				1235	1400e 1505		1815
uffalo ...d.	2230	2330	2345	2310	0230		0430	0540			0745			0915			1100	1135	1310	1315	1430	1445	1630 1730		2015
ochester ...d.	0005		0040	0405				0740			0925			1105			1235	1315			1610	1620	1820 1910		2205c
yracuse ...d.	0215	0225	0230d	0230d	0600d			0750	0925d 0935		1145		1245	1315d			1430d 1500	1520	1600d 1630		1815d 1845	2020d 2050			2359c
ica ...d.			0335d	0705d				0855	1040d 1040		1250		1420d				1535d 1620	1625			1930d 1950	2125d			
chenectady ...d.			0505d	0850d				1035	1220d 1220		1430		1555d				1800	1805			2105d 2130	2300d			
bany ...a.	0530		0550d	0915d	0930		1145	1245d 1300	1250	1530	1545		1625d 1640				1825	1900			2200d 2200	2300d			
ew York ...a.		0815	0725	0730d	0905d	1250d	1420	1550d 1550			1820		1745 1950d		2000d		2150 2100d	2145			0105d 0105			
ttsfield ⊠ ...d.				0655d		1030			1355			1645			1740										
oringfield ⊠ ...d.	0725			0815g		1140	1340		1515	1725	1800			1915			2055								
orcester ⊠ ...d.	0830									1830				2015											
oston ⊠ ...a.	0940			1000g		1400g	1525			1700	1940			2120			2240								

-Runs on ⑤† (ex on ⑦ of holiday weekends).
-⑤⑦. b–①⑥. c–ETW. d–ADT. e–LFL. f–⑥ only. g–PPB.
–Complete service (PPB) Boston-Springfield and v.v.; from Boston: 0015, 0340, 0540, 00, 1000, 1100, 1200, 1400, 1500, 1615, 1715, 1830, 1930, 2015®, 2115, 2215†; from

Springfield: 0230, 0615, 0645, 0815, 0915, 1015, 1215, 1315, 1415, 1515, 1610, 1715, 1815®, 1915, 2130, 2330. ADT–Adirondack Trailways. BZ–Bonanza Bus Lines. ETW–Empire Trailways. GL–Greyhound Lines. LFL–Lake Front Trailways. PPB–Peter Pan Trailways.

Table 325 ALBANY - BINGHAMTON

VT

US$			9669		km			9670		
0.00	....	....	1445	....	0	d.**Albany** ....a.	....	1355	....	....
	....	....	1515	....		d.Schenectady .....d.	....	1325	....	....
	....	....	1650	....		d.Oneonta ....d.	....	1150	....	....
	....	....	1805	....		a.**Binghamton** .....d.	....	1030	....	....

VT– Vermont Transit.

Table 328 UTICA - BINGHAMTON

CVB

US $	11			13	km			10		12
0.00	1105	....	....	1705	0	d.**Utica** ....a.	....	0950	....	1700
8.55	1355	....	....	1955	148	a.**Binghamton** .....d.	....	0700	....	1410

CVB– Chenango Valley Bus Lines Inc.

Table 330 BUFFALO - PITTSBURGH

FAB

US $	600	815	530	730	km		705	510	805	605
0.00	....	....	1450	....	0	d.**Buffalo**.............a.	....	1255	....	....
	0635	1725	│	....		d. State College ..a.	....	│	0955	....
28.00	0810	1910	1915	1925		d.DuBois ....d.	0810	0825	0825	1845
32.00	0840	....	....	1955		d.Punxsutawney ...d.	0735	....	....	1810
35.00	0925	....	....	2040		d.Indiana ....d.	0650	....	....	1725
39.00	1010	....	....	2125		d.Vandergrift.........d.	0605	....	....	1640
39.00	1115	....	....	2235		a.**Pittsburgh** ....d.	0500	....	....	1530

FAB– Fullington Trailways.

Table 331 NEW YORK - CANTON

ADT

US $	↓	km	102A	106B	108A	114	116A ⑤	618A	122	126
0.00	**New York** ....d.	0	0700	1000	1300	1400	1600	1745	2000	233
	Ridgewood (**u**)......d.		0730	1030	1330	1430	1630	1815	2030	235
23.05	**Albany** ....d.	226	1010	1315	1610	1730	1915	2040	2305	023
29.60	Saratoga Springs .d.	275	1055	1400	1700	1825	2000	2125	2350	....
31.85	Glens Falls ....d.	323	1120	1445	1730	1900	2025	2150	0015	....
46.20	Lake Placid ....d.	451	....	1700	....	....	....	....	....	....
47.70	Saranac Lake ....d.	466	....	1730	....	....	....	....	....	....
52.90	Malone ....d.	541	....	1845	....	....	....	....	....	....
	Potsdam..............a.	605	....	2000	....	....	....	....	....	....
	Canton ....a.	621	....	2015	....	....	....	....	....	....

↓	101	103 ex⑥⑦	109	111	115	119	123	125	627 P	129
Canton ....d.	....	....	....	....	....	0830	....	....	....	....
Potsdam.......................d.	....	....	....	....	....	0855	....	....	....	....
Malone ....d.	....	....	....	....	....	1015	....	....	....	....
Saranac Lake...............d.	....	....	....	....	....	1115	....	....	1630	....
Lake Placid ....d.	....	....	....	....	....	1135	....	....	1650	....
Glens Falls...................d.	....	0545	0825	....	1130	1420	1515	....	1905	203
Saratoga Springs ....d.	....	0615	0850	....	1201	1450	1540	....	1930	210
Albany ....d.	0600	0715	0940	1100	1250	1535	1630	1845	2015	214
Ridgewood (**s**)............a.	s	s	s	s	s	s	s	s	s	s
New York ....a.	0905	1055	1250	1350	1550	1850	1950	2205	2320	010

P– Runs on † (ex on ⑦ of holiday weekends).
ADT– Adirondack Trailways.

Table 332 NEW YORK - MONTRÉAL

GL

US $	4002 ♣	4181	4008 ♣	4006 ♣	4024 ♣⑤⑦	4014 ♣	4074	4012 ⑤⑦	4076 ♣	4020 ♣⑤	4010 ♣	km	↓ ↑	4021 ♣	4001 ♣	4073	4075	4007 ♣		4003 ♣	4009 ♣		4013 ♣	408 ⑤⑦
0.00	0015	0600	0900	1130	1315	1315	1530	1730	1830	2100	2100	0	d.**New York**...............a.	0645	0815	1150	1420	1530	....	1705	1850	....	2150	010
	0050u	0635u	0935u	1205u	│	1350u	1605u	1805u	1905u	│	2135u		d.Ridgewood ....d.	│	0730s	1105s	1335s	1445s	....	1620s	1805s	....	2105s	002
26.00	0330	0850	1220	1450	│	1635	1820	2020	2205	│	0020	250	d.**Albany** ◇ ....d.	│	0525	0900	1130	1240	....	1415	1600	....	1900	221
32.00	0435	....	1315	1545	1715	1735	....	....	2255	0100	0110	300	d.Saratoga Springs ◇ ..d.	0315	0415	....	....	1125	....	1305	1450	....	1750	....
34.00	│	....	1350	1620	│	│	....	....	│	│	│	348	d.Glens Falls ◇ ....d.	│	│	....	....	1035	....	│	1405	....	│	....
53.00	0655	....	1610	1840	1940	2000	....	....	0115	│	0330	508	d.Plattsburgh ....d.	│	0135	....	....	0835	....	1040	1155	....	1520	....
	│	....	│	│	│	│	....	....	│	│	│		a. Lake Placid ....d.	│	│	....	....	│	....	│	│	....	│	....
	│	....	│	│	│	│	....	....	│	│	│		a. Saranac Lake..........d.	│	│	....	....	│	....	│	│	....	│	....
61.00	0840	....	1755	2025	2125	2145	....	....	0300	0445	0515	610	a.**Montréal** ....d.	2300	2345	....	....	0645	....	0845	1000	....	1330	....

◇– Local traffic not carried between Albany and Glens Falls.
GL– Greyhound Lines.

Table 333 NEW YORK - BINGHAMTON - BUFFALO

ADT CPB CVB ETW GCL GL HTL

US $	↓	km	GL 4260		ETW 501 ⚒		GL 4256	ETW 505 †	ADT 510 ♣	CPB 1	HTL 101	GL 4268	CVB 103	HTL 103	GL 4304	GL 4250	CPB 3	CPB 193		HTL 107	GL 4278	HTL 111	GL 4252	GL 4306	HTL 113	GL 4264	GL 4280	ADT 518	GL 3500	CPB 5	HTL 119	CPB 7	ADT 508 ♣	HTL 12
0.00	**New York** d.	0	0100	....	....	....	0730	....	0845	....	0830	0945	....	1015	....	1145	....	....	....	1230	1330	1430	1445	....	1630	1630	1830	1930	....	....	1830	....	2215	230
❖	**Washington** d.		│	....	....	....	│	....	│	0300	│	│	....	│	0650	│	....	0845	....	│	│	│	│	1030	│	│	│	│	1315	....	│	1710	│	│
❖	Mahwah.. d.		│	....	....	....	│	....	│	│	0910	│	....	1055	│	│	....	│	....	1310	│	1510	│	│	│	│	│	│	│	....	1910	│	│	│
❖	**Baltimore** d.		│	....	....	....	│	....	│	0400	│	│	....	│	0800	│	....	0940	....	│	│	│	│	1201	│	│	│	│	1420	....	│	1810	│	│
❖	York...... d.		│	....	....	....	│	....	│	0510	│	│	....	│	0910	│	....	1110	....	│	│	│	│	1310	│	│	│	│	1530	....	│	1920	│	│
❖	Harrisburg d.		│	....	....	....	│	....	│	0605	│	│	....	│	1005	│	1201	1201	....	│	│	│	│	1430	│	│	│	│	1640	1700	│	2015	│	│
❖	Pottsville d.		│	....	....	....	│	....	│	0745	│	│	....	│	│	│	1325	│	....	│	│	│	│	│	│	│	│	│	│	1825	│	2205	│	│
❖	Sunbury d.		│	....	....	....	│	....	│	│	│	│	....	│	1110	│	│	│	....	│	│	│	│	│	│	│	│	│	1810	│	│	│	│	│
❖	Hazleton d.		│	....	....	....	│	....	│	0845	│	│	....	│	│	│	1425	│	....	│	│	│	│	│	│	│	│	│	│	1925	│	2250	│	│
❖	Wilkes Barre d.		│	....	....	....	│	....	│	0930	│	│	....	│	1325	│	1505	│	....	│	│	│	│	1645	│	│	│	│	2005	2005	│	2330	│	│
❖	Scranton d.		│	....	....	....	0945	....	│	1020	│	│	....	│	1415	│	1535	│	....	│	│	│	1700	1730	│	│	│	│	2055	2040	│	0015	│	│
24.40	Monticello d.	200	│	....	....	....	│	....	│	│	1025	│	....	1210	│	│	....	│	....	1425	│	1625	│	│	1825	│	│	│	│	│	2025	│	│	010
27.95	Liberty .... d.	220	│	....	....	....	│	....	│	│	│	│	....	│	│	│	....	│	....	│	│	│	│	│	│	│	│	│	│	│	2045	│	│	012
32.00	Binghamton d.	309	0435	....	....	....	1115	....	│	1135	1235e	1330	1405	1410	1540	1540	....	│	....	1620e	1710	1825	1825	1855	2015e	2015	2210	│	2225	│	2225	0125	│	030
33.00	Cortland d.		│	....	....	....	│	....	│	1225	│	1420	│	│	1630	│	....	│	....	│	1800	│	│	1945	│	2105	2300	│	2310s	│	│	s	│	│
42.00	**Syracuse** a.	435	│	....	....	....	│	....	1345	1310	│	1505	│	│	1715	│	....	│	....	│	1845	│	│	2030	│	2150	2345	2359	2355	│	│	0255	│	│
39.00	Ithaca..... d.	396	0600	....	....	....	1235	....	│	....	1340e	│	1515	│	....	1655	....	│	....	1730e	....	│	1940	....	2125e	....	....	│	....	│	│	....	0255	041
48.90	Geneva.... d.	468	0655	....	....	....	1330	....	│	....	....	│	....	│	....	1750	....	│	....	....	....	│	2035	....	....	....	....	│	....	│	│	....	│	....
	Canandaigua d.		0725	....	....	....	1400	....	│	....	....	│	....	│	....	1820	....	│	....	....	....	│	2105	....	....	....	....	│	....	│	│	....	│	....
37.00	Elmira. d.	427	│	....	0915	....	│	1215	│	....	....	│	....	1540	....	│	....	1615a	....	....	....	1955	│	....	....	....	....	│	....	2315	2350	....	│	....
37.00	Corning d.	453	│	....	0940	....	│	1240	│	....	....	│	....	1610	....	│	....	1640a	....	....	....	2015	│	....	....	....	....	│	....	....	0010	....	│	....
53.00	Rochester a.	544	0815	....	1230	....	1440	1530	1530a	....	....	│	....	....	....	1900	....	1925a	....	....	....	....	2145	....	....	....	....	0210a	....	....	....	....	0440a	....
59.00	**Buffalo**... a.	662	1000	....	....	....	1640	....	1710a	....	....	1815	....	....	....	2045	....	....	....	....	....	....	2325	....	....	....	....	0340a	....	....	....	....	0605a	....
❖	*Toronto* 108 a.	815	....	....	....	....	....	....	2000f	....	....	....	....	....	....	....	....	....	....	....	....	....	....	....	....	....	....	0750f	....	....	....	....	0905f	....

↓		ETW 614 ♣	HTL 100	GL 4261	CPB 6	GL 4305	CVB 102	GL 4307	GL 4251	GL 4271	CVB 104	HTL 104	CPB 8	CPB 198		CVB 108	HTL 108	CPB 10	GL 4311	GL 4253	GL 4273	GL 4257		CVB 116	ETW 616 ♣	HTL 118	ETW 502 ⚒	GL 4269	GL 4313	CVB 122	GL 4263	ETW 504 †		ETW 61 ♣
Toronto 108 d.	....	2100f	....	....	....	....	....	....	....	....	....	....	....	....	....	....	....	....	....	....	....	....	....	....	0745f	....	....	....	....	....	....	....	....	170
Buffalo...... d.	....	2345	....	....	....	....	....	....	....	....	....	....	....	....	....	....	....	....	....	0845	....	1030	....	....	1100	....	1310	1315	....	....	1445	....	....	203
Rochester... d.	....	│	....	....	....	....	....	....	0545	....	....	....	....	0850	....	....	....	....	....	1030	....	1215	....	....	│	....	1505	│	....	....	1645	1820	....	222
Corning. d.	....	│	....	....	....	....	....	....	│	....	....	0840	....	1130	....	....	1133	....	....	│	....	│	....	....	│	1530	1750	│	....	....	│	2120	....	│
Elmira.... d.	....	│	....	....	0440	....	....	....	│	....	....	0915	....	1215	....	....	1220	....	....	│	....	│	....	....	│	1600	1820	│	....	....	│	2150	....	│
Canandaigua d.	....	│	....	....	│	....	....	....	0625	....	....	│	....	│	....	....	│	....	....	1110	....	1255	....	....	│	│	....	│	....	....	1725	....	....	│
Geneva...... d.	....	│	....	....	│	....	....	....	0705	....	....	│	....	│	....	....	│	....	....	1150	....	1335	....	....	│	│	....	│	....	....	1805	....	....	│
Ithaca........ d.	....	│	....	....	│	....	0715	....	0800	....	0940	│	....	│	....	1240	│	....	....	1300	....	1435	....	1450	│	│	....	│	....	1840	1905	....	....	│
Syracuse d.	....	0230h	....	....	│	....	│	0730	│	0900	│	│	0935	│	....	│	│	....	1245	│	1400	│	....	│	1430h	│	....	1630	1815	│	│	....	....	003
Cortland .. d.	....	│	....	....	│	....	│	0815	│	0945	│	│	1020	│	....	│	│	....	1330	│	1445	│	....	│	│	│	....	1715	1900	│	│	....	....	011
Binghamton d.	....	│	0550	0800	│	0725	0840g	0920	0935	1045	1050	1110	1115	│	....	1350	1410	....	1430	1445	1545	1600	....	1615g	│	1750	....	1815	1950	2005g	2030	....	....	021
Liberty .... d.	....	│	0735	│	│	│	│	│	│	│	....	│	│	│	....	....	│	....	│	│	│	│	....	│	│	1935	....	│	....	2140g	│	....	....	│
Monticello... d.	....	│	0800	│	│	│	1030g	│	│	│	....	1300	│	│	....	....	1600	....	│	│	│	│	....	1800g	│	2000	....	│	....	2200g	│	....	....	│
Scranton ... d.	....	│	│	│	0725	0845	│	1045	│	│	....	│	1240	│	....	....	│	1555	1600	│	│	│	....	│	│	│	....	│	....	│	│	....	....	033
Wilkes Barre d.	....	│	│	│	0800	0920	│	1120	│	│	....	│	1315	│	....	....	│	1630	1635	│	│	│	....	│	│	│	....	│	....	│	│	....	....	041
Hazleton ... d.	....	│	│	│	0845	│	│	│	│	│	....	│	1400	│	....	....	│	1715	│	│	│	│	....	│	│	│	....	│	....	│	│	....	....	045
Sunbury ... d.	....	│	│	│	│	│	│	1330	│	│	....	│	│	│	....	....	│	│	1840	│	│	│	....	│	│	│	....	│	....	│	│	....	....	│
Pottsville ... d.	....	│	│	│	0940	│	│	│	│	│	....	│	1500	│	....	....	│	1810	│	│	│	│	....	│	│	│	....	│	....	│	│	....	....	055
Harrisburg . d.	....	│	│	│	1055	1145	│	1450	│	│	....	│	1640	1650	....	....	│	1945	2010	│	│	│	....	│	│	│	....	│	....	│	│	....	....	074
York......... d.	....	│	│	│	....	1225	│	1530	│	│	....	│	....	1740	....	....	│	2025	2050	│	│	│	....	│	│	│	....	│	....	│	│	....	....	083
Baltimore . d.	....	│	│	│	....	1340	│	1645	│	│	....	│	....	1850	....	....	│	2140	2205	│	│	│	....	│	│	│	....	│	....	│	│	....	....	095
Mahwah..... a.	....	│	0905s	│	....	│	1135gs	│	│	│	....	1405s	....	│	....	....	1705s	│	│	│	│	│	....	1905g	│	2105	....	│	....	2317gs	│	....	....	│
Washington a.	....	│	│	│	....	1500	│	1755	│	│	....	│	....	2005	....	....	│	2255	2300	│	│	│	....	│	│	│	....	│	....	│	│	....	....	110
New York .. a.	....	0730h	0950	1130	....	....	1220g	....	1305	1415	....	1450	....	....	....	....	1755	....	....	1815	1915	1930	....	1955g	2000h	2150	....	2145	....	2359g	2359	....	....	....

a– *ETW.*
c– *CPB.*
e– *CVB.*
f– *GCL.*
g– *HTL.*
h– *ADT.*
ADT– Adirondack Trailways.
CPB– Capitol Trailways.
CVB– Chenango Valley Bus Lines Inc.
ETW– Empire Trailways.
GCL– Gray Coach Lines.
GL– Greyhound Lines.
HTL– The Short Line.

Table 335 — SYRACUSE - GENEVA (ONC)

US $	400 Ⓐ	402 Ⓐ	404	406	408	410	412	414	416 ★☆	418/20	422 ☆	km	
0.00	0720	0720	0745	0830	0945	1215	1500	1600	1700	1710	1815	0	d.Syracuse ....a.
2.30	0810	0820	0845	0930	1045	1315	1600	1700	1800	1815	1915	40	a.Auburn ....d.
3.70	....	....	....	....	1110	....	....	....	....	1840	....	66	a.Seneca Falls ....d.
4.45	....	....	....	....	1130	....	....	....	....	1900	....	84	a.Geneva ....d.

	401	403 Ⓐ	405	407	409	411 ☆☆	413 ☆☆	415 ☆☆	417 ☆☆	419	421/3 ☆☆
d.Syracuse ....a.	0715	0745	0820	0930	1200	1430	1530	1630	1650	1810	2100
a.Auburn ....d.	0610	0640	0710	0830	1100	1330	1430	1530	1600	1710	2000
a.Seneca Falls ...d.	....	....	....	....	....	....	....	....	1450	....	1925
a.Geneva ....d.	....	....	....	....	....	....	....	....	1430	....	1910

>—Additional trip: 2110.   ONC–Onondaga Coach Corporation.

Table 337 — BUFFALO - PITTSBURGH (CRTS FAB GL LCL NSB)

US $	GL 7929 Ⓐ	CRTS 7 Ⓐ	NSB 1001	NSB 1003	GL 4637	FAB 570 ⑦	NSB 1005	GL 4641	NSB 1007	NSB 1009 ★	km	
0.00	0730	....	0815	1110	1255	....	1400	1700	1715	2130	0	d.Buffalo ....a.
9.00	....	0910	0915	1210	....	1458	....	1815	....	2240	73	d.Dunkirk ....d.
	....	0930	0940	1240	....	1524	....	1845	....	2310	40	d. Cassadaga ....d.
18.00	0930	....	....	1500	1515	....	2010	....	....	....	159	d.Erie ....d.
23.00	1030	....	....	1555	1615	....	2105	....	....	....	225	d.Meadville ....d.
28.00	1115	....	....	1640	....	....	2150	....	....	....	279	d.Mercer ....d.
12.70	....	1020	1010	1310	....	1600	....	1915	....	2335	115	d. Jamestown ....d.
26.00	....	....	....	....	....	1700	....	....	....	....	237	d. Franklin ....d.
28.00	....	....	....	....	....	1715	....	....	....	....	254	d. Oil City ....d.
	....	....	....	....	....	1845	....	....	....	....		a. DuBois ◇ ....d.
34.00	....	....	....	....	....	....	....	....	....	....	324	d. Butler ◇ ....d.
39.00	1330	....	....	1815	....	....	2315	....	....	....	376	a.Pittsburgh ◇ ....d.

US $	NSB 1000	NSB 1002 Ⓐ	NSB 1004	NSB 1006	FAB 550	GL 4646 ⑥⑦	CRTS 8 Ⓐ	NSB 1008	GL 4640	GL 7928	km	
0.00	....	0800	1045	1300	1600	....	1700	....	1950	2145	0	d.Buffalo ....a.
9.00	....	0659	0935	1130	1455	....	1700	1840	....	....	73	d.Dunkirk ....d.
	....	0630	0910	1105	1425	....	r	1810	....	....	40	d. Cassadaga ....d.
18.00	....	....	....	....	1145	1440	....	....	1850	2230	159	d.Erie ....d.
23.00	....	....	....	....	1045	1340	....	....	1755	2130	225	d.Meadville ....d.
28.00	....	....	....	....	1255	....	....	....	1710	2045	279	d.Mercer ....d.
12.70	0605	0845	1040	1400	....	....	1605	1745	....	....	115	d. Jamestown ....d.
26.00	....	....	....	....	1000	....	....	....	....	....	237	d. Franklin ....d.
28.00	....	....	....	....	0945	....	....	....	....	....	254	d. Oil City ....d.
	....	....	....	....	0825	....	....	....	....	....		a. DuBois ◇ ....d.
34.00	....	....	....	....	....	....	....	....	....	....	324	d. Butler ◇ ....d.
39.00	....	....	....	....	1130	....	....	....	1545	1830	376	a.Pittsburgh ◇ ....d.

>— Local service (LCL) operates Pittsburgh-Butler and v.v., from Pittsburgh: 0730Ⓐ, 1040⑥, 1220Ⓐ, 1455⑥, 1500⑥, 1605Ⓐ, 1630⑦, 1710⑥, 1730⑥, 1740⑥, 2015⑥; from Butler: 0600–, 0650Ⓐ, 0900Ⓐ, 0915Ⓐ, 1330⑥, 1335Ⓐ, 1615⑥, 1620Ⓐ, 1845⑥, 1900⑥.
GL– Greyhound Lines.   LCL– Lincoln Coach Lines.   NSB– Niagara Scenic Bus Lines.
CRTS– Chautauqua Area Rural Transit System.   FAB– Fullington Trailways.

Table 338 — BOSTON - LITTLETON (CLI)

US $	2 ⑤	2A ex⑤	4	6	8 ⑥⑦Ⓐ	8 ex⑦	14 ⑦	20	26	34 ⑤⑦	34 ex⑤⑦	km	
	0800	0800	0915	1115	1245	1245	1500	1600	1630	1915	1915	7	d.Boston Logan Airport..a.
0.00	0845	0845	1000	1201	1330	1330	1615	1715	1745	2015	2015	0	d.Boston ....a.
8.35	0945	0945	1105	1330	1430	1430	....	1820	....	2120	2120	113	d.Manchester ....d.
9.90	1015	1015	1135	1330	1505	1505	1740	1855	1900	2140s	2140	140	d.Concord ....d.
12.70	1045	....	1205	1400	1530s	1530s	1805	1920s	....	2205s	....	171	d.Franklin (Tilton Junction)..d.
13.50	1100	....	1225	1225	1545	1545s	....	1940	....	2225	....	190	d. Laconia ....d.
	1210	....	....	....	1655	....	....	....	2055	....	....	256	d. Conway ....d.
18.10	....	....	....	....	....	....	....	2105s	....	....	....	256	d. North Conway ....d.
22.15	....	....	....	....	....	....	....	2155	....	....	....	312	a. Berlin ....a.
14.40	....	....	1430	....	1830	....	....	....	....	....	....	203	d.Plymouth ....d.
17.55	....	....	1520	....	1920s	....	....	....	....	....	....	258	d.Franconia ....d.
18.60	....	....	1530	....	1930	....	....	....	....	....	....	271	a.Littleton ◇ ....d.

	21 ex⑤	23 ⑤	25	8	31A ex⑥⑦Ⓐ	31 ⑤⑥⑦	33	35A ⑤⑥⑦	35	37 ⑦	km	
d.Boston Logan Airport..a.	1045	1145	1250	1520	1700	1700	1900	1945	1945	2145	7	
d.Boston ....a.	1030	1125	1230	1500	1630	1630	1840	1930	1930	2130	0	
d.Manchester ....d.	0930	....	1130	1400	1530	1530	1730	1830	1830	2030	113	
d.Concord ....d.	0900	1000	1100	1330	1500	1500	1700	1800	1800	2000	140	
d.Franklin ....d.	0825	....	1030	1300	....	....	1625	....	1725	1925	171	
d.Laconia ....d.	0810	....	....	1245	....	....	1610	....	....	1910	190	
d.Conway ....d.	....	0750	....	....	....	1250	....	....	....	1750	256	
a.Berlin ....a.	....	0650	....	....	....	....	....	....	....	....	312	
d.Plymouth ....d.	....	....	1000	....	....	....	1700	....	....	....	203	
d.Franconia ....d.	....	....	0900	....	....	....	1550	....	....	....	258	
a.Littleton ◇ ....d.	....	....	0850	....	....	....	1545	....	....	....	271	

>—For Mt. Washington Cog Railway.   CLI–Concord Trailways.

Table 340 — CLEVELAND - CHARLESTON - JACKSONVILLE (GL LFL)

US $	GL 1093	GL 1099	LFL 13	GL 1097	LFL 11	km	
0.00	....	1045	1615	1715	1925	0	d.Cleveland ....a.
8.00	....	1201	1700	1830	2010	55	d.Akron ....d.
12.00	....	1235	....	1910	....	94	d.Canton ....d.
24.00	....	1450	....	2045	....	293	d.Cambridge ....d.
34.00	....	1620	....	2210	....	397	d.Parkersburg ....d.
43.00	0630	1815	....	0005	....	518	d.Charleston ....d.
	0825	2000	....	0110	....		d.Beckley ....d.
61.00	0930	2105	....	0210	....	658	d.Bluefield ....d.
67.00	1115	2230	....	0325	....	758	d.Wytheville ....d.
77.00	1340	0045	....	....	....	887	d.Winston Salem ....d.
82.00	1615	0315	0700	....	....	1002	d.Charlotte ....d.
92.00	1830	0545	0930	....	....	1146	d.Columbia ....d.
	1925	....	1025	....	....		d.Orangeburg ....d.
04.00	2330	0925	1355	....	....	1381	d.Savannah ....d.
		1045	1515	....	....		d.Brunswick ....d.
18.00	0150	1215	1645	....	....	1618	a.Jacksonville ....d.

US $	LFL 12	GL 1096	LFL 10	GL 1090	GL 1092	km	
0.00	1110	....	1550	1745	0115	0	d.Cleveland ....a.
8.00	1005	....	1445	1635	0030	55	d.Akron ....d.
12.00	....	....	....	1550	2350	94	d.Canton ....d.
24.00	....	....	....	1420	2220	293	d.Cambridge ....d.
34.00	....	....	....	1220	2045	397	d.Parkersburg ....d.
43.00	0300	....	....	1045	1915	518	d.Charleston ....d.
	0150	....	....	0900	1730		d.Beckley ....d.
61.00	0040	....	....	0700	1540	658	d.Bluefield ....d.
67.00	2340	....	....	0600	1440	758	d.Wytheville ....d.
77.00	2125	....	....	....	1230	887	d.Winston Salem ....d.
82.00	1915	....	....	0315	1015	1002	d.Charlotte ....d.
92.00	1700	....	....	0035	0730	1146	d.Columbia ....d.
	1500	....	....	2310	....		d.Orangeburg ....d.
04.00	1130	....	....	2020	....	1381	d.Savannah ....d.
	0830	....	....	1845	0200		d.Brunswick ....d.
18.00	0715	....	....	1715	0030	1618	a.Jacksonville ....d.

GL–Greyhound Lines.   LFL–Lake Front Trailways.

Table 341 — RICHMOND - NORFOLK (CCC GL)

US $	CCC 552	GL 3463	GL 3465	CCC 546	CCC 542	CCC 544	GL 3467	CCC 548	km	
0.00	0045	0645	0945	1255	1545	1600	1845	2245	0	d.Richmond ....a.
	0145	0745	1045	1355	....	1700	1945	2345		d.Williamsburg ....d.
	s	0845	1150	1455	....	1800	2050	0040		d.Newport News ....d.
	s	0905	1210	1515	....	1820	2105	0055		d.Hampton ....d.
20.00	....	1010	....	....	1835	....	....	0140		a.Portsmouth ....d.
20.00	0310	0940	1240	1550	1850	1850	2135	0120	151	a.Norfolk ....d.

	CCC 547	CCC 541	CCC 545	GL 3468	GL 3470	CCC 549	CCC 543	GL 3472	km	
d.Richmond ....a.	0940	1045	1340	1445	1800	2040	2345	0210	0	
d.Williamsburg ....d.	0840	....	1240	1345	1700	1940	2245	0110		
d.Newport News ....d.	0740	....	1140	1245	1600	1845	2150	0020		
d.Hampton ....d.	0720	....	1120	1225	1540	1825	2130	2359		
a.Portsmouth ....d.	....	0755	1030	....	....	2030	....	....		
a.Norfolk ....d.	0645	0745	1050	1155	1510	1755	2100	2330	151	

CCC– Carolina Trailways.   GL– Greyhound Lines.

Table 342 — NEW YORK/PHILADELPHIA - WILLIAMSPORT 🚌 FMT SHT

US $	SHT 23	SHT 13	FMT 3	FMT 5	FMT 61	FMT 15	FMT 21	SHT 11	SHT 15	FMT 35	FMT 39	km	↓ ↑	FMT 16	SHT 20	SHT 10	FMT 20	SHT 22	FMT 14	SHT 60	FMT 22	SHT 12	FMT 40	FMT 44
					☆				⑤⑦										⑤⑦				ex⑦	⑦
30.00	....	0730	0830	1100	1320	1515	....	1600	1840	1900	2300	389	d.New York..........a.	1000	....	1215	1255	1545	1630	1715	....	2100	2120	2355
29.00	....	0800			1350		....					373	d.Newark..............d.		....				1636		....	2020s		
23.00	....	0845			1440		....	1710				327	d.Somerville ....d.		....	1100s			s		....	1945s		
	....	0935					....	1800				323	d.Easton.................d.		....	s					....	1900		
20.70	0745				1630		....					323	d. Philadelphia..........a.	1155	....					2035	....			
20.70	r				s		....					310	d. Quakertown ....a.		....					1850s	....			
17.50	0945				1810		....					226	d. Allentown ....d.	1025	....					1835	....			
16.35	1050	1050			1910	1910	....					190	d.Lehighton ....d.	0915	0915					1730	1730			
			1020	1230	1600	1700			2015	2020	0035		d. Stroudsburg........d.	0830		1110	1405	1500	1430			1940	2215
		1130						1945	2115				d.Hazleton...............d.		0840		1355			1715			
5.90	1305					2105	s	s				65	d. Sunbury ....d.		0700		1205	1515					
0.00	1355	1330					2130	2300				0	d.Williamsport..........d.		0630		1125	1415	1500				

FMT–Martz Trailways.   SHT–Susquehanna Trailways.

Table 345 — NORFOLK - RALEIGH 🚌 CCC

US $	551	105	303	309	305	343	559	311	km	↓ ↑	304	554	340	310	104	312	300
0.00	....	....	0800	1115	1600	....	....	1800	0	d.Norfolk...............a.	....	1410	....	1755	....	2240	0500
	....	....	0810	1125	1610	....	....	1810		d.Portsmouth.........d.	....	1355	....	1740	....	s	s
12.00	....	....	1300			....	....			d.Murfreesboro........d.	....		....	1620	....		
28.00	0340	....	1120	1450	1915	....	2115	2110		d.Rocky Mount........d.	....	1105	1445	1445	....	1920	0205
31.00	....	1110		1520	1940	....	....			d.Wilson................d.	....	1030		1740	....		0130
	....	....				1705	....			d. Cedar Island........d.	....				....		
	....	....				1810	....			d. Morehead City.......a.	....	1635			....		
	0505	....				1905	2300			d. New Bern...........d.	....	1535			....		
	....	....				1945	....			d. Kinston...............d.	....	1255	1435		....		
33.00	....	1230	1230	1620	2040	2105	....	2220		d. Goldsboro...........d.	....		1355		....		
										a.Raleigh...............d.	....	0930		1230	1315	1630	1800	0030

CCC– Carolina Trailways.

Table 347 — BETHLEHEM/READING - PHILADELPHIA 🚌 BI CPB

US $		km		CPB 42	BI 301	BI 303	CPB 30	BI 401	BI 305	CPB 32	BI 307	BI 403	BI 405	CPB 34	BI 309	BI 407
				Ⓐ	Ⓐ	Ⓐ		Ⓒ	Ⓐ		Ⓐ	Ⓒ	Ⓒ	Ⓐ	Ⓐ	Ⓒ
18.00	Pottsville ....d.	155	....	0500			0620			1010			1520			
12.00	Reading ◇......d.	100	....	0600		0530	0730	0700	0735	1120	1030	1100	1500	1640		1900
8.00	Pottstown ....d.	65	....	0625			0755			1145			1715			
	King of Prussia a.		....				0835			1220			1750			
9.00	Kutztown ◇.......d.	126	....		0500	0600		0730	0800		1100	1130	1530		1655	1930
6.00	Allentown ◇.......d.	97	....		0535	0640		0810	0840		1140	1210	1610		1740	2010
6.00	Bethlehem ....d.	87	....		0550	0655		0825	0855		1155	1225	1625		1755	2025
5.50	Quakertown ....d.	68	....		0615	0720		0850	0920		1220	1250	1650		1820	2050
0.00	Philadelphia......a.	0	....	0730	0735	0840	0910	1000	1040	1255	1340	1400	1800	1825	1940	2200

			BI 302	CPB 29	BI 402		BI 304	BI 404	CPB 33	BI 306		CPB 43	BI 308	BI 406	CPB 37	BI 310	BI 408
			Ⓐ		Ⓒ		Ⓐ	Ⓐ	Ⓒ	Ⓐ			Ⓐ	Ⓒ	Ⓐ	Ⓒ	Ⓒ
Philadelphia..........d.		....	0900	0935	1050	....	1400	1450	1510	1600	....	1645	1730	1850	1915	2100	2250
Quakertown...........d.		....	1020		1210	....	1520	1610		1720	....		1825	2010		2220	0010
Bethlehem............a.		....	1045		1235	....	1545	1635		1745	....		1915	2035		2245	0035
Allentown.............a.		....	1100		1250	....	1600	1650		1800	....		1930	2050		2300	0050
Kutztown ◇ ....a.		....	1140		1330	....	1655	1730		1840	....		2000	2130		2340	0130
King of Prussia ......d.		....		1010		....				1550	....			1950		
Pottstown............d.		....		1045		....				1630	....	1735		2025		
Reading ◇...........a.		....	1230	1115	1400	....		1800		1700	1930	1805	2030	2200	2055	0030	0200
Pottsville ....a.		....		1230		....				1805	....	1910		2155		

◇– BI also operate an express Reading-Kutztown-New York service (203 km; journey: 3 hours; fare: US $: 6.50) **from Reading** at 0500Ⓒ, 0530Ⓐ, 0630Ⓐ, 0700, 0730Ⓐ, 0900Ⓢ, 0930Ⓐ, 1030Ⓐ, 1100Ⓒ, 1200Ⓐ, 1300Ⓒ, 1330Ⓐ, 1500Ⓒ, 1530Ⓐ, 1700Ⓒ, 1730Ⓐ, 1900; **from New York** at 0830Ⓐ, 0930Ⓐ, 1100Ⓒ, 1200Ⓐ, 1300Ⓒ, 1330Ⓐ,

1500Ⓒ, 1530Ⓐ, 1630Ⓐ, 1700, 1730Ⓐ, 1830Ⓐ, 1900Ⓒ, 1930Ⓐ, 2100Ⓒ, 2130Ⓐ, 2330
BI– Carl R. Bieber Tourways.
CPB– Capitol Trailways.

Table 348 — NEW YORK - ALLENTOWN 🚌 NJTB OAE TBR

US$	TBR		102/202	204	104/206	208	106/210	108/212	110/214	114/216	116	118	120/218	122	126/220	128	130	132	134/222	136/224	138/226	140/228	230	142/232	234
		km	☆	Ⓒ	☆	Ⓒ					Ⓐ	Ⓐ	Ⓐ	Ⓐ	Ⓐ	Ⓐ	Ⓐ						†		⑦
	New York Kennedy Airport .d.													1545				1730	1845					
0.00	New York ★......d.	0	0800	0900	1000	1050	1200	1400	1500	1600	1630	1640	1710	1720	1730	1740	1750	1810	1830	1900	2000	2125	2215	2330	2359
2.15	Newark Intl. Airport ★d.	17	0830	0930	1030		1230	1430		1630							1855		2155		2000		0040
	Clinton.................d.		0920	1020	1120	1205	1325	1525	1610	1725	1740		1820		1840	1900	1920	1950	2010	2110	2245	2325	2350	0050	0140
	Easton.................d.		0940	1040	1140	1220	1345	1545	1635	1745	1805s		1845		1900b		1945	2010	2030	2135	2305	2345	0110	0200
9.55	Bethlehem..........a.	153	1000	1100	1200	1240	1405	1605	1655	1805		1835		1900s	1910	1920b	1940	1955	2005	2030	2050e	2155e	2325e	0005	0130s	0220s
9.95	Allentown..........a.	161	1030	1130	1240a	1310	1435	1620	1725	1835	1835		1930c		1940d		2100	2120	2225	2355		0200	s

	TBR		101	103/201	105	109	113	111	115/203	121	123/205	207	125/209	211	127/213	129/215	131/217	219	133/221	223	135/225	227	137/229	231	233	139/235	237
			Ⓐ	Ⓐ	☆	Ⓐ	Ⓒ	Ⓐ		Ⓐ		Ⓐ		Ⓐ	Ⓐ		Ⓐ	Ⓐ	Ⓐ	Ⓐ	Ⓐ	Ⓐ	Ⓐ	Ⓐ	Ⓐ	Ⓐ	Ⓐ
Allentown.............d.			0515		0550		0605	0600b		0715	0745	0800	0830	0915	1030	1210	1315	1330	1445	1515	1630	1715	1800	1900	1925	2130
Bethlehem............d.			0510	0530	0555		0615		0630	0725	0745	0800	0830	0900	0930	1100	1245	1330	1400	1500	1545	1645	1750	1830	1930	1955	2200
Easton.................d.			0525	0550		0625		0650		0805		0850	0920	0950	1120	1305	1350	1420	1520	1605	1705	1810	1850	1950	2015	2215
Clinton.................d.			0550	0615		0650	0705	0715		0830	0845	0915	1005	1015	1145	1335	1415	1445	1545	1630	1730	1815	1915	2010	2040	2235
Newark Intl. Airport ★..a.				0710s					0810bs		0925s		1040s		1240s		1510s		1640s	1725s	1825s	1930s		2135s	2325s
New York ★.........a.			0710	0740	0755	0810	0815	0825	0840f	0925	0955	1000	1110	1130	1310	1430	1540	1610	1710	1755	1855	2000	2030	2135	2205	2355
New York Kennedy Airport a.													1240		1600		1720					

US $	2	4	302/6	6	8	12	16	310	22	24	312	km	↓ TBR ↑	7	301	13	303	15	17	307	19	21	311	313
	Ⓐ	Ⓐ	Ⓒ	Ⓑ	Ⓢ	Ⓐ	Ⓒ	Ⓐ	Ⓒ	Ⓐ	Ⓒ			Ⓐ	Ⓒ	Ⓐ	Ⓒ	Ⓐ	Ⓐ	Ⓒ	Ⓐ	Ⓐ	Ⓒ	Ⓒ
0.00	0735	0945	1015	1300	1530	1640	1715	1730	1900	2015	2015	0	d.New York................a.	0820	1000	1110	1325	1410	1600	1755	1805	1940	1950	2110
		1015	1045	1330			1800		2045	2045		17	d.Newark International Airport a.		0930s	1035s	1255s	1340s	1530s	1725s		1910s	1920s	2040s
	0910	1140	1210g	1450	1740	1830	1900	1925	2045	2205	s		d.Lambertville.............d.	0630	0805	0915	1125	1220	1405	1530	1550	1750	1725	1900
	0940	1210	1240g	1525	1810	1900	1930	1955	2115	2235	s		d.Doylestown.............d.	0600	0735	0845	1055	1150	1335	1500	1520	1720	1655	1830
			1305g	1550	1835	1925	1955	2020	2140	s			d.Quakertown............d.	0535	0710	0810	1030		1435	1455	1655	1630	1805
			1340g	1625	1910	2000	2030	2055	2215	s	s		a.Bethlehem.............a.		0640	0735	1000		1405	1420	1620	1600	1735

a–1230 on Ⓐ.   **b**–Ⓒ only.   **c**–1920 on Ⓐ.   **d**–Ⓐ only.   **e**–Note **s** applies on Ⓒ.   frequent to 2359.   **NJTB**–New Jersey Transit.
f–0830 on Ⓐ.   **g**–30 mins. later on Ⓒ.   ★–Local services (NJTB 300) New York-Newark   **OAE**– Olympia Airport Express.
International Airport and v.v. every 15 mins (30-90 mins. at night); also by OAE at 0500 and   **TBR**– Trans-Bridge Lines.

Table 349   PHILADELPHIA - ATLANTIC CITY   GL NJTB

services operate Philadelphia-Camden (*NJTB* only)-Sicklerville (*NJTB* only)-Atlantic City and v v *94* km. Journey: 1½-2 hours. Fare: US $: 12.00

rom Philadelphia: *GL* at 0700, 0930, 1015, 1130, 1330, 1400, 1515, 1745, 1845, 2000, 2030, 2130, 2230⑤⑥; *NJTB* **551/5** at 0050, 0220, 0350, 0450, 0550, 0620, 0650, 0720, 0750, 0820,
0850, 0920, 0950, 1020, 1050, 1120, 1150, 1220, 1250, 1320, 1350, 1420, 1450, 1520, 1550, 1620, 1650, 1720⑥, 1750, 1820, 1850, 1920, 1950, 2020, 2050, 2120, 2150, 2220, 2250, 2350.

rom Atlantic City: *GL* at 0130, 0400, 0645⑥⑦, 0830, 1130, 1430, 1730, 1745, 1815, 1930, 2010, 2115, 2245, 2115, 2215; *NJTB* **551** at 0040, 0140, 0240, 0340, 0410, 0440, 0510, 0540,
0610⑥, 0640, 0710⑥, 0740, 0810, 0840, 0910, 0940, 1040, 1110, 1140, 1210, 1240, 1310, 1340, 1410, 1440, 1510, 1540, 1610, 1640, 1710, 1740, 1840, 1910, 1940, 2010, 2040,
2140, 2240, 2340.

GL–Greyhound Lines.   *NJTB*–New Jersey Transit.

Table 350   NEW YORK - ATLANTIC CITY   GL NJTB

US $	421	435	447	km	*NJTB* 319	316	334	315
0.00	.... 1300	1800	2200	0	d.New York............a.	.... 1125	1625	2025 ....
	.... 1425	1925	2325	118	d.Tom's River............d.	.... 1000	1500	1900 ....
23.00	.... 1535	2035	0035	206	d.Atlantic City............d.	.... 0900	1400	1800 ....
	.... 1605	2105	0105	222	d.Ocean City............d.	.... 0819	1319	1719 ....
	.... 1702	2202	0202	264	d.Wildwood............d.	.... 0722	1222	1622 ....
	.... 1732	2232	0232	274	a.Cape May............d.	.... 0652	1152	1552 ....

service *(GL)* operates New York - Atlantic City and v.v. *207* km. Journey: 2½-3 hours. Fare: US $: 23.00.
rom New York: 0745, 0815, 0845⑦, 0900, 0930ex③④, 1000, 1030, 1045⑥⑦, 1100, 1130ex④⑤, 1201, 1230, 1300ex②③, 1330, 1400, 1430⑥, 1500, 1530, 1600, 1630, 1700, 1730, 1800, 1830⑤⑥, 1900, 1930, 2000, 2030, 2115, 2200⑤⑥, 2230⑤⑥, 2330⑤⑥.
rom Atlantic City: 0030, 0100, 0200, 0230, 0330, 0400⑥⑦, 0430, 0500, 0600⑧⑦, 0615⑥⑦, 0700⑧⑦, 0800, 1000, 1130, 1230, 1330⑥⑦, 1430, 1530, 1630, 1700ex④③, 1730, 1800⑦, 1830ex③④, 1900, 1930, 2000⑧⑦, 2030, 2100ex④⑤, 2130ex②③, 2200, 2300, 2330⑥.

service *(NJTB 319)* operates New York-Tom's River-Atlantic City and v.v. *206* km. Journey: 2½ hours. Fare: US $: 23.00.
rom New York: 0000, 0800, 0900⑥, 1000, 1100, 1200, 1300, 1400, 1500, 1600, 1700, 1800, 1900, 2000, 2100, 2130, 2200, 2300⑻.
rom Atlantic City: 0030, 0415, 0600, 0630ex⑦, 0700, 0800, 0900, 1000, 1100, 1200, 1300, 1400, 1500, 1600, 1700, 1800, 2000, 2200, 2300.

service *(NJTB 102)* operates Atlantic City-Wildwood-Cape May and v.v. *65* km. Journey: 1½-2 hours. Fare: US $: ❖.
rom Atlantic City: 0020, 0820, 1020, 1220, 1420, 1620, 1820, 2020, 2220.
rom Cape May: 0601, 0759, 1001, 1201, 1401, 1601, 1801, 2001, 2203.

service *(NJTB A7)* operates Atlantic City-Ocean City and v.v. *15* km. Journey: 45 mins. Fare: US $: ❖.
From Atlantic City: 0010⑧, 0040©, 0110⑧, 0210, 0310, 0410©, 0415⑧, 0510©, 0527⑧, 0540©, 0607⑧, 0640©, 0707⑧, 0727©, 0740©, 0752⑧, 0840©, 0910⑧, 0940©, 1010⑧, 1040©, 1110⑧, 1140©, 1210⑧, 1240©, 1310⑧, 1340©, 1410⑧, 1440©, 1525⑧, 1540©, 1630⑧, 1640©, 1725⑧, 1740©, 1810⑧, 1840©, 1910⑧, 1940©, 2010⑧, 2040©, 2110⑧, 2210⑧, 2240©, 2310⑧, 2340©.
rom Ocean City: 0017⑧, 0044©, 0105⑧, 0141©, 0210⑧, 0305©, 0310⑧, 0404©, 0410⑧, 0510, 0604©, 0605⑧, 0644©, 0700⑧, 0739©, 0800⑧, 0828©, 0842©, 0900⑧, 0941©, 1010⑧, 1044©, 1100⑧, 1141©, 1211⑧, 1244©, 1309⑧, 1341©, 1421⑧, 1444©, 1521⑧, 1541©, 1621⑧, 1644©, 1726⑧, 1742©, 1819⑧, 1844©, 1914⑧, 1941©, 2014⑧, 2044©, 2114⑧, 2141©, 2215⑧, 2245©, 2341©.

GL–Greyhound Lines.   *NJTB*–New Jersey Transit.

Table 351   NEW YORK - GREENPORT   SE

US $	▽	Λ		☆		①③⑤	x	km		▽	Λ		☆	†	☆		①③⑤	x	
0.00	....	0830 0930	....	1100	....	1430	....	1830 2030 2145	0	d.New York............a.	....	0815 0845	....	1000 1030 1330 1700		2000 2130	....		....	
15.00	....	1100 1200	....	1330	....	1700	....	2100 2300 2345		a.Greenport............d.	....	0545 0545	....	0730 0800 1100 1430 1730		1900	....		....	

⑦–⑥ June 1-mid October.   x–† (also ⑥ June 1-mid October).   Λ–① June 1-Sept. 1.   *SE*–Sunrise Express.

Table 352   CLEVELAND - CINCINNATI   GL LFL

US $				GL	GL	GL	GL	GL	GL	LFL	GL
			km	1165	1167	1171	1173	1115	1109	11	589
0.00	Cleveland............d.	↓	0	0130	0530	0915	1300	1700	1900	1925	2230
20.00	Mansfield............d.		125			1445		2100			
25.00	Columbus............d.		219	0430	0845	1250	1645	2010	2300	2230	0125
40.00	Cincinnati............a.		394	0635	1035	1440	1900	2200	0050	0040	0315

93		GL	LFL	GL	GL	LFL	GL	GL	GL	GL
		580	12	1176	1152	10	1170	1174	4816	592
Cincinnati............d.		0145	0530	0610	0830	1020	1100	1515		1815	2115
Columbus............d.		0400	0750	0900	1100	1230	1315	1800		2050	0010
Mansfield............d.				1020						2205	
Cleveland............a.		0625	1110	1159	1325	1550	1610	2040		2330	0235

GL–Greyhound Lines.   *LFL*–Lake Front Trailways.

Table 353   AUGUSTA - SAVANNAH   SES

US $	301		121		km	↓	↑		100	200
0.00	1130	....	1510	....	0	d.Augusta............a.	....	1115	1715	....
	1305	....	1630	....		d.Sylvania............a.	....	0940	1545	....
	1415	....	1740	....		a.Savannah............d.	....	0830	1445	....

SES– Southeastern Stages.

Table 354   WASHINGTON - NORFOLK   JRB

US $					km	↓	↑			
0.00	....	....	....	....	0	d.Washington......a.	....			
20.00	....	....	....	....	161	d.Warsaw............d.	....			
28.00	....	....	....	....	276	d.Yorktown............d.	....			
32.00	....	....	....	....	309	a.Newport News...d.	....			
35.00	....	....	....	....	351	a.Norfolk............d.	....			
35.00	....	....	....	....	365	a.Portsmouth............d.	....			

JRB– James River Bus Lines.

Table 355   DULUTH - ST. IGNACE   DTA JJL WPT

US$	JJL		WPT	JJL		km	↓	↑		JJL	WPT	JJL
			1502								1501	
0.00	....	....	1915	....		0	d.Duluth ◇............a.		0720	....	....
24.00	....	....	1925	....		7	d.Superior ◇............a.		0710	....	....
13.00	....	....	2055	....		112	d.Ashland............d.		0540	....	....
22.00	....	....	2145	....		174	d.Ironwood............d.		0450	....	....
	....	....	2350	....			d.Iron River............d.		0305	....	....
40.00	....	....	0050	....		379	d.Iron Mountain...d.		0210	....	....
50.00	....	....	0250	....		462	d.Escanaba............d.		0205	....	....
67.00	2215	....	0600	0700		462	a.St Ignace............d.	2200	2245	....	0650
	2315	....		0750			a.Sault Ste. Marie M...d.	2115		....	0600

◇–Regular local service *(DTA 16)* operates between Duluth and Superior 0536⑧/
⑥10⑥–1825⑥/1848⑥. ☒–$0.60 by DTA.   *DTA*–Duluth Transit Authority.   *JJL*–J&J
imo.   *WPT*–White Pine Bus Service.

Table 356   GETTYSBURG   CPB GL

US $	CPB	GL	CPB	CPB			CPB	GL	CPB	GL
	201	7933	203	205	km		202	7932	204	208
						↓				
	0745		1315	1725		d.New York............a.	1055	....	1450	2005
						d.Newark Intnl Airport...a.				
0.00		1215			225	d. Philadelphia............a.		1225		
3.45	1010	1250	1545	1950	191	d.King of Prussia...a.	0830	1150s	1220	1745
13.00	1125	1440	1700	2105	97	d.Lancaster............d.	0715	1005	1105	1625
19.00	1205	1545	1740	2140	58	d.York............d.	0635	0910	1025	1540
22.00		1605			0	d.Gettysburg............d.		0755		
	1240	1740	1815	2210		a.Harrisburg............d.	0600	0700	0950	1500

CPB–Capitol Trailways.   *GL*–Greyhound Lines.

Table 357   VALLEY FORGE   SEPTA

service Philadelphia-King of Prussia-Valley Forge and v.v. *30* km. Journey: 1 hour 10
mins. Fare: US $: 3.10.
From Philadelphia to King of Prussia: 0510④/0600© and every 30 mins. (hourly on †
evenings) to 2100†/2130④/2300④.
From Philadelphia to Valley Forge: 0530④/0600© and about hourly to 2100©/2230④.
From King of Prussia: 0010②–⑥, 0020©, 0030②–⑥, 0550④/0700© and every 30 mins.
(hourly on † evenings) to 2335©/2350④.
From Valley Forge ◇: 0004②–⑥, 0643©, 0654© and about hourly to 1844④, 1854©,
1954☆, 2054, 2159④, 2205©, 2304④.
◇–Early morning and late evening (all day on ©) operates to/from Valley Forge Sheraton,
and **not** Valley Forge National Park.
SEPTA–Southeastern Pennsylvania Transportation Authority.

Table 358   GRAND RAPIDS - DETROIT   GL

US $	5095	5089	5091	5093			5088	5090	5092	5094
					km	↓	↑			
0.00	0600	1015	1315	1700	0	d.Muskegon............a.	1245	1635	1940	2335
8.00					58	d. Holland............d.				
10.00	0710	1140	1440	1810	64	d.Grand Rapids ..d.	1130	1530	1840	2235
21.00	0830	1305	1605	1930	170	d.Lansing............d.	1010	1410	1715	2115
21.00	0840	1315	1615	1940	176	d.East Lansing............d.	0950	1350	1700	2100
33.00	1040	1515	1815	2140	302	a.Detroit............d.	0745	1145	1500	1900

GL– Greyhound Lines.

Table 359   ST. LOUIS - NASHVILLE   GL

US $	1231	1233	1235	1237			1236	1230	1232	1234
					km	↓	↑			
0.00	0030	0615	1345	1930	0	d.St. Louis............a.	1645	2210	0120	0605
1.90					6	d.East St. Louis............a.				
4.00		0650	1420		27	d.Belleville............d.	1610			0530
14.75	0200	0840	1610		132	d.Mount Vernon............d.	1450	2045		0410
33.00	0400	1140	1900		277	d.Evansville............d.	1205	1850		0210
	0745	1530	2245	0235		a.Nashville............d.	0745	1445	1830	2215

GL– Greyhound Lines.

Table 360 ANNAPOLIS — MTA

service Baltimore◇-Patapsco-Annapolis and v.v. *41* km. Journey: 1¼ hours. Fare: US $: 1.50.
From Patapsco: 0532Ⓐ/0610⑥ and frequent (about hourly on ⑥) to 2110⑥/2237Ⓐ.
From Annapolis: 0554Ⓐ/0754⑥ and frequent (about hourly on ⑥) to 2242⑥/2359Ⓐ.
Direct Baltimore-Annapolis and v.v.
From Baltimore: 0543Ⓐ, 0613Ⓐ, 0635†, 0805†, 0935†, 1105†, 1235†, 1405†, 1535†, 1603Ⓐ, 1626Ⓐ, 1641Ⓐ, 1703Ⓐ, 1705†, 1746Ⓐ, 1835†.
From Annapolis: 0620Ⓐ, 0640Ⓐ, 0700Ⓐ, 0720Ⓐ, 0745Ⓐ, 0810†, 0940†, 1110†, 1240†, 1410†, 1540†, 1710†, 1716Ⓐ, 1840†, 2010†.

◇– By between Baltimore and Patapsco on ⚒.
MTA– Maryland Mass Transit Administration.

Table 361 RICHMOND - JACKSONVILLE — GL

US $	1043	1045	1047		km	↓ ↑	1048		1046	1044
		⑥					⑦			
0.00	0105	0410	0930	....	*0*	d.**Richmond**........a.	1740	....	2030	0245
6.00	|	|	1010	....	*36*	d.Petersburg.........d.	1700	....	1950	|
	0330	0645	1240	....		d.Rocky Mount.....d.	1500	....	1750	0025
◇10.00	|	|	|	....	★*128*	d. **Raleigh**...........a.	|	....	|	|
36.00	0435	0800	1355	....	*258*	d.Goldsboro..........d.	1345	....	1635	2320
	0515	0910	1435	....		d.Warsaw.............d.	1255	....	1540	2235
50.00	0630	1035	1600	....	*409*	d.Wilmington........d.	1130	....	1430	2125
53.00	0915	1315	1845	....	*524*	d.Myrtle Beach.....d.	0845	....	1145	1840
64.00	1145	1530	2115	....	*676*	d.North Charlestond.	0615	....	0915	1615
77.00	1500	....	0020	....	*846*	a.Savannah..........d.	....	....	0615	....
92.00	1830	....	0345	....	*1061*	a.**Jacksonville**.....d.	....	....	0315	....

◇–Fare ex Goldsboro. ★–Km ex Goldsboro. *GL*–Greyhound Lines.

Table 362 JACKSONVILLE - ST. PETERSBURG — GL

US $	3741	3737	3743	3739	3733	3745	3731	3747	1005	3751	3753	km	↓ ↑	3748	3680	3730	3734	3742	3736	3744	3740	3738	3750	3746
0.00	0220	0415	0415	0700	1000	1300	1315	1300	....	1730	1930	*0*	d.**Jacksonville**............a.	0645	1305	1315	1630	1630	2050	2050	....	2315	2330	0230
13.00	|	0550	|	|	|	|	1455	|	....	|	|		d. Gainesville.............d.	|	|	1135	|	|	|	|	....	2140	|	|
19.00	|	|	0610	0845	1155	|	|	1535	....	1940	2130		d.Daytona Beach.........d.	0455	1100	|	1430	|	1820	1910	....	|	2140	|
21.00	|	0710	|	|	|	|	1615	|	....	|	|		d. Ocala.....................d.	|	|	1045	|	|	|	|	....	2050	|	|
26.00	0525	|	0800	1045	1330	1600	|	1730	1815	2130	2300		d.Orlando *(Disney World)*.d.	0345	0900	|	1230	1345	1615	1800	1945	|	2030	0001
	|	|	|	1125	|	1640	|	....	|	|	....		d.Kissimmee................d.	|	....	|	1105	|	....	|	|	|	|	|
	0630	|	0900	1220	|	1730	|	....	|	2235	....		d.Winter Haven............d.	0155	....	|	1010	|	....	|	1830	|	|	|
35.00	0700	|	0930	1250	|	1800	|	....	|	2305	....		d.Lakeland...................d.	0120	....	|	0940	|	....	|	1800	|	|	|
36.00	0800	1045	1030	1350	1510	1845	1835	....	1955	2359	....		a.**Tampa**.......................d.	0030	....	0645	0845	1120	....	1530	1700	1800	1800	2130
39.00	*0930*	1015	|	*1500*	|	1945	*1930*	....	|	|	....		a.Clearwater.................d.	....	....	0715	0800	....	....	|	1615	|	|	2045
39.00	*1000*	*1135*	1135	*1530*	1635	2015	*2000*	....	2045	*0100*	....		a.**St. Petersburg**..........d.	....	....	....	0730	....	....	1440	1545	*1645*	1645	2015

GL– Greyhound Lines.

Table 363 PHILADELPHIA - NORFOLK — CCC GL HCS

US $	↓	km		CCC 903	CCC 923	HCS 15 ex②③④		CCC 925	CCC 901	
	New York...........d.		....	0830**a**	*1100***a**	....	....	*1500***a**	2100**a**	....
0.00	**Philadelphia**........d.	*0*	....	*1015*	1330	....	....	1730	*2230*	....
6.00	Wilmington...........d.	*46*	....	1135	1445	....	....	1845	2350	....
	State Road...........d.		....	**r**	**r**	1615	....	**r**	**r**	....
13.00	Dover...................d.	*120*	....	1250	1605	|	....	2000	0105	....
17.00	Harrington............d.	*149*	....	1320	1635	|	....	2025	0130	....
22.00	Salisbury..............d.	*212*	....	1430	1745	1945	....	2145	0235	....
40.00	**Norfolk**................a.	*404*	....	1740	2055	....	....	0035	0520	....

↓			HCS ex②③④	CCC 904	CCC 920		CCC 924			CCC 902
Norfolk.......................d.	....	....	....	0900	1430	....	1815	....	....	2300
Salisbury.....................d.	....	....	1100	1220	1750	....	2130	....	....	0200
Harrington...................d.	....	....	|	1320	1850	....	2230	....	....	|
Dover...........................d.	....	....	|	1350	1920	....	2300	....	....	**s**
State Road...................a.	....	....	1425	**r**	**r**	....	**r**	....	....	**r**
Wilmington...................a.	....	....	....	1505	2035	....	0015	....	....	0410
Philadelphia..............a.	....	....	....	*1615*	2135	....	0115	....	....	*0520*
New York...................a.	....	....	....	1805**a**	....	....	....	....	....	0710**a**

US $	957	953	971	955	km	CCC ↓ ↑	950	970	952	954
24.00	....	....	1815	....	*0*	d.**Washington**......a.	....	1555	....	....
20.00	0915	1435	|	1830		d. **Baltimore**.......a.	1130	|	1540	2045
18.00	|	|	1855	|	*31*	d.Annapolis..........d.	|	1505	|	|
	1020	1540	1935	1935		d.Stevensville.......d.	1025	1440	1440	1945
5.00	1225	1740	|	2125	*167*	d.Salisbury...........d.	0830	|	1245	1750
11.00	|	|	2035	....	*122*	d. Harrington.....d.	|	1320	....	|
7.00	|	|	**s**	....	*177*	d. Lewes...........d.	|	**r**	....	|
6.00	|	|	2125	....	*190*	d. Rehoboth Beachd.	|	1205	....	|
0.00	1305	1830	2210	....	*232*	a.**Ocean City**.......d.	0730	1120	....	1700

a–*GL*. *CCC*–Carolina Trailways. *GL*–Greyhound Lines. *HCS*–Handy's Charter Service.

Table 364 BALTIMORE - PITTSBURGH — GL

US $		4705 ex④	4621 ex②	4709 ex③	km	↓ ↑	4704 ex③	4620 ex④	4706 ex②	
0.00	....	0540	....	1115	*0*	d.**Baltimore**..........a.	1450	....	2055	....
13.00	....	0745	....	1315	*148*	d.Hagerstown.......d.	1300	....	1905	....
24.00	....	0910	....	1440	*214*	d.Cumberland.......d.	1120	....	1725	....
	....	0950	....	1520		d.Grantsville.........d.	1035	....	1640	....
34.00	....	|	....	1625	*306*	a.Uniontown.........d.	0935	....	|	....
37.00	....	|	1100	1740	*371*	a.**Pittsburgh**........d.	0815	1530	|	....
	....	|	1215	....		d. Uniontown.......d.	....	1420	|	....
	....	1100	1310	....		d. Morgantown....d.	....	1325	1535	....
	....	1205	1415	....		a. **Clarksburg**.....d.	....	1215	1430	....

GL– Greyhound Lines.

Table 365 ST. IGNACE - DETROIT — GL

US $	5137	5129	5139	5169	km	↓ ↑	5130	5166	5128	5140
50.00	....	....	0525	....	*486*	d.St. Ignace..........a.	1755	....	....	....
50.00	....	....	0540	....	*475*	d.**Mackinaw City**.a.	1740	....	....	....
	....	....	0620	....		d.Petoskey...........d.	1655	....	....	....
	....	....	0810	1201		d.Traverse City.....d.	1525	2240	....	....
	....	....	0915	1305		d.Cadillac.............d.	1410	2135	....	....
	....	....	1030	1430		d.Clare.................d.	1255	2030	....	....
	....	....	|	1700		d. Lansing...........d.	|	1750	....	....
	....	....	|	1745		d. Jackson...........d.	|	1705	....	....
	....	....	|	1835		d. Ann Arbor.......d.	|	1610	....	....
	....	....	|	1900		d. Ypsilanti..........d.	|	1540	....	....
20.00	0745	0930	1220	|	*185*	d.Bay City............d.	1110	|	1800	2230
18.00	0810	0955	1245	|	*165*	d.Saginaw............d.	1035	|	1735	2205**s**
11.00	0900	1045	1335	|	*105*	d.Flint..................d.	0950	|	1650	2120
6.00	0950	1135	1425	|	*42*	d.Pontiac..............d.	0855	|	1555	2025
0.00	1050	1230	1520	1955	*0*	a.**Detroit**.............d.	0800	1445	1500	1930

GL– Greyhound Lines.

Table 366 RALEIGH - WINSTON SALEM - ASHEVILLE — CCC GL

US $	CCC 21		CCC 571	CCC 23		CCC 25		CCC 579	GL	CCC 39	CCC 525	km	↓ ↑		CCC 22	CCC 20	GL	CCC 576		CCC 12	CCC 38	CCC 524	GL 572	
0.00	2245	....	0800	1100	....	1400	....	1715	....	2120	....	*0*	d.**Raleigh**....................a.	....	0905	1215	....	1605	....	2130	2240	....	2350**b**	....
7.00	2320	....	0840	1140	....	1440	....	1755	....	2150	2155	*33*	d.Durham.....................d.	....	0825	1135	....	1525	....	2050	2200	2330	2310**b**	....
17.00	0045	....	1050	1345	....	1645	....	2000	....	....	2315	*130*	d.Greensboro...............d.	....	0635	0945	1245	1335	....	1910	....	2210	2200**b**	....
21.00	....	....	1215**a**	|	....	|	....	2040	2115	....	|	*159*	d.Winston Salem..........d.	....	|	|	|	1230	....	|	....	|	2115**b**	....
33.00	....	....	1340**a**	|	....	|	....	....	|	....	|		d.Hickory......................d.	....	|	|	|	....	....	|	....	|	1845	....
42.00	....	....	1525**a**	|	....	|	....	....	|	....	|	*389*	a.**Asheville**..................d.	....	|	|	|	....	....	|	....	|	1730	....
	....	....	....	1410	....	1710	....	....	|	....	2340		d. High Point...............d.	....	0600	0905	1215	....	....	1840	....	2130	....	....
	....	....	....	1505	....	1800	....	....	2205	....	....		d. Salisbury.................d.	....	....	0815	1125	....	....	1755	....	2040	....	....
	....	....	....	1530	....	1825	....	....	2230	....	....		d. Concord ϕ...............d.	....	....	0750	1100	....	....	1730	....	2015	....	....
	....	....	....	1600	....	1855	....	....	2300	....	....		a. **Charlotte**...............d.	....	....	0720	1030	....	....	1700	....	1945	....	....

a–*GL*. **b**–*CCC*. ϕ–Kannapolis. *CCC*–Carolina Trailways. *GL*–Greyhound Lines.

Table 367 NORFOLK - WILMINGTON — CCC

US $	551	387	557	559	km	↓ ↑	550	554	382	556
0.00	....	0545	....	....	*0*	d.**Norfolk**.............a.	....	....	2240	....
4.00	....	0555	....	....	*16*	d.Portsmouth........a.	....	....	2225	....
	0100	|	1140	1815		d. **Richmond**....a.	1350	1745	|	2330
	0135	|	1215	1850		d. Petersburg....a.	1315	1710	|	2255
11.00	|	0655	|	|	*84*	d.Elizabeth City....d.	|	|	2125	|
	|	0915	|	|		d.Washington........d.	|	|	1915	|
33.00	|	1005	|	|	*280*	d.New Bern..........d.	|	|	1815	|
	0600	1201	1730	2359		d.Jacksonville.......d.	0815	1201	1725	1800
	0630	|	1755	0025		a. Camp LeJeuned.	0745	1130	1630	....
43.00	....	1315	....	....	*424*	a.**Wilmington**......d.	....	....	1500	....

CCC– Carolina Trailways.

Table 368 KNOXVILLE - FAYETTEVILLE — GL

US $	4844	1111	589	4840	km	↓ ↑	4841	571	4843	4845
0.00	0150	0645	0910	1500	*0*	d.**Knoxville**..........a.	1250	1750	2215	0600
13.40	0355	0900	1120	1720	*168*	d.Asheville............d.	1040	1545	2010	0350
35.00	0750	1400	....	2100	*350*	d.Charlotte............d.	0700	....	1630	0040
48.00	**r**	**r**	....	....	*480*	d.Hamlet...............d.	....	....	**r**	**r**
56.00	1230	1840	....	....	*575*	d.**Fayetteville**.......d.	....	....	1215	2015
	r	**r**	....	....		d.Warsaw.............d.	....	....	**r**	**r**
	1455	2105	....	....		a.Jacksonville.......d.	....	....	0900	1715
	1525	2135	....	....		a.Camp LeJeune..d.	....	....	0830	1645

GL– Greyhound Lines.

Table 370 — STATE COLLEGE — GL

US $	4693	4691	4695		km	↓	↑	4694	4690	4692	4696
0.00	....	0715	1020	1315	0	d.Philadelphia ....a.		1225	1625	2140	....
4.00	....	0800	1100	1355	34	d.King of Prussia...a.		1145	1545	2100	....
2.00	....	1030	1400	1645	179	d.Harrisburg ....d.		1000	1400	1915	....
2.00	....	1145	1515	1755	244	d.Lewistown ....d.		0830	1210	1730	....
6.00	....	1235	1610	1840	277	d.State College......d.		0745	1125	1645	....
0.00	....	1340	1715	....	342	d.Altoona..............d.		....	1005	1530	....
0.00	....	1500	1835	....	407	d.Johnstown ....d.		....	0845	1405	....
0.00	....	1655	2030	....	496	a.Pittsburgh ....d.		....	0645	1215	....

L– Greyhound Lines.

Table 371 — DULUTH - THUNDER BAY — HTL

US $	20		km	↓	↑	21	
0.00	....	1300	0	d.Duluth ....a.		1205	....
	....	1600		d.Grand Marais ....d.		0930	....
	....	1815		d.Pigeon River ▩..d.		0830	....
	....	1900		a.Thunder Bay ....d.		0830	....

HTL– HT Leasing Thunder Bay Ltd.

Table 373 — DETROIT - TOLEDO - COLUMBUS/CINCINNATI — ABL GL

US $		GL 8153	ABL 213	GL 4601	GL 585	GL 4440	ABL 217	ABL 601	GL 1149	GL 4603	GL 8155	GL 1151	ABL 215	GL 8157		GL 1153	GL 1185		GL 4809	GL 1157		GL 1093	GL 1161	GL 4807
																			⑤⑦					
0.00	Detroit ....d.	0	....	0510	....	0745	0900	0930	....	1130	1130	....	1335	1400	....	1600	1600	....	1915	1915	....	2030	2200	2200
8.00	Lincoln Park ......d.	50	....		....	0805	0920	0950	....		1150	....	1355	1420	....		1620	....		1935	....	2050		
1.00	Toledo ....d.	99	....	0620	....	0915	1020	1050	....	1250	1300	....	1505	1520	....		1730	....		2045	....	2205		2315
20.95	Findlay ....d.	180	....		....	1020		....	....		1410	....	1555		....		1835	....		2135	....	2310		0001
24.00	Lima ....d.	237	....		....	1115		....	1330			....	1645		....		1925	....			....			
26.00	Marion ....d.	265	....		....			....	1500		1520	....			....			....			....	0015s		
33.00	Columbus ....d.	330	....	1000	....			....	1610		1750	....			....			....			....	0200		
39.00	Chillicothe ....d.	408	....	1110	....			....			1900	....			....			....			....	0250		
43.00	Portsmouth ......a.	479	....	1210	....			....			2000	....			....			....			....	0350		
34.00	Dayton ....d.	363	1045		....	1315		....			....	1600	1820	....	1830	2010	2110	....	2325	2350	....		0205	0215
41.00	Cincinnati ....a.	430	1155		....	1430		....	1645		....	1715	1925	....	1935	2120	2215	....	0035	0100	....		0310	0320

	GL 1160	GL 1146	ABL 210	GL 1162	GL 1168		GL 4804		GL 598	GL 1154	GL 1096		GL 8152	ABL 214	GL 4810	GL 4802	ABL 602	GL 8156	GL 1158	ABL 216	GL 4600	GL 4449	GL 4606	GL 8158
								⑥							⑤⑥⑦									
incinnati..............d.	1815	2115	....	0001	0145	....	0600		0600	0830	....		0915	....	1115	1115	....	1445	1500	....			1700	....
ayton ....d.		2230	....	0115	0255	....			0730		....		1035	....	1240	1555	1615			....			1820	....
Portsmouth ....d.			....			....					0600	....						1425		....	1820			....
Chillicothe ....d.			....			....					0705	....						1525		....	1920			....
Columbus ....d.			....			....					0915	....				1330		1730		....	2020			....
Marion ....d.			....			....					1020	....				1500		1840		....				....
Lima ....d.			....			....			0915		....				1430	1615		1725		....				....
Findlay ....d.		0050	....		0510	....			1020		1150	....			1530			1900	2015	....				....
Toledo ....d.	2220	0135	0200	0410	0600	....	1005		1120	1235	1250	....	1500	1515	1635			2005	2010	2150				....
Lincoln Park ....d.		0252s	....			....					1350s	....	1600		1740			2105	2110s	2210s	2245s			....
Detroit ....a.	2330	0245	0310	0520	0710	....	1115		1230	1345	1410	....	1620	1625	1800			2125	2130	2230	2305			....

ABL– American Trailways. GL– Greyhound Lines.

Table 374 — PITTSBURGH - ST. LOUIS — GL

US $	1375		1377	1363	1379		1369	1361	1371	1373		km	↓	↑	1368	1358	1370		1372		1374	1376	1362	1366
	....	1400		1700	2130	2045	....	0015	0445	0700	1000		d.New York 311 ......a.		0410	0540	0820	....	1120	....	1520	1715	2020	0020
	....	1700		2040		0001	....	0300	0715	1020	1315		d.Philadelphia 311....a.		0145	0305	0535	....	0835	....	1425	1845	2140	
0.00	....	0045		0410	0600	0730	....	1145	1530	1830	2130	0	d.Pittsburgh ....a.		1725	2015	2230	....	0015	....	0355	0715	1115	1325
	....					1235							d.Washington ....d.		1635			....						
9.00	....				0835				1940			70	d.Steubenville ....d.				2125	....						1230
12.00	....				0920		1325	1645	2020			91	d. Wheeling............d.		1550		2045	....						1150
21.00	....				1030		1430	1740	2115			177	d.Cambridge............d.		1455		1950	....						1100
24.00	....				1100		1500	1810	2145			219	d. Zanesville ....d.		1415		1915	....						1015
32.00	....	0430		0825	0945	1245	1645	2015	2320	0130		299	d.Columbus ....d.		1315	1700	1815	....	2100	....	0040	0400	0800	0915
37.00	....			0920		1340	1745	2115				362	d.Springfield ....d.		1120		1630	....	1915	....	2255			0740
40.00	....	0600		1010		1435	1835	2205		0300		406	d.Dayton..............d.		1040		1550	....	1835	....	2205	0140		0655
44.00	....	0555		1005		1430	1830					474	d.Richmond............d.		0835		1345	....	1630	....		2340s		
56.00	....	0800		1210	1250	1645	....	2130	0045	0230	0500	584	d.Indianapolis ....d.		0710	1220	1220	....	1505	....	1900	2215	0315	0340
64.00	....	0935		1340		1820	2300				0630	694	d.Terre Haute..........d.		0455		1020	....	1305	....	1655	2010		
73.00	....	1100		1455		1945	....				0745	810	d.Effingham............d.		0345		0910	....	1155	....	1545	1900		
	....	1140		1535									d.Vandalia............d.					....	1110	....				
82.00	....	1300		1655	1710	2135	....	0145	0510	0655	0940	990	a.St. Louis..............a.		0145	0715	0715	....	0945	....	1345	1700	2230	2230

L– Greyhound Lines.

Table 375 — ST. LOUIS - HOUSTON — GL

US $	1397			1395		km	↓	↑	1396	1394
0.00	0745	....	....	2215		0	d.St. Louis..............a.		2200	0615
30.00	1100	....	....	0120			d.Poplar Bluff..........d.		1845	0300
37.00	r	....	....	r			d.Walnut Ridge......d.		r	r
37.00	1310	....	....	0310			d.Hoxie................d.		1645	0105
59.00	1640	....	....	0630			d.Little Rock..........d.		1345	2200
	1730	....	....	0720			d.Pine Bluff..........d.		1225	2050
	2130	....	....	1130			d.Monroe..............d.		0830	1700
	2350	....	....	1345			d.Alexandria..........d.		0615	1445
	0210	....	....	1615			d.Lake Charles......d.		0400	1215
	0320	....	....	1740			d.Beaumont..........d.			1040
	0500	....	....	1930			a.Houston ....d.		0045	0900

L– Greyhound Lines.

Table 376 — TEXARKANA - HOUSTON — GL

US $	7231	7233		km	↓	↑	7232		7230
0.00	0750	....	1500	0	d.Texarkana ....a.		2025	....	0615
	0935	....	1645		d.Marshall ....d.		1840	....	0430
	1010	....	1720		d.Longview ....d.		1805	....	0355
	1135	....	1845		d.Tyler................d.		1705	....	0255
	1250	....	2000		d.Palestine ....d.		1535	....	0125
	1455	....	2200		d.Huntsville..........d.		1330	....	2325
	1630	....	2330		a.Houston ....d.		1201	....	2200

GL– Greyhound Lines.

Table 377 — BUFFALO - NIAGARA FALLS — NF

▭▭ service (40) Buffalo-Niagara Falls and v.v. 40 km. Journey: 55 mins. Fare: US $: 1.40.

From Buffalo: 0527④, 0605④, 0645✗, 0733④, 0750©, 0900, 1010④, 1020©, 1130④, 1135©, 1300, 1415✗, 1420†, 1510④, 1530©, 1610④, 1640†, 1643④, 1645⑥, 1705④, 1725④, 1800©, 1815④, 1930©, 2105④, 2110†, 2115④, 2205†, 2315⑥, 2320†, 2330④.

From Niagara Falls: 0020④, 0545④, 0627④, 0650✗, 0710④, 0750④, 0755④, 0855④, 0905©, 1020④, 1025④, 1130†, 1135©, 1140④, 1250④, 1305©, 1410④, 1415©, 1535©, 1540④, 1625④, 1640④, 1650④, 1712④, 1803④, 1805④, 1830④, 1933©, 1935©, 2050④, 2105†, 2215④, 2220†, 2228④.

NF– Niagara Frontier Transit Metro.

Table 378 — COLUMBUS — ABL GL

US $	GL 4351	GL 4361	GL 4355	GL 4357	km	↓	↑	GL 4360	GL 4350	GL 4358	ABL 605
32.00	0800	....	1500	....	0	d.Cleveland ....a.	1345	....	1645	....
22.00	0855	0855	1545	1615		d.Akron ....d.	1250	1550	1600	....
22.00	0925	0935	▬▬	1700		d.Canton ....d.	1150	1520	▬▬	....
18.00	....	1015	ABL	1740		d.Wooster ....d.	1100	1440	....	....
13.00	....	1100	ABL	1825		d.Mansfield ....d.	1020	1400	ABL	....
0.00	....	1215	602	1940	0	a.}Columbus....{d.	0900	1245	601	....
	....	....	1330			a.	....	....	1610	....
9.00	....	....	1500		66	d.Marion ....d.	....	....	1500	....
19.00	ABL	....	1620		150	d.Lima ....d.	....	....	1330	....
	604	....	1705			d.Van Wert ....d.	....	....	1240	....
30.00	0840	....	1700		246	d.Fort Wayne ....d.	....	....	1055	1945
	1000	....	1845			d.Bourbon ....d.	....	....	0930	1840s
	1025	....	1905			d.Plymouth ....d.	....	....	0850	1820
44.00	1120	....	2000		450	d.Valparaiso ....d.	....	....	0755	1920
44.00	1201	....	2040		480	a.Gary ....d.	....	....	0715	1640
50.00	1220	....	2100		495	a.Hammond ....d.	....	....	0655	1620
53.00	1315	....	2130		520	a.Chicago ....d.	....	....	0605	1650

ABL–American Trailways.   GL–Greyhound Lines.

Table 380 — SHREVEPORT - LAKE CHARLES — ABCD

US $	6135	6137		km	↓	↑	6134	6136
0.00	....	0730	1315	....	0	d.Shreveport ......a.	1645	....	2315
24.00	....	1055	1640	....		d.De Ridder ....d.	1320	....	1950
32.00	....	1159	1745	....		a.Lake Charles ....d.	1215	....	1845

GL– Greyhound Lines.

Table 381 — ALLIANCE - CANTON — ABCD

US $	Ⓐ	Ⓐ	Ⓐ		km	↓	↑	Ⓐ	Ⓐ	Ⓐ
0.00	0730	1030	1415	....	0	d.Alliance ....a.	0845	1205	1545
5.00	0805	1105	1500	....		a.Canton............d.	0815	1130	1515

ABCD–ABCD Transportation Services.

Table 382 — RICHMOND - CINCINNATI/EVANSVILLE — GL

US $	1096	4515	4600	4606	3921	km	↓	↑	4601	4516	4603	1093	3920
56.00	....	....	....	....	1140	0	d.Richmond ....a.	....	....	....	....	1435
41.00	....	....	....	....	1325	127	d.Charlottesville...........d.	....	....	....	....	1310
36.00	....	....	....	....	1420	176	d.Staunton...............d.	....	....	....	....	1155
32.00	....	....	....	....	1505	215	d.Lexington ....d.	....	....	....	....	1110
26.00	....	....	....	....	1550	271	d.Clifton Forge ....d.	....	....	....	....	1025
21.00	....	....	....	....	1645	329	d.White Sulphur Springs ..d.	....	....	....	....	0930
	....	....	....	....	1945		a.}Charleston....{d.	....	....	....	....	0645
0.00	....	0330	1000	1130	1540	490	a.	1455	2220	2240	0630
10.00	....	0425	1100	1230	1640	568	d.Huntington ....d.	1350	2120	2140	0530
13.00	....	0510	1201	1330	1730	605	d.Ashland ....d.	1315	2045	2105	0455
20.00	....	0600		1425	1815	663	d.Portsmouth ....d.	1215	....	2005	0355
59.00	....	1410		....	2230	1142	a. Detroit 373 ....d.	....	....	1130	2030
34.00	....	....		....	....	728	a.Cincinnati ....d.	....	....			
	....	....	1450				d. Lexington ....d.	....	1800			
	....	....	1525				d. Frankfort ....d.	....	1705			
	....	....	1745				d. Louisville ....d.	....	1545			
	....	....					d. Fort Knox ....d.	....				
	....	....					d. Owensboro ....d.	....				
	....	....	1845				a. Evansville ....d.	....	1201			

GL– Greyhound Lines.

Table 383 — CINCINNATI - LOUISVILLE/KNOXVILLE — ET GL SET

US $			GL 1109	GL 1111	GL 1157	GL 1161	GL 1159	SET 589	GL 1123	ET 17	SET 581	GL 1165	GL 1167	GL 539	GL 1171	SET 585	GL 599	GL 1149	GL 1151	GL 1173	SET 593	GL 1155	GL 1115	GL 1185
	Chicago 415......d.		....	....	....	....	....	....	2300	④	0001b	....	0800	....	....	1115a	....	....	....	1730	....	....	....	
0.00	Cincinnati........d.	0	0130	0130	0135	0400	0400	0400			0730	0730	1215		1515	1545		1745	2015	2015		2245	2300	
4.00	Covington........d.	12				0410					0740	0740	1225		1525	1555		1755		2025	2025			2310	
20.00	Louisville ......d.	165			0410		0640		0640			1030	1440	1605	1800		1915	2025	2240	2240		0110		
17.00	Lexington........d.	135		0300				0530			0915					1745					2200		0040	
32.00	London ....d.	250									1105					1950					2335			
33.00	Corbin ....d.	290						0645			1125					2010					2350			
◇3.00	Oak Ridge........d.									0930														
44.00	Knoxville ....a.	415	0555	0555				0825		1000	1305					2150				0130		0335	
56.00	Chattanooga .....a.	600	0905							1605b					0055b				0420b		0625	
	Fort Knox........d.	224													2015							
33.00	Cave City........d.	295						0721			1111		1645	1846		2033s						
37.00	Bowling Green ...d.	349			0510s			0805			1155		1725	1930		2110		2340				
44.00	Nashville........d.	436			0630	0730	0850	0930			1320	1645	1845	2055		2230	2230	0045	0100		0315	0215	

	SET 598	SET 594	GL 1148	GL 1150	GL 1154	GL 1152	GL 1114	GL 1170	GL 4802	GL 584	GL 586	GL 5018	GL 1156	GL 1158	GL 4816	GL 1160	SET 592	ET 18	GL 1172	GL 1146	GL 1166	SET 596	GL 1168	GL 1164	SET 580
Nashville............d.	....	2230	2230	0045	0200	0200	....	....	0345	....	0545	0630	0630	1015	1201	....	④	1330		1445	....	1815	1815	....
Bowling Green ......d.	....	....	2350				....	0505s	....	0710		0750	1140		....		1610		1940	....
Cave City...........d.	....	....					....	....	0748		0830	1220		....		1650		2015	....
Fort Knox...........d.	....	....					....	....	1015					....					....
Chattanooga.........d.	2130b	....					0135	....	0500				1050b					1520b	
Knoxville...........d.	0030	0030					0420	....	0815				1405	1500			1835		1835	
Oak Ridge...........d.														1530					
Corbin ....d.							0600	....	0955				1545					2015	
London ....d.							0620	....	1045				1620					2110	
Lexington...........d.				0330			0820	....	1225				1800			2145		2255	
Louisville ....d.				0320	0330	0530		0645		0830	0900		1120	1145	1201	1530			1735	1815	2030		2305	2315	
Covington...........a.		0440	0455	0510		0715			0945	1025		1350		1350	1720		1925		2005		2310	0050s		0020
Cincinnati..........a.					0730	0730			0955	1035		1400		1400	1730	1730	1940		2015		2320	0100		0030
Chicago 415.........a.		1115		0915			1230			1455	2140a	1750					2330		0135	0535		0430	

a–SET.   b–GL.   ◇–Fare ex Knoxville.   ET–East Tennessee Human Resources Agency.   GL–Greyhound Lines.   SET–Southeastern Trailways.

Table 385 — TOLEDO - INDIANAPOLIS — ABL

US $	213	217	215		km	↓	↑	214	216	210
43.00	0510	0930	1400	....		d.Detroit 373 ....a.	1620	2130	0310
36.00	0625	1100	1530	....	0	d.Toledo ....a.	1455	2005	0200
22.00	0810	1245	1700	....	138	d.Fort Wayne ....d.	1055	1610	2230
	0915	1400	1835	....	211	d.Marion ....d.	0930	1445	2105
	1020	1505	1935	....		d.Muncie ....d.	0830	1345	2005
13.00	1050	1535	2005	....		d.Anderson ....d.	0750	1305	1935
0.00	1145	1630	2100	....	306	a.Indianapolis .....d.	0655	1210	1840

ABL– American Trailways.

Table 386 — ASHEVILLE - ATLANTA — BRI

US $				km	↓	↑			
	....	....	....	0	d.Asheville ....a.			
	....	....	....	218	d.Gainesville........d.			
0.00	....	....	....	307	a.Atlanta ....d.			

BRI– Blue Ridge Trailways.

Table 387 — CHARLOTTE - BOONE — BRI

US $	102	2	4	104		km	↓	↑	1	3	101	103
0.00	1100	....	....	1915		0	d.Charlotte ....a.	....	....	1710	2030
11.00	1230	....	....	2030		96	d.Hickory ....d.	....	....	1535	1905
	1305	1310	1550	....			d.Lenoir ....d.	1255	1450	1500	....
21.00		1355	1505	....		176	a. Boone ....d.	1215	1410	....	....
	1450	....	....	2205			a.Asheville ....d.	....	....	1315	1720

BRI– Blue Ridge Trailways.

ble 388 — WASHINGTON - ROANOKE - KNOXVILLE   GL

1539	1531	1537	1511	3927	1533	3929	1535	km	Station	1534	3924	1536	1532	1538	1518	1530	3922
	1300		1600	1800	2100	0400	0900		d.New York a.	0300		0450	0755	1555	1835	2120	2120
1830	2135	2345	0200	0930	1000		1445	0	d.Washington a.	2030		0100	0200	1015	1215	1600	1630
			0445			1715		175	d.Richmond a.			1800	2115				
		2245			1115				d.Fredericksburg d.					1050	1440		
		0025	0630		1315		1805	185	d.Charlottesville d.	1725		1950				0925	1315
2015					1150			106	d.Winchester d.						0800		1415
2200			0220		1340			216	d.Harrisonburg d.						0610		1230
2230			0255s		1415			260	d.Staunton d.						0525		1145
2310			0335		1455			314	d.Lexington d.					2215	0445		1100
						1920			d. Appomattox d.				1555				
				0815	1500	1955	1945		d. Lynchburg d.				1520	1525	1805	0720	1120
0045	0300	0515	1000	1600	1645	2110	2125	406	d.Roanoke d.	1400	1400	1645	2115	0345	0600	1000	1000
0230	0440	0725	1215		1905		2330	486	d.Wytheville d.	1145		1435	1925	0210	0410	0750	
		0850	1340	2030			0055s	570	d.Abingdon d.			0940	1240	0010			
	0610	0920	1410	2100			0120	591	d.Bristol d.			0915	1215	2345		0535	
	0715	1000		2140				627	d.Johnson City d.			0830		2300			
	0845	1130	1610					724	d.Morristown d.			0700	1015	2130			
0610	0945	1230	1710	2355		0320		800	a.Knoxville d.	0600		0915	1515	2030	0015	0315	
0940	1310	1545	2040	0315		0615			a.Nashville 426 d.			0045	0345	1015	1500	1845	2200
	1800	2040	0125	0745					a.Memphis 426 d.			2315	0600	0930	1315	1700	
									a.Dallas 426 d.								

Greyhound Lines.

ble 390 — KNOXVILLE - COLUMBIA - CHARLESTON   BRI GL SES

SES 405	GL 1183	SES 131	BRI 607	SES 401	GL 589	SES 403	BRI 101	GL 4853	km	Station	SES 130	BRI 602	GL 1182	SES 400	BRI 104	GL 594	SES 136	GL 1184	SES 402
	0400				0910			1340	0	d.Knoxville a.		1715	1700			0010		2330		0330
	0605		0715		1135		1315	1550	168	d.Asheville d.		1515	1435		2210		2125		0125
	0735		0855		1330			1745	262	d.Greenville d.		1325	1245			1945		2345	
			0036							d. Spartanburg d.			1235						
		0345								d. Atlanta a.	1530						0045		
		0630								d. Augusta a.	1100						2200		
0400		0845	1220	1330	1700	1730	2115	2000	417	d.Columbia d.	0930	1015		1530	1600	1615	2030	2115	2345
										d. Sumter d.									
0455		0940	1320	1425	1815	1825	2210		482	d.Orangeburg d.	0815			1438		1915			2245
0615		1100	1500	1545		1945	2325		596	a.Charleston a.	0700	0800		1315	1330	1800			2130

BRI. b-GL.
Blue Ridge Trailways.
GL- Greyhound Lines.
SES- Southeastern Stages.

ble 391 — CHATTANOOGA - ATLANTA - JACKSONVILLE   GL

585	1149	593	1185	1155	1109	5359	1123	581	1233	539	km	Station	5356	592	580	1164	598	594	5358	588	1114	1116	1174
	0130			0400		0830	1015		1615	1945	0	d.Nashville a.	1340		1715	2110				0115	0300	0545	
0115		0440	0700	0745	0930	1330	1430	1630	2015	2330	215	d.Chattanooga a.	1030	1030	1500	1500	1900	2100	2215	2340	0125		0440
						1510					330	d.Rome d.	0845						2035				
0315	0645	0655	0915	1000	1145	1700	1645	1845	2230	0145	405	⟩Atlanta⟨ a.	0700	0815	1245	1245	1645	1845	2130	2315	0230		0230

5381	5393	5383	5387	5397	5389	5399	5391	5395	km	Station	5380	5394	5384	5386	5382	5398	5388	5392	5390
0415	0800	0800		1100	1245		1800	1945	2315 0245	d.Atlanta	0715	1115	1130	1530	1600		2000	2215	2215 0130
									471 d.Griffin d.									
0605	0940	1000		1300	1445		2000	2145	0115 0430	540 d.Macon d.	0515	0945	0945	1345	1415		1830	2030	2045 2345
	1201			1715			2355		0655	d.Tifton d.	0305	0630			1105		1525		1815
									d. Alma d.				0500	0915				
1025		1410		1655			2350		0430	790 d.Waycross d.			0500	0915			1550		1905
	1255			1820			0050		0800	785 d. Valdosta d.	0210	0535			1000		1420	1720	
	1415			1945			0205		0925	831 d. Lake City d.		0425		0850			1310	1610	
1215		1600		1845			0135	0315	0615	930 a.Jacksonville d.	0001		0315	0730	0730			1400	1715
				2330						a. Tampa d.			0030				0900		
	1745									a. St. Petersburg d.								1240	
	2325								1355	a. Orlando d.									
									1505	a.Miami 400 d.	1230		1730					0700	

Greyhound Lines.

ble 392 — BIRMINGHAM - JACKSONVILLE   GL

$ 5003		km	Station	5004	
2020			d.Memphis 431 a.	0145	
0550		0	d.Birmingham a.	1630	
0650		81	d.Sylacauga d.	1525	
0835		196	d.Opelika d.	1340	
1030		245	d.Columbus d.	1400	
1240		360	d.Albany d.	1145	
1340			d.Tifton d.	1030	
1510		544	d.Waycross d.	0900	
		515	d. Valdosta d.		
		576	d. Lake City d.		
1700		675	a.Jacksonville d.	0715	

Greyhound Lines.

Table 396 — ATLANTA - TALLAHASSEE   CHL GL

US $	Station	km	CHL 2100	GL 5365	GL 5363	GL 5361
0.00	Atlanta d.	0	0735	1115	1715	2300
9.00	Griffin d.	65		1215		
19.00	Macon d.	133			1915	0100
24.00	Americus d.	220		1420	2040	0225
30.00	Albany d.	280		1530	2145	0330
36.00	Thomasville d.	377		1700	2310	0455
44.00	Tallahassee a.	426	1435	1745	2355	0540

Station	GL 5360	GL 5362	CHL 2300	GL 5364
Tallahassee d.	0915	1300	1515	1830
Thomasville d.	1000	1345	1915	
Albany d.	1201	1530		2100
Americus d.	1255	1625		2150
Macon d.		1830		2345
Griffin d.	1500			
Atlanta a.	1600	2015	2220	0130

CHL- C & H Bus Lines.
GL- Greyhound Lines.

ble 393 — ATLANTA - SAVANNAH   GL GTY

$ GTY 8202	GTY 8204	GL 5059	km	Station	GL 5054	GTY 8201	GTY 8203
0800b	1100b	1800	0	d.Atlanta a.	1730	2015b	0130b
1005	1345	2030	125	d.Macon a.	1510	1745	2330
1100	1500	2130	209	d.Dublin d.	1410	1645	2230
1145	1550		320	d. Vidalia d.		1605	2140
1340	1750	2359	476	a.Savannah d.	1130	1415	1910

GL.
Greyhound Lines.
Georgia Trailways.

Table 397 — WASHINGTON - ATLANTA - NEW ORLEANS

CCC COT G…

US $	GL 1055		GL 1057	CCC 527	CCC 525	GL 1063	CCC 529	COT 65	GL 1071	GL 1051	GL 1053	km	↓ ↑	GL 1070	CCC 524	GL 1056	GL 1072	GL 528	GL 492	GL 1058	GL 1050	GL 1052	COT 26	G 10…
0.00	0200	....	0830	1100b	1100b	1400	1600b	....	1730	1900	2300		d. New York a.	0805	1020b	1135	1135	1305	....	1840	2120	0300	....	04
37.00	0730	....	1220	1530b	1530b	|	2100b	....	|	0015	0340		d. **Washington** a.	|	0545b	|	|	0845	....	1500	1620	2110	....	00
	|	....	|	|	|	|	|	....	|	|	|		d. Fredericksburg d.	|	|	|	|	|	....	|	|	|	....	
	|	....	|	|	|	|	|	....	|	|	|		d. Charlottesville d.	|	|	|	|	|	....	|	|	|	....	
	|	....	|	|	|	|	|	....	|	|	|		d. Lynchburg d.	|	|	|	|	|	....	|	|	|	....	
53.00	1115	....	1600	1845	1845	2130	0015	....	0100	0315	0615		d. **Richmond** a.	2230	0210	0415	0400	0510d	....	1030	1330	1745	....	21
56.00	|	....	|	|	1925	|	|	....	|	|	|		d. Petersburg a.	|	0130	|	|	|	....	|	|	|	....	
70.00	1450	....	1925	2200	|	|	0255	....	|	0555	0950		d. Danville d.	|	|	|	|	0220d	....	0735	1045	1450	...	18
73.00	|	....	|	|	2155	|	|	....	|	|	|		d. Durham d.	|	2310	|	|	|	....	|	|	|	....	
73.00	1610	....	2045	2320	2315	|	0410	....	|	0710	1110		d. Greensboro d.	|	2140	|	|	0115d	....	0545	0900	1255	....	16
77.00	1720	....	|	0020	|	|	|	....	|	0810	1220		d. Winston Salem d.	|	|	0015	|	|	....	|	0815	|	....	15
77.00	|	....	2150	|	s	|	0520	....	|	0905	|		d. Salisbury d.	|	2010	|	|	|	....	|	|	1125	....	
85.00	1945	....	2330	0245b	0115	0315	0645b	....	0645	1035	1445		d. Charlotte d.	1715	1915	2225	2300	2315d	....	0345	0600	1030	....	14
	2125	....	|	|	▬	0445	|	....	0815	1220	1635		d. Spartanburg d.	|	....	2015	2045	|	....	|	0300	0755	....	11
92.00	2215	....	|	|	....	0535	0855b	....	|	1310	1730		d. Greenville *SC* d.	|	....	1935	|	2035	....	|	|	0715	....	11
	0045	....	0345	0700b	....	0930	1145b	....	1130	1645	2100		a. **Atlanta 466** d.	1201	....	1600	1800	1800	....	2245	0030	0345	....	07
104.00	GL 1555		GL 533		GL 1559	GL 1563	GL 1565		GL 513	GL 531	GL 1553	0	**Atlanta 466**	GL 1560		COT 2	GL 1564			COT 4	GL 1550	GL 1552		G 15…
	0145	....	0500	....	0800	1030	1245	....	1245	1745	2145		d. **Atlanta 466** a.	1115	....	1530b	1700	....	2100	2115b	2315	0245	0630b	06
118.00	0300	....	0615	....	|	1155	|	....	|	1900	|	105	d. La Grange d.	0945	....	1400b	|	....	1915	1945b	|	|	0510b	
118.00	|	....	0725	....	|	|	|	....	1530	2010	|	135	d. Columbus **466** d.	|	....	1300b	|	....	1815	|	2100	0045	0410b	
118.00	0300	....	|	....	0845	1155	1335	....	|	|	2230	167	d. Opelika d.	0745	....	|	1415	....	....	1745b	|	|	|	
118.00	0515	....	0830a	....	1030	1400	1545	1700	1645	2130a	0015	280	d. **Montgomery 466** d.	0615	....	1005b	1300	....	....	1615b	1800	2150	0120b	02
118.00	0600	....	0920a	....	|	1450	|	|	....	2215a	|	358	d. Greenville *AL* d.	|	....	|	|	....	....	1435	1625	2030	2359	
131.00	0735	....	1055a	....	|	1625	|	|	....	|	|	478	d. Flomaton d.	|	....	|	|	....	....	1300	1450	|	|	
131.00	|	....	|	....	|	|	|	|	....	|	|	553	a. Pensacola d.	|	....	|	|	....	....	|	|	|	|	
131.00	0930	....	1250a	....	1400	1830	1930	2210	....	0140a	0330	593	d. Mobile d.	0230	....	0515	0915	....	....	1130	1330	1800	2120	23
131.00	|	....	1335a	....	|	1920	|	2255	....	0220a	|	658	d. Pascagoula d.	0120	....	0355	|	....	....	1015	1205	1650	2010	
142.00	|	....	1400a	....	|	1950	|	2325	....	0250a	|	793	d. Biloxi d.	0055	....	0325	|	....	....	0945	1140	1625	1940	
142.00	|	....	1425a	....	|	2015	|	2350	....	0315a	|	813	d. Gulfport d.	0025	....	0300	|	....	....	0920	1110	1555	1915	
142.00	1159	....	1610a	....	1630	2200	2200	0115	....	0500a	0600	933	a. **New Orleans** d.	2245	....	0140	0615	....	....	0730	0950	1400	1720	20

a–*COT*. **b**–*GL*. **d**–*CCC*. *CCC*–Carolina Trailways. *COT*–Colonial Trailways. *GL*–Greyhound Lines.

Table 398 — HOUSTON - JACKSONVILLE/MIAMI

COT G…

US $	GL 1248	GL 1244	GL 1262	GL 1564	GL 5414	GL 1246	GL 1250	GL 1252	GL 1254	GL 1240	GL 1260	km	↓ ↑	GL 5431	GL 1253	GL 1565	GL 1241	GL 1259	GL 1255	GL 1261	GL 1257	GL 1239	GL 1263	12…
82.00	1130	1645	1715	....	....	2030	0001	....	0830	0405	0830		d. *San Antonio* **544** a.	....	0650	1120	1610	1100	2130	1900	2345	0210	0810	05
59.00	1700	2100	2200	2200	....	0130	0445	0800	1300	1000	1315	523	d. **Houston** a.	....	0245	0600	1130	0630	1545	1430	1830	2130	2320	01
50.00	1850	|	|	2330	....	0305	0625	0940	|	1150	1455	388	d. Beaumont d.	....	|	|	0940	|	|	|	1640	1955	2145	23
39.00	2035	|	|	0100	....	0430	0800	1130	|	1410	1635	297	d. Lake Charles d.	....	|	0325	0815	|	1230	1150	1530	1830	2035	22
24.00	2200	|	0140	0215	0320	0600	0950	1305	|	1545	1825	177	d. Lafayette d.	2335	|	0145	0600	|	1040	|	1345	1600	1900	20
17.00	2325	0200	0330	0345	|	0740	1245	1445	1830	1730	2000	116	d. Baton Rouge d.	|	2215	0035	0445	0200	0930	0915	1230	1445	1745	19
18.00	|	|	|	|	0515	|	|	|	|	|	|		d. Morgan City d.	2140	|	|	|	|	|	|	|	|	|	
	0100	|	|	0530	0830	0930	|	1645	|	1920	2135		a. **New Orleans** d.	1830	|	2245	0300	|	0730	|	1000	1230	1515	17
0.00	|	|	|	|	▬ GL1242	GL 1256	|	GL 1264	|		COT 12	0	**New Orleans**	▬	|	|	|	|	GL 1243	|	GL 1249	GL 483	GL 1245	C 2
	0140b	|	|	0615	0615	1215	|	1720	|	....	2200		d. **New Orleans** a.	....	|	2155	0130	|	0630	|	0900	1135b	1425	16
14.00	|	|	|	|	0755	1410	|	|	|	....	2335	120	d. Gulfport d.	....	|	|	|	|	0500	|	0700	0945b	|	14
18.00	|	|	|	|	0825	1435	|	|	|	....	2359	140	d. Biloxi d.	....	|	|	|	|	0435	|	0635	0920b	|	14
21.00	|	|	|	|	0850	1505	|	|	|	....	0030	275	d. Pascagoula d.	....	|	|	|	|	0405	|	0605	0850b	|	13
26.00	0450	0600	0730	0840	1010	1630	1630	2030	2240	....	0140	340	d. Mobile d.	GL	1830	1930	2305	2215	0320	0520	0520	0805b	1201	12
35.00	0610	0745	0845	....	1145	1805	1805	2145	2350	....	0320c	420	d. Pensacola d.	5014	1645	....	2115	|	0145	0330b	0345	0600b	1015	.
56.00	|	|	|	....	|	|	|	|	|	....	|	660	d. Marianna d.	0850	|	....	|	|	2310	|	|	|	|	.
53.00	0850	|	1120	....	1420	1905	|	|	|	....	|	595	d. Panama City d.	|	1345	....	1910	|	|	|	|	|	0725	.
59.00	|	|	|	....	|	|	|	|	|	....	|	740	d. Chattahoochee d.	0915	|	....	|	|	|	|	|	|	|	.
64.00	1300	1245	1530	....	1815	2300	0045	0200	0445	....	0810c	800	d. Tallahassee d.	0815	1230	....	1800	1815	2245	0100	0115	0330	0615	.
73.00	1530	|	|	....	|	|	|	....	|	....	|	965	d. Lake City d.	....	0915	....	1520	|	|	|	2245	0105	|	.
82.00	1640	|	|	....	|	0145	|	....	|	....	|	1064	a. **Jacksonville** d.	....	0800	...	1400	|	|	|	2130	0001	|	.
77.00	....	1525	1810	....	2055	....	0325	....	0725	....	1050c	1040	a. Gainesville d.	....	....	....	....	1505	1920	2135	....	....	|	.
82.00	....	1610	1900	....	2140	....	0410	....	0845	....	1135c	1100	a. Ocala d.	....	....	....	....	1420	1835	2050	....	....	|	.
92.00	....	1745	2100	....	2330	....	0615	....	|	....	1420c	1235	a. Orlando (*Disney World*) d.	....	....	....	....	1245	1600	1815	....	....	|	.
92.00	....	|	....	....	....	....	|	....	1030	....	|	1240	a. **Tampa** d.	....	....	....	....	|	|	|	....	....	0030	.
92.00	....	|	....	....	....	....	|	....	1135	....	|	1273	a. St. Petersburg d.	....	....	....	....	|	|	|	....	....	2325	.
104.00	....	2325	....	....	....	....	1300	....	....	....	2115c	1615	a. **Miami** d.	....	....	....	....	0700	0815	1115	....	....	1540	.

b–*COT*. **c**–*GL*. *COT*–Colonial Trailways. *GL*–Greyhound Lines.

Table 400 — JACKSONVILLE - MIAMI

C…

US $	↓	km	3681	3673	507	1250	1264	5015	1001	3685	1013	1254	3687	3739	3797	490	1017	3689	5393	3733	3691	1262	3693	3695	37…
0.00	**Jacksonville** d.	0	0220	....	0415	....	....	....	....	0700	1000	....	1000	....	....	....	1315	1315	....	....	1730	....	2030	2330	...
9.00	St. Augustine d.	39	0305s	....	|	....	....	....	....	0800	|	....	1100	....	....	....	|	1415	....	....	|	....	2115	0015s	...
19.00	Daytona Beach d.	125	0415	....	|	....	....	....	....	|	|	....	1215	....	....	....	|	1530	....	....	|	....	2230	0125	...
26.00	Orlando (*Disney World*) d.	214	|	....	|	0700	0900	....	1045	|	|	....	|	....	....	1600	|	|	1815	....	|	2130	0015	0300	...
28.00	Cocoa d.	250	0550	....	|	|	|	....	|	1150	|	....	1355	....	....	|	|	1710	|	....	|	2235	|	|	...
32.00	Melbourne d.	286	0620	....	|	|	|	....	|	1220	|	....	1425	....	....	|	|	1740	|	....	|	2305	|	|	...
36.00	Fort Pierce d.	335	0825	....	0830	1000	1150	....	1330	1355	1420	....	1615	....	....	|	1730	1930	|	....	2145	0040	0240	0540	...
44.00	West Palm Beach d.	419	0950	1000	|	1110	1300	....	|	1505	|	....	1740	....	1745	2000	|	2055	2130	....	|	0150	0350	0650	...
53.00	Fort Lauderdale d.	490	1105	1225	1030	1225	1415	1415	1530	1620	1620	1625	1855	2900	2000	2115	1930	2210	2245	2245	2345	0305	0505	0805	08
56.00	**North Miami Beach** a.	539	|	1305	|	|	|	1455	|	1700	|	|	|	|	2040	|	|	|	|	2325	|	0345s	|	|	08
56.00	**Miami** a.		1210	1400	1130	1330	1520	1545	1635	1805	1725	1730	2000	2100	2125	2155	2010	2250	2325	2355	0025	0415	0545	0915	09

↓	3680	3682	5392	3796	3750	516	1243	3684		5010	1261		5380	1024	3686	3674	5396	3748	3688	5012	5384	1265	500	3692	50…
Miami d.	0100	0545	0700	0745	0830	0915	0915	1000	....	1100	1115	....	1230	1330	1330	1430	1510	1540	1600	1700	1730	1730	1900	2030	21
North Miami Beach d.	0125	0650	|	0850	|	|	|	1105	....	|	|	....	1335	|	|	1535	|	|	1710	|	|	|	1945	2135	
Fort Lauderdale d.	0210	0745	0755	0945	0935	1015	1015	1201	....	1201	1220	....	1430	1430	1430	1635	1630	1645	1815	1805	1830	1850	2030	2230	22
West Palm Beach d.	0315	0850	0900	1145	....	|	1120	1305	....	1305	....	....	1535	|	1535	1835	1735	....	1920	....	1935	|	|	2335	..
Fort Pierce d.	0515	1050	|	....	....	1245	1310	1505	....	|	....	....	1735	1700	1730	....	1920	....	2115	....	2115	2115	2245	0105	..
Melbourne d.	0630	1210	|	....	....	|	|	1630	....	|	....	....	1900	|	|	....	|	....	|	....	2230	|	|	|	..
Cocoa d.	0700	1240	|	....	....	|	|	1705	....	|	....	....	1935	|	|	....	|	....	|	....	2300	|	|	|	..
Orlando (*Disney World*) d.	0915	|	1210	....	....	|	1530	|	....	1730	....	....	|	|	2030	....	2130	....	0001	....	|	2325	|	0345	..
Daytona Beach d.	1045	1435	....	....	....	|	....	1855	....	....	....	....	2125	|	|	....	....	....	|	...	0035	....	|	|	..
St. Augustine d.	|	|	....	....	....	|	....	2000	....	....	....	....	2230	|	|	....	....	....	|	....	|	....	|	|	..
Jacksonville a.	1230	1625	....	....	....	1630	....	2045	....	....	....	....	2315	2045	2330	....	....	....	0230	....	0215	...	0230	0615	..

GL– Greyhound Lines.

Check update notes to timetables and with operator before starting your journey

Table 403 — SAVANNAH - TALLAHASSEE — GL

$	5379			km	↓	↑			5378	
.00	0615	....	....	0	d.**Savannah** ....a.		....	....	1830	....
.00	0840	....	....	169	d.Waycross ....d.		....	....	1605	....
.54	1010	....	....	268	d.Valdosta ....d.		....	....	1445	....
.14	1110	....	....		d.Thomasville ......d.		....	....	1335	....
.75	1215	....	....	378	a.**Tallahassee** ......d.		....	....	1230	....

– Greyhound Lines.

Table 404 — MIAMI - KEY WEST — GL

US $	3713	3715		km	↓	↑		3712	3714
0.00	0910	1810	....	0	d.**Miami** ....a.		....	1215	1900
4.00			....	6	d.Miami International Apt. ..a.		....		
4.00			....	7	d.Coral Gables ......a.		....		
7.00	1025	1925	....	49	d.Homestead ....d.		....	1055	1740
	1300	2145	....		d.Big Pine Key .....d.		....	0815	1500
28.00	1345	2230	....	264	a.**Key West**..........d.		....	0730	1415

GL– Greyhound Lines.

Table 405 — TAMPA - NAPLES - MIAMI — GL

$	5011	5015				1254	3743	3797	3729	3733	3745	km	↓	↑		3742		3744	3750	3796	3742a	1261	3746	5012	5016
.00	0030	0615	....	....	....	1100	1100	1115	1530	1600	1915	0	d.**Tampa** ....a.		....	1035	1515	1720	1800	1800	2115	2359	0500	
.00	0105	0700	....	....	....		1145			1645	2025	33	d. St. Petersburg ......a.		....		1430	1635			2005	2315	0420	
.00		0815	....	....	....		1300	1700			2135	92	d.Sarasota................d.		....	0905	1315	1520			1850	2200		
		0935	....	....	....		1420	1820			2250		d.Port Charlotte..........d.		....	0745	1125	1400			1730			
.00	0320	1020	....	....	....	1325	1505		1905	1930	2330	212	d.Fort Myers...........d.		....	0700	1040	1315		1535	1645	1955	0205	
.00	0445	1201	....	....	....					2025	0025	270	d.**Naples**..................d.		....		0945	1145			1855		0040	
			....	....	....			1210					d. Lakeland ....d.		....			1705						
			....	....	....			1240					d. Winter Haven........d.		....			1635						
			....	....	....			1445					d. Sebring ....d.		....			1500						
			....	....	....			1715					a. West Palm Beach.d.		....			1201						
.00	0645	1400	....	....	....	1625			1945		2225	430	d.Fort Lauderdale........d.		....		0950	0945	1235			1700	2245	
.00	0740	1455	....	....	....				2040		2325	432	a.**North Miami Beach**..d.		....			0850						
.00	0825	1525	....	....	....	1725			2125		2355		a.**Miami**...................d.		....		0850	0745	1135			1600	2145	

– Greyhound Lines.

Table 406 — CHICAGO - BAY CITY — IT

$	62	64	10	14		68	24	52	84	26	28	km	↓	↑	17	61	21	25	85	27	63	65	33	53	67
								⑤																⑤	
.00	....	....	0200	0600	....	....	1000		....	1315	1700	0	d.**Chicago**..............a.		1210	....	1550	1800	....	1950	....	....	2340	....	....
.00	....	....		0640	....	....	1040		....	1355	1740	34	d.Hammond.............d.			....	1450	1705	....		....	....		....	....
.00	....	....	0230	0705	....	....			....	1420	1805	49	d.Gary....................d.		1125	....	1435	1645	....	s	....	....		....	....
.00	....	....			....	1131			....	1450			d. Michigan City ....d.		1055	....		1615	....		....	....		....	....
.00	....	....	0450	0930	....	1330			....	1645	2030	151	d.Benton Harbor......d.		1110	....	1420	1630	....	1850	....	....	2235	....	....
.00	....	....	0600	1100	....	1445	1500		....	1820	2140	230	d.Kalamazoo...........d.		1000	....	1305	1520	....	1745	....	....	2135	2130	....
.00	....	....	0700	1145	....	1530	1545		....	1905	2240	269	d.Battle Creek........d.		0855	....	1215	1425	....	1640	....	....	2035	2050	....
.00	....	....	0805	1255	....	1635	1650		....	2010	2340	342	d.Lansing................d.		0750	....	1110	1320	....	1535	....	....	1935	1945	....
.00	....	....	0820	1310	....	1650	1705		....	2025	2350	349	d.East Lansing........d.		0715	....	1055	1305	....	1520	....	....	1920	1930	....
.90	0500	0805		1355	....	1700			....		0025	394	d.Owosso...............d.			0645	1010		....		1600	1850		....	....
.90	0520	0825			....				....			399	d.Durand.................d.						....		1545			....	....
.10	0600	0855	0915	1435	....	1740	1745	1800	....	2120	0110	428	a.**Flint**...................a.		0600	0605	0925	1201	....	1415	1500	1810	1815	1825	2120
.40					....				....		0300		a. Port Huron..........d.		0415	....	1110		....		....	....		....	....
.00			1010	1550	....		1835		....			483	a. Saginaw..............d.			....	1045		....	1255	....	....	1725	....	....
.00			1035	1615	....		1900		1905			504	a. **Bay City**............d.			....		1220	1230	....	1600	....		....	....
.00					....				2155				a. Alpena ....d.			....			0930	....		....		....	....

– Indian Trails.

Table 407 — CALUMET - GREEN BAY - MILWAUKEE - CHICAGO — GL LAB NSB WPT

WPT 1401	GL 5787	GL 5791	WPT 1201	NSB 1101	GL 5813	LAB 211		GL 5783	GL 5811	GL 5771		km	↓	↑	GL 5784	WPT 1404	GL 5772	GL 5788	GL 5810	WPT 1202	NSB 1102		GL 5770	LAB 210	GL 5790		WPT 1402
									⑨⑦																⑨⑦		
2120	....	....	....	....	....	....		....	....	....		◊159	d.**Calumet** ....a.		....	....	....	....	....	....	....		....	....	....	0710	....
2152	....	....	....	....	....	....		....	....	....		◊138	d.Houghton ....d.		....	....	....	....	....	....	....		....	....	....	0650	....
2350	....	....	....	....	....	....		....	....	....		0	d.Ishpeming ....d.		....	....	....	....	....	....	....		....	....	....	0510	....
0018	....	....	0800	....	....	....		....	....	....		25	d.Marquette ....d.		....	....	....	....	2220	....	....		....	....	....	0450	....
0145	....	....	0935	....	....	....		....	....	....		135	d.Escanaba ....d.		....	....	....	....	2055	....	....		....	....	....	0315	....
0245	....	....	1014	....	....	....		....	....	....		226	d.Marinette/Menominee d.		....	....	....	....	1810	....	....		....	....	....	0015	....
	....	....		0630	....	....		....	1240	....			d. Ironwood ....a.		....	....	....	....	....	2150	....		....	....	....		....
	....	....		0830	....	....		....	1405	....			d. Rhinelander ....a.		....	1600	....	....	....	1955	....		....	....	....		....
	....	0650			....	0910		....	1505	....			d. Wausau ....a.		....	1435	....	....	....		....		1945	....	....		....
	....			1000	....	0955		....		....			d. Stevens Point ....a.		....	1340	....	....	....		....			2115	....		....
	....				....			....		....			d. Wittenberg ....d.		....		....	....	....	1830	....		1905	....	....		....
	....				....			....		....			d. Sturgeon Bay ... d.		....		....	....	....		....				....		....
0405	....	0900	1120	1140	1145			....	1750	1715		310	d.**Green Bay** ....d.			1125	1335	1645	1635	1700	1700		1745	....	....	2310	....
0450	....							....				367	d.Manitowoc ....d.			1040	....	....	....	....	....		....	....	....		....
	....	0945			1125	1655		....	1800			412	d. Plymouth ....d.				....	....	....	....	....		....	....	....		....
	....				1215	1740		....	1845			359	d. Appleton ....d.			1120	1250	1600	....	1700	1720		1945	....	....		....
	0825	1030			1250	1820		....	1925			390	d. Oshkosh ....d.			1205	1515	....	....	1615	1640		1900	....	....		....
	0905	1110						....				421	d. Fond du Lac ....d.			0955	1130	1440	....	1540	1600		1825	....	....		....
0535	....				1350	1405		....	1955	1955	2050	412	d.Sheboygan ....d.		0955		....	....	....	....	....		....	....	....		....
0640	1040	1245			1625	1625a		....				597	a.**Milwaukee** Ω ....d.		0815	0845	1000	1300	1430	....	....		1415	1450	1650		....
	1245	1530			1630	1615a		....	2200	2200	2330	730	a.Chicago O'Hare Airport d.				....	....	....	....	....		....	....	....		....
								....				742	a.**Chicago** Ω...........d.		0550		0700	1030	1201	....	....		1201	1201a	1330		....

GL.
† only.
☼ only.
Km ex Ishpeming.
Complete GL service Milwaukee-Chicago and v.v.; **from Milwaukee**: 0330, 0700, 0800, 1000, 1100, 1300, 1415, 1615, 1730, 2015, 2145, 2320; **from Chicago**: 0035, 0550, 0730, 0900, 1030, 1201, 1330, 1500, 1630, 1800, 1930, 2100, 2230⑨⑦.
Fare ex Green Bay.
Greyhound Lines.
Lamers Bus Lines.

WPT– White Pine Bus Service.

Check update notes to timetables and with operator before starting your journey

Table 408 — DETROIT LOCAL SERVICES 🚌 DDT SEMTA WT

Local 🚌 services operate in the Detroit area as follows:

Dearborn (SEMTA) (11 km, US $: 1.50). From Detroit: 0050, 0525④, 0600④, 0610ex①/0815† and frequent to 2000⑥, 2035, 2135④, 2136④, 2245⑤⚡, 2250†, 2346⑤⚡, returning at 0023, 0457⑤, 0528⑥, 0546⑥/ 0901† and frequent to 2107⑥, 2109⑥, 2217⑤⚡, 2225†, 2320④, 2321④. Journey: 40 mins.
East Detroit (DDT) (⟡ km, US $: ⟡). From Detroit: ⟡, returning at ⟡. Journey: ⟡.
Ecorse (SEMTA) (⟡ km, US $: 1.00). From Detroit: 0518④, 0550④, 0625④ and about hourly to 1705④, 1737④, 1812④, returning at 0551④, 0641④, 0712④ and about hourly to 1832④. Journey: 30 mins.
Ferndale (SEMTA) (⟡ km, US $: 1.25). From Detroit: 0000†, 0100ex①④, 0449④, 0516④, 0530④, 0539④, 0559④, 0600†, 0605④ and frequent (hourly on †) to 2000†, 2020④, 2203S④, 2100†, 2110S⚡, 2200†, 2220④, 2232④, 2300†, 2330④, returning at 0008④, 0020ex①⑦, 0023⑦, 0500④, 0523④, 0530④, 0550④, 0558④, 0600④, 0622† and frequent (about hourly on †) to 2020†, 2031S⚡, 2120†, 2142④, 2146④, 2220†, 2242④, 2321④. Journey: 40 mins.
Gross Pointe Farms (DDT) (⟡ km, US $: ⟡). From Detroit: ⟡, returning at ⟡. Journey: ⟡.
Gross Pointe Park (DDT) (⟡ km, US $: ⟡). From Detroit: ⟡, returning at ⟡. Journey: ⟡.
Gross Pointe Woods (DDT) (⟡ km, US $: ⟡). From Detroit: ⟡, returning at ⟡. Journey: ⟡.
Hamtramck (DDT) (⟡ km, US $: ⟡). From Detroit: ⟡, returning at ⟡. Journey: ⟡.
Hazel Park (DDT) (⟡ km, US $: ⟡). From Detroit: ⟡, returning at ⟡. Journey: ⟡.
Highland Park (DDT) (⟡ km, US $: ⟡). From Detroit: ⟡, returning at ⟡. Journey: ⟡.
Lincoln Park (SEMTA) (⟡ km, US $: 1.25). From Detroit: 0603④, 0635④/0818④/1118† and frequent (hourly on ©) to 1818©, 1825④, 2025④, returning at 0529④, 0559④, 0619④, 0639④/0730④/1030† and frequent (hourly on ©) to 1830©, 1840④, 1959④. Journey: 30 mins.
Melvindale (SEMTA) (⟡ km, US $: 1.25). From Detroit: 0620④, 0716④, 0742④ and about hourly to 1709④, 1734④, 1808④, returning at 0545④, 0614④, 0644④ and about hourly to 1759④, 1845④. Journey: 40 mins.
Oak Park (SEMTA) (⟡ km, US $: 1.50). From Detroit: 0739④, 1235④, 1445④, 1600④, 1630④, 1703④,

1750④, returning at 0613④, 0643④, 0713④, 0743④, 0848④, 0953④, 1455④. Journey: 50 mins.
River Rouge (SEMTA) (⟡ km, US $: 1.00). From Detroit: 0518④, 0550④, 0625④ and about hourly 1737④, 1812④, returning at 0600④, 0652④, 0723④ and about hourly to 1747④, 1841④. Journey: mins.
Royal Oak (SEMTA) (⟡ km, US $: 1.50). From Detroit: 0000⑦, 0100ex①⑦, 0449④, 0516④, 0530 0539④, 0559④, 0600† and frequent (hourly on †) to 2000⑥, 2020④, 2035④, 2100†, 2110S⚡, 220 2220④, 2232④, 2300†, 2330④, returning at 0002⑦, 0015ex①⑦, 0017⑦, 0454④, 0517④, 0523④, 0543 0553④,0616† and frequent (about hourly on †) to 2014†, 2023S⚡, 2114†, 2134④, 2138④, 2214†, 2234 2313④. Journey: 50 mins.
St Clair (DDT) (⟡ km, US $: ⟡). From Detroit: 0700⚡ and frequent to 2000⚡, returning at 0730⚡ a frequent to 2030⚡. Journey: ⟡.
Warren (DDT) (⟡ km, US $: ⟡). From Detroit: ⟡, returning at ⟡. Journey: ⟡.
🚢 **Windsor** (WT) (3 km, US $: 2.00). From Detroit: 0550⚡/0810† and frequent to 2330†/0050⚡, retur at 0540⚡/0800† and frequent to 2320†/0040⚡.

DDT–	Detroit Department of Transportation.	WT– Transit Windsor (Chartabus).
SEMTA–	South East Michigan Transportation Authority.	

Table 412 — CHICAGO - MADISON 🚌

US$		km	5631	5633	5748	5639	1347			5635		5858		5686	5621	5641		5688			5643
0.00	Chicago ....d.	0	0030	0500	0615	0700	0700	....	1000	....	1210	....	1410	1500	1500	....	1615	....	....	2100
	O'Hare Airport (u) ....d.	12		0530	0700						1305		1500				1730			
8.00	Elgin ....d.				0750								1550							
18.00	Rockford East ......d.	145			0840		0900a	....		....	1430	....	1640			....	1855			
21.00	Beloit ....d.	174			0905						1455		1705				1920			
22.00	Janesville ....d.	195			0935						1525		1735				1950			
25.00	Madison ....a.	260		0355	0925	1025	1110	....	1415	....	1615	....	1825	1750	1920	....	2040			0050

			5640		5622	5642	5681					5630	5649		5614		5767	5634		1306		5743	5636	563
	Madison ....d.			....	0145	....	0530	0610	0840			1225	1220	....	1335		....	1525	1615	....			1845	1955	214
	Janesville ....d.							0925				1305						1610				1930		
	Beloit ....d.							0955				1335						1640				2000		
	Rockford East .....d.							1025				1405						1710		1955a		2030		
	Elgin...............d.							1115				1455						1800				2120		
	O'Hare Airport (s)......a.			....	0455	....		1155				1535					....	1840				2200		
	Chicago ....a.			....	0520	....	0830	1015	1230			1630	1610	....	1625		....	1920	2030	....	2125		2230	2330	01

a–Rockford.   GL–Greyhound Lines.

Table 413 — GREEN BAY - MADISON 🚌 GL

US$	5849	5787	5791	5802		km					5801	5788	5790	5858
0.00	0630	....	0925	....		0	d.**Green Bay** ....a.	....	1615	....	2055
7.00	0715	....	1010	1655		49	d.Appleton ....d.	1300	1530	2010	2010
10.00	0800	0805	1055	1740		85	d.Oshkosh ....d.	1215	1445	1925	1930
13.00	0840	0840	1130	1815		116	d.Fond du Lac ....d.	1140	1410	1850	1855
20.00	0930	....	....	....		166	d.Beaver Dam ....d.	....	....	....	1805
25.00	1045	....	....	....		227	a.**Madison** ....d.	....	....	....	1655

GL– Greyhound Lines.

Table 414 — LA CROSSE - GREEN BAY 🚌 NSB RCSB SC

US$	NSB 1101	SCE 532	RCSB 603	SCE		km				RCSB 604	SCE 531	SCE 11	NS
0.00	....	0900	....			0	d.**La Crosse**..........d.	....	2015	....	
	....	1100	....	1125			d.Eau Claire ....d.	....	1715	1830	....
			....	1330			d.Abbotsford ....d.	....	1540	....	
			1245				d. Marshfield ....a.	1545	....		
	....		1345	1430			d.Wausau ....d.	1445	1450	....	
1000	....		....	1510			d.Wittenberg ....d.	....	1335	18	
1140	....		....	1650			a.**Green Bay** ....d.	....	1215	17	

NSB–North Star Bus Service.   SCE–Scenic Trailways.

Table 415 — CHICAGO - INDIANAPOLIS/LOUISVILLE 🚌 ABL GL S

US$		km	GL 1163	ABL 601	GL 583	GL 539	ABL 101		SET 591	SET 599		ABL 105	SET 595		4923	GL 1111	ABL 605	GL 1155	ABL 107	GL 1135⑤	GL 1123	ABL 581
0.00	Chicago ....d.	0	0145	0605	0700	0800	....		1020	1115		....	1330		1500	1700	1550	1730	....	2030	2300	0001
6.00	Hammond ....d.	35		0655	0755		....		1115			....	1425			1810	1620					
7.00	Gary ....d.	41	0230	0715	0815		....		1135			....	1445			1830	1640		....	2359	0040	
	Valparaiso ....d.	230		0755													1720					
23.00	Lafayette ....d.		0410		0955		....		1325			....	1635		2015							
	Elkhart ....d.	▼271				0700						1330				1700						
	South Bend ....d.					0735						1410				1735						
	Plymouth ....d.	▼230		0850		0815						1455			1815	1820						
	Logansport ....d.	191				0910						1545				1925						
	Peru ....d.	▼125				0950										1950						
	Kokomo ....d.	232				1020						1630										
33.00	Indianapolis ....{a.	335	0530		1115	1115	1140		1445	1430		1750	1755		1815	2125		2055	2110	2345	0235	0315
	Indianapolis ....{d.		0600		1201a	1201a			1600	1505b		1900b			1900	2200		2145		0030	0310	0400a
50.00	Louisville ....d.	520	0945			1545a				1840b		2200					0045			0330	0610	
50.00	Cincinnati ....d.	510			1510a				1910			....	2200b			0100						0700a

		SET 596	GL 1150	ABL 102	SET 594	GL 1114	ABL 604	SET 584		ABL 104	GL 4922	GL 1156		ABL 602	GL 586		ABL 106		GL 1172		SET 588	GL 1166	GL 1164
Cincinnati ....d.		0100	....		0530					1020				1525					2000		....		
Louisville ....d.			0330			0645		0900			1145				1830						2030	2315	
Indianapolis ....{a.			0200	0430		0640	0745	1045		1130	1320			1625			1930		2110		2130	0015	
Indianapolis ....{d.		0225	0500	0700	0800	0810		1115b		1201	1201	1400		1740a	1840		2020		....		2145	0040	
Kokomo ....d.		....		0820				1325							1955								
Peru ....d.		....		0900											2020								
Logansport ....d.		....		0925				1400															
Plymouth ....d.				1025		1025		1455						1905			2115						
South Bend ....a.				1105				1535									2155						
Elkhart ....a.				1140				1610									2225						
Lafayette ....d.			0620		0930		1245b			1520		1900a							2305				
Valparaiso ....d.					1120							2000										
Gary ....d.			0805		1120	1201	1415b			1705		2040	2050a									0320	
Hammond ....d.			0825		1140	1220						2100s	2110as									0340	
Chicago ....a.		0535	0915		1115	1230	1315	1455b		1510	1750	2133	2140a		2330					0135	0430		

a–SET.   b–GL.   ▼–Km ex Indianapolis.   ABL–American Trailways.   GL–Greyhound Lines.   SET–Southeastern Trailways.

Table 416 — CHICAGO - DES MOINES - OMAHA

BTW GL JL KCO

S $		km	GL 1305	BTW 1302	BTW 1201	GL 1347		GL 5737	KCO 52	GL 1315	GL 1349			GL 1301		GL 1311	BTW 1306	GL 1343
.00	Chicago........d.	0	....	0030	....	0700	....	....	....	1400	1230	....	....	1630	....	2100	....	2100
.00	Aurora ....d.	65	....		....		....	0755	....	....	1320	....	....	1730	....		....	2140s
0.00	Burlington......d.	415	....	0930	0945	....	....	....	....			....	....		....	....	2300	
8.00	Ottumwa ....d.	535	....		1135	....	....	....	1710			....	....		....	....		
2.00	Muscatine .....d.		....		1040	....	....	....	....			....	....		....	....	0005	
	Moline ....d.		....	0335		....	....	1140	....	....	1605	....	....	2100	....		....	0030s
00	Davenport ......d.	290	....	0350	1135	....	....	1205	....	....	1645	....	....	2135	....	0055	0100	
00	Iowa City.......d.	377	....	0455	1250	....	....	1350	....	1815	1800	....	....	2245	....	0200	0210	
00	Clinton...........d.	220	....			....	....	....	....			....	....		....			
00	Rockford.......d.	138	....			0900	....	....	....			....	....		....			
00	Freeport ....d.	183	....			1005	....	....	....			....	....		....			
00	Dubuque ......d.	293	....			1210	....	....	....			....	....		....			
00	Cedar Rapids d.	360	....	0545	1425a	....	....	1440	....	....	1850	....	....		....	0245		
00	Waterloo....d.		....		1520a	1435	....	....	....			....	....		....			
00	Tama ....d.	433	....	0715		....	....	1540	....	....	2030	....	....		....			
00	Marshalltown .d.	470	....	0750		1615	....	1615	....	....	2105	....	....		....			
00	Ames ......d.	530	....			....	....	1700	....	....		....	....		....			
00	Des Moines...{a.	572	....	0855	1005	1710	....	1740	1910	2125	2210	....	....	0110	....	0330	0455
00	Des Moines...{d.		....	0910		1800	....	....	....	2150	2235	....	....	0130	....	0400	0520
00	Omaha............d.	792	....	1125		2040	....	....	....	0005	0050	....	....	0345	....	0615	0800
00	Denver 476 ...a.	1667	....			0640	....	....	....	....	1330	....	....		....	1740	2100
00	Cheyenne 476 a.	1592	....	2255		....	....	....	....	1045		....	....	1650	....		
.00	Salt Lake City 476 a.	2342	....	0815		....	....	....	....	2030		....	....	0200	....		

		BTW 1301		GL 1340	GL 1342	KCO 53	GL 1314	GL 1316		JL 405	GL 5738			GL 1306	BTW 1202		GL 1346			GL 1308
	Salt Lake City 476 .d.	....	....	....	....	0745	....	....	....	....	....	....	....	1130	....	....		....	....	1845
	Cheyenne 476 ......d.	....	....	....	....	1715	....	....	....	....	....	....	....	2130	....	....		....	....	0420
	Denver 476 ......d.	....	....	1120	1440		1815	....	....	....	....	....	....		....	2210		....	....	
	Omaha...............d.	....	....	0115	0320	....	0515	0610	....	....	....	....	....	0850	....	1240		....	....	1945
	Des Moines.......{a.	....	....	0330	0600	....	0730	0825	....	....	....	....	....	1105	....	1520		....	....	2200
	Des Moines.......{d.	....	....	0350	0630	0735	0745	0845	....	....	1115	....	....	1145	1430	1610		....	....	2215
	Ames............d	....	....	....	....	....	....	....	....	....	1155	....	....		....			....	....	
	Marshalltown ......d.	....	....	....	0725				....	....	1235	....	....	1240	....	1705		....	....	
	Tama ....d.	....	....	....	0845				....	....	1310	....	....		....	1805		....	....	
	Waterloo.......d.	....	....	....					....	1255		....	....	1430	....			....	....	
	Cedar Rapids...d.	0545	....	....	1010				....	1420b	1420	....	....	1715	....	1920		....	....	
	Dubuque ....d.		....	....					....	....		....	....	1850	....			....	....	
	Freeport ....d.		....	....					....	....		....	....	1955	....			....	....	
	Rockford.........d.		....	....					....	....		....	....		....			....	....	
	Clinton............d.		....	....					....	....		....	....		....			....	....	
	Iowa City.........d.	0625	....	....	0635	1055		1055	....	1505b	1500	....	....		....	2000		....	....	0045
	Davenport........d.	0745	....	....	0755	1215			....	1630b	1700	....	....		....	2120		....	....	0155
	Moline ....d.		....	....	0815	1235			....	1720		....	....		....	2135		....	....	0210
	Muscatine.........d.	0830	....	....			0935		....	1715b		....	....		....			....	....	
	Ottumwa...........d.		....	....					....	1825b		....	....	1700	....			....	....	
	Burlington.........a.	0940	....	....			1435		....			....	....	1845	....			....	....	
	Aurora...........d.		....	....	1145	1605		1520	1530	....	2100	....	....		....			....	....	0520
	Chicago...........a.		....	....	1230	1605		1520	1530	....	2140	....	....	2125	....	0045		....	....	0520

.. b–BTW. ◇–Fare ex Des Moines. ★–Fare ex Cedar Rapids. *BTW*–Burlington Trailways. *GL*–Greyhound Lines. *JL*–Jefferson Lines. *KCO*–Kincaid Coach Lines.

Table 417 — CHICAGO - PEORIA

BSC

® $		®		km	↓		®		®	
00	....	1230	....	1820	0	d.Chicago...........a.	1140	....	1750	....
00	....	1605	....	2220	253	a.Peoria..............d.	0745	....	1415	....

® – Blue Star Coaches.

Table 418 — INDIANAPOLIS - PEORIA

ISL

$	24 ®	6	14	8	km	↓		5 ®	5 ©	15	9
00	....	0915	1210	1645	0	d.Indianapolis ....a.	1525	1525	2020	0040
70	....	0920	1310	1800	73	d.Crawfordsville....d.	1405	1405	1915		
20	....	1035	1415	1910	139	d.Danville ....d.	1250	1250	1810	2310
45	....	1150	1510	2005	196	d.Champaign ......d.	1150	1150	1700	2210
75	0850	1305	1645	2130	278	d.Bloomington ......d.	1000	1000	1535	2115
25	1420	1745	2220		345	d.Peoria ....d.	0845	0845	1415	2010
25	0955	1530	1855	....	426	d.Galesburg.........d.	0730	....	1255	1850
25	1050	1630	2000	....	510	d.Moline Ω...........d.	0625	....	1144	1740
55	1105	1645	2010	....	515	a.Davenport ....d.	0610	....	1130	1725

Ω–For Rock Island. *ISL*–Illini Swallow Lines.

Table 420 — CHICAGO - EVANSVILLE

RAT

US $		①③⑤			km	↓			①③⑤	
0.00	....	....	....	....	0	d.Chicago...........a.	....	....	....	
6.00	....	....	....	....	35	d.Hammond.........a.	....	....	....	
11.00	....	....	....	....	92	d.Kankakee ....d.	....	....	....	
24.00	....	....	....	....	208	d.Champaign ......d.	....	....	....	
25.00	....	....	....	....	220	d.Danville ....d.	....	....	....	
33.00	....	....	0830	....	325	d.Terre Haute ......d.	....	....	1430	
40.00	....	....	0945	....	411	d.Vincennes ....d.	....	....	1315	
50.00	....	....	1110	....	497	a.Evansville.........d.	....	....	1201	

RAT– Red Arrow Transportation.

Table 421 — MILWAUKEE - ROCKFORD

US $				km	↓		↑	
0.00	....	....	....	0	d.Milwaukee ....a.		....	
17.00	....	....	....		a.Rockford ....d.		....	

Table 422 — CHICAGO - ST. LOUIS

GL

$	5211	5203	5205	5201	5207	5213	5209	km	↓		5212	5200	5202	5214	5204	5206	5208
00	0100	0600	....	0800	1201	1330	....	1500	....	2030	0	d.Chicago ....a.	0750	1300	....	1520	....	1530	....	2015	....	2320	0520
00		0710	....		1310		....		....		70	d.Joliet ....d.	0645	1145	....		....		....	1905	....		
00			....	0935		1505	....		....		90	d. Kankakee..............d.			....	1350	....		....		....	2205	0410
00			....	1120		1645	....		....		218	d. Champaign ....d.			....	1205	....		....		....	2030	0240
00			....	1245		1815	....		....		285	d. Decatur ....d.			....	1030	....		....		....	1920	0150
00		0800	....		1400		....	1625	....		165	d.Dwight ....d.	0555	1055	....		....		....	1815	....		
00		0825	....				....	1650	....			d.Pontiac ....d.		1030	....		....		....	1750	....		
00	0320	0945	....		1530		....	1820	....	2250	217	d.Bloomington ....d.	0435	0915	....		....	1235	....	1630	....		
00		1025	....				....	1900	....		261	d.Lincoln ....d.		0830	....		....		....	1545	....		
00	0435	1110	....	1340	1645	1910	....	1945	....	0001	318	d.Springfield ....d.	0325	0750	....	0935	1120	....	1505	....	1825	0045
00			....				....		....		464	a.East St. Louis...........d.			....		....		....		....		
00	0620	1255	....	1530	1830	2100	....	2130	....	0145	474	a.St. Louis................d.	0140	0600	....	0745	0930	....	1315	....	1630	2300
	....	....	....	....	....	....	....		....		1274	a.Oklahoma City 458....d.	....	....	....	....	....		....		....		
	....	....	....	....	....	....	....		....		1611	a.Dallas 458 ....d.	....	....	....	....	....		....		....		
	....	....	....	....	....	....	....		....		2074	a.Houston 483 ....d.	....	....	....	....	....		....		....		
	....	....	....	....	....	....	....		....			a.San Antonio 481.......d.	....	....	....	....	....		....		....		
	....	....	....	....	....	....	....		....			a.Laredo 481.............d.	....	....	....	....	....		....		....		

Greyhound Lines.

Table 423 NASHVILLE - TALLAHASSEE/NEW ORLEANS

CML ·

US $	GL 5003	CML 51	GL 5011	GL 5013	CML 63	GL 5015	GL 5023	CML 55	GL 5017	GL 5019	GL 5021	km	↓ ↑	GL 5024	GL 5010	GL 5010	GL 5012	GL 5014	CML 81	CML 62	GL 5022	GL 5016		CM 85
★73.00	....	....	*2245*	*0130*	....	*0400*	....	....	....	....	....	*0*	d. *Cincinnati* **383** ...a.	....	*1400*	....	*0100*	....	....	....	....	*0730*	....	....
0.00	....	....	*1730*	|	....	*2300*	....	....	....	*1115*	....		d. *Chicago* **415** ...a.	....	*1750*	*2350*	*0430*	*0915*	....	....	....	*1230*	....	....
50.00	....	....	*0110*	*0400*	....	*0640*	....	....	....	*1915*	....	*185*	d. *Louisville* **383** ...a.	....	*1110*	*1735*	*2245*	*0235*	....	....	....	*0605*	....	....
70.00	0145	....	0345	0715	....	1000	....	....	1715	2315	....	*350*	d. **Nashville** ...a.	....	0520	1245	1730	2145	....	....	2145	0115	....	....
73.00	|	....	|	|	....	|	....	....	1850	|	....	*470*	d. Pulaski ...d.	....	|	|	1555	|	....	....	|	|	....	....
◇14.00	|	....	|	|	....	|	....	....	|	|	....		d. Lawrenceburg ...d.	....	|	|	|	|	....	....	|	|	....	....
◇33.00	|	....	|	|	....	|	....	....	|	|	....		d. Florence ...d.	....	|	|	|	|	....	....	|	|	....	....
85.00	|	....	|	0900	....	|	....	....	|	0055	....	*520*	d. Athens ...d.	....	|	|	|	|	....	....	1950	|	....	....
82.00	|	....	0555	0945	1030	1215	....	....	1955	|	....	*505*	d. Huntsville ...d.	....	|	1045	1505	1945	....	2200	|	2315	....	....
85.00	0505	....	0815	1220	|	1435	....	....	2215	0240	....	*665*	a. **Birmingham** ...d.	....	0200	0800	1230	1700	....	|	1800	2040	....	....
	....	0550	0900	1300	|	1525	1545	1815	2305	0315	0330		d. **Birmingham** ...a.	0120	0115	0645	1159	1515	1740	|	1710	1945	....	231
98.00	....	0800	1105	1515	1645	1750	|	2015	0135	0530	|	*820*	d. Montgomery ...d.	|	2330	0500	1000	1315	1540	1630	|	1745	....	21
104.00	....	1115	1415	1820	2015	2045	|	....	0355	0830	|	*985*	d. Dothan ...d.	|	1955	0215	0710	0945	1215	....	|	1415	....	17
104.00	....	|	1505	1910	|	2135	|	....	|	0920	|	*1051*	d. Marianna ...d.	|	1910	|	0615	0855	|	....	|	1325	....	|
118.00	....	1435	1745	2145	2340	2359	|	....	0710	1155	|	*1181*	a. **Tallahassee** ...d.	|	1830	0105	0545	0815	1050	....	|	1245	....	154
142.00	....	....	....	....	....	....	|	....	....	....	|	*2031*	a. *Miami* **398** ...d.	|	....	....	....	....	....	....	|	....	....	....
91.00	....	....	....	....	....	....	1705	....	....	....	0450		d. Tuscaloosa ...d.	0005	....	....	....	....	....	....	1540	....	....	....
98.00	....	....	....	....	....	....	1925	....	....	....	0710		d. Meridian ...d.	2200	....	....	....	....	....	....	1335	....	....	....
104.00	....	....	....	....	....	....	2035	....	....	....	0820		d. Laurel ...d.	2040	....	....	....	....	....	....	1210	....	....	....
104.00	....	....	....	....	....	....	2130	....	....	....	0915		d. Hattiesburg ...d.	2000	....	....	....	....	....	....	1130	....	....	....
104.00	....	....	....	....	....	....	2359	....	....	....	1155		a. **New Orleans** ...d.	1715	....	....	....	....	....	....	0840	....	....	....

◇–Fare ex Nashville. ★–Fare ex Birmingham. *CML*–Capital Motor Lines. *GL*–Greyhound Lines.

Table 425 DETROIT - GRAND RAPIDS - MACKINAW CITY/CHICAGO

GL

US $	GL 5181	GL 5115	GL 5171	GL 5109	GL 5168	GL 5130	GL 5173	GL 5111	GL 5175	IT 80	GL 5166	GL 5128	IT 86	GL 5179		km	↓ ↑	GL 5170	GL 5167	GL 5137	GL 5172	GL 5108	IT 81	GL 5180	GL 5139	GL 5169	GL 5176	GL 5110	GL 5178	IT 87	GL 5112	G 51
25.00	0050	....	0530	....	0700	0800	0815	....	1045	....	1300	1330	....	1645	....	*238*	d. **Detroit** ... a.	1050	1340	1050	1540	....	....	1415	1810	1855	1945	....	2140	....	....	07
24.00	|	....	0640	....	0800	|	0925	....	1201	....	1355	|	....	1800	....	*229*	d. Ypsilanti ... d.	0940	1245	|	1430	....	....	|	|	1800	1850	....	|	....	....	06
23.00	|	....	0705	....	0825	|	0950	....	1225	....	1420	|	....	1825	....	*211*	d. Ann Arbor ... d.	0915	1220	|	1400	....	....	|	|	1735	1825	....	2030	....	....	05
19.00	|	....	0820	....	0920	|	1045	....	1325	....	1515	|	....	1920	....	*182*	d. Jackson ... d.	0820	1130	|	1310	....	....	|	|	1645	1730	....	1940	....	....	04
12.00	|	....	|	....	1010	|	|	....	|	....	1605	|	....	|	....	*113*	d. Lansing ... d.	|	1045	|	|	....	....	|	|	1600	|	....	|	....	....	
12.00	|	....	|	....	1020	|	|	....	|	....	1615	|	....	|	....	*106*	d. East Lansing ... d.	|	1030	|	|	....	....	|	|	1530	|	....	|	....	....	
12.00	|	....	0930	....	|	|	1155	....	1435	....	|	|	....	2030	....		d. Battle Creek ... d.	0705	|	|	1135	....	....	|	|	|	1615	....	1845	....	....	
10.00	|	....	1010	....	|	|	1230	....	1510	*1445*	|	|	1900	2110	....		d. Kalamazoo ... d.	0615	|	|	1100	....	*1425*	|	|	|	1530	....	1810	2125	....	
0.00	|	0715	....	1815	|	|	....	1600	....	1600	|	|	2000	....	....	*0*	d. **Grand Rapids** ... d.	....	|	|	....	1245	1305	|	|	|	....	1520	....	2025	2225	
	|	0750	....	1855	|	|	....	1640	....	|	|	|	....	....	....	*45*	d. Holland ... d.	....	|	|	....	1210	|	|	|	|	....	1445	....	....	2150	
	|	0920	....	2000	|	|	....	1750	....	|	|	|	....	....	....	*129*	d. Benton Harbor ... d.	....	|	|	....	1055	|	|	|	|	....	1320	....	....	2040	
	|	0950	....	|	|	|	....	1820	....	|	|	|	....	....	....	*230*	d. Gary ... d.	....	|	|	....	0815	|	|	|	|	....	1155	....	....	|	
	|	1010	....	2035	|	|	....	**1840s**	....	|	|	|	....	....	....	*236*	d. Hammond ... d.	....	|	|	....	0755	|	|	|	|	....	1035	....	....	|	
31.00	0520	1045	....	2110	|	|	....	1930	....	|	|	|	....	....	....	*271*	a. **Chicago** ... a.	....	|	|	....	0700	|	0745	|	|	....	0945	....	....	1730	12
11.00	....	....	....	....	|	|	....	....	....	1714	|	|	....	....	....	*91*	d. Big Rapids ... d.	....	|	|	....	....	1151	....	|	|	....	....	....	....	....	..
13.00	....	....	....	....	|	|	....	....	....	1731	|	|	....	....	....	*109*	d. Reed City ... d.	....	|	|	....	....	1134	....	|	|	....	....	....	....	....	..
	....	....	....	....	1250	1255	....	....	....	|	1845	1825	....	....	....		d. Clare ... d.	....	0830	0910	....	....	|	....	1330	1330	....	....	....	....	....	..
19.00	....	....	....	....	1355	1400	....	....	....	1820	1950	|	....	....	....	*157*	d. Cadillac ... d.	....	0705	0755	....	....	1045	....	|	1205	....	....	....	....	....	..
19.00	....	....	....	....	1500	1515	....	....	....	1930	2055	|	....	....	....	*238*	d. Traverse City ... d.	....	0600	0720	....	....	0940	....	|	1100	....	....	....	....	....	..
35.00	....	....	....	....	....	1655	....	....	....	2100	....	2115	....	....	....	*316*	d. Petoskey ... d.	....	....	0530	....	....	0800	....	1040	....	....	....	....	....	....	..
40.00	....	....	....	....	....	1825	....	....	....	2145	....	2200	....	....	....	*379*	a. **Mackinaw City** ... d.	....	....	0450	....	....	0715	....	0955	....	....	....	....	....	....	..
41.00	....	....	....	....	....	1840	....	....	....	2200	....	2215	....	....	....	*390*	a. St. Ignace ... d.	....	....	0435	....	....	0700	....	0940	....	....	....	....	....	....	..

GL–Greyhound Lines. *IT*–Indian Trails.

Table 426 KNOXVILLE - NASHVILLE - MEMPHIS - DALLAS

GL K

US $	↓	km	GL 1173	GL 1505		GL 1533		GL 1513	KBC 602	GL 1535	GL 1515		GL 1539	GL 1519	GL 6143		GL 1531	GL 1509			GL 1537	GL 1507	GL 1511	GL 1501	
0.00	**Knoxville** ...d.	*0*	....	....	....	0055	....	....	....	0405	....	....	0700	....	....	....	1045	....	....	....	1320	....	1815	....	...
	Cookeville ...d.		....	....	....	**0145s**	....	....	....	|	....	....	0810	....	....	....	1140	....	....	....	1415	....	1910	....	...
	Nashville ...d.		0145	....	....	0345	....	....	....	0615	0700	....	0940	1015	....	....	1400	....	....	....	1630	....	2040	2135	...
	Jackson ...d.		|	....	....	0555	....	....	....	....	0930	....	....	1230	....	....	1615	....	....	....	1850	....	....	2345	...
	Memphis ...a.		0530	....	....	0745	....	....	....	....	1115	....	....	1410	....	....	1800	....	....	....	2040	....	....	0125	...
	Memphis ...d.		....	0630	....	....	....	0830	1145	....	1201	....	....	1500	1845	....	....	1900	....	....	....	2145	....	0230	...
	Little Rock ...d.		....	0915	....	....	....	1201	|	....	1440	....	....	1820	2130	....	....	2145	....	....	....	0030	....	0510	..
	Pine Bluff ...d.		....	|	....	....	....	|	1505	....	|	....	....	|	....	....	....	|	....	....	....	|	....	|	..
	Hot Springs ...d.		....	1035	....	....	....	|	|	....	|	....	....	1940	....	....	....	|	....	....	....	|	....	|	..
	Malvern ...d.		....	|	....	....	....	1245	|	....	1535	....	....	|	....	....	....	|	....	....	....	|	....	|	..
	Arkadelphia ...d.		....	1125	....	....	....	|	|	....	1610	....	....	2030	....	....	....	|	....	....	....	|	....	|	..
	Camden ...d.		....	|	....	....	....	|	1640	....	|	....	....	|	....	....	....	|	....	....	....	|	....	|	..
	Texarkana ...d.		....	1325	....	....	....	1505	1840	....	1830	....	....	2220	....	....	....	0030	....	....	....	0315	....	0815	..
	Dallas ...a.		....	1700	....	....	....	1815	....	....	2215	....	....	0130	....	....	....	0340	....	....	....	0640	....	1210	..

↓			GL 6142	GL 1502	GL 1532			GL 1516	GL 1538		GL 1514		GL 1518	KBC 601	GL 1510	GL 1530			GL 1504	GL 1534	GL 1506	GL 1536		GL 1508	
Dallas ...d.	....	....	....	2000	....	....	....	0001	....	....	0230	....	....	....	0530	....	....	....	0845	....	1230	....	....	1645	..
Texarkana ...d.	....	....	....	0005	....	....	....	0320	....	....	0615	....	....	0755	0940	....	....	....	1300	....	1640	....	....	2100	..
Camden ...d.	....	....	....	|	....	....	....	|	....	....	|	....	....	0950	|	....	....	....	|	....	|	....	....	|	..
Arkadelphia ...d.	....	....	....	|	....	....	....	|	....	....	|	....	....	|	1105	....	....	....	1430	....	|	....	....	2230	..
Malvern ...d.	....	....	....	|	....	....	....	|	....	....	|	....	....	|	|	....	....	....	1505	....	|	....	....	2305	..
Hot Springs ...d.	....	....	....	|	....	....	....	|	....	....	|	....	....	|	1201	....	....	....	|	....	1840	....	....	|	..
Pine Bluff ...d.	....	....	....	|	....	....	....	|	....	....	|	....	....	1150	|	....	....	....	|	....	|	....	....	|	..
Little Rock ...d.	....	....	0250	0250	....	....	....	0615	....	....	0900	....	....	|	1345	....	....	....	1625	....	2010	....	....	0025	..
Memphis ...a.	....	....	0510	0510	....	....	....	0900	....	....	1159	....	....	1500	1610	....	....	....	1915	....	2230	....	....	0245	..
Memphis ...d.	....	....	....	....	0600	....	....	....	0930	....	1315	....	....	....	....	1700	....	....	2000	....	....	2315	....	0330	..
Jackson ...d.	....	....	....	....	|	....	....	....	1115	....	1500	....	....	....	....	1900	....	....	2140	....	....	|	....	0505	..
Nashville ...d.	....	....	....	....	1015	....	....	....	1500	....	1730	....	1845	....	....	2200	....	....	2355	0045	....	0345	....	0715	..
Cookeville ...d.	....	....	....	....	1135	....	....	....	1630	....	....	....	2020	....	....	**2335s**	....	....	....	**0220s**	....	**0520s**	....	....	..
Knoxville ...a.	....	....	....	....	1425	....	....	....	1940	....	....	....	2315	....	...	0230	....	....	....	0515	....	0815	....	....	..

GL–Greyhound Lines. *KBC*–Kerrville Bus Co.

Table 428 HUTCHINSON

H

US $	6 Ⓐ	2 ⑥		4 Ⓐ	km	↓ ↑	1 ⑥	3 Ⓐ	5 Ⓐ¶	
0.00	....	0630	....	1315	*0*	d. **Wichita** ...a.	0630	1145	....	..
	0730	0800	....	1420		d. Hutchinson ...d.	0515	1000	1700	..
	0830	....	....	1545¶		d. Great Bend ...d.	....	0830	1545	..
	....	....	....	....		a. **Salina** ...d.	....	....	....	..

HSS– Hutchinson Bus Line.

ble 430   CHICAGO - MEMPHIS - NEW ORLEANS   COT DEA GL

$	GL 1215	GL 7901	GL 1223	GL 1217	GL 5226	GL 1219	GL 1221	GL 1213	GL 1425	GL 7903	GL 1211		km			GL 1208	GL 7900	GL 5221	GL 1222	GL 1224	GL 7902	GL 5227	GL 1220	GL 1214	GL 1206	GL 1218
.00	0215	1045	1201	1430	1700	1745	1930	2000	2100	2300	0001		0	d.Chicago............a.		1155	1345	1515	1720	2120	1930	2350	0430	0625	0600	0830
.00	0320s				1840			2135					92	d.Kankakee ....d.		0950		1345				2220		0505		
.00	0445		1450	1720	2015	2045	2215	2305			0245		208	d.Champaign.............d.		0820		1201	1445	1845		2045		0340		
.00	0630		1655	1910		2225	0020	0040			0420		323	d.Effingham..............d.		0630			1300	1700			0055	0220	0215	0445
.00	0830	1615	1850	2040	....			0200	0215	0415			433	d.Mount Vernon..........d.		0430	0845	....	1120	1500	1430		....	0035		
.00					....						0720		590	d. Cairo ....d.									2150			
.00	0950		2005								0825		629	d.Carbondale.............d.					0935	1305			....			
.00				GL	0150						0940		739	d. Sikeston ....d.		0230						GL	2120		2245	0115
.00				1191									739	d. Blytheville ....d.								1190	1945			
.00	1201		2155	0440		0430							613	d.Paducah 433............d.				0805	1135		2155		2220		
.00	1240		2225	0520		0510							651	d.Mayfield 433...........d.				0710	1040		2115		2115s		
.00						0755								d. Jackson TN ....d.							1905				
.00						0925								d. Corinth................d.							1720				
.00						1055								d. Tupelo ....d.							1605				
.00	1325		2320	0605									705	d.Union City 433.........d.				0620	0950		2025				
.00	1405		2359	0645									762	d.Dyersburg 433..........d.				0535	0905		1940				
.00	1610	2045	0200	0110	0845	0415	0545		0645	0845	1115			a.............d.		2345	0345	....	0345	0715	0930	1750	1815		2000	2230

$	DEA 005	GL 1201	DEA 001	GL 1203	DEA 003		GL 1207			GL 1209	GL 1205		km			DEA 004	GL 1226	DEA 006	GL 1202	GL 1204	COT 70	DEA 002	GL 1210		GL 1212	
.00	1645	2115	0515	0230	0915	0500	0700			0915	1145		912	Memphis 433............		1930	2245	2245	0300	0615	....	1600	1720		1810	2145
.00	1830		0655		1100		0830				1315		1038	d.j..................a.		1755	2115	2115			....	1420			1635	
.00	2000		0845		1300								1143	d.Clarksdale.............d.		1605		1930			....	1230				
.00	....				1455						1450		1283	d. Greenville...........d.				1720							1500	
.00	....						1015						1133	a. Vicksburg ....d.			2000									
.00	....	0020								1245			1107	d.Greenwood..............d.					2359				1350			
.00	....	0100						COT	1330				1164	d. Durant...............d.					2320				1305			
.00								1315	73					d. Canton ....d.										1345		
.00	....	0220	1140	0700		0930	1250	1700	1740	1445	1740		1242	d.Jackson MS ....d.		1250	1800		2250	0230	1210		1230	0920	1250	1800
.00	....	0400											1329	d. Columbia ....d.					2015							
.00	....	0445											1384	d. Bogalusa .....d.					1930							
.00	....	0520											1433	d. Covington .....d.					1850							
.00					1100	1445					1935		1367	d.McComb................d.						0015			0950			1505
.00					1220	1615					2055		1453	d.Hammond...............d.						2300			0830			1350
.00				0910						1650				d. Hattiesburg..d.			1510					1020			0955	
.00									1935					d. Laurel ....d.												
.00			1040							1820				d. Gulfport....d.			1325							0810		
.00			1105							1845				d. Biloxi .....d.			1300							0745		
.00			1220						2200	2000				a. Mobile .....d.			1145				0745			0630		
.00			0630		1340	1735					2225		1531	a.New Orleans ....d.				1745	2145			0715			1201

Fare ex Memphis.
T– Colonial Trailways.
4– Delta Bus Lines.
- Greyhound Lines.

ble 431   MEMPHIS - CHATTANOOGA/ATLANTA   GL

$	1140	1558	1138		1142	1546	1132	1136	1554	1134		km			1557	1143	1545	1137	1561	1131		1145	1141	1551	1147
00	....	0140	....	0400	0615	....	0945	1645	....	2020		0	d.Memphis ....a.		....	1415	....	1745	....	1930		2110	0200	....	0655
75	....			0605			1205					145	d.Corinth ....d.				1535		1725						
00	....				0715			1745	....	2120			d. Holly Springs.........d.			1315						2005	0105	....	0555
00	....							1835		2210		120	d. New Albany...........d.									1920	0020		0505
00	....	0350			0925			1925	....	2300		160	d. Tupelo ....d.			1120						1845	2345	....	0435
90	....			0730			1330					236	d.Florence ....d.				1410		1600						
00	....	0730	1100		1315	1515	1715	2235	2315	0300		445	d.Birmingham ....d.		0640	0745	0930		1205	1245		1530	2035	2040	0140
85	....			0925				....				341	d. Huntsville ....d.					1215							
80	....											516	a. Chattanooga...........d.												
00	....	0810	1210	1210	1425	....	1905	....	....	0410			d.Anniston ....d.				0820	0915	....			1335	1820	....	2340
00	....	1130	1450	1500	1715	1855	2145	....	0255	0650			a.Atlanta ....d.		0500		0730	0830	1015			1245	1730	1900	2300

-Greyhound Lines.

ble 432   ST. LOUIS - MEMPHIS   GL

$	5237	5231	5233	5235		km			5232	5234	5230	5236
00	0030	0830	1400	1815		0	d.St. Louis..........a.		0615	1300	1740	0115
00		1110		2053		210	d.Cape Girardeau.d.		0348		1505	2305
00	0320	1230	1645	2155		264	d.Sikeston ....d.		0305	1030	1420	2220
00	0440	1400	1800	2320		374	d.Blytheville ....d.		0137	0900	1235	2035
00	0632	1535	1910	0050		494	a.Memphis ....d.		0015	0730	1100	1900

- Greyhound Lines.

ble 433   INDIANAPOLIS - MEMPHIS   ABL

$	401	213	405	215		km			402	210	408	214
00	0705	1300	1830	2145		0	d.Indianapolis ....a.		0945	1700	2105	0625
00	0815	1420	1945	2300		126	d.Bloomington ......d.		0830	1545	1950	0510
00	....	1656		....		183	d.Vincennes ....d.		....	1305		....
00	....	1900		0200		313	d.Evansville ....d.		....	1150		0210
00	....	1920		0215		330	d.Henderson ....d.		....	1100		0105
00	....	2000		0248			d.Morganfield ......d.		....	1015		0030
00	....	2155		0440		495	d.Paducah 430...d.		....	0840		2250
00	....	2225		0520		533	d.Mayfield 430.....d.		....	0740		2125
00	....	2320		0605		587	d.Union City 430 ..d.		....	0650		2035
00	....	2359		0645		644	d.Dyersburg 430...d.		....	0605		1950
00	....	0200		0845		794	a.Memphis 430....d.		....	0415		1800

- American Trailways.

Table 436   BIRMINGHAM - MOBILE   GL

US $	5043	5045		km			5042	5044
		⑤⑥						⑥⑦
					d.Chattanooga ...a.			
	....	....			d.Gadsden ....d.			
0.00	0745	1300		0	d.Birmingham ....d.		1155	1920
11.00				100	d. Tuscaloosa ....d.			
				155	d. Eutaw..........d.			
22.00				215	d. Demopolis .....d.			
24.00	1020	1535		140	d.Selma ....d.		0855	1625
32.00	1140	1655		239	d.Thomasville ....d.		0735	1505
43.00	1330	1845		399	a.Mobile ....d.		0545	1315

GL– Greyhound Lines.

Table 437   OMAHA - MEMPHIS   GL

US $	6101	6131	6103	5879		km			5880	6102	6132
0.00	....	0820	....	1955		0	d.Omaha...............a.		0330	....	1815
		0930					d.Nebraska City......d.				1710
26.80				2215		192	d. Maryville..........d.		0110		
13.00	0957					100	d. Auburn ....d.			1643	
19.35	1040					157	d. Falls City ....d.			1600	
33 40	1220			2310		242	d.St.Joseph ....d.		0015	1425	
40.85	1325			0010			a....................d.		2315	1315	
						308	Kansas City..{		6100		
0.00	0700		....	1800			d...................a.		2040	0545	....
15.85	0845		....	1945		438	d.Clinton ....d.		1855	0400	....
30.57	1120		....	2220		648	d.Springfield ....d.		1645	0205	....
35.20			r	....		907	d.Walnut Ridge....d.		r		
67.85	1705		0315	....			d.Hoxie ....d.		1030	2055	....
73.15	1730		0335	....		948	d.Jonesboro ....d.		1005	2030	....
131.45	1920		0530	....		1063	a.Memphis ....d.		0815	1840	....

GL–Greyhound Lines.

Check update notes to timetables and with operator before starting your journey

Table 439 — CAPE CANAVERAL 🚌 BTA

Regular local 🚌 services link Cocoa, Rockledge, Melbourne, Cape Canaveral and Port Canaveral.

BTA– Brevard Transportation Authority.

Table 440 — MINNEAPOLIS - DULUTH 🚌 GL

US $	5900	5908			km	↓	↑			5907	5909
0.00	0700	1520	....		0	d.**Minneapolis** .....a.		....		1605	2230
11.00	0730	1545	....		16	d.**St. Paul**..........a.		....		1545	2205
18.00	0910	1700	....		150	d.Hinckley ....d.		....		1355	2020
30.00	1055	1835	....		270	d.**Duluth** ....d.		....		1210	1915
30.00	....	....	....		278	a.Superior ....d.		....		....	....
	....	....	....			d. Virginia ....d.		....		....	....
	....	....	....			a. Hibbing ....d.		....		....	....

GL– Greyhound Lines.

Table 441 — INTERNATIONAL FALLS 🚌 TRT

US $	302			km	↓	↑		301	
0.00	0800	....	....	0	d.International Falls a.		....	2030	....
9.60	1010	....	....		d.Virginia ....d.		....	1830	....
16.15	1135	....	....		a.**Duluth**............d.		....	1700	....

TRT– Triangle Transportation.

Table 442 — DULUTH - GRAND FORKS 🚌 TRT

US $	3			km	↓	↑		2	
0.00	....	1230	....	0	d.Duluth ....a.		1645	....	
10.75	....	1435	....		d.Grand Rapids....d.		1435	....	
15.90	....	1625	....	200	d.Bemidji ....d.		1310	....	
24.10	....	1830	....	340	d.Crookston..........d.		1050	....	
32.85	....	1920	....	384	a.**Grand Forks**.....d.		1010	....	

TRT– Triangle Transportation.

Table 443 — MINNEAPOLIS - ST. PAUL 🚌 MTC

🚌 service (16, 94L) Minneapolis-St. Paul and v.v. 17 km. Journey: 25-45 mins. Fare: US $: 1.00.

From Minneapolis: 0412⑥/0413†/0502④ and frequent to 0104①/0106⑦/0107②–⑥.

From St. Paul: 0458④/0501① and frequent to 0109①/0112ex①.

AMTRAK's Midway rail station is served by route 16. Bus stop is two blocks south of station on University Avenue.

MTC– Metropolitan Transit Commission. 📞 Minneapolis 827 7733.

Table 445 — MINNEAPOLIS - KANSAS CITY 🚌 JL

US $		↓	km	405	817		803	905	811
0.00	**Minneapolis** ....d.		0	....	0600	0730	....	1201	1730	1855
3.20	**St. Paul** ....d.		16	....	0620		....		1750	
12.75	Owatonna...............d.		121	....	0815	0835	1340			2045
19.10	Albert Lea ....d.		176	....	0920s	0910		1415	2125	2125
30.00	Mason City ....d.		233	....	1015	1015	1520			2235
40.60	Iowa Falls..............d.		309		1115					
47.85	Ames ....d.		376		1225		1700			
52.00	**Des Moines** ......{a./d.		424		1310 / 1330		1745 / 1830		0050 / 0125	
70.75	Eagleville...............d.				1545		2045		0330	
70.75	Bethany.................d.		634		1605		2105			
91.55	**Kansas City** ......{a./d.		709		1750 / 1820		2250 / 2355		0520 / 0615	
42.65	Waterloo ....d.		296	1240						
54.10	**Cedar Rapids**......a.		406	1340						
96.75	Lawrence ....d.					1920		0050	0710	
106.10	Iola ....d.					2105		0240	0900	
109.20	Coffeyville ....d.		951			2235		0435	1045	
113.40	Tulsa ....a.		1167			0015		0630	1245	
123.80	**Oklahoma City** .....a.		1470			0220		0915	1445	

		↓	493	734	724	910	730	408
Oklahoma City........d.			0830	....	1245	....	2230	....
Tulsa ....d.			1100	....	1600	....	0035	....
Coffeyville ....d.			1250	....	1750	....	0215	....
Iola ....d.			1510	....	2010	....	0355	....
Lawrence ....d.			1700	....	2200	....		....
Cedar Rapids..........d.							1400	
Waterloo ....d.							1500	
Kansas City ....{a./d.			1800 / 1900	....	2300 / 2345		0630 / 0700	
Bethany..................d.			2045	....			0835	
Eagleville................d.			2145	0145			0920	
Des Moines ....{a./d.			2340 / 0005	0330 / 0350			1105 / 1120	
Ames......................d.			0050				1205	
Iowa Falls...............d.					0525			
Mason City..............d.				0645		....	1405	1715
Albert Lea ....d.			0325	0740		0745	1450	1800
Owatonna................d.			0400	0820		1	1525	1905
St. Paul ....a.						1100as		2050s
Minneapolis ....a.			0600		1015	1115	1720	2105

a– Note ⓐ applies.
JL– Jefferson Lines.

Table 446 — MINNEAPOLIS - ASHLAND 🚌 NLI WNT

US $	NLI	WNT		km	↓	↑	NLI	WNT
	201	**102**					**200**	**101**
		▲						▲
0.00	....	1300		0	d.**Minneapolis** .....a.		1140	....
2.00	....	1325		16	d.**St. Paul**.............a.		1120	....
0.00	....	1852			d. Eau Claire........a.			1110
◇7.95	....	1605	2003	174	d.Rice Lake ....d.		0855	0935
◇11.20	....	1635	2032		d.Spooner ....d.		0810	0850
◇22.95	....		2202		a. **Duluth** ....d.			0710
◇22.95	....		2212		a. Superior ....d.			0700
18.75	....	1710		257	d.Hayward ....d.		0735	....
26.20	....	1825		352	a.**Ashland** ....d.		0620	....
31.45	....	1915		414	a.Ironwood ....d.		0535	....

◇–Fare ex Eau Claire. NLI–Northfield Lines Inc. WNT–Wisconsin Northern.

Table 447 — MINNEAPOLIS - OMAHA 🚌 GL MLA SQTR

US $	GL	SQTR	MLA	GL	km	↓	↑	MLA	SQTR	GL	GL
	5879	**61**		**5881**				**60**		**5880**	**588?**
0.00	0845	....	1405	1615	0	d.**Minneapolis** .....a.		1125	....	1455	222?
		0800				d. Winona ....d.			1535		
		0900				d. Rochester ......d.			1425		
		1000				d. Owatonna ......d.			1325		
17.00	1115	1100	1605	1840	131	d.**Mankato** ....d.		0925	1225	1225	202?
25.50	1400	....		2130	256	d.Worthington ....d.		....		0935	173?
						d. Storm Lake ......d.					
						d. Cherokee ....d.					
74.00	1530	....		2300	428	d.Sioux Falls ....d.		....		0815	161?
95.00	1735	....		0045	525	d.Sioux City ....d.		....		0615	132?
98.00	1920	....		0220	602	a.**Omaha** ....d.		....		0430	114?

US $	22		km		MLA			21	
	⑤							⑤	
0.00	1615		0	d.**Mankato** ....a.			1840		
	1735			a.**Fairmont**..........d.			1740		

GL–Greyhound Lines. MLA–Mankato Land to Air Inc. SQTR–Speciality Tours.

Table 448 — BURLINGTON - ST. LOUIS 🚌 BT?

US $	1307		km	↓	↑	1302	
0.00	....	1850	0	d.**Burlington** ....a.		0845	....
8.40	....	1955	73	d.Keokuk ....d.		0735	....
16.80	....	2055	133	d.Quincy ....d.		0625	....
21.00	....	2130	182	d.Hannibal ....d.		0505	....
36.75	....	2359	362	a.**St. Louis** ....d.		0230	....

BTW– Burlington Trailways.

Table 449 — BEMIDJI/HIBBING 🚌 GL TIQ?

US $		GL	TIQU	km	↓	↑	TIQU	GL	TIQ
		5654	**101**				**100**	**5657**	**10?**
			▲				▲☆		▲
0.00		1035	1715	0	d.**Minneapolis** .....a.		1145	....	1430	162?
11.50		1230			d.St. Cloud ....d.			....	1235	
15.50		1330			d.Little Falls..........d.			....	1140	
18.00		1405			d.Brainerd ....d.			....	1050	
			2110		d.**Hibbing** ....d.		0800			121?
			2145		d.Virginia ....d.		0710			112?
34.50		1620			a. Bemidji ....d.		....		0835	

GL–Greyhound Lines. TIQU–Tri-Action Tours Inc.

Table 450 — MINNEAPOLIS - ABERDEEN 🚌 JRL QU?

US $	QUC	QUC	JRL		km	↓	↑	QUC		QUC	JR?
	①③⑤	②④	**5613**					②④		①③⑤	**56?**
0.00	....	....	1530		0	d.**Minneapolis** .....a.		....		....	145?
28.00	1440	1440	1755		150	d.Willmar ....d.		1220		1225	124?
43.00			1955		275	d.Ortonville ....d.				1110	
	1505	1505				d. Clara City ....d.		1140		1200	
	1545					d. Granite Falls ....d.				1130	
	1800					a. Marshall ....d.				0900	
		1710				a. Madison ....d.		0950			
		1800				a. Ivanhoe ....d.		0900			
59.00			2205		440	a.**Aberdeen**..........d.		....			08?

JRL– Jack Rabbit Lines. QUC–Quality Carriers.

Table 451 — SIOUX FALLS - RAPID CITY 🚌 JR?

US $	11		15	13		km	↓	↑	12		10	1?
0.00	0845		1630	....		0	d.**Sioux Falls** ......a.		....		1445	214?
21.00	....		1755	1755		91	d.Mitchell ....d.		1300		1300	
						174	d. Chamberlain ....d.					
33.00	1125			1855		190	d.Huron ....d.		1145			18?
56.00	1415					380	d.Pierre ....d.		....			15?
68.00	1510						d.Wall ....d.		....			12?
75.00	1630					514	a.**Rapid City** ◇ ...d.		....			11?

◇– A special 9-hour tour of the Black Hills is operated daily June 15-Sept. 15, dep. Ra? City 0800.

JRL– Jack Rabbit Lines.

MYSTIFIED
by all the symbols?
See page 61 for an explanation!

Table 452 — MILWAUKEE - MADISON — BGC GL

service Milwaukee-Madison and v.v. 124 km. Journey: 1½-2 hours. Fare: US $: 8.00.
from Milwaukee: BGC at 0700, 1000, 1230, 1500, 1730, 1845⑦, 2000, 2230†, 1300, 1745, 2315. GL at 0805,
from Madison: BGC at 0700, 1000, 1230, 1500, 1615⑤, 1730, 2000, 2230†; GL at 0145, 0605, 1415, 1940, 2130.
BGC–Badger Coaches.   GL–Greyhound Lines.

Table 453 — ▲ WICHITA FALLS - ABILENE ▲ — SKYK

US $		401 ☆▲		km	↓	↑		414 ☆▲	
0.00	....	0845	....	0	d.Wichita Falls ....a.		....	1745	....
	....	0950	....	82	d.Seymour..........d.		....	1640	....
	....	1240	....	245	a.Abilene ....d.		....	1400	....

SKYK– Skylark Transportation.

Table 454 — ST. LOUIS - MEMPHIS — SOV

US $	1	3	5	km	↓	↑	2	4	
0.00	....	1345	1800	0	d.St. Louis...........a.	1205	....	....	1740
	0800	1635	2145		d. Farmington......d.	0800	....	....	1430
25.00	0950	....	....	223	d.Cape Girardeau..d.		....	....	1230
	....	....	....	461	d.Jonesboro ....d.		....	....	
33.00	....	....	....	579	a.Memphis ....d.		....	....	

SOV– Shumakes Ozark Village.

Table 456 — DES MOINES - SPRINGFIELD — SMC

US $		01		km	↓	↑		02	
	....	....		0	d.Des Moines......a.		....	....	
	....	....		162	d.Ottumwa.........d.		....	....	
	....	....		265	d.Kirksville........d.		....	....	
	....	....		320	d.Macon ....d.		....	....	
	....	....		356	d.Moberly ....d.		....	....	
		1630		413	d.Columbia ....d.			0955	
		1720		462	d.Jefferson City ....d.			0850	
		1925		600	d.Lebanon ....d.			0650	
0.00		2020		685	a.Springfield ....d.			0545	

SMC– Sho-Me Coaches Inc.

Table 457 — NORFOLK - CHADRON — KSE

US $		22 ②④		km	↓	↑		21 ③⑤	
0.00	....	1530		0	d.Norfolk ....a.		0730	....	
					d.O'Neill ....d.				
					d.Bassett ....d.				
					d.Ainsworth ....d.				
		1915			d.Valentine ....d.		0330		
		2045			d.Gordon ....d.		0030		
		2100			d.Rushville..........d.		0015		
		2130			a.Chadron ....d.		2330		

KSE– K&S Expressway Inc.

Table 458 — ST. LOUIS - OKLAHOMA CITY - DALLAS — CPL GL JL

US $		GL 1351	JL 467	GL 6425	GI 6427	GI 473	GL 6207	JL 737	GL 1367	GL 6423	GL 1355		GL 6253 Ⓐ	GL 6255		GL 6209	GL 475			GL 1385	
	km																				
35.00	Chicago 422.....d.	2030	....	....	0010	....	0600	....	0830	....	....	....	....	....	....	1530	....	....	1530	....
0.00	St. Louis..........d.	0	0245	....	....	0730	....	1400	....	1730	....	1845	2000	....	....	2300		....	....	2300	....
18.25	Rolla...............d.	166	0440	....	....	1010	....	1640	....		....	2100	2235	....	....			....	....	0115	....
31.00	Lebanon ....d.	250	0617	....	....	1135	....	1822	....	2105	....			....	....			....	....		....
37.00	Springfield ....d.	331	0800	....	....	1315	....	2010	....	2210	....			....	....	0310		....	....	0340	....
46.26	Carthage ....d.		0910	....	....	1425	....		....		....			....	....			....	....		....
50.00	Joplin.............d.	442	0945	....	....	1505	....	2145	....		....			....	....	0455		....	....		....
70.50	Tulsa ◇ ....d.	627	1315	....	1315	1815	1835	....	0030	0115	0200	0300		....	....	0800		....	....	0830	....
88.50	Oklahoma City ◇ .{a.	800	1510	....	....	2030	....	0220	0310	....	0455			....	....	0955		....	....		....
	{d.		1515	1600	....	2045c	0001	0300	0325	....	0515			....	1015	1030c		....	....		....
76.50	Muskogee.......d.	665		....	1420	1920	....		....		....			....	....			....	....	0935	....
88.50	McAlester.........d.	752		....	1600	2055	....		....		....			....	....			....	....	1115	....
95.00	Ardmore ....d.	940		....	1830a	....	....	0220	0530a	....	....			....	1215			....	....	1250	....
95.00	Durant.............d.	882		....	1735	2225	....		....		....			....	....			....	....	1250	....
95.00	Sherman ....d.	932		....	1820	2310	....		....	0540	....			....	....			....	....	1335	....
92.00	Gainesville.........d.	1003		....	1920a	....	....	0310	0640a	....	....			....	1325			....	....		....
94.00	Denton ....d.	1050		....	1955a	....	....	0345	0715a	....	....			....	1400			....	....		....
94.00	Dallas.............a.	1037		....	2055a	2015	0100	0430	0815a	....	0745			....	1500			....	....	1530	....
19.00	*Albuquerque 545* a.	1700	0150	....	....	....	0730	....	1245	....	1515			....	....	2130		....	....		....
39.00	*Los Angeles 545* a.	3050	....	....	....	....	0130	....	....	....	....			....	....	1605		....	....		....

		GL 6208 ④⑥⑥	GL 6256		GL 1356	GL 6200 Ⓐ	GL 6250	GL 6422		GL 474			GL 1382	GL 468	GL 1352		GL 6424	GL 464	GL 470		GL 6426		GL 6252 ⑤⑥	GL 1364
	Los Angeles 545..d.	....	....		1915	....	....	....		....			....	....	....		....	0900		....	....		....	....
	Albuquerque 545 .d.	....	....		1600	....	....	2045		....			....	0350	....		....	0600		....	....		....	1145
	Dallas................d.	1915	....			0200	....	2345		....			0630	0715	....		1230	1330		1715	....		....	
	Denton ....d.	2015	....			0250	....			....				0815	....			1430			....		....	
	Gainesville............d.	2050	....			0325	....			....				0905	....			1505			....		....	
	Sherman ....d.		....				0130			....			0820		....		1420			1920	....		....	
	Durant.................d.		....				0225			....			0910		....		1510			2010	....		....	
	Ardmore ....d.	2240	....			0415	....			....				0955b	....			1555b			....		....	
	McAlester..............d.		....				0410			....			1105		....		1725			2200	....		....	
	Muskogee..............d.		....							....			1230		....		1835			2310	....		....	
	Oklahoma City ◇ .{a.	2359	....			0325	0630			0830c				1215b	1615			1820b	1845c	....	....		....	2345
	{d.		....			0350	....			0905				1700				1915			....		....	0015
	Tulsa ◇ ....d.		....			0645	....	0615		1201			1455	2000	....	1940		2210		0015	....		....	0310
	Joplin..................d.		....			0920	....			1415			1715	2230	....						....		....	0520
	Carthage ....d.		....										1745		....						....		....	0550
	Springfield ....d.		....			1120	....			1620			1930	0015	....			0155			....		....	0730
	Lebanon ....d.		....			1220	....			1725			2030		....						....		....	0835
	Rolla...................d.		1320			1345	1505			1855			2205		....			0420			....	0955		1015
	St. Louis...............d.		1545			1600	1720			2140			0020	0435	....			0640			....	1210		1300
	Chicago 422...........a.		2325			2325	....			0520			0750	1300	....			1520			....		....	2015

–GL. b–JL. c–CPL. ◇–Local service (JL) Tulsa-Oklahoma City and v.v.; Tulsa dep.: 0030, 0715, 1300, 2100; Oklahoma City dep.: 0830, 1245, 1845, 2300. CPL–Panhandle railways.   GL–Greyhound Lines.   JL–Jefferson Lines.

Table 459 — ABILENE - DEL RIO — SSS

US $	101	102	100		km	↓	↑	106	104	105	
0.00	0625	1435	2330	....	0	d.Abilene ....a.		0330	1330	....	1955
7.90	0920	1730	0130	....	150	d.San Angelo ......d.		0130	1125	....	1750
11.20	1100	1910	0300	....	255	d.Sonora ....d.		0001	1005	....	1530
18.00	1300	2110	0455	....	405	a.Del Rio ....d.		2200	0815	....	1330

SSS– Sun Set Stages.

Table 460 — AUSTIN - VICTORIA — KBC

US $		604	608		km	↓	↑		601	607	
18.00			1620			d.Bryan.............a.		....	1400	....	
0.00	....	0935	1825		0	d.Austin.............d.		1630	1155	....	
7.00	....	1040			70	d.Luling ....d.		1530		....	
21.00	....	1245			197	a.Victoria ....d.		1315		....	

KBC– Kerrville Bus Co.

Table 461 — LITTLE ROCK - SHREVEPORT — KBC

US $		704		km	↓	↑		703	
0.00	....	1445		0	d.Little Rock........a.		....	0230	
	....	....			d. Pine Bluff ....d.		....		
18.00	....	1640		125	d.Camden ....d.		....	0035	
23.00	....	1730		177	d.El Dorado ....d.		....	2350	
31.25	....	....		228	d.Magnolia ....d.		....	2305	
40.75	....	1855		282	d.Minden ....d.		....	2135	
40.75	....	1935		324	a.Shreveport ....d.		....	2100	

KTO– Kerrville Bus Co.

Table 462 MONROE - NATCHEZ

RAM

US$		22 ⚒			km	↓	↑				21 ⚒
0.00	....	0955	....	....	0	d.**Monroe**	a.	....	....	....	1900
	....	1225	....	....	240	a.**Natchez**	d.	....	....	....	1645

RAM–Ramsey's Trailways.

Table 463 VICKSBURG - NEW ORLEANS

DEA GL RAM

US$		*RAM* 22 ⚒	*DEA* 003		km	↓	↑			*DEA* 6	*RAM* 21 ⚒
0.00	....	....	1505	....	116	d.**Vicksburg**	a.	....	....	1715	....
13.75	....	1230	1700	....	0	d.Natchez	d.	....	....	1540	1635
24.00	....	1340	1810	....	297	d.St. Francisville	d.	....	....	1410	1520
32.75	....	1415	1845	....	138	d.Baton Rouge	d.	....	....	1330	1445
41.25	....	*1645***a**	*2135***a**	....	263	a.**New Orleans**	d.	....	....	*0945***a**	*1230***a**

a–*GL*. *DEA*–Delta Bus Lines. *GL*–Greyhound Lines. *RAM*–Ramsey's Trailways.

Table 465 SHREVEPORT - NEW ORLEANS

GL KBC

US$					*GL* 710					*GL* 712	*GL* 714	km	↓	↑			*GL* 711		*GL* 713					*GL* 715	
	....	....	....	....	0530**b**	....	....	....	....	1201**b**	1700**b**		d.*Dallas* **466**	a.	....	....	2145**b**	....	0130**b**	....	....	....	....	1130**b**	....
0.00	....	....	....	....	1100	....	....	....	....	1730	2230	0	d.**Shreveport**	a.	....	....	1615	....	2030	....	....	....	....	0600	....
14.30	....	....	....	....	1400	....	....	....	....	2045	0130	185	d.Alexandria	d.	....	....	1310	....	1750	....	....	....	....	0310	....
29.80	....	....	....	....	1715	....	....	....	....	2345	0355	365	d.Baton Rouge	d.	....	....	1000	....	1445	....	....	....	....	0040	....
39.95	....	....	....	....	1925	....	....	....	....	0120	0530	490	a.**New Orleans**	d.	....	....	0715	....	1230	....	....	....	....	2245	....

b–*KTO*. *GL*–Greyhound Lines. *KBC*–Kerrville Bus Co.

Table 466 COLUMBIA - MONTGOMERY - DALLAS

CML GL IBL KBC SES

US$	↓	km	*KBC* 704		*GL* 1561	*GL* 5023	*SES* 120	*GL* 513	*SES* 100	*IBL* 32 ⑤	*SES* 132	*CML* 73	*KBC* 511	*GL* 1551	*SES* 408		*KBC* 402	*SES* 134	*GL* 1549	*GL* 1149		*GL* 1557	*SES* 142	*SES* 138	*KBC* 515
0.00	**Columbia** d.	0	....	....	....	....	0530	....	....	....	1215	....	....	....	....	....	....	1615	....	....	....	....	2045	0030	....
	Aiken d.		....	....	....	....	0635	....	....	....	1320	....	....	....	....	....	....	1720	....	....	....	....	2150	0140	....
	Augusta d.	93	....	....	....	....	0730	....	1130	....	1400	1415	....	....	1730	....	....	1800	....	....	....	....	2230	0200	....
	Athens d.		....	....	....	....	0945	....	1345	....	│	│	....	....	1920	....	....	│	....	....	....	....	│	│	....
	Atlanta 397 d.		....	....	0730	....	1130	1245	1530	....	1715	│	....	1745	2100	....	....	2100	2145	....	....	0445	0100	0430	....
	Milledgeville d.		....	....	│	....	....	│	....	....	....	1655	....	│	....	....	....	....	│	....	....	│	....	....	....
	Macon d.	333	....	....	│	....	....	│	....	....	....	1745	....	│	....	....	....	....	│	....	....	│	....	....	....
	Columbus **397** d.	493	....	....	│	....	....	1530f	....	1930	....	2010	....	│	....	....	....	....	0020	....	....	│	....	....	....
	Montgomery 397 d.	623	....	....	│	....	....	1715f	....	2045	....	2115	....	│	....	....	....	....	0130	....	....	│	....	....	....
	Anniston d.		....	....	0820	....	....	│	....	....	....	│	....	1835	....	....	....	....	│	....	....	│	....	....	....
	Birmingham d.		....	....	1015	1545	....	│	....	....	....	│	....	2115	....	....	....	....	│	0330	....	0715	....	....	....
	Tuscaloosa d.		....	....	1130	1705	....	│	....	....	....	│	....	2230	....	....	....	....	│	0450	....	0825	....	....	....
	Selma d.	725	....	....	│	│	....	1815f	....	....	....	2215	....	│	....	....	....	....	0230	│	....	│	....	....	....
	Uniontown d.		....	....	│	│	....	1850f	....	....	....	2248	....	│	....	....	....	....	0305	│	....	│	....	....	....
	Demopolis d.	784	....	....	│	│	....	1915f	....	....	....	2310	....	│	....	....	....	....	0330	│	....	│	....	....	....
	Meridian d.	871	....	....	│	1910	....	2045	....	....	....	0010	....	0015	....	....	....	....	0445	0655	....	1015	....	....	....
	Jackson d.	1021	....	....	1830	....	....	2330	....	....	....	....	....	0245	....	....	....	....	0715	▬	....	1245	....	....	....
	Vicksburg d.	1094	....	....	1920	....	....	0020	....	....	....	....	....	0335	....	....	....	....	0805	....	....	1335	....	....	....
	Tallulah d.	1125	....	....	1955	....	....	│	....	....	....	....	....	│	....	....	....	....	0840	....	....	1400	....	....	....
	Monroe d.	1220	....	....	2140	....	....	0135	....	....	....	....	....	0500	....	....	....	....	1010	....	....	1515	....	....	....
	Minden d.	1330	1855	....	│	....	....	│	....	....	....	....	....	0630	....	....	....	....	1150	*KBC*	....	1650	....	....	....
	Shreveport a.	1372	1935	....	2345	....	....	0325	....	....	....	....	....	0710	....	....	....	....	1230	**513**	....	1730	....	....	....
	Shreveport d.		....	....	0020	....	....	0345	....	....	....	....	0630	0800	....	....	....	....	1300	1700	....	1800	....	....	2115
	Marshall d.	1442	....	....	0110	....	....	│	....	....	....	....	0720	0850	....	....	....	....	1350	1755	....	1850	....	....	2200
	Longview d.	1484	....	....	0145	....	....	│	....	....	....	....	0755	0925	....	....	....	....	1425	1830	....	1925	....	....	2235
	Tyler d.	1560	....	....	0240	....	....	0535	....	....	....	....	0900	1020	....	....	1520	....	1520	1935	....	2035	....	....	2335
	Dallas a.	1705	....	....	0430	....	....	0730	....	....	....	....	1130	1220	....	....	1800	....	1725	2145	....	2230	....	....	0130

↓		*IBL* 31 ⑤		*GL* 1546	*GL* 5022	*GL* 1548	*SES* 133	*KBC* 703		*KBC* 516	*GL* 1158	*GL* 1554	*KBC* 401	*GL* 1158	*GL* 514	*KBC* 512	*SES* 143	*KBC* 514		*GL* 1558	*SES* 139		*CML* 2	*SES* 103	
Dallas d.	....	....	....	2315	....	0300	....	....	....	0530	....	0800	1015	....	1230	1201	....	1700	....	1915	....	....	....	....	....
Tyler d.	....	....	....	0120	....	0500	....	....	....	0800	....	1000	1255	....	│	1425	....	1945	....	2130	....	....	....	....	....
Longview d.	....	....	....	0210	....	│	....	....	....	0900	....	1050	▬	....	1510	1525	....	2045	....	2220	....	....	....	....	....
Marshall d.	....	....	....	0245	....	│	....	....	....	0935	....	1125	....	....	1545	1600	....	2120	....	2255	....	....	....	....	....
Shreveport a.	....	....	....	0335	....	0645	....	....	....	1035	....	1215	....	....	1635	1655	....	2210	....	2345	....	....	....	....	....
Shreveport d.	....	....	....	0355	....	0715	....	0645	....	....	....	1245	....	....	1710	▬	....	....	....	0015	....	....	....	....	....
Minden d.	....	....	....	│	....	0750	....	0725	....	....	....	1320	....	....	1745	....	....	....	....	│	....	....	....	....	....
Monroe d.	....	....	....	0600	....	0940	....	....	....	....	....	1505	....	....	1935	....	....	....	....	0225	....	....	....	....	....
Tallulah d.	....	....	....	0720	....	1100	....	....	....	....	....	1605	....	....	2035	....	....	....	....	│	....	....	....	....	....
Vicksburg d.	....	....	....	0745	....	1125	....	....	....	....	....	1630	....	....	2100	....	....	....	....	0340	....	....	....	....	....
Jackson d.	....	....	....	0920	....	1300	....	....	....	....	....	1800	....	....	2235	....	....	....	....	0515	....	....	....	....	....
Meridian d.	....	....	....	│	1335	1515	....	....	....	....	2200	1955	....	2200	0025f	....	....	....	....	0710	....	....	0720	....	....
Demopolis d.	....	....	....	│	│	1625	....	....	....	....	│	│	....	│	0130f	....	....	....	....	│	....	....	0845	....	....
Uniontown d.	....	....	....	│	│	1650	....	....	....	....	│	│	....	│	0155f	....	....	....	....	│	....	....	0910	....	....
Selma d.	....	....	....	│	│	1725	....	....	....	....	│	│	....	│	0230f	....	....	....	....	│	....	....	0945	....	....
Tuscaloosa d.	....	....	....	1500	1540	│	....	....	....	....	0005	2125	....	0005	│	....	....	....	....	0900	....	....	│	....	....
Birmingham d.	....	....	....	1715	1710	│	....	....	....	....	0120	2315	....	0120	│	....	....	....	....	1115	....	....	│	....	....
Anniston d.	....	....	....	1905	....	│	....	....	....	....	....	│	....	▬	│	....	....	....	....	1225	....	....	│	....	....
Montgomery 397 d.	....	1600	....	│	....	1915	....	....	....	....	....	│	....	....	0445f	....	....	....	....	│	....	....	1245	....	....
Columbus **397** d.	....	1915	....	│	....	│	....	....	....	....	....	│	....	....	0815	....	....	....	....	│	....	....	1615	....	....
Macon d.	....	....	....	│	....	│	....	....	....	....	....	│	*SES*	*SES*	│	*SES*	....	....	....	│	....	....	1845	....	....
Milledgeville d.	....	....	....	│	....	│	....	....	....	....	....	│	**131**	**205**	│	**121**	....	....	....	│	....	....	1935	....	....
Atlanta 397 d.	....	....	....	2150	....	2315	2345	....	....	....	....	0255	0345	0730	1100	1100	1215	....	....	1515	1600	....	│	1830	....
Athens d.	....	....	....	....	....	....	│	....	....	....	....	....	│	0915	....	1245	│	....	....	....	│	....	│	2015	....
Augusta d.	....	....	....	....	....	....	0220	....	....	....	....	....	0645	1145	....	1455	1510	....	....	....	1915	....	2205	2230	....
Aiken d.	....	....	....	....	....	....	│	....	....	....	....	....	0705	1205	....	....	1530	....	....	....	1935	....	....	2250	....
Columbia a.	....	....	....	....	....	....	0340	....	....	....	....	....	0815	1315	....	....	1640	....	....	....	2045	....	....	2359	....

f–*CML*. *GL*–Greyhound Lines. *CML*–Capital Motor Lines. *IBL*–Ingram Bus Lines. *KBC*–Kerrville Bus Co. *SES*–Southeastern Stages.

Table 467 LA CROSSE

GL JL

US$	901	903	905	911	km	↓ *JL*	↑	912	910	904	906
0.00	0715	1201	1730	1830	0	d.**Minneapolis**	a.	1110	1115	1640	2210
4.00	0740	1220	1750	1850**b**	17	d.**St. Paul**	a.	1025**b**	1100bs	│	2150**s**
12.00	│	│	│	2018	87	d.Red Wing	d.	0920	│	│	│
19.00	0955	1425	2005	│	134	d. Rochester	d.	│	0900	1430	2000
	│	│	2125	│		a. Albert Lea	d.	│	0745	│	│
23.00	1105	1530	....	2150	188	d.Winona	d.	0800	....	1310	1850
26.00	1145	1610	....	2225	232	d.La Crosse	d.	0710	....	1230	1815
	│	1705	....	2330		d.Tomah	d.	0600	....	....	1715
	*1510***a**	*1945***a**	....	*0140***a**		a.**Madison**	d.	*0400***a**	....	....	*1430***a**

a–*GL*. **b**–Ex ⑥. *GL*–Greyhound Lines. *JL*–Jefferson Lines.

Table 468 FARGO - SIOUX FALLS

JRL

US $	30				km	↓	↑			35	
41.00	0815	....	....	....	0	d.**Fargo**	a.	....	....	2305	....
	s	....	....	....	8	d.Moorhead	d.	....	....	**s**	....
	0915	....	....	....	79	d.Breckenridge	d.	....	....	2205	....
	1100	....	....	....	194	d.Ortonville	d.	....	....	2040	....
	1210	....	....	....		d.Watertown	d.	....	....	1900	....
	1310	....	....	....		d.Brookings	d.	....	....	1805	....
0.00	1445	....	....	....	451	a.**Sioux Falls**	d.	....	....	1630	....

JRL– Jack Rabbit Lines.

Table 470 — CHICAGO - WINNIPEG/SEATTLE (EMP GL NWS RRS TRT)

Westbound (read down)

US $	GL 5631	GL 5633	RRS 3	GL 5645	GL 5639	GL 5768	TRT 322 ♣	GL 5635	GL 5641	GL 5643	km	
0.00	0035	0550		0700	0700			1000	1500	2100	0	d.Chicago
19.00	0235	0805			0940			1235	1745	2315	140	d. Milwaukee
26.00	0405	0955	1000	1120	1130			1420	1930	0100	260	d.Madison
33.00		1115				1527					320	d.Baraboo
34.00		1135		1255				1545	2055	0205	338	d.Wisconsin Dells
40.00	0625	1315		1225				1715	2150	0310	406	d.Tomah
						1445						d. La Crosse
53.00	0810	1500		1510				1855	2325	0440	536	d.Eau Claire
64.00	1000	1650	1455	1645	1820			2045	0110s	0615	708	d.St. Paul
	1020	1710	1520	1705	1845			2105	0130	0640		a. ↕
64.00	*GL 1293*	*GL 1275*	▬	▬	▬	▬	▬	▬	▬	*GL 1273*	725	Minneapolis
	1130	1745								0715		d.
73.00	1250	1940								0845	830	d.St. Cloud
		2040								1005		d.Little Falls
		2115								1037		d.Brainerd
		2150								1115		d.Motley
85.00	1700	0034								1404	1092	d.Moorhead
85.00	1745	0110			0820					1450	1100	d.Fargo
92.00	1915				1025						1235	d. Grand Forks
					1240						1360	d. Emerson 🚉
					1315						1402	d. Morris
104.00					1410						1470	a. Winnipeg
92.00			0215							1605	1197	d.Valley City
92.00			0255							1650	1265	d.Jamestown
98.00			0455							1935	1430	d.Bismarck
98.00											1438	d.Mandan
104.00			0610							2100	1583	d.Dickinson
										2125		d.Belfield
118.00			0810							2310	1738	d.Glendive
118.00		RRS	0950				RRS			0100s	1868	d.Miles City
	3		1145				5			0235s	2008	d.Custer
131.00		1410	1340						2145	0430	2118	d.Billings
143.00		1640	1625						0015	0730	2308	d.Livingston
143.00		1720	1705						0100	0815	2355	d.Bozeman
			1950									d. Helena
143.00		1930	2020						0255	1100	2500	d.Butte
155.00		2020							0345	1150	2566	d.Deer Lodge
155.00		2205	2205		EMP				0530	1340	2696	d.Missoula
164.00		0035				602 NWS			0835	1630	2981	d.Coeur d'Alene
164.00		0115			Σ		736	5599	0930	1725	3035	a. ↕ Spokane d.
164.00		0205	GL	0700	1100	1040	1030		1415	1815		d.
164.00		0530	5563		1440				1415	2220	3315	d.Ellensburg
164.00			0730	1125		1455					3310	d. Wenatchee
164.00			1035	1425		1805					3510	d. Everett
164.00			0730	1115	1540	1715	1845	1630		0020	3475	a.Seattle

Eastbound (read up)

km		TRT 321 ♣	GL 5638	GL 5630	GL 5767	GL 5634	GL 5636	NWS 5564	GL 5632	GL 5640	GL 5642
0	a.Chicago		1450	1630	1915	2030	2330		0100	0515	1015
140	a. Milwaukee			1400		1750	2130		2300	0320	0740
260	d.Madison		1145	1215	1510	1605	1945		2120	0140	0555
320	d.Baraboo					1455					0450
338	d.Wisconsin Dells			1110		1430			2015		0430
406	d.Tomah		0955	0950		1325	1740		1920	2350	0340
	d. La Crosse			1205							
536	d.Eau Claire		0815			1115	1525		1720	2200	0155
708	d.St. Paul		0640	0640	0830	0910	1330		1525	2010	0020s
	a. ↕		0615	0615	0800	0845	1305		1500	1945	0001
725	Minneapolis								*GL 1272*	*GL 1290*	*GL 1274*
	d.								1350	1800	2305
830	d.St. Cloud								1235	1620	2150
	d.Little Falls									1150	2107
	d.Brainerd									1115	2030
	d.Motley									1010	1925
1092	d.Moorhead								0721	1201	1636
1100	d.Fargo	2315							0715	1155	1625
1235	d. Grand Forks	2145								1000	▬
1360	d. Emerson 🚉	1800									
1402	d. Morris	1730									
1470	a. Winnipeg	1630									
1197	d.Valley City									0540	1440
1265	d.Jamestown									0500	1400
1430	d.Bismarck									0305	1130
1438	d.Mandan										
1583	d.Dickinson									0015	0810
	d.Belfield									r	0715
1738	d.Glendive									2205	0535
1868	d.Miles City						RRS			2036	0350s
2008	d.Custer						6			1825	0215s
2118	d.Billings	0745							0005	1720	0120
2308	d.Livingston	0525							2140	1350	2210
2355	d.Bozeman	0435							2100	1300	2120
	d. Helena									1840	
2500	d.Butte	0255								1100	1925
2566	d.Deer Lodge	0150								0935	1635
2696	d.Missoula	EMP 0030							1600	0800	1500
2981	d.Coeur d'Alene	601	1945	GL	NWS					0305	0945
3035	a. ↕ Spokane d.	Σ 1900		5596	737					0225	0850
	d.	1515	1845	1745	1910					0140	0800
3315	d.Ellensburg		1530		1530					2220	0355
3310	d. Wenatchee	1115		1345					2150		
3510	d. Everett	0745		1015					1840		
3475	a.Seattle	0630	1300	0930	1240			1755	2015		0130

EMP–Empire Trailways. GL–Greyhound Lines. NWS–Northwestern Trailways. RRS–Rimrock Trailways. TRT–Triangle Transportation.

Table 472 — ABERDEEN (JRL)

US $	50				km		51
0.00		0930			0	d.Aberdeen a.	2100
		1025			66	d.Redfield d.	2000
		1145			145	d.Huron d.	1900
		1300			231	d.Mitchell d.	1755
		1445			322	a.Sioux Falls d.	1630

JRL– Jack Rabbit Lines.

Table 473 — OMAHA - NORFOLK ♿ (BHL)

US $	41 Ⓐ		km		42 Ⓐ
0.00	1205		0	d.Omaha a.	1830
4.55	1300		54	d.Fremont d.	1735
	1410			d.Columbus d.	1630
	◇143			d. Sioux City a.	
12.20	1510		174	a.Norfolk d.	1530

◇–Km ex Norfolk. BHL–Black Hills Stage Line.

Table 474 — OSOYOOS - YAKIMA (EMP)

US $	1022	102	104	km		103	1011	101 ♣
		0745		0	d.Osoyoos 🚉 a.			2300
0.00	0950	0955	2045		d.Brewster d.	0915	2025	1925
	1055				d. Grand Coulee d.			1925
	1245				a. Spokane d.			1715
		1215	2220		d.Wenatchee d.	0720	1855	
		1425			d.Ellensburg d.		1630	
		1510			a.Yakima d.		1540	

EMP– Empire Trailways.

Table 475 — ROCHESTER - CEDAR RAPIDS (HKS)

US $	18	20	km		17	19
0.00	0945	2000	0	d.Rochester a.	0850	1900
	1130	2135		d.Decorah d.	0715	1720
	1410			a.Cedar Rapids d.		1430

HKS– Hawkeye Stages Inc.

Table 476 — OMAHA - DENVER/SALT LAKE CITY (BHL GL STS)

US $	GL 1315	GL 1301	GL 1343	STS 7 ④	BHL 41 Ⓐ	GL 1305	GL 1347	km		STS 8 ④	GL 1340	GL 1314	GL 1306	GL 1346	BHL 42 Ⓐ	GL 1308
	1400		1630		2130	0100	0700	416	d.Chicago a.	1230		1545	2125	0045		0520
0.00	0115		0500	0925	1220	1250	2140	0	d.Omaha a.	0005		0420	0750	1050	1110	1800
8.00					1315			70	d. Fremont d.					1005		
11.00	0220		0610	1030	1355	2245		87	d.Lincoln d.	2305		0320	0650	0950		1700
18.00					1425			148	d. Columbus d.					0900		
26.00			0830	1300	1620			232	d.Grand Island d.	2040			0725			1510
33.00			0935	1355	1600	1715		305	d.Kearney d.	1400	1945		0620			1320
43.00	0635		1155	1610		1910		460	d.North Platte d.		1750	2310	0435			1110
				1740			0335	247	d. Julesburg d.		1420		0130			
28.00								299	d. Hastings d.	1300						
				1700				452	d. Minden d.							
50.00									d. McCook d.							
			1840				0435		d. Sterling d.		1320		0030			
70.00			1935				0530	722	d. Fort Morgan d.		1220		2335			
77.00			2100				0655	852	a. Denver d.		1100		2210			
	0935		1530			2145			d.Kimball d.			1840				0540
73.00	1150		1800			2355		820	d.Cheyenne d.		1730		2130			0420
	1255		1900			0055		907	d.Laramie d.		1515		1930			0220
85.00	1445		2045			0240		1069	d.Rawlins d.		1325		1740			0035
	1645		2245			0440		1244	d.Rock Springs d.		1135		1550			2250
104.00	2030		0200			0815		1595	a.Salt Lake City d.		0745		1130			1845
142.00								2795	a. Los Angeles 543 d.							
142.00	1230		1840			0235		2845	a.San Francisco 542 d.				1315		1735	0001

BHL–Black Hills Stage Line. GL–Greyhound Lines. STS–Senlow Transportation.

Check update notes to timetables and with operator before starting your journey

Table 477 WICHITA *GL*

US $	6209	467	6207		km	↓ ↑	6208	6200	468	
0.00	0030	0710	1345	....	*0*	d.**Kansas City** .....a.	0915	1725	2235	....
10.00	0120	0810	1445	....	*50*	d.Lawrence..........d.	0810	1620	2140	....
14.00	0155	0845	1525	....	*92*	d.Topeka.............d.	0735	1545	2105	....
	|	|	|	....		d. Salina ....d.	|	|	|	....
	|	|	|	....		d. Newton ....d.	|	|	|	....
✣	0515	1210	1855	....	✣	d.Wichita ....d.	0350	1210	1750	....
✣	0740	|	2105	....	✣	d.Ponca City.........d.	|	0945	1535	....
	|	1323	|	....		d. Blackwell........d.	0222	|	|	....
	0835	|	2200	....		d.Stillwater ....d.	|	0850	1440	....
✣	1015	1525	2325	....	✣	a.**Oklahoma City**.d.	0030	0710	1250	....

GL– Greyhound Lines.

Table 478 ST. LOUIS - DENVER *GL PDR*

US $	↓	km	*GL* 6228	*GL* 1331	*GL* 6201	*PDR* 120	*GL* 1333	*PDR* 122	*GL* 1335	*GL* 6230
	St. Louis..............d.	*414*	....	0220	0730	....	1330	....	1800	....
	Kingdom City........d.		....	0410	0935	....	1550	....	2015	....
	Columbia..............d.	*210*	....	0440	1005	....	1620	....	2045	....
	Jefferson City.....d.	*235*	....	|	|	....	|	....	|	....
	Sedalia...............d.	*139*	....	|	|	....	|	....	|	....
0.00	**Kansas City** ...... a.	*0*	....	0650	1250	....	1830	....	2255	....
	d.		....	0750	....	....	1925	....	0001	....
10.00	Lawrence ....d.	*50*	....	0850	....	....	2025	....	0050	....
14.00	Topeka ....d.	*92*	....	0925	....	....	2105	....	0125	....
23.00	Manhattan ....d.	*170*	....	1040	....	....	2210	....	0230	....
33.00	Salina ....d.	*285*	....	1300	....	....	0015	....	0445	....
50.00	Hays.....................d.	*435*	....	1450	....	....	0200	....	0630	....
	WaKeeney ....d.		....	1540	....	....	0245	....	0720	....
	Oakley..................d.		....	1645	....	....	|	....	0825	....
41.00	Beloit ....d.	*345*	....	|	....	....	|	....	|	....
	Stockton ....d.		....	|	....	....	|	....	|	....
77.00	Limon ....d.	*845*	....	1935	....	....	0535	....	1100	....
85.00	**Denver**.................d.	*1010*	1800	2125	....	2230	0725	0800	1300	1345
	Greeley ....d.		1925	....	....	2350	....	0920	....	1540
	Fort Collins....d.		2010	....	....	0030	....	1030	....	1620
	Cheyenne...........a.		2105	....	....	0150	....	1125	....	1715

↓	*PDR* 41	*GL* 1330	*PDR* 45	*GL* 1332	*GL* 6229		*GL* 6231		*GL* 1334	*GL* 6204
Cheyenne..................d.	0340	....	0630	....	1100	....	1830	....	....	....
Fort Collins..........d.	0435	....	0730	....	1201	....	1930	....	....	....
Greeley ....d.	0515	....	0840	....	1235	....	2015	....	....	....
Denver.......................d.	0640	0815	1000	1500	1430	....	2140	....	2215	....
Limon ....d.	....	1005	....	1705	....	....	....	....	2345	....
Stockton ....d.	....	|	....	|	....	....	....	....	|	....
Beloit ....d.	....	|	....	|	....	....	....	....	|	....
Oakley.........................d.	....	1455	....	2155	....	....	....	....	|	....
WaKeeney ....d.	....	1600	....	2300	....	....	....	....	0455	....
Hays.............................d.	....	1650	....	2345	....	....	....	....	0545	....
Salina ....d.	....	1920	....	0140	....	....	....	....	0830	....
Manhattan ....d.	....	2100	....	0340	....	....	....	....	1010	....
Topeka ....d.	....	2205	....	0445	....	....	....	....	1115	....
Lawrence ....d.	....	2240	....	0520	....	....	....	....	1150	....
Kansas City .... a.	....	2330	....	0615	....	....	....	....	1255	....
d.	....	0040	....	0730	....	....	....	....	1355	1845
Sedalia.....................d.	....	|	....	|	....	....	....	....	|	|
Jefferson City...........d.	....	|	....	|	....	....	....	....	|	|
Columbia.....................d.	....	0250	....	1005	....	....	....	....	1620	2125
Kingdom City...............d.	....	0320	....	1035	....	....	....	....	1650	2155
St. Louis....................a.	....	0515	....	1240	....	....	....	....	1855	2350

GL– Greyhound Lines. *PDR*–Powder River Transportation.

Table 480 HOUSTON - ABILENE *ARO KBC SSS*

US $	*ARO* 101	*KBC* 904	*ARO* 105	*ARO* 107	km	↓ ↑	*SSS* 110	*ARO* 100	*ARO* 104	*ARO* 106
0.00	0645	1500	2250	0030	*0*	d.**Houston** ◇.......a.	1205**b**	1555	2130	2400
	0925	|	|	0250		d. Bryan...........d.	|	1320	|	|
	0950	|	|	**r**		d. Hearne..........d.	|	1245	|	|
	|	|	|	|		d.Brenham ....d.	1025**b**	|	|	|
30.00	|	1815	0300	|	*264*	d.Austin ◇ ....d.	|	|	1830	2100
37.00	1200	|	|	0440	*291*	d. Temple...........d.	0830**b**	1130	|	|
40.00	1315	1945**a**	0430	0530	*325*	d.Killeen ....d.	0750**b**	1035	1710	1930
44.00	1405	2035**a**	....	....	*380*	d.Lampasas..........d.	0655	0945	....	....
59.00	1605	2200**a**	....	....	*492*	d.Brownwood ....d.	0530	0820	....	....
	1645	|	....	....		d. Coleman.....d.	|	0735	....	....
67.00	1750	2325**a**	....	....	*570*	a.**Abilene**............d.	0350	0630	....	....

a–*SSS*. **b**–*KBC*. ◇–Local trips operate Houston-Austin and v.v.; from Houston *(KBC)* at 0715, 0900, 1130, 1330, 1500, 1630, 2030; from Austin *(KBC)* at 0900, 1155, 1330, 1445, 1600, 1940. *ARO*–Arrow Trailways of Texas. *KBC*–Kerrville Bus Co. *SSS*–Sun Set Stages.

Table 481 DALLAS - LAREDO *ARO CTX GL*

US $	↓	km	*GL* 7265	*GL* 7901	*CTX* 561	*GL* 7271	*CTX* 563	*GL* 6471	*CTX* 565	*GL* 7907
	Chicago **458**.........d.		....	1045	....	....	....	....	....	....
	St. Louis **458**........d.		....	|	....	....	....	....	....	....
0.00	**Dallas** ....d.	*0*	0500	0700	0700	0815	1315	1600	1800	2215
19.00	Waco......................d.		0655	|	0915**a**	1010	1530**a**	1745	2015**a**	|
24.00	Temple ....d.		0740	|	1000**a**	1055	1615**a**	1830	2100**a**	|
	Killeen ....d.		|	|	1050**a**	|	1710**a**	|	2150**a**	|
34.00	Austin....................d.		0900	|	1225**b**	1215	1850**b**	2005	2325**b**	|
37.00	San Marcos..........d.		0940	|	1305**b**	|	1930**b**	2045	0005**b**	|
42.00	San Antonio ....d.		1130	1230	1515**b**	1430	2130**b**	2145	0110**b**	0300
64.00	**Laredo** 🏛 ....a.		1410	1515	1815**b**	1710	0010**b**	*0110*	*0510***b**	0610

293 ↓	*GL* 7246	*GL* 7252	*GL* 7256	*GL* 560	*GL* 562	*GL* 7264	*GL* 564	*GL* 7902	*GL* 7280	*GL* 7908
Laredo 🏛 ....d.	0200	0500	0700	*0800*	*1000*	1100	1400	1500	1900	2100
San Antonio ....d.	0515	0830	1030	1115	1315	1430	1700	1830	2215	0015
San Marcos................d.	0620	0945	|	1230	1430	|	1805	|	2320	|
Austin.........................d.	0730	1055	1220	1325**a**	1530**a**	1620	1900**a**	|	0015	|
Killeen......................d.	|	1215	|	1445**a**	1710**a**	|	2020**a**	|	0135	|
Temple ....d.	0855	1300	|	1530**a**	1755**a**	|	|	|	0215	|
Waco..........................d.	1000	1400	|	1630**c**	1845**c**	|	2145**c**	|	0315	|
Dallas ....a.	1159	1600	1545	1830**c**	2045**c**	1945	2330**c**	2315	0455	0500
St. Louis **458**.............a.	....	....	....	....	....	....	....	|	....	....
Chicago **458**...............a.	....	....	....	....	....	....	....	1930	....	....

a–*ARO*. **b**–*GL*. **c**–*CTX*. *ARO*–Arrow Trailways of Texas. *CTX*–Central Texas Trailways. *GL*–Greyhound Lines.

Table 482 LIBERAL - AMARILLO *CPL*

US $	105	109	121		km	↓ ↑	120	110		
	....	....	1205	....		d.**Liberal** ....a.	1145	....	....	....
	....	....	1305	....		d.Perryton ....d.	1045	....	....	....
	....	....	1345	....		d.Spearman..........a.	1005	....	....	....
	....	....	1430	....		d.Stinnett.............d.	0915	....	....	....
	0135	1020	1455	....		d.Borger ....d.	0855	1320	....	....
	|	|	1520	....		d.Panhandle ....d.	|	|	....	....
	r	1040	|	....		d. Fritch..............d.	0835	1300	....	....
0.00	0255	1130	1610	....	*0*	a.**Amarillo**...........d.	0750	1215	....	....

CPL– Panhandle Trailways.

Table 483 DALLAS/FORT WORTH - HOUSTON *ARO CTX GL*

US $	↓	km	*GL* 7233	*GL* 7257	*GL* 7201	*GL* 7259	*GL* 7265	*GL* 7205	*CTX* 30	*GL* 7207	*GL* 7203	*GL* 7271	*ARO* 100	*CTX* 3231	*GL* 6485	*GL* 17A	*CTX* 5	*CTX* 6489	*GL* 6471	*GL* 6487	*GL* 19A	*CTX* 34	*CTX* 6491	*GL* 18A	*CTX*
	Fort Worth....d.	★*120*	....	....	....	....	....	....	....	....	....	....	....	....	....	....	1245	....	....	....	....	1750	....	....	2030
0.00	**Dallas** ....d.	*0*	....	0001	0200	0215	0500	0530	0700	0715	0815	0815	....	1315	....	1315	|	....	....	1600	1645	|	1800	1915	|
19.00	Waco..................d.	*150*	....	0140	|	0355	0640	0745	0900	|	|	0955	....	1515	....	|	1510	1630	1645	1740	|	1950	2000	|	2240
30.00	Hearne ....d.	*270*	....	....	|	....	....	0905	....	|	|	....	1255	....	....	|	....	|	1805	....	|	....	....	|	....
32.00	Bryan ....d.	*303*	....	....	|	....	....	0940	....	|	|	....	1320	....	....	|	....	|	1840	....	|	....	....	|	....
11.00	Corsicana.........d.	*91*	....	....	|	....	....	|	....	0825	|	....	|	....	....	1425	....	1750	|	....	1800	....	....	|	....
	Buffalo ....d.		....	....	|	....	....	|	....	|	|	....	|	....	....	1530	....	....	|	....	|	....	....	|	....
31.00	Huntsville ....d.	*276*	0100	....	|	....	....	|	....	1050	1100	....	|	....	1445	|	....	....	|	....	2005	....	....	2215	....
39.00	**Houston** ....a.	*463*	0230	....	0600	....	....	1215	....	1230	1230	....	1615	....	1615	1810	....	....	2115	....	2130	....	....	2345	....

↓		*GL* 7208	*GL* 7280	*CTX* 17	*GL* 7246	*ARO* 101	*GL* 7202	*GL* 7232	*GL* 7204	*GL* 7252	*GL* 6490	*GL* 6488	*CTX* 18	*CTX* 31	*CTX* 33		*GL* 6494	*GL* 6492	*CTX* 19	*CTX* 35	*CTX* 5A		*GL* 6496	*GL* 7230	
Houston ....d.	....	0045	....	....	....	0630	0630	0745	0800	....	1201	1300	....	....	....	....	1600	1700	....	....	....	....	2045	2145	....
Huntsville ....d.	....	|	....	....	....	|	0805	0915	0930	....	|	1430	....	....	....	....	|	1845	....	....	....	....	2215	2315	....
Buffalo ....d.	....	|	....	....	....	|	0940	....	|	....	|	|	....	....	....	....	|	2015	....	....	....	....	|	....	....
Corsicana..............d.	....	|	....	....	....	|	1045	....	|	....	|	1645	....	....	....	....	|	2120	....	....	2125	....	0025	....	....
Bryan ....d.	....	|	....	....	....	0855	|	....	|	....	1430	|	....	....	....	....	1845	|	....	....	|	....	|	....	....
Hearne ....d.	....	|	....	....	....	0915	|	....	|	....	1455	|	....	....	....	....	1910	|	....	....	|	....	|	....	....
Waco.........................d.	....	|	0315	1000	1000	....	|	....	|	1400	1615	|	1630	1630	1845	....	2045	|	2145	2145	2235	....	|	....	....
Dallas ....a.	....	0445	0455	|	1159	....	1159	....	1215	1600	....	1800	|	1830	2045	....	2225	2230	|	2330	....	....	0130	....	....
Fort Worth..........a.	....	....	....	1230	....	....	....	....	....	....	....	....	1850	....	....	....	....	....	2335	....	....	....	....	....	....

b– *GL*.
c– *CTX*.
★– Km ex Waco.
ARO– Arrow Trailways of Texas.
CTX– Central Texas Trailways.
GL– Greyhound Lines.

Table 485   DALLAS - FORT WORTH - ABILENE - EL PASO   GL

US$	1419	1409	1407	1411	1435	1413	1415	km		1402	1418	1416	1408	1412	1404	1406
0.00	....	0245	0530	0800	....	1315	1800	1915	2330	0 ↓	d.Dallas ....a.	1605	1845	2240	0130	0430		0730		1125	....
7.00	....	0335	0620	0905	....	1410	1910	2005	0020	50	d.Fort Worth...........d.	1510	1735	2145	0035	0335		0620		1015	....
17.00	....		0725			1515				126	d.Mineral Wells..........d.		1630					0910	
			0857								d.Albany....................d.		1457						
25.00	....			1102		1627		2202		215	d. Eastland..................d.			1958				0758	
34.00	....	0645	1000	1240		1805	2205	2330	0320	321	d.Abilene..................d.	1235	1415	1850	2215	0100	0345		0645	....
39.00	....	0735	1050	1330		1900				389	d.Sweetwater............d.		1250	1720	as			0520	
50.00	....	0855	1215	1455		2025		0135	0520	471	d.Big Spring..............d.		1130	1600	2000	2240	0135		0410	....
56.00	....	0945	1305	1550		2115		0225	0610	534	d.Midland..................d.		1030	1505	1910	2140	0040		0315	....
56.00	....	1030	1415	1635		2200		0310	0720	567	d.Odessa....................d.		1000	1435	1840	2110	0010		0245	....
64.00	....	1210	1555	1815		2340	0220	0445	0900	687	d.Pecos.....................d.	0750	0805	1240	1700	1905	2225		0055	....
73.00	....	1410	1755	2020		0125	0405	0640	1050	827	d.Van Horn................d.	0630	0630	1105	1530	1735	2055		2330	....
85.00	....	1535	1850	2125		0225	0505	0740	1150	1027	a.El Paso...................d.	0300	0300	0735	1201	1400	1735		2015	....
118.00	....	1159		0545		1100	1315	1635	2045	1677	a.Phoenix 544............d.	1630		2130	0130	0330	0640		0845	....
142.00	....	0800		1635		2100				2327	a.Los Angeles 544.......d.	0700		1800	2000		2200		....

a–Calls on ⑦ only.   GL–Greyhound Lines.

Table 486   DALLAS - DENVER   TNO

US$		km		458	438		436	434	430	440
0.00	Dallas ....d.	0		....	0215		1300	1845	2300	....
4.45	Fort Worth..............d.	50		....	0300		1400	1950	2345	....
16.85	Wichita Falls............d.	225		....	0540		1630	2230	0220	....
	Vernon ....d.			....	0645		1735	2335	0325	....
	Quanah ....d.			....	0725		1815	0015	0405	....
41.10	Amarillo..................d.	585		....	1130		2225	0400	0700	0800
	Wichita ....d.	◇490	0515							
	Pratt......................d.		0657							
	Dodge City ....d.	◇240	0845							
	Garden City ....d.	◇157	1000							
65.60	Lamar.....................d.	944	1110	1445		0205	0715			
72.50	La Junta..................d.	1035	1240	1625		0320	0855			
79.40	Pueblo.....................a.	1145	1415	1750		0430	1030		1415
82.85	Denver 513 ....a.	1294		2045		0720	1330		1730

		441	437		431	459	439		435
Denver 513 ....d.		1600			2200	....	0715		1045
Pueblo.....................d.		1910			0040	0040	1005		1410
La Junta..................d.		2030			0200		1125		1535
Lamar.....................d.		2150			0310		1305		1700
Garden City ....d.					0615				
Dodge City ....d.					0800				
Pratt......................d.					0930				
Wichita ....a.					1110				
Amarillo..................d.		0310	0350		0950		1915		2300
Quanah ....d.			0637		1240		2210		s
Vernon ....d.			0720		1320		2250		s
Wichita Falls............d.			0840		1450		0005		0325
Fort Worth..............a.			1100		1720		0215		0545
Dallas ....a.			1159		1830		0300		0645

◇–Km ex Lamar.   TNO–TNM&O Coaches.

Table 487   DALLAS - FORT WORTH
COMPLETE SERVICE   GL KBC TNO

service Dallas-Fort Worth and v.v. 50 km. Journey: ¾-1¼ hours. Fare: US$: 7.00.
From Dallas: GL at 0245, 0530, 0800, 1315, 1800, 1915, 2230⑨, 2330; KBC at 0800, 1230; TNO at 0215, 1300, 1845, 2300.
From Fort Worth: GL at 0045, 0345, 0630, 1025, 1520, 1745, 2155; KBC at 1505, 2120; TNO at 0220, 0550, 1105, 1730.

GL– Greyhound Lines.
KBC– Kerrville Bus Co.
TNO– TNM&O Coaches.

Table 489   HOUSTON - GALVESTON   TXB

service Houston-Galveston and v.v. 81 km. Journey: 1¼-1¾ hours. Fare: US$: 4.50.
From Houston: 0700, 1000, 1300, 1700, 2030.
From Galveston: 0830, 1130, 1500, 1845, 2200.

TXB– Texas Bus Lines.

Table 490   TUCSON - DOUGLAS   BWTS

US$	2	4		6	km		5	3	1
0.00	0700	1300	....	1800	0 ↓	d.Tucson ....a. ↑	1230	1830	2245
	0830	1430	....	1930	122	d.Sierra Vista ....d.	1100	1700		
	0945	1530	....	2030	227	a.Douglas................d.	1000	1600	2045

BWTS–Bridgewater Transport.

Table 494   AMARILLO - SAN ANTONIO   KBC TNO

US$	TNO	TNO		TNO				KBC	KBC	KBC
	441	443		447	km			703	705	707
0.00	0400	0900	....	1900	0 ↓	d.Amarillo..........a. ↑		2105b	0215b	0650b
	0550	1050	....	2105		d.Plainview.........d.		1905b	0035b	0515b
	0745	1215	....	2305		d.Lubbock..........d.		1800b	2345b	0425b
	0915	1345	....	0025		d.Lamesa...........d.		1600b	2130b	0240b
	1025a	1500a	....	0140a		d.Big Spring ....d.		1500b	2030b	0150b
	1230a	1710a	....	0330a		d.San Angelo ......d.		1235	1810	2335
	1410a	1840a	....	0505a		d.Brady ....d.		1045	1615	2155
	1725a	2140a	....	0810a		a.San Antonio....d.		0730	1300	1830

a–KBC.   b–TNO.   KBC–Kerrville Bus Co.   TNO–TNM&O Coaches.

Table 491   MEMPHIS - OKLAHOMA CITY   GL JL

US$			JL	GL	JL		JL	GL
			710	6141	714		702	6143
		km						
0.00	Memphis.................d.	0	....	0230				1845
24.00	Little Rock...............d.	220	0545	0545	1125		1800	2200
44.00	Fort Smith...............d.	456	0845	0945	1530		2100	0145
56.00	Muskogee................d.	551	1010	1120				
	Tulsa.....................a.		1130					
	McAlester ....d.	590			1800			*
73.00	Oklahoma City.........a.	766	....	1430	2045		0015	0455

		JL		GL		JL		GL	JL
		120		6140		126		6142	174
Oklahoma City..........d.	↓	0400		0945		....		1900	0005
McAlester ....d.		0715				....			
Tulsa......................d.						1415			
Muskogee ....d.				1300		1535		2150	
Fort Smith ....d.		1000		1500		1710		2330	0320
Little Rock ....d.		1330		1840		2000		0230	0600
Memphis ....a.				2230				0515	

GL–Greyhound Lines.
JL–Jefferson Lines.

Table 492   SHREVEPORT - HOUSTON   KBC

US$		km	808	810		806	802		804
0.00	Texarkana ....d.						0745		....
	Shreveport ....d.	0	....	0001	0715		0950	1315		1800
	Nacogdoches............d.	145	....	0235	0950		1215	1545		2030
	Houston ....a.	342	....	0550	1300		1600	1920		2355

			801	803	805		807	809	807	809
Houston ....d.	↓		0630	0945	1415		1915	0045	....	
Nacogdoches...............d.			0940	1325	1750		2240	0335	....	
Shreveport ....d.			1345	1600	2025		0100	0545	0615	0745
Texarkana ....a.			1600					0745		0915

KBC–Kerrville Bus Co.

Table 493   NORTON - DODGE CITY   BLB

US $	101			km			102	
	ex⑦			0	↓	↑	ex⑦	
0.00	0800	....		0	d.Norton...........a.		1620	
10.90	0910	....			d.WaKeeney......d.		1500	
29.05	1105	....			a.Dodge City.....d.		1230	

BLB– Bickel Bus Line.

Table 496   KANSAS CITY - TEXARKANA   JL KBC

US$	JL	JL		JL		km			KBC	JL	KBC
	103	111		117					803	312	809
0.00	0015	0700	....	1830		0	↓	d.Kansas City ......a. ↑	0710b	1815	2255b
	0300	0945	....					d.Fort Scott ....d.	0420b		2010b
	0515	1120	....	2240		242		d.Joplin...............d.	0300b	1435	1850b
	1000a	1530	....	0330a		458		d.Fort Smith ....d.	2230b	0945	1430b
	1435a		....	0730a		761		a.Texarkana ....d.	1835	....	0950

a–KBC.   b–JL.   JL–Jefferson Lines.   KBC–Kerrville Bus Co.

Table 497   EAGLE PASS   KBC

US$	201	203	205	207		km			202	204	206	208
0.00	0850	1230	1830	2200		0	↓	d.San Antonio......d. ↑	1000	1620	2000	0115
				2350		125		d.Uvalde..............d.				2325
	1150	1530	2130	0115		225		a.Eagle Pass.........d.	0700	1320	1700	2200

KBC–Kerrville Bus Co.

Check update notes to timetables and with operator before starting your journey

Table 498 — HOUSTON - BROWNSVILLE 🚌 GL NTI VTC

US$	GL 1247	VTC 201	GL 202	VTC 7213	GL 203	VTC 7211	GL 204	VTC 205	VTC 206	NTI 101	GL 7209	VTC 207	GL 7217	VTC 208	km		GL 7210	VTC 7200	GL 101	NTI 102	VTC 102	VTC 103	GL 7212	VTC 104	VTC 7208	GL 105	VTC 7214	GL 106	VTC 107	VTC 108
0.00	0020	0145	0615	0715	1115	1300	1300	1530	1645	1830	1900	2000	2200	2230	0	d.Houston...a.	0515	1230	1515	1615	1845	2000	2015	2120	2300	2320	0015	0120	0345	0530
15.30	0245	....	0855	1005	....	1530	1530	1855	....	2130	2300	0030	0130		115	d.Victoria...d.	0230	0915	1235	....	1545	....	1700	1840	2000	2040	2145	2255	....	0300
		0505			1500					2145						d.Port Lavaca...d.			1300		1610									0025
25.85	0500	0715	1100	1245	1705	1845	1800	2100	2210	2340	2330	0115	0230	0315	320	d.Corpus Christi...d.	0045	0715	1020	1115	1345	1415	1515	1620	1800	1815	2000	2030	2230	0045
	0610		1250		2000					0045						d.Alice...d.	2225				1350			1720	1825					
	0810		1505				0245								550	a.Laredo...d.	2030				1145			1500	1630					
32.95	0810	1230	1245	1345	1750	....	1910s	2155	2305s	....	0210s	0330	0425s		383	d.Kingsville...d.	2310	0920			1230	1315	....	1500	1625	1710	....	1910	2110	
	1010	1415	1545	1940	....	2100	2400	0050	....	0400	0530	0610		538	d.Harlingen...d.	2115	0715			1030	1115	....	1315	1430	1515	....	1715	1915	2130
	1145	1540	1700	....	....	2240	....	0230	....	0515	....	0730		587	a.McAllen ◇...d.	2000	0545			0845	0945	....	....	1345	....	1545	1745	1950	
43.70	1145	1625	2045	....	....	0140	....	0610	0710						608	a.Brownsville...d.	2030	0615			0915	1015	....	1215	1345	1415	....	1615	1815	2045

◇– Regular 🚌 service (VTC) McAllen-Reynosa 0530 and every 15 mins to 2230; VTC– Valley Transit Co.
Reynosa-McAllen 0545 and every 15 mins to 2300.
GL– Greyhound Lines.
NTI– National Tours Inc.

Table 500 — MIDLAND - PRESIDIO/SAN ANGELO 🚌 CCI IBU

US$	CCI 4 ◇	CCI 6 ◇	IBU 2	CCI 8 ⓐ	km		CCI 3 ◇	IBU 1	CCI 5 ◇	CCI 7 ⓐ
	0745	1245	....	1800		d.San Angelo...a.	1550	....	1930	0030
0.00	0945	1445	1740	2000	0	d.Midland...d.	1345	1510	1730	
2.30	1020	1515	1840	2050	33	d.Odessa...d.	1310	1430	1700	2110
8.75	....	....	2100	....	173	d.Fort Stockton...d.	1235	....	....	....
13.70	....	2230			278	d.Alpine...d.	1105			
15.60	....	2300			333	d.Marfa...d.	1030			
19.90	....	0015			428	a.Presidio 🏛...d.	0915			

◇–Daily except holidays. CCI–Concho Coaches. IBU–All American Travels.

Table 501 — DEL RIO - BROWNSVILLE 🚌 GL VTC

US$	GL 1470	VTC 2D	VTC 63	GL 1472	km		GL 1473	VTC 2K	VTC 4K	GL 1471
51.00	0245	....	....	1300	0	d.Del Rio...a.	1605	....	....	0015
43.00	0350	....	....	1405		d.Eagle Pass...d.	1500	....	....	2310
29.00	0645	1000	1615	1700		d.Laredo...d.	1225	1455	2005	2035
23.50	0805	1100	1715	1820		d.Zapata...d.	1055	1405	1905	1900
8.00	1030	1345	1950	2045		d.McAllen ★...d.	0840	1145	1645	1645
8.00	s	1410	2015	s		d.Alamo ★...d.	s	1115	1615	s
4.00	1140	1515	2105	2155		d.Harlingen ★...d.	0730	1015	1515	1530
0.00	1225	1610	2210	2235		a.Brownsville ★...d.	0645	0915	1415	1445

★–Regular 🚌 service (VTC), 0545 and hourly to 1745, 1950, 2355 McAllen-Brownsville,
returning 0015, 0515, 0600, 0700, 0815 and hourly to 1715, 2045. GL–Greyhound Lines.
VTC–Valley Transit Co.

Table 502 — DENVER - SALT LAKE CITY 🚌 GL

US$	6241	6243	km		6240	6242
0.00	0830	2200	0	d.Denver...a.	1945	0640
10.00	1025	2340	120	d.Winter Park...d.	1800	0505
13.00	1050	0020	150	d.Granby...d.	1735	0440
27.50	1335	0240	280	d.Steamboat Springs...d.	1520	0245
35.25	1440	0340	348	d.Craig...d.	1410	0130
45.75	1620	0520	493	d.Dinosaur...d.	1225	2350
45.75	1730	0630	548	d.Vernal...d.	1145	2310
65.00	1955	0855	822	d.Heber City...d.	0850	2020
65.00	2055	0955	888	a.Salt Lake City...d.	0745	1915

GL– Greyhound Lines.

Table 503 — GRAND FORKS - BISMARCK 🚌 TRT

US$	501	km		500
25.15	1015		d.Grand Forks...a.	2130
14.90	1245		d.Devil's Lake...d.	1925
0.00	1600	0	d.Minot...d.	1630
6.10	1715	82	d.Coleharbor Ω...d.	1400
14.30	1845	185	a.Bismarck...d.	1230
		275	a.Jamestown...d.	

Ω– For Audobon Wildlife Refuge and Lake Sakakawea.
TRT– Triangle Transportation.

Table 505 — RAPID CITY - DENVER 🚌 GL PDR

US$	45	43	13	15	km		12	40	42
75.00	....	....	1705	....	0	d.Rapid City ⊠...a.	1100	....	....
					70	d.Deadwood...d.			
73.00	....	....	1835	....		d.Sundance...d.	0845	....	....
73.00						d.Buffalo...a.		0930	2130
73.00	0430					d.Casper...d.		0715	1700
73.00	0715	1400				d.Gillette...d.	0745		
51.00	0815	1500	2245		164	d.Douglas...d.	0430	0450	1530
						a.New Castle...d.			
28.00	1045	1745	0100		498	a.)Cheyenne (d.	0200	....	1215
	1100a	1800a	0340	0630		d.) (a.	0125	....	1125a
10.50	1201a	1900a	0435	0730		d.Fort Collins...d.	0030	....	1030a
10.00		1940a	0515	0840		d.Greeley...d.	2350	....	0920a
0.00	1350a	2100a	0640	1000		a.Denver...d.	2230	....	0800a

a-GL. ⊠–For Mount Rushmore. GL–Greyhound Lines. PDR–Powder River
Transportation.

Table 506 — DEL RIO 🚌 KBC

US$	101	103	205	105	km		102	104	208	206
0.00	0815	1310	1830	2200	0	d.San Antonio...a.	1035	1650	2120	0125
❖	1030	1510	2030	0000	128	d.Uvalde...d.	0835	1445	1910	2335
❖	1155	1640	2200	0125	244	a.Del Rio...d.	0700	1300	1730	2210

KBC– Kerrville Bus Co.

Table 507 — DENVER - GRAND JUNCTION 🚌 GL

US$	1307	km		1309	1313	1303
		20	Denver Stapleton Airport...d.			
0.00	0830	0	d.Denver...d.	1500	1830	2215
20.00	1045	179	d.Vail...d.	1720	2105	0050
34.00	1235	256	d.Glenwood Springs...d.	1900	2230	0210
	1310		d.Rifle...d.	1935	2305	0245
39.00		324	d.Aspen...a.			
44.00	1425	395	a.Grand Junction...a.	2050	0005	0350

	1310		1312	1300	1304
Grand Junction...d.	0435		0745	1155	1500
Aspen...d.					
Rifle...d.	0548		0858	1303	1613
Glenwood Springs...d.	0625		0935	1340	1650
Vail...d.	0755		1115	1510	1815
Denver...a.	1005		1325	1715	2025
Denver Stapleton Airport a.					

GL– Greyhound Lines.

Table 508 — OKLAHOMA CITY - EL PASO 🚌 CCC JL SWT TNO

US$	JL 329	JL 335	JL 325	km		JL 350	JL 352	JL 354
0.00	2155	....	1000	1545	0	d.Oklahoma City...a.	2210	0805	1159
	2255	....	1105	1645	78	d.Chickasha...d.	2110	0705	1100
			1715		107	d.Anadarko...d.		0635	
	0010	1250	1820	144	d.Lawton (Fort Sill)...d.	2010	0535	1000
	0115	1350	2035		a....d.	1755	0315	0855

	TNO 351		TNO 353	km			TNO 352		TNO 354
				228	Wichita Falls				
	0210	....	1700		d....a.		....	0130	0835
	0310	....	1800	311	d.Seymour...d.		....	0020	0730
	r	....	1920	413	d.Guthrie...d.		2305	r	
	r	....	2000		d.Dickens...d.		2230	0545	
	0700	....	2230	563	d.Lubbock...d.		2100	0430	
	0750	....	0001		d.Brownfield...d.		1850	0305	
	0840			687	d.Seminole...d.			0205	
	0820	0100		734	d.Hobbs...d.		1555	0035	
	0940	0230		845	d.Carlsbad...d.		1430	2315	
	r	r		874	d.Whites City...d.		r	r	
	1255	0545		1138	a.El Paso...d.		1100	1930	

US$	①③⑤	①③⑤	km		①③⑤	①③⑤
				SWT		
0.00	1010	2010	0	d.Lawton...a.	1000	1815
	1115	2125		a.Altus...d.	0830	1645

R.T. US$		km			
			CCC		
0.00	1050	0	d.Whites City...a.	1120	
5.00	1105	10	a.Carlsbad Caverns...d.	1110	

CCC– Carlsbad Caverns Coaches.
JL– Jefferson Lines.
SWT– Southwest Transit.
TNO– TNM&O Coaches.

Table 510 — CARLSBAD 🚌 TNO

US$	203 ex⑥⑦	201	km		204 ex①⑦	202
0.00	0830	1715	0	d.Albuquerque...a.	1115	1645
	1030	1940	170	d.Vaughn...d.	0905	1445
	1245	2135	320	d.Roswell...d.	0715	1245
	1345	2230	391	d.Artesia...d.	0535	1105
	1430	2315	449	d.Carlsbad...d.	0445	1015
			588	d.Pecos...d.		
			672	a.Fort Stockton...d.		

TNO– TNM&O Coaches.

Table 511 — ALBUQUERQUE - ABILENE 🚌 TNO

US$	379	km		378
0.00	1515	0	d.Albuquerque...d.	0030
8.75	1715	170	d.Santa Rosa...d.	2230
			d.Vaughn...d.	
			d.Portales...d.	2020
18.00	1945	355	d.Clovis...d.	1955
50.35	2330	515	d.Lubbock...d.	1825
	0230	699	d.Sweetwater...d.	1405
74.90	0315	765	a.Abilene...d.	1315

TNO– TNM&O Coaches.

Table 512 — DENVER - BOULDER 🚌 RTD

🚌 service Denver-Boulder and v.v. *49 km. Journey: 50 mins. Fare: US$: 1.75.*
From Denver 16th & Market ◇: 0007, 0107, 0537④, 0607④, 0637⑥, 0652④, 0707☆, 0710⑥, 0722④, 0737④, 0752④, 0807④, 0907, 0937☆, 1007, 1037☆, 1107, 1137☆, 1207, 1237☆, 1307, 1337☆, 1407, 1437☆, 1507, 1525④, 1535④, 1537④, 1545④, 1600④, 1605④, 1607④, 1615④, 1630④, 1635④, 1637④, 1638④, 1648④, 1657④, 1700④, 1705④, 1707, 1713④, 1714④, 1722④, 1731④, 1735④, 1737④, 1740④, 1755④, 1800④, 1807④, 1815④, 1820④, 1837④, 1840④, 1850④, 1907, 1942④, 2007, 2042④, 2107, 2142④, 2207, 2307.
From Boulder ◇: 0440④, 0500☆, 0515④, 0530④, 0554④, 0600, 0608④, 0618④, 0628④, 0630④, 0633④, 0642④, 0656④, 0700, 0701④, 0712④, 0722④, 0725④, 0731④, 0741④, 0750④, 0800, 0830☆, 0900, 0930☆, 1000, 1030☆, 1100, 1130☆, 1200, 1230☆, 1300, 1330☆, 1400, 1430☆, 1500, 1530☆, 1600, 1615④, 1630④, 1700, 1730☆, 1800, 1830☆, 1900, 1930☆, 2000, 2030④, 2100, 2200, 2300.
RTD operates frequent bus services throughout the Denver Metropolitan area.

◇–Most trips are extended to serve Stapleton Airport.
RTD– Regional Transportation District.

Table 513 — DENVER - ALBUQUERQUE 🚍 TNO

US$		↓ km	439	427	425	423	441	429	431	421
0.00	**Denver** d.	0	0715	0715	1045	1450	1600	1600	2200	2200
	Aurora d.		0740				1625			
14.00	Colorado Springs d.	115	0910	0915	1245	1650	1800	1800	2335	2335
22.00	Pueblo d.	185	1000	1015	1350	1755	1855	1900	0040	0050
	Walsenburg d.			1110	1445	1850		1955	0130	
	Alamosa d.					2030				
	Antonito d.					2105				
34.00	Trinidad d.	320		1155	1530			2035		0215
37.99	Raton d.	353		1255	1615			2115	0245	0300
	Capulin d.	400						r		
	Dalhart d.	553						0630		
	Amarillo d.	715						0830		
	Springer d.	423		1335	1700					
53.00	Las Vegas d.	535		1455	1815			2315		
47.30	Taos d.	467			2230					0515
61.00	Santa Fe d.	633		1605	1930	0005		0020		0645
70.00	**Albuquerque** a.	733		1715	2045	0125		0135		0815

		426	436	428		434	422	440	438	420	424
Albuquerque d.		2000		0100		0645			1130	1530
Santa Fe d.		2135		0210		0755			1305	1700
Taos d.						0925			1435	
Las Vegas d.		2245		0325						1815
Springer d.		0001		s						1930
Amarillo d.							0800			
Dalhart d.							0955			
Capulin d.							r			
Raton d.		0110		0530		1215	1201			2045
Trinidad d.		0140		0600		1245	1230			2115
Antonito d.								1555		
Alamosa d.								1635		
Walsenburg d.		0220		0645		1320			1810	2205
Pueblo d.		0330	0450	0745		1040	1440	1440	1810	1915	2310
Colorado Springs d.		0430	0545	0845		1140	1540	1540	1900	2015	0010
Aurora d.							1700			
Denver a.		0605	0720	1035		1330	1730	1730	2045	2140	0130

TNO–TNM&O Coaches.

Table 515 — ALAMOGORDO 🚍 TNO

US$	429	421		km ↓		426	428
0.00	0215	0900	....	0	d.**Albuquerque** ↑ a.	1830	0001
12.16	0520	1205	....	280	d.Carrizozo d.	1520	2050
16.66	0640	1320	....	375	d.Alamogordo d.	1405	1940
	0810	1440	....		a.Las Cruces d.		
38.75	0905	1555	....	515	a.**El Paso** d.	1215	1730

TNO–TNM&O Coaches.

Table 516 — BILLINGS - CHEYENNE 🚌 CDY PDR

US$		↓ km	PDR 125/45	PDR 10		PDR 101		PDR 121/41	CDY 15 ④	
0.00	**Billings** d.	0	0100	....	1300		1400	1730	....
	Crow Agency d.	102		....					
22.00	Sheridan d.	225	0315	....	1630		1630		
	Buffalo d.		0400		1705				
	Cody a.					2030		
	Powell a.					2100		
	Worland d.			1630				
	Shoshoni d.			1800				
	Gillette ★ d.	391	0600	0800		1930			
	New Castle d.							
	Moorcroft d.			0830				
	Sundance d.			0900				
	Spearfish d.			1010				
	Deadwood d.							
44.00	Rapid City 505 a.			1110				
	Casper d.	450			1955			
	Rawlins a.							
61.00	Douglas 505 d.		0820		2045		2140		
	Cheyenne 505 a.	725	1005				2359		

		CDY 10 ④	PDR 120	PDR 102 ex①		PDR 13	PDR 122
Cheyenne 505 d.		....	0130	....		....	1215
Douglas 505 d.		....	0405	0550		....	1430
Rawlins d.							
Casper d.		....	0700			....	1700
Rapid City 505 d.						1630	1630
Deadwood d.							
Spearfish d.						1735	
Sundance d.						1810	
Moorcroft d.						1850	
New Castle d.							
Gillette ★ d.		....	0830			1920	1930
Shoshoni d.				0845			
Worland d.				1015			
Powell d.		0800					
Cody d.		0845					
Buffalo d.			0940				2040
Sheridan d.			1030				2130
Crow Agency d.							
Billings a.		1145	1245	1335			2345

★–For Devils Tower. *CDY*–Cody Bus Line. *PDR*–Powder River Transportation.

Table 517 — AMARILLO - EL PASO 🚍 TNO

US$		451	453	455		km ↓		450	452	454
0.00	....	0330	1150	1835	....	0	d.**Amarillo** ↑ a.	1825	2220	0345
	....	0430	1250	1935	....		d.Hereford d.	1725	2115	0250
14.65	....	0505	1320	2000	....	170	d.Clovis d.	1505	1855	0035
	....	0530	1345	2025	....	201	d.Portales d.	1430	1820	0005
27.35	....	0730	1545	2230	....	350	d.Roswell d.	1245	1640	2225
44.00	....	1000	1830	0055	....	535	d.Alamogordo d.	0930	1355	1945
52.40	....	1120	2000	....	....	645	a.Las Cruces d.		1215	1810
52.40	....	1215	2055	0245	....	703	a.**El Paso** d.	0730	1110	1715

TNO–TNM&O Coaches.

Table 518 — HOBBS - ODESSA 🚍 TNO

US$	207	211 ex⑦		km ↓		206 ex⑦	210
0.00	0700	....	....	0	d.**Hobbs** a.	1310	....
		1215	....		d. Lubbock a.		2205
		1350	....		d. Brownfield d.		2110
	0850	1450	....	47	d.Seminole d.		2010
	1005	1620	....		d.**Odessa** d.	1130	1845

TNO–TNM&O Coaches.

Table 520 — SALT LAKE CITY - ALBUQUERQUE 🚍 GL TNO UTA

US$	GL 1304	TNO 381 ex⑧⑦			GL 379	GL 1310	TNO 457	GL 1312	GL 1300	km ↓		TNO 378		GL 1307	TNO 382 ex⑧⑦	TNO 456	GL 1309	GL 1313	GL 1303
0.00	....	....	....	....	2145	....	....	....	....	0	d.**Salt Lake City** Ω a.	2020c	....	....	....	....	....	....	....
9.00	....	....	....	....	2240	....	....	....	....	65	d.Provo Ω d.	1930c	....	....	....	....	....	....	....
	....	....	....	....	0015	....	....	....	....		d.Price d.	1755c	....	....	....	....	....	....	....
32.00	1245	....	....	....	0200	0225	....	0525	0940	289	d.Green River d.	1625c	....	1640	....	....	2315	0205	0605
44.00	1500	....	....	....	0420a	0435	0705	0745	1155	469	d. Grand Junction d.	1430c	....	1500	....	2135	2125	0025	0425
77.00	2025	....	....	....		1005	....	1325	1715	889	d. *Denver 507* d.		....	0830	....	....	1500	1830	2215
56.00	....	....	....	....	0535a	....	0820	....	....	569	d. Montrose d.	1205	....	....	....	....	2015	....	....
61.00	....	....	....	....		....	0940	....	....	679	d. Gunnison d.		....	....	....	....	1850	....	....
73.00	....	....	....	....		....	1140	....	....	829	d. Salida d.		....	....	....	....	1650	....	....
77.00	....	....	....	....		....	1255	....	....	931	d. Canon City d.		....	....	....	....	1530	....	....
92.00	....	....	....	....		....	1345	....	....	989	d. **Pueblo** d.		....	....	....	....	1440	....	....
59.00	....	....	....	....	ra	....	....	....	....	629	d.Ouray d.	r	....	....	....	....	....	....	....
61.00	....	....	....	....	0745a	....	....	....	....	666	d.Silverton d.	1015	....	....	....	....	....	....	....
	....	....	....	....		....	....	....	....		d. Mesa Verde a.		....	....	....	....	....	....	....
	....	....	....	....		....	....	....	....		d. Dove Creek a.		....	....	....	....	....	....	....
56.00	....	....	....	....		....	....	....	....	528	d. Cortez d.		....	....	....	....	....	....	....
67.00	....	1645	....	....	0925a	....	....	....	....	747	d.**Durango** d.	0800	....	1620	....	....	....	....	....
73.00	....	s	....	....	sa	....	....	....	....	805	d.Aztec d.	s	....	s	....	....	....	....	....
73.00	....	1805	....	....	1050a	....	....	....	....	828	d.Farmington d.	0625	....	1505	....	....	....	....	....
88.00	....	2010	....	....	1255a	....	....	....	....	983	d.Cuba d.	0340	....	1255	....	....	....	....	....
118.00	....	2145	....	....	1430a	....	....	....	....	1118	a.**Albuquerque** d.	0215	....	1130	....	....	....	....	....

a–TNO. c–GL. Ω–Frequent local service (UTA routes 1/801) Salt Lake City-Provo and v.v. GL–Greyhound Lines. TNO–TNM&O Coaches. UTA–Utah Transit Authority.

Check update notes to timetables and with operator before starting your journey

Table 523   GREAT FALLS - BILLINGS   🚌 RRS

US$			2			km	↓	↑			1	
0.00	....	....	1830	....	....	0	d.Great Falls ....a.		....	....	1800	....
12.00	....	....	2100	....	....	175	d.Lewistown ....d.		....	....	1545	....
17.60	....	....	2225	....	....	305	d.Roundup ....d.		....	....	1400	....
22.50	....	....	2330	....	....	391	a.Billings ....d.		....	....	1300	....

RRS–Rimrock Trailways.

Table 525   ALAMOSA - WALSENBURG   🚌 SLV

US$		🎿		km	↓	↑		🎿	
		1600	....	0	d.Alamosa ....a.		....	2000	....
0.00	....	1630	....		d.Fort Garland ....d.		....	1930	....
		r			d.La Veta ....d.			r	
22.00	....	1730	....		a.Walsenburg ....d.		....	1830	....

SLV– SLV Van Lines Inc.

Table 526   ALBUQUERQUE - EL PASO   🚌 TNO

US$	419	425		km	↓	↑		422	424
0.00	1515	2200		0	d.Albuquerque ....a.		0530	1430
13.00	1640	2325		105	d.Socorro ....d.		0440	1255
25.00	1815	0040		225	d.Truth or Consequences d.		0240	1115
38.75	1945	0210		350	d.Las Cruces ....d.		0110	0945
38.75	2050	0305		408	a.El Paso ....d.		0015	0845

TNO– TNM&O Coaches.

Table 527   SALMON   🚌 BSG SBL

US $	BSG 4	SBL ①②④⑤	BSG 8	BSG 6 ex⑦		km	↓	↑		BSG 3	SBL ①④	SBL ②⑤
			1500	1630		0	d.Missoula ....a.		1230	—	—
	0530		1615	1815			d.Hamilton ....d.		1100	—	—
0.00	0800	0800	....				d.Salmon ....d.		0815	1830	1930
		0930a		....		98	d.Challis ....d.				1800
		1045a		....		181	d.Mackay ....d.				1700
		1130a		....		223	d.Arco ◇ ....d.				1620
						324	d.Blackfoot ....d.					
15.90						352	a.Pocatello ....d.					
14.10		1300b				264	a. Idaho Falls ....d.				1500	1500

a–②⑤ only.   b–1130 on ①④.   ◇–For Craters of the Moon.   BSG–Bitterroot Stages.   SBL–Salmon Bus Lines Inc.

Table 528   BUTTE - SWEETGRASS   🚌 INM RRS

US$			INM 5	RRS 7		INM 3	RRS 9
		↓ km					
16.35	Butte ....d.	0	....	0330	....	1130	....
10.80	Helena ....d.	110	....	0510	....	1315	....
0.00	Great Falls ....d.	260	....	0700	0715	1505	1820
12.55	Havre ....a.	445	....				2045
	Shelby ....d.	410	....		1010		
13.15	Sweetgrass 🏛 ....d.	467	....		1100		

			INM 4	RRS 8	RRS 10	INM 2
		↓				
Sweetgrass 🏛 ....d.		....		1145		
Shelby ....d.		....		1240		
Havre ....d.		....			1245	
Great Falls ....d.		0715	1435	1515	1530	
Helena ....d.		0900			1730	
Butte ....a.		1045			1850	

INM– Intermountain Transportation.
RRS– Rimrock Stages.

Table 530   BUTTE - SALT LAKE CITY   🚌 GL INM

US$	INM 4	GL 5921	INM 2	GL 5919	km	↓	↑		GL 5920	INM 1	GL 5918	INM 5
67.00	1045	....	1915	....	617	d.Butte ....a.		....	1900	....	0300
59.00	1155	....	2020	....	522	d.Dillon ....d.		....	1740	....	0200
67.00					631	d. Bozeman ....a.					
56.00					486	d. West Yellowstone d.					
70.00					363	d. St. Anthony ....d.					
37.00	1445	1515	2315	2345	312	d.Idaho Falls ....d.		1445	1500	2310	2320
32.00		1630		0100	250	d.Pocatello ....d.		1340		2200	
12.00		1935		0335	85	d.Brigham City ....d.		1015		1900	
8.00		2015		0405	48	d.Ogden ....d.		0945		1830	
0.00		2105		0500	0	a.Salt Lake City ....d.		0845		1730	

GL– Greyhound Lines.   INM–Intermountain Transportation.

Table 531   PRESCOTT   🚌 NHT PTA

US$	NHT 8004	PTA	NHT 8554	NHT 8504	km	↓	↑		NHT 8553	PTA	NHT 8503	NHT 8003
0.00	0305		1145	1730	0	d.Phoenix ....a.		1035		1545	0100
		0915				d. Prescott ....a.		1215			
	0445	1015	1405	1950		d.Camp Verde ....d.		0825	1115	1340	2310
						a.Williams ....d.					
	0610		1525	2110		a.Flagstaff ....d.		0720		1230	2150
						a.Grand Canyon ......d.					

NHT–Nava Hopi Tours.   PTA–Prescott Transit Authority.

Table 532   AJO - TUCSON   🚌 PP

US$	①③⑤		km	↓	↑			①③⑤	
0.00	0600		0	d.Ajo ....a.		....		1845	....
7.50	0900		225	a.Tucson ....d.		....		1520	....

PP– La Tortuga Transit.

Table 533   DEL RIO - EL PASO   🚌 GL

US $	1471	1473		km	↓	↑		1472	1470
0.00	0020	1600		0	d.Del Rio ....a.		1230	0255
	0445	2025			d.Alpine ....d.		0750	2230
	0520	2100			d.Marfa ....d.		0715	2155
	0715	2240			a. Van Horn ....d.		0550	2030
	0815	2335			a.El Paso ....d.		0225	1715

GL– Greyhound Lines.

Table 535   BUTTE - WHITEFISH   🚌 INM

US$	41	41	45		km	↓	↑		44	40
0.00	....	1045	1915		0	d.Butte ....a.		1030	1730
	....	1125	1945		44	d.Anaconda ....d.		1000	1700
	....	1330	1745		218	d.Missoula ....d.		1445	....
	....	1915			322	d.Polson ....d.		1200	....
	....	2035			408	d.Kalispell ....d.		1045	....
	....	2135				a. Whitefish ....d.		1005	....

INM– Intermountain Transportation.

Table 536   YELLOWSTONE PARK   🚌 CDY GL PDR TSL YP

🚌 (YP) services operate on all major routes within the park. They link the main resort areas and principal monuments within the park with the main gateways at West Yellowstone (GL to Idaho Falls), Jackson Lake (TSL to Idaho Falls), Grand Teton National Park, Cody (CDY/PDR to Billings), Bozeman (GL to Billings/Butte), Livingston (GL to Billings/Butte), Billings (GL to Fargo).

CDY–Cody Bus Line.   GL–Greyhound Lines.   PDR–Powder River Transportation.   TSL–Teton Stage Line.   YP–Yellowstone Park Co.

Table 537   PARK CITY/SNOWBIRD   🚌 LB UTA

🚌 (LB) service Salt Lake City-Park City and v.v. 48 km. Journey: 1 hour. Fare: US$: 6.00 ($14.00 to Airport) 🅱.
From Park City to Salt Lake City: 1000, 1700.
From Park City to Salt Lake City Airport: 0600 and every 30 mins. to 2100.
From Salt Lake City to Park City: 0820, 1515, 2245.
From Salt Lake City Airport to Park City: 0930 and every 30 mins. to 2330, 2359.

🚌 (LB) service Park City-Snowbird-Alta and v.v. 72 km. Journey: 1½ hours. Fare: US$: 10.00 🅱.
From Park City: 0800.   **From Alta:** 1700.

🚌 (UTA) service Salt Lake City-Alta and v.v. 30 km. Journey: 1 hour. Fare: US$: 3.00 ($6.00 from Airport) (routes 92/93/94/98).
From Salt Lake City: 0545, 0715, 0725, 0734, 0752ⓒ, 0754, 0814, 0834, 0854, 0945, 1045, 1059, 1145ⓒ, 1200, 1515, 1545, 1630.
From Alta: 0900ⓒ, 0917, 0930, 1000, 1015, 1047, 1145, 1200, 1230, 1310, 1400, 1430, 1515, 1600ⓒ, 1615, 1620ⓒ, 1630, 1645, 1650, 1700, 1710, 1715, 1730, 1800.
From Salt Lake City Airport: 1100, 1200, 1500.
From Alta (to Airport): 0900, 1315.

LB–Lewis Bros. Stages.   UTA–Utah Transit Authority.

Table 538   AUSTIN   🚌 TNS

US$		①③⑤	②④	km	↓	↑		②④	①③⑤
0.00	....		0900	0	d.Reno ....a.		1645	....	....
	....		1315		d.Austin ....d.		1315	....	....
	....	0800	1615		d.Ely ....d.		0915	2200	....
	....	1230			a.Las Vegas ....d.		0845	1730	....

TNS– TransNevada Stages.

Table 540   GRAND CANYON   🚌 NHT

US$	8633	8603		km	↓	↑		8604	8634
0.00	....	1020	1725	0	d.Grand Canyon ....a.		0955	....	1710
9.00	....		1830	92	a. Williams ....d.		0840	....	....
12.50	....	1230	1910	130	a.Flagstaff 🅧 ....d.		0750	....	1515

🅧– NHT operates a day tour in summer on ①③⑤⑥ (subject to a minimum of 5 passengers) from Flagstaff at 0730 to Kayenta and Monument Valley (return to Flagstaff at 1900).
NHT– Nava Hopi Tours.

Table 541   SEATTLE - WALLA WALLA   🚌 GL

US$	5560	1421	5594		km	↓	↑		5559	1422	5561	5557
0.00	0725	1130	1645		0	d.Seattle ....a.		1130	....	1855	2025
22.00	1000	1405	1920		160	d.Ellensburg ....d.		0920	....	1625	1755
28.00	1135	1515	2025		223	d.Yakima ....d.		0825	1525	1530	1700
31.00	1210	1550	2100		254	d.Toppenish ....d.		0735	1450	1440	....
37.00	1340		2230		349	d.Richland ....d.		0610	....	1305	....
39.00	1405		2250		362	d.Pasco ....d.		0545	....	1245	....
44.00	1515		0001		438	a. Walla Walla ....d.		0350	....	1130	....
	1620		0105			a.Pendleton ....d.		0245	....	1025	....

GL– Greyhound Lines.

able 542 SALT LAKE CITY - SAN FRANCISCO

GL ST

S $	GL 8301	ST 35	ST 34	GL 1311	GL 1315	GL 8331	ST 37	GL 8313	ST 30	GL 8319	GL 1301	GL 8309	GL 8321	GL 8325	GL 1305	km	↓ ↑
.00	....	....	....	2145	2145	....	....	....	....	....	0320	....	....	....	1040	0	d.**Salt Lake City** ..... a.
	....	....	....	│	│	....	....	....	....	....	│	....	....	....	│		d.Wendover .... d.
.00	....	....	....	│	2355	....	....	....	....	....	0530	....	....	....	1250	290	d.Wells .. .. d.
.00	....	....	....	0055	0105	....	....	....	....	....	0705	....	....	....	1415	364	d.Elko.... .... d.
.00	....	....	....	0320	0350	....	....	....	....	....	0950	....	....	....	1700	504	d.Winnemucca........ d.
.00	....	....	....	│	│	....	....	....	....	....	1105	....	....	....	1815	659	d.Lovelock............. d.
.00	0001	0200	0530	0640	0715	0645	0830	0905	1130	1240	1320	1500	1650	1905	2030	814	d.**Reno** .. .. d.
.00	│	│	│	│	│	│	│	│	│	│	│	│	│	│	│	819	d.Sparks .... d.
.00	0125**s**	│	│	│	│	0810	│	1030	│	1405	│	│	1755	│	2115	870	d.Truckee.............. d.
00	0230**s**	│	│	│	│	0925	│	1201	│	1520	│	│	1905	│	2225	975	d.Colfax . ... d.
	0255**s**	0430	0800	│	│	0950	│	1225	1400	1545	│	│	1930	│	2250		d.Auburn .... d.
.00	0425	0505	0840	0930	1030	1130	1140	1430	1440	1730	1630	1830	2130	2245	0005	1034	d.**Sacramento**........ d.
.00	0540	0630	1000	│	│	│	1300	1620	1540	│	│	│	│	2350**s**	0120**s**	1155	a.Vallejo. .... d.
	│	│	│	│	│	│	│	│	│	│	│	│	│	│	│		a.Richmond............ d.
00	0630	0710	1050	│	1159	1300	1350	1720	1630	1900	1800	2000	2300	0025	0205	1168	a.**Oakland**............ d.
00	0715	0735	1120	1115	1230	1330	1420	1805	1645	1930	1840	2030	2330	0055	0235	1179	a.**San Francisco** .... d.

↓ ↑	GL 1308	GL 8310	GL 8314	GL 8316	ST 32	ST 34	GL 8312	GL 1314	GL 1316	ST 37	GL 8326	GL 1306	ST 30	GL 8306	GL 8338
d.**Salt Lake City** ..... a.	1700	....	....	....	....	....	....	0630	0630	....	....	1015	....	....	....
d.Wendover .... d.	│	....	....	....	....	....	....	│	│	....	....	│	....	....	....
d.Wells .. .. d.	1240	....	....	....	....	....	....	│	│	....	....	0610	....	....	....
d.Elko.... .... d.	1145	....	....	....	....	....	....	0125	0135	....	....	0515	....	....	....
d.Winnemucca........ d.	0840	....	....	....	....	....	....	2240	2300	....	....	0230	....	....	....
d.Lovelock............. d.	0710	....	....	....	....	....	....	2105	│	....	....	│	....	....	....
d.**Reno** .. .. d.	0535	1230	1420	1540	1615	1800	1840	1930	2020	2115	2250	2340	2300	2320	0205
d.Sparks .... d.	│	│	│	│	│	│	│	│	│	│	│	│	│	│	│
d.Truckee.............. d.	│	│	1320	│	│	│	│	│	│	│	2155	│	│	│	│
d.Colfax . ... d.	│	│	1215	│	│	│	│	│	│	│	2050	│	│	│	0005**s**
d.Auburn .... d.	│	│	1145	│	1355	│	│	│	│	1910**a**	2015	│	│	│	2340**s**
d.**Sacramento**........ d.	0215	0920	1030	1230	1300	1500	1520	1550	1700	1830	1900	2020	2040	2030	2230
a.Vallejo. .... d.	│	│	│	│	1140	1335	│	│	│	1650	│	│	1920	│	│
a.Richmond............ d.	│	│	│	│	│	│	│	│	│	│	│	│	│	│	│
a.**Oakland**............ d.	0030	0730	0830	1030	1100	1300	1330	1350	1500	1600	1640	1820	1830	1835	2030
a.**San Francisco** .... d.	0001	0700	0800	1000	1040	1240	1300	1315	1430	1540	1600	1735	1800	1800	2000

⑤⑦ only.
– Greyhound Lines.
– Sierra Trailways.

able 543 SALT LAKE CITY - LAS VEGAS

GL

S $	1313	1303		6027			1307		6051	1309		km	↓ ↑
0.00	....	....	....	0845	....	....	....	....	2215	....	....	0	d.**Salt Lake City** ....a.
9.00	....	....	....	0940	....	....	....	....	2310	....	....	65	d.Provo ....d.
18.00	1800	2245	....	│	....	....	0810	....	│	1500	....	★892	d. *Denver* **520** ....a.
9.00	│	0640	....	│	....	....	1645	....	│	2325	....	★292	d. **Green River** ....a.
2.00	│	0905	....	│	....	....	1910	....	│	0145	....	★94	d. Richfield..................d.
4.00	0425	1035	....	1310	....	....	2045	....	0235	0310	....	309	d.Beaver........................d.
1.00	│	1135	....	1420	....	....	2145	....	0340	0410	....	392	d.Cedar City..................d.
	│	1250	....	1530	....	....	2240	....	0430	0505	....		d.St. George..................d.
4.00	0715	1355	....	1645	....	....	2345	....	0545	0610	....	687	a.**Las Vegas** ....d.
2.00	1310	2015	....	2355	....	....	0710	....	1340	1300	....	1147	a.*Los Angeles* **570** ....d.

↓ ↑		1302		1304	6022				1310	1312	6050
d.**Salt Lake City** ....a.	....	....	....	....	1650	....	....	....	....	....	0705
d.Provo ....d.	....	....	....	....	1545	....	....	....	....	....	0605
d. *Denver* **520** ....a.	....	1635	....	2030	│	....	....	....	1005	1325	│
d. **Green River** ....a.	....	│	....	1220	│	....	....	....	0205	0505	│
d. Richfield..................d.	....	0710	....	0955	│	....	....	....	2345	0245	│
d.Beaver........................d.	....	0600	....	0845	1230	....	....	....	2235	0135	0315
d.Cedar City..................d.	....	│	....	0725	1125	....	....	....	2115	0020	0150
d.St. George..................d.	....	│	....	0630	1030	....	....	....	2020	2325	0100
a.**Las Vegas** ....d.	....	0030	....	0250	0630		....	....	1710	2015	2135
a.*Los Angeles* **570** ....d.	....	1800	....	2000	2330	....	....	....	0900	1400	1400

–Fare ex Las Vegas. ★–Km ex Beaver. *GL*–Greyhound Lines.

able 544 EL PASO - SAN DIEGO

BWTS GL

S $	↓	km	GL 6315	GL 6373	GL 1411	BWTS	GL 6331	GL 1435	GL 407	GL 1413	GL 6379	GL 6313	GL 401	GL 1415	GL 6349	BWTS	GL 1419		GL 403	GL 6343	GL 6341	GL 1407	GL 6345	GL 405	GL 6353
	Dallas **485**.d.		....	....	1315	....	....	1800	....	1915	....	....	....	2330	....	....	0245	....	....	....	....	0800	....	....	....
0.00	*Houston* **588**.......d.	0	....	....	│	....	....	│	....	│	....	....	2000	│	....	....	│	....	....	....	....	│	....	0730	....
2.00	Van Horn............d.	960	....	....	0125	....	....	0405	....	0640	....	....	0945	1050	....	....	1410	....	....	....	....	2020	....	2155**s**	....
4.00	**El Paso**............a.	1160	....	....	0225	....	....	0505	....	0740	....	....	1045	1150	....	....	1535	....	....	....	....	2125	....	2250	....
	El Paso............d.		....	....	0315	....	....	0600	0645	0845	....	....	1201	1300	....	....	1630	....	1915	....	....	2225	....	2350	....
4.00	Las Cruces.........d.	1238	....	....	0405	....	....	│	│	0940	....	....	1255	1355	....	....	1730	....	2010	....	....	2320	....	│	....
3.00	Lordsburg...........d.	1418	....	....	0655	....	....	0905	0945	1230	....	....	1520	1610	....	....	1950	....	2230	....	....	0135	....	0255	....
	Benson Ω...........d.		....	....	0755	....	....	│	│	1330	....	....	│	1715	....	....	│	....	│	....	....	│	....	│	....
1.00	Tucson...............d.	1678	....	0800	0900	0900	....	1100	│	1435	1600	....	│	1845	....	1900	2145	....	0025	....	....	0330	....	│	....
	Casa Grande .d.		....	0915	│	│	....	│	│	│	1725	....	│	│	....	│	│	....	│	....	....	│	....	│	....
1.00	Globe ....d.	1663	....	│	│	│	....	│	1230	│	│	GL	1800	│	....	│	│	....	│	....	....	│	....	0510	....
1.00	**Phoenix**...........a.	1863	....	1015	1100	1200	....	1315	1500	1635	1830	**6313**	2025	2045	....	2200	2359	....	0225	....	....	0545	....	0750	....
	Phoenix...........d.		0830	....	▬	....	1215	1400	▬	▬	....	1815	....	....	....	....	0045	....	▬	....	....	0630	....	....	....
2.00	Gila Bend...........d.	1968	0955	....	GL	....	1350	│	GL	GL	....	1930	....	....	....	....	│	....	GL	....	....	│	....	....	....
2.00	Yuma ....d.	2168	1159	....	**6351**	....	1610	│	**6363**	**7092**	....	2130	....	....	....	....	│	....	**6325**	....	....	│	....	....	....
2.00	Calexico ....d.	2251	1345	....	1445	....	1800	│	1830	2040	....	2310	....	....	0001	....	│	....	0630	0645	0910	│	1015	....	1215
2.00	El Centro............d.	2269	1410	....	1510	....	1830	│	1900	│	....	2340	....	....	0030	....	│	....	0705	0710	0945	│	1050	....	1300
2.00	**San Diego** ....a.	2474	1640	....	│	....	2055	│	│	2305	....	0200	....	....	│	....	│	....	0935	│	│	│	│	....	│
2.00	*Los Angeles* **545** d.	2488	....	....	2010	....	....	2100	0015	0225	....	....	....	....	0600	....	0800	....	....	1340	1450	1635	1700	....	1940

↓	GL 6339	GL 6312	GL 6346	GL 1402	GL 404	BWTS	GL 6326	GL 1416	GL 6348	GL 6366	GL 6356	GL 406	GL 6314		GL 6352	GL 1408	GL 6354		GL 1412	GL 1404	GL 6332	GL 402	GL 1406	BWTS	GL 6380
Los Angeles **545**..d.	0030	....	0530	0700	....	....	....	....	1045	1201	1400	1415	....	....	1540	1800	1915	....	2000	2200	....	....	....	....	....
n Diego ....d.	│	0645	│	│	....	....	1040	....	│	1530	│	│	1700	....	│	│	│	....	│	│	2145	....	....	....	....
Centro..................d.	0555	0945	1255	│	....	....	1335	....	1745	1825	2010	│	1935	....	2140	│	0145	....	│	│	0015	....	....	....	....
exico ....d.	0620	1015	1320	│	....	....	1305	....	1805	1755	2040	│	2005	....	2205	│	0205	....	│	│	0045	....	....	....	....
na ....d.	▬	1130	▬	│	....	....	▬	....	....	▬	....	│	2120	....	....	│	▬	....	│	│	0200	....	....	....	....
a Bend ....d.	....	1405	GL	│	....	....	....	....	....	....	....	│	2340	....	....	│	GL	....	│	│	0430	....	....	....	....
oenix.................a.	BWTS	1530	**6378**	1525	....	....	BWTS	....	....	BWTS	....	2225	0100	....	....	0045	**408**	....	0245	0555	0615	....	....	....	....
oenix.................d.	1400	....	1555	1630	1600	1800	2000	2130	....	2200	....	2315	....	....	....	0130	0315	....	0330	0645	....	0845	0845	1200	1230
Globe ....d.	│	....	│	│	1900	│	│	│	....	│	....	│	....	....	....	│	0545	....	│	│	....	1140	│	│	│
Casa Grande d.	│	....	1755	│	│	│	│	│	....	│	....	│	....	....	....	│	│	....	│	│	....	│	0945	│	1330
son ....d.	1630	....	1920	1900	│	2040	2240	2345	....	0040	....	0145	....	....	....	0400	│	....	0630	0915	....	│	1145	1440	1445
nson Ω.................d.	....	....	....	1945	│	....	....	│	....	....	....	│	....	....	....	│	│	....	│	1005	....	│	1235	....	....
dsburg.................d.	....	....	....	2305	2315	....	....	0340	....	....	....	0540	....	....	....	0815	1030	....	1015	1335	....	1600	1550	....	....
Cruces...............d.	....	....	....	0110	0120	....	....	0545	....	....	....	0745	....	....	....	1010	1240	....	│	1545	....	1810	1755	....	....
Paso.................a.	....	....	....	0200	0210	....	....	0635	....	....	....	0835	....	....	....	1100	1330	....	1300	1635	....	1900	1845	....	....
Paso.................d.	....	....	....	0300	0335	....	....	0735	....	....	....	....	....	....	....	1201	1445	....	1400	1735	....	....	2015	....	....
Horn.................d.	....	....	....	0630	0705	....	....	1105	....	....	....	....	....	....	....	1530	1835	....	1735	2055	....	....	2330	....	....
ston ....a.	....		....	│	2115	....	....	│	....	....	....	....	....	....	....	│	0815	....	│	│	....	....	│	....	....
Dallas **485**.......a.	....	....	....	1605	....	....	....	2240	....	....	....	....	....	....	....	0130	....	....	0430	0730	....	....	1125	....	....

For Tombstone.
TS–Bridgewater Transport.
- Greyhound Lines.

Table 545 OKLAHOMA CITY - ALBUQUERQUE - PHOENIX - LOS ANGELES

CPL GL NHT

US $		km	GL 6323	NHT 8503 ⑤⑦	GL 473	GL 1435	GL 6307	GL 1415		GL 6349	GL 1419	NHT 8003	GL 1367	GL 403	GL 1409	GL 6343	GL 6322	GL 475	GL 6355	NHT 8553	GL 405	GL 1351	GL 1411	GL 6351	
	St. Louis **458** d.		....	....	0730	....	....	....	....	....	....	....	1730	....	....	....	....	2230	....	....	....	0230	....	....	....
0.00	**Oklahoma City** d.	0	....	....	2100**a**	....	....	....	....	....	....	....	0545	....	....	....	....	1030**a**	....	....	....	1545	....	....	....
	Sayre d.		....	....	|	....	....	....	....	....	....	....	0840	....	....	....	....	1335**a**	....	....	....	1850	....	....	....
	Pampa d.		....	....	0110**a**	....	....	....	....	....	....	....	|	....	....	....	....	1515**a**	....	....	....	|	....	....	....
41.00	Amarillo d.	420	....	....	0340	....	....	....	....	....	....	....	1145	....	....	....	....	1720	....	....	....	2155	....	....	....
	Vega d.		....	....	|	....	....	....	....	....	....	....	1225	....	....	....	....	|	....	....	....	|	....	....	....
59.00	Tucumcari d.	605	....	....	|	....	....	....	....	....	....	....	1245	....	....	....	....	1835	....	....	....	2250	....	....	....
	Santa Rosa d.	704	....	....	|	....	....	....	....	....	....	....	1415	....	....	....	....	1940	....	....	....	|	....	....	....
77.00	**Albuquerque** d.	890	....	....	0830	....	....	....	....	....	....	....	1715	....	....	....	....	2230	....	....	....	0250	....	....	....
82.00	Grants d.	1015	....	....	1000	....	....	....	....	....	....	....	1845	....	....	....	....	0001	....	....	....	0420	....	....	....
98.00	Gallup d.	1114	....	....	1110	....	....	....	....	....	....	....	1955	....	....	....	....	0105	....	....	....	0525	....	....	....
	Houck d.		....	....	1220	....	....	....	....	....	....	....	2110	....	....	....	....	|	....	....	....	0620	....	....	....
98.00	Holbrook d.	1269	....	....	1330	....	....	....	....	....	....	....	2220	....	....	....	....	0310**s**	....	....	....	0730	....	....	....
98.00	Winslow d.	1356	....	....	1415	....	....	....	....	....	....	....	2305	....	....	....	....	0355	....	....	....	0815	....	....	....
98.00	**Flagstaff** d.	1437	....	1230	1545	....	1600	....	....	....	....	2315	0030	....	....	....	0520	0530	....	0720	....	1000	....	....	....
104.00	Williams d.	1482	....	|	1630	....	|	....	....	....	....	|	|	....	....	....	|	0605	....	|	....	|	....	....	....
118.00	Kingman d.	1707	....	|	1905	....	|	....	....	....	....	|	|	....	....	....	|	0850	....	|	....	|	....	....	....
118.00	Needles d.	1812	....	|	1945	....	|	....	....	....	....	|	|	....	....	....	|	0930	....	|	....	|	....	....	....
118.00	Barstow d.	2042	....	|	2215	....	|	....	....	....	....	|	|	....	....	....	|	1210	....	|	....	|	....	....	....
◇27.00	**Phoenix** a.	1777	....	1545	|	....	1900	....	....	....	....	0210	0315	....	....	....	0820	|	....	1035	....	1245	....	....	....
	Phoenix d.		1700	....	|	1700	▬	2300	....	....	0145	▬	....	0415	0415	....	▬	|	0745	▬	0945	▬	1315	....	....
	Wickenburg d.	1865	|	....	|	|	*GL*	|	....	....	|	*GL*	....	|	|	....	*GL*	|	0925	*GL*	|	*GL*	|	....	....
131.00	Blythe d.	2017	1845	....	|	1900	**6363**	0050	....	....	0330	**6991**	....	0615	0615	....	**6341**	|	1105	**6345**	1210	**6353**	1500	....	....
131.00	Indio d.	2187	|	....	|	2100	2115	|	....	0240	0515	0530	....	|	0810	0915	1210	|	1300	1315	1405	1530	1705	1710	....
131.00	Palm Springs d.	2236	|	....	|	|	2150	|	....	|	|	0605	....	|	0845	0950	1245	|	1335	1350	1435	1605	|	1745	....
131.00	San Bernardino d.	2167	|	....	0001	2225	|	|	....	|	|	0715	....	|	0950	1130	|	1430	1450	1520	1540	1735	1840	|	....
131.00	Riverside d.	2182	|	....	|	2245	2300	|	....	0430	|	0735	....	|	|	|	|	1445	1510	|	|	1800	|	1855	....
131.00	Claremont *(Pomona)* d.	2218	|	....	0030	2330	|	|	....	0505	|	0810	....	|	|	|	|	1525	|	1555	|	1835	|	|	....
142.00	El Monte *(Alhambra)* d.	2263	2215	....	0100	|	|	|	....	0540	|	0850	....	|	|	1210	1440	|	|	1630	|	1910	|	|	....
142.00	Pasadena d.	2248	|	....	|	|	|	|	....	|	|	|	....	|	|	|	|	|	|	|	|	|	|	|	....
142.00	**Los Angeles** a.	2288	2245	....	0130	0010	0100	0450	....	0610	0755	0920	....	1015	1100	1240	1510	1605	1620	1700	1705	1940	1945	2010	....

	GL 6339	GL 1414	GL 474	NHT 8554 ⑤⑦	GL 6306	GL 6346	GL 1418		NHT 8504	GL 470		GL 6348	GL 1416	GL 6994		GL 406		GL 1364	GL 6352	GL 1400	GL 6324	GL 6354	GL 1356	GL 1412	GL 1404
Los Angeles d.	0030	0045	....	....	....	0530	0700	....	....	0950	....	1045	1120	1201	....	1430	....	....	1540	1800	1800	1915	1915	2000	2200
Pasadena d.	|	|	....	....	....	|	|	....	....	|	....	|	|	|	....	|	....	....	|	|	|	|	|	|	|
El Monte *(Alhambra)* d.	|	|	....	....	....	0600	0730	....	....	|	....	1115	|	1225	....	|	....	....	1610	|	1830	|	1945	|	|
Claremont *(Pomona)* d.	|	|	....	....	....	0635	0805	....	....	1030	....	1150	|	1305	....	|	....	....	1645	|	1905	|	2020	|	|
Riverside d.	|	|	....	....	....	0720	0845	....	....	|	....	1235	1235	1350	....	|	....	....	1730	|	1950	|	2105	|	|
San Bernardino d.	|	|	....	....	....	0745	0910	....	....	1120	....	1300	1300	1415	....	1550	....	....	1755	|	2025	2040	2135	|	2325
Palm Springs d.	|	|	....	....	....	0915	|	....	....	|	....	1400	1400	1540	....	|	....	....	1905	|	|	2200	|	|	|
Indio d.	0300	|	....	....	....	1000	1045	....	....	|	....	1435	1450	1615	....	1730	....	....	1940	|	2200	2235	|	|	0050
Blythe d.	....	0500	....	....	....	....	1300	....	....	|	....	▬	1700	....	....	1940	....	....	....	2215	0001	▬	|	0015	0250
Wickenburg d.	....	|	....	....	....	....	|	....	....	|	....	*GL*	2005	....	....	|	....	....	....	|	|	*NHT*	|	|	|
Phoenix a.	....	0830	....	....	....	....	1630	....	....	|	....	**6308**	2140	....	....	2315	....	....	....	0145	0330	**8004**	|	0345	0620
Phoenix d.	....	....	0945	1145	1230	....	....	....	1730	|	....	1905	....	....	....	....	....	0035	....	....	....	0405	|	....	....
Barstow d.	....	....	|	|	|	....	....	....	|	1330	....	|	....	....	....	....	....	|	....	....	....	|	2330	....	....
Needles d.	....	....	|	|	|	....	....	....	|	1605	....	|	....	....	....	....	....	|	....	....	....	|	0200	....	....
Kingman d.	....	....	|	|	|	....	....	....	|	1930	....	|	....	....	....	....	....	|	....	....	....	|	0455	....	....
Williams d.	....	....	|	|	|	....	....	....	|	|	....	|	....	....	....	....	....	|	....	....	....	|	0705	....	....
Flagstaff d.	....	....	1310	1525	1530	....	....	....	2100	2225	....	2200	....	....	....	....	....	0345	....	....	....	0655	0820	....	....
Winslow d.	....	....	1415	....	....	....	....	....	....	2330	....	....	....	....	....	....	....	0450	....	....	....	....	0925	....	....
Holbrook d.	....	....	1500	....	....	....	....	....	....	0015	....	....	....	....	....	....	....	|	....	....	....	....	1010	....	....
Houck d.	....	....	1625	....	....	....	....	....	....	|	....	....	....	....	....	....	....	0725	....	....	....	....	1140	....	....
Gallup d.	....	....	1710	....	....	....	....	....	....	0220	....	....	....	....	....	....	....	0810	....	....	....	....	1225	....	....
Grants d.	....	....	1815	....	....	....	....	....	....	|	....	....	....	....	....	....	....	0915	....	....	....	....	1330	....	....
Albuquerque d.	....	....	2030	....	....	....	....	....	....	0530	....	....	....	....	....	....	....	1130	....	....	....	....	1545	....	....
Santa Rosa d.	....	....	2225	....	....	....	....	....	....	|	....	....	....	....	....	....	....	1325	....	....	....	....	1740**s**	....	....
Tucumcari d.	....	....	0005	....	....	....	....	....	....	0845	....	....	....	....	....	....	....	1505	....	....	....	....	1915	....	....
Vega d.	....	....	|	....	....	....	....	....	....	1110	....	....	....	....	....	....	....	|	....	....	....	....	|	....	....
Amarillo d.	....	....	0355**a**	....	....	....	....	....	....	1230**a**	....	....	....	....	....	....	....	1855	....	....	....	....	2300	....	....
Pampa d.	....	....	0505**a**	....	....	....	....	....	....	1355**a**	....	....	....	....	....	....	....	|	....	....	....	....	|	....	....
Sayre d.	....	....	|	....	....	....	....	....	....	1545**a**	....	....	....	....	....	....	....	2115	....	....	....	....	|	....	....
Oklahoma City a.	....	....	0910**a**	....	....	....	....	....	....	1830**a**	....	....	....	....	....	....	....	2355	....	....	....	....	0325	....	....
St. Louis **458** a.	....	....	2055	....	....	....	....	....	....	0620	....	....	....	....	....	....	....	1230	....	....	....	....	1600	....	....

a–*CPL*. ◇–Fare ex Flagstaff. *CPL*–Panhandle Trailways. *GL*–Greyhound Lines. *NHT*–Nava Hopi Tours.

Table 546 TUCSON - NOGALES

CAS

service Tucson-Nogales 🏛 and v.v. *105* km. Journey: 1¾ hours. Fare: US $: 5.60.
From Tucson: 0700, 0900, 1000, 1100, 1200, 1300, 1500⑤⑥⑦, 1530, 1700, 1800, 2000.
From Nogales: 0700, 0900, 1000, 1100, 1200, 1300, 1430, 1600, 1700⑤⑥⑦, 1800, 2000.

CAS– Citizen Auto Stage Co.

Table 547 DALLAS - PALESTINE

US $					km					
						↓ ↑				
0.00	....	....	....	....	0	d.**Dallas** a.	....	....	....	....
13.35	....	....	....	....	140	a.**Palestine** d.	....	....	....	....

Table 556 SAN DIEGO - TIJUANA ♣

GL MC

service San Diego-San Ysidro 🏛-Tijuana and v.v. *20* km. Journey: 45 mins.-1 hour. Fare: US $: 5.25.
From San Diego Greyhound Terminal *(GL)*: 0515, 0610, 0715, 0720, 0820, 0840, 0940, 1040, 1210, 1340, 1440, 1540, 1640, 1810, 1955, 2040, 2210, 2340.
From San Diego Amtrak *(MC)*: 0900, 1100, 1400, 1600, 1800.
From Tijuana (to San Diego Greyhound Terminal) *(GL)*: 0050, 0510, 0615, 0720, 0815, 0920, 1015, 1120, 1215, 1320, 1450, 1620, 1700, 1750, 1905, 2050, 2135, 2305.
From Tijuana (to San Diego Amtrak) *(MC)*: 0800, 1000, 1200, 1500, 1700, 1845, 2100©.

GL–Greyhound Lines. *MC*–Mexicoach.

Table 560 BISMARCK - RAPID CITY

BSI

US $		1			km		2			
						↓ ↑				
0.00	....	1200	....	....	0	d.**Bismarck** a.	1730	....	....	....
	....	1420	....	....		d.Hettinger d.	1345	....	....	....
	....	1600	....	....		d.Buffalo d.	1110	....	....	....
	....	1745	....	....		d.Belle Fourche d.	0950	....	....	....
	....	1800	....	....		d.Spearfish d.	0930	....	....	....
	....	1845	....	....		d.Deadwood d.	0905	....	....	....
	....	2000	....	....		a.**Rapid City** d.	0800	....	....	....

BSI– Bus Services Inc.

Table 561 BARSTOW - BAKERSFIELD

OR[illegible]

US $		1ATC		475	km				2ATC	20[illegible]
						↓ ↑				
0.00	....	1210	....	2215	0	d.**Barstow** a.	....	....	1630	214[illegible]
10.15	....	1340	....	2330	100	d.Mojave d.	....	....	1455	200[illegible]
10.15	....	1530	....	0110	213	a.**Bakersfield** d.	....	....	1345	184[illegible]

ORB– Orange Belt Stages.

Table 562 — BOISE (BW NWS STM)

US$	NWS 730 ⑧	STM 6	BW 1	NWS 734	km	↓	↑	STM 5 ④	NWS 735	BW 2	NWS 731
19.00	1015	1600	....	1830	172	d.**Spokane**..............a.		1015	1705	....	0045
		1700				d. Coeur d'Alene ....a.		0935			
>0.00	1210	1900	....	2025		d.Moscow..............d.		0740	1500	....	2245
	1300	2000	....	2115	0	a.}Lewiston............{d.		0630	1410	....	2155
17.00	1310	....	....	2125		d.}		....	1400	....	2145
		....	....	2340	160	a. Walla Walla ....d.		....	1145		
		....	....	0040	233	a. Pendleton ......d.		....	1035		
6.70	1450	....	....	....	130	d.Grangeville ....d.		....	....	....	2015
17.20	1830	....	....	....	285	d.McCall ....d.		....	....	....	1830
25.60	2100	....	2115	....	460	d.**Boise**..............d.		....	....	1530	1545
>1.90	....	....	2140	....	488	d.Nampa ....d.		....	....	1500	....
>2.40	....	....	2210	....	522	d.Caldwell ....d.		....	....	1440	....
>22.50	....	....	0145	....	942	a.**Winnemucca**......d.		....	....	0900	....

>–Fare ex Boise. BW–Boise-Winnemucca Stages. NWS–Northwestern Trailways. STM–St. Maries Bus Lines.

Table 563 — YOSEMITE PARK ♿ (GLN YTS)

US$	YTS		GLN	YTS	km	↓	↑	GLN	YTS	YTS
0.00	0800	....	....	1445	125	d.**Merced** ....a.		....	1310	1940
		1320			130	d. Fresno ....d.		1120		
13.00	1030	....	1700	1715	0	a.**Yosemite Lodge** d.		0745	1100	1720

GLN–Gray Line. YTS–Yosemite Transportation Service.

Table 564 — PORTLAND - ASTORIA (RAZ)

US$	16	18	km	↓	↑	17	19
0.00	....	0630 1630	0	d.**Portland** ....d.		1225 2215	
			43	d. Glenwood........d.			
14.00			105	d. Tillamook ....d.			
14.00	....	0845	125	d. Seaside ....d.			2000
7.00	....	1715	49	d.St. Helens ....d.		1135	
20.00	....	0915 1915	165	a.**Astoria**............d.		0930 1930	

RAZ–Raz Transportation.

Table 565 — RENO - PHOENIX (GL KTS)

US$	GL 6531	KTS 411	GL 6361	KTS 409	KTS 507	GL 6369	km	↓	↑	KTS 506	GL 6358	KTS 508	GL 6530	GL 6362	KTS 510
	0045	....	....	....	....	....	445	d.Klamath Falls ....a.		....	....	1455	....	....
	0305	....	....	....	....	....		d.Alturas ....d.		....	....	1250	....	....
0.00	0650	0745	....	....	2000	....	0	d.**Reno**..............a.		....	0805	0830	....	1820
	....	0825	....	....	2050	....		d.Carson City ....d.		....	0710		....	1740
6.95	....	1030	....	....	2235	....	150	d.Schurz..............d.		....	0510		....	1530
14.75	....	1340	....	0115	....	....	370	d.Tonopah ....d.		....	0240		....	1230
16.30	....	1415	....	0145	....	....	412	d.Goldfield ....d.		....	0155		....	1120
20.15	....	1535	....	0305	....	....	520	d.Beatty..............d.		....	0045		....	1010
26.40	....	1800	....	0535	....	....	705	a.**Las Vegas** ....d.		....	2150		....	0715
26.40	....	1830	0015	0630	1100	1430	705	d.**Las Vegas** ....a.		1615	1620	2200	0205	0515
26.60	....	1940		0740	1210		742	d.Boulder City ....d.		1520		2105		0420
	....				1500			d. Needles............d.		1230				
	....				1630			d. Lake Havasu City....d.		1130				
30.10	....	2300	0405	1100		1815	863	d.Kingman ....d.			1305	1815	2230	0130
	....	0120	0630	1320	1920	2035		d.Wickenburg ....d.		0810	1005	1525	1950	2240
37.20	....	0300	0805	1500	2100	2205	1168	a.**Phoenix**............d.		0630	0830	1345	1815	2100

GL–Greyhound Lines. KTS–K-T Services.

Table 570 — LAS VEGAS - LOS ANGELES (GL GLSN)

US$	GL		6049	1307		6051	1309	6041	6031		1313		1303	6047		6035	6027
0.00	**Las Vegas** ★ ....d.	0	0045	0045	....	0630	0645	0800	1015	....	1130	....	1445	1445	....	1735 †	1735
28.00	Barstow ....d.	255	....	0350	....	0950	1000	1140	1340	....	1500	....	1755	1815	....	2115	2050
37.00	San Bernardino ....d.	380	....	0500	....	1125		1515		....		....		1950	....		2225
39.00	Riverside ....d.	395	....	0515	....	1150				....		....			....		2245
41.00	Claremont (Pomona) .d.	431	....	0550	....		1125		1550	....		....	2025		....		2335
47.75	Anaheim (D'land) ....d.	439	....		....	1245				....		....			....		
43.00	El Monte (Alhambra) .d.	476	....	0625	....		1159			....		....	2100		....		
43.00	Pasadena ....d.	461	....		....				1630	....		....			....		
40.00	Los Angeles..........a.	501	0630	0655	....	1340	1230	1400	1730	....	1720	....	2000	2130	....	2325	0025

	GL		6024		6040		1310	6042	1312		6050	6048	1300			6068 ⑤		1304	6060	6022
	Los Angeles..........d.		....	....	0600	....	0900	....	0900	1030	1400	....	1400	1615	1800	....	....	1945	....	2000	2330	2330
	Pasadena ....d.		....	....		....		....				....				....	....	2010	....			
	Monte (Alhambra) ...d.		....	....		....		....	0930			....	1430			....	....		....	2030		
	Anaheim (D'land) ....d.		....	....	0645	....		....				....		1820		....	....		....			
	Claremont (Pomona) ....d.		....	....		....		....	1005			....	1505			....	....	2105	....			
	Riverside..........d.		....	....	0745	....		....	1050			....		1955		....	....		....			
	San Bernardino ....d.		....	....	0805	....		....	1115			....	1550	2025		....	....	2145	....		0040	
	Barstow ....d.		....	....	1010	....	1125	....	1305	1255	1630	....	1745	2215	2025	....	....	2220	....	2310	0200	
	Las Vegas ★ ....a.		....	....	1320	....	1450	....	1610	1610	1925	....	2045	0130	2335	....	....	0135	....	0205	0450	0515

★–Charter (GLSN) service Las Vegas-Death Valley Junction-Furnace Creek Ranch-Scotty's Castle and v.v. GL–Greyhound Lines. GLSN–Gray Line of Southern Nevada.

Table 575 — PORTLAND - SALT LAKE CITY (GL PUT RAZ UTA)

US$	GL 5548	GL 5530	GL 5544	RAZ	GL 1421	GL 5534	GL 5532	PUT 102	km	↓	↑	GL 1422	GL 5533	GL 5537	GL 5549	PUT 101	GL 5543	GL 5547
0.00	0020	....	1015	1025	....	....	2245	....	0	d.**Portland** ....a.		....	1440	1605	1950	....	0450	1020
9.00	0210	....	1145	1210	....	1820	0025	....	136	d.The Dalles............d.		....		1410	1805	....	0320	0835
	0235	....	1255	1235	....	1750	0045	....	172	d.Biggs..............d.		1255		1340	1735	....	0255	0810
7.00	....	....	1530		....	....	0250	....	340	d.Pendleton............d.				1045		....	0045	....
4.00	....	....	1635		....	....	0355	....	425	d.La Grande ....d.				0905		....	2320	....
3.00	....	....	1815		....	....	0520	....	488	d.Baker..............d.				0805		....	2230	....
1.00	....	....			....	2025		....	91	d. Government Camp....d.		1315				....		
2.00	....	....		1100	....			....	▼205	d. Eugene ....a.						....		
3.00	....	....		1350	....	2125	2325	....	276	d.Bend ....d.		1000	1005			....		
	....	....			....			....	470	d.Burns ....d.						....		
7.00	....	....	2045		....	....	0750	....	⊠600	d.Ontario ....d.				0700		....	2135	....
0.00	....	....	2130		....	....	0830	....	⊠766	d.Caldwell ....d.				0625		....	2100	....
0.00	....	....	2150		....	....	0850	....	⊠800	d.Nampa ....d.				0555		....	2035	....
0.00	....	....	2250		....	....	0940	....	⊠828	d.**Boise**..............d.				0525		....	2005	....
0.00	....	....	0125		....	1305		....	⊠1013	d.Twin Falls............d.				0225		....	1600	....
5.00	....	....	0230		....	1400	1435	....	⊠1114	d.Burley..............d.				0120		....	1430	1505
2.00	....	....			....			1615	⊠1244	a. Pocatello ....d.						1300		
8.00	....	....	0500		....	....	1645	....	⊠1279	d.Brigham City ....d.				2250		....	1215	....
8.00	....	....	0535		....	....	1720	....	⊠1316	d.Ogden ►............d.				2220		....	1145	....
8.00	....	....	0630		....	....	1815	....	⊠1374	a.**Salt Lake City** ►....d.				2125		....	1045	....

–Fare ex Bend. ⊠–Km via Bend. ▼–Km ex Bend. ►–Local (UTA 55/70/71/170) operates Salt Lake City-Ogden and v.v. 0600 and frequent (hourly after 1800) to 2307⑥/
37④. GL–Greyhound Lines. PUT–Pocatello Urban Transit. RAZ–Raz Transportation. UTA–Utah Transit Authority.

Check update notes to timetables and with operator before starting your journey

Table 580 — VANCOUVER - SEATTLE
🚌 GL GLC QUS TNW

US $			TNW 101 ♣	GL 6547	GLC 191 ♣	GL 6529	GLC 197		QUS 107 ♣	GLC 193	TNW 107 ♣	GL 6577		QUS 109 ♣		QUS 111 ♣	GLC 189 ♣	GL 6537	GLC 195
28.00	Vancouver........d.	km 0	0515	....	....	0715	....	1000	....	1200	1300	1300	....	....	1500	....	....	1730 1730	....	1930
25.00	New Westminster (u)d.	19		....	....	0740	....	1025	....		1325		....	....		....	....	1755	....	1955
21.00	Blaine 🏛 ◇......d.	58	0620	....	....	0920	....		....	1410			....	....		....	....	2015		
18.00	Bellingham ....d.	93	0655	....	0800	0955	s		....	1445	1500	s	....	....		....	....	2055	s	
	Mount Vernon ....d.		0735	....	0850	1030	....		....	1525	1535		....	....		....	....	2130		
7.00	Everett ....d.	198	0815	....	0945	1120	....		....	1605	1630		....	....		....	....	2220		
0.00	Seattle ....a.	250	0915	1025	1045	1159	1325		1510	1630	1655	1715	....	1810	....	2040	2100	2300	2300
	Seattle/Tacoma Airport.a.		....	....	1115	....	1355	....	1700				....	....	....	....	2130	....	2330

			GL 6524		QUS 100 ♣	GLC 194 ♣	GL 6526 ♣	GLC 190 ♣	QUS 104 ♣	TNW 110 ♣		GLC 196 ♣	QUS 110 ♣		GL 6532 ♣	QUS 112 ♣	GLC 188 ♣		QUS 114 ♣	TNW 114 ♣	GLC 198 ♣		GL 6540
	Seattle/Tacoma Airport.d.		....	....	0900	....	....	1045	....	....		1230	....	....	....	....	1630	....		2000	....	....	
	Seattle ....d.		0525	....	0900	0930	1115	1115	1145	1230		1300	1500	....	1610	1700	1715	....	1900	2020	2030	....	2050
	Everett ....d.		0610	....			1201			1320				....	1655			....		2120		....	2135
	Mount Vernon ....d.		0700	....			1250			1400				....	1745			....		2205		....	2225
	Bellingham ....d.		0745	....			1325	1255		1440		1440		....	1830		1855	....		2240	2210	....	2300
	Blaine 🏛 ◇...........a.		0815	....						1510				....	1900			....		2315		....	
	New Westminster (s)a.		....	....			1230		1420			1605		....			2020	....		2330		....	
	Vancouver ....a.		....	....	1215	1255		1230	1445	1500	1645		1630	1815	....		2015	2045	....	2215	0020	2355	....	

◇–For Semi-Ah-Moo.   GL–Greyhound Lines.   GLC–Greyhound Lines of Canada.   QUS–Quick Shuttle.   TNW–Trailways Northwest.

Table 581 — PORT ANGELES
🚌 GL JT

US $	5581				GL	km	↓	↑	5578	
0.00	1045	....	....	....		0	d.Seattle ....a.	....	1900	....
7.00	1225	....	....	....		65	d.Port Ludlow ......d.	....	1705	....
	1330	....	....	....		90	a. Port Towsend ★d.	....	1610	....
10.00	1315	....	....	....		115	d.Sequim ....d.	....	1615	....
12.00	1340	....	....	....		145	a.Port Angeles ....d.	....	1550	....

★–   Connecting 🚌 Port Ludlow-Port Townsend and v.v. by JT.
GL–   Greyhound Lines.   JT–   Jefferson Transit.

Table 582 — HOQUIAM - OLYMPIA
🚌 GHT

US $	1	3	7	9	km	↓	↑	2	4	8	10
0.00	0605	1105	1510	1845	0	d.Hoquiam..........a.	0935	1445	1850	2210
0.75	0615	1120	1530	1900	7	d.Aberdeen.........d.	0925	1430	1840	2200
0.75	0745	1250	1700	2025	84	a.Olympia...........d.	0800	1300	1715	2035

GHT–   Grays Harbor Transportation Authority.

Table 583 — SEATTLE - PORTLAND
🚌 GL

US $	6539	6547	6551	1447	6535	6527	6533	6549	6579	6545	6541	km	↓	↑	6520	1430	6552	6546	6528	6548	6588	6544	6578	6542	6556
0.00	0100	0650	0800	1045	1201	1215	1345	1630	1745	1745	2015	0	d.Seattle ....a.		0445	1015	0915	1345	1530	1725	1935	1815	2135	2345	0205
					1225					1810			d.Seattle/Tacoma Airport...a.			0950			1505		1910				
	0150	0740		1135	1305			1730		1845		52	d.Tacoma ....d.		0405	0935		1435	1640	1840		2050	2300	0120
		0810						1800		1915			d.Fort Lewis ....d.			0900		1400	1605	1805				
	0230	0845		1225	1405			1830		1945		93	d.Olympia ....d.		0315	0830		1335	1540	1740		2000	2210	0030
					1445					2025		131	d.Centralia (Chehalis)...d.			0745			1455	1655				
	0345	1000		1340	1535			1945		2115		201	d.Longview ....d.		0155	0655		1205	1405	1605		2040		
		1050			1625			2035				266	d.Vancouver ....d.			0605		1115	1315	1515		1755	1950	
	0445	1110	1115	1450	1700	1530	1700	2055	2100	2215	2330	278	a.Portland ....d.		0050	0545	0600	1030	1055	1255	1450	1500	1730	1930	2205

GL–   Greyhound Lines.

Table 587 — PORTLAND - SAN FRANCISCO
🚌 GL

US $	1441	1439	6521	1443		1427	6531	1421	1423	1453	1429	km	↓	↑	1424	6536	6530	1428	1450	1434		1438	1420	1442	1422
0.00	....	0515	0920	1145	....	1645	1800	....	1900	2255	2345	674	d.Portland ....a.	1800	1900	2215	2350	....	0500	....	0955	1159	1420	....
❖	....	0625	1055	1310	....	1805	1910	....	2005	0001	....	598	d.Salem ....d.	1655	1800	2120	2250	....	0400	....	0855		1255	....
	....	0705	1140		....	1845		....		0040		565	d.Albany ....d.		1720	2043		....		....	0815		1215	....
❖	....	0840	1330	1430	....	2025	2045	....	2140	0215	0155	500	d.Eugene..............d.	1535	1545	1925	2130	....	0240	....	0650	0945	1050	....
❖	....	1015	1520		....	2200		....			0325	390	d.Roseburg.............d.		1330		1945	....	0110	....	0455		0905	....
❖	....				....			1515					d. Yakima ....a.					....		....				1525
❖	....				....			1750					d. Biggs ....d.					....		....				1330
❖	....				....			1820					d. The Dalles ....d.					....		....				1000
❖	....				....			2140					d. Bend ....d.					....		....				
❖	....	1205	1655		....	2320					0455	284	d.Grants Pass ....d.		1155		1825	....	2325	....	0340		0705	....
❖	....	1300	1735	1830	....	0020		0055			0545	238	d.Medford...............d.		1125		1745	....	2245	....	0305	0600	0625	....
❖	....	1450		2020	....		0025	0040		0610			d. Klamath Falls Ω....d.	1100		1510		....		....				0650
❖	....	1520		2050	....					0740	0740		d.Weed ....d.	0915			1510	....	2040	....				0440
❖	1400	1715		2215	....	0405		0415	0415	1000	1000	0	d.Dunsmuir..............d.	0845			1440	....	2010	....	0045s			
❖	1450	1805			....	0445		0505	0505	1050	1045		d.Redding ....d.	0735		1330	1835	1900	....	2350	0250	0300	0305
❖	1600	1910			....			0625			1145		d.Red Bluff ....d.			1205	1755	1725	....	2240			0200
❖	1735	2040			....			0820			1310		d.Chico ....d.			1115	1705		....	2155			0115
❖	1900	2130	....	0100	....			0910	0750		1430		d.Marysville............d.			0930	1525		....	2030			2355
❖	....				....					1455			a.Sacramento ....d.	0400		0800	1430		....	1900	2300		2300
❖	....				....		0750			1530			d. Vallejo ....d.				1325		....				
❖	....				....		0830			1605			a. Richmond ....d.				1250		....				
❖	....				....								a. Oakland.............d.				1230		....		2245		
❖	....				....								a. San Francisco...d.				1201		....		2215		

Ω–   For Crater Lake.
GL–   Greyhound Lines.

Table 588 — HOUSTON - EL PASO
🚌 GL KBC

US $	GL 1251	GL 1253	KBC 403		GL 405	GL 7220	GL 1261	KBC 407	GL 1255	GL 401	GL 1239	km	↓	↑	GL 1258	GL 408		GL 402	GL 1260	GL 1248	GL 7223	GL 1244	GL 404	GL 1246	GL 406
0.00	0145	0315	....		0730	1230	1515	....	1700	2000	2245	0	d.Houston ....a.	0330	0815	....	1230	1550	1845	2015	2115	0005	....
							2015						d.Luling ....d.			0945			1830				
34.00	0510	0650	0730		1300a	1610	1900	2030	2130	0100a	0210	305	d.San Antonio..............d.	0001	0405	0715a	0830	1130	1500	1645	1715	2030	2115
			0905		1440a		2150		0215a			417	d.Kerrville ....d.		0130a	0600a			1420a			2020
59.00	....	1110			1640a		2345		0411a			585	d.Sonora ....d.	2330a	0357a			1210a				1810
73.00	....	1410b			1930		0230b		0700			875	d.Fort Stockton..............d.	2100a	0130a			0930a				1540
92.00	....	1700b			2155s				0945			960	d.Van Horn ....d.	1835	2315			0705				1315
104.00	....	1800b			2250		0525b		1045			1160	a.El Paso......................d.	1445	2000			0335				0935

a–   KBC.
b–   GL.
GL–   Greyhound Lines.   KBC–   Kerrville Bus Co.

Table 891 PORTLAND - SAN FRANCISCO · FBL GL

US $	GL	FBL	GL	GL	km		GL	GL	GL	FBL
	1486	1	6642	1483		↓	1487	6643	1482	2
2.00	0830	a	....	2115	0	d.Portland ....a.	2015	....	0905	b
2.00	1230	....	0110	190	d.Newport.........d.	1655	....	0530	....
	1420	....	0305		d.Reedsport......d.	1455	....	0310	....
3.00	1515	....	0405	365	d.Coos Bay ....d.	1400	....	0220	....
9.00	1930	....	0800	585	d.Crescent City ....d.	1100	....	2245	....
3.00	2145	....	1010	720	d.Eureka.............d.	0745	....	2025	....
5.00	2315	....	1150	820	d.Garberville ......d.	0540	....	1830	....
5.00	0050	....	1320	970	d.Willits ....d.	0405	....	1655	....
2.00	0135	....	1420	1007	d.Ukiah................d.	0335	....	1630	....
		0730			d. Fort Bragg ....a.				2030
	0240	1020	....	1525	d.Healdsburg ....d.	0215	....	1445	1750
1.00	0305	1040	1615	1555	1099	d.Santa Rosa ......d.	0155	1530	1425	1730
8.00	0330	1100	....	1620	1125	d.Petaluma..........d.	0130	....	1355	1655
4.00	0400	1140	....	1650	1167	d.San Rafael ....d.	0110	....	1325	1620
			1915			a. Sacramento ...d.		1230		....
0.00	0440	1215	....	1730	1195	a.San Francisco..d.	0030	....	1245	1540

4½ hours later on †. b–1¼ hours later on †.
BL– Falcon Bus Lines.
L– Greyhound Lines. RAZ–Raz Transportation.

Table 895 SACRAMENTO - SAN JOSE · GL ST

US $		ST	GL	GL	GL	ST	GL		ST
		14/35	8393	6805	6809	11/31	6817		36/32
			km						
	South Lake Tahoe.d.	◇ 299	0230	0345	....	1445	....		2000
6.00	Sacramento........d.	0	0510	0650	1045	1510	1745	1800	2245
4.00	Stockton ....d.	79	....	0810	1145	1640				
	Tracy...................d.		....	0840	1220	1720			
	Oakland..............d.		0710				1930		0030
	San Francisco a.		0736				1945		0050
	Palo Alto (Mountain View).d.		....						
0.00	San Jose ....a.	209	....	1040	1330	1845	....	2050	

		ST	ST	GL	GL	ST	GL	GL
		11	35/36	6806	6810	37/14	8392	6804
	San Jose..................d.							
	Palo Alto (Mountain View).d.							
	San Francisco....d.		....	0840	1105	....	1500	1740
	Oakland...............d.		....	0840			1540		
	racy...................d.		....	0900			1600		
	ockton................d.		....	1010	1220		1630		
	acramento..........a.		....	1045	1255		1705		
	South Lake Tahoe ..a.		0725	1050	1205	1400	1815	1820	2050
			1100	1400			1945		

–Km ex Stockton. GL–Greyhound Lines. ST–Sierra Trailways.

Table 897 SEATTLE - VICTORIA · GLS WIC

US $	GLS	WIC				WIC	GLS
	114	1B				1A	114
	♣	①③⑤		km	↓	①③⑤	♣
0.00	0555	1030	....	0	d.Seattle ....a.	0945	1635
			....	52	d.Everett..............d.		
	0700	1430	....	❖	d.Mount Vernon...d.	0530	s
0.75	0730	1355	....	157	a.Anacortes ....d.	0555	1500
0.75	0745	....	....	157	d.Anacortes ....d.	....	1450
7.60	1100	....	....	250	a.Sidney ....d.	....	1100
7.60	1115	....	....	250	d.Sidney ....a.	....	1055
1.00	1240	....	....	280	a.Victoria ....d.	....	0930

LS– Gray Line of Seattle (Evergreen Trails Inc).
C– Whidbey Island Coach.

Table 909 SAN FRANCISCO · ACT GGT GL

service (ACT) San Francisco-Oakland-Berkeley-Richmond-San Pablo and v.v. (and throughout Alameda and Contra Costa counties). ❖ km. Journey: 1½ hours. Fare: US $: 1.75. ♿.
om San Francisco: 0600✕/0800† and frequent to 2300.
om San Pablo: 0600✕/0800† and frequent to 2300.

service (GL) San Francisco-Oakland-Richmond-Vallejo-Calistoga/Sacramento and v.v. 145 km. Journey: 2¼ hours. Fare: US $: ❖.

To/from Calistoga, not Sacramento. ACT–AC Transit. GGT–Golden Gate Transit. GL–Greyhound Lines.

Table 892 RENO - LOS ANGELES · GL

US $	6007	6005		km	↓			6002	6008
0.00	....	0730	....	0	d.Reno................a.	....	....	....	0520
7.00	....	0820	....	49	d.Carson City ......d.	....	....	....	0430
33.00	....	1335	....	329	d.Bishop.............d.	....	....	....	0005
59.00	0700	1800	....	679	d.Mojave.............d.	....	....	1440	2010
67.00	0930	2030	....	821	d.Hollywood........d.	....	....	1210	1645
73.00	0955	2055	....	845	d.Los Angeles.....d.	....	....	1150	1615

GL– Greyhound Lines.

Table 893 AUSTIN - KERRVILLE · KBC

US $		608		km	↓		607	
0.00	....	1840	....	0	d.Austin ....a.	....	1045	....
❖	....	2015	....	❖	d.Fredericksburg ..d.	....	0905	....
❖	....	2055	....	❖	a.Kerrville ....d.	....	0830	....

KBC– Kerrville Bus Co.

Table 905 OAKLAND - SANTA CRUZ · PLS

US $		441		km	↓		432	
0.00	....	1215	....	0	d.Oakland............a.	....	1240	....
	....	1345	....		d.San Jose ....d.	....	1135	....
	....	1455	....		a.Santa Cruz ....d.	....	1030	....

PLS– Peerless Stages.

Table 906 TACOMA - BREMERTON · BTA

US $	301	303	305		km	↓		300	302	304
	ⓐ	ⓐ	ⓐ					ⓐ	ⓐ	ⓐ
0.00	0610	0845	1315	....	0	d.Tacoma ....a.	....	0830	1045	1745
	0700	0945	1415	....		a.Bremerton.......d.	....	0745	1000	1625

BTA– Cascade Trailways.

Table 907 LOS ANGELES · SCRTD

service Los Angeles-Long Beach and v.v. 15 km. Journey: 1 hour. Fare: US $: 1.25.
From Los Angeles: frequent service, day and night.
From Long Beach: frequent service, day and night.
Frequent daily services operate between Los Angeles and Hollywood, North Hollywood, Beverly Hills, Burbank, Pasadena, Alhambra, Buena Park, El Monte, San Pedro, Newport Beach, Anaheim (Disneyland), Pomona and all points in metropolitan Los Angeles.
SCRTD–Southern California Rapid Transit District.

Table 908 SALINAS - MONTEREY ♿ · MST

service Salinas-Monterey and v.v. 30 km. Journey: 50 mins. Fare: US $: 1.50.
From Monterey: 0630④, 0645④, 0700④, 0715④, 0730④, 0745✕, 0800④, 0830④, 0845✕, 0915✕, 0945, 1015✕, 1045, 1115✕, 1245, 1315✕, 1345, 1415✕, 1445, 1515✕, 1545, 1615✕, 1645, 1715✕, 1745, 1815✕, 1915✕, 2015✕, 2115✕.
From Salinas: 0645④, 0655④, 0712④, 0725④, 0745④, 0825④, 0845✕, 0915✕, 0945✕, 1015✕, 1045, 1115✕, 1145, 1215✕, 1245, 1315✕, 1345, 1415✕, 1440Ω, 1445, 1500Ω, 1515✕, 1545, 1615✕, 1645, 1705④, 1715✕, 1745, 1815✕, 1915✕, 2015✕, 2115✕, 2215✕.
Ω– Schooldays only.
MST– Monterey Salinas Transit.

From San Francisco: 0001, 0530, 0700, 0900, 1100, 1201, 1300, 1315, 1400, 1530, 1550a, 1600, 1645, 1700, 1735, 1800⑤, 1900⑤, 2000, 2230.
From Sacramento: 0005, 0425, 0630, 0730, 0830, 0905a, 0930, 1030, 1230, 1330, 1530, 1630, 1730, 1830⑥⑦, 2020, 2130.
service (GGT) San Francisco-San Rafael-Petaluma-Santa Rosa and v.v. ❖ km. Journey: 1½ hours. Fare: US $: 1.50. ♿.
From San Francisco: 0500 and frequent (about hourly on ©) to 0203.
From Santa Rosa: 0406 and frequent (about hourly on ©) to 0100.

Check update notes to timetables and with operator before starting your journey

Table 910 SAN FRANCISCO - LOS ANGELES

GL IC ST

US $	km		GL 6747	GL 6863		GL 6865	GL 6753	GL 6821	GL 6869	GL 6757	GL 1447	GL 6729	GL 6861	GL 6771	GL 6837	GL 6779	GL 6881	GL 6879	GL 6845
0.00	0	San Francisco d.	....	....	....	....	....	....	....	....	....	0545	....	0800	....	....	....	....	1000
4.00	40	S Francisco Intnl Apt d.	....	....	....	....	....	....	....	....	....	|	....	|	....	....	....	....	|
7.00	49	P Alto (Mtn View) d.	....	....	....	....	....	....	....	....	....	|	....	|	....	....	....	....	|
		Santa Cruz d.	....	....	....	....	....	....	....	....	....	|	....	|	....	....	....	....	|
10.00	76	San Jose d.	....	....	....	....	....	....	....	....	....	0655	....	0915	....	0745	....	....	|
		Gilroy ..... d.	....	....	....	....	....	....	....	....	....	0740	....	1000	....	0835	....	....	|
		Los Banos d.	....	....	....	....	....	....	....	....	....	|	....	|	....	0945	....	....	|
		Watsonville d.	....	....	....	....	....	....	....	....	....	|	....	|	....	|	....	....	|
21.00	170	Salinas ... d.	....	....	....	....	....	....	....	....	....	0835	....	|	....	|	....	....	|
23.00	196	Monterey d.	....	....	....	....	....	....	....	....	....	|	....	|	....	|	....	....	|
37.00	380	San Luis Obispo d.	....	....	....	....	0600	....	....	....	....	1145	....	|	....	|	....	....	|
53.00	585	Santa Barbara d.	0700	....	....	....	0925	....	....	0930	....	1400	....	|	....	|	....	....	|
		Ventura... d.	0740	....	....	....	|	....	....	1015	....	|	....	|	....	|	....	....	|
4.00	11	**Oakland** . d.	|	....	....	....	|	....	....	|	....	|	....	|	....	|	....	....	1035
		Tracy ... d.	|	....	....	....	|	....	....	|	....	|	....	|	....	|	....	....	|
◇14.00	⊠130	**Sacramento** . d.	|	0200	....	....	|	....	....	|	0615	|	0830	|	....	|	0830	1040	|
18.00	⊠47	Stockton . d.	|	0300	....	....	|	....	....	|	0715	|	0950	|	....	|	0930	|	|
19.00	166	Modesto d.	|	0345	....	....	|	....	....	|	0800	|	|	|	....	|	1015	|	|
24.00	231	Merced . d.	|	0430	....	....	|	....	....	|	0855	|	|	|	....	|	1110	|	|
33.00	310	Fresno .. d.	|	0615	....	....	|	0630	0815	|	1030	|	|	|	1015	1150	1250	1415	|
		Visalia d.	|	|	....	....	|	0735	|	|	|	|	|	|	|	|	|	|	|
44.00	505	Bakersfield d.	|	|	....	0715	|	0925	1025	|	|	|	|	|	1255	1425	|	|	|
59.00	640	Oxnard ... d.	0810	|	....	|	1010	|	|	1040	|	|	|	|	|	|	|	|	|
61.00	695	Glendale★ d.	|	|	....	|	|	|	|	|	|	|	|	1600	|	1650	|	|	|
61.00	714	Malibu Beach d.	|	|	....	|	|	|	|	|	|	|	|	|	|	|	|	|	|
61.00	734	Santa Monica a.	|	|	....	|	1140	|	|	|	|	|	|	|	|	|	|	|	|
61.00	730	Hollywood a.	0945	|	....	0950	|	1155	|	1225	|	|	1625	|	1540	|	|	|	1745
61.00	750	**Los Angeles** a.	1005	1025	....	1015	1205	1215	1250	1255	1440	1615	1650	1645	1605	1715	1725	1825	1805

	GL 6751	ST 103 ⊠	IC ⊠	GL 6725	GL 6806	GL 6833	GL 6705	GL 6777	GL 6745	GL 6897	GL 6893	GL 6887	GL 6885 ⑤⑥⑦	GL 6889	GL 6731
San Francisco d.	....	....	....	....	....	0815	0825	0930	1230	1300	0925	1035	....	....	1030
S Francisco Intnl Apt d.	....	....	....	....	....	|	|	|	|	|	|	|	....	....	|
P Alto (Mtn View) d.	....	....	....	....	....	|	0915	1020	|	|	|	|	....	....	|
Santa Cruz d.	....	....	....	....	....	|	1045	|	|	|	|	|	....	....	|
San Jose d.	....	....	....	....	0840	|	|	1120	1340	|	|	|	....	....	1140
Gilroy ..... d.	....	....	....	....	|	|	|	1210	|	|	|	|	....	....	1225
Los Banos d.	....	....	....	....	|	|	|	1345	|	|	|	|	....	....	|
Watsonville d.	....	....	....	....	|	|	1110	|	|	|	|	|	....	....	|
Salinas ... d.	....	....	....	....	|	|	1240	|	|	|	|	|	....	....	1315
Monterey d.	....	....	....	....	|	|	1210	|	|	|	|	|	....	....	|
San Luis Obispo d.	....	....	....	1400	|	|	[redacted]	|	|	|	|	|	....	....	1655
Santa Barbara d.	1400	....	....	1630	|	|	....	|	|	|	|	|	....	....	2020
Ventura... d.	1440	....	....	1710	|	|	....	|	|	|	|	|	....	....	2100
Oakland . d.	|	....	....	|	|	0845	*GL*	|	|	1330	0955	1110	....	....	|
Tracy ... d.	|	....	....	|	1015	1020	**6883**	|	|	|	1130	1250	....	....	|
Sacramento . d.	|	0945	....	|	1040	|	1040	|	|	|	|	|	1535	1535	|
Stockton . d.	|	1045	....	|	....	|	1159	|	|	|	1159	|	1635	1635	|
Modesto d.	|	1130	....	|	....	1125	1300	|	|	1520	....	1355	|	1720	|
Merced . d.	|	1230	....	|	....	1235	1400	|	|	|	....	1500	|	|	|
Fresno .. d.	|	1330	1330	|	....	1415	1540	1540	|	1740	....	1645	|	1920	|
Visalia d.	|	....	|	|	....	1520	|	|	|	|	....	|	|	|	|
Bakersfield d.	|	....	|	|	....	1710	|	1825	|	|	....	1855	|	|	|
Oxnard ... d.	1505	....	|	1735	....	|	|	|	|	|	....	|	|	|	2125
Glendale★ d.	|	....	|	|	....	|	|	|	|	|	....	|	|	|	|
Malibu Beach d.	r	....	|	|	....	|	|	|	|	|	....	|	|	|	|
Santa Monica a.	1635	....	|	|	....	|	|	|	|	|	....	|	|	|	2245
Hollywood a.	|	....	|	1850	....	1945	|	|	2020	|	....	2135	|	|	|
Los Angeles a.	1710	....	1730	1920	....	2005	1950	2050	2040	2150	....	2200	2245	2330	2310

	GL 6871	GL 6703	GL 8326 ⑤⑥	GL 8392	GL 6870	GL 6867	GL 6735	GL 6781	GL 6841	GL 6909	GL 6839	GL 6709	GL 6891	GL 6737	GL 6847	GL 6877	GL 6873		GL 6849	GL 6739		GL 6743
San Francisco d.	....	1230	....	....	1530	1425	1430	1700	....	....	1645	1715	1820	1800	2130	....	....	....	2230	2000	....	2230
San Francisco Intnl. Apt. d.	....	1255	....	....	|	|	|	|	....	....	|	1740	|	|	|	....	....	....	|	|	....	|
Palo Alto (Mountain View) d.	....	1345	....	....	|	|	|	|	....	....	|	|	|	|	|	....	....	....	|	|	....	|
Santa Cruz d.	....	1525	....	....	|	|	|	|	....	....	|	1945	|	|	|	....	....	....	|	|	....	|
San Jose ... d.	....	|	1245	1500	|	|	1545	1840	....	1745	|	|	|	1915	|	....	....	....	|	2115	....	2345
Gilroy .... d.	....	|	|	|	|	|	1630	1930	....	|	|	|	|	2010	|	....	....	....	|	|	....	|
Los Banos .. d.	....	|	|	|	|	|	|	2040	....	|	|	|	|	|	|	....	....	....	|	|	....	|
Watsonville d.	....	1550	|	|	|	|	|	|	....	|	|	2015	|	|	|	....	....	....	|	|	....	|
Salinas ...... d.	....	1710	|	|	|	|	1725	|	....	|	|	2135	|	2055	|	....	....	....	|	2230	....	|
Monterey... a.	....	1640	|	|	|	|	|	|	....	|	|	2105	|	|	|	....	....	....	|	|	....	|
San Luis Obispo d.	....	....	|	|	|	|	2115	|	....	|	|	[redacted]	|	0005	|	....	....	....	|	0105	....	|
Santa Barbara d.	....	....	|	|	|	|	2335	|	....	|	|	....	|	0225	|	....	....	....	|	0330	....	|
Ventura...... d.	....	....	|	|	|	|	0015	|	....	|	|	....	|	0305	|	....	....	....	|	|	....	|
Oakland .. d.	....	....	|	|	1550	1455	|	|	....	|	1730	....	1845	|	2210	....	....	....	2310	|	....	|
Tracy ...... d.	....	....	|	1645	|	1640	|	|	....	1915	1915	....	2025	|	|	....	....	....	|	|	....	|
Sacramento d.	1245	....	|	|	|	|	|	|	1730	|	|	....	|	|	|	2015	2245	....	|	|	....	|
Stockton... d.	1405	....	1430	1715	|	|	|	|	1850	1945	|	....	2055	|	|	2135	2345	....	|	|	....	|
Modesto... d.	1500	....	....	....	|	1740	|	|	2000	....	2010	*GL*	....	|	|	2220	|	....	|	|	....	|
Merced .... d.	1600	....	....	....	|	1840	|	|	2055	....	2105	**6875**	....	|	|	2320	|	....	|	|	....	|
Fresno..... d.	1740	....	....	....	|	2015	|	2210	2245	....	2245	2245	....	|	|	0045	|	....	|	|	....	|
Visalia . d.	|	....	....	....	|	2120	|	....	|	....	|	|	....	|	|	|	|	....	|	|	....	|
Bakersfield d.	2035	....	....	....	|	2315	|	....	0055	....	0110	0100	....	|	|	0320	|	....	|	|	....	|
Oxnard ...... d.	|	....	....	....	|	|	0040	....	....	....	|	|	....	0330	|	|	|	....	|	|	....	|
Glendale ★ d.	2315	....	....	....	|	|	|	....	....	....	|	|	....	|	0450**s**	|	|	....	|	|	....	0620
Malibu Beach d.	|	....	....	....	|	|	|	....	....	....	|	|	....	|	|	|	|	....	|	|	....	|
Santa Monica a.	|	....	....	....	|	|	|	....	....	....	|	|	....	0450	|	|	|	....	|	|	....	|
Hollywood a.	|	....	....	....	2255	0135	0150	....	....	....	|	|	....	|	|	0540	0555	....	0605**s**	|	....	|
Los Angeles a.	2340	....	....	....	2315	0155	0205	....	....	....	0340	0325	....	0515	0515	0610	0620	....	0625	0525	....	0645

	GL 6894	GL 8393	GL 6708	GL 6704	GL 6838	GL 6850		GL 6774	GL 6706	GL 6840	GL 6724	GL 6908	GL 6890	GL 6780	GL 6726	GL 1430	GL 6858	IC ⊠	GL 6770	GL 6809	ST 102 ⊠	GL 6886	GL 6766	GL 6836	GL 1438	GL 6844		GL 8329 ⑤⑦		GL 6730
Los Angeles d.	....	....	....	....	0100	0100	....	....	....	0315	0325	....	....	....	0625	0700	0700	0930	0830	....	....	0830	1025	1030	1030	1400	....	....	....	1145
Hollywood d.	....	....	....	....	0120	|	....	....	....	|	|	....	....	....	0650	|	0725	|	|	....	....	0855	|	|	|	1425	....	....	....	|
Santa Monica d.	....	....	....	....	|	|	....	....	....	|	|	....	....	....	|	|	|	|	|	....	....	|	1100	|	|	|	....	....	....	|
Malibu Beach d.	....	....	....	....	|	|	....	....	....	|	|	....	....	....	|	|	|	|	|	....	....	|	|	|	|	|	....	....	....	|
Glendale ★ d.	....	....	....	....	|	|	....	....	....	|	|	....	....	....	|	0725	|	|	0855	....	....	|	|	|	|	|	....	....	....	|
Oxnard ...... d.	....	....	....	....	|	|	....	....	....	|	0445	....	....	....	0840	|	|	|	|	....	....	|	1225	|	|	|	....	....	....	|
Bakersfield d.	....	....	....	....	0345	0345	....	....	....	0555	|	....	....	....	|	0955	1025	|	|	....	....	1205	|	|	1310	|	....	....	....	|
Visalia . d.	....	....	....	....	|	0520	....	....	....	0735	|	....	....	....	|	|	|	|	|	....	....	|	|	|	|	|	....	....	....	|
Fresno..... d.	....	....	....	....	0630	0650	....	0900	....	0900	|	....	....	1330	|	1225	1330	1330	|	....	1400	1435	|	1510	1535	|	....	....	....	|
Merced .... d.	....	....	....	....	0745	0815	....	|	....	1015	|	....	....	|	|	1340	1445	....	|	....	1505	1545	|	|	|	|	....	....	....	|
Modesto... d.	....	....	....	....	0855	0915	....	|	....	1130	|	....	....	|	|	1440	1555	....	|	....	1600	1645	|	1700	|	|	....	....	....	|
Stockton... d.	0700	0810	....	....	1000	|	....	|	....	1230	|	1230	1530	|	|	1520	|	....	|	1640	1640	1725	|	|	|	|	....	1830	....	|
Sacramento a.	|	|	....	....	1055	|	....	|	....	1345	|	|	|	|	|	1635	|	....	|	|	1745	1830	|	|	1840	|	....	|	....	|
Tracy ...... d.	0730	0840	....	....	....	1010	....	|	....	....	|	|	1605	|	|	....	1650	....	|	1720	....	....	|	|	....	|	....	|	....	|
Oakland .. a.	0905	|	....	....	....	1145	....	|	....	....	|	|	1745	|	|	....	1820	....	|	|	....	....	|	1830	....	2140	....	|	....	|
Ventura...... d.	|	|	....	....	....	|	....	|	....	....	0505	|	|	|	0900	....	|	....	|	|	....	....	1245	|	....	|	....	|	....	|
Santa Barbara d.	|	|	....	....	....	|	....	|	....	....	0605	|	|	|	0950	....	|	....	|	|	....	....	1335	|	....	|	....	|	....	1355
San Luis Obispo d.	|	|	....	....	....	|	....	|	....	....	0925	|	|	|	1250	....	|	....	|	|	....	....	....	|	....	|	....	|	....	1630
Monterey... d.	|	|	....	0715	....	|	....	|	1105	....	|	|	|	|	|	....	|	....	|	|	....	....	....	|	....	|	....	|	....	|
Salinas ...... d.	|	|	....	0640	....	|	....	|	1025	....	1315	|	|	|	1555	....	|	....	|	|	....	....	....	|	....	|	....	|	....	1925
Watsonville d.	|	|	....	0815	....	|	....	|	|	....	|	|	|	|	|	....	|	....	|	|	....	....	....	|	....	|	....	|	....	|
Los Banos .. d.	|	|	....	|	....	|	....	1030	|	....	|	|	|	1520	|	....	|	....	|	|	....	....	....	|	....	|	....	|	....	|
Gilroy .... d.	|	|	....	|	....	|	....	1135	1210	....	1355	|	|	1635	1635	....	|	....	|	|	....	....	....	|	....	|	....	|	....	2000
San Jose ... d.	|	1005	1030	|	....	|	....	1235	1310	....	1500	1525	|	1720	1735	....	|	....	1550	1845	....	....	....	|	....	|	....	2025	....	2100
Santa Cruz d.	|	....	|	0850	....	|	....	|	|	....	|	....	|	....	|	....	|	....	|	....	....	....	....	|	....	|	....	....	....	|
Palo Alto (Mountain View) a.	|	....	|	1020	....	|	....	1305	|	....	1545	....	|	....	|	....	|	....	|	....	....	....	....	|	....	|	....	....	....	|
San Francisco Intnl. Apt. a.	|	....	|	1110	....	|	....	|	1405	....	|	....	|	....	1825	....	|	....	|	....	....	....	....	|	....	|	....	....	....	|
San Francisco a.	0930	....	1130	1135	....	1210	....	1405	1430	....	1630	....	1815	....	1850	....	1850	....	1700	....	....	....	....	1900	....	2220	....	....	....	2200

	GL 6710	GL 6734		GL 6820	GL 6842			GL 6874	GL 6826	GL 6866	GL 6736	GL 6772	GL 6896	GL 6888	GL 6876	GL 6754	GL 6852	GL 6732	GL 6844	GL 6878	GL 6856 ⑤⑦	GL 6882		GL 6872	GL 6834	GL 6756		GL 6868	GL 6740	GL 6848	GL 6846	GL 6880	GL 6755
Los Angeles d.	....	1235	....	1230	1230	....	....	1415	1415	1415	1430	1530	1700	1600	1700	1630	1700	1800	1800	1845	1845	1845	....	2045	2130	2100	....	2200	2230	2300	2300	2345	0045
Hollywood d.	....	1300	....	1255	|	....	....	|	|	1435	1455	1555	1730	|	|	|	1730	1830	|	|	|	1910	....	2110	|	|	....	2225	2250	2325	2325	|	|
Santa Monica d.	....	|	....	|	|	....	....	|	|	|	|	|	|	|	|	1715	|	|	|	|	|	|	....	|	|	|	....	|	|	|	|	|	|
Malibu Beach d.	....	|	....	|	|	....	....	|	|	|	|	|	|	|	|	r	|	|	|	|	|	|	....	|	|	|	....	|	|	|	|	|	|
Glendale ★ d.	....	|	....	|	1315	....	....	|	1445	|	|	|	|	|	|	|	|	|	1830	|	|	|	....	|	|	|	....	|	|	|	|	0010	0110
Oxnard ...... d.	....	1440	....	|	|	....	....	|	|	|	1650	|	|	|	|	1840	|	2020	|	|	|	|	....	|	|	|	....	|	0030	|	|	|	|
Bakersfield d.	....	|	....	1550	1550	....	....	|	|	1730	|	|	|	1845	1945	|	2040	|	2055	|	|	2155	....	2350	|	|	....	0110	|	|	|	|	|
Visalia . d.	....	|	....	|	|	....	....	|	|	|	|	|	|	|	|	|	2220	|	....	|	|	|	....	|	|	|	....	|	|	|	|	|	|
Fresno..... d.	....	|	....	1815	1840	....	....	1900	|	1950	|	|	|	2040	2150	|	2315	|	....	2255	|	0005	....	0205	0220	|	....	0340	|	|	|	|	|
Merced .... d.	....	|	....	1930	1955	....	....	|	|	....	|	|	|	....	|	|	....	|	....	....	|	0115	....	....	|	|	....	0450	|	|	|	|	|
Modesto... d.	....	|	....	2025	2050	....	....	|	|	....	|	|	|	....	2345	|	....	|	....	....	|	0205	....	....	0410	|	....	0545	|	|	|	|	|
Stockton... d.	....	|	....	2115	|	....	....	|	2115	....	|	|	|	....	0030	|	....	|	....	....	0050	0250	....	....	|	|	....	0625	|	|	|	0630	|
Sacramento a.	....	|	....	2225	|	....	....	|	2210	....	|	|	|	....	0125	|	....	|	....	....	0145	0345	....	....	|	|	....	0720	|	|	|	0745	|
Tracy ...... d.	....	|	....	....	2135	....	....	|	....	....	|	|	|	....	....	|	....	|	....	....	....	....	....	....	|	|	....	....	|	|	|	....	|
Oakland .. a.	....	|	....	....	2250	....	....	|	....	....	|	|	0030	....	....	|	....	|	....	....	....	....	....	....	0540	|	....	....	|	0615	|	....	|
Ventura...... d.	....	1500	....	....	|	....	....	|	....	....	1705	|	|	....	....	1905	....	2040	....	....	....	....	....	....	|	|	....	....	|	|	|	....	|
Santa Barbara d.	....	1540	....	....	|	....	....	|	....	....	1800	|	|	....	....	1950	....	2130	....	....	....	....	....	....	|	2310	....	....	0140	|	|	....	|
San Luis Obispo d.	....	....	....	....	|	....	....	|	....	....	2045	|	|	....	....	....	....	2350	....	....	....	....	....	....	|	0130	....	....	0400	|	|	....	|
Monterey... d.	1655	....	....	....	|	....	....	|	....	....	....	|	|	....	....	....	....	....	....	....	....	....	....	....	|	|	....	....	|	|	|	....	|
Salinas ...... d.	1615	....	....	....	|	....	....	|	....	....	....	|	|	....	....	....	....	....	....	....	....	....	....	....	|	0420	....	....	0645	|	|	....	|
Watsonville d.	1745	....	....	....	|	....	....	|	....	....	....	|	|	....	....	....	....	....	....	....	....	....	....	....	|	|	....	....	|	|	|	....	|
Los Banos .. d.	|	....	....	....	|	....	....	2030	....	....	....	|	|	....	....	....	....	....	....	....	....	....	....	....	|	|	....	....	|	|	|	....	|
Gilroy .... d.	|	....	....	....	|	....	....	2140	....	....	....	|	|	....	....	....	....	....	....	....	....	....	....	....	|	|	....	....	0725	|	|	....	0705**s**
San Jose ... d.	|	....	....	....	|	....	....	2225	....	....	....	2300	|	....	....	....	....	....	....	....	....	....	....	....	|	0545	....	....	0835	|	0610	....	0800
Santa Cruz d.	1825	....	....	....	|	....	....	....	....	....	....	|	|	....	....	....	....	....	....	....	....	....	....	....	|	|	....	....	|	|	|	....	|
Palo Alto (Mountain View) a.	1940	....	....	....	|	....	....	....	....	....	....	|	|	....	....	....	....	....	....	....	....	....	....	....	|	|	....	....	|	|	|	....	|
San Francisco Intnl. Apt. a.	2020	....	....	....	|	....	....	....	....	....	....	|	|	....	....	....	....	....	....	....	....	....	....	....	|	|	....	....	0925	|	|	....	|
San Francisco a.	2045	....	....	....	2320	....	....	....	....	....	....	2359	0055	....	....	....	....	....	....	....	....	....	....	....	0610	0645	....	....	0950	0655	0710	....	0900

★– Burbank. ⊠–Apr. 1-Jan. 6. ◇–Fare ex Modesto. ⊠–Km ex Modesto. *GL*–Greyhound Lines. *IC*–Intercalifornias. *ST*–Sierra Trailways.

Table 920 — ALALASKA — ADB ADT AYM SBL VAB

US $	ADB	ADT 002A T	ADT 002 U	km	↓	↑	ADB	ADT 001 U	ADT 001A T
	①③⑥						①③⑥		
9.00	0230	....	....	0900	0	d.Fairbanks ....a.	1500	1730	....
5.00	0500	....	....	1430	195	d.Denali Park ......d.	1230	1330	....
		....	....		229	d.Cantwell ....d.			....
5.00		....	1730		392	d. Talkeetna ....a.			1030
0.00	1130	....	2000	2000	572	a.Anchorage ......d.	0600	0800	0800

US $		R ex②		km	↓	↑	AYM	R ex②	
0.00		0900		....	0	d.Fairbanks ....a.	2000		
5.00		1200		....	158	d.Delta ....d.	1745		
		1430		....		a. Tok ....d.	1500		
47.00				....	424	d.Copper Center...d.	....		
				....	586	a.Valdez..............d.	....		

US $	SBL	AYM W	SBL	SBL	km	↓	↑	SBL	SBL	SBL	AYM W
0.00	....	0800	1000	1430	0	d.Anchorage ......a.	1200	....	1530	2200
5.00	....	0900			80	d.Portage ◇ ....d.		....		2100
5.00	....					a. Whittier ◇ ......d.		....		
9.00	1130	1130		1730	212	a.Seward ....d.	0900	1400		1800
5.00	1615	....	1615		365	a. Homer.............d.	....	0900	0900	

US $		VAB ex①	AYM 2 V		km	↓	↑	VAB ex①	AYM 1 Q	
0.00	....		0900	0800	0	d.Valdez.............a.	1715	1800	
8.00	....		1330		184	d.Glenallen ....d.	1330		
9.00	....		1700	1800	412	a.Anchorage ....d.	0930	0800	

R.T. US $		007		km	↓	↑	ADT	007	
45.00	....	★		0	d.Prudhoe Bay....a.	....	★	
	....	★			d.Wiseman ....d.	....	★	
	....	★			d.Fairbanks ....d.	....	★	
40.00	....	★			a.Anchorage ....d.	....	★	

–②③⑤⑦ May 21-Sept. 14.   R–May 16-Sept. 17.   S–May 22-Sept. 16.   T–May 1-31.
–June 1-Sept. 21.   V–②④⑤⑦ May 23-Sept. 17.   W–May 29-Sept. 6.   ◇–┼┼┼┼ service
ily (see Table 272).   ★–Special 7-day excursion service; from Anchorage on June 18,
ly 18, Aug. 15.   ADB–Alaska Direct Bus Line Inc.   ADT–Alaska-Denali Transit.   AYM–
laskon Express.   SBL–Seward Bus Lines.   VAB–Valdez-Anchorage Bus Line.

Table 921 — WHITEHORSE - SKAGWAY — ADB AYM SD

US $	ADB	SD	AYM Q	km	↓	↑	AYM P♣	SD Q		ADB
			P♣							
0.00	1200	1400	....	1630	0	d.Whitehorse......a.	1130	1230	....	1900
21.00		1500	....	1730	69	d.Carcross..........d.	1030	1130	....	
53.00	1430	1600	....	1830	179	a.Skagway...........d.	0730	0830	....	1530

P–May 17-Sept. 19.   Q–Runs daily May 1-Sept. 30; daily subject to a minimumu of 3
passengers Oct. 1-Apr. 30..   ADB–Alaska Direct Bus Line Inc.   AYM–Alaskon Express.
SD–Sourdough Co.

Table 922 — ANCHORAGE - HAINES — ADB AYM NWS

US $	AYM 6 S	NWS R	ADB ②⑨⑦	ADB ①③⑥	km	↓	↑	NWS R	ADB ③⑤⑦	ADB ②⑨⑦	AYM 7 Q
0.00	0700	....	1000	0600	0	d.Anchorage ......a.	....	1130	0600	1915
60.00	1230	....	1130		301	d.Glenallen ....d.	....		0430	1430
0.00		....			⊠409	d. Valdez.............a.	....			
		....			⊠247	d. Copper Center d.	....			
	0900	....		1500		d. Fairbanks ..a.	....	0230		2000
	1200	....		1830		d. Delta.............d.	....	2300		1745
99.00	1500	....	1800	2030	528	a.Tok.................d.	....	2100	2200	1100
99.00	1600	....	▬▬	2030	528	d.Tok.................d.	....	2100	▬▬	1100
▼126.00	1930	....		2300	708	a.Beaver Creek 🚐d.	....	1830		0900
▼126.00	0930	1615	....	2300	708	d.Beaver Creek 🚐a.	1545	1830		1930
◇35.00	1230	1830	....	0130	884	d.Burwash Landing d.	1320	1600	....	1700
◇33.00		1900	ADB			d.Destruction Bay.d.	1300		ADB	
◇30.00		1925	②⑨⑦			d.Kluane Park ►..d.	1215		②⑨⑦	
▼161.00	1500	2030	1330	0345	1018	d.Haines Junction.d.	1115	1345	1245	1500
189.00	1830		1730		1250	a. Haines...........d.			0745	0815
▼195.00	1630	2245	....	0600		a.Whitehorse......d.	0900	1130	....	1200

Q– ②③⑤⑦ May 18-Sept. 19.   R–③⑥ (also ① May 31-Aug. 30).
S– ①③⑤⑦ May 16-Sept. 17.
⊠– Km ex Tok.   ▼–Fare ex Valdez.   ◇–Fare ex Whitehorse.
►– Sheep Mountain.   ADB–Alaska Direct Bus Line Inc.
AYM– Alaskon Express.
NWS– North West Stage Lines.

The Thomas Cook Worldwide Network

BUNAC... *Working Adventures Abroad*

Bunac (British Universities North America Club) is a non-profit, co-operative, educational student club, which enables thousands of students (and non-students) each year to enjoy self-financing working vacations in North America and other parts of the world.

Most universities have local club committees or reps who can supply you with full programme brochures and give you the benefit of first hand advice. They hold regular lunchtime and evening stalls, and informational or social events at which you can meet others and build up contacts. In addition, local committees arrange the orientations for *Work America* and *Work Canada*. BUNAC also administers a scholarship fund for post-graduate study in North America and has reciprocal incoming programmes for American, Canadian and Jamaican Students wishing to work and travel in Britain.

BUNAC, 16 Bowling Green Lane, London, EC1R 0BD
BUNAC Travel Services Ltd. ATOL No. 1364
Telephone: (071) 251-3472 Telex: 24605
Fax: (071) 251-0215

INDEX

ADVERTISEMENTS

If you would like to place an advertisement in future editions of the *Thomas Cook North American Rail & Bus Guide*, please contact:

The Advertisement Co-ordinator
Thomas Cook Publishing
PO Box 227
PETERBOROUGH PE3 6SB
United Kingdom
☎(0733) 269610. Fax: (0733) 267052

READER SURVEY
Fill in this form and you can win a full-colour guidebook!

If you enjoyed using this book – or if you didn't – please help us to improve future editions, by taking part in our reader survey. Every returned form will be acknowledged, and to show our appreciation for your help we will give you the chance to win a Thomas Cook illustrated guidebook for your travel bookshelf. Just take a few minutes to complete and return this form to us.

When did you buy this book?

Where did you buy it? (Please give town/city and if possible name of retailer)

Did you/do you intend to travel in America by train/bus this year?
☐ Have travelled   ☐ Will travel this year   ☐ Not this year

If so, which cities, states or other destinations did you/do you intend to visit?

In which month did you/do you intend to travel?

For how long (approx.)?

Did you/will you travel on: ☐ An Amtrak pass? ☐ A VIA Rail
pass?   ☐ A Greyhound pass?   ☐ Other
passes or ticket(s)? Please specify:

Did you/do you intend to use this book:
☐ For planning your trip?   ☐ During the trip itself?   ☐ Both?

Did you/do you intend to also purchase any other guidebooks/maps for your trip?
If so, please specify:

Please rate the following features of North American Rail and Bus Guide for their value to you (circle the 1 for "little or no use," 2 for "useful," 3 for "very useful"):

Travelling North America (pages 6–11)	1	2	3
Atlantic Air Deals (pages 12–15)	1	2	3
Deals on Wheels (pages 16–18)	1	2	3
Train and Bus Accommodation (pages 19–22)	1	2	3
Country Information (page 23)	1	2	3
Gateway Airports (pages 24–39)	1	2	3
City Information (pages 40–55)	1	2	3
How to Use the Timetable (pages 59–61)	1	2	3
The Timetables (pages 63–135)	1	2	3
Index to Timetable Places (pages 137–141)	1	2	3

Please use this space to tell us about any features that in your opinion could be changed, improved, or added in future editions of the book, or any other comments you would like to make concerning the book:

Your age category:
☐ Under 26   ☐ 26–50   ☐ over 50

Your name: Mr/Mrs/Ms (First name or initials)
(Last name)

Your full address (please include postal code):

Your daytime telephone number:

Please detach this page and send it to: The Project Editor, North American Rail and Bus Guide, Thomas Cook Publishing, PO Box 227, Peterborough PE3 6SB, United Kingdom.

Guidebooks to be won!

All surveys returned to us before the closing date of 31 October 1994 will be entered for a prize draw on that date. The senders of the first **five** replies drawn will each be invited to make their personal selection of any book from the *Thomas Cook Travellers* range of guidebooks (retail price £6.99), to be sent to them free of charge. With 24 cities and countries to choose from, this new, full colour series of guides covers the major tourist destinations of the world. Each book offers 192 pages of sightseeing, background information, and travel tips.

Prizewinners will be notified as soon as possible after the closing date and asked to select from the list of titles. Offer is subject to availability of titles at 1 November 1994. A list of winners will be available on receipt of a stamped self-addressed envelope.